CHAPTER 13 (pp. 295–297, 299–300)
Independent-sample t, pooled S^2, and effect size r:

$$t = \frac{M_1 - M_2}{\sqrt{\left(\frac{1}{n_1} + \frac{1}{n_2}\right)S^2}} \qquad S^2 = \frac{\Sigma(X_1 - M_1)^2 + \Sigma(X_2 - M_2)^2}{n_1 + n_2 - 2} \qquad r_{\text{effect size}} = \sqrt{\frac{t^2}{t^2 + df}}$$

CHAPTER 13 (pp. 301–302)
Cohen's d and pooled population standard deviation: $\quad d = \frac{M_1 - M_2}{\sigma_{\text{pooled}}} \qquad \sigma_{\text{pooled}} = S_{\text{pooled}}\left(\sqrt{\frac{df}{N}}\right)$

CHAPTER 13 (pp. 302–303)
Cohen's d from t and harmonic mean sample size (n_h) when $n_1 \neq n_2$:

$$d = \frac{2t}{\sqrt{df}}\left(\sqrt{\frac{\bar{n}}{n_h}}\right) \qquad n_h = \frac{2(n_1 n_2)}{n_1 + n_2}$$

which, when $n_1 = n_2$, simplifies to: $\quad d = \frac{2t}{\sqrt{df}}$

CHAPTER 13 (p. 303)
Cohen's d converted to r when $n_1 \neq n_2$: $\qquad r = \dfrac{d}{\sqrt{d^2 + 4\left(\dfrac{\bar{n}}{n_h}\right)}}$

which, when $n_1 = n_2$, simplifies to: $\quad r = \dfrac{d}{\sqrt{d^2 + 4}}$

CHAPTER 13 (p. 305)
95% CI for Cohen's d on independent means:

$$d \pm t_{(.05)}(S_{\text{Cohen's d}})$$

where $S_{\text{Cohen's d}}$ is the square root of:

$$S^2_{\text{Cohen's d}} = \left[\frac{n_1 + n_2}{n_1 n_2} + \frac{d^2}{2(df)}\right]\frac{n_1 + n_2}{df}$$

CHAPTER 13 (pp. 306–308)
Paired (correlated) t and population variance estimate:

$$t = \frac{M_D}{\sqrt{\left(\frac{1}{N}\right)S_D^2}} \qquad S_D^2 = \frac{\Sigma(D - M_D)^2}{N - 1}$$

Beginning Behavioral Research

SIXTH
EDITION

Beginning Behavioral Research
A Conceptual Primer

RALPH L. ROSNOW
Emeritus, Temple University

ROBERT ROSENTHAL
University of California, Riverside

PEARSON
Prentice
Hall

Upper Saddle River, New Jersey 07458

Editorial Director: Leah Jewell
Executive Editor: Jeff Marshall
Project Manager (Editorial): LeeAnn Doherty
Editorial Assistant: Jennifer Puma
Senior Marketing Manager: Jeanette Moyer
Marketing Assistant: Laura Kennedy
Production Liaison: Marianne Peters-Riordan
Permissions Supervisor: Kathleen Karcher
Manufacturing Buyer: Sherry Lewis
Cover Art Director: Jayne Conte

Cover Design: Bruce Kenselaar
Cover Illustration: Getty Images, Inc.
Director, Image Resource Center: Melinda Patelli
Manager, Cover Visual Research & Permissions: Karen Sanatar
Composition/Full-Service Project Management: Donna Leik/Aptara, Inc.
Printer/Binder: Courier Companies, Inc.
Cover Printer: Coral Graphics

> *To our students and colleagues*
> *in research methods*
> *past, present, and future*

Credits and acknowledgments borrowed from other sources and reproduced, with permission, in this textbook appear on appropriate page within text.

Pearson Education LTD.
Pearson Education Singapore, Pte. Ltd
Pearson Education, Canada, Ltd
Pearson Education–Japan
Pearson Education Australia PTY, Limited

Pearson Education North Asia Ltd
Pearson Educación de Mexico, S.A. de C.V.
Pearson Education Malaysia, Pte. Ltd
Pearson Education, Upper Saddle River, New Jersey

10 9 8 7 6 5 4 3 2 1

Contents

PART II OBSERVATION AND MEASUREMENT

4 Strategies of Systematic Observational Research   74

5 Methods for Looking Within Ourselves   95

9   Survey Research and Subject Recruitment   198

PART IV DESCRIBING DATA AND MAKING INFERENCES

10   Summarizing the Data   225

14 Comparisons on More Than Two Conditions   315

15 The Analysis of Frequency Tables   351

Appendix A   Communicating Your Research Findings   368

Preface

Welcome to the sixth edition of *Beginning Behavioral Research*. This book was conceived as an undergraduate text for students who, as part of a course in research methods, are required to plan an empirical study, to analyze and interpret the data, and to present their findings and conclusions in a written report. Although there is much that is new in this edition, it is about the same length as the previous edition because we have tightened and refocused all of the material. Every chapter has some changes, but we have not tinkered with the basic structure, so that instructors who have used this book will have no difficulty integrating the sixth edition into their syllabuses and lectures.

As in the previous edition, the chapters follow a linear sequence corresponding to the steps involved in conceptualizing and conducting an empirical study and then analyzing and reporting the results. The beginning researcher is led step by step through the following process:

1. *Crafting a research idea that can be empirically tested.* Understanding empirical reasoning, the scientific method, levels of empirical investigation, and the characteristics of good researchers (Chapter 1); creating, shaping, and polishing the research idea, doing a search of the literature, and writing the research proposal (Chapter 2); weighing and balancing ethical considerations, and preparing for an ethics review (Chapter 3)

2. *Choosing methods of data collection and measurement.* Knowing the range of observational methods available for watching and recording behavior in lab and field settings, using archival data and outside observers or judges, and knowing the limitations of these methods (Chapter 4); knowing how to collect data in which the participants describe their own behavior or state of mind, and having a sense of the limitations of self-report methods (Chapter 5); assessing the reliability and validity of measuring tools and the validity of research designs (Chapter 6)

3. *Designing and implementing the research study.* Knowing about design options for randomized experiments, the nature and limits of causal reasoning, and how certain artifacts are anticipated and addressed (Chapter 7); understanding the nature and limits of causal reasoning in research that does not use random assignment, including nonequivalent-groups designs (and a statistical adjustment using propensity scores), interrupted time-series designs, single-case experimental research, and longitudinal research (Chapter 8); understanding the logic and the limitations of probability sampling in survey research and the rationale and limitations of using opportunity samples in experimental research, and knowing how nonresponse bias and volunteer bias may be addressed (Chapter 9)

4. *Approaching the research data.* Using graphics, statistical summaries, and confidence intervals to give an overall picture of the results, and using z-score transformations on raw data (Chapter 10); correlating and interpreting relationships between variables based on raw scores, dummy-coded variables, or a combination of both (Chapter 11); testing hypotheses, understanding the effect size, creating a confidence interval around effect size correlations, using the BESD when assessing practical importance, doing a power analysis, and consulting p_{rep} to estimate the likelihood of replication (Chapter 12)

5. *Testing hypotheses and exploring the results.* Using t and r or d to compare two independent groups, understanding what circumstances maximize t, using the paired t for two correlated conditions, and knowing about the assumptions of t (Chapter 13); understanding how F and t are related, using F in designs with more than two conditions and using t and r to examine simple effects, understanding factorial ANOVA and how obtained interactions are interpreted from residuals, computing F and t contrasts and r-type effect sizes in focused comparisons on more than two conditions, and understanding what focused analyses on repeated measures can tell us (Chapter 14); analyzing and interpreting 2×2 and larger tables of independent counts by chi-square, computing phi (ϕ) as an effect size index for $1\text{-}df\ \chi^2$, using Mosteller's standardization procedure to interpret larger chi-square tables (Chapter 15); comparing and combining r-type effect sizes in meta-analyses, obtaining overall significance levels, estimating the tolerance for future null results, and using the null-counternull interval as protection against Type II errors (Appendix C)

6. *Reporting the research project in a paper or in a poster.* Writing up the research findings and conclusions in the style of the APA publication manual and preparing a poster (Appendix A)

Even though this book was conceived as an undergraduate text for students planning to do empirical research, it has also been used in ways that go beyond that original purpose. For example, it has been used in methods courses in which the production of a research project was not a major goal, as well as by master's degree students in several fields as a primary text and by doctoral students to ease themselves into our advanced text, *Essentials of Behavioral Research* (Rosenthal & Rosnow, 1991, 2008). *Beginning Behavioral Research* has also been used to teach research methods and data analysis to several thousand students in distance learning programs. Although the vast majority of students who have used this book had not planned to pursue a career in research, most recognized the vitality and ubiquitousness of scientific research in their daily lives. Thus, we have tried to anticipate and confront questions and uncertainties from the student's perspective not as a potential producer of empirical research, but as an intelligent consumer of scientific findings. Our hope is that this book will teach students to understand the difference between good science and pseudoscience and the exacting standards of sound research.

Our Approach

We are not wedded to any single scientific method, theory, or unit of analysis. The mantra of this book—as well as of our advanced text—is "methodological pluralism and theoretical ecumenism." As Donald T. Campbell argued so eloquently, all research methods are limited in some ways, and therefore it is essential not to foreclose on the use of tools and techniques that enable us to study phenomena from more than one relevant vantage point and to triangulate on questions of interest (see Overman, 1988). Because human behavior is complex and multifaceted, there is often more than one plausible theoretical answer, each answer anchored in an experiential context that is constrained by a particular frame of reference (cf. Rosnow, 1981; Rosnow & Georgoudi, 1986) and, as David Hume argued, circumscribed by our individual mental states.

The primary emphasis of this text is on psychological research, but we have also tried to connect this approach with the empirical reasoning used in other fields to accentuate the broad base of scientific thinking. The discussion is punctuated by both classic and contemporary examples. We want to give a sense not only of traditional ways of doing, analyzing, and thinking about research, but also of continuity, which, we believe, will encourage the idea that each generation of researchers builds on the important findings of previous researchers in a chain of discovery and understanding. Continuity is also implicit in our discussion of data analysis, for example, the conceptual idea that significance tests can be parsed into one or more definitions of effect size multiplied by one or more definitions of study size. Once students have a good grasp of this relationship, they should begin to perceive that statistical procedures are interconnected at some level.

We assume that most students will already have had some exposure to basic statistics in an introductory course and that most students dread the thought of having to wrestle again with statistics. However, on the assumption that few students have total recall of introductory statistics or have come away from a statistics course with an intuitive understanding of what was taught, we review basic aspects of data analysis. We purposely avoid the use of any mathematics beyond the high school level. We illustrate the use of simple statistical procedures not only in the context of the student's research, but also outside a research course so that the student will see and understand what is behind the research reported in newspaper, TV, and Internet stories of scientific results and claims. Although the main focus of our discussion is the most popular statistical procedures, we discuss many recent developments that may not be as well known: contrast t and F tests; r-type indices of effect size for use with contrasts; subclassification on propensity scores; intrinsic and nonintrinsic repeated measures; meta-analysis and the tolerance for future null results; the counternull statistic and the interpretation of the null-counternull interval; Killeen's (2005) p_{rep} statistic, and so on. The emphasis of the statistical discussions is intended to resonate with the spirit and substance of the guidelines recommended by the APA's Task Force on Statistical Inference (Wilkinson et al., 1999).

Guided by the instructor's lectures, even students with little or no training in statistics should find they can master basic data-analytic skills by reading the chapters and repeating the exercises in the order in which they are presented. In this age of the computer, the speediest method of doing complex calculations is with the aid of SPSS, SAS, SYSTAT, Minitab, or some other program. As John W. Tukey (1977) counseled, we can also learn much by simply changing our point of view and exploring the data in different ways. Our own philosophy of data analysis is to treat statistics (in Chapters 10–15 and Appendix C) by showing, through intuitive reasoning and clear examples, what the results tell us. Instructors who plan to teach students to perform their main calculations on a computer will find that our emphasis on the concrete and arithmetical aspects of data analysis will complement any statistics program they choose. We also describe useful data-analytic procedures that might not yet be available in basic computer packages but can be easily performed on a good calculator.

Throughout this book, we have sought to communicate the richness, diversity, utility, and excitement of good research, which we ourselves find so challenging and stimulating. In an effort to make this book useful and user-friendly to a wide variety of students, we have incorporated a number of pedagogical devices. Each chapter begins with a set of *preview questions,* which then appear as section headings in the chapter. The introduction to each chapter states the purpose of the chapter and gives an overview of its content. *Box discussions* highlight and enliven concepts with practical examples and illustrations. Each chapter ends with a *summary* of the main themes, followed by a list of *key terms* pegged to the particular pages on which those terms are set off in boldface print. Each chapter concludes with a set of *review questions* intended to stimulate thought and discussion, with answers given at the end of the chapter. A *glossary* at the back of the book lists and defines all key terms (in boldface) as well as other terms (in italics) in the text and notes the primary chapter(s) where each of those terms is discussed. A test bank and instructional materials are available to instructors, and a research methods website (www.prenhall.com/rosnow) is available to students.

Acknowledgments

Once again, Margaret Ritchie did the copyediting. She has edited so many of our books for several different publishers that, although we have lost count, we count our blessings each time Margaret agrees to work with us. We have enjoyed working with our editors at Prentice Hall, Jeff Marshall and LeeAnn Doherty, whose enthusiasm for this book has carried us along on a cloud of positive energy; it was Jeff who came up with the idea of repeating the preview questions at the beginning of each chapter as section headings in the chapters. We thank Bruce Rind (Temple University) for again allowing us to use his unpublished research in Appendix A and to represent it as a study by a fictitious student named "Mary Jones." We thank MaryLu Rosenthal for preparing the indexes. We thank the following reviewers whose insights and suggestions were helpful in preparing this edition of *Beginning Behavioral Research*: Canan Karatekin (University of Minnesota), Thomas Malloy (Rhode xvi | Preface

Island College), Brenda Russell (Castleton State College), Carey S. Ryan (University of Nebraska at Omaha), Mark R. Seely (Saint Joseph's College), Pamela Stuntz (Texas Christian University), and Joseph R. Troisi II (Saint Anselm College). Certain tables and figures (noted in the text) have by permission been reproduced in part or in their entirety, for which we thank the authors, representatives, and publishers cited as sources in footnotes. And finally, we thank Mimi Rosnow and MaryLu Rosenthal for constructive feedback and counseling in ways too numerous to mention.

This is our 17th book together, and we have had terrific fun throughout the course of this 40-year-old collaboration.

Ralph L. Rosnow
Robert Rosenthal

About the Authors

Robert Rosenthal   Ralph L. Rosnow

Photo by Mimi Rosnow

Ralph L. Rosnow is Thaddeus Bolton Professor Emeritus at Temple University, where he taught for 34 years and directed the graduate program in social and organizational psychology. He has also taught research methods at Boston University and Harvard University and does consulting on research and data analysis. The overarching theme of his scholarly work is how people make sense of, and impose meaning on, their experiential world, called the "will to meaning" by Viktor Frankl. Rosnow has explored aspects of this construct in research and theory within the framework of contextualism, the psychology of rumor and gossip, attitude and social cognition, the structure of interpersonal acumen, artifacts and ethical dilemmas in human research, and the statistical justification of scientific conclusions. He has authored and coauthored many articles and books on these topics and, with Mimi Rosnow, coauthored *Writing Papers in Psychology: A Student Guide to Research Reports, Literature Reviews, Proposals, Posters, and Handouts* (7th ed., Thomson Wadsworth, 2006). He has served on the editorial boards of journals and encyclopedias, was (with R. E. Lana) General Editor of the Reconstruction of Society Series published by Oxford University Press, and chaired the Committee on Standards in Research of the American Psychological Association (APA). He is a fellow of the American Association for the Advancement of Science, the APA, and the Association for Psychological Science; was a recipient of the Society of General Psychology's George A. Miller Award; and was recently honored with a Festschrift book edited by D. A. Hantula, *Advances in Social and Organizational Psychology* (Erlbaum, 2006).

Robert Rosenthal is Distinguished Professor at the University of California at Riverside, and Edgar Pierce Professor of Psychology, Emeritus, Harvard University. His research has centered for nearly 50 years on the role of the self-fulfilling prophecy in everyday life and in laboratory situations. Special interests include the effects of teachers' expectations on students' performance, the effects of experimenters' expectations on the results of their research, and the effects of clinicians' expectations on their patients' mental and physical health. He also has strong interests in sources of artifact in behavioral research and in various quantitative procedures. In the realm of data analysis, his special interests are in experimental design and analysis, contrast analysis, and meta-analysis. His most recent books and articles are about these areas of data analysis and about the nature of nonverbal communication in teacher-student, doctor-patient, manager-employee, judge-jury, and psychotherapist-client interaction. He has been cochair of the Task Force on Statistical Inference of the American Psychological Association and has served as chair of the Research Committee of the Bayer Institute for Health Care Communication. He was a corecipient of two behavioral science awards of the American Association for the Advancement of Science (1960, 1993) and recipient of the James McKeen Cattell Award of the American Psychological Society, the Distinguished Scientist Award of the Society of Experimental Social Psychology, the Samuel J. Messick Distinguished Scientific Contributions Award of APA's Division 5—Evaluation, Measurement, and Statistics, and APA's Distinguished Scientific Award for Applications of Psychology.

Rosenthal and Rosnow have collaborated on articles and other books on research methods and data analysis, including *Artifact in Behavioral Research* (Academic Press, 1969); *The Volunteer Subject* (Wiley, 1975); *Primer of Methods for the Behavioral Sciences* (Wiley, 1975); *Understanding Behavioral Science: Research Methods for Research Consumers* (McGraw-Hill, 1984); *Contrast Analysis: Focused Comparisons in the Analysis of Variance* (Cambridge University Press, 1985); *People Studying People: Artifacts and Ethics in Behavioral Research* (W. H. Freeman, 1997); (with D. B. Rubin) *Contrasts and Effect Sizes in Behavioral Research: A Correlational Approach* (Cambridge University Press, 2000); and *Essentials of Behavioral Research: Methods and Data Analysis* (3rd ed., McGraw-Hill, 2008).

CHAPTER 1

Behavioral Research and the Scientific Method

Preview Questions

- Why study research methods and data analysis?
- What rival alternatives are there to the scientific method?
- What is empirical reasoning?
- How is empirical reasoning used in psychological science?
- How do extraempirical factors play a role?
- What does behavioral science encompass?
- What do methodological pluralism and theoretical ecumenism connote?
- How does research go from descriptive to relational to experimental?
- What are the characteristics of good researchers?

Why Study Research Methods and Data Analysis?

Reading, 'riting, and 'rithmetic—the three Rs—have been traditionally viewed as the fundamentals of education that we have been taught since grade school. A fourth R, "researching" (or exploring a question systematically), is now regarded as another crucial skill for any educated person (Hult, 1996). In high school, you were introduced to the steps involved in "researching" a term paper. In college science courses, the term *researching* implies the use of an approach traditionally called the **scientific method**. Embracing all branches of science, the applications of this approach vary from one research discipline to another. Researchers in disciplines as varied as psychology, biomedicine, business, education, communication, economics, sociology, anthropology, physics, biology, and chemistry all use some variation of this approach. However, you may be wondering why you need to know about the scientific method or to study techniques of research and data analysis if becoming a researcher in one of the above-mentioned areas is not your ultimate goal. There are at least five good reasons.

One is that our modern way of life is largely the creation of science and technology, and we enhance our understanding of the full range of this influence by learning about the logic and evidence used by researchers to open up the world to scrutiny and explanation. By analogy, viewing paintings, drawings, and sculpture in a museum becomes more meaningful when we know something about the processes and creative ideas that were involved in producing the works of art. Similarly, when we understand how the conclusions were reached, we can attach more meaning to reading that a scientific poll of likely voters found Candidate X ahead of Candidate Y by 4 percentage points with a 5% margin of error, or that a longitudinal study found that higher quality child care is related to advanced cognitive and language skills, or that an epidemiological study found a significant relationship between health problems and exposure to some environmental substance, or that a randomized trial showed a new drug to be effective in treating depression.

Besides the richer appreciation of the information that science brings to our lives, a second reason for studying research methods is that *not* clearly understanding how researchers cast and address questions sometimes costs us dearly. Doctors, teachers, lawyers, the clergy, and politicians have an influence on our daily lives, and most of us are familiar with how people in these fields go about their work. But few of us seem to have even a vague idea of how researchers create and test hypotheses and theories that enlarge our understanding of the world. As a consequence, people often give credence to misleading recommendations based on bogus data or succumb to claims for cure-all remedies or panaceas for warding off diseases when there is not a shred of reliable evidence of their effectiveness apart from the power of the placebo effect. Studying the conceptual bases of various research methods, and having the opportunity to conduct an empirical study and to analyze and interpret the data under the watchful eye of an experienced guide, will begin to sensitize you to the difference between well-grounded scientific conclusions and dubious claims masquerading as generalizable facts.

A third reason is to acquire information and skills you can use later. For example, once you have mastered the discussions of data analysis in the later chapters of this book, you should be able to raise and address statistical questions of your own choosing. A case in point is news reports about dramatic findings in randomized trials of new drugs. Once you have mastered the analysis of 2×2 frequency tables in Chapter 15, you will be able to use a calculator to estimate the magnitude of the outcome results in the population even when all you have are limited raw ingredients. In Chapter 12, you will learn that the "statistical significance" of a result does not actually tell us the degree to which the phenomenon is present in the population. If you are preparing for a career in health care, it is important that you understand the difference between statistical and practical significance. However, such understanding is not limited just to careers in health care. In business or government and policymaking, or in any other decision-making field, you will be served well by a conceptual understanding of basic methods of data analysis and what they can and cannot tell us, of how it is possible statistically to generalize from the known to the unknown, and of the risk of seeing something that is not there, balanced against the risk of *not* seeing something that *is* there.

A fourth reason for studying (and doing) research is to learn about the limits of particular studies and methods. All studies are limited in some way, but an important question is the degree to which the meaning and generalizability of the results are circumscribed by specific constraints. For example, correlations in epidemiological studies may be partly (or sometimes entirely) due to variables other than those measured, and results in experimental trials of new drugs administered to young, healthy, mobile volunteer subjects may not apply to aged, infirm, hospitalized patients with advanced diseases (Brody, 2002). Both of those limits are explored later in this book. In Chapter 3, we discuss the limits imposed by review boards that are charged with overseeing the ethical responsibilities of scientific researchers. In research with human participants, another limitation occurs when those whose behavior is being studied know they are being observed for some scientific purpose; they may behave quite differently from those who don't know. In Chapter 7, we describe techniques used by researchers to overcome this problem, although these techniques are also limited in some ways. However, despite limitations, behavioral and social researchers have formulated empirically grounded answers to questions about how and why humans feel, think, and behave as they do (see also Box 1.1).

A final reason for studying and doing research is that some students will find this activity so much fun and so absorbing that they may want to make a career of it!

What Rival Alternatives Are There to the Scientific Method?

The scientific method is not the only approach commonly used to make sense of things and give us information. Philosophers, novelists, and theologians seek to give us a coherent picture of our world, but they do not use the scientific method

---

BOX 1.1 The Provisional Nature of Scientific Knowledge

Because even the most carefully designed study is limited in some way, scientific knowledge is in a constant state of development. For many years, philosophers and historians of science have speculated on the pattern of this development. Thomas S. Kuhn (1962, 1977), a physicist turned scientific historian, believed that major advances in science appear as "paradigm shifts" resulting from revolutionary insights. Karl Popper (1963, 1972), an Austrian-born British philosopher of science, compared progress in science with Charles Darwin's theory of "survival of the fittest." Popper's idea was that the fittest scientific formulations withstand falsification in what resembles an evolutionary process of competition and survival. No matter whether the development of science is viewed as revolutionary or evolutionary, on one point all seem to agree: Scientific knowledge is relative and provisional. As one researcher put it, "Scientists know that questions are not settled; rather, they are given provisional answers for which it is contingent upon the imagination of followers to find more illuminating solutions" (Baltimore, 1997, p. 8).

to organize ideas and explain things. What is distinctive about the different approaches used by scientists and nonscientists to formulate a sense of understanding and belief? One scholar who was fascinated by this question was the American philosopher Charles Sanders Peirce (1839–1914). Peirce conceived of the scientific method as being one among four distinctive approaches to explaining things and providing a foundation for strongly held beliefs; he called this process "the fixation of beliefs." Peirce (pronounced "purse") called the other three approaches the *method of tenacity,* the *method of authority,* and the *a priori method.* Each, he argued, is characterized by a particular formulaic way of thinking and behaving (Peirce, 1966).

Peirce thought the **method of tenacity** was the most primitive approach of all, because it is bound by tradition and involves clinging stubbornly (tenaciously) and mindlessly to claims or beliefs because they have been around for a while. People who exhibit this kind of knee-jerk behavior are like the ostrich that buries its head in the sand, he said, because they go through life excluding anything that might challenge or alter their beliefs. Sometimes it seems that a whole society has fallen victim to some outlandish notion merely because it has been around for a long time, and it is not easy to shake fixed beliefs or to open up closed minds (Mitchell, 1985). For example, beginning with the Ptolemaic treatise in the 2nd century A.D., people were convinced that the earth was fixed, immobile, and at the center of the universe. It was one of the ancient astronomer Ptolemy's few misconceptions, but it was a whopper that endured for over a thousand years. It was not until Copernicus's insight that the sun, not the earth, is the center of the universe that the geocentric (i.e., earth-centered) design was challenged, although the Copernican system also left much room for improvement (it neglected to show that the sun is a center of force). Indeed, it was not until the advent of modern astronomy, or what one historian called the "witness of the naked eye" (Boorstein, 1985, p. 305), that the geocentric design was finally swept away by the scientific method.

In our own time, the method of tenacity still has a pernicious hold on many people's convictions and superstitions (see, e.g., Box 1.2). Peirce thought that superstitions and other dogmatic beliefs are like the cadence that concludes a musical phrase in a symphony and provides closure. Sometimes this closure seems to be based on what social psychologists call a "false consensus" or "pluralistic ignorance"; it means that people have a tendency to misperceive, and frequently to overestimate, the extent to which others believe the same thing (Kelley & Thibaut, 1969; Ross, Greene, & House, 1977). Telling themselves that only their beliefs are correct, they dismiss counterarguments as deviant and seek out information that is consistent with their own biases about how the world should be understood (Marks & Miller, 1987; Ross et al., 1977; Sherman, Presson, & Chassin, 1984). Classic research by psychologist Milton Rokeach (1960) resulted in measures of the degree of dogmatism, or closed-mindedness, showing that people who score high on dogmatism are not only highly defensive about their beliefs but less likely to act on the plausible merits of information independent of their subjective impression of the source (Powell, 1962).

BOX 1.2 Flying Saucers, Big Foot, and Other Odd Beliefs

Myth, folklore, and superstition illustrate the method of tenacity's powerful hold on beliefs that can endure for centuries. The noted Swiss psychiatrist and psychologist Carl G. Jung (1910, 1959)—one of Sigmund Freud's students—theorized about the persistence of stories of "flying saucers," unidentified flying objects (UFOs) piloted by extraterrestrials. This stubborn myth, he argued, is a projection of people's fears and uncertainties about the world situation and their wish for a redeeming supernatural force. Interestingly, the UFO story usually takes one of two forms: It is said either that benevolent superior beings from another planet have come to save humanity (as represented in the 1951 movie *The Day the Earth Stood Still*), or that menacing creatures threaten humanity and this threat will unify people of diverse ideologies to make a stand against a common foe (represented in the 1996 movie *Independence Day*). There are also people who still insist that the earth is flat, that sunrise and sunset are optical illusions, and that the 1969 moon landing was an elaborate hoax staged in a hangar in Arizona (D. Martin, 2001). In a fascinating case, it was revealed a few years ago that a prankster named Ray L. Wallace had created the modern myth of Bigfoot (or Sasquatch), the name for the giant, hairy, upright biped rumored to be living in the woods of the Pacific Northwest. After Wallace's death in 2002, his family displayed the carved wooden feet that he had used to stamp a track of oversized footprints. Despite all evidence to the contrary, Bigfoot defenders still insist that the creature exists (Egan, 2003).

The **method of authority** was Peirce's term for the presumption that something is true because someone in a position of authority says it is. Peirce saw that blind obedience to authority is similar in some ways to the method of tenacity (both imply conformity), but he thought the method of authority superior in some ways, although flawed. To illustrate the negative side, he described the violence that resulted when ordinary people obeyed the word of authority to cruelly punish those accused of witchcraft. Unimaginable atrocities committed in the Holocaust during World War II and "ethnic-cleansing" carnage occurring even today are instances of the heights of cruelty that can be reached in the name of a malevolent authority. Other present-day examples on the negative side include unscrupulous people who pose as authorities, preying on human weakness by using fakery. Think of medical quacks, food faddists, faith healers, TV psychics, cult leaders, and eccentric sexual theorists (M. Gardner, 1957; Shermer, 1997). The authority of these fakers and hucksters is in the eyes of their victims, however, so that it behooves the buyer to beware.

Peirce thought the method of authority was at least a small improvement on the method of tenacity because civilized society would cease to exist without people's willingness to obey just laws and to carry out reasonable orders. Researchers are subject to the benevolent authority of an ever-evolving social contract between science and society concerning the rights of research participants and the privileges granted to researchers (Rosnow, 1997). Other examples on the positive side are the astute physician who prescribes a drug or regimen to cure an illness, the skilled electrician who advises the replacement of wiring that is about to burn out, and the expert mechanic who warns that the brakes on a car are worn and need replacing. We depend on their honesty and the authority of their expertise. On the other hand, not everyone perceives the same source as credible, and thus some people are quite willing to accept claims that others reject as preposterous. One writer discussed consumers who reject the medical establishment but often unquestionably accept the authority of someone without the slightest medical expertise or qualification, who, in their minds, makes a "credible" case for the medicinal value of a health supplement that was never critically tested (R. Walker, 2006).

Even if we know very little about medicine, wiring, or brakes, we can use a third strategy of Peirce's to ask questions to help us better understand the authoritative recommendations. The defining characteristic of this third strategy—the **a priori method**—is that people rely primarily on their individual powers of reason and logic to make sense of the world and to explain it to others. This strategy, Peirce (1966) argued, is "far more intellectual and respectable" than the previous two (p. 106); it has proved itself quite robust in the hands of mathematicians and philosophers. In fact, we use the a priori method all the time. When we balance our checkbooks, ruminate on what career path to take, or figure out the amount of a tip in a restaurant, we bring reason and logic into play. Thinking rationally and logically is an effective defense against hoaxes and hucksters who depend on human gullibility. We can approach dubious claims with a questioning mind that, as one psychologist put it, "resists being overly impressed" (Gilovich, 1991, p. 187). Similarly, when people pass on malicious gossip, we can ask where they heard it and how they know it is true. The person who tells it to us may be dependable, but we may question the objectivity of the person who originated it.

It is hard to find fault with the a priori method, but Peirce cautioned that it is constrained by the limits of pure reason. Suppose you conclude that A causes B, and I disagree. Do we just have to let it go at that? What we need, Peirce said, is a way of drawing on nature to help us resolve our dispute. This is the role of the scientific method, to provide a framework for drawing on independent realities to evaluate claims rather than to depend only on tradition, authority, or armchair reasoning. As a noted researcher once said, we use the scientific method in psychology to help us sort out what we know about human nature from what we only think we know (Milgram, 1977). The scientific method depends heavily on the use of empirical research (**empirical** means "based on observation"). The term *scientific method* is actually a misnomer, however, because it is not synonymous with just a single, fixed empirical method; instead, it embraces a great many procedures and empirical techniques. In particular, it can be distinguished by what we define next as *empirical reasoning*.

What Is Empirical Reasoning?

By **empirical reasoning**, we mean a combination of careful logic, organized observation, and measurement that is open to scrutiny by others. One scientist used the following analogy to describe how this idealized process works: Suppose someone is trying to unlock a door with a set of previously untried keys. The person reasons, "If this key fits the lock, then the lock will spring when I turn the key" (Conant, 1957, p. xii). Similarly, the scientist has a choice of "keys" in the form of hunches and empirical techniques, logically decides on one, and then says, "Let's try it." The same "key" is available to other researchers with the knowledge, resources, and skill to use it to open up the world for scrutiny and measurement. In theory, it is this dependence on accessible logic, observation, and measurement (i.e., on empirical reasoning) that unifies research scientists, no matter their specialized field or the focus of their research.

The use of empirical reasoning goes back centuries (see Box 1.3). If you took a physics course in high school, you will recall the story of how Galileo, in the 16th century, reasoned that dropping two objects of different weights from the Leaning Tower of Pisa would prove Aristotle was wrong when he insisted that heavier objects fall faster than lighter ones. (When American astronauts landed on the moon, they successfully conducted an experiment showing that Galileo's principle worked on the moon.) Another early example of empirical reasoning is Newton's use of a prism to show that white light is a combination of different colors

BOX 1.3 Empirical Reasoning in Ancient Times

An early illustration of empirical reasoning was described in a work by Athenaeus of Naucratis (in Egypt), a 2nd-century Greek philosopher (Yonge, 1854). Athenaeus had been convinced by the governor of Egypt that citron ingested before any kind of food was an antidote for "the evil effects from poison" (p. 141). It seems the governor had condemned some robbers to being given to wild beasts and bitten by asps. On their way to the theater where the execution was to be carried out, they passed a woman who was selling fruit and, taking pity on them, gave them citron to eat. When they were later bitten by the beasts and asps, they suffered no injury. When told about the episode in the marketplace, the governor reasoned that it must have been the citron that had saved their lives. He ordered the sentence to be carried again the next day, but that citron be given to some of the prisoners before they were bitten. Those who ate the citron survived when they were bitten, but the others perished immediately. According to Athenaeus, this grotesque experiment was replicated several times and included various ways of preparing the citron.

(not a pure form of light, as Aristotle had claimed), and that each color remains pure when refracted through a second prism. If you have visited a science museum, you may have seen a perpetually swinging iron ball suspended from a wire, with a stylus on the ball tracing a slightly different clockwise pattern in the sand beneath it with each revolution. This construction goes back to the mid-19th century and the idea of a French scientist, Jean-Bernard-Léon Foucault, who wanted to show convincingly that the earth revolves on its axis. (Incidentally, in the Southern Hemisphere the rotation of Foucault's pendulum is counterclockwise, and on the equator, it does not move at all.)

How Is Empirical Reasoning Used in Psychological Science?

Empirical reasoning entered into the scientific study of behavior at the end of the 19th century when the creative advances inspired by the applications of the scientific method in physics and biology led to the development of psychology as a distinct science. In Leipzig, Germany, Wilhelm Wundt (1832–1920), trained in medicine and experimental physiology, built the first formal experimental laboratory for studying psychological behavior. Around the same time, William James (1843–1910), who had a background in philosophy and physiology, announced a graduate course in psychology at Harvard University in which the students participated in experiments that he arranged. Empirical reasoning was not practiced only in the laboratory or only experimentally. In Britain, Sir Francis Galton (1822–1911) demonstrated its application to questions that had been previously thought to lie completely outside science (Forrest, 1974).

In one of his many fascinating studies, Galton explored empirical grounds for the belief that prayers are answered. In England, the health and longevity of the royal family were prayed for weekly or monthly nationwide. Galton asked: Do members of royal families live longer than individuals of humbler birth? In 1872, in an article entitled "Statistical Inquiries Into the Efficacy of Prayer," published by the *Fortnightly Review,* Galton reported that, of 97 members of royal families, the mean age attained by males had been 64.04 years. Compared to 945 members of the clergy, who had lived to a mean age of 69.49; 294 lawyers who had lived to 68.14; 244 doctors who had lived to 67.31; 366 officers in the Royal Navy who had lived to 68.40; 569 officers of the Army who had lived to 67.07; and 1,632 "gentry" who had lived to 70.22, members of royal families had fared worse than expected based on the many prayers on their behalf (Medawar, 1969, p. 4). Galton could not, of course, control for any differences in the sincerity of all those prayers, nor did he reject the idea that religious faith can have a powerful effect in other ways. Prayer, he observed, may strengthen people's resolution to face hardships and bring serenity in distress (Medawar, 1969, p. 5), although for some it may also be a source of stress or confusion (cf. Exline, 2002; Myers, 2000; Pargament, 2002).

Since the time of Wundt, James, and Galton, there has been phenomenal growth in the application of empirical reasoning to questions about human nature, cognition, perception, and behavior. Open any introductory psychology text, and you will find hundreds of contemporary and classic examples, and there are also hundreds of research journals in the behavioral sciences that regularly publish reams of empirical studies. Throughout this text we mention examples of classic and contemporary applications. To begin, let us look at two fascinating experiments: one by Stephen J. Ceci and his coworkers at Cornell University in developmental psychology, the second by Solomon Asch in social psychology. Each study illustrates the application of empirical reasoning in a context of tightly controlled observation and measurement. Each was also seminal in expanding our theoretical understanding of human suggestibility as well as in setting a course for follow-up studies by other researchers. Each also used a form of deception, a topic explored in depth in Chapter 3.

Ceci and his colleagues focused on the accuracy of children's eyewitness testimony. They designed an experiment in which a character named "Sam Stone" was described to 3- to 6-year-olds as someone who was very clumsy and broke things (Ceci & Bruck, 1993, 1995; White, Leichtman, & Ceci, 1997). A person identified as Sam Stone visited the children's nursery school, where he chatted briefly with them during a storytelling session, but he did not behave clumsily or break anything. The next day, the children were shown a ripped book and a soiled teddy bear and were asked if they knew how the objects had been damaged. Over the course of the next 10 weeks, the children were reinterviewed. Each time, the interviewer planted stereotypical information about Sam Stone, such as "I wonder whether Sam Stone was wearing long pants or short pants when he ripped the book?" or "I wonder if Sam Stone got the teddy bear dirty on purpose or by accident?" The result of this manipulation was that the planted stereotype of Sam Stone carried over into the children's eyewitness reports. When asked, 72% of the 3- to 4-year-olds said that Sam Stone had ruined either the book or the teddy bear, and 45% of these children claimed that they had actually seen him do it (and they embellished their accounts with other details). The researchers used a comparison (*control*) group against which to assess the effect of their experimental manipulation. Children in the control group underwent the suggestive interviews, but they received no planted stereotypical information about Sam Stone. Ceci's finding was that the children in the control group made fewer false claims than the children in whom the stereotype had been planted.

Asch (1952) was interested in the degree to which people with normal intelligence will resist mindlessly conforming to a consensus view when faced with an objective reality that shows the consensus view to be false. In this famous experiment, a subject arrived at the psychology lab along with several other participants, who were actually accomplices of the experimenter. Seated together at the same table, all of the participants were told by the experimenter that they would be asked to make judgments about the length of several lines. Each person was to judge which of three lines was closest in length to a standard line. The accomplices always stated their opinions first, after which the subject expressed an opinion. The accomplices, instructed by the experimenter to act in collusion, sometimes gave obviously incorrect opinions, but they were unanimous. A third of the subjects, Asch found, gave the same opinion as the accomplices. When interviewed later, these subjects gave different reasons for yielding to the pressure exerted by the incorrect majority: (a) unawareness of being incorrect; (b) uneasiness about their own perceptions; and (c) wanting to appear the same as the majority. The predominant response of all the subjects, however, was to respond with what was objectively true rather than to go along with the false majority. The theoretical and moral implications of this classic study continue to be amplified in social psychology (Hodges & Geyer, 2006).

How Do Extraempirical Factors Play a Role?

In Asch's experiment, the idea was to see whether people would depend on their own independent observations and resist a majority consensus that was clearly false. The reliance of the scientific method on empirical data and logical reasoning also emphasizes the *primary* role of independent observation to ascertain what is true, but extraempirical factors play a role in science just as they do in everyday life. One reason is that universal laws require a leap of faith because of the limitations of human observation. As an illustration, one of the most powerful laws of science is Newton's first law of motion, which asserts that a body not acted on by any force will continue in a state of rest or, if the body is moving, remain in uniform motion in a straight line forever. Belief in this law is based partly on a leap of faith, however, because obviously no scientist can claim to have *observed* "a body not acted on by any force" (e.g., friction or gravity), much less *observed* a body moving "in a straight line forever." Empirical reasoning thus concedes that there are aspects of reality that are beyond the bounds of our ability to observe them, but this does not abrogate the ideal of generating far-reaching theories and laws based on what we *can* observe.

Philosophers of science have argued that one of several extraempirical factors in science is a sense of beauty or elegance, described as the **aesthetic aspect of science** (Chandrasekhar, 1987; Garfield, 1989a, 1989b; Gombrich, 1963; Hineline, 2005; Nisbet, 1976; Wechler, 1978). For example, it is not uncommon to hear a scientist say that some study or finding or theory is "beautiful." A famous case was Albert Einstein's theory of general relativity, which an eminent mathematician (Paul Dirac) said was so beautiful that it *had* to be true (Kragh, 2002). As another example, several years ago, a science magazine invited readers to nominate the *most beautiful experiments in physics*. The top 10 included Galileo's Tower of Pisa hypothetical experiment, Newton's prism experiment, and Foucault's pendulum. The respondents also offered a range of definitions of beauty in science, including the "economy" of the procedure and what they called "deep play" (meaning that the experiment was incredibly absorbing and engaging). The top 10 experiments were thought to epitomize beauty in the classical sense, in that the logic and simplicity of the apparatus or analysis in each case seemed "as inevitable and pure as the lines of a Greek monument" (G. Johnson, 2002, p. F3).

Another extraempirical factor that has been discussed is frequently called *visualization,* but we prefer a more general term **perceptibility**, by which we mean that scientists often use images in the form of analogies and metaphors to explain the operation of complex phenomena. Analogies and metaphors, in which we try to imagine one thing in terms of another, offer a way of trying to make complex ideas more digestible (an analogy!) without, as one writer put it, "slipping into trivia and meaninglessness" (Perloff, 2006, p. 315). Much has been written about the use of analogies and metaphors not only in science but also in everyday life (Barker, 1996; Billow, 1977; Gentner, Holyoak, & Kokinov, 2001; Gentner & Markman, 1997; Gigerenzer, 1991; Holyoak & Thagard, 1997; Kolodner, 1997; Lakoff & Johnson, 1980; Leary, 1990; A. I. Miller, 1986, 1996; Oppenheimer, 1956; Randhawa & Coffman, 1978; Weiner, 1991). "Her life was an uphill climb" and "He is between a rock and a hard place" are everyday examples of this usage. In physics, a famous case occurred when the quantum theorists first tried to convince colleagues that, given a great many atoms, all capable of certain definite changes, the proportion of atoms undergoing each change could be estimated, but not the specific changes that any given atoms would undergo. Einstein's pungent metaphor to express his visceral dislike of that theory was that God "does not play dice with the world" (Clark, 1971; Jammer, 1966). What makes this imagery so affecting is that we perceive in our "mind's eye" what Einstein meant (see also Bauer & Johnson-Laird, 1993; Johnson-Laird, 1983; Johnson-Laird & Byrne, 1991; Robin, 1993).

Another extraempirical factor is the **rhetoric of justification** that is used to build a case in support of some conclusion. As Yale psychologist William J. McGuire (2006) put it, "Because researchers are verbal people, they usually express their knowledge in the verbal modality, oral or written" (p. 356). Indeed, every specialized field has its own rhetoric of justification (A. G. Gross, 1990; Pera & Shea, 1991): Lawyers sound like lawyers, philosophers like philosophers, doctors like doctors, scientists like scientists, and so on. To understand what people in different fields are saying, we must understand the terms and concepts they are using. For example, McGuire (2006) went on to say, "When the verbalization is formally scientific (rather than colloquial), it typically takes the form of a hypothesis (proposition, statement) expressing the relation among the two or more variables, usually either a main-effect, interactional, or mediating relation" (p. 356). What are a *hypothesis,* a *main-effect* relation, an *interactional* relation, and a *mediating* relation, and what do behavioral and social researchers mean when they say they have done *debriefing of subjects* or have done a *participant observation study* or used *back translation,* or that *intercoder reliability* was a particular value? We define these and many other specialized terms throughout this book.

Another aspect of this rhetoric is that professional researchers are expected to publish their empirical results in *peer-reviewed journals* (i.e., before the articles are actually accepted for publication, they undergo reviews by experts in the field). In Appendix A, you will find a sample report that is structured in the way that many research reports are in psychology and other areas that have adopted the "APA style" (the style recommended in the latest edition of the *Publication Manual of the American Psychological Association*). This structure, which evolved over many years, currently consists of an abstract (or summary), an introduction, a method section, a results section, a discussion section, and a list of the references cited in the report. The purpose of having a standardized organization is that it enables busy researchers to read research articles more easily (because they conform to a similar structure) and it encourages authors to organize their thoughts in a systematic way as they report their research to others.

What Does Behavioral Science Encompass?

The examples we have mentioned cover a range of disciplines, including psychology, physics, and astronomy. However, this book is not just a trip into the realm of science in general; it is a journey into the domain of behavioral science in particular. **Behavior** is what you do and how you act; **behavioral science** is an umbrella term that covers cognitive and emotional functioning as well as social behavior (social science) and behavioral economics. As the term is defined in this broad way, the range of interests of behavioral scientists includes the study of early primitive humans, and of humans as political animals, financial animals, social animals, talking animals, and logicians. These aspects of human nature are the concern of psychologists (e.g., clinical, cognitive, counseling, developmental, educational, experimental, organizational, personality, and social), mass communication researchers, sociologists, cultural anthropologists, behavioral economists, psycholinguists, behavioral biologists, neuroscientists, and even some statisticians. The objective in all these branches of behavioral and social science is the same: to describe and explain how and why humans think, feel, and behave as they do (Kimble, 1989).

For many purposes, it may not matter much whether we can distinguish among the various branches, but there are differences nonetheless. In experimental psychology, researchers often study human experiences in controlled laboratory settings. Social and organizational psychologists, particularly those trained in a psychology graduate program, frequently conduct experiments, but they can be performed either in a field environment or a lab setting. By contrast, sociologists are more likely to perform survey studies in the field. Nonetheless, behavioral and social scientists borrow from one another's storehouse of methods: Sociologists and some economists also conduct experiments, and some psychologists perform survey research. Though these researchers teach in different departments in colleges and universities, the boundary lines in behavioral and social science are by no means rigid. As one illustration, there is a project called TESS (Time-Sharing Experiments for the Social Sciences, funded by the National Science Foundation), which allows experimenters in the social sciences to compete for the opportunity to replicate their lab findings in large populations by using telephone and Internet-based survey interviews.

Some research questions seem especially suitable to experimental investigation in the lab and also have real-life applications. For example, in psychophysics (the study of the relationship between physical stimuli and our human experience of them), experimenters working in the lab discovered many years ago that the amount by which stimulus intensity must be increased to produce a just-noticeable change in the perception of the stimulus is a constant proportion of the intensity of the original stimulus. Following this line of empirical investigation, they showed that it is possible to write a mathematical statement of the theoretical relationship between the intensity of a stimulus and the intensity of a sensation, a statement that can then be applied to a range of real-life situations. If, say, your room is lighted by a 100-watt bulb, and if 15 watts of light must be added before you can just detect a difference in the amount of the light, then in a room with a 50-watt bulb, 7.5 watts must be added to make the difference detectable.

What Do Methodological Pluralism and Theoretical Ecumenism Connote?

The philosopher Hans Reichenbach noted how scientists, inspired by different ideas and often using different techniques, amass "concatenations of evidence" to explain things. This description applies as well to behavioral and social scientists. In many areas, research has evolved since the early 1970s to embrace what we describe as *methodological pluralism and theoretical ecumenism* (Jaeger & Rosnow, 1988; Rosnow, 1981, 1986; cf. Houts, Cook, & Shadish, 1986). By **methodological pluralism**, we mean that behavioral scientists frequently use more than one method to zero in on phenomena of interest, on the assumption that any single method is limited in some ways. Using multiple methods is a way of attempting to have one method's strengths compensate for another's limitations. The TESS project noted above is an example, in that it allows researchers to use large populations, thereby compensating for the small, highly select samples originally used in their lab experiments. By **theoretical ecumenism**, we mean there is often more than one "right way" to view the causes of behavior, because human nature is quite complex and behavior may be motivated by more than one cause or the pursuit of more than one objective. As scientists in different fields strive to develop a more complete and integrated picture of human behavior, we have begun to see more interdisciplinary research. Sometimes a whole new field is created. Familiar examples include behavioral medicine, psycholinguistics, and, perhaps most broadly, cognitive neuroscience.

Another prime example recently has been the application of psychological principles to the understanding of economic behavior. Psychologists Daniel Kahneman (who was awarded a Nobel Prize in economics in 2002) and his coworker for many years, the late Amos Tversky, did seminal research on how people commonly use information-processing rules of thumb (called *cognitive heuristics*) to quickly make judgments that not only defy logic but are often wrong (Kahneman & Tversky, 1973; Tversky & Kahneman, 1974). Later on in this book (Chapter 11), we refer to risk judgments, which show that laypeople frequently think things are more risky or less risky than experts do (Kahneman, Slovic, & Tversky, 1982). When people frame an event in their minds, they frequently make predictions and then behave in ways that are generally consistent with their expectations, such as overestimating the likelihood of a particular economic outcome merely because instances of it are salient at that moment. Previously, we mentioned the false consensus effect (Ross et al., 1977), which is another example of a cognitive heuristic (in this case, overestimating the extent to which others share your beliefs). Once people behave in accordance with their predictions, their predictions become what the sociologist Robert Merton (1948, 1968) called a *self-fulfilling prophecy* (we will refer to this term again). Thus, we see how hybrid branches of behavioral science grow creatively from new interdisciplinary ventures.

Other examples of the range of methodological pluralism in psychology were mentioned previously, including Galton's use of actuarial data to study the efficacy of prayer, Ceci et al.'s use of the "Sam Stone" manipulation to study children's eyewitness testimony, and Asch's laboratory simulation of conformity. But even a cursory glance at any of the hundreds of different journals in psychology will reveal that there are countless techniques of empirical inquiry. To create a general overview, we will lump together the orientations of behavioral and social research into three general types: descriptive, relational, and experimental. As you become better acquainted with the literature in your area of interest, you will see that the research usually involves more than one line of attack, although a given study can often be described as primarily one of these three in terms of its main orientation. Frequently, as illustrated next, the progression of empirical reasoning and research is from descriptive to relational to experimental.

How Does Research Go From Descriptive to Relational to Experimental?

In **descriptive research**, the goal of the investigation is the careful mapping out of a situation or a set of events, that is, a description of what is happening behaviorally. Causal explanations are not of direct concern except perhaps speculatively. For example, if we are interested in the study of children's failure in school, we might spend a good deal of time measuring and evaluating the classroom behavior of children who are doing poorly. We would then describe as carefully as possible what we have observed. Our careful observation of failing students might lead to some revision of traditional concepts of classroom failure, to suggestions about factors that contribute to the development of failure, and perhaps to speculative ideas for the remediation of failure.

This descriptive orientation is often considered a necessary first step in the development of a program of research because it establishes the foundation of any future undertaking. But it is rarely regarded as sufficient, because sooner or later someone will want to know *why* something happens or *how* what happens is related to other events. If our interest is in children's classroom failure, we are not likely to be satisfied for very long with even the most careful description of that failure. We will want to know the antecedents of the failure and the outcomes of procedures designed to reduce it. Even if we were not motivated directly by the practical implications of knowing the causes and cures of failure, we would believe our understanding to be considerably improved if we knew the conditions that increase and decrease its likelihood. To learn about the increase or decrease of failure, or any other behavior, we must focus on at least two variables at the same time. That is, we must make two sets of observations and assess the degree of relationship between the two sets.

At this point, the second broad type of approach, **relational research**, begins. Research is relational (or **correlational**) when two or more variables or conditions are measured and their degree of relationship to each other is estimated. As we continue with the classroom example, let us suppose we noted that the teachers of many of the failing students rarely looked at or addressed the students and seldom exposed them to new academic information. At this stage, we may have an impression about the relation between learning failure and teaching behavior. Such impressions are a frequent, and often valuable, by-product of descriptive research. If they are to be taken seriously, however, they cannot be left at the impressionistic level for very long.

Because we want to find out whether the researcher's impressions are accurate, we now arrange a series of coordinated observations on a sample of students who effectively represent the *target population* (i.e., the students to whom we would like to generalize our findings). We note whether or not each student in the sample has been learning anything or to what degree the student has been learning; we also note to what degree the teacher has been exposing the student to the material to be learned. From these coordinated observations, we should be able to make a quantitative statement concerning the relationship (or *degree of correlation*) between the amount of the student's exposure to the material to be learned and the amount of this material the student has in fact learned. We will then indicate not just (a) whether "X and Y are significantly related" (i.e., whether this nonzero relationship is unlikely to have occurred by chance alone), but also (b) the pattern of the relationship (e.g., linear or nonlinear) and (c) the strength of the relationship in terms of the size of the correlation between X and Y. (Later in this book, we will illustrate in a more precise way what these statistical terms mean.)

To carry the example into the third general approach, suppose that the students exposed to less information were also those who tended to learn less. The discovery of this relationship might tempt us to conclude that children learn less because they are taught less. Such an **ad hoc hypothesis** (a conjecture or supposition developed on the spot "for this" special result), although plausible, is not warranted by the relationship reported. It may be that teachers teach less to those they know to be less able to learn; that is, differences in teaching behavior may be a result of the students' learning as much as a determinant of that learning. To pursue this idea, we will need to make further observations that will allow us to infer whether differences in the information presented to the students, apart from any individual differences among them, affect their learning. We can best answer such questions by manipulating the conditions that we think are responsible for the effect. In other words, we introduce some change into the situation, or we interrupt or terminate the situation in order to identify causes.

This process is what is generally meant by the term **experimental research**, the objective of which is the identification of causes (i.e., what leads to what). Relational research only rarely provides such information, and then only under very special conditions. The difference between the degree of focus on a causal explanation in relational and experimental research can be expressed in the difference between the statements "X is *related* to Y" (relational research) and "X is *responsible* for Y"

BOX 1.4   Random Sampling and Random Assignment

Two important concepts that students new to research methods may find confusing are *random sampling* and *random assignment*. In the relational example, we described arranging for a series of observations on a sample of students who represented the target population. To increase the likelihood that the sample will be representative of the population, we use a **random sampling** procedure (the procedure used by professional survey researchers) to select the sample. In the experimental example just discussed, we described dividing a sample of students into two groups by tossing a coin to decide which condition each student would be assigned to. An unbiased randomizing procedure (a coin toss, for example) to allocate subjects to different conditions is called **random assignment** and is characteristic of *randomized experiments* (or *randomized trials,* the term that is commonly used to describe randomized experiments with new drugs in biomedical research). We will have more to say about these concepts and terms later in this book.

(experimental research). In our example, teaching is X and learning is Y. Our experiment will be designed to reveal the effects of teaching on student learning. We will select a sample of youngsters and, by tossing a coin, or by some other unbiased method of selection, randomly assign them to two groups (see Box 1.4). The teachers will give more information to one of these groups (the experimental group) and will give the other group (the control group) less information. We can then assess whether the experimental group surpassed the control group in learning achievement. If we find this to be true, we can say that giving the experimental group more information was *responsible* for the outcome.

There might still be a question of what it was about the better procedure that led to the improvement. Indeed, it is characteristic of research that, when a new procedure is shown to be effective, many questions arise about what elements of the procedure are producing the benefits. In the case of increased teaching, we may wonder whether the improvement was due to (a) the nature of the additional material; (b) the teacher's increased attention to the student while presenting the additional material; (c) any accompanying increases in eye contact, smiles, or warmth; or (d) other possible correlates of increased teaching behavior. These alternatives have been empirically investigated, and it has been observed that the amount of new material teachers present to their students is sometimes predictable not so much by the student's learning ability as by the teachers' beliefs or expectations about their students' learning ability. In other words, teachers' expectations about their students' performance sometimes becomes a self-fulfilling prophecy, in which teachers' expectations become responsible for their students' performance (Babad, 1993; Raudenbush, 1984; R. Rosenthal, 1966, 1976, 1985, 1991; R. Rosenthal & Jacobson, 1968; R. Rosenthal & Rubin, 1978).

As a final illustration of the distinction between descriptive, relational, and experimental research, Table 1.1 shows empirically grounded conclusions in psycholinguistics, the psychology of rumor, and research on a methodological issue. As you study these conclusions, you will see that descriptive research tells us

---

Table 1.1 Descriptive, Relational, and Experimental Conclusions in Three Research Areas

---

Psycholinguistics

Descriptive: When a 2-year-old child listens to a message spoken by his or her mother and is asked to repeat it, the child typically repeats only part of the message (R. Brown, 1965).
Relational: On the average, frequently used words tend to be shorter than infrequently used words; this statement is called *Zipf's law* (G. A. Miller & Newman, 1958; Zipf, 1935, 1949).
Experimental: When interfering background noise is present, a speaker tends to use more words and fewer abbreviations than when there is no interfering background noise (Heise & Miller, 1951).

Psychology of Rumor

Descriptive: In rumor chat groups on the Internet, the participants tend to adopt changing roles, described as the skeptical disbeliever, the positivist, the apprehensive believer, the curious, the anxious, the prudent initiator, and the investigator (Bordia & Rosnow, 1998). In network studies of rumors in organizations, it has been found that there are usually a few well-connected opinion leaders or liaisons who spread rumors (Hellweg, 1987).
Relational: In some circumstances, rumors forecasting unpleasant consequences are passed to others with greater frequency than rumors forecasting pleasant consequences (Rosnow, Esposito, & Gibney, 1987; C. J. Walker & Blaine, 1991).
Experimental: Children 3–5 years old who overheard a rumor were as likely to report that they had experienced the rumored, but not experienced, event as were children who actually experienced it (Principe, Kanaya, Ceci, & Singh, 2006).

Methodological Research

Descriptive: It has been estimated that perhaps 80% of psychological research on normal adults has used college and university students as research participants (Higbee & Wells, 1972; J. Jung, 1969; McNemar, 1946; Schultz, 1969; Sears, 1986; Sieber & Saks, 1989; Smart, 1966).
Relational: People who volunteer to participate in behavioral and social research are usually higher than nonvolunteers in education, social class, intelligence, and the need for social approval (Rosenthal & Rosnow, 1975b; Rosnow & Rosenthal, 1997).
Experimental: Research participants made to experience a conflict between "looking good" and cooperating with the experimenter are likely to try to look good, whereas participants not made to experience such a conflict are likely to help the experimenter (Rosnow, Goodstadt, Suls, & Gitter, 1973; Sigall, Aronson, & Van Hoose, 1970).

how things are; relational research tells us *how things are in relation to other things;* and experimental research tells us *how things are and how they got to be that way.*

What Are the Characteristics of Good Researchers?

Some people are better at what they do than others, whether students, teachers, spouses, parents, workers, and so on. This is no less true of researchers, many of whom excel in what they do. Judith A. Hall (1984), a Northeastern University psychology professor, observed that many textbooks are filled with guidelines for good research but rarely mention what makes a good researcher. We will end this chapter by borrowing her list and adding a little to it, because these characteristics should also serve you well in everyday life:

1. *Enthusiasm.* Being enthusiastic about what you do is contagious and self-motivating, whereas being apathetic can also sap the passion and zeal of everyone around you. This is also true in science. As a wise researcher, Edward C. Tolman (1959), astutely commented, "In the end, the only sure criterion is to have fun" (p. 152). He did not mean that the good researcher views science as just fun and games without any ethical or societal implications or consequences. What he meant was that for researchers who excel in what they do, choosing a topic, doing research, and analyzing and reporting the results are as absorbing and as much fun as any game that requires skill and concentration and that fills a person with enthusiasm.

2. *Open-mindedness.* It is also more satisfying to be with someone who is open-minded, listens to what you have to say, and, when responding, is reasonable rather than dogmatic or a know-it-all. The good researcher is open-minded because it is by experiencing the world with a keen, attentive, inquisitive, and open mind that scientists come to perceive the world in novel ways. Another characteristic of an open mind is the ability to learn from one's mistakes and from the sensible advice and keen insights of others.

3. *Common sense.* Common sense is a prized characteristic in every aspect of life. There is an old story about "the drunkard's search": A drunkard lost his house key and began searching for it under a street lamp although he had dropped the key some distance away. Asked why he didn't look where he had dropped it, he answered, "There is more light here." Much effort is lost when researchers fail to use common sense and instead look in a convenient place, rather than in the most likely place (the place where common sense would lead them), for the answers to their questions. Similarly, Hall (1984) mentioned that many students ask only whether their research plan is technically correct, not whether it makes good sense.

4. *Role-taking ability.* The ability to see things from others' viewpoints is crucial to success in a wide variety of situations. In behavioral and social research, it means being able to see your study from the viewpoint of the participants. It

also means seeing it from the viewpoint of the person who will evaluate it (in this case, the instructor who will grade it). For students who plan to present their results in a poster, role-taking ability means seeing it from the vantage point of those who will view the poster.

5. *Creativity and inventiveness.* The good researcher is creative and inventive, that is, adept at finding solutions to problems of financial resources, equipment, recruitment, research space, and scheduling participants. The good researcher responds appropriately in emergencies and, of course, raises interesting questions.

6. *Confidence in one's own judgment.* Since there is seldom only one right way to do things, as Hall (1984) also noted, "There is no inherent reason why you must do as others in a research tradition have done" (p. v). As another writer put it, "You have to believe that by the simple application of your own mind to the facts of experience, you can discover the truth—a little part of it anyway" (Regis, 1987, p. 209).

7. *Ability to communicate.* Given the provisional nature of scientific truths (Box 1.1), the end of one study may very well be the starting point for another study. Therefore, it is essential to be able to communicate clearly so that one's findings will be plain to others (Barrass, 1978). As Hall (1984) commented, "Research is not just the doing, it's the telling. If no one knows about your study, or if they can't figure out or remember your results, then you might as well never have done it" (p. vi).

8. *Care about details.* Being careful about details is another characteristic that can serve us well, because others know they can have confidence in our conscientiousness, thoroughness, and the accuracy of our work. The good researcher is always careful about details, whether preparing a poster for a meeting, a paper for a course, or an article for a scientific journal. It means keeping complete records, carefully organizing the data, copying and adding numbers correctly, stating facts accurately, and proofreading patiently.

9. *Integrity and honest scholarship.* Every good researcher knows that integrity and honesty are paramount. Because "rigged" experiments or the presentation of faked results undermines the basic respect for the literature on which the advancement of science depends, either one is devastating to science. It is the duty of all scientists to guard against dishonesty, and this responsibility is taken very seriously (e.g., American Association for the Advancement of Science, 1988; American Psychological Association, 1973, 1982; Bridgstock, 1982; Koshland, 1988; R. Rosenthal, 1994b). (As you think about ethical problems in research, you are also forced to confront your own moral presuppositions.)

Summary of Ideas

1. Five reasons for studying research methods are (a) to provide a richer appreciation of the information that science and technology bring to modern life; (b) to avoid falling prey to hucksters and imposters whose showy claims are counterfeit; (c) to learn information and skills that are transferable beyond the research setting; (d) to learn that scientific knowledge is relative and provisional (Box 1.1); and (f) to consider research as a career.

2. Peirce's four methods for the "fixation of belief" (the formation of strong beliefs) are (a) the *method of tenacity* (stubbornly and mindlessly clinging to myth, folklore, and superstition, like believing in UFOs or the geocentric design; Box 1.2); (b) the *method of authority* (complying with the word of authority, like Peirce's witchcraft example on the negative side or, on the positive side, obeying reasonable laws that are the basis of civilized society); (c) the *a priori method* (the use of reason and logic to make sense of things and debunk hoaxes); and (d) the *scientific method*.

3. The *scientific method* is a misnomer, in that it is not a single, fixed method but is an approach that depends heavily on *empirical reasoning* (a combination of logic and the use of careful observation and measurement that is accessible to other researchers, e.g., Galton's study of prayer, Ceci's experimental study of children's eyewitness testimony, Asch's use of accomplices in his experimental study of whether a person will conform with a false consensus, and the early example in Box 1.3).

4. One illustration of how empirical methods are limited is that universal laws are based partly on a leap of faith because we simply cannot observe everything (e.g., that objects in motion will stay in motion forever).

5. Three extraempirical factors are (a) the beauty or elegance (the *aesthetic aspect*) of science (e.g., Einstein's general theory of relativity); (b) visualizations in the form of analogies and metaphors to make complex ideas more digestible; and (c) the informative and persuasive language (the *rhetoric of justification*) of science, which takes the form of written reports that conform to an accepted basic structure (illustrated in Appendix A).

6. *Behavioral science* comprises a variety of different fields, which enlist the use of multiple methods and theories (called *methodological pluralism* and *theoretical ecumenism*) to explain things by zeroing in (converging) on phenomena of interest. These fields are concerned with how and why people behave, feel, and think as they do.

7. *Descriptive research* tells us "how things are" (e.g., describes children's failure in school; other examples are given in Table 1.1).

8. *Relational research* tells us "how things are in relation to other things" (e.g., describes the relation between student failure and teaching behavior; see other examples in Table 1.1).

9. *Experimental research* tells us "how things are and how they got to be that way" (e.g., in studying the effects of teaching on student learning by manipulating the hypothesized causes of student failure; see other examples in Table 1.1).

10. *Random sampling* refers to choosing an unbiased sample that is representative of a targeted population, whereas *random assignment* refers to how subjects are allocated by an unbiased procedure to different groups or conditions in a randomized experiment (Box 1.4).

11. J. A. Hall listed nine traits of good researchers: enthusiasm, open-mindedness, common sense, role-taking ability, a combination of creativity and inventiveness, confidence in one's own judgment, the ability to communicate, care about details, and integrity and honest scholarship.

Key Terms

ad hoc hypothesis   p. 15
aesthetic aspect of science
  p. 10
a priori method   p. 6
behavior   p. 12
behavioral science   p. 12
correlational research   p. 15
descriptive research   p. 14

empirical   p. 6
empirical reasoning   p. 7
experimental research   p. 15
method of authority   p. 5
method of tenacity   p. 4
methodological pluralism
  p. 13
perceptibility   p. 10

random assignment   p. 16
random sampling   p. 16
relational research   p. 15
rhetoric of justification
  p. 11
scientific method   p. 1
theoretical ecumenism
  p. 13

Multiple-Choice Questions for Review
(answers appear at the end of this chapter) _____

1. John believes that women are more emotionally expressive than men. When asked why he believes this, John says it is because he has "always" believed it, and because "everybody knows it is true." John is using the (a) method of tenacity; (b) scientific method; (c) a priori method; (d) method of authority.

2. Miles, a student at California State University at Sacramento, tells another student, Sasha, that "numbers are infinite," to which she responds, "Prove it!" Miles says, "Would you agree that any number doubled will result in a new number twice the size?" When Sasha answers "yes," Miles responds, "Aha, you have just proved that numbers are infinite, because there must be a limitless number of numbers if you are correct." Miles is using the (a) method of tenacity; (b) scientific method; (c) a priori method; (d) method of authority.

3. Julie believes that everyone dreams every night, because her psychology professor told her this is true. Julie is using the (a) method of tenacity; (b) scientific method; (c) a priori method; (d) method of authority.

4. Dr. Smith believes that psychotherapy is generally very effective in treating mental disorders. She claims that her belief is based on empirical research in which therapy was given to some patients but not others, and in which the degree of mental disorder was carefully measured. Dr. Smith's belief is based on the (a) method of tenacity; (b) scientific method; (c) a priori method; (d) method of authority.

5. Which of the following is the *most* distinctive characteristic of science? (a) empirical inquiry and empirical reasoning; (b) images and metaphors; (c) the rhetoric of science; (d) statistical explanation

6. Behavioral science (a) encompasses many scientific fields that study behavior; (b) emphasizes multiple methods of observation and explanation; (c) has seen a growth in the number of interdisciplinary fields; (d) all of the above.

7. Which empirical approach is often considered a necessary first step in conducting research but is rarely considered sufficient by itself? (a) relational research; (b) experimental research; (c) descriptive research; (d) none of the above

8. A researcher at the College of the Southwest conducts a research project on the study habits of students. She reports that, on average, college students study 20 hours per week. This is an example of (a) relational research; (b) experimental research; (c) descriptive research; (d) none of the above.

9. Experimental research (a) can support cause-effect conclusions; (b) involves the manipulation of variables; (c) often involves randomly assigning subjects to conditions; (d) all of the above.

10. A researcher at Grand Valley State University flips a coin to decide whether each person in a sample of research participants will be assigned to the experimental group or the control group. This is an illustration of (a) random sampling; (b) random assignment; (c) both random assignment and randomization because they are synonyms; (d) none of the above.

Discussion Questions for Review
(answers appear at the end of this chapter) _____

1. Philosopher Charles Sanders Peirce described four distinctive approaches (he called them *methods*) on which strongly held beliefs are based. What are these "methods"? Give an example of a belief based on each method.

2. In addition to the use of empirical observation, three other (extraempirical) factors were said to play a role in science. What are those factors? Which of the four is traditionally considered "more fundamental" than the others in science?

3. A Wayne State researcher is interested in the effects of children's viewing TV violence on the children's level of aggression on the playground. The amount and type of viewing will be assessed through a standard procedure: TV diaries sent to parents. Aggression will be rated by two judges. The researcher hypothesizes that children who spend more time watching violent TV at home are more aggressive on the playground than their peers who watch relatively little violent TV at home. Of the three general research types (descriptive, relational, and experimental), which type is this, and why?

4. A Wichita State researcher plans to assign fifth-grade children to one of two conditions. Half the children (Group A) will be shown a relatively violent movie at 10:30, and half (Group B) will be shown a nonviolent movie at the same time. Each film will be equally engaging. Two observers will code the children's behavior when both groups are brought back together on the playground for their 11:00 recess. This procedure will continue daily for six weeks. The researcher predicts that Group A will be more aggressive on the playground than Group B. Which type of research is this, and why?

5. A researcher at the University of New Hampshire wants to measure the prevalence of shyness in the undergraduate community. She administers the well-standardized Shyness Scale to volunteers in a main dining hall, collecting data on a respectable 35% of all undergraduates. Which type of research is this, and why?

6. A North Dakota State student wants to study other students' creativity, and he wants to use all three types of research approaches (descriptive, relational, and experimental) in this project. Think of a concrete example of each type that he could use.

7. A student at Foothill College claims that it is not possible to study such nonscientific concepts as prayer because prayer falls in the domain of theology rather than of science. Is the student correct?

8. Alan Turing, who conceived of the computer and was also primarily responsible for breaking the German code (called Enigma) during World War II, proposed a way of demonstrating that a computer simulation of human intelligence actually works. Called the *Turing test,* it consists of people having a dialogue with the computer and seeing whether the computer can fool them into thinking that they are interacting with a human being. How is this an example of empirical reasoning?

9. The chapter ended by describing psychologist Judith Hall's nine "traits of good researchers." List as many as you can recall.

Answers to Review Questions

Multiple-Choice Questions

1. a	**3.** d	**5.** a	**7.** c	**9.** d
2. c	**4.** b	**6.** d	**8.** c	**10.** b

Discussion Questions

1. First, the method of tenacity: believing something because it is an idea that has been around for a long time (e.g., Elvis is alive). Second, the method of authority: believing something said by an expert in the field (e.g., cutting back on fatty foods because the doctor told you to do so and you believe doctors know about this). Third, the a priori method: using pure reason as a basis of belief (e.g., reasoning that $12 \times 100 = 120 \times 10 = 1 \times 1200$). Fourth, the scientific method: using empirical reasoning as a basis of belief (e.g., believing the earth is round because you have circled the globe by foot, boat, and vehicle and not fallen off).

2. The three extraempirical factors are aesthetics (the beauty of science), perceptibility (the use of images and metaphors), and rhetoric (the technical concepts and persuasive language used in

science). Empirical reasoning and empirical methods are considered the "most fundamental" in science.

3. This is relational research because the relationship between two sets of observations (TV diary entries and playground aggression) is examined. It is not experimental because neither of the variables is manipulated by the investigator.

4. This is experimental research because the investigator has manipulated the type of movie shown.

5. This is descriptive research because the data are collected on student shyness, but these scores are not examined for their relationship with any other variable.

6. For his descriptive research, he might collect data on the creativity scores of other students. For his relational research, he might examine the relationship between creativity scores and SAT (Scholastic Assessment Test) scores. For his experimental research, he might experimentally manipulate the type of music being played in the background while the students' creativity is being measured to see whether Mozart makes students more creative than does hard rock.

7. No, it certainly *is* possible to study the concept of prayer, and Galton conducted a relational study of prayer and longevity. An experimental study might use prayer for a randomly chosen half of 50 people who are ill and no prayer for the remaining people to see whether prayer brings about faster recovery.

8. It is an example of empirical reasoning because it involves logic, observation, and even a kind of measurement. The logic is Turing's reasoning that it may be possible for a computer to trick a person into mistaking it for a human being. The observation is the test itself, and the kind of measurement might consist of judgments made by people at different points in their interaction with the computer, and then a final judgment about whether they were interacting with a person or a computer.

9. The nine traits are (a) being enthusiastic about the topic and process of research; (b) being open-minded so as not to miss a promising lead, and so as to learn from your mistakes and others' criticisms; (c) using good sense rather than doing something only because it is convenient; (d) taking the role of the research participant, the person who grades your paper, and, if you are presenting a poster, the poster's viewers; (e) being inventive and creative during the planning and implementation of your research and in asking interesting questions; (f) having confidence in your own judgment after applying your mind to the facts; (g) learning to communicate clearly; (h) being careful about details in all phases of your research; and (i) being honest in every aspect of the research.

CHAPTER 2

Creative Ideas and Working Hypotheses

Preview Questions

- What is the "discovery phase" of scientific inquiry?
- What are hypothesis-generating heuristics?
- What belongs in my research proposal?
- How can I do a literature search?
- How should I go about defining variables?
- What identifies "good" theories and working hypotheses?
- What is meant by *independent variable* and *dependent variable*?

What Is the "Discovery Phase" of Scientific Inquiry?

The purpose of this chapter is to begin to give you a sense of what philosopher Hans Reichenbach (1938) called the **discovery phase** of scientific inquiry. He chose this term to capture the idea of the scientist as a kind of "Christopher Columbus" who is venturing into the unknown. This phase typically includes coming up with an idea, doing a background search of the literature, defining concepts and variables, formulating hypotheses, crafting the research materials, and developing a study design and a plan to implement it. In this chapter, we examine the first four steps; in subsequent chapters, we will discuss aspects of the remaining steps. Reichenbach's idea was that the discovery phase is followed by the **justification phase**. The justification phase takes its name from the assumption that the scientist's report of the research will include a rationale for the plan of the study and the data analysis, as well as a logical argument for the conclusions reached. However, this classic distinction between discovery and justification is not without controversy in the philosophy of science. For example, there is no rule stating that research must proceed in a linear or formulaic fashion, and scientists who do *exploratory research* are frequently guided by questions rather than specific working hypotheses. But even in exploratory research, scientists usually have implicit expectations based on a theory or a hunch.

Thus, another purpose of this chapter is to get you thinking about a research question and a working hypothesis. Later on in this chapter, we will describe four standard criteria of scientific hypotheses as plausibility, testability, refutability, and succinctness. If you have not yet looked at the sample report in Appendix A, now is the time to read it, as the appendix also provides tips that will help you organize your time. The name of the student shown on the report ("Mary Jones") is fictitious, but the study and results are real (from an unpublished study done by social psychologist Bruce Rind, who gave us permission to use these data). The report begins by describing how "Mary" got the idea for her research from watching lawyers on TV who were at loggerheads on a controversial issue. The report describes her design, her empirical findings and the results of her calculations, and then her interpretation of the results and the overall study. Notice also that there is a special section at the end of the report (an appendix) that contains her raw data and gives an overview of her statistical analyses. Not all instructors require students to include such an appendix, but many now do. However, even if you are not asked to report the raw scores and your calculations, it is important that you keep all your notes and raw data, at least until the instructor has returned your report and you have received a grade in the course—just in case there are any questions about your work.

As Mary's introduction illustrates, suitable leads for research questions and hypotheses are all around us, and keeping our eyes, ears, and minds open can lead to interesting questions, fresh insights, or innovative applications. For example, clinical psychologist Leo Kanner (1943) made a discovery while he was working with disturbed children. He noticed a striking similarity in their behavior. Not only did they tend to be socially isolated, but they had failed to develop appropriate language skills. Calling this *syndrome* (i.e., a set of symptoms) "infantile autism," Kanner and others began to do research on it, and it is now listed in the diagnostic manual used by clinical psychologists and psychiatrists. Kanner's felicitous discovery is an example of *serendipity* (which we discuss later in this chapter). Reading the literature is another way to generate ideas for research, and we will explore the literature retrieval process. Still another way to learn about important issues that need further scientific probing is to attend public lectures at your college and paper and poster presentations at professional meetings.

To organize our discussion of strategies and circumstances that lead scientists to initial ideas, we borrow from the work of Yale University psychologist William J. McGuire (whom we briefly mentioned in the previous chapter in connection with the rhetoric of science). McGuire (1973, 1997) described more than four dozen "hypothesis-generating heuristics," and we will sample six of them: (a) the use of an intensive case study; (b) the effort to make psychological sense of a paradoxical incident; (c) the use of analogies, metaphors, figures of speech, and other assorted imagery; (d) the resolution of conflicting results; (e) the effort to improve on older ideas; and (f) serendipity. Another strategy, which we discuss in a later chapter, is to *replicate* (repeat) a published study with a new twist (described as a *varied replication*). It can be especially valuable early in the history of a research question (R. Rosenthal, 1990c). Suppose that all replications are weighted equally, in which case the first replication doubles the amount of empirical information on the topic found in the original research. Once the number of replications becomes substantial, researchers frequently use a quantitative approach called *meta-analysis* (introduced in Appendix C) to develop an overall picture and to explore for conditions (known as **moderator variables**) that may strengthen or weaken the relationships between independent and dependent variables (defined later in this chapter).

What Are Hypothesis-Generating Heuristics?

The word *heuristic* means stimulating interest as a means of furthering investigation, and a classic hypothesis-generating heuristic is the *intensive case study,* or in-depth examination of something (e.g., Davison, 2000; Ragin, 1992; Ragin & Becker, 1992). For example, in the work of Sigmund Freud (1856–1939), psychoanalytic ideas about human motivation usually came from case studies based on the free association method (i.e., the patient stated whatever passed through his or her mind) to tease out the concealed psychological bases of neurotic symptoms that apparently had no organic cause. Intensive case studies are currently used in educational research, policymaking, organizational and management analysis, and city and regional planning as a strategy for creating ideas and hypotheses (Merriam, 1991; Yin, 1989). In Chapter 8, we will describe an experimental variant of the intensive case study that is called *single-case experimental research* (see also Box 2.1). Single-case studies have spawned new insights and inspired hypotheses and further research in such diverse areas as memory, animal behavior, and cognitive development (Kazdin, 1980, 1992).

In a second hypothesis-generating heuristic, researchers develop ideas to help them make sense of a *paradoxical incident* (i.e., a seemingly contradictory event).

BOX 2.1   XOT, BOK, LUM, ZAT

An early example of single-case experimental research was an investigation by Hermann Ebbinghaus (1850–1909). Using himself as the case studied, Ebbinghaus developed theoretical curves to describe the rates at which certain information is learned and forgotten. To do this, he measured his own ability to learn and relearn thousands of nonsense syllables, each consisting of a random combination of two consonants and a middle vowel, pronounceable as words but uniformly lacking in meaning (e.g., *xot, bok, lum, zat*). With himself as the sole subject, he first recorded how long it took him to master a list of nonsense syllables. He waited until he had forgotten the syllables and then relearned the list. He then repeated the procedure, each time making a careful record of his learning and forgetting.

A modern classic was the bystander helping research done by social psychologists Bibb Latané and John Darley. They had been puzzled by contradictory aspects of the circumstances surrounding a lurid murder in Queens, New York, in the spring of 1964. A 28-year-old nurse was coming home from work at 3 a.m. when she was attacked by a man who stabbed her repeatedly. When they heard her cries of terror, more than three dozen of her neighbors came to their windows to see what was happening, but no one went to her aid, even though it took the stalker over half an hour to murder her. Latané and Darley were struck by the paradox that, even though there were many witnesses, none bothered to phone the police. The social psychologists wondered whether *so many* people failed to intervene because each believed someone else was likely to. On the basis of this idea, they developed a concept they called the "diffusion of responsibility" and hypothesized that the more the bystander witnesses to an emergency, the less likely it is that any one of them will offer help.

Latané and Darley (1970) then went on to test the diffusion-of-responsibility hypothesis in a series of experiments. For example, in a study at Columbia University, they demonstrated that the larger the number of the students present, the less likely any of them was to volunteer to help in an emergency. The students in this experiment had agreed to take part in a discussion of problems related to life at an urban university. As the discussion progressed, a stream of smoke began to puff into the room through a wall vent. The researchers observed that, when one student was in the room, she or he was about twice as likely to report the emergency as when the student was in the room with as few as three others. Instead of reporting the emergency, students in a group tended to be passive and to dismiss their fears through rationalization (Latané & Darley, 1968). In a similar study with introductory psychology students at New York University, who had also agreed to take part in a discussion group, each was much more likely to report a (simulated) epileptic seizure that he or she happened to hear if alone than if he or she believed that others were also aware of the emergency (Darley & Latané, 1968).

A third hypothesis-generating heuristic involves the use of analogies, metaphors, figures of speech, or other *analogical thinking* (mentioned in Chapter 1; see also Box 2.2). For example, McGuire (1964) used an inoculation metaphor to come up with ideas for inducing resistance to propaganda messages. He assumed that some beliefs (cultural truisms) are so widely accepted in American society that they are perceived as indisputably true. Examples of cultural truisms are "Mental illness is not contagious," "It's a good idea to brush your teeth after every meal," and "Cigarette smoking is bad for your health." Using the inoculation metaphor as a point of departure, McGuire reasoned that beliefs like these should be vulnerable to counterpropaganda for two reasons. First, recipients of propaganda attacking cultural truisms, seldom having been called on to defend their beliefs, are unpracticed in mustering a defense. Second, they may not be motivated to develop a defense because they view such beliefs as established and unassailable.

McGuire drew an analogy between believing some cultural truisms and not having been vaccinated for smallpox. Like the unvaccinated person, who is highly

BOX 2.2 The Spiral in Nature and Analogy

A favorite analogy is the spiral, because it seems to have such a prominent place in nature. For example, economists speak of "inflationary spirals," and in football, we have "spiral passes." A noted developmental psychologist, Heinz Werner, proposed a "psychogenetic principle of spirality," which he derived from an earlier philosophical analogy about the unfolding of historical events (Werner & Kaplan, 1963). In nature, of course, there are many examples of spirality: Storms that arise in the Northern Hemisphere typically display a counterclockwise spiral rotation, whereas those that arise in the Southern Hemisphere typically display a clockwise rotation. Human hair forms a spiral pattern on the scalp that is generally clockwise in men and counterclockwise in women. Recently, auditory researchers theorized that the spiral shape of the cochlea (the bony sound-perceiving organ in the inner ear) serves to increase sensitivity to low-frequency sounds (Cho, 2006). Spiral forms are also found in pinecones and other varieties of plants. One author told of a researcher who blindfolded a right-handed friend and told him to walk a straight line across a country field; the man walked in a clockwise spiral—that is, until he stumbled on a tree stump (Robin, 1993).

vulnerable to an attack of the smallpox virus, a person who has not given very much thought to *why* he or she believes that something is true may also be highly vulnerable to a massive attack of counterpropaganda. Just as vaccinating a person with a weakened dose of smallpox virus stimulates the person's defenses so that he or she can later overcome an attack, perhaps a similar kind of technique would work to "immunize" people's attitudes. Extrapolating from this idea, McGuire theorized that, to immunize people against "viral-like" counterpropaganda, we can simply expose them to some small form of the counterpropaganda in advance, thus stimulating them to build up their own "logical defenses" by rehearsing arguments against the counterpropaganda. Exposing them to too much preliminary counterpropaganda may, however, produce the opposite effect, causing them to reverse their attitude (i.e., it would be like accidentally giving them the disease). The problem, which McGuire worked out in a systematic program of research studies, was to establish the amount of "live virus" in an "inoculation" that, without giving people the "disease," would help build a defense against a future massive attack of the same "virus."

In a fourth hypothesis-generating heuristic, the researcher develops insights by trying to *account for conflicting results*. A prominent case in psychology involved the work of Robert Zajonc (pronounced "zy-ence," rhymes with *science*). He proposed a hypothesis that he termed "social facilitation" (Zajonc, 1965) to account for some conflicting published data: Some earlier reports had indicated that performance in humans and animals improved when passive observers were present, whereas other reports had showed performance becoming poorer in the presence of others. For instance, in one experiment, the participants were required to learn a list of nonsense syllables, either alone or in the presence of others. The number of trials needed to learn the list was the criterion variable. Those participants who learned the list alone averaged more than 9 trials, and those who learned the syllables before an audience averaged more than 11 trials (Pessin, 1933). In other experiments, participants who performed a familiar task in groups did better than when they performed the task alone (Bergum & Lehr, 1963). Thus, it seemed that the presence of others enhanced the performance of some tasks but not of others.

How could these seemingly inconsistent results be explained? One important finding in experimental psychology is that a high drive level causes people to give the dominant response to a stimulus. When the task is familiar and well learned, the dominant response is usually the right one. However, when the task is novel and the correct responses are unknown or not well learned, the dominant response will probably be wrong. Zajonc started with the idea that the presence of others serves to increase the individual's drive level and this increase leads to dominant responses. Therefore, Zajonc hypothesized, the presence of others must inhibit the learning of new responses but facilitate the performance of well-learned responses. In other words, students should study alone, preferably in an isolated cubicle, and then (having learned all the correct responses) take exams with many other students on a stage before a large audience.

A fifth hypothesis-generating heuristic involves *improving on older ideas*. For example, Daryl Bem thought of inverting a traditional principle in social psychology stating that attitudes shape behavior. Bem reasoned that people's behavior sometimes also shapes their attitudes about what they believe is true. For example, a politician who repeatedly defends a position for the sake of expediency then thinks, "I guess I really believe this," or suppose you wolfed down a sandwich and *then* you thought, "Gee, I must have been starving" (Brehm & Kassin, 1996). Bem's (1965, 1972) formulation, which he called "self-perception theory," became the basis of a program of empirical research that provided support for his initial idea.

Another example of this heuristic was B. F. Skinner's improvement on two older theories of conditioning. In the 1930s, two popular conceptualizations were those of Russian physiologist Ivan Pavlov and American psychologist E. L. Thorndike. Skinner's distinction between these two conceptualizations opened the way to a long series of studies by Skinner and others (Ferster & Skinner, 1957; Skinner, 1938). Pavlov had done pioneering research on "classical conditioning." In the experimental procedure that produces this type of conditioning, a neutral stimulus is paired with one that consistently brings about some desired behavior or response. Suppose that we, like Pavlov, wish to condition a hungry dog to salivate at the sound of a bell. Once the dog becomes accustomed to the apparatus, we sound the bell to make sure that the dog does not automatically salivate to it. The dog pricks up its ears or barks, but it does not salivate. We now know that the bell will not cause the animal to respond as it does to food. The next step is to ring the bell and present meat to the dog. If we do this a number of times, we find that the dog begins to salivate at the sound of the bell, before we present the meat. In contrast,

Thorndike, who experimented at about the same time as Pavlov, in the early 1900s, worked with "trial-and-error learning." For example, Thorndike studied how cats learned to escape from a puzzle box to gain food. He was convinced that the cats did not reason out a solution, but that their getting out and eating the food he provided somehow strengthened the connection between successful escape movements and the actual escape.

Skinner recognized that, in Pavlovian conditioning, the major factor is the stimulus that precedes the response. In other words, the response is elicited reflexively. In Thorndike's trial-and-error conditioning, the major factor is the stimulus consequence (i.e., the reinforcement of escaping the puzzle box), which follows the response. Skinner focused his own research on the latter type of conditioning, which he called *operant* or *instrumental*. In this type of conditioning, first, the organism responds to a stimulus, and then something is done that will either increase or decrease the probability of the organism's making the same response again. Say that we wish to train a dog to sit on command, and we prepare the animal by withholding food for a time. An operant-conditioning procedure requires that we reward the dog *after* it sits (or approximates sitting) following the command. The laboratory research on operant conditioning paved the way for applications in the military, in educational institutions, and in the treatment of behavior disorders. In his novel, *Walden II,* Skinner (1948b) described a whole society organized according to known principles of conditioning.

Serendipity (defined as a felicitous or lucky discovery) is a sixth hypothesis-generating heuristic. An example, mentioned previously, was clinical psychologist Leo Kanner's discovery of what he named "infantile autism." In a famous practical application of serendipity, George deMestral was picking cockleburs from his jacket after a stroll in the Swiss countryside when he noticed that they were covered with tiny hooks that had become embedded in the loops of the fabric of his jacket. Suddenly he perceived a way to create something useful out of a nuisance: the Velcro fastener (Roberts, 1989). Everyone has an opportunity to benefit from serendipity at one time or another, and like many other researchers, we have benefited from it in our own research.

In Chapter 1, we mentioned the finding that teachers' expectations about their students' performance may become a self-fulfilling prophecy, in that the expectations become responsible for the students' behavior (Babad, 1993; Raudenbush, 1984; R. Rosenthal, 1966, 1976, 1985, 1991; Rosenthal & Jacobson, 1968; Rosenthal & Rubin, 1978). In a later chapter, we discuss another implication of self-fulfilling prophecies in research, now called the *experimenter expectancy effect*. A series of focused studies of this phenomenon was inspired by an unexpected result in Rosenthal's dissertation research (which at the time did not seem so felicitous). Rosenthal had been studying the defense mechanism of projection (i.e., ascribing to another person one's own feelings or thoughts) in college men and women as well as in a group of hospitalized patients with paranoid symptomatology. Each of these groups was divided into three subgroups that received a success, failure, or neutral experience on a task structured to seem like a test of intelligence. Before the participants' treatment conditions were imposed, they were asked to rate the degree to which they perceived success or failure in the faces of individuals pictured in photographs. Immediately after the experiment, the participants rated another set of faces on their degree of success or failure. Rosenthal's dissertation hypothesis was that being in the success condition would lead the participants to perceive other people as prone to success, and that being in the failure condition would lead those participants to perceive other people as prone to failure (as measured by the difference between the preratings and postratings). Digging into the results, Rosenthal did a number of statistical analyses, and in one of these, to his great surprise and dismay, he found that the *preratings* (i.e., the ratings made *before* the treatment was implemented) were biased in favor of his hypothesis. After discussing the problem with his research adviser, Rosenthal began a frantic search of journals and books for references to this problem, which he called "unconscious experimenter bias." He learned that, as far back as Ebbinghaus (1885), psychologists had alluded to something like this problem, though no one had explicitly designed and conducted experiments to test the hypothesis of unconscious experimenter bias. In a long series of studies of how experimenters' hypotheses may unwittingly influence their results, the concept of unconscious experimenter bias evolved into the concept of experimenter expectancy bias (R. Rosenthal, 1966, 1976, 1993).

Rosnow's brush with serendipity happened in 1969, when the Beatles were at the height of their popularity and a rumor about them began to circulate. The rumor alleged that, leaving the recording studio tired and dejected, Paul McCartney had been decapitated in a car accident; to maintain the group, the accident had been covered up, and he had been replaced by a double. The Paul-is-dead rumor, although a preposterous fiction, swept across U.S. colleges with numerous variants and deviations (Rosnow & Fine, 1974, 1976). What made the rumor intriguing was that it was not at all like the rumors that had been previously studied by psychologists and sociologists. A prominent text on the psychology of rumor had concluded that, in view of the porosity of human memory, rumors *always* become shorter (Allport & Postman, 1947). The Paul-is-dead rumor was not shrinking, however, but instead was growing by leaps and bounds as students improvised details and the "clues" multiplied. Rosnow wondered whether the traditional view of rumor was limited, perhaps wrong, in other respects as well. Pursuing this question opened the way to new hypotheses, further research, and ultimately to a modified theory in which rumormongering can be viewed as an attempt to deal with emotional stresses and cognitive uncertainties by generating and passing stories and suppositions that explain nebulous events, address anxieties, and provide a rationale for behavior. Another addendum is that people have a tendency to pass rumors that they regard as "credible" (even the most ridiculous stories), but when anxieties are intense, rumormongers are less likely to monitor the logic or plausibility of what they pass on to others (Rosnow, 1991, 2001). Other researchers have uncovered additional patterns in both the content and the level of individual participation in rumor networks, providing further insights into rumors and their possible control (DiFonzo & Bordia, 2006, 2007; Fine & Turner, 2001; Kimmel, 2004).

What Belongs in My Research Proposal?

Let us assume you have an initial inspiration for a research study. The next step is to decide whether your idea makes sense and is worth investigating. As you search and retrieve the relevant literature and discuss your idea with your instructor, you will begin to get a better awareness of how to develop a rationale for hypotheses (in the way that Mary Jones explains the basis of her hypothesis in Appendix A). Once you have retrieved relevant work, developed your hypothesis, and have a design and a plan to implement it, you must tell your instructor what you would like to study and how you propose to go about it, including how you propose to deal with ethical issues (discussed in the next chapter). We will have more to say in this chapter about criteria that are used to assess good hypotheses, but Exhibit 2.1 will give you an idea of what a research proposal might look like. Think of it not as a one-way communication, but as a mutual understanding between you and the instructor. Your instructor may require additional information or some variation on the sample proposal. Once your proposal has been approved, it is expected that you will first consult with your instructor should you wish to make changes, because the proposal constitutes a formal agreement you have made with the instructor.

Notice that Mary's proposal begins with an obviously tentative title, which provides a focus for her ideas but can be changed when she writes her final report. Next, she tells how she came up with her initial idea, so that its originality is not in question. She then cites the basis of her hypothesis. The next section describes her proposed design (including details and technical terms that we will explain later in this book). She describes the experimental manipulation, making clear that it is closely tied to her hypothesis. She tells how she proposes to measure the responses and why she chose this range of responses. In describing her proposed data analysis, she mentions her intention to meet with the instructor to "go over the planned analysis" once she has the raw data and has done some preliminary calculations. Mary implies that she has given more than just cursory attention to ethical issues. The proposal concludes with a couple of references, a list that Mary will presumably expand as she gets further into the study, resumes her literature search if she (or the instructor) feels it is necessary to do so, and begins to sketch out her final report.

How Can I Do a Literature Search?

Because you will be using resources physically located in your college library, or accessible via an online link, now is the time to familiarize yourself with what is available. College libraries have fact sheets that indicate where books, journals, and other work are stored in the *stacks* (the shelves in the library). You also need information on the material that has restricted access and the books and periodicals that are available for *browsing* (they can be read in the library, but not checked out), which you can ask about at the information desk or by going online to the library's Web page. All of the library's material is referenced in its automated card catalog, which not only gives you basic information but also tells you

(*text continues on p. 36*)

Mary Jones 1

Research Proposal for Psych 333

Mary Jones (e-mail address or other contact information)

(Date the proposal is submitted)

Working Title of Proposed Research

Is There a Biasing Effect of Drug-Testing Results on Bail Judgments?

Objective of the Research

While watching television one evening, I happened to see two lawyers disagreeing about whether judges impose higher bail on defendants who test positive for drug usage. One lawyer insisted that, even when positive information from mandatory drug testing is not directly related to the crime in question, it will nevertheless bias the judge's bail decision. This lawyer further argued that mandatory drug testing is therefore a serious threat to the criminal justice system's ideal of being just and unbiased in all its aspects. Moved by this dispute, I began perusing texts and searching PsycINFO for some relevant literature.

Hypotheses and Predictions

To develop a directional hypothesis, I have been thinking about Jones and Davis's (1965) correspondent inference theory, which states that observers focus on certain types of behavior to infer traits since they believe that only certain behaviors are indicative of traits. Among the questions that observers presumably ask themselves is whether the behavior is low in social desirability. Baron and Byrne (1987) also mentioned that observers have a tendency to focus on socially undesirable behavior in judging the actor's traits and, once having inferred these traits, use this information to predict the actor's future behavior. On the assumption that drug usage is generally considered low in social desirability in our society, my working hypothesis is that positive results from a drug test will result in harsher bail judgments than when no such information is made available.

Exhibit 2.1   Sample Research Proposal

(continued)

Mary Jones 2

Proposed Method

I propose to use a randomized design in which the participants are assigned to one of two conditions. The sample will consist of approximately 30 students in an undergraduate class. I have been given permission by the course instructor to invite the students to participate. I have also developed a "crime scenario" that the participants will read; it describes a man seen running from a burglarized house.

In the experimental condition, the scenario will state that the suspect tested positive for drugs while in custody:

A man was arrested as a suspected burglar. He fit the description of a man seen running from the burglarized house. While in custody the man submitted to a blood test, and it was determined that he had very recently used drugs.

In the control condition, neutral information (i.e., the suspect ate and phoned someone) will be presented in lieu of the information about having tested positive for drugs:

A man was arrested as a suspected burglar. He fit the description of a man seen running from the burglarized house. The man spent enough time in custody to receive two meals and make three phone calls.

Following these conditions, I will measure the dependent variable by asking the participants to respond to the following question:

If you were the bail judge, what would you set the bail to be? Choose a dollar amount from $0 to $50,000.

My reason for specifying a range is to give the participants a common metric, and I chose this range because it seemed realistic and sufficiently wide to produce differences between the experimental and control groups. At the beginning of the questionnaire, the

Exhibit 2.1   (*continued*)

Mary Jones 3

participants will be asked their age, sex, year in college, and estimated GPA. No name will be asked for, because I believe that the participants will be more forthcoming if they know they are responding anonymously.

Proposed Data Analysis

I plan to analyze the results using an independent t test and to report not only the associated p value but also the effect size and its 95% confidence interval. As these calculations are pretty simple, I expect to do them by hand using my calculator. As a precaution, I will go over the planned analysis with Professor Rind once I have the raw data and have calculated the means and standard deviations.

Ethical Considerations

Though I have obtained permission to run my study in another instructor's class, I will emphasize at the outset (as part of the informed-consent procedure) that students who do not wish to participate may decline to respond. I will point out that all responses will be anonymous. The study does not involve deception; nevertheless, I will debrief the students and answer any questions at the end of the study.

Preliminary List of References

Baron, R. A., & Byrne, D. (1987). *Social psychology: Understanding human interaction.* Boston: Allyn & Bacon.

Jones, E. E., & Davis, K. E. (1965). From acts to dispositions: The attribution process in person perception. In L. Berkowitz (Ed.), *Advances in experimental social psychology* (Vol. 2, pp. 219-266). New York: Academic Press.

Exhibit 2.1 (*continued*)

where things can be found. It is easy to use the automated catalog, but if you have a question, click on the "Help" key (or icon) or ask for assistance at the information desk. Information librarians like to be helpful, and they will know the right answer or know where to send you for the answer. Because it is a lot easier (and more accurate) to print out pages from full-text journal articles than to copy lengthy passages by hand, ask whether you can do this at the library or through your own computer. It is also easier (and more accurate) to photocopy pages or paragraphs from books than to copy lengthy passages, so you will want to know where copying machines are located and whether you need to bring coins or purchase a debit card to use them.

For psychology students, a common way of searching the literature is to use PsycINFO, an extensive reference database maintained by the American Psychological Association, to which your library subscribes. The PsycINFO database now goes back to 1872 and contains abstracts as well as full-text materials. You can typically access PsycINFO in your college library using one of its desktop computers, and you may also be able to do so outside the library using your own computer. Once you are into PsycINFO, you use search terms (sets of words or phrases, generally called *descriptors*) to pull up relevant abstracts. PsycINFO has a list of its own special descriptors, which you can find by clicking on its "Thesaurus" key. However, experts in data retrieval suggest not limiting searches to only the special descriptors (or controlled vocabulary) associated with each database but also to do *free-text searching,* which means using the terms that we intuitively think are relevant to our interest (M. C. Rosenthal, 2006). The reason for doing free-text searching is that a database-linked thesaurus may not contain the keywords or key phrases we need, and not finding what we are looking for does not mean that the material does not exist in the database. The trick in using PsycINFO is not to get too much or too little information; you will have to use patience in combining keywords and key phrases until you feel you have all the records you need. There is a tiny box at the beginning of each record that you can check for later printing or saving, or you can save the whole file without checking any of the boxes.

Once you feel comfortable using PsycINFO, other computerized databases will be a snap. By going to your library's Web page, you will be able to find out what other reference and *full-text databases* (i.e., databases that contain the entire article, not just an abstract) are available to you online. You will find reference databases for just about anything you can think of, including census data (Census Lookup), free government publications (GPO Access), medical information, news reports by topic areas (LEXIS-NEXIS), and dictionaries and encyclopedias. Another database is the Web of Science, which will provide you access to the Social Sciences Citation Index (SSCI) and the Science Citation Index (SCI). The SSCI and SCI are used by meta-analysts to do a very thorough *ancestry search,* which means tracking "ancestral" citations of an article or a book back to a specified year. Even hard-to-find material (called the *fugitive literature*)—like technical reports, dissertations, and master's theses—can often be identified and later retrieved once you know what reference databases are available to you (M. C. Rosenthal, 1985, 1994, 2006). Box 2.3 provides some tips to help you get started.

BOX 2.3   Tips on Retrieving Literature

Here are three tips that we borrowed from a librarian and information retrieval expert, MaryLu C. Rosenthal (2006, pp. 90–91), which should help you get started on your literature search:

- Use several free-text descriptor words or phrases. Even though this broad search may turn up more than is relevant, it is easier to limit the search *after* you have looked at what turned up than to try to anticipate the perfect descriptor.

- Search not only PsycINFO but also other reference databases. There may be a lot of overlap, but you never know whether something new will turn up, and it will take only a little extra time to do this search online.

- Keep a running list so that you don't waste effort in accidentally retracing your steps. Note down the databases searched, the dates you used them, and the search terms or strategies you used.

Once you have turned up relevant abstracts, it is important not to stop with the abstract but to go to the work itself and read it. Full-text databases provide these works, including PsycARTICLES (the American Psychological Association's database of APA journal articles) and other full-text databases that are available over a specified period of time to students who purchase a textbook from a particular publisher. There are also emerging databases with full-text access to books that are no longer copyright-protected. Our advice about going to the original work applies even to a summary of a classic work that you find consistently cited and described by many authors. Mark Twain once defined a *classic* as a book that people praise and don't read. Read what you are citing, if only to make sure that you are not passing on a misreported account in a secondary source (cf. Treadway & McCloskey, 1989). Another reason to go to the original work, particularly in the case of a research article, is to make sure you agree with the researchers' conclusions: No rule says you *must* agree with something just because it is in print.

It is particularly important not to depend on media accounts of research as the final word; scientific findings reported in the media are often oversimplified. Go to the original and examine the findings yourself. Similarly, in a public lecture, the speaker does not have the opportunity to provide the minute details that are required by scientific journals. By the time an article has been published in a quality journal, the report has gone through a review by independent consultants. Nevertheless, published research reports are not guaranteed to be error-free, even though the aim of the review process is to detect errors and to raise questions that the author is required to address. There is also a "pecking order" of journals, and when a manuscript is rejected by a high-prestige journal, the author usually tries a somewhat lesser journal that may be willing to overlook some flaws (Sternberg, 2000). As the philosopher Francis Bacon advised more than 350 years ago, "Read not to contradict and confute; nor to believe and take for granted . . . but to weigh and consider" (Vickers, 1996, p. 438). As you study the material you have gathered, think carefully about the plausibility of your initial idea in the context of the published work.

How Should I Go About Defining Variables?

At this juncture, you also need to think about naming and defining the variables in which you are interested, since how you describe something tells others how you conceptualize it and whether you see it the same way they do. We will have more to say about the term *variable* in a moment, but researchers frequently distinguish between two types of definitions, called *operational* and *theoretical*. First, **operational definitions** identify variables on the basis of empirical conditions (the *operations*) used to measure or to manipulate the variables. For example, an experimental psychologist interested in the variable of *hunger* might define it operationally by the degree of stomach contractions. A social psychologist interested in *prejudice* might define it operationally by respondents' scores on an attitude scale designed to measure stereotyping and other elements of attitudinal biases. A child psychologist interested in studying *frustration* might define it operationally by an intervention that thwarts children in some way, such as interrupting play with a set of attractive new toys. A clinical psychologist interested in studying *depression* might define it operationally in terms of scores on a test, such as the Beck Depression Inventory (BDI).

Theoretical definitions define variables in more abstract or more general terms, such as defining *hunger* by a connection between the reported feeling of being hungry and the sensory experience of certain internal and external cues. After consulting the unabridged *Oxford English Dictionary* (which gives the etymology of words), the social psychologist interested in prejudice might discuss how the word *prejudice* derived from the Latin *praejudicium,* meaning a precedent, or judgment, based on prior decisions, and how through centuries of English it has come to mean a "premature judgment, or readiness to prejudge." The child psychologist interested in *frustration* might conceptualize it as "the condition that exists when people feel their goals are blocked by internal or external barriers." After consulting the latest edition of the *Diagnostic and Statistical Manual of Mental Disorders* (published by the American Psychiatric Association), the clinical psychologist interested in *depression* might emphasize symptoms that are clinically associated with it, such as a feeling of sadness or despair, sleep problems, loss of interest in things that were once pleasurable, weight changes, the inability to concentrate, and feelings of hopelessness and death.

How can you get started in your quest for good operational and theoretical definitions of the variables you want to study? Before you find yourself reinventing the wheel, you might also look in standard references to see how others have conceptualized those variables (see Box 2.4). As an illustration, suppose a student is

BOX 2.4 Don't Reinvent the Wheel!

Whatever concept you are interested in, some psychologist or other behavioral or social scientist has probably written about it somewhere. Concise definitions of the language of psychology can be found in the *APA Dictionary of Psychology* (VandenBos, 2007). Major concepts are discussed in legions of sourcebooks, monographs, and encyclopedias, such as Kazdin's *Encyclopedia of Psychology* (2000), Smelser and Baltes's *International Encyclopedia of the Social and Behavioral Sciences* (2002), Lewis-Beck, Bryman, and Liao's *Encyclopedia of Research Methods for the Social Sciences* (2003), and H. Friedman's *Encyclopedia of Mental Health* (1998). Your library may also have earlier encyclopedic works, such as Ramachandran's *Encyclopedia of Human Behavior* (1994), Harré and Lamb's *Encyclopedic Dictionary of Psychology* (1983), Wolman's *International Encyclopedia of Psychiatry, Psychology, Psychoanalysis, and Neurology* (1977), and Corsini's *Encyclopedia of Psychology* (1984). Another valuable source of information is the *Annual Review of Psychology,* which has integrative literature reviews in various specialized areas. Other literature reviews can be found in the *Psychological Bulletin,* the *Review of General Psychology, Behavioral and Brain Sciences, Personality and Social Psychology Review,* and *Psychological Science in the Public Interest.*

interested in developing a three-item test that could serve as a quick measure of feelings of depression not in a clinical or psychiatric sample but in ordinary college students. The instructor suggests that the student think about correlating summed scores on the three-item test with the BDI as an indicator of the three-item test's *construct validity.* We will have more to say about construct validity in Chapter 6, but **construct** is another name for a "concept" formulated ("constructed") to serve as a causal or descriptive explanation. By *construct validation,* the instructor means establishing the relation of a concept to variables with which it should, theoretically, be associated positively, negatively, or practically not at all (Cronbach & Meehl, 1955). In this case, the idea would be to show that the three-item test actually correlates positively with the BDI. For a theoretical definition of depression, the instructor recommends that the student read what the author of the BDI, Aaron T. Beck (e.g., Beck, Rush, Shaw, & Emery, 1979; Beck, Steer, & Garbin, 1988), has written about it. There will be no problem using this material in the student's paper, as long as the source of any material used is properly cited, and when quoting someone, the page numbers of the quoted passage are given.

Once the preliminary reading and note taking have been completed, the student is ready to draft the three sample items for the instructor to evaluate *before* the student administers them to anyone. One item might focus on sleep problems in depression: "I just don't want to get out of bed in the morning." A second item might focus on procrastination: "I can't get my work done, knowing that it will be really inferior." A third item might ask whether the person has thought about seeking help: "I have been so blue that maybe I should talk to someone about it." These are preliminary items. Expect to be asked to revise and polish your preliminary work based on the instructor's feedback and guidance.

What Identifies "Good" Theories and Working Hypotheses?

We have used the terms *theory* and *hypothesis,* but we haven't distinguished between these two concepts. To help you understand this difference, let us look at another example, a formulation created by Leon Festinger (1954) called social comparison theory. Basically, this theory assumes that all people need to evaluate their opinions and abilities. People want to know whether they are like or unlike others, or better or worse than others. There are objective standards for many opinions and abilities to help people decide where they stand in relation to others. But for many others, such as opinions about ethnic or racial groups, religion, sex, or environmental pollution, it is not easy to find objective criteria. It follows, Festinger reasoned, that when no immediate objective standard exists, people attempt to evaluate their opinions and abilities by comparing themselves to others. He also theorized that the tendency to compare oneself with another person will decrease as the expected difference between oneself and another increases. Thus, if you wanted to evaluate your opinions about the existence of God, you would be more likely to compare yourself with another student than with a member of the clergy. The theory also states that you will be less attracted to groups in which the members' way of thinking is very different from your own than to groups in which the members think more as you do. One reason, according to Festinger, is that people are motivated to elicit reinforcement of the legitimacy of their own opinions.

We see what a "theory" can look like (at least in social psychology), and now let us see what **working hypotheses** look like (frequently called **experimental hypotheses** in experimental psychology). Karl Popper (the philosopher mentioned in the previous chapter in Box 1.1) pointed out that the purpose of scientific hypotheses is to "select" what the researcher will be looking for. To illustrate this function in his lectures, Popper told students, "Take pencil and paper; carefully observe, and write down what you have observed." They immediately asked *what* it was that he wanted them to observe, because a directed observation needs a chosen object, a definite task, an interest, a point of view, and a problem. Popper (1934, 1963) explained to them that this is why scientists need hypotheses, because a direction for their observations is something they cannot do without in their empirical research. Here are two of Festinger's (1954) hypotheses: "The tendency to compare oneself with some other specific person decreases as the difference between his opinion or ability and one's own increases" (p. 120) and "The existence of a discrepancy in a group with respect to opinions or abilities will lead to action on the part of the members of that group to reduce the discrepancy" (p. 124).

What does this illustration teach us so far about scientific theories and hypotheses? First, it illustrates that a **hypothesis** is a conjectural statement or supposition, and a **theory** is a larger set of such statements in the context of certain assumptions, or presuppositions. Second, we see that hypotheses can be derived from a good theory and that they give direction to researchers' observations. Third, we see that a theory postulates a kind of conceptual pattern, which can then serve as a logical framework for the interpretation of the larger meaning of our observations (Hoover & Donovan, 1995). Finally, it is true of *seminal theories* (i.e., those that shape or stimulate other work) that they are constantly evolving as new findings, hypotheses, and interpretations emerge. Good scientific theories are also described as *generative,* which means they encourage others to generate additional hypotheses; social comparison theory measures up well to this standard (e.g., Buunk & Gibbons, 1997; Suls, Martin, & Wheeler, 2000; Suls & Miller, 1977; Wheeler, Martin, & Suls, 1997; Wood, 1989).

Good working hypotheses also have certain identifiable characteristics. First, they are *plausible,* or credible; that is, they are consistent with respected theories and reliable data. Traditionally, the working hypotheses that correspond most closely to accepted scientific truths are assumed to have good "payoff potential" when subjected to empirical jeopardy. That is to say, such hypotheses are expected to be more easily corroborated than conjectures that come out of the blue. It is impossible to be absolutely certain that a working hypothesis will pay off when tested, but the idea is to maximize the odds by ensuring that the hypothesis is credible. Second, good working hypotheses are *testable* in some empirical way. Third, they are *refutable,* or what Popper (1934, 1961) called *falsifiable.* Realizing that it is possible for those with a fertile imagination to find or concoct support for even the most preposterous claims, Popper argued that **falsifiability** is the most essential scientific standard of all. Conjectures that cannot, in principle, be refuted by *any* means are not within the realm of science, he argued. For example, "Behavior is a product of the good and evil lying within us" is not refutable empirically and, therefore, is not within the realm of science.

Finally, a fourth characteristic of good working hypotheses is that they are *succinct.* Traditionally, this requirement implies a combination of **coherence**, which means that the statement of the hypothesis "sticks together" in a logical way, and **parsimony**, which means the statement is not overly wordy or unduly complex. Most scientists believe that, to be acceptable, hypotheses must be only as complex and wordy as is absolutely necessary. Therefore, they "cut away" what is superfluous by means of a ruminative and winnowing process figuratively known as **Occam's razor** after a 14th-century Franciscan philosopher named William of Occam (also Ockham, known to his fellow friars as "doctor invincibilis"), who insisted that we cut away what is unwieldy. What can be stated or explained in fewer words or on the basis of fewer principles is stated or explained needlessly by more, he argued. A word of caution, however: Occam's razor is not a description of nature (because nature is often very complicated); it is a prescription for the *wording* of hypotheses. It is important not to cut off too much—"beards" but not "chins." How can you find out whether your working hypothesis cuts off too much or does not cut off enough? The best way is to ask the instructor for feedback and suggestions.

What Is Meant by Independent Variable and Dependent Variable?

We have referred to *variables,* and a **variable** is simply an event or condition that the researcher observes or measures or plans to investigate that is likely to vary (or change). The rhetoric of behavioral and social science also recognizes a further distinction between dependent variables and independent variables (R. A. Fisher, 1973, p. 129). The **dependent variable** (usually symbolized as Y) is the "effect" (or the outcome) in which the researcher is interested. The **independent variable** (usually symbolized as X) is the presumed "cause," changes in which lead to or predict changes in the dependent variable. For example, in the statement "Jogging makes you feel better," the independent variable (X) would be *jogging or not jogging,* and the dependent variable (Y) would be *feeling better or not feeling better.* This does not mean that particular variables are always either dependent or independent variables but is simply another conceptual convenience in the rhetoric of behavioral science. In fact, *any* event or condition may be an independent variable *or* a dependent variable.

For example, it is easy to imagine how some independent variable might be transformed into a dependent variable, and vice versa, because a variable derives its label from its context. By way of illustration, in the 1960s, a commission was established by President Lyndon B. Johnson to study the roots of racial rioting in the United States. It was called the Kerner Commission (after its chairman, Governor Otto Kerner of Illinois), and one of its chief conclusions was that rumors had significantly aggravated tensions and disorder in a substantial proportion of civil disorders (Kerner et al., 1968, p. 136). Earlier in this chapter, we mentioned the idea that rumors are triggered by a combination of anxiety and uncertainty; in that context, anxiety and uncertainty were independent variables, and rumor was the dependent variable. In the Kerner Commission's conclusion, rumors are the independent variable (i.e., the aggravating condition) and anxiety and uncertainty are the dependent variables (i.e., the aggravated tension). In the blink of an eye, the independent and dependent variables have switched places. Thus, the causal pattern is no longer linear (i.e., cause leads to effect); it now becomes a vicious circle in which some rumors can be viewed as "causes" (independent variables) one moment and "effects" (dependent variables) the next (Rosnow, 2001).

You may be wondering whether there is an agreed-upon way of classifying independent and dependent variables in behavioral and social research, in the way, for instance, that chemists can turn to the periodic table to find out how an element is classified. The answer is no. There are, in fact, scores of independent and dependent variables in the literature of behavioral and social research. As simply an illustration, two general categories of independent variables that encompass a great many specific forms are biological and social variables. We will use eating behavior to illustrate these two categories.

In one classic example, a biological independent variable is seen when blood from a well-fed animal, as compared to the blood of a hungry animal, is injected into another animal that is hungry. The hungry animal stops feeding (Davis, Gallagher, & Ladove, 1967). This finding suggested that a biological independent variable for satiation is somehow carried by the blood: Information about a cell need must be transmitted to a part of the central nervous system that is well supplied with blood and that can control and organize the food-getting activities of the whole animal. Another classic example of a biological independent variable affecting eating behavior was first identified by physicians who observed that tumors in the region of the brain near the hypothalamus and the pituitary gland caused the symptoms (described as *Froehlich's syndrome*) of atrophy of the genital organs and tremendous obesity. It was unclear, before experiments on animals were conducted, whether the syndrome was due to damage of the pituitary gland or to damage of the hypothalamus by the tumor. When the pituitary gland of normal animals was surgically removed, no obesity resulted, but later damage to the hypothalamus was followed by obesity (Bailey & Bremer, 1921). The status of the hypothalamus, not the pituitary gland, was the independent biological variable involved in the physiological regulation of food intake.

There are also many examples of social variables affecting eating behavior. The reason, of course, is that feeding by both humans and other species is affected not only by internal factors but also by many external conditions, including attitudes toward food in different cultures. For example, when people in Flemish Belgium, France, the United States, and Japan were surveyed for their beliefs about the diet-health link, whether they worried about food, and other issues related to the consumption of foods perceived as "healthier," the results revealed clear country differences in all domains except the importance of diet to health. Interestingly, among these cultural groups, Americans associated food most with health and least with pleasure (Rozin, Fischler, Imada, Sarubin, & Wrzesniewski, 1999). Having learned to eat at particular times of the day is another social variable that affects one's experiences of hunger (e.g., Schachter, 1968), as anyone who has ever crossed several time zones during an airplane trip can testify. Taste, appearance, and consistency are other obvious independent variables that strongly influence what foods humans prefer and how much food they will eat.

Independent variables can also occur in combinations, or *interactions* (more about this in Chapter 14). For example, approximately half of the 40%–50% of North American women who crave chocolate or sweets do so primarily during the part of the menstrual cycle surrounding the onset of menstruation, but it is not clear whether this craving is due to biological or social factors, or maybe to a combination of both (Michener, Rozin, Freeman, & Gale, 1999). Another example implying an interaction is that, if ice cream is adulterated with quinine in increasing quantities, obese people tend to refuse it before normal-weight people refuse it. Experiments have also found that obese people eat more of an expensive, good-tasting ice cream than do normal-weight people, but obese people do not work as hard as normal-weight or underweight people to obtain the food (Schachter, 1968).

Dependent variables also have no single classification system. Suppose a behavioral researcher wants to study pain avoidance as a source of *drive* somewhat different from the appetitive drives of hunger, thirst, and sex. (A drive is another example of a construct; it is a theoretical idea referring to the state of readiness of an organism to engage in physiologically connected behavior.) As no distinct element is characteristic of pain avoidance and compares with the drive for food, water, or a mate, what should the researcher choose as the dependent measure? Imagining yourself quickly withdrawing your hand from a shock-producing stimulus suggests that measuring the time it takes to withdraw from the stimulus (i.e., the *latency,* or delay, of withdrawal) is a good dependent measure. However, suppose the researcher is interested instead in the pain connected with extreme sexual deprivation. This topic seems more complex than food or water deprivation, though similarities certainly exist. If the subjects are hungry, sexually deprived male rats, the researcher might record their actions as they are faced with choosing between food and a female rat in heat.

When you peruse the journal literature in your field, you will see that these examples barely scratch the surface of the many kinds of dependent variables examined by behavioral scientists. Here is a more exotic example from the field of developmental psychology: Infants have always fascinated their parents by balancing precariously on the edge of a chair or table in apparent imitation of a tightrope walker. The parents' fascination is usually liberally mixed with fear for the safety of the infant. Obviously, an infant is not yet a fully competent and accurate judge of size and distance in its exploration of the space around it. The child's ability to perceive depth was a subject of intense interest to Eleanor J. Gibson and Richard D. Walk. These investigators worked with a "visual cliff," a board laid across a large sheet of glass that was raised a foot or more above the floor. A checkerboard pattern covered half the glass. On the other half, the same checkerboard pattern appeared on the floor directly under the glass. The visual cliff was created by the perceptual experience of the difference between the two sides. In one study, Gibson and Walk (1960) tested infants ranging in age from 6 to 14 months on the visual cliff. Each child was placed on the central board and was called by its mother from the "cliff" side and the "shallow" side successively. Most of the infants moved off the central board onto the glass, and all of these crawled out to the "shallow" side at least once. Only a few moved to the glass suspended above the pattern on the floor; most infants would not cross the apparent chasm to their mothers. The dependent variable was *crossing versus not crossing the apparent chasm.* As a consequence of having developed this not-so-ordinary dependent variable, Gibson and Walk discovered that most human infants discriminate depth as soon as they are able to crawl.

In this chapter, we have considered the initial part of the discovery phase as a process of creative insight, library research, and critical rumination leading to one or more good hypotheses. However, we began by cautioning against thinking that research *must* proceed in a formulaic way. One philosopher asserted that "successful research . . . relies now on one trick, now on another; the moves that advance it and the standards that define what counts as an advance are not always known to the movers" (Feyerabend, 1988, p. 1). Although a lot of what scientists do is perhaps based on myriad phenomena and a kind of surface intuition, there are also many tried-and-true methods. Before we resume our discussion of these methods, it is essential to have an understanding of the ethical considerations and guidelines that are now considered an essential component of the scientific method in behavioral and social research, and it is to this subject that we turn in the next chapter.

Summary of Ideas

1. Reichenbach's *discovery phase* of scientific inquiry includes coming up with a testable idea (in the form of a *working hypothesis*), crafting the research materials, and developing a study design and a plan to implement it. The *justification phase* creates the rationale for the plan of study and the data analysis, as well as the logic behind conclusions put forward.

2. Studying the sample research report in Appendix A, as well as the research proposal in this chapter (Exhibit 2.1), will give you a useful overview of these phases.

3. Besides getting good ideas for hypotheses and research from the relevant literature, colloquia, and poster presentations, six hypothesis-generating heuristics that were discussed are (a) the use of an intensive case study (Ebbinghaus's studies with nonsense syllables in Box 2.1); (b) making sense of a paradoxical incident (Latané and Darley's work on bystander intervention); (c) the use of analogical thinking (McGuire's inoculation model of propaganda resistance); (d) the resolution of conflicting results (Zajonc's social facilitation hypothesis); (e) the effort to improve on older ideas (Bem's idea of turning the old attitudes-shape-behavior principle on its head, and Skinner's distinction between Pavlovian conditioning and Thorndikian learning); and (f) serendipity (Rosenthal's work on the self-fulfilling nature of interpersonal expectations, and Rosnow's on rumor).

4. The research proposal is an agreement made between the student and the instructor regarding the student's plans to do a research study; it describes (a) the rationale and hypotheses of the proposed investigation, (b) the proposed method and data analysis, and (c) the ethics of the proposed plan of investigation.

5. The literature search can be facilitated by computerized databases, including full-text databases, which can be accessed online (see also Box 2.3).

6. *Operational definitions* identify variables on the basis of the empirical conditions (*operations*) that are used to measure or manipulate the variables, whereas *theoretical definitions* assign the meaning of terms abstractly or generally. Before you find yourself reinventing the wheel, look in standard references (e.g., Box 2.4) to see how concepts and variables are defined in the area in which you propose to do research.

7. *Theories* are sets of statements, generally including some hypotheses, connected by a logical argument (Festinger's social comparison theory). "Good" *working hypotheses* are plausible, testable, refutable (Popper's falsifiability criterion), and succinct (coherent and parsimonious, using "Occam's razor" to cut away what is superfluous).

8. *Constructs* are explanatory concepts that provide a scaffold or theoretical connection between variables.

9. *Variables* are what the researcher observes or measures, and as the term implies, they are likely to vary.

10. The *independent variable* (X) is the status of the determining or predictive event or condition, and countless types of events and conditions can qualify as independent variables in different situations. The *dependent variable* (Y) is the status of the effect or consequence, and there is also an infinite variety of dependent variables. Furthermore, the same event or condition may qualify as an independent variable in one situation and as a dependent variable in another, all depending on our particular interest (e.g., anxiety, uncertainty, and rumor). The events or conditions may also occur in combinations.

Key Terms

coherence p. 41
construct p. 39
dependent variable p. 42
discovery phase p. 24
experimental hypotheses
 p. 40
falsifiability p. 41

hypothesis p. 40
independent variable p. 42
justification phase p. 24
moderator variables p. 26
Occam's razor p. 41
operational definitions
 p. 38

parsimony p. 41
serendipity p. 30
theoretical definitions
 p. 38
theory p. 41
variable p. 42
working hypotheses p. 40

Multiple-Choice Questions for Review

1. Paul has suffered brain damage in a car accident. Dr. Thaler, a specialist in internal medicine, studies Paul intensively, giving him many clinical interviews and tests to measure his cognitive functioning. Based on his work with Paul, Dr. Thaler comes up with a brilliant new hypothesis, which he and others can test further in empirical research. From what we know so far, we would say that the doctor's hypothesis came about primarily through (a) serendipity; (b) analogical thinking; (c) an intensive case study; (d) the examination of a paradoxical incident.

2. A researcher at the University of Colorado is interested in studying dynamics in small groups (typically consisting of two to five people). She begins by thinking that people in small groups relate to each other much as the governments of large countries relate to each other. She develops hypotheses about small-group dynamics by thinking about how people in small groups are similar to diplomats at the United Nations. Her hypothesis came about through (a) attempting to resolve conflicting results; (b) improving on older ideas; (c) using analogical thinking; (d) serendipity.

3. A researcher at Monmouth University conducts a study of high school students and finds there is no relationship between the amount of time spent watching TV and grade point average. A researcher at Emporia University conducts a study of elementary school students and finds that those who watch a lot of TV tend to have very low grades. A third researcher, from Providence College, now develops a new theory stating that the relationship between watching TV and grade point average depends on other variables, including the age of the subject. This third researcher's theory has come about through (a) serendipity; (b) using analogical thinking; (c) attempting to resolve conflicting results; (d) examining intensive case studies.

4. A medical researcher at the University of Minnesota sets out to find a new treatment for cancerous brain tumors. She accidentally discovers a treatment for Parkinson's disease, a disease that is totally unrelated to cancer. Her new discovery has come about through (a) improving on older ideas; (b) using analogical thinking; (c) examining intensive case studies; (d) serendipity.

5. Edwin H. Land was with his 3-year-old daughter when she asked him why a camera could not produce pictures instantly. Thinking about her question while out for a walk, he hit on the idea for the Polaroid Land Camera. This is an illustration of how (a) circumstances can evoke ideas; (b) ideas are all around us if we keep our eyes, ears, and minds open to discovery; (c) creativity is not limited to art or music; (d) all of the above.

6. A researcher at the Baltimore campus of the University of Maryland is studying *intelligence* and defines it as "a person's general ability to adapt to his or her environment." This statement is (a) an operational definition; (b) a theoretical definition; (c) a dimensional definition; (d) none of the above.

7. The same researcher will be measuring the intelligence of high school students at the Baltimore City College. For this aspect of his study, the researcher defines *intelligence* as "a score on the

WAIS (Wechsler Adult Intelligence Scale)," an example of (a) an operational definition; (b) a theoretical definition; (c) a dimensional definition; (d) none of the above.

8. _____ is to operational definition as _____ is to theoretical definition. (a) Construct, variable; (b) Coherence, parsimony; (c) Parsimony, coherence; (d) Variable, construct

9. A researcher at Saint Anselm College conducts an experiment with volunteers. Half of them are given 1 ounce of colored water and told it is bourbon; the other half are given 4 ounces of the same liquid and told that it is bourbon. The researcher then gives all the participants a test of motor coordination. In this experiment, the test of motor coordination is the _____ variable. (a) control; (b) dependent; (c) independent; (d) none of the above

10. A researcher at the University of South Carolina, who is collaborating with the researcher at Saint Anselm College, conducts the same experiment with high schoolers in Columbia, South Carolina. In this experiment, the colored water the participants receive is the _____ variable. (a) control; (b) dependent; (c) independent; (d) none of the above

Discussion Questions for Review

1. A Rowan University student wants to see whether self-esteem affects academic performance. He asks 30 randomly selected students from his dormitory to fill out a self-esteem measure, and he divides the students into groups having high and low self-esteem on the basis of their test scores. He then compares the self-reported grade point average (GPA) of the two groups and concludes that high self-esteem does lead to a higher GPA. How has he operationalized his independent and dependent variables? If he finds these variables to be highly related, how well justified will he be in claiming that self-esteem affects academic performance?

2. A Virginia Tech student is interested in the personality trait of extraversion. Give an example of both an operational and a theoretical definition of this construct that she can use.

3. A friend tells a George Washington University student that astrology is accurate and reminds her that President Ronald Reagan consulted an astrologer. How should the student respond to her friend? Can you think of a way for her to do an empirical study to test her friend's assertion?

4. A San Diego State student is interested in studying revenge. Can you devise a causal hypothesis for her to test? How can you assess whether your hypothesis is "good" before passing it to her?

5. A "wolf boy" was discovered in Alaska and brought to a learned doctor for study. The doctor conducted many exploratory tests to determine the boy's reactions. The doctor slammed the door, and though everyone else flinched, the boy remained calm and unmoving. The doctor called out to his secretary, who was taking notes, "Write: Does not respond to noise." A nurse who was looking after the boy protested, "But, sir, I have seen the boy startle at the sound of a cracking nut in the woods 30 feet away!" The doctor paused and then instructed his secretary, "Write: Does not respond to *significant* noise." How was the doctor's explanatory observation flawed? How would you instead propose to study the wolf boy?

Answers to Review Questions

Multiple-Choice Questions

1. c	3. c	5. d	7. a	9. b
2. c	4. d	6. b	8. d	10. c

Discussion Questions

1. His independent variable was operationalized by scores on the self-esteem scale; his dependent variable was operationalized by self-reported GPA. Because this is a relational study rather than an experimental study, he would not be justified in drawing the causal inference that either variable led to or affected the other.

2. An operational definition could be the score earned on a standard psychological test purported to measure extraversion. A theoretical definition might be "the degree of social ease and smoothness shown in a group setting."

3. One study of the accuracy of astrological forecasts might ask a panel of "expert" astrologers to prepare a brief description of the personality of persons born under each of the 12 signs of the zodiac. A large number of students would then be asked to rate each of these 12 descriptions on the extent to which each of the descriptions applied to them. As long as the students know nothing about astrology, evidence for the accuracy of astrology would be obtained if the students rated the personality descriptions of their sign as more characteristic of them than the average of the other 11 descriptions. These students' roommates or friends could also rate the students, assuming the roommates or friends also knew nothing about astrology.

4. A causal hypothesis might be that revenge is more likely to occur when people feel they have been harmed intentionally by another. To evaluate this hypothesis, we can assess its plausibility (Is it consistent with accepted truths?); testability (Can it be subjected to empirical scrutiny?); credibility; refutability (Is it falsifiable if wrong?); and succinctness (Is the statement of the hypothesis coherent and parsimonious?).

5. The doctor did not take the boy's cultural background or context into account. We might study the boy by administering standard medical, neurological, and psychological evaluations; by giving him a wide choice of cultural artifacts (toys, tools, foods, pictures, videos, etc.) to observe, use, and explore; and by accompanying him to settings (e.g., parks, lakes, and forests) more like those in which he grew up in order to observe his behavior in a habitat to which he was more accustomed.

CHAPTER 3

Ethical Considerations and Guidelines

Preview Questions

- How do ethical guidelines in research function?
- What is informed consent, and when is it used?
- How are ethics reviews done and acted on?
- What are obstacles to the rendering of "full justice"?
- How can a "relationship of trust" be established?
- How do scientific quality and ethical quality intertwine?
- Is deception ever justified?
- What is the purpose of debriefing, and how do I do it?
- How is animal research governed by ethical rules?
- What are my ethical responsibilities when writing up my research?

How Do Ethical Guidelines in Research Function?

In Chapter 1, we discussed three general research approaches (descriptive, relational, and experimental), and you learned that any single study may be focused on one objective of these three types (to describe, to identify relationships, or to infer causality) or that the study might involve more than one approach. We noted that, within these three approaches, there are many different strategies and options (some of which are further illustrated in the next two chapters). In Chapter 2, we examined the "discovery phase" of scientific inquiry, in which credible, tightly reasoned, falsifiable hypotheses are created. In the sample proposal (pp. 33–35), under the heading "Ethical Considerations," Mary Jones stated her intention to use an informed-consent procedure, to tell the participants that their responses would be anonymous, and, at the end of the study, to debrief them and answer any of their questions. Once your instructor is satisfied that your research question is satisfactory and that it can be formulated in a scientifically testable way, you are ready to consider the ethics of the empirical strategy that you will pursue. The purpose of this chapter is to get you thinking about this challenge and to acquaint you with other ethical issues in empirical research with human or animal subjects.

The term **ethics** (from the Greek *ethos*, meaning "character" or "disposition") generally refers to the values by which people morally (from the Latin *moralis*, meaning "custom" or "manner") evaluate character or behavior. As the term is used in modern science, *ethics* refers to the values by which the conduct of researchers, as well as the morality of the various strategies they use, is evaluated. Thinking about ethical issues in research with human or animal subjects also forces us to confront our own moral presuppositions. For example, how would you answer the following three questions?

1. Is it right to withhold information from participants if I think that a full disclosure will bias their responses?

2. Am I justified in misleading participants by using a deception if it is necessary to study an important issue?

3. Is it permissible for me to invade the privacy of participants if there is no other way to gather essential facts?

Ethicists and researchers in behavioral science wrestle with questions like these all the time (e.g., Blanck, Bellack, Rosnow, Rotheram-Borus, & Schooler, 1992; Kimmel, 1981, 1988, 1991, 1996; Parloff, 1995; Rosenthal, 1994b; Rosnow, Rotheram-Borus, Ceci, Blanck, & Koocher, 1993; Schuler, 1982; Sieber, 1982a, 1982b, 1983, 1992, 1994; Stanley, Sieber, & Melton, 1987). As one writer commented, one thing that is sure is that research with human subjects always treads "on thin moral ice" inasmuch as we "are constantly in danger of violating someone's basic rights, if only the right of privacy" (Atwell, 1981, p. 89).

To help us in this process, we can consult legal, institutional, and professional **ethical guidelines** that contain rules and specifications pertaining to the question "Should I conduct this study?" when conducting the study involves a moral issue (Kimmel, 1996, p. 5). The guidelines that have figured most prominently in psychological research in the United States are those adopted by the American Psychological Association (APA; American Psychological Association, 1973, 1982, 1992). A few years ago, an APA task force addressed emerging ethical issues; the results of those deliberations were published in an informative book edited by Bruce D. Sales and Susan Folkman (2000); it also contains (a) the APA's 1992 ethical principles and code of conduct, (b) the U.S. government's regulations for the protection of human subjects, and (c) a government document that is well known to researchers, the Belmont Report (see Box 3.1). The Sales and Folkman book is not an official statement of the APA but does recommend five broad principles to organize researchers' thinking about ethical issues (M. B. Smith, 2000).

Principle I is respect for persons and their autonomy. *Autonomy* connotes "independence" and, in the context of research ethics, refers to a prospective participant's right as well as ability to choose whether to take part or to continue in the study. Potential participants are informed about what they will be getting into

BOX 3.1 The Belmont Report and the Tuskegee Study

The **Belmont Report** was developed in 1974 by a national commission that was given the task of formulating guidelines that would protect the rights and welfare of participants in biomedical and behavioral research. The document takes its name from discussions that were held in Washington, DC, at the Smithsonian Institution's Belmont Conference Center (National Commission for the Protection of Human Subjects of Biomedical and Behavioral Research, 1979). Before this report, there had been some safeguards to protect subjects in medical research, but serious violations had occurred nonetheless. In a notorious study done by the U.S. Public Health Service from 1932 to 1973, the course of syphilis in more than 400 low-income African-American men in Tuskegee, Alabama, had been monitored without the researchers' informing the men they had syphilis (they were told only that they had "bad blood") or giving them penicillin when, in 1947, it was found to effectively treat syphilis. Although given free health care and a free annual medical exam, they were warned that they would be dropped from the study if they sought treatment elsewhere; the researchers even got local doctors to promise not to provide antibiotics to subjects in the study (Stryker, 1997). The Tuskegee study was terminated after details were made public by a lawyer who had once been an epidemiologist for the U.S. Public Health Service. By this time, however, the disease had progressed in its predictable form without treatment: The men had experienced skeletal, cardiovascular, and central nervous system damage, and, in some cases, death (J. H. Jones, 1993). As a consequence of this horrendous episode, there remains a "legacy of mistrust" of government and medicine in many minority communities (Stryker, 1997, p. F4).

and are asked to provide their written consent if they choose to participate. Principle II is reminiscent of the Hippocratic oath that physicians take, in that researchers must also agree to "do no harm" (called **nonmaleficence**, or "not doing harm") and to try to maximize the benefits of their research (called **beneficence**, or the "doing of good"). Principle III is the pursuit and promotion of *justice,* which means that the burdens as well as the benefits of research are distributed equitably and without favoritism. Principle IV refers to the establishment of a relationship of *trust* with the research participants. Principle V is the fostering of fidelity and scientific integrity. In the following discussion, we will flesh out each principle, discuss how ethical guidelines are overseen, and raise questions for you to ponder. Of course, no set of guidelines can possibly anticipate every case, but these five general principles can provide a focal point from which to examine "matters of right or wrong, ought or ought not, a good action or a bad one" (Kimmel, 1996, p. 5).

What Is Informed Consent, and When Is It Used?

Principle I (respect for persons and their autonomy) proceeds from the idea that the researcher's ethical and legal responsibility is to ensure that each potential participant knows what the study involves and is free to decide whether or not to participate. In practice, the way this works is to tell prospective subjects about the research and to obtain their written agreement to participate (called **informed consent**). There are, however, situations in which obtaining informed consent is unnecessary or impossible, such as archival studies that use public records (illustrated in the next chapter). Another exempt case would be risk-free experiments in which informed consent would be counterproductive. For example, a team of social psychologists who were interested in tipping behavior had servers in a restaurant-diner draw or not draw a happy face on the back of customer checks before presenting them (Rind & Bordia, 1996). Before initiating the study, the researchers explained everything to the servers and the owner of the restaurant and obtained their permission to proceed. No effort was made to inform the customers (the subjects in this study) or to get them to sign a consent form, as telling them about the research would have destroyed the credibility of the manipulation and rendered the study meaningless. (Incidentally, the results were that drawing the happy face was associated with increased tips for the female server but did not increase tips for the male server.)

In most cases, however, informed consent is a requirement of the research procedure. In clinical trials to test new drugs in which the subjects are randomly assigned to a treatment group that receives the drug or a control group that receives a **placebo** (a fake "pill" masquerading as the real thing), they are all told that they will be blindly given an active drug or a placebo but are not told which one they will receive. In the recruitment of subjects for psychological experiments, the prospective participants are given a form that describes (a) the nature of the study, (b) any potential risk or inconvenience to them, (c) the procedure for ensuring the confidentiality of the data, and (d) the voluntary nature of their cooperation and their freedom to withdraw at any time without prejudice or consequence. The person is asked to sign a form in order to indicate that he or she understands the research and is willing to participate. Figure 3.1 shows in Section A an example of the consent portion of an informed-consent agreement and, in Section B, a form on which the participant may be asked about being *debriefed* after the study has been completed. (We will return to debriefing later in this chapter.) However, because of increased scrutiny by regulatory groups, the disclosure form and procedure in some studies have become so detailed and cumbersome that they could defeat the purpose for which they were intended (Imber et al., 1986). If the participants are confused about the nature of their participation, it cannot be said that the researcher complied with the spirit of the law.

Suppose the prospective participants have a limited or diminished capacity to understand the consent form. For example, young children may have difficulty understanding the consent agreement (e.g., Dorn, Susman, & Fletcher, 1995; Susman, Dorn, & Fletcher, 1992). Whenever research calls for children or adolescents to participate, the researcher is required to obtain parental consent before proceeding and is not permitted to make appeals to children to participate before this consent is obtained (Scott-Jones & Rosnow, 1998). If the children do not live with their parents

---

Instructions to participant: Before you participate in this study, please print and then sign your name in the space provided in Section A. Once the study is over and you have been debriefed, you will be asked to initial the three statements in Section B to indicate your agreement.

Section A

I, _____, voluntarily give my consent to participate in this project. I have been informed about, and feel that I understand, the basic nature of the project. I understand that I may leave at any time and that my anonymity will be protected.

_____   _____

Signature of Research Participant   Date

Section B

Please initial each of the following statements once the study has been completed and you have been debriefed:

_____I have been debriefed.

_____I was not forced to stay to complete the study.

_____All my questions have been answered satisfactorily.

Figure 3.1   Example of the written-consent portion of the informed-consent agreement.

(e.g., they may be wards of some agency), the researcher can speak with an advocate who is appointed to act in the best interests of the child. Once the informed consent of the parent or advocate has been obtained, the researcher asks the child on the day of the study whether he or she wishes to participate—assuming the child is mature enough to be asked about participation. Incidentally, some participants may mistakenly assume that, by signing an informed-consent agreement, they have relinquished their legal right to sue the researcher for negligence (T. Mann, 1994). In fact, the right to sue is protected by federal regulations on the use of human subjects (U.S. Department of Health and Human Services, 1983).

Because college and university students are so readily available, they are used frequently in studies by psychologists. Students as research subjects have taught us a tremendous amount about cognition, perception, and social behavior. Nonetheless, concerns have been raised about generalizing from students to the population in general. In Chapter 7, we will discuss the problem that some participants may be especially sensitive and responsive to uncontrolled task-orienting cues (called *demand characteristics*), raising a question about the degree to which observed results are due to the experimental treatment rather than to demand characteristics. There are techniques for dealing with this issue, which we will discuss in the later chapter. In many departments, students are required to participate in a certain number of hours of research. Researchers must still factor in the freedom-of-choice ethical requirement, typically by giving students a choice whether to participate in the study or to select some alternative requirement. There must be an educational benefit to the students who participate in the research (e.g., a deeper understanding of the research process and, presumably, the material they are learning in the course). To prevent coercion or the appearance of coercion, the alternative requirement must be educational and no more arduous than the research participation (e.g. reading one or more journal papers or attending a special lecture).

How Are Ethics Reviews Done and Acted On?

Implicit in Principle II (beneficence and nonmaleficence) is the idea that researchers will attempt to maximize the benefits of their research. The researcher affiliated with an academic institution submits a detailed written proposal of the planned research to a panel of evaluators, called an **institutional review board (IRB)**, which provides an oversight mechanism by performing a **risk-benefit analysis** of the proposed study. Research classified by the IRB as of **minimal risk** (i.e., the likelihood and extent of harm to participants is no greater than that typically experienced in everyday life) is eligible for an **expedited review** (i.e., it can be evaluated without undue delay). Research involving more than minimal risk automatically raises a red flag that signals the need for a detailed assessment by the IRB. Student projects in research courses typically fall in the no-risk category and are typically evaluated by either the instructor or a surrogate committee responsible to the IRB.

Figure 3.2 shows a "decision-plane model" that helps us conceptualize how this review process is supposed to work (Rosenthal & Rosnow, 1984). After reviewing a detailed description of the proposed study, and after the researchers have responded to specific questions, the IRB members consider aspects of the study that may have risk-benefit implications. The questions that researchers must answer vary from one institution to another (see Table 3.1 for sample questions). Basically, the risks and

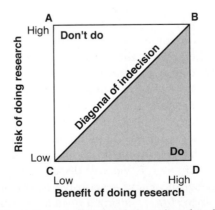

Figure 3.2   Representation of an idealized risk-benefit ethical evaluation. Studies falling at A are unlikely to be approved by an IRB; studies falling at D are likely to be approved; and studies falling along the B–C diagonal are likely to be returned to the investigators for further elaboration and possible modifications.

Table 3.1   Sample Questions for Ethics Review

Investigator

1. Who is the primary investigator, and who is supervising the study?
2. Will anyone be assisting you in this investigation?
3. Have you or the others whose names are listed above had any experience with this kind of research?

Nature of the Study

4. What is the purpose of this research? What is it about?
5. What will the research participants be asked to do, or what will be done to them?
6. Will deception be used? If the answer is yes, why is it necessary?
7. What is the nature of the deception, and when will the debriefing take place?
8. Will the participants risk any harm (physical, psychological, legal, or social) by taking part in this research?
9. If there are any risks, how do you justify them? How will you minimize the risks?

Research Participants

10. How will you recruit the research participants?
11. How do you plan to explain the research to your potential participants and obtain their informed consent?
12. What should be the general characteristics of your research participants (e.g., age range, sex, institutional affiliation, and the projected number of participants)?
13. What, if any, are the special characteristics you need in your research participants (e.g., children, pregnant women, racial or ethnic minorities, mentally retarded persons, prisoners, or alcoholics)?
14. Are other institutions or individuals cooperating in or cosponsoring the study?
15. Do the participants have to be in a particular mental or physical state to participate usefully?

Material

16. If electrical or mechanical equipment will be used, how has it been checked for safety?
17. What standardized tests, if any, will be used? What information will be provided to the participants about their scores on these tests?

Confidentiality

18. What procedure will you use to ensure the confidentiality of the data?

Debriefing

19. How do you plan to debrief the participants?

benefits of doing a particular study are evaluated on scales of perceived methodological and societal values or interests. "Risks" of doing the research might include annoyances or inconveniences to the subjects and the loss of privacy, whereas the "benefits" of doing the research might include the advance of scientific knowledge and educational or psychological advantages to the participants or to other people at other times and places. Studies that are well thought out and are of minimal risk, and that address important issues, will be judged more beneficial than studies that are not well thought out, that involve physical or psychological risks, or that address trivial issues. In Figure 3.2, studies falling in the upper left area (labeled A) are *not* approved because the risks are high and the benefits low; studies falling in the lower right area (labeled D) *are* approved since the benefits are high and the risks low. Studies falling along the B–C diagonal (the "diagonal of indecision") are too hard to decide about and are returned to the researchers for changes or further information.

A limitation of this idealized assessment is that it focuses only on the risks and benefits of *doing research* and ignores the societal and scientific costs of *not doing research*. In view of this limitation, critics have argued that IRBs are typically held to a less rigorous standard of accountability than are researchers (Haywood, 1976; Rosnow, 1997). Bureaucrats and pressure groups may also obstruct important scientific research (Brooks-Gunn & Rotheram-Borus, 1994). For example, a study involving a sexual survey of adolescents was terminated prematurely on the grounds that it "violated community norms," but stopping this research deprived the community of fundamental data that were needed to address vital health problems (Wilcox & Gardner, 1993). Another issue is that IRBs may ignore potential benefits altogether and use only a "risk analysis" as the basis of their decision making. Not surprisingly, given the subjectivity of an ethical review, there is considerable variability in the decision making of different IRBs. Researchers argue that getting a sensitive proposal approved is often a matter of the luck of drawing a particular group of IRB members whose values happen to be similar to the values of the researchers (Ceci, Peters, & Plotkin, 1985; Kimmel, 1991).

What Are Obstacles to the Rendering of "Full Justice"?

The spirit of Principle III (justice) is that the burdens and benefits of the study are supposed to be distributed fairly. In the case of the Tuskegee study (Box 3.1), none of the men who participated could have benefited in any significant way; they alone bore the awful burdens. In the model in Figure 3.2, this study would clearly fall at A. But suppose it had been a medical experiment to test the effectiveness of a new drug to cure syphilis, and suppose the strategy was to give half the men at random the new drug and the other half a placebo. Do you think it is acceptable to deprive some people (those in the control group) of the benefits of a potentially lifesaving drug? This is a divisive question in our society, but one alternative that has been used is to give the control group the best available medicine, so that the comparison is between the new drug and the best available option. (In 2000, the World Medical Association adopted the principle that a placebo should be used only when no other effective treatment is available for comparison with the therapeutic intervention being tested.)

Justice also implies fair-mindedness, or impartiality, but this is usually a matter of one's perception or subjective judgment. Even if the objective is desirable, some people might see the study as unfair. For example, in the 1970s, there was a field experiment, known as the *Rushton study,* that was designed to improve the quality of work life in a mining operation owned by the Rushton Mining Company in Pennsylvania (Blumberg & Pringle, 1983). After months of careful preparation by the researchers and the managers of the mine, an appeal was made for volunteers for a work group that would have direct responsibility for the production in one section of the mine. The experiment called for the workers in this group to abandon their traditional roles and to coordinate their own activities after extensive training in safety laws, good mining practices, and job safety analysis. They were also given the top-rate wages, those paid for the highest skilled job classification in that section. Not surprisingly, they were enthusiastic proponents of "our way of working." Unfortunately, trouble soon reared its head. Workers in the rest of the mine (who were the control group) were resentful of the "injustice" of the situation: "Why should inexperienced volunteers receive special treatment and higher pay than other miners with many more years on the job?" Rumors circulated through the mine that the volunteers were "riding the gravy train" and being "spoon-fed," and that the project was a "communist plot" because all the volunteers received the same rate and the company was "making out" at their expense. As a consequence, the study had to be terminated prematurely.

Yet, is it reasonable to expect *full justice* to be achieved in any research situation? As life constantly reminds us, it is not always easy to distribute benefits and burdens equally. For example, a drug company announces a new medicine that slows the course of multiple sclerosis, but the company is unable to produce enough of the new medicine to treat everyone who wants it (Lewin, 1994). The ethical question is how to select people for treatment. The company's answer is to have people register for a lottery and then to draw names at random as the medicine becomes available. Each person in the lottery has the same likelihood of being chosen—in the same way, for example, that a lottery was used in the United States in World War II, the Korean War, and the Vietnam War to select conscripts for the American military. Is this a "just" procedure because everyone who is eligible has an equal chance of being selected for life or death? Suppose people are selected to receive the new medicine not randomly, but on the grounds of who is most likely to benefit from it. Suppose there is a draft but conscripts for the military are selected on the basis of who is the biggest and strongest (Broome, 1984). Which approach, in your view, is *more ethical*—a random lottery or selection on the basis of who is more likely to benefit or survive? The point is that the principle of justice is an ideal that is unlikely to be fully achieved in a world that is never fully just (Sales & Folkman, 2000).

How Can a "Relationship of Trust" Be Established?

Principle IV (the establishment of a relationship of trust with the research participants) proceeds on the assumption that there is informed consent and that nothing will happen to jeopardize this agreement. And yet we asked you earlier, "Is it right to withhold information from participants if I think that a full disclosure will bias their responses?" To deal with this situation, researchers *debrief* people after their participation in the study (described later in this chapter). Promising subjects that their disclosures will be held in strict confidence is another way of establishing trust. **Confidentiality** means that the participants' disclosures are "protected against unwarranted access"; it is a way of ensuring their privacy and may be a way of improving the data they provide, since it seems to lead to more open and honest responses (e.g., Esposito, Agard, & Rosnow, 1984).

To maintain confidentiality in your research, you need to seek advice from your instructor to set procedures in place that will protect your data. For example, you can devise a coding system in which the names of your participants are represented by a sequence of numbers that no one else can identify. When participants are not asked to give any personal information that would identify them, their privacy is automatically protected. In government-funded biomedical and behavioral research, it may be possible for the researcher to obtain a "certificate of confidentiality," which is a formal agreement that requires the researcher to keep the data confidential (and exempts the data from subpoena). The extent to which such a certificate can actually provide legal protection has not been established in the courts, however, and is complicated by the existence of laws that require the reporting of certain sensitive information.

For example, the Child Abuse Prevention and Treatment Act of 1974 and its revisions and amendments mandate that each state pass laws to require the reporting of child abuse and neglect. The nature and wording of such statutes is left to the discretion of the states, but the lists of people who are now obligated to report suspected cases in each state have expanded over the years (Liss, 1994). Suppose you are a member of a team of developmental researchers studying child abuse, and you want to protect the privacy and confidentiality of your respondents. Your legal responsibility is to report suspected cases of child abuse, but reporting a suspected culprit means violating the trust you established with the respondents when you promised to hold their disclosures confidential. Furthermore, it is possible that charges of abuse will not be proven, although this possibility does not excuse you from your legal responsibility (Liss, 1994).

How Do Scientific Quality and Ethical Quality Intertwine?

The essence of Principle V (fidelity and scientific integrity) is that there is a close relationship between scientific quality and ethical quality (R. Rosenthal, 1994b). One obvious example is that poor-quality research is wasteful of resources. Badly designed or sloppily implemented studies, mindlessly analyzed data, and exaggerated conclusions (called *hyperclaiming*) may be not only wasteful but misleading, even potentially damaging to society. Inadequately reported studies are especially difficult to evaluate for the legitimacy of the research claims, which in turn could have profound ramifications for policymaking decisions (Blanck, Schartz, Ritchie, & Rosenthal, 2006). As a case in point, randomized clinical trials in medical research have been criticized as being vague in the reporting of vital details about how the participants were allocated to conditions. Despite efforts to correct this problem, it was noted recently that many medical studies reported information ambiguously, and the result could be biased estimates of the effectiveness of the clinical treatments (Moher, Schulz, & Altman, 2001). The deliberate omission of results that contradict the researcher's hypothesis is another violation of the fidelity and scientific integrity principle. The most blatant of deliberate misrepresentations is the reporting of "results" that never were, which constitutes fraud. That behavior, if detected, ends (or ought to end) the scientific career of the perpetrator. In the same way that the career of a scientist who falsifies data or fabricates results is compromised, the consequences will be harsh for a student writing a research report in which the data or results are fabricated.

There is another way in which inaccuracy is wasteful of resources, and it is a common problem in students' research reports (Rosnow & Rosnow, 2006). It concerns what might be described as "missing the forest for the p," because it pertains to how "p values" can cloud students' perceptions. We will have more to say about p values in later chapters, but the point is not to behave as if there were some special place in the instructor's heart for students with p values less than .05, or to think that a nonsignificant p means there was zero effect or no obtained relationship between an independent and a dependent variable. Your instructor will have just as much admiration for a "statistically nonsignificant" result as for a "statistically significant" result, as long as the data are reported accurately and honestly, and appropriate conclusions are drawn. In Chapter 12, we will discuss the concepts of statistical significance, effect size, and power, all essential to fostering an understanding of the interpretation of statistical tests such as t (Chapter 13), F (Chapter 14), and chi-square (Chapter 15).

Another problem that instructors frequently see in students' reports is implying a causal relationship where the data do not support it. Is this also an "ethical issue" and not just a design issue? Suppose an IRB receives a proposal for a study that, according to the researchers' own statement, "will test whether private schools, more than public schools, improve children's intellectual functioning." Children from randomly selected private and public schools will be tested extensively, and the hypothesis will be tested by a comparison of the scores earned by students from private and public schools. The research design and proposal raise ethical problems because the design does not permit reasonable causal inference ("intellectual functioning" might be due to intrinsic differences in the different populations). Resources will be wasted (e.g., money will be wasted, and people's time will be taken from potentially more beneficial educational experiences), and conclusions that are unwarranted and inaccurate will result. Were it not an ethical and practical absurdity, an alternative would be to propose an experiment in which children would be randomly assigned to either private or public schools. Another choice, which is both practical and ethical, is to accurately state in the proposal exactly what the study design can tell us. If the research proposal had stated that the purpose of the investigation was to learn about *performance differences* between students in private and public schools, then the original design would have been quite suitable (Rosenthal, 1994b).

Is Deception Ever Justified?

Another example of the interrelationship between ethics and scientific integrity involves the use of deception. Although deception is commonly used in everyday life, it is considered an ethical problem in science. Recall that Mary Jones (sample proposal in Chapter 2) made a point of noting that her proposed study design did not involve deception. As an illustration of its use by investigative journalists, CBS-TV's news program *60 Minutes* used an elaborate deception to study claims made by polygraph examiners (Saxe, 1991). On the pretense that they represented a photography magazine owned by CBS, the *60 Minutes* people recruited four polygraph examiners randomly chosen from the telephone directory and asked each of them to identify which of the magazine's employees had stolen more than $500 worth of camera equipment. No one, in fact, had stolen anything, and a different person was "fingered" by the *60 Minutes* staff for each of the polygraphers. The "culprits" were confederates who were paid $50 by the program staff if they could convince the polygrapher of their innocence. A hidden camera filmed the testing situation without the polygraphers' knowing they were being recorded. The film record showed each polygraph examiner *trying* to get the "guilty" person to confess. Dramatically, the *60 Minutes* report showed that the polygraphers did not necessarily "read" the psychophysiological polygraph information to make their diagnoses of deception.

If this had been a scientific study, problems would have arisen because of the moral conflict between the respect for persons and their autonomy (Principle I) and a duty to scientific integrity (Principle V). As one researcher put it, "The demonstration was very clever, but dishonest: CBS lied to the polygraphers. The four polygraphers unwittingly starred in a television drama viewed by millions . . . yet it is hard to think of a way to do this study without deception" (Saxe, 1991, p. 409). Informing the polygraphers that they were the subjects of a *60 Minutes* exposé would have made the study—and no doubt the results—quite different. Were this study to be submitted for approval to an IRB, it is unlikely that it would be approved in this form. Would you say that the deception used was justified by the study's purpose (i.e., to expose fraud), or would you instead argue that the ends did not justify the means? Do you think using any form of deception is ever justified in scientific research? In fact, its use by leading social psychologists in a number of classic studies has been a source of controversy for years (cf. Gross & Fleming, 1982; Kelman, 1968; Menges, 1973; Z. Rubin, 1974; I. Silverman, 1977). The most famous example was the research conducted by Stanley Milgram (1974) on obedience to authority.

Milgram's research, which was inspired in part by Solomon Asch's work on conformity (discussed in Chapter 1), also stemmed from Milgram's profound dismay about the horrifying results of blind obedience to Nazi commands in World War II (see also Box 3.2). During that nightmarish period, the unthinkable became a reality when millions of innocent men, women, and children were systematically slaughtered. Milgram's purpose in performing his experiments was to study the psychological mechanism that links blind obedience to destructive behavior. In particular, he

BOX 3.2 Milgram's Inspiration for His Obedience Experiments

As Milgram (1977) explained, he had wanted to make the classic work done by Solomon Asch "more humanly significant" (p. 12). Asch had designed his investigation to determine under what conditions people will remain independent of their groups and when they will conform. It will be recalled that Asch used accomplices to influence an individual subject's expressed judgment concerning which of three lines was closest in length to a standard line. Milgram (1977) recalled the moment when he suddenly hit on the idea for his own experiments:

> I was dissatisfied that the test of conformity was judgments about *lines*. I wondered whether groups could pressure a person into performing an act whose human import was more readily apparent, perhaps behaving aggressively toward another person, say by administering increasingly severe shocks to him. But to study the group effect you would also need an experimental control; you'd have to know how the subject performed without any group pressure. At that instant, my thought shifted, zeroing in on this experimental control. Just how far *would* a person go under the experimenter's orders? It was an incandescent moment, the fusion of a general idea on obedience with a specific technical procedure. Within a few minutes, dozens of ideas on relevant variables emerged, and the only problem was to get them all down on paper. (p. 12)

wanted to see how far *ordinary adults* would go in carrying out the orders of a legitimate authority to act against a third person. To study this question, Milgram tricked volunteer participants, placed in the role of the "teacher," into believing that they would be giving varying degrees of painful electric shock to a third person (the "learner") each time the learner made a mistake in a certain task. Milgram also varied the distance between the teacher and the learner, to see whether the teachers would be less ruthless in administering the electric shocks as they got closer and the learner pressed the teacher to quit. The results were, to Milgram as well as to others, almost beyond belief. A great many participants (the "teachers") unhesitatingly obeyed the experimenter's "Please continue" or "You have no choice, you must go on" and continued to increase the level of the shocks no matter how much the learner pleaded with the "teacher" to stop. What especially surprised Milgram was that no one ever walked out of the room in disgust or protest. This remarkable obedience was seen time and time again in a number of different settings where the experiment was repeated. "It is the extreme willingness of adults to go to almost any lengths on the command of an authority that constitutes the chief finding of the study and the fact most urgently demanding explanation," Milgram wrote (1974, p. 5).

Although the "learner" in these studies was a confederate of Milgram's and no electrical shocks were really administered by the "teacher," concerns about ethics and values have dogged these studies ever since they were first reported. Psychologist Diane Baumrind (1964) quoted Milgram's descriptions of the reactions of some of his subjects—such as "a twitching, stuttering wreck, who was rapidly approaching a point of nervous collapse" (Milgram, 1963, p. 377). Baumrind argued that once Milgram had seen how stressful his deception was, he should have immediately terminated the research on moral grounds. She insisted that there was "no rational basis" for ever using this kind of manipulation, unless the participants were fully aware of the psychological dangers to themselves and effective steps were taken to ensure the restoration of their well-being afterward.

Milgram responded that the chief horror was not that a stressful deception was carried out, but instead that the participants obeyed. The signs of extreme tension in some participants were quite unexpected, but his intention had not been to create anxiety, he explained. Indeed, before carrying out the research, he had asked professional colleagues about their expectations, and none of the experts had anticipated the blind obedience that resulted. Like the experts, he had thought the participants would refuse to follow orders. Moreover, he was skeptical about Baumrind's contention that there had been psychologically injurious effects on the participants, in spite of the dramatic appearance of anxiety in some of them. To ensure that the participants would not feel worse after the experiment than before, he had taken elaborate precautions to debrief them. They were given an opportunity for a friendly reconciliation with the "learner" after the experiment was concluded and were shown that the "learner" had not received dangerous electric shocks but had only pretended to receive them. To find out whether there were any delayed negative effects, Milgram sent questionnaires to the participants to elicit their reactions after they had read a full report of his investigation. Less than 1% of those who received this questionnaire said they regretted having participated; 15% were neutral or ambivalent, and over 80% said they were glad to have participated. Milgram interpreted these results as providing another good reason for his research:

> The central moral justification for allowing my experiment is that it was judged acceptable by those who took part in it. Criticism of the experiment that does not take account of the tolerant reaction of the participants has always seemed to me hollow. This applies particularly to criticism centering on the use of false illusion (or "deception," as the critics prefer to say) that fails to relate this detail to the central fact that subjects find the device acceptable. The participants, rather than the external critics, must be the ultimate source of judgment in these matters. (Milgram, 1977, p. 93)

In arguing that research participants, not the experimenter, are the ultimate arbiters of whether a particular deception is morally acceptable, Milgram was speaking before the advent of IRBs. In fact, *when* Milgram did his work, it was well within the norms of deception then in use. But suppose the study had never been done, and it was you who wanted to do it. The IRB rejects your proposal and responds that the use of deception in any form is unacceptable. "Be open and honest

with your participants, and have them sign an informed-consent agreement that indicates they fully understand what the research is about," the IRB admonishes you.
Is getting rid of the deception, and being open and honest, a reasonable requirement in this case, or could it present a further ethical dilemma? Before you answer,
imagine an experiment like Milgram's in which the experimenter instead greeted
the participants by saying something like the following:

> Hello. Today we are going to do a study on blind obedience to a malevolent au-
> thority, particularly emphasizing the effects of physical distance from the victim on
> willingness to inflict pain on her or him. You will be in the "close" condition,
> which means that you are expected to be somewhat less ruthless in your behavior.
> In addition, you will be asked to fill out a test of your fascist tendencies because
> we believe there is a positive relation between scores on our fascism test and blind
> obedience to an authority who requests that we hurt others. Any questions?

A completely open and honest statement to a research participant of the intention of the experiment might involve a briefing of this kind, but would it result in
fewer problems? Clearly, such a briefing would be absurd if you were serious in
your wish to learn about blind obedience to authority. If the participants had full
information about your experimental purpose, plans, procedures, and hypotheses,
it seems unlikely they would behave as Milgram's participants did. They might instead base their behavior on what they *thought* the world was like or what they
believed *you* thought the world was like. This is not to say that any scientists would
advocate the use of deception merely for its own sake. At the same time, however,
there may be few who feel that they can do entirely without certain minimal risk
deceptions (e.g., disguising the name of the "California Fascism Scale" by calling it
the "Personal Reaction Inventory"). For example, surely no social psychologist
would advocate giving up the study of prejudice or discrimination. But would it be
worth the effort and expenditure if all measures of prejudice and discrimination
had to be openly labeled? If you answered yes, what about the ethical dilemma of
reporting results that would be misleading because the subjects were not open and
honest regarding their beliefs and behavior? Adopting an uncompromising moral
orientation that decries deception as wrong would mean banishing *all forms* of deception or producing misleading results in some cases.

Some argue that deception in *any* form is morally wrong, whereas others
argue that there are special circumstances in which it is needed to ensure the integrity of important scientific data (Principle V). In general, we can distinguish between two forms of deception: active and passive. In **active deception** (sometimes
described as *deception by commission*), the participants are actively misled, as
when they are given false information about the purpose of the research, or when
they unwittingly interact with confederates, or when they are secretly given a
placebo. In **passive deception** (sometimes described as *deception by omission*),
information is withheld from the participants, as when they are not informed of the
meaning of their responses when they are given a projective test or when they are
not told the full details of the research (Arellano-Galdames, 1972). Surely, most
people—most scientists included—would be willing to weigh and measure the "sins"

of commission and omission resulting from the use of deception, and to judge some to be larger than others (e.g., Kimmel, 2006).

For example, refraining from telling diners that you are doing a study of tipping behavior, or not telling a participant that an "experiment in the learning of verbal materials is designed to show whether earlier, later, or intermediate material is better remembered," does not seem to be an especially heinous deception. The reason most of us would probably not view these deceptions with alarm seems, on first glance, to be that they involve an omission (a passive deception) rather than a commission (an active deception). A truth is left unspoken; a lie is not told. But what if the verbal learning experiment were instead represented as a "study of the effects of the meaningfulness of verbal material on retention or recall"? That is a direct lie, designed to misdirect the participant's attention from a crucial aspect of the experimental treatment to another factor that really does not interest the scientist. Even this change, however, does not seem to make the deception appalling, though the "sin" is now one of commission and the scientist has not withheld information from, but actively lied to, the participant. It is not simply the active or passive style of a deception that is its measure, but its effect on the participant. Few people would care whether participants focused on a noncrucial aspect of verbal material rather than on a crucial aspect, because this deception seems to have no perilous consequence. Similarly, not telling diners they are participating in an experiment on tipping behavior does not seem shocking in any way. It is not deception so much as it is potentially *harmful* deception that we would like to minimize. But how shall we decide what is potentially harmful? Does it come down to someone's opinion, and if so, whose opinions should prevail? Individual investigators, their colleagues, IRBs, and, to some extent, ultimately, the general society that supports the research must decide whether a particular deception is worth a possible increase in knowledge.

What Is the Purpose of Debriefing, and How Do I Do It?

We mentioned that Milgram's research participants were given the opportunity to have a friendly reconciliation with the "learner." They were also given an opportunity to engage in an extended discussion with the experimenter about the purpose of the study (i.e., a **debriefing**), and about why it was necessary to use the particular deception (see also Box 3.3). The debriefing session gives us an opportunity to remove any misconceptions and anxieties the participants may have, so that their sense of dignity remains intact and they feel that their time has not been wasted (Blanck et al., 1992; Harris, 1988). If deception has been used in the study, it is also important to remove any "detrimental impact on the participant's feeling of trust in interpersonal relationships" (APA, 1973, p. 77). However, just as there were research situations in which informed consent seemed impossible or counterproductive, there are also situations in which the use of debriefing seems impossible or inadvisable. For example, a full debriefing is inadvisable if it would produce stress or be ineffective, such as when the subjects are children, are mentally ill, or are retarded (Blanck et al., 1992).

In many instances, however, debriefings not only are ethically essential but can also provide an opportunity to explore what the participants thought about the

BOX 3.3 Debriefing

The word *debrief* was first used by the British military in World War II to describe the procedure used by Royal Air Force (RAF) interrogators of pilots who had returned from bombing missions. Before the mission, the RAF pilot was "briefed" and, after the mission, "debriefed." You can see that the term *debriefing,* when it refers to informing research subjects of the nature and purpose of the deception used in a study is a misnomer; such a session should be called a *briefing session*. On the other hand, when researchers use this opportunity to interrogate the subjects about their perceptions, the term *debriefing session* is more appropriate (Harris, 1988).

study, providing the researcher with an experiential context in which to interpret the data and with good ideas for further investigation (Blanck et al., 1992; Jones & Gerard, 1967). Milgram's debriefings were unusually extensive, far more so, in fact, than is characteristic of most experiments. Because he duped the participants into believing that they were administering painful electric shocks to another person, Milgram felt it necessary to go to elaborate lengths to remove any lingering stresses or anxieties. He told the participants that their behavior was normal and that any conflict or tension that they may have experienced had been felt by other participants. At the conclusion of the research, all received a comprehensive written report detailing the experimental procedures and findings and, of course, treating the participants' own part in the research with dignity. They were also administered a questionnaire that asked them again to express their thoughts and feelings about their behavior in the research. A year later, a psychiatrist experienced in outpatient treatment interviewed 40 of the participants, to identify any possible injurious effects resulting from the experiment, and found no evidence of any traumatic reactions.

Most studies do not require debriefing covering so wide an area or so great a span of time as Milgram's study, but the debriefing procedure used should be sufficiently focused to satisfy the participants about having cooperated in the investigation. The following four guidelines (Aronson & Carlsmith, 1968; Sieber, 1982a, 1983) may be incorporated into more typical debriefings:

1. If your study involved some form of deception, you should give whatever explanation is needed to reveal the truth about the research and your carefully considered use of the deception. You might explain that science is the search for truth and that it is sometimes necessary to resort to deception to uncover truth.

2. Despite your sincere wish to treat your participants responsibly, some of them may have left the study feeling gullible, as if they have been "had" by a fraudulent procedure. Whatever kind of deception you used, you should clearly explain it and assure your participants that being taken in does not reflect in any way on their intelligence or character but simply shows the validity or effectiveness of the study's design. You presumably went to some pains to achieve

an effective scientific design in order not to waste the participants' time and effort in your search for truth.

3. You should proceed gradually and patiently, with the chief aim of gently unfolding the details of any deception that you used. A patient discussion will go far to reduce the subjects' negative feelings. Instead of thinking of themselves as "victims," they may more correctly realize that they have been "coinvestigators" in the search for truth.

4. Never use a **double deception**, that is, a second deception in what the participant thinks is the official debriefing. Double deception can be terribly damaging: Instead of restoring your participants to the frame of mind in which they entered the study, you are leaving them with a lie. It is also unethical.

How Is Animal Research Governed by Ethical Rules?

Although the primary focus of this book is on research with human subjects, we did mention in Chapter 2 the Pavlovian conditioning of a dog and Thorndike's studies of cats in puzzle boxes. Given the biological continuities between animals and human beings, animals are used as research subjects in about 8% of psychological research (Kimmel, 1996). The use of animals in experiments has been vigorously debated (Slife & Rubinstein, 1992) because the very assumption of biological continuity raises ethical dilemmas. That is, it should follow that animals, like humans, must experience some measure of pain and suffering. As a consequence of concerns about the treatment of animals, federal laws and licensing requirements now spell out the responsibilities of researchers and animal facilities to protect the well-being of experimental animals, consistent with advancements made possible by research.

For example, the Animal Welfare Act sets specific standards for the use of animals in research, such as their handling, housing, feeding, and use in the study of drugs. Research institutions are also subject to unannounced inspections by the U.S. Department of Agriculture at any time, and if violations are uncovered, the institution's license to run animal facilities may be revoked. Beyond these federal regulations, animal researchers are subject to institutional and professional requirements. Institutions with animal care facilities make a point of underscoring the experimenter's responsibilities, and any proposed animal research also routinely undergoes ethical review. In addition, the APA and other professional and scientific organizations around the world have elaborated on the ethical obligations of investigators of animal behavior. For example, the APA insists that researchers make every effort to minimize discomfort, illness, and pain in their experimental animals. Any procedure that subjects animals to pain, stress, or privation may be used only when no alternative procedure is available and the goal of the research is justified by its prospective scientific, educational, or applied value.

Nevertheless, the confrontation between those who argue for and those who argue against experiments using animals is often quite heated. One point of disagreement concerns whether the interests of human beings supersede the interests of animals. At one extreme, many animal rights activists argue that animals and humans have equal rights and that benefits to humans are not a justification for animal experimentation. On the other side, it has been argued that animals have often benefited from the research, such as from discoveries in veterinary medicine (e.g., vaccines for deadly diseases) and experimental insights that have helped to preserve some species from extinction (e.g., the wild condor). Scientists point out that the use of animals in a variety of behavioral and biomedical studies has directly benefited humans in a great many ways. In medical research, the development of vaccines for rabies and yellow fever was made possible by the use of animal proxies (Paul, Miller, & Paul, 2000).

In behavioral science, research with animals has led to advances in the rehabilitation of persons suffering from spinal cord injuries, in the treatment of disease and eating disorders, and in improvements in communication with the severely retarded. For example, Roger Sperry, who won a Nobel Prize for his work, did experiments with cats and monkeys that demonstrated that severing the fibers connecting the right and left hemispheres of the brain (resulting in a so-called split brain) did not impair a variety of functions, including learning and memory. This important discovery led to a split-brain treatment for severe epilepsy and made it possible for people who would have been confined to hospitals to lead a normal life (Gazzaniga & LeDoux, 1978; Sperry, 1968).

Animal rights activists argue that enterprising researchers would be forced to think of alternative methods if they were banned from using animals (see Box 3.4). In fact, such advances have been made without any ban on animal experimentation. It has been possible, for example, to use anthropomorphic "dummies" (e.g., in car crash tests), to simulate tissue and bodily fluids in research situations, to use computer models of human beings, to use lower order species (e.g., fruit flies in experiments on genetics), and to study animals in their natural habitats (such as Dian Fossey's studies of gorillas; Fossey, 1981, 1983) or else in zoos, rather than to breed animals for laboratory research. In a fascinating set of studies, comparative psychologists were able to generate new theoretical insights into the functions of yawning behavior simply by comparing Siamese fighting fish in the lab, lions and baboons in the zoo, and students who kept daily logs of yawning behavior (Baenninger, 1987; Baenninger, Binkley, & Baenninger, 1996; Greco, Baenninger, & Govern, 1993).

BOX 3.4   Another Three Rs

Some years ago, the British zoologist William M. S. Russell and microbiologist Rex L. Burch made the argument that, given scientists' own interest in the humane treatment of the animals used in research, it would be prudent to search for ways to (a) *reduce* the number of animals used in research, (b) *refine* the experiments so that there was less suffering, and (c) *replace* animals with other procedures whenever possible. Called the **three Rs principle** by Russell and Burch (1959), this argument defines modern research on animal subjects.

In sum, just as the scientific community recognizes both an ethical and a scientific responsibility for the general welfare of human subjects, it also assumes responsibility for the humane care and treatment of animals used in research. There are laws and ethical guidelines to protect animals in research, and it is also evident that humans and animals have benefited by discoveries made in experiments with animals. Thus, even though there is a heated debate about the use of animals in research, it is clear that society has benefited in terms of biomedical and behavioral advances and that the ethical consciousness of science and society has been raised with regard to the conduct of this research.

What Are My Ethical Responsibilities When Writing Up My Research?

In this chapter, we have concentrated on the data collection phase of the research process, but ethical guidelines have implications for all aspects of the research process. As mentioned in Chapter 1, the most fundamental ethical principle of good researchers is integrity and honesty, an essential aspect of the research process, from the implementation of the study to the final report of the procedures used, the results, and their implications. As we have also tried to show, many of the ethical guidelines discussed in this chapter, although directed specifically at professional researchers, have implications for students who are conducting research to satisfy a requirement in a methods course.

Some ethical rules have implications for the final phase of the process, in which you will be writing up your results (Rosnow & Rosnow, 2006). For example, professional researchers are responsible for making available the data on which their conclusions are based. The implication for students writing research reports is that they are expected to produce all of their raw data as required by the instructor. It is also considered unethical to misrepresent original research by publishing it in more than one journal and implying that each report represents a different study. The implication for students is that it is unethical to submit the same work for additional credit in different courses. Also, authors of published articles are expected to give credit where it is due, and the implication for the student is that if someone gave you an idea, you should credit that person in a footnote. Should your research become part of an article authored by your instructor, the decision about whether you will be listed as a coauthor or in a footnote acknowledgment will depend on the nature of your contribution to the research. Analyzing data that the instructor provided may be a minor contribution deserving a footnote acknowledgment, but if the article is substantially based on your individual efforts, you will usually be listed as a coauthor, possibly as the principal author of a multiple-authored piece (if the circumstances warrant this and at the discretion of the instructor).

The most nagging ethical concern of most instructors, however, is conveying to students the meaning and consequences of **plagiarism** and how to avoid it. The term *plagiarism* comes from a Latin word meaning "kidnapper," and to plagiarize means to kidnap another person's idea or work and to pass it off as one's own. "Accidental plagiarism" occurs when one copies someone else's work but "forgets" to credit it or to put it in quotes. It is crucial that you know what constitutes plagiarism, because it is not an acceptable defense to claim that you do not understand what plagiarism is, nor is it ethically defensible to lift a passage (without putting it in quotes) because it was not easy to think of a way to express a thought or concept in your own words. Even if the plagiarism was "accidental," it is important to understand that stealing someone else's work is wrong and that, even if it is unintentional, the penalty may be severe.

Of course, you can quote other's people's ideas or work in your research and writing, but you must always give the author of that material full credit for originality and not misrepresent (intentionally or accidentally) that material as your own original work. For example, suppose a student did a study on cognitive dissonance and then turned in a report that, without a citation, contained the following passage:

> Dissonance—that is, the existence of nonfitting relations among cognitions—is a motivating factor in its own right. By *cognition* is generally meant any knowledge, opinion, or belief about the environment, about oneself, or about one's behavior. Cognitive dissonance can be seen as an antecedent condition that leads to activity oriented toward dissonance reduction, just as hunger leads to activity oriented toward hunger reduction.

The student has cheated by committing plagiarism and will pay the consequences: an F in the course. The reason is that, except for a changed word here and there, the student has lifted this passage directly from Leon Festinger's *Theory of Cognitive Dissonance* (1962). On page 5 of that book, Festinger wrote:

> In short, I am proposing that dissonance, that is, the existence of nonfitting relations among cognitions, is a motivating factor in its own right. By the term *cognition*, here and in the remainder of the book, I mean any knowledge, opinion, or belief about the environment, about oneself, or about one's behavior. Cognitive dissonance can be seen as an antecedent condition which leads to activity oriented toward dissonance reduction just as hunger leads to activity oriented toward hunger reduction.

How might the student have used Festinger's work without falling into plagiarism? The student would indicate what is his or hers and what is Festinger's. For example, this student could have written:

> In his book *A Theory of Cognitive Dissonance,* Festinger (1962) described cognition as "any knowledge, opinion, or belief about the environment, about oneself, or about one's behavior" and defined cognitive dissonance as "the existence of nonfitting relations among cognitions" (p. 5). He added, "Cognitive dissonance can be seen as an antecedent condition which leads to activity oriented toward dissonance reduction" (p. 5).

If you find something on the Internet you want to use, the same considerations of honesty apply. Electronic plagiarizing is no more acceptable than plagiarizing from printed matter, and given the ready availability and effectiveness of dedicated search engines, it is easier for instructors to catch perpetrators.

One final word of advice: Some students, on hearing that cited material is not construed by definition as plagiarism, submit papers that are saturated with quoted material. However, such papers are viewed by instructors as **lazy writing**. Although the penalty for lazy writing is not as severe as that for plagiarism, often it means a reduced grade. You may need to quote or paraphrase some material (with a citation, of course), but your written work is expected to result from your own individual effort. Quoting a simple sentence that can easily be paraphrased signals lazy writing.

Summary of Ideas

1. Legal, institutional, and professional *ethical guidelines* help us evaluate the moral "rights" and "wrongs" of particular strategies of doing and reporting research. Horrendous cases, such as the Tuskegee study (Box 3.1), are a reminder of why there is a "legacy of distrust" of medical research in some communities. In general, scientific researchers are ethically obligated *not to do* physical or psychological harm to research participants and *to do* research in a way that is most likely to produce valid results of benefit to society.

2. Principle I of the APA's task force on ethics in research with human participants underscores respect for persons and their autonomy, which means telling prospective participants what they will be getting into (the *informed-consent* agreement) and respecting their right to decide whether they want to participate in the study and remain in the study. There are situations in which obtaining informed consent may be unnecessary or impossible (e.g., studies that use public records or risk-free studies in which informed consent would be counterproductive to the purpose of the research).

3. If the subjects have diminished capacity to understand the consent form, a legally responsible person may speak on their behalf, but this does not mean that these subjects relinquish their right to sue the researcher for negligence. Freedom of choice must also be factored in when students are required to participate as subjects, in which case there must be an educational benefit to their participation and, if they choose not to participate, an alternative requirement that is no more arduous than the research participation.

4. Principle II (beneficence and nonmaleficence) instructs us to maximize benefits and minimize risks of research, as assessed by a review board (e.g., an *IRB*) that, in theory, weighs the risks and benefits of the proposed research. *Minimal risk* studies are eligible for *expedited review*. A limitation of the idealized assessment is that it focuses only on the risks and benefits of the *doing* of research and ignores the societal and scientific costs of *not doing* the research.

5. Principle III (justice) underscores the idea that the benefits and burdens of research be distributed as fairly as possible, though (as is true of life itself) full justice can seldom be achieved. One reason is that justice (or fair-mindedness, or impartiality) is usually a matter of each person's perspective or subjective judgment (e.g., the Rushton study).

6. Principle IV (relationship of trust) reminds researchers not to do anything that may jeopardize the trusting relationship participants have entered into and to protect the disclosures of the participants against unwarranted access (i.e., to maintain *confidentiality*).

7. Principle V (fidelity and scientific integrity) defines the promulgation of valid knowledge as an ethical pursuit. Violations of this principle include badly designed or carelessly conducted studies, poorly analyzed data, exaggerated conclusions, ambiguously reported studies, and the deliberate omission or fabrication of data.

8. Assuming Milgram's research on obedience to authority was worth doing, he had no alternative but to use *active deception,* because being open and honest with the participants would probably have

jeopardized the validity of the results. It also does not seem to be the *active* or *passive* nature of deception that is most problematic but whether a deception could be potentially harmful in some way.

9. *Debriefing* subjects after the data have been collected is the final step in the data collection process and is considered essential when there has been a deception or when there is likely to be any residual anxiety. Deceiving the subject during the debriefing (a *double deception*) is never permissible.

10. Just as the scientific community has an ethical and scientific responsibility for the general welfare of human subjects, it also assumes responsibility for the humane care and treatment of animals used in research. The *three Rs principle* emphasizes the *reduction* of the number of animals used in research, the *refinement* of experiments so there is less suffering, and the *replacement* of the use of animals with other procedures whenever possible.

11. Ethical guidelines during the reporting stage also require that researchers (a) make available the data on which their conclusions are based (while protecting the confidentiality of their participants); (b) not imply that a study published in more than one journal represents different studies; and (c) give credit where it is due.

12. *Plagiarism* means lifting another person's idea or work, and it is severely punished. To avoid "accidental plagiarism," it is essential to make careful notes and to cite the sources of any ideas, work, or quotations used in your report. Also avoid the *lazy writing* of repeatedly quoting sentences that can be paraphrased in your own words (and referenced, of course). Do not buy "scientific" reports on the Internet.

Key Terms

active deception (deception by commission) p. 63
Belmont Report p. 51
beneficence p. 51
confidentiality p. 58
debriefing p. 64
double deception p. 66
ethical guidelines p. 50

ethics p. 50
expedited review p. 54
informed consent p. 52
institutional review board (IRB) p. 54
lazy writing p. 70
minimal risk p. 54
nonmaleficence p. 51

passive deception (deception by omission) p. 63
placebo p. 52
plagiarism p. 68
risk-benefit analysis p. 54
three Rs principle p. 67

Multiple-Choice Questions for Review

1. Which of the following methodological procedures can cause moral conflicts to arise? (a) invasion of privacy; (b) deception; (c) withholding information from research participants; (d) all of the above

2. Deliberately withholding information from research participants is called _____; deliberately misinforming participants is called _____. (a) active deception, passive deception; (b) active deception, double deception; (c) double deception, passive deception; (d) passive deception, active deception

3. In the Milgram experiments, which of the following actually received electrical shocks? (a) the "teacher"; (b) the "learner"; (c) both a and b; (d) neither a nor b

4. Ethical questions were raised about the Milgram experiments because (a) participants were deceived and apparently stressed; (b) some participants received severe shocks; (c) some participants were physically injured; (d) all of the above.

5. The Rushton study, conducted in a mining company, raised the ethical issue of (a) deception; (b) fair-mindedness; (c) invasion of privacy; (d) all of the above.

6. The participants who objected to the Rushton study were (a) in the control group; (b) in the experimental group; (c) in both the experimental and control groups; (d) subjected to severe shocks.

7. According to the decision-plane diagram in the text, if the risks of doing a research project are equal to the benefits of doing the research, then the study is said to fall on (a) the diagonal of ambivalence; (b) the diagonal of equality; (c) the diagonal of indecision; (d) none of the above.

8. Research at virtually all colleges and universities has to be approved by (a) the president of the institution; (b) the U.S. government; (c) professors in the psychology department; (d) an IRB.

9. The procedure of disclosing the full purpose of a study after individuals have participated is called (a) debriefing; (b) peer review; (c) the Milgram procedure; (d) double deception.

10. Which of the following help ensure that animals used as subjects in research are treated ethically? (a) federal laws; (b) professional codes of conduct; (c) institutional (e.g., university) policies; (d) all of the above

Discussion Questions for Review

1. A study proposal is submitted to the Tufts University IRB for review. The researchers propose to administer a two-hour-long questionnaire to people hanging out on the street in the red light district in Boston. The questionnaire contains items asking about these people's lifestyles and attitudes toward criminal behavior. What are some potential risks to the subjects for their participation in the study?

2. A University of Richmond student is interested in studying helping behavior. She designs an experiment to take place in a corner drugstore. Enlisting the aid of the owner, the student has confederates, varying in age and manner of dress, commit a robbery at the store. Another confederate, posing as a customer, observes the real customers, noting which of them help, what they do, how long it takes, and so on. What are some ethical problems in this research? What risks and benefits would you consider in deciding whether this project should be done?

3. A student at California State–Fullerton wants to run a study in which he will deceive subjects into believing that they have done poorly on a test of their sensitivity to others. At the end of the experimental session, he plans to pay the subjects, thank them for participating, and tell them they can call him later if they have questions about the study. How does the student fail in his ethical responsibilities to the participants? What should he do?

4. An instructor at the University of Nebraska tells a student in her research methods class that, in her view, the student's proposed study falls on the "diagonal of indecision." What does the instructor mean, and what are the implications for the student?

5. An Arlington University researcher proposes to use Texas students to replicate Asch's classic experiment. The IRB requires an informed-consent agreement from the prospective subjects. What does this mean, and what are the implications for the researcher?

6. A Whittier College student is interested in conducting a study of the effects of various financial incentive programs in a large organization. Because his research involves no deception or invasion of privacy, he tells his adviser that no ethical issues are raised by his research. The adviser's reply is "Remember the Rushton study!" What does she mean?

7. An instructor at the University of Utah tells her students that they have ethical responsibilities when writing up their research? What are those responsibilities?

Answers to Review Questions

Multiple-Choice Questions

1. d	**3.** d	**5.** b	**7.** c	**9.** a
2. d	**4.** a	**6.** a	**8.** d	**10.** d

Discussion Questions

1. Two possible risks include (a) embarrassment at "being studied" in an unsavory location or occupation and (b) the danger of discovery of subjects' criminal behavior because someone in law enforcement obtains the questionnaire and can link it to the respondents.

2. Observing the thefts might be quite upsetting to the real customers, who may be put at risk of, say, anxiety reactions or heart attacks. The confederate "robbers" may also be put at risk of being shot by a neighboring armed shopkeeper or attacked by a customer trying to foil the robbery. We need to ask whether what we might be able to learn from this research is really worth the risk to the real customers, the shopkeeper, and the confederate "robbers."

3. The student has failed to debrief the participants, so that they may leave feeling that they are really insensitive to others. He should, of course, debrief them.

4. The instructor means that the risks and benefits are in such balance that it is very difficult for her to reach a decision on whether to let the student go ahead with the research. For removal of the study from the diagonal of indecision, the student needs to decrease the risks of the study, increase the benefits, or both. If there are significant risks, however, the student should start by eliminating them.

5. The IRB requires that the participant must understand what the research will require from her or him, that she or he may leave at any time, and that she or he will remain anonymous. Fully informing the participants about the nature of the Asch experiment would, however, make it impossible to replicate because they would see through the manipulation.

6. The Rushton study also raised no questions of deception or invasion of privacy. However, the issue of fair-mindedness was raised. Were some of the company's workers going to be "treated specially," or would they get to ride "the gravy train" in the eyes of other workers?

7. Their responsibilities include (a) producing all of their raw data if the instructor asks for it, (b) not submitting the paper for credit in another course, (c) giving credit to anyone who helped, and (d) not committing plagiarism, even accidentally.

CHAPTER 4

Strategies of Systematic Observational Research

Preview Questions

- What is systematic observational research?
- How do researchers simultaneously participate and observe?
- What can be learned from quantifying observations?
- How is a content analysis done?
- How are raters or coders chosen for a judgment study?
- How are situations simulated in experimental research?
- How do I identify rival interpretations or rival hypotheses?
- What is the distinction between reactive and nonreactive observation?

What Is Systematic Observational Research?

The term **systematic observational research** differentiates the research strategies described in this chapter from the self-report methods described in the next chapter. *Observation* means that the researcher is viewing or noting a fact or an occurrence for a scientific purpose, and *systematic* implies that this observation follows a particular plan or involves a system that can be evaluated on the basis of technical standards (as contrasted with the casual or haphazard nature of most of our daily observations). Within this broad definition, systematic observational research typically calls for resourcefulness in the spirit of a "let's-try-it-and-see" attitude (see Box 4.1) and also the use of more than just one observational or self-report method. Because all empirical methods are limited in some ways, the use of a single empirical method would confine our observations to a narrow range of facts or occurrences. Hence, as discussed earlier, *methodological pluralism* (the use of multiple methods) is an underlying thread that runs throughout this book and also ties the various methods together. That is, by using multiple methods, researchers zero in on phenomena from more than one perspective, a process called **methodological triangulation** (Campbell & Fiske, 1959), and thereby arrive at a more comprehensive picture.

BOX 4.1 Does Anything Go?

At the conclusion of Chapter 2, we quoted a philosopher of science, Paul Feyerabend (1988), who said that "successful research. . . relies now on one trick, now on another" (p. 1). Feyerabend's idea, described by others as the "anything-goes" philosophy of science, is that scientists do whatever works. It does not mean, however, that there are no accepted criteria for weeding out bad science or pseudoscience. All it means is that doing research *does* seem to involve a "let's-try-it-and-see" attitude. Like the person trying to figure out which key opened the door (discussed in Chapter 1), the scientist may experiment with different empirical techniques before deciding that a theoretical prediction is correct or should be junked. The continuing challenge is to choose (or create) and properly implement methods that precisely address the theoretical question or hypothesis, while conceding that no method is perfect in every way.

There are many more observational techniques than we could possibly cover in this chapter, the purpose of which is to sample some of the ways that observational research is done. Within the descriptive, relational, and experimental framework that we outlined in Chapter 1, a further distinction in the social sciences is between quantitative and qualitative research. The term **quantitative research** simply means that the data exist in a numerical or graphic form, and **qualitative research** means that the data exist in a narrative form (spoken words, recorded conversations) or a pictorial form. This distinction is not unambiguous, however, because we can always figure out ways to enumerate and graph aspects of qualitative data (e.g., using judges as raters or as counters of events, or having a computer systematically decompose written messages or pictorial documents). Furthermore, the two classes are not mutually exclusive, as it is possible to use quantitative and qualitative methods in the same study (e.g., interviewing some participants in a rigorously quantified lab experiment in order to get their impressions of their participation). It may also be informative to systematically observe and then describe in a narrative the demeanor of the subjects. Were they attentive and focused on the instructions and the experimental task, or did they seem uninterested and distracted? Did they appear calm and composed, or were they anxious and unsettled and possibly concerned about how they would be evaluated?

If we think of qualitative and quantitative as the two ends of a continuum, at one end would be naturalistic studies in which the researchers are part of the scene and are also observers and recorders. We begin with two classic psychological cases, although there are also many more famous examples in the annals of social psychology as well as examples in modern organizational psychology. Moving along the qualitative-quantitative continuum, we then use two cases to illustrate how qualitative data might be quantified. One case involves a set of procedures (rooted in classic work but modernized in recent years, and of growing interest to social scientists, mathematicians, and economists) for studying network relations; the second case is a classic demonstration of the use of judges to rate and classify qualitative actions in discussion groups. We next describe how the content of narrative information in books, pictorial information, or some other qualitative communication can be sorted and classified by judges or, if relevant, how a computer can be used to do the sorting and counting (and we describe three ways of selecting judges). We then turn to experimental research cases, which anchor the quantitative end of the qualitative-quantitative continuum, and we raise the issue of plausible rival interpretations or rival hypotheses. Finally, we illustrate studies in which people's behavior is observed unobtrusively or by using some form of nonreactive procedure or measurement.

How Do Researchers Simultaneously Participate and Observe?

In one traditional form of qualitative research, the procedure is called **participant observation** (where the term *participant* refers to the investigator as opposed to the research participants, or *informants* as they are commonly called by sociologists). For example, in a classic study in psychology, a team of social psychologists observed a cult from within (as members) for approximately two months before and one month after the date that the cult leader had predicted that the world would end (Festinger, Schachter, & Riecken, 1956). The leader told her followers, who fervently believed every word, that she had received written messages from extraterrestrials about gods and spiritual vibrations on other planets, and that, on a specified day, just before dawn, a flood would engulf most of the continent. In the days before this predicted cataclysm, many members quit their jobs, discarded their possessions, and were careless about their money, believing they would have no need for these things. What gave them emotional consolation was the leader's word that they would be evacuated by a flying saucer that would land in her backyard at 4:00 p.m. on a particular day to transport the "chosen ones" to another planet. Although they waited in anticipation with coats in hand, no flying saucer arrived and the world did not end. Nonetheless, they did not lose faith but instead reinterpreted their experience as a drill and a rehearsal for the real pickup. Leon Festinger (1957) discussed this study in his book on cognitive dissonance, using it as evidence of how people cling to beliefs even in the face of disconfirmation by, for example, seeking out new reasons to justify their beliefs.

In another famous participant observation study, clinical psychologist David Rosenhan (1973) was interested in how people who are labeled as "mentally ill" get to be stigmatized and what determines how they are treated. Rosenhan and a number of volunteer coworkers gained secret admission to psychiatric hospitals in five states on the East and West Coasts by feigning psychiatric symptoms (e.g., complaining of hearing voices). Once admitted, however, they all behaved quite normally, responded honestly to questions about significant life events, and also attempted to interact normally with the staff members (psychiatrists, psychologists, and resident physicians). The staff members were not told that it was *their* behavior that was being studied by Rosenhan and his team of pseudopatients. The reason the staff was not told was that Rosenhan believed that, sensitive to their loss of privacy, staff members would have become selective in cooperating with the researchers. None of the pseudopatients was detected, and all but one was diagnosed as schizophrenic. Notes about ward life were kept by the pseudopatient researchers, one of whom (Lando, 1976) reported positive aspects of his experience. In contrast, Rosenhan strongly emphasized a feeling of depersonalization and powerlessness. Rosenhan (1973) also reported a follow-up study in which hospital staff were alerted to the possibility of pseudopatients. In that study, about 10%–20% of new admissions were judged to be faking, even though none of the patients was an experimental pseudopatient. As you might guess, these results were immediately a lightning rod for a heated discussion on the accuracy of the diagnostic labeling of psychiatric patients. One beneficial consequence, however, was that the American Psychiatric Association's diagnostic manual was revised in an effort to reduce the likelihood of future misdiagnoses.

As these cases illustrate, participant observation lets the researcher investigate complex social interactions as they occur rather than relying on public records of past events. It is also a way of watching natural events in their "wholeness," particularly those that would be impossible to simulate in a lab, or that might be too sensitive or too risky to try to manipulate experimentally (Weick, 1968). Some have argued that participant observers approach the field of observation without any preconceived ideas (Taylor & Bogdan, 1998). However, it is hard to believe that researchers would realistically know where, when, how, or what to study without having at least a hunch or theoretical preconception, even if the purpose of the research were exploratory and descriptive. If for no other reason, having some ideas in advance encourages serendipity, or as social scientists Fine and Deegan (1996) noted, "The prepared participant observer hoping to maximize the chances of obtaining data selects just the right time and just the right place" (p. 439). Suppose a researcher wants to observe barroom brawls. Clearly, the researcher is more likely to witness such behavior by visiting bars on weekend nights rather than during afternoons in the middle of the week. As Fine and Deegan advised, "Courting serendipity involves planned insight married to unplanned events" (p. 435).

In the early development of this research approach, there was not yet a tradition of how to obtain the most credible qualitative data. Nowadays, participant observers typically work in teams and use checks and balances to try to control for individually biased observations, known as **observer bias**. It occurs when observers overestimate or underestimate the occurrence of events or "see" things that are not really there because they think things exist in a particular way. As one writer commented, scientists, like all human beings, sometimes associate what they *believe* they see, and what they may *want* to see, with what is actually happening (Lane, 1960). One way to identify observer bias is to compare the field notes of two or more independent observers for discrepancies. When taking field notes, several conventions are used. One rule of thumb is to indicate for every written note referring to a conversation whether it is based on a verbatim quote or is instead the observer's paraphrase. The risk of paraphrases is that observers may distort what the informants meant. Whenever possible, researchers also make audio or video recordings (with the permission of the informants), though this would have been impossible in the Rosenhan (1973) study without jeopardizing the integrity of the investigation (see also Box 4.2).

BOX 4.2 Translation and Back Translation

When people are to be interviewed or given questionnaires to answer, it is important that items be phrased accurately in those people's own language or dialect. When the language of those observed is not the native language of the researchers, translation and back translation are used: One bilingual person first translates the questions from the source to the target language, and then another bilingual person translates the questions back into the source language. As a result, the researchers can compare the original with the twice-translated version (i.e., the *back translation*) to see whether anything has been lost in the translation.

What Can Be Learned From Quantifying Observations?

Social scientists and mathematicians have developed special methods for measuring and graphing qualitative data. For example, in the 1950s, *sociometric methods* were created by Jacob Moreno (1953) for charting networks of interpersonal behavior in social, psychological, and occupational situations. The further development of those early procedures (e.g., Wasserman & Faust, 1994), as well as the creation of computer programs that enable researchers to measure and graph large networks (Borgatti, Everett, & Freeman, 2002), has stimulated renewed interest in this approach, known as **social network analysis (SNA)**. For example, Kossinets and Watts (2006) recently examined the e-mail traffic of 43,553 students, faculty, and staff at a large university and found that, although there was variability at the individual level, the overall network approached a kind of equilibrium state. SNA graphs (called *maps*) connect individuals *(nodes)* by lines *(links)* that reflect some defined relationship or interaction. For example, the relationship might be "who *communicates* with whom" or "who *passes gossip* to whom" or "whom you would choose as a *working partner*". In this way, qualitative patterns and social roles are operationalized in terms that can be quantified and graphed. We can map out, for instance, which people are chosen most often (the "stars"), or which people are hardly ever chosen (the "isolates"), or which people form cliques within the network, and we can also measure group cohesiveness and other characteristics of the network and observe changing patterns of relationships over time.

As a simplified example, Part A of Figure 4.1 shows an SNA "map" that represents a cult network (Foster & Rosnow, 2006). Typical of cults is that the leader achieves absolute control over the cult members by essentially walling them off from the world. The cult leader is the intermediary who speaks to the cult members about the "other" (spiritual) world and the real world of kin, reporters, and so on. Writing in another context, journalism professor David Manning White (1950) coined the term *gatekeeper* to describe a reporter who controls the flow of news. The cult leader is not only the self-appointed guardian of how the cult members are permitted to think and behave but also (as depicted in the figure's map) the sole keeper at the gate.

A. Hypothetical cult network   **B. Hypothetical corporate network**

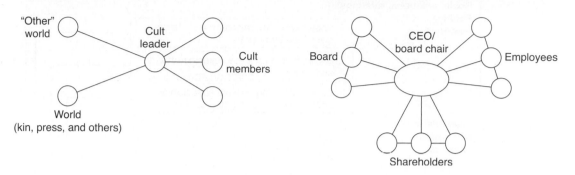

Figure 4.1   Illustrations of social network analysis (SNA) maps (Foster & Rosnow, 2006, pp. 172, 173).

A parallel (if less pathological) situation would be a company in which the top executive is both the CEO and the chair of the company board (Foster & Rosnow, 2006). Part B of Figure 4.1 shows a hypothetical case in which the top executive controls the information flow to each of the three constituent groups (i.e., the board, the employees, and the shareholders). It is a powerful executive role because this gatekeeper can keep each constituent group in the dark about what is happening in the other groups. For example, if there is dissension among board members, and if formal communications have to pass through the top executive, the shareholders may be unaware of this situation (unless the news is leaked). A few years ago, two large corporations underwent major makeovers in which the CEO and board chair positions were separated because the vested constituencies perceived that the power of the top executive had become too centralized (Foster & Rosnow, 2006).

Another strategy for quantifying qualitative observational data is to use judges or raters in what is called a **judgment study**. The advantage of such studies is that we can measure the judge-to-judge reliability (discussed in Chapter 6); also we can use basic statistics (e.g., those discussed in Chapter 10) to enumerate summary characteristics of the data. Continuing with our interest in interpersonal behavior, a classic set of judgment studies was performed by Robert F. Bales (1950a, 1950b, Bales & Cohen, 1979). In the previous cases, the analyses were of existing groups, whereas in Bales's studies, the analyses were of groups that were purposely created by the researchers. When people engage in a group discussion, some contribute more than their fair share of communications or ideas, and others rarely contribute anything. Some members may be more influential, may be considered more expert, or may in some other way exert more influence on the group than others. Bales had judges categorize every observable act—an *act* being defined as a single statement, question, or gesture.

For his research, Bales brought several people together and had them discuss a complex human relations problem. Through a one-way screen, trained observers recorded every act that occurred. Figure 4.2 contains the 12 categories developed by Bales for the observers (the judges) to classify the acts. Note that the acts are

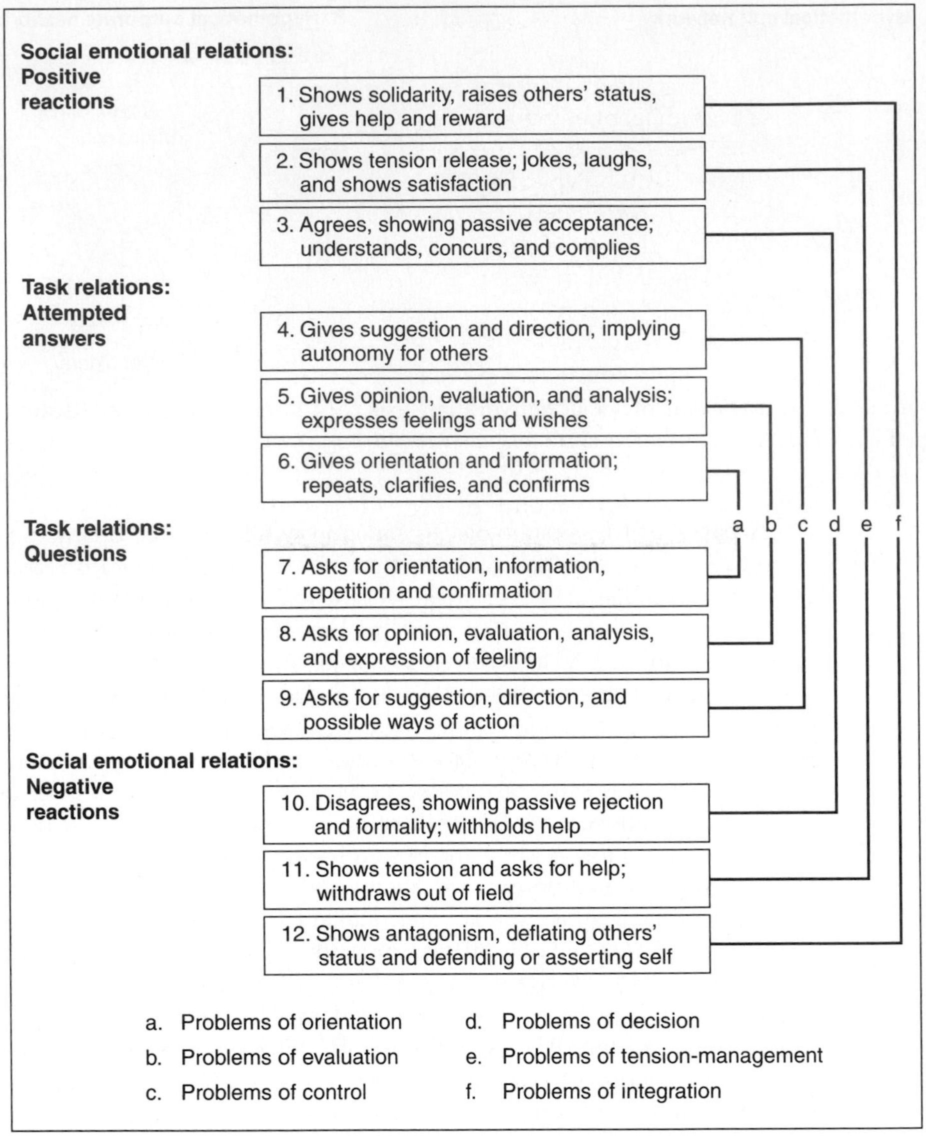

Social emotional relations:
Positive reactions

1. Shows solidarity, raises others' status, gives help and reward

2. Shows tension release; jokes, laughs, and shows satisfaction

3. Agrees, showing passive acceptance; understands, concurs, and complies

Task relations:
Attempted answers

4. Gives suggestion and direction, implying autonomy for others

5. Gives opinion, evaluation, and analysis; expresses feelings and wishes

6. Gives orientation and information; repeats, clarifies, and confirms

Task relations:
Questions

a b c d e f

7. Asks for orientation, information, repetition and confirmation

8. Asks for opinion, evaluation, analysis, and expression of feeling

9. Asks for suggestion, direction, and possible ways of action

Social emotional relations:
Negative reactions

10. Disagrees, showing passive rejection and formality; withholds help

11. Shows tension and asks for help; withdraws out of field

12. Shows antagonism, deflating others' status and defending or asserting self

a. Problems of orientation   d. Problems of decision

b. Problems of evaluation   e. Problems of tension-management

c. Problems of control   f. Problems of integration

Figure 4.2 Categories of socioemotional (directed at friendship and emotional needs) and task-related (directed at achieving concrete problem solving) interactions in small groups.

Source: R. F. Bales, "A Set of Categories for Analysis of Small Group Interaction," *American Sociological Review,* 1950, *15,* 257–263. Reprinted by permission of the American Sociological Association.

divided into *socioemotional relations* and *task relations* classifications, the former term referring to positive and negative reactions, and the latter term referring to questions and attempted answers. The subjects in these studies read a factual information sheet containing material related to a problem. Then they discussed the problem for a period of time, usually about 40 minutes, meeting as a group in four different sessions. Typically, there were between 15 and 20 acts per minute, about half of which were rated as problem-solving attempts. The remaining acts consisted of positive and negative reactions and questions. In the first third of a session, giving information tended to be the most frequent act. Opinions tended to be given most during the middle portion of a meeting, and offering suggestions was most frequent in the last third. Of particular interest to Bales was a consistent finding that the acts alternated between socioemotional and task or problem-solving attempts. When too much emphasis is given to a problem, socioemotional relations between members become strained; emphasis is then placed on this area until member relations are again harmonious. Then there is a return to the problem, and thereafter activities are directed back and forth between these two areas.

In the next chapter, we turn to self-report methods, and such a method (a questionnaire) was also used by Bales in this study. After each meeting, the discussion group members were given a questionnaire asking them to rank other members in terms of the quality of their ideas, those members liked best, and so forth. Bales (1955) observed that the person ranked as having the best ideas was often the one who did the most talking and who offered more than the average number of suggestions and opinions. Bales also noted that, whereas one person would become a specialist in advancing ideas, another would develop a specialization on the socioemotional side. Those most commonly rated "best liked" also had higher-than-average rates of showing tension release and showing agreement. It was not impossible for a person who was ranked at the top in ideas also to be the best liked, but it was rare.

How Is a Content Analysis Done?

Observational methods sometimes involve the use of public records (**archival material**) rather than firsthand observations of behavior. Convenient sources of public records in libraries include encyclopedias, biographical dictionaries, histories, anthologies, print collections, manuscripts, and a wide variety of computerized databases (M. C. Rosenthal, 1985, 1994, 2006; Simonton, 2000). Database material accessible by computer includes (a) actuarial records (birth, marriage, and death records); (b) political and judicial records (e.g., voting records of legislators and speeches printed in the *Congressional Record*); (c) other government records (weather reports, invention records, and crime reports); and (d) information from the mass media (stories, news reports, advertising, and editorials). Other useful sources of archival material are (e) sales records (e.g., sales at airport bars, sales of trip insurance policies, and decreased sales of airline tickets, which might serve as plausible indicators of increased anxiety); (f) industrial and institutional records (e.g., sicknesses and absences, complaints, unsolicited commendations from the public, and accident reports); and (g) various other written documents (e.g., diaries and letters of captured soldiers in wartime or letters of protest to large companies). The use of archival material falls into a category known as **secondary observation**, which means that the information is twice removed from the source. That is, the person who originally recorded the information is once removed from the source, and the social scientist is removed from the recorder by another degree.

In work with archival material, a popular method of sorting through the material and categorizing the contents is called **content analysis**. As an illustration, Crabb and Bielawski (1994) used content analysis to explore how visual presentations in influential books for children portrayed female and male roles. They chose for their study all picture books that had received a prestigious award (the Caldecott Medal) over a 53-year period, on the assumption that the books must have had a high profile in libraries and bookstores. The books contained 1,613 illustrations, including 416 of female characters and 1,197 of male characters. Instead of content-analyzing *all* this material by hand, the researchers drew a sample of 300 representative illustrations of gender and decade. The judges, who were first rehearsed in the use of the coding system, coded the sex of the characters shown in the pictures, the nature of any household tools (such as those used in food preparation, cleaning, repair, and family care), nonhousehold tools (such as those used in construction, agriculture, and transportation), tools not falling into the above two groups, and features of the characters using the tools and the situation (such as the age of the character, coded as child, teenager, or adult). The ratings had strong judge-to-judge reliability (discussed in Chapter 6). One finding was that household tools were associated more with female characters, whereas nonhousehold tools were associated more with male characters. However, the proportion of male characters shown using household tools had increased over time, though the proportion of female characters using nonhousehold tools had not changed much over time.

In this content analysis, judges were used to rate and tabulate aspects of the material, but there are also computer programs specially created for content analysis research (P. Stone, 1997, 2000). These programs can sort through written material according to particular research specifications. Sourcebooks on content analysis are quite detailed (C. W. Roberts, 1997; C. P. Smith, 1992), but there are three general guidelines to keep in mind:

1. If you are planning to use judges (or raters or coders), it is important that the analysis of content be reasonably consistent among the judges. That is, the different coders should produce similar results (i.e., there should be good judge-to-judge reliability). Assuming that each category and unit has been precisely defined, and that the judges were properly trained, the consistency among the judges should be satisfactorily high.

2. It is essential that the specific categories and units be relevant to the questions or hypotheses of the study. In choosing categories for written records, for example, it is a good idea to ask, "What is the communication about?" and "How is it said?" Questions like these help to focus the analysis on the substance (the *what*) and the form (the *how*) of the subject matter. It is also prudent to consider

several different units of analysis before settling on any one unit. For example, you might consider coding words and word compounds (or phrases) or perhaps themes (or assertions), as illustrated by the pictorial themes in the Crabb and Bielawski study.

3. If you are not planning to analyze the entire universe of data, it is important to decide on a good sampling procedure. We will have more to say about different sampling plans later in this book, including approaches that call for (a) random sampling from listings of all relevant units; (b) stratified samples, which break up units into subgroups and then sample from the subgroups; and (c) systematic samples, in which every *n*th unit of a list is selected.

As we said before, all strategies and procedures are limited in some ways, and the method of content analysis is no exception. Most basically, it is limited by the quality, dependability, and relevance of the material to be analyzed. However, it also has four definite advantages when used properly (Woodrum, 1984). First, developing a coding system and then implementing it requires little more than commonsense logic. Second, content analysis is a "shoestring" methodology in that, although labor-intensive when done by hand, it does not require much capital investment. Third, it is a "safe" methodology, because you can add necessary information if it is missed or incorrectly coded or if there are changes in what is being measured over time. These additions and corrections are far more difficult to implement in the typical experimental or survey study. Fourth, it forces researchers to think carefully about the material to be evaluated and classified.

How Are Raters or Coders Chosen for a Judgment Study?

Judges for a content analysis or some other kind of judgment study may be chosen in one of three ways: (a) by using intuition, (b) by consulting the research literature for criteria relevant to the choice; or (c) by doing pilot testing.

The first approach is to decide intuitively on the type of judges needed (e.g., graduate students, community members, college students, clinical psychologists, linguists, mothers) and then to regard each judge within that sample as equivalent to (or interchangeable with) any other judge within the sample. Suppose we want a sample of raters educated at a certain level; we might be content to select college students. If we want ratings of nonverbal expressions of psychopathology, we might choose as our judges experienced professionals, such as clinical psychologists, psychiatrists, or psychiatric social workers. If we want ratings of nonverbal expressions of discomfort in infants, we might select pediatricians, developmental psychologists, or mothers. If we want ratings of nonverbal cues of persuasion, we might invite trial lawyers, Fundamentalist ministers, or salespersons. We would also want to make sure that the judges are not relying on stereotypes (e.g., salespersons recruited to watch people give persuasive messages might rely on stereotypes to tell us which nonverbal cues were most persuasive).

A second approach is to consult the relevant research literature, in which case we might do even better by making a special selection of judges. For example, if we want to obtain the highest possible general accuracy in judgments of nonverbal cues, our selection of judges might be based on prior research that identified the characteristics of people who are most sensitive to nonverbal cues. This research suggests that, to optimize overall sensitivity to nonverbal cues, we should select judges who are (a) female, (b) college-aged, and (as measured by psychological tests) both (c) cognitively complex and (d) psychiatrically unimpaired (Rosenthal, Hall, DiMatteo, Rogers, & Archer, 1979). One study found that people high in *field independence* (as measured by a psychological test) are more accurate raters than field-dependent persons (Härtel, 1993).

A third way to select judges is to do a "pilot test" in which we compare all recruits in our pool of potential judges for their accuracy of judgments on some relevant criterion. Suppose we are interested in selecting raters for a study in which they will have to categorize the emotions expressed by adolescents in tutoring sessions. We might begin by showing all the potential raters pictures of people exhibiting different emotions (anger, disgust, fear, happiness, sadness, surprise, and so on). We would ask them to identify the emotion expressed in each picture, score their answers, and then use the most accurate judges in our study.

How Are Situations Simulated in Experimental Research?

In Chapter 2, we mentioned examples of laboratory experimental observation, including the use of animals in learning and conditioning studies. It is frequently possible to *simulate* (or mimic) a causal relationship in a controlled experimental setting in which we can manipulate the causal condition (the independent variable). Suppose we are interested in why people's ears buzz and tickle as they listen to a hard rock band up close. We could position a loudspeaker next to one or more subjects in a lab, manipulate the carefully calibrated sounds, and ask the subjects to report the sensations they feel. If they report that their ears buzz and tickle, the sound pressure is probably well above 120 decibels, which can produce feelings of discomfort, prickling, and pain. After each exposure to such high-decibel sounds, the sensitivity of the ear may be temporarily reduced. (If we want to find out whether people who have a steady diet of hard rock have more hearing difficulties than those who do not listen to hard rock, we can design a relational study in which we sample a population of people and record the minimal audible noise detected by those who say they routinely listened either to a lot of hard rock or to no hard rock at all.)

Experimental simulations have also involved scripted role playing. For example, social psychologists Irving Janis and Leon Mann (1965; Mann, 1967; Mann & Janis, 1968) studied how to use the "saying-is-believing" principle to get heavy smokers to modify their smoking behavior. In this research, Janis and Mann experimented with a scripted simulation designed to increase the participants' emotional involvement. The volunteer participants were young women, all between the ages of 18 and 23, none of whom knew that the objective of the research involved modifying their smoking habits and attitudes toward smoking. Before the study began, the participants had averaged approximately a pack of cigarettes a day. Randomly assigned to an experimental or a control group, they were told at the beginning of the study that the purpose of the research was to examine two important problems about the human side of medical practice: (a) how patients react to bad news and (b) how they feel when a physician tells them to quit smoking.

Each participant in the experimental condition was told to imagine that the experimenter was a physician who had been treating her for a persistent cough, and on this "third visit" he was going to give her the results of X-rays and other diagnostic tests. The experimenter then outlined five different scenes, and he instructed the participant to "act out" each scene as realistically as possible. The first scene took place in the doctor's office while the patient awaited the diagnosis. She was asked to imagine and express aloud her thoughts, her concerns, her feelings about whether to give up cigarettes. The second scene was the imagined interaction with the physician. The participant was told that according to the results of the diagnostic tests, there was a small malignant mass in her right lung. She was also told that there was only a moderate chance of surgical success in treating this condition. She was then encouraged to ask questions. In the next scene she was instructed to express her feelings about her misfortune. The physician could be overheard in the background phoning for a hospital bed. In the fourth scene the physician described the details of imminent hospitalization. He told the participant that chest surgery typically requires a long convalescent period, at least 6 weeks. He then raised questions about the woman's smoking history and asked whether she was aware of the relationship between smoking and cancer. He stressed the urgent need for her to stop smoking and encouraged her to talk freely about the problems she felt she might encounter in trying to break the smoking habit.

Participants assigned to the control group were exposed to similar information about lung cancer in a tape recording of one of the experimental sessions. However, they were not given an opportunity to engage in emotional role playing. As Janis and Mann hypothesized, the impact of the experimental manipulation in the role-play condition exceeded that in the control condition. There was greater fear of personal harm from smoking, a stronger belief that smoking causes lung cancer, and a much greater willingness and intent to quit smoking in the experimental group. To find out about long-term effects, the researchers conducted follow-up interviews at different points over 18 months. The results were essentially as before. On the average, the women in the scripted role-play sessions reported that they had reduced their daily cigarette consumption by more than twice the amount of those randomly assigned to the control group; this difference persisted even after a year and a half.

In many cases, doing research in an artificial setting is a convenient and effective way of studying a phenomenon of interest in behavioral science (Mook, 1983). However, it is important to proceed with some caution when generalizing from simulations to real-world situations. For example, suppose we were interested in the effect of frustration on aggression in a controlled laboratory setting. Because frustration can make a person display hostile behavior, we might design a simulation experiment in which two subjects engage in a competitive task and are given an opportunity to administer a mild electric shock to one another. We frustrate one

BOX 4.3 Microworlds for Experimental Research

So-called *microworld simulations,* which use computer-generated environments, are intended to reduce concerns about realism and generalizability (Brehmer & Dörner, 1993; DiFonzo, Hantula, & Bordia, 1998; Funke, 1991; Omodei & Wearing, 1995). Simulations of perceptual and social phenomena might be improved, for example, by the use of virtual-reality technology similar to that found in some arcades (Biocca & Levy, 1995; Carr & England, 1995; Loomis, Blascovich, & Beall, 1999; Steuer, 1992). The person wears a helmet with a 3-D video card that displays and receives tactile, motion, and audio stimulation designed to immerse the person in a "world" that feels the same as the real world. This approach has been used for years by the U.S. military and aerospace programs to train pilots and astronauts. There are time constraints on this methodology, as many subjects in psychology studies find the simulation uncomfortable after a period of time. Still, the potential advantages are that (a) subjects may be made to "feel" the same way they do in a real-world setting; (b) naturally occurring variables can be manipulated in a controlled setting; (c) the situation is dynamic (rather than static), in the way that real-world settings are; and (d) we can study questions that may be too sensitive to study in other than passive observational studies or in experiments using written vignettes or videotapes (Pierce & Aguinis, 1997).

subject by withdrawing some desired object and then see whether the person administers shock to the other participant. Meta-analytic findings suggest that simulating aggression in the lab yields a faithful representation of certain effects in the real world, but these lab simulations of aggression may overestimate the effects of situational variables (e.g., media violence) and underestimate the effects of individual differences (C. A. Anderson & Bushman, 1997). Efforts to improve the generalizability of experimental simulations are currently under way in a number of areas of psychology (see Box 4.3).

How Do I Identify Rival Interpretations or Rival Hypotheses?

Later in this book, we will discuss how to anticipate and control for certain experimental design problems. However, it is not too soon to begin to sharpen your intuitive skills or to get an idea of what your instructor may expect as you begin to put together a background review of the literature on your research topic or to write the discussion section of your research report. The instructor will expect you to think carefully about flaws and alternative explanations (also called **rival interpretations** or **rival hypotheses**) for the reported results and about possible ways of improving the studies you review. To get you thinking about rival interpretations, let us look at two more examples of lab research (although the process of critical evaluation is typical of the scrutiny given all research studies). The first example focuses on how life experience influences what people select from their perceptual environment as significant objects and events.

Several classic studies in psychology have shown that individuals' personal values affect how they perceive aspects of their environment. In one study, the researchers began by giving a questionnaire to a group of participants to measure each person's values, for example, whether the person's value orientation was predominantly aesthetic, theoretical, economic, social, political, or religious (Postman, Bruner, & McGinnies, 1948). Participants who valued the search for truth above most other things received a high "theoretical" score, and participants whose values were dominated by the usefulness of things had a high "economic" score. The "political" participants were concerned about power, "social" participants about the needs of others, "aesthetic" participants about criteria of beauty, and "religious" participants about the meaning of life as it related to their conception of God. All participants were then presented with a series of words through a tachistoscope projector, a device (used before the computer had been invented) that briefly presented various stimuli by flashing them on a screen for a fraction of a second. The words chosen reflected the six value orientations of the participants. On the whole, participants identified words associated with their own value orientation more rapidly than words not so associated. This outcome was taken as evidence of "subliminal perception" but was then challenged by experimenters (Solomon & Howes, 1951) who proposed a rival interpretation: People with a specific value orientation may have been exposed to these words in print more often than other people (presumably, individuals read more literature relevant to their own values). Thus, people oriented to "political" words would recognize them more rapidly than other words because of their familiarity and not because they were perceived more quickly subliminally. This rival hypothesis paved the way for follow-up studies that were specifically designed to reconcile such differences in interpretation.

Here is another example on which to practice identifying the flaws and thinking of plausible rival interpretations. Although a great deal is now known about how marijuana acts (e.g., L. L. Iversen, 2000), in the 1960s, when this experiment was done, there were volumes of statistics on the relationship between alcohol use and accident rates, but comparable data for marijuana use were unavailable. A study of the effects of drugs on simulated driving performance was deemed ethically acceptable and could be tightly controlled. What was lost, however, was the actual stress of driving in traffic. In this study (Crancer, Dille, Delay, Wallace, & Haybin, 1969), the effects of marijuana, alcohol, and no drug were compared in three simulated driving tests. In all three driving tests, the participant sat in a specially constructed console mock-up of a car and observed a large screen on which a driver's-eye motion picture was projected. Normal and emergency situations on urban and suburban streets appeared on the screen, and the subject was instructed to respond to them by operating the accelerator, brake, turn signals, and steering, and by checking the speedometer.

In the first driving test, experienced marijuana smokers were tested for 30 minutes on the console mock-up after smoking two marijuana cigarettes, and the same people were tested when their blood alcohol concentration reached 0.10% (the legally defined intoxication level in 1969), the equivalent of about 6 ounces of 86-proof liquor in a 120-pound person. In the no-drug control condition, neither marijuana nor alcohol was given. The second driving test was taken $2\frac{1}{2}$ hours after the first test, and the third driving test was taken $1\frac{1}{2}$ hours after the second test. All tests were the same, and on each test it was possible to make up to 405 errors. Under the effects of alcohol, the participants did worse than in either the marijuana or no-drug condition. In the alcohol condition over all three tests, they made a mean of 97 errors, compared with a mean of 85 errors in the control condition. In the marijuana condition, compared to the control condition, the only bad effect was an increase in speedometer errors. Under the effects of alcohol, there was an increase in all types of errors except steering errors. What problems do you see in this study? Compare your answer with the footnote at the bottom of this page.*

What Is the Distinction Between Reactive and Nonreactive Observation?

Another important distinction in observational research is between *reactive* and *nonreactive* observation. These two terms are used to differentiate between observations that do (**reactive**) from those that do not (**nonreactive**) affect the behavior or phenomenon that is being observed. For example, in a clinical experiment on therapy for weight control, the initial weigh-in observation might be a reactive stimulus to weight reduction, even without the therapeutic intervention (Campbell & Stanley, 1963). In a recent case, the researchers demonstrated experimentally that simply asking students (executive M.B.A. students and college undergraduate students) about their intent to engage in a certain behavior increased the likelihood of their subsequently engaging in that behavior (Levav & Fitzsimons, 2006). Any use of **concealed measurement** illustrates nonreactive observation, such as using a hidden recording device to eavesdrop on conversations. A variant of concealed measurement is also sometimes called **partial concealment**; the researcher does not conceal the fact that he or she is making observations but does conceal who or what is being observed. For example, in studies of mother-child interaction, the researcher implies that it is the child who is being observed when *both* the mother and the child are being studied (Weick, 1968). In the previous chapter, we discussed some ethical concerns and methodological nuances associated with the use of active and passive deceptions, and the use of concealment and partial concealment raises another ethical red flag.

---

* The research subjects were experienced marijuana users, were probably motivated to do well in the marijuana condition, and may even have been motivated to do poorly in the alcohol condition. A second problem is that the drug doses may not have been comparable. Two marijuana cigarettes may not have made the participants nearly as "high" as 6 ounces of 86-proof alcohol. Moreover, if the alcohol and marijuana treatments had made the participants equally "high," the errors might have been more nearly equal, and both might have been greater than those accumulated in the no-drug condition.

In a classic example of a field experiment that used nonreactive observation, psychologist George W. Hartmann (1936) examined the role of emotional and rational persuasive communications in an actual voting campaign and election. Hartmann was struck by the fact that much of the persuasive communication to which we are subjected in advertisements and political speeches is designed to appeal more to our emotions than to our reason. The purpose of such communication is to arouse certain needs and to offer simple solutions that, if we adopt them, will satisfy those needs. Every day we are bombarded by a host of advertisements on TV, radio, and so forth, each commercial in its own way claiming it will make us feel better because we will be more sexually appealing or more companionable or more sweet-smelling. Around election time, political commercials become a complex fusion of excitement, resentment, vague enthusiasm, aroused fears, and hopes. While he was working at Columbia University in the 1930s as a postdoctoral fellow, Hartmann decided to test whether emotional or rational advertisements are more persuasive in politics.

During the 1935 statewide election campaign in Pennsylvania, Hartmann's name had been placed on the ballot as a Socialist Party candidate in Allentown. To study the effects of emotional and rational messages, he created two political leaflets, one designed to appeal to Allentown voters' reason and the other to appeal to their emotions. The leaflets were distributed in different wards matched on the basis of their size, population density, assessed property valuation, previous voting habits, and socioeconomic status. The nonreactive observation in this study was the objective record of the polls. The results of Hartmann's analysis of these data were that the wards that had received the emotional leaflet increased their Socialist votes more than did the wards receiving the rational leaflet. In a more in-depth comparison, Hartmann found that even the "rational" wards showed a greater increase in Socialist votes than a number of control wards that had received neither leaflet.

Another classic example of a nonreactive measurement, called the *lost-letter technique,* involves dropping addressed, stamped, but unposted letters in public places. The person who comes across such a letter must decide whether to read it, mail it, disregard it, or destroy it. In the first field experiment that used this technique (Merritt & Fowler, 1948), two kinds of stamped, fully addressed envelopes, one containing a trivial message and the other a lead slug about the size of a half-dollar, were "lost." By recording the return rates, the experimenters attempted to gauge the honesty of various samples of respondents in large cities around the country without the respondents' suspecting that they were participating in an experiment. The result was that fewer letters with slugs than without them were mailed. Other researchers have used variations on this strategy, including lost letters (Milgram, Mann, & Harter, 1965) and lost e-mail to study attitudinal responses (Stern & Faber, 1997) and have used lost postcards to study the spread of rumors (Walker & Blaine, 1991).

Hartmann's use of voting behavior and the lost-letter technique are also two examples of what is termed **unobtrusive observation**, so called because those being studied are unaware that they are being observed for the purpose of research.

Unobtrusive observation, because it involves the use of concealment, causes ethical conflicts that need to be carefully considered. For example, the threat to privacy is made worse by the lack of permission in this situation, and debriefing is not typically used. The defense of unobtrusive observation usually assumes that the individuals observed are anonymous, so that their privacy is protected. That is, the researcher's goal (unlike, for example, the investigative reporter's) is not to obtain individually identified information. The code of ethics that governs psychological researchers (Chapter 3) reminds us that individual researchers are responsible for protecting the dignity of those they study. Thus, the ethical obligation of researchers who use unobtrusive observation is to ensure that information to be published or reported in a poster or talk will not damage a person by subjecting him or her to ridicule or scorn (see also Box 4.4).

You have seen from the wide variety of examples in this chapter (and in previous ones) that systematic observational methods provide much of the empirical content of behavioral and social science, yet our discussion has barely scratched the surface of what is possible. Before we turn to strategies in which the observations are directed "inward" rather than "outward," we want to reiterate an earlier point, which is that scientists, like all humans, are susceptible to the errors and biases

BOX 4.4 Four Types of Unobtrusive Observations

A major work on unobtrusive observation was written by a team of psychologists and sociologists headed by Eugene J. Webb (Webb, Campbell, Schwartz, & Sechrest, 1966; updated by Webb, Campbell, Schwartz, Sechrest, & Grove, 1981). It is a fascinating gem of a book that contains hundreds of unobtrusive measures collected by Webb and his group, and classified into four broad categories: (a) archival records (discussed previously), (b) physical traces, (c) simple observations, and (d) contrived observations. **Physical traces** are the kind of material evidence that a detective might consider clues to solving a crime. For example, in one detective case, a car's radio buttons were clues to the driver's geographic location. By studying the commercial station frequencies to which the buttons were tuned, the detective could identify the general area where the car had been garaged. **Simple observation** is unobtrusive observation that does not in any way affect what is being observed. For example, Webb's group told of finding a correlation between the methodological and theoretical disposition of psychologists and the length of their hair; the "tough-minded" psychologists had shorter hair than the "tender-minded" psychologists. In **contrived observation**, the researcher introduces some variable of interest into a situation and unobtrusively observes its effects, as Hartmann did in his field experiment, or as in assessing the degree of fear induced by a ghost story by observing the shrinking diameter of a circle of seated children.

imposed by limitations of perception and cognition. This is why scientists encourage independent replications as a way of checking on the accuracy of any single observation or set of observations. We will have more to say about this topic in Chapter 6, when we discuss the role of replication in research. We began by urging that you not harbor illusions about the power of any single research method or tool but instead be mindful that all are limited in some ways. It is a constant challenge to attempt to figure out ways of opening up our world for scientific scrutiny, to evaluate the validity and reliability of these strategies, and, ultimately, to make sensible generalizations that do not mislead by exaggerating what we think we know.

Summary of Ideas

1. Systematic observation is characterized by a plan of action and by preexisting questions or hypotheses in naturalistic and simulation studies, direct and secondary observational research, and qualitative and quantitative research. Feyerabend's "anything-goes" view of science (Box 4.1) means that doing research *does* involve a "let's-try-it-and-see" attitude. Because every method is limited in some ways, we use multiple methods to try to fill in the gaps through *methodological triangulation,* that is, by converging on the phenomenon or research question from more than one perspective.

2. Participant observers study a social situation from within by watching and recording how people behave and what they talk about (e.g., Festinger et al.'s observational study of a cult that predicted the end of the world on a specified date and Rosenhan's study of patients in mental hospitals). One possible limitation of this research (not limited only to this research) is called *observer bias* because the observer overestimates or underestimates an event or "sees" something that is not there. Using more than one independent observer is a traditional way of identifying discrepancies in observations.

3. *Social network analysts* (SNA) can be used to quantify and graph networks of relationships (Figure 4.1). Bales's judgment study of socioemotional relations and task relations in discussion groups also illustrates what can be learned from quantifying qualitative behavior.

4. *Content analysts* (an example of *secondary observation*) can be used to enumerate variables in *archival material* (e.g., Crabb and Bielawski's content analysis of pictorial representations of gender roles in children's books). Three important guidelines for content analysis are (a) checking for intercoder reliability, (b) using relevant categories, and (c) using a good sampling procedure.

5. Choosing judges might be done (a) by using intuition, (b) by consulting the literature for relevant empirical criteria, and (c) by doing pilot testing.

6. Simulating a real-world event or phenomenon in the lab can in many cases be a convenient and effective way of studying the event or phenomenon in a more controlled situation (see also Box 4.3).

7. All research studies, including tightly controlled laboratory experiments, are subject to critical reexamination for flaws, *rival interpretations,* and *rival hypotheses* (e.g., the tachistoscopic study of word recognition and the mock-driving study of the effects of marijuana smoking).

8. *Nonreactive observation* includes *concealed measurement* (hidden recording devices), *partial concealment* (not revealing who or what is being observed), and *unobtrusive observation* (e.g., Hartmann's study and the lost-letter technique). Besides archival records, three additional types of unobtrusive observation used are *physical traces, simple observation,* and *contrived observation* (Box 4.4).

Key Terms

archival material   p. 81
concealed measurement
   p. 88
content analysis   p. 82
contrived observation   p. 90
judgment study   p. 79
methodological triangulation
   p. 74
nonreactive observation
   p. 88

observer bias   p. 77
partial concealment   p. 88
participant observation
   p. 76
physical traces   p. 90
qualitative research   p. 75
quantitative research   p. 75
reactive observation   p. 88
rival hypotheses   p. 86
rival interpretations   p. 86

secondary observation
   p. 82
simple observation   p. 90
social network analysis (SNA)
   p. 78
systematic observational
   research   p. 74
unobtrusive observation
   p. 89

Multiple-Choice Questions for Review

1. In a classic study, several social psychologists "joined" a religious cult that believed that the world would soon end. After they were accepted as members of the group, they made careful observations of the behavior of the group. This type of research is known as (a) a field experiment; (b) participant observation; (c) ethnocentric research; (d) back translation.

2. A student at the University of Hawaii wants to study gossip and rumor among Asian cultures. In this research, interview questions must be translated from English into other languages. To ensure that the translations are accurate, the researcher must use (a) ethnographic research; (b) linguistic relativism; (c) back translation; (d) dual translation.

3. In 1935, psychologist George Hartmann ran for political office in Pennsylvania. In some areas, he distributed leaflets with an emotional appeal to voters. In other areas, he distributed leaflets with a rational appeal. He then observed the voting records for these different areas. In this study, the type of leaflet was the _____ variable, and the voting records were the _____ variable. (a) independent, experimental; (b) experimental, independent; (c) dependent, independent; (d) independent, dependent

4. Suppose you are conducting an observational study, and you want judges (or raters) who are very sensitive to nonverbal cues. You should choose judges who are (a) psychiatrically unimpaired; (b) college-aged; (c) female; (d) all of the above.

5. A researcher at Montclair State University carefully observes whether or not people lock their car doors when parked in the university's parking lot. The people do not realize that they are being observed for a research study. This is an example of (a) reactive observation; (b) partial conceal-ment; (c) unobtrusive observation; (d) none of the above.

6. A researcher at Florida International University conducts an observational study of job satisfaction in a large corporation. She tells the research participants that she is studying their behavior but does not tell them what aspect of their behavior she will be observing. This is an example of (a) quasi disclosure; (b) partial concealment; (c) unobtrusive observation; (d) residual disclosure.

7. To determine which classrooms are used most heavily at Akron University, a researcher measures the amount of wear on floor tiles. This is an example of the use of (a) physical traces; (b) simple observations; (c) contrived observations; (d) archival records.

8. A researcher at Colby College observes how far apart people stand from each other at a party. This is an example of the use of (a) physical traces; (b) simple observations; (c) contrived observations; (d) archival records.

9. A researcher at the University of Colorado at Denver reports that marriage rates are associated with the size of the city. She obtained both the marriage rates and the population estimates from government statistics available in the library. This is an example of the use of (a) physical traces; (b) simple observations; (c) contrived observations; (d) archival research.

10. Which of the following is not an unobtrusive measure? (a) physical traces; (b) simple observations; (c) contrived observations; (d) interviewing people

Discussion Questions for Review

1. An Iowa State student is given the task of describing two possible uses of archival measures not mentioned in this chapter. Can you suggest some possibilities?

2. An Arizona State student wants to test the hypothesis that people's level of aggression predicts their preference of sports; that is, more aggressive people like more aggressive sports. How might the student test this hypothesis using nonreactive measures?

3. A Towson State student wants to use content analysis to study the comic pages in the *Baltimore Sun*. Can you think of a particular hypothesis to guide the data collection? What steps would you advise the student to take in carrying out her study?

4. A Fitchburg State College student wants to do a participant-observer study of tourists and local residents in Provincetown. What advice would you give him about systematizing his observations?

5. A student at the University of Massachusetts at Boston wants to illustrate the application of methodological triangulation to the question of whether inhaling cigarette smoke is unhealthy. Can you help by giving an example of a descriptive, a relational, and an experimental study, all addressing the same question?

6. An Ohio State University student has found that teachers' ratings of their students' intellectual ability are highly correlated with the students' IQ test scores and concludes that this correlation reflects the effects of teachers' expectations on students' intellectual performance. What might be a plausible rival hypothesis to that interpretation?

Answers to Review Questions

Multiple-Choice Questions

1. b	3. d	5. c	7. a	9. d
2. c	4. d	6. b	8. b	10. d

Discussion Questions

1. Archival materials could be used as follows: to learn the "effects" of legislation on some outcome behavior (e.g., drunk driving) by comparing the change in behavior in states (or counties) enacting new laws with the change in behavior in states not enacting new laws; to predict legislators' votes from an analysis of their past votes or the style of communication revealed in their earlier speeches; to predict future intelligence, personality, and psychopathology from archived early childhood drawings.

2. The student could correlate the frequency of reported fights, stampedes, and riots with the aggressiveness of various sports as defined by the average number of injuries per player sustained in each sport.

3. The student could examine the hypothesis that comic strips featuring children are designed for a younger readership. The mean word length in comic strips featuring children could be compared to the mean word length in comic strips not featuring children. The student should check the reliability of two judges' (a) classifying the strips as featuring or not featuring children and (b) counting the word lengths and computing their average. The student might also want to sample the comic strips over a period of several weeks or months.

4. The most important advice is that he should be clear about what he wants to learn from this research. He should pay heed to the problems of interpreter bias and observer bias.

5. A descriptive study may reveal a high rate of wheezing, coughing, illness, and death among those exposed to cigarette smoke. A relational study may show that those who are exposed to greater amounts of cigarette smoke suffer from higher rates of illness and death. An experimental study may show that animals experimentally exposed to higher dosages of cigarette smoke have higher rates of illness and death than do animals exposed to lower dosages.

6. A rival hypothesis might be that the teachers' ratings of their students' intellectual ability were nothing more than the teachers' accurate diagnosing of IQ. It would take an experimental manipulation of teachers' expectations to demonstrate that they played a causal role.

CHAPTER 5

Methods for Looking Within Ourselves

Preview Questions

- What are the uses and limitations of self-report measures?
- What are open-ended and fixed-choice items?
- How are personality and projective tests used?
- What are numerical, forced-choice, and graphic ratings?
- What are rating errors, and how do I control them?
- What are semantic differentials, Likert scales, and Thurstone scales?
- How do I prepare items for a questionnaire or an interview?
- How are face-to-face and telephone interviews done?
- How are behavioral diaries used in research?

What Are the Uses and Limitations of Self-Report Measures?

Researchers who study human behavior not only watch and record, frequently calling on judges (raters or coders) to make systematic observations, but they also often ask people to look within themselves and disclose their own attitudes, feelings, perceptions, and beliefs in order to elicit a kind of information that is unique (Baldwin, 2000). These inner-directed observations are described as **self-report measures**, and their use in behavioral and social research goes back more than a century. In the formative years of psychology, experimental researchers had subjects reflect and verbally report on their sensations and perceptions (a process known as *introspection*). Later on, with the development of behavioral methodology, verbal reports fell out of favor in experimental psychology and were largely replaced by behavioral responses and observational methods.

Nonetheless, self-report is used quite regularly in many areas. When you go to the eye doctor to be fitted for glasses, after you are shown the letter chart you are shown a series of paired images and asked which of the two you find easier to see. When you go to your family doctor, you are asked how you feel. In a similar way, psychological researchers who use **standardized measures** (i.e., the measures

BOX 5.1 Personality Testing of Professional Athletes

Psychologists have shown that it is possible to estimate future performance in some occupations from well-constructed measures of normal personality, given to potential employees before employment (Hogan, Hogan, & Roberts, 1996). Some National Football League teams even give personality tests to prospective draft choices to help in judging the draftees. The New York Giants organization gives its own test to prospective players, including asking them to answer true or false to statements like "When a person 'pads' an income tax report so as to get out of some taxes, it is just as bad as stealing money from the Government," and "I am often said to be hotheaded" (T. W. Smith, 1997, p. 11). The prospective player's responses to these and other items are used to create a personality profile. These profiles are believed to be as informative as the required physicals.

were developed and are administered and scored according to certain rules, or standards) to study subjective well-being also ask people how they feel (e.g., Diener, 2000). Many behavioral and social researchers use a variety of self-report measures in their work (A. A. Stone et al., 2000), including personality inventories that estimate future performance (see Box 5.1), attitude and opinion questionnaires, and procedures in which people are asked to reflect on their inner feelings or to "think aloud" (Ericsson & Simon, 1993). In research on pain, self-report measures are used to gather specific information about the duration, intensity, and kind of pain (Turk & Melzack, 1992).

The purpose of this chapter is to acquaint you with a range of self-report methods and to discuss the uses and limitations of each. Most of the instruments described are readily available to student researchers, but some require supervised training and certification. If you are looking for a specialized psychological measure in the public domain to use in your research, a good place to begin is the *Directory of Unpublished Experimental Mental Measures,* edited by B. A. Goldman, D. Mitchell, and their colleagues (1995, 1996, 1996, 1997, 2003). This series of volumes contains brief descriptions of several thousand noncommercial psychological instruments for use in research situations, including various measures of aptitude, attitude, concept meaning, creativity, personality, problem solving, status, and so on. Another huge database (created by Evelyn and Linda Perloff) is Health and Psychosocial Instruments (HaPI), available on the Ovid database; it includes questionnaires, checklists, rating scales, interview schedules, and specialized tests for use in research. In this chapter, we also discuss different forms of rating scales, questionnaires that measure attitudes, the use of interviews and behavioral diaries, and rating errors and how they are controlled. In addition, we illustrate three traditional scaling procedures that use rating methods (the semantic differential, the

Likert item-analysis procedure, and the Thurstone equal-appearing interval procedure). In the use of any of these tools as self-report measures, there are four important issues to consider.

One issue is the dependability of self-report data. A basic assumption when self-report measures are used is that what people say about themselves is true and not merely a strategy to "look good." However, when people feel apprehensive about being evaluated, they are often evasive or not completely forthcoming. Called **evaluation apprehension** (Rosenberg, 1969), this anxious state may be reduced somewhat if respondents are allowed to answer privately (Schaeffer, 2000), anonymously (Thomas, Hall, Miller, et al., 1979), or confidentially (Esposito et al., 1984; Singer, Von Thurn, & Miller 1995). In survey research, however, there is evidence that the more elaborate the assurance of confidentiality, the more expectations may increase that the questions will touch on highly sensitive topics that the person is reluctant to talk about (Frey, 1986; Singer, Hippler, & Schwarz 1992). In experiments that contain an element of surprise or have an aura of mystery, the level of evaluation apprehension may also be intensified (Rosenberg, 1969).

A second issue is the right to privacy, as people have the right to withhold information and also the right not to have the information they disclose made public or used against them (Bersoff & Bersoff, 2000). However, suppose we are studying young children or adolescents, and we learn that the child has a suicidal tendency or that the parents are abusing the child (LaGreca, 1990). Obviously the moral, clinical, and legal implications are profound. Because such situations are possible, a concern of ethicists is whether it is appropriate for an untrained researcher (such as a college student) to ask people about such things as depression, anxiety, sexuality, and traumatic life experiences (Bersoff & Bersoff, 2000). As we discussed in Chapter 3, proposed research is subject to an ethical evaluation. Your instructor will be sensitive to ethical considerations and potential conflicts that may not even occur to beginning researchers.

A third issue is whether research participants, even the most well-intentioned, can provide information that is as valid and reliable as other behavioral data. Some psychologists have argued that people simply cannot look within themselves or have a clear sense of themselves apart from the immediate situation (Nisbett & Wilson, 1977). For example, some views that people hold about themselves are accurate, but people also generally have a tendency to overvalue themselves. Cornell University psychologist David Dunning, coauthor of a detailed review of self-assessment measures (Dunning, Heath, & Suls, 2004), mentioned in an interview in the Association of Psychological Science's August 2005 *Observer* (p. 9) that, defying statistical probability, 94% of college professors rate themselves as doing "above average" work! In a study in which parents were interviewed as they were leaving an HMO immediately after their children had received one or more vaccinations, the parents' reports of what had occurred a few minutes earlier were riddled with errors of recall (Willis, Brittingham, Lee, Tourangeau, & Ching, 1999). In another study, men were asked about particular experiences they had reported 30 years earlier when they were adolescents (Offer, Kaiz, Howard, & Bennett, 2000). Whereas 61% of them, as adolescents, had reported that sports and other physical

---

BOX 5.2 The Seven Sins of Memory

Daniel L. Schacter (1999), a Harvard cognitive psychologist, described what he called the "seven sins of memory." Three of them refer to types of forgetting: (a) absent-mindedness, (b) blocking out certain information, and (c) the gradual deterioration of details over time. Another three refer to different kinds of distortions or inaccuracies: (d) attributing something to the wrong source, (e) unconscious biases due to stereotypes and prejudices, and (f) human suggestibility to implanted ideas. The final memory "sin" does not refer to forgetting or memory gaps, but instead to (g) the nagging persistence of images that are instantaneously, and seemingly forever, imprinted in our memory (like the shocking images of September 11, 2001). Schacter theorized that these sins of memory are like "spandrels," an architectural term referring to the leftover spaces in structural components of buildings, except that these memory spandrels are leftover effects gone astray in an evolutionary process that is imperfect.

---

activities were their favorite pastimes, only 23% of them as adults gave the same answer when asked to recollect their favorite pastimes. When they were young, 28% of them had reported that they disliked schoolwork, but 58%, as adults, "remembered" they hated it. As adolescents, 70% had said they found religion personally helpful, but as adults, only 26% of them remembered it the same way (see also Box 5.2).

A fourth issue has to do with the interpretation of individual scores. Suppose we were using a standardized test for which there were **norm-referenced** values of respondents in some specified population (such as the Scholastic Assessment Test that many high school seniors take, and that is used by many colleges and universities in their selection process). By comparing a person's score with those of the normative group, we can estimate the percentile in which the person's score falls (more about percentiles in a later chapter). But what if we constructed our own rating instrument? It might be misleading to compare the rating scores of one person with those of another person (Bartoshuk, 2002). Suppose that Persons A and B independently rated the extent to which they were "feeling stress" as 3 on a scale from 0 (no stress) to 7 (extreme stress). Although both gave the same response, how do we know that A's score means the same thing as B's? Suppose they have different thresholds of stress. On the other hand, if all we want to know is whether each person's feeling of stress has changed over time, we have the original scores as base rates in a repeated-measures design (more about repeated-measures designs later in this book). Similarly, there is no problem if all we want to do is compare the average rating scores for stress in two randomly assigned groups, because we presume that randomly occurring differences (called *random errors* in the next chapter) will cancel out (Norwick, Choi, & Ben-Shachar, 2002).

What Are Open-Ended and Fixed-Choice Items?

All of the methods that are described in this chapter, whatever their limitations, have been used in basic and applied behavioral research. In fact, few people escape the opportunity to participate in one of these two types of research, although not everyone agrees to participate. Suppose you receive the following telephone call:

> Hello, is this _____? My name is _____, and I'm calling from the Survey Institute at Central University. We are conducting a short random survey to determine how people feel about gun control issues so that we can get a true picture of people's attitudes. It will only take about 5 minutes, and we would greatly appreciate your help. May I ask you some questions?

If you answer yes, you will be a participant in a study using self-report data to measure people's behavior or state of mind.

You will be read a series of questions and asked to say how you personally behave, feel, or think (Lavrakas, 1987). Some of the questions you are asked may be **open-ended items**, so called because they offer you an opportunity to express your feelings and impressions spontaneously. The doctor's asking "How do you feel?" is an example of an open-ended question. Your answer not only gives the doctor a clue to *what* to observe or diagnose but also gives her or him a sense of how *you* (as an individual) experience things. In the telephone survey example, the researcher is looking for individual responses, although the goal is to generalize (cautiously) about similar individuals in some specified population. An example of an open-ended question that the researcher might ask is "How do you feel about the National Rifle Association?" When analyzing the data, the researcher will categorize responses to this question and then correlate the coded data with the responses to other questions (another example of relational research).

Like any observational or self-report method, an open-ended format has advantages and disadvantages (Scott, 1968). The advantages of open-ended items are that (a) they do not lead the respondent by suggesting specific answers; (b) their approach is exploratory, allowing the researcher to find out whether the person has anything at all to say; and (c) they invite the person to answer in his or her own language, a procedure that sometimes helps to increase rapport. The disadvantages of open-ended items are that (a) they are time-consuming for both the researcher (who must code and analyze the responses) and the respondents; (b) they often elicit rambling and off-the-mark responses that may never actually touch on the topic the researcher is interested in; and (c) they may be hard to assess for reliability (discussed in the next chapter).

Thus, another approach is to use **fixed-choice items** (also called *structured, precoded,* or *closed*), which take their name from the fact that they use a more controlled format, giving the respondent specified options such as yes-no or multiple-choice alternatives. An example of a fixed-choice item would be "How do you feel about a 10-day waiting period for permission to buy a gun? Would you say you are strongly in favor, moderately in favor, moderately against, or strongly against this idea?" A response that would not be read to you is "Don't know," but if that is your spontaneous answer, the interviewer would note it down. In general, the advantages and disadvantages of fixed-choice items are the reverse of those of open-ended items. For most researchers, the major advantage of the fixed-choice format is that it forces the respondents' answers into the dimensions of interest to the researcher rather than producing irrelevant or uncodable answers (Scott, 1968). Later on, we will describe how open-ended and fixed-choice methods are used in personality inventories, attitude and survey questionnaires, interviews, and behavioral diaries. The rule of thumb is that the measures chosen should match the dimensions of interest and the kind of information that is desired.

How Are Personality and Projective Tests Used?

As ideas of personality have developed, from the time of Sigmund Freud to the present, methods of assessing various personality characteristics, particularly as part of the therapeutic process, have also evolved. Much of the early testing of personality consisted of diagnosing the mental state of the individual by examining that part of the personality relevant to therapy, a process that led to the development of a variety of personality measures. The particular configuration of an individual's personality is believed to have profound consequences for her or his behavior. Although there is disagreement about the factors that are most influential in a given situation, there is theoretical speculation that a small number of factors may transcend cultural differences (McCrae & Costa, 1997). That is, there is presumed to be a human universal in the structure of personality, similar to the universality of the human skeletal structure—even though individuals differ from one another in, for example, their girth and height (see also Box 5.3).

BOX 5.3 OCEAN: The Big Five

Current thinking in personality assessment generally supports the idea of five broad domains of individual personality, often referred to as the *Big Five factors* (Goldberg, 1993; McCrae & Costa, 1997; Wiggins, 1996). The acronym *OCEAN* is an easy way to remember these five factors, although each factor may be made up of hundreds of specific traits:

1. *Openness to experience* (O), or the degree of imagination, curiosity, and creativity.
2. *Conscientiousness* (C), or the degree of organization, thoroughness, and reliability.
3. *Extraversion* (E), or the degree of talkativeness, assertiveness, and activity.
4. *Agreeableness* (A), or the degree of kindness, trust, and warmth.
5. *Neuroticism* (N), or the degree of nervousness, moodiness, and temperamentality.

Measures of the structure of personality take many different forms, including the use of open-ended and fixed-choice formats. One of the oldest psychological measures of personality is the **projective test**. This class of instruments, of which the **Rorschach test** is perhaps the most familiar name, uses an open-ended format. The Rorschach comprises 10 inkblots, shown one by one to the respondent in a standard order, each for as long as the respondent likes. The Rorschach test is open-ended because the presenter instructs the respondent to describe whatever he or she sees in the blot. The presenter keeps a verbatim record of everything the person says, also noting any peculiarity of facial expression or bodily movement. Once the person has responded to all the test plates, the task of scoring begins. The 10 test plates were originally created by psychiatrist Hermann Rorschach, who also provided a scoring method. Interpreting the Rorschach has been modified and expanded by other researchers over the years (e.g., S. J. Beck, Beck, Levitt, & Molish, 1961; Exner, 1993; Huprich, 2006; Kleinmuntz, 1982; I. B. Weiner, 2003). Scoring and interpreting the Rorschach calls for professionally supervised experience, so the Rorschach is out of the reach of undergraduate students doing research. Illustrative of its use in research was a study that used a scoring system that the researchers developed to assess the verbal responses of Japanese, Algerian Arabs, and Apache Native Americans in order to identify certain universal concepts and symbols (De Vos & Boyer, 1989). (We discuss the validity and reliability of the Rorschach test in the next chapter.)

Another open-ended projective test, not as well known to the general public, is the **Thematic Apperception Test (TAT)**. Created by Henry Murray, it consists of a number of picture cards of people in various life contexts, and the respondent is asked to make up a story explaining each picture. Because the situations depicted are adaptable to a large number of interpretations, different stories are appropriate. The cards include different subsets for men, women, boys, and girls. The stories the respondent tells are presumed to disclose the respondent's perception of interpersonal relationships. In a classic study in personality research, David McClelland and his coworkers (McClelland, Atkinson, Clark, & Lowell, 1953) used the TAT to profile people who were high and low in the "need to achieve." The researchers asked college students to construct a story from TAT pictures. As each picture was presented, the student was asked: (a) What is happening? Who are the persons? (b) What has led up to this situation? That is, what has happened in the past? (c) What is being thought? What is wanted? By whom? and (d) What will happen? What will be done? Once the students had made up their stories, they were scored on the need for achievement. The researchers also used other tools of personality measurement to elicit the respondents' high and low levels of need for achievement. McClelland and his colleagues described the structure and intensity of the need for achievement in each respondent and also developed a model of the situational factors that, they theorized, might increase or decrease a need for achievement.

Another widely used measure of personality that you may come across in your reading is the **Minnesota Multiphasic Personality Inventory (MMPI)**. The MMPI, which uses a fixed-choice format, contains several hundred statements such as "I often cross the street to avoid meeting people," "I am afraid of losing my mind," "I believe I am no more nervous than most others," and "I have a great deal of stomach trouble." The test taker responds "true" or "false" to each statement. The statements were originally selected by researchers after studies had revealed which items best differentiated normal individuals from various types of psychiatric patients. Some statements were also selected to reflect general health, sexual attitudes, emotional states, and so on. From these statements, clinical scales were created, which are related to diagnostic categories such as depression, paranoia, and schizophrenia. Those taking the MMPI are usually scored on all scales, and the scores are then compared with those of normal control respondents (e.g., A. F. Friedman, Lewak, Nichols, & Webb, 2001). All of the tools described in the remainder of this chapter can be used routinely by most students (with the ethical stipulation noted previously), but the availability of the MMPI (like the Rorschach and the TAT) is restricted to testers who have had supervised training. (See Box 5.4 for an approach that is more generally available to all researchers.) Students who are interested in learning more about professional testing principles will find a detailed discussion in the most recent edition of the American Psychological Association's *Standards for Educational and Psychological Testing*. (We discuss the validity and reliability of the MMPI in the next chapter.)

BOX 5.4 The Three Faces of Eve

Although access to the Rorschach test and the TAT is limited to those with supervised training and experience, there are (as cited at the beginning of this chapter) many instruments that are in the public domain. It is also possible to construct our own measures using the scaling procedures discussed in this chapter. One such procedure, discussed later in this chapter, is the *semantic differential,* which has been employed in a wide variety of experimental and applied contexts, including clarifying the meaning of the Rorschach (Otten & Van de Castle, 1963) and the TAT (Friedman, Johnson, & Fode, 1964) and as a diagnostic test. If you are an old movie buff who has seen the 1957 film *The Three Faces of Eve,* you will be particularly interested in a classic article by Osgood and Luria (1954) in which they describe how they used the semantic differential in a blind analysis of Eve's multiple personality. The article also contains a set of graphics resembling a Tinkertoy, where the circles are descriptive words, and the sticklike lines that connect the circles are the quantified psychological distances that Osgood and Luria calculated. The graphics are representations of each of Eve's three personalities ("Eve White," "Eve Black," and "Jane") based on her responses on a semantic differential created by the researchers for this specific research. If you enjoyed the movie, you will be fascinated by the researchers' diagnostic interpretations of the semantic differential graphics.

What Are Numerical, Forced-Choice, and Graphic Ratings?

Researchers who want to have people rate themselves (or to have judges rate others, as discussed in the previous chapter) often create their own **rating scales**. The most commonly used scales in behavioral and social research are the numerical and graphic kinds, but we will also describe a third kind, the forced-choice rating scale. Whether you are testing people and scoring the results yourself or are using a computer to administer and score rating scales, you will find these three types easy to use, easy to score, and widely applicable. Standardized questionnaires also typically use one of these three formats. Where there are response options that are labeled with **cue words** (guiding labels), it is prudent to give the respondent an example (illustrated later in this chapter).

Numerical scales, which are the most popular of these three types, take their name from the fact that respondents work with a sequence of defined numbers. The numbers may be stated for the person to see and use, or they may be implicit (e.g., 1 vs. 0 for "yes" vs. "no"). To illustrate, here is a 5-point item from a questionnaire that was designed to measure attitudes toward mathematics (Aiken, 1963):

My mind goes blank, and I am unable to think clearly when working with math.

_____strongly disagree

_____disagree

_____undecided

_____agree

_____strongly agree

In this example, the numbers are implicit rather than explicit. For instance, we can score *strongly disagree* as -2, *disagree* as -1, *undecided* as 0, *agree* as $+1$, and *strongly agree* as $+2$. Or we can score *strongly disagree* as 1, *disagree* as 2, *undecided* as 3, *agree* as 4, and *strongly agree* as 5. Either way, we will get equivalent results when we analyze the data.

Notice in the item above that the respondent is given the option to answer "undecided" (neutral). However, some researchers prefer pushing respondents to one or the other side rather than giving them the neutral option, for example:

My mind goes blank, and I am unable to think clearly when working with math.

_____strongly disagree

_____disagree

_____agree

_____strongly agree

Most survey researchers regard neutral responses as a form of missing data that reduces their ability to detect statistical differences (Schuman & Presser, 1996). In the illustrative item above, the positive and negative scoring will remain the same, but there is no zero. Alternatively, we can score *strongly disagree* as 1, *disagree* as 2, *agree* as 3, and *strongly agree* as 4.

To illustrate the second form of rating scales, called **forced-choice scales**, suppose you were asked to respond to the following question:

Which characteristic *best* describes your best friend—honest or intelligent?

This question forces you to choose between two positive attributes (thereby implying that the one you did not choose is less characteristic of your friend). Since many people dislike having to make such a choice, you might ask why use forced-choice scales at all? The answer is that they were created to overcome a type of response bias called the **halo effect**, which occurs when the person doing the rating of someone (the target person) forms a very favorable impression of the target person based on one central trait and extends that impression to the target person's other characteristics. For example, suppose a target person who is athletic and good-looking is judged to be far more popular than she or he really is. A numerical scale would allow the rater to pile up favorable scores, but on a forced-choice scale the rater is required to make a difficult choice. The forced-choice format that seems to arouse the least antagonism (and produces the most valid results) presents four positively valenced options and asks respondents to select the two *most descriptive ones* in this group (Guilford, 1954).

Suppose we are interested in evaluating a new incentive program designed to improve the reward system and morale in a company. As a way of experimentally assessing the effectiveness of the program, we expose a sample of workers (the experimental group) to a 1-month treatment condition and compare their reactions with those of other workers (the control group) who did not receive the experimental treatment. In the spirit of methodological pluralism, our dependent measures consist of self-ratings, ratings by managers, and nonreactive measures of performance, which we will use to triangulate on the effectiveness of the new program. Among the self-ratings are some forced-choice items, such as:

Circle the *two* characteristics that *best describe* how you feel in your work:

rewarded   relaxed   appreciated   trusting

Our hypothesis is that, if the incentive program has the effect of improving the reward system and morale, the experimental group is more likely than the control group to circle characteristics such as "rewarded" and "appreciated."

Finally, **graphic scales** are a third basic type of rating scale. Usually a graphic scale is a straight line resembling a thermometer, presented either horizontally or vertically. It can be used as either an observational or a self-report method (just as numerical and forced-choice scales can be used in both situations). For example, teachers might be asked to use the following items to rate each student in their homeroom (an observational method), or students might be asked to rate themselves (a self-report method):

Unpopular _____ Popular
Shy _____ Outgoing
Solitary _____ Gregarious

The respondent makes a check mark, and the scorer then transforms that mark into a number by placing a ruler under the line and reading the number from the ruler. Of course, it would be a lot easier to present the items on a computer so that the responding and scoring are both done quite automatically. Notice in this case that the items above are what would be described as *bipolar,* which in this context means that the cue words at the ends of these scales are extreme opposites. (Using bipolar items can be a problem, however, when respondents have mixed emotions about what they are rating. In that situation, we generally recommend that researchers use unipolar rather than bipolar items, where *unipolar* means that the scores run from a low amount to a high amount on a particular dimension.)

For scoring purposes, it is also usually preferable to divide the straight line into segments. In the case above, dividing the straight line into six segments would transform the "thermometer scale" into a numerical rating scale (or what also may be described as a *segmented graphic scale*):

Unpopular _____:_____:_____:_____:_____:_____ Popular

Shy _____:_____:_____:_____:_____:_____ Outgoing

Solitary _____:_____:_____:_____:_____:_____ Gregarious

Here, the researcher asks the teacher or student to make a decision that reflects only positively or negatively on the person being rated, because a scale with an even number of segments does not allow for an undecided response. This example is reminiscent of a forced-choice measure, except that it gives the person a range of positive and negative options.

What Are Rating Errors, and How Do I Control Them?

The use of rating scales assumes that respondents are capable of an acceptable degree of rating precision and objectivity. In constructing questionnaires that use such measures, it is important to think about how to overcome certain **rating errors** (also called *response biases* or *rater biases*), such as the halo effect mentioned above. In recent years, some researchers have questioned the seriousness of the halo effect and whether it is as prevalent as earlier researchers claimed (Murphy, Jako, & Anhalt, 1993). Should it occur, it may be likely to do so when the rater relies on global impressions rather than on recently observed behavior. Halo errors may also occur when the rater is only casually acquainted with the person being rated, or when earlier judgments involve dimensions that are logically related to the rater's global evaluation of the person. Early research suggested other situations in which halo errors might occur, such as when the trait or characteristic to be rated cannot be easily observed, or is not clearly defined, or involves relations with other people, or is of some moral importance (Symonds, 1925). When there is concern about halo effects, the forced-choice procedure is the traditional control.

For other suspected rating errors, statistical adjustments are often possible (Hoyt, 2000), but there are also simpler ways of attempting to overcome the biases by choosing or modifying a particular numerical or graphic rating scale. For example, another type of rating error is called **leniency bias** because it occurs when judges rate someone who is very familiar, or someone with whom they are ego-involved, in an unrealistically positive manner. If we were using a graphic scale, a way to overcome this bias would be to give only one unfavorable cue word (e.g., *poor*); the rest of the range is then made up of favorable responses in different degrees (e.g., *fairly good, good, very good, excellent*), as in the following extended scale:

Poor	Fairly good	Good	Very good	Excellent

However, we treat or analyze the cue words numerically so that *Good* is only a 3 on a 5-point scale from *Poor* (scored 1) to *Excellent* (scored 5).

Another type of rating error, **central tendency bias**, occurs when respondents hesitate to give extreme ratings and instead cluster their responses around the center choice. This potential bias can be addressed in the same way that the positive range was expanded in the case above. Suppose we want to have a range of at least 5 points in a segmented-graphic scale, in which case we might use a 7-point scale, on the assumption that some respondents are reluctant to use the end points under any circumstances. Similarly, if we want to have a range of at least 7 points, we might use a 9-point scale.

Another circumstance is a rating scale used as a before-and-after measure. Suppose we want to use 5-point numerical or segmented-graphic scales as before-and-after measures (or "tests") in an experiment using a manipulation designed to move the participants' responses in a given direction. If the participants make extremely high or extremely low scores on the *pretest* (i.e., the measure taken before the manipulation), there will be a problem if we then want to produce further change in that direction. That is, we will have a **ceiling effect** or a **floor effect**, which restricts the amount of change that can be produced. We could try extending the ends of the scale after pilot-testing it, so that a 5-point scale becomes a 9-point or an 11-point scale. If we find no changes from pretest to posttest we must make sure the data were not artificially restricted by a ceiling or floor effect, that is, that there really was no room for the respondents to move their scores on the after measure.

In another type of response bias, the **logical error in rating**, the respondents give similar ratings for variables or traits that they themselves feel to be logically related but that may not occur together in the person being rated. This bias is similar, in a way, to the halo effect in that both erroneously intercorrelate variables or traits that are being rated. The difference between the two is that, in the halo effect, the respondent extends one favorable trait to the person as a whole, whereas in the logical error, the respondent interrelates certain variables or traits irrespective of the individual being rated. The standard way to overcome a logical error in rating is to construct very precise definitions and to make the instructions as explicit as possible.

In still another type of response bias, the **acquiescent response set**, some respondents (sometimes called *yea-sayers*) are overly agreeable. Rather than weighing each statement on its merits, they go along with almost any statement. If they are asked whether they agree or disagree with even the most unlikely item, they will almost invariably agree with it. This bias is addressed by the use of both anti and pro items so that the yea-sayers can easily be identified by their agreement with both types of items and dropped from the study or at least considered separately. In reporting the results, we would indicate the number of such subjects identified and how we decided to deal with them. Our expectation is that there will be few if any yea-sayers, although if there are many of them, we need to figure out why our questionnaire is so vulnerable to the acquiescent response set.

The examples above give a flavor of response biases and their control, but there are other possibilities as well. In the next chapter, we will describe classic research on "socially desirable responding," in which the person answering has a tendency to give responses that will make him or her look good. The MMPI, mentioned earlier in this chapter, has a set of items (called the *L Scale,* or *Lie Scale*) that was designed to identify respondents who are *trying* to appear socially desirable. Socially desirable responding was originally seen by researchers as simply a nuisance variable to be controlled or eliminated in some way (R. J. Fisher, 1993), but it is also now viewed as a personality variable of interest in a wide variety of settings (Crowne, 1979; Nouri, Blau, & Shahid, 1995; Ones, Viswesvaran, & Reiss, 1996). We now turn to three traditional approaches that have often been used to develop specialized attitude questionnaires: the semantic differential method, the Likert method of item analysis, and the Thurstone equal-appearing interval method.

What Are Semantic Differentials, Likert Scales, and Thurstone Scales?

In Box 5.4, we mentioned the **semantic differential method**, which was created for the study of the subjective (or representational) meaning of things (Osgood, Suci, & Tannenbaum, 1957; Snider & Osgood, 1969). For example, your open-ended, subjective associations about a "puppy" might be "a warm, furry animal that shows unconditional acceptance of its master." The semantic differential, however, uses not an open-ended format, but a fixed-choice format with segmented-graphic scales. The developers of this method found that most things in life (puppies, kittens, chairs, continents, ethnic groups, flowers, undergraduate majors, and so forth) are universally perceived in terms of three primary dimensions of subjective meaning, which they named *evaluation, potency,* and *activity,* and which they defined in terms of bipolar cue words (Osgood et al., 1957). There are some other dimensions, but they usually account for only a tiny portion of people's subjective associations.

Suppose we want to compare people's attitudinal associations about two music groups in terms of their respective evaluative, potency, and activity meanings to samples of different age groups. To tap the evaluative dimension, we can choose from among the following bipolar anchors: *bad-good, unpleasant-pleasant, negative-positive, ugly-beautiful, cruel-kind, unfair-fair,* and *worthless-valuable.* To measure the potency dimension, we can choose from among *weak-strong, light-heavy, small-large, soft-hard,* and *thin-heavy.* For the activity dimension, any of the following can be used: *slow-fast, passive-active,* and *dull-sharp.*

The 7-point bipolar scales might look as follows, though we want to use more than just these three items (because, as explained in the next chapter, increasing the number of items increases the reliability of the instrument as a whole):

Ugly ____:____:____:____:____:____:____ Beautiful

Soft ____:____:____:____:____:____:____ Hard

Dull ____:____:____:____:____:____:____ Sharp

We instruct the participants to rate each music group by checking the appropriate space. To score people's responses, we assign numbers to their ratings as follows:

Ugly ____:____:____:____:____:____:____ Beautiful

$\qquad$ -3 $\quad -2$ $\quad -1$ $\quad 0$ $\quad +1$ $\quad +2$ $\quad +3$

We can then compute a composite index such as a median (the midmost score) or mean (reviewed in Chapter 10).

Previously, we noted the importance of ensuring that the participants understand what each response category signifies, particularly when the segments in graphic scales are unlabeled. In this example, the numbers above stand for something like "extremely beautiful music" (+3), "quite beautiful music" (+2), "slightly beautiful music" (+1), "neutral" (0), "slightly ugly music" (−1), "quite ugly music" (−2), and "extremely ugly music" (−3). If these labels make sense to you in terms of the purpose of your study, then the rating scale will do. Figure 5.1 shows a typical set of instructions, based on those provided by the inventors of the semantic differential, which would appear on the front page of our questionnaire booklet. Notice that these instructions incorporate a number of examples so that the respondents will know what each checkmark is intended to represent. In reporting the results, we can create profiles of the stimuli being rated by showing the median ratings on each dimension (evaluation, potency, and activity) or on each pair of adjectives. For example, marketing researchers have used the semantic differential procedure to develop profiles of products and advertising campaigns. If you are interested in seeing how it has been used in the past and how the data might be presented in interesting ways, you will find a collection of useful articles in Snider and Osgood's (1969) anthology.

The semantic differential gives us a multidimensional picture (evaluation, potency, and activity) of what is being evaluated. Another traditional scaling procedure, the **summated ratings method**, provides a one-dimensional picture of attitudes on controversial issues. The summated ratings method was created by Rensis Likert (1932); attitude questionnaires that are developed by this method are known as **Likert scales**. Some researchers use the term *Likert items* to describe any 5-point numerical items ranging from *strongly agree* to *strongly disagree,* but this usage is misleading if the summated ratings method is not also used. Though most students will not have occasion to create their own Likert scales, it is useful to know how they are constructed in case you refer to a Likert questionnaire in your work. The first step is to compose a large number of statements on the controversial issue. These statements are given to a sample of people from the target population, who indicate their evaluations of each statement, usually by means of a 5-point scale *(strongly agree,*

The purpose of this questionnaire is to measure the *meanings* of some music groups to various people by having them judge these groups against a set of descriptive scales. We would like you to judge each group on the basis of what the group listed means *to you*. On each page of this booklet, you will find a different group to be judged and beneath it a set of scales. You are to rate the group on each of these scales in order.

If you feel that the group at the top of the page is *very accurately described* by the word at one end of the scale, place your check mark as follows:

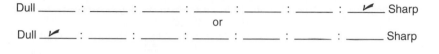

If you feel that the group is quite (but not extremely) *accurately described* at one end of the scale, place your check mark as follows:

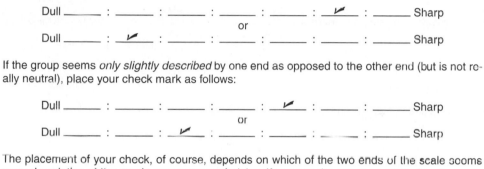

If the group seems *only slightly described* by one end as opposed to the other end (but is not really neutral), place your check mark as follows:

Dull _____ : _____ : _____ : _____ : ✔ : _____ : _____ Sharp

or

Dull _____ : _____ : ✔ : _____ : _____ : _____ : _____ Sharp

The placement of your check, of course, depends on which of the two ends of the scale seems more descriptive of the music group you are judging. If you see the group as *neutral* on the scale (that is, if both ends of the scale are *equally descriptive* of the group), or if the scale is *completely irrelevant* (that is, unrelated to the group), place your check mark in the middle space:

Dull _____ : _____ : _____ : ✔ : _____ : _____ : _____ Sharp

Figure 5.1 Semantic differential instructions.

agree, undecided, disagree, strongly disagree). The researcher then sorts through the data in order to select the best 20 or so statements for the final questionnaire. This selection involves observing the extent to which the individual responses to individual statements are correlated with the total score (the sum of the scores for all the items). Statements that correlate well with (show a strong relationship to) the total score are prospects for the final Likert questionnaire. The theory behind the summated ratings method is that statements that have low correlations with the total score will not discriminate those people with positive attitudes from those with negative attitudes.

The result of using this method is illustrated in Figure 5.2. It shows a questionnaire that was pared down to 20 items (Mahler, 1953). Items 2, 4, 6, 9, 10, 11, 14, and 15 (called "pro-socialized medicine" statements

Instructions to Subjects

Please indicate your reaction to the following statements, using these alternatives (circle your choice):

Strongly agree = SA
Agree = A
Undecided = U
Disagree = D
Strongly disagree = SD

1. The quality of medical care under the system of private practice is superior to that under a system of compulsory health insurance.

    SA   A   U   D   SD

2. A compulsory health program will produce a healthier and more productive population.

    SA   A   U   D   SD

3. Under a compulsory health program there would be less incentive for young men and women to become doctors.

    SA   A   U   D   SD

4. A compulsory health program is necessary because it brings the greatest good to the greatest number of people.

    SA   A   U   D   SD

5. Treatment under a compulsory health program would be mechanical and superficial.

    SA   A   U   D   SD

6. A compulsory health program would be a realization of one of the true aims of a democracy.

    SA   A   U   D   SD

7. Compulsory medical care would upset the traditional relationship between the family doctor and the patient.

    SA   A   U   D   SD

8. I feel that I would get better care from a doctor whom I am paying than from a doctor who is being paid by the government.

    SA   A   U   D   SD

9. Despite many practical objections, I feel that compulsory health insurance is a real need of the American people.

    SA   A   U   D   SD

10. A compulsory health program could be administered quite efficiently if the doctors would cooperate.

    SA   A   U   D   SD

11. There is no reason why the traditional relationship between doctor and patient cannot be continued under a compulsory health program.

    SA   A   U   D   SD

12. If a compulsory health program were enacted, politicians would have control over doctors.

    SA   A   U   D   SD

13. The present system of private medical practice is the one best adapted to the liberal philosophy of democracy.

    SA   A   U   D   SD

14. There is no reason why doctors should not be able to work just as well under a compulsory health program as they do now.

    SA   A   U   D   SD

15. More and better care will be obtained under a compulsory program.

    SA   A   U   D   SD

16. The atmosphere of a compulsory health program would destroy the initiative and the ambition of young doctors.

    SA   A   U   D   SD

17. Politicians are trying to force a compulsory health program upon the people without giving them the true facts.

    SA   A   U   D   SD

18. Administrative costs under a compulsory health program would be exorbitant.

    SA   A   U   D   SD

19. Red tape and bureaucratic problems would make a compulsory health program grossly inefficient.

    SA   A   U   D   SD

20. Any system of compulsory insurance would invade the privacy of the individual.

    SA   A   U   D   SD

Figure 5.2   The Socialized Medicine Attitude Scale.

Source: Reproduced from "Attitudes Toward Socialized Medicine" by I. Mahler, 1953, *Journal of Social Psychology, 38,* 273–282. Copyright © 1953. Used by permission of the Helen Dwight Reid Educational Foundation. Published by Heldref Publications, 1319 Eighteenth Street NW, Washington, DC 20036-1802.

by the author of this scale) are in favor of a compulsory health program and against the system of private practice. Items 1, 3, 5, 7, 8, 12, 13, 16, 17, 18, 19, and 20 (called "anti-socialized medicine" statements) are against a compulsory health program and in favor of the system of private practice. In using this attitude scale, we weight the responses to the pro-socialized-medicine statements from 5 *(strongly agree)* to 1 *(strongly disagree)*. For the anti-socialized-medicine statements, we simply reverse this scoring procedure. A person's score is the sum of the weighted responses, a high score indicating an accepting attitude toward a compulsory health program and a low score indicating an unaccepting attitude toward a compulsory health program. In this example, the highest and lowest possible scores, respectively, are 100 (most strongly in favor of a compulsory health program) and 20 (most strongly against a compulsory health program).

Another traditional scaling procedure for developing an attitude questionnaire was called the **method of equal-appearing intervals** by its inventor, L. L. Thurstone (1929, 1929–1934). It takes its name from the idea that judges, who are asked to sort statements into different piles, are able to keep the piles psychologically equidistant. Attitude questionnaires developed by this method are often known as **Thurstone scales**. Thurstone also invented other scaling methods and conceptualized theoretical rationales for all these methods, and his ideas have been absorbed into modern scaling methodology and theory (a field known as *psychometrics*). However, when you see some reference to a "Thurstone attitude scale," you can usually assume that the writer means the questionnaire was constructed by the method of equal-appearing intervals. This method also begins with a large number of statements, each one printed on a separate slip of paper or an index card. Judges (not the people to be given the questionnaire) then sort the statements into 11 piles, numbered from 1 (labeled "most unfavorable statements") to 11 ("most favorable statements"). The judges are allowed to place as many statements as they wish in any pile. A scale value is obtained for each statement and is usually calculated as the median of the responses of all the judges to that item. In selecting statements for the final questionnaire, the idea is to try to choose those (a) that are most consistently rated by the judges and (b) that are spread relatively evenly along the entire attitude range.

Shown in Figure 5.3 is an attitude questionnaire that, although developed during World War II, is still topical (Day & Quackenbush, 1942). Notice that respondents are asked to reply to each statement three times, that is, once for each type of war. Using the method of equal-appearing intervals, Shaw and Wright (1967) obtained scale values for these 13 items by having 15 women and 35 men respond to each statement; these values are shown in Table 5.1. The lowest scale value (0.8 for Statement 3) corresponds to the most "promilitaristic" item, and the highest scale value (8.4 for Statement 6) to the most "antimilitaristic" item in this set. If we decided to use this scale in research, the attitude score for each referent (defensive war, cooperative war, and aggressive war) would be the median scale value of the statements endorsed (i.e., checked) by the respondent for the referent. The higher the median, the more unfavorable the respondent's attitude toward that particular war referent. For example, if the respondent checks Statements 2, 4, 6, and 11 under Roman numeral I, we know that the person is very strongly opposed to

Instructions to Subjects

This is a study of attitudes toward war. Below you will find a number of statements expressing various degrees of attitudes toward war or tendencies to act in case of war.

In expressing your agreement or disagreement with the statements, please put yourself in three possible situations. First, imagine that the United States had declared a *Defensive War* (war for the purpose of defending the United States in case of an attack). Please indicate in the first set of parentheses, designated by Roman numeral I, your agreement, disagreement, or doubt. Put a check mark (✓) if you agree with the statement, put a minus sign (−) if you disagree with the statement, and a question mark (?) if you are in doubt about the statement.

Second, imagine that the United States has declared a *Cooperative War* (war in cooperation with the democratic countries of Europe for the defense of democracy). Go over the statements again and indicate in the second set of parentheses, designated by Roman II, your agreement, disagreement, or doubt in a similar way.

Third, imagine that the United States has declared an *Aggressive War* (war for the purpose of gaining more territory). Read the statements again and indicate in the third set of parentheses, designated by Roman III, your agreement, disagreement, or doubt by a similar method.

I	II	III	
( )	( )	( )	1. I would support my country even against my convictions.
( )	( )	( )	2. I would immediately attempt to find some technicality on which to evade going to war.
( )	( )	( )	3. I would immediately go to war and would do everything in my power to influence others to do the same.
( )	( )	( )	4. I would rather be called a coward than go to war.
( )	( )	( )	5. I would offer my services in whatever capacity I can.
( )	( )	( )	6. I would not only refuse to participate in any way in war but also attempt to influence public opinion against war.
( )	( )	( )	7. I would take part in war only to avoid social ostracism.
( )	( )	( )	8. I would not go to war unless I were drafted.
( )	( )	( )	9. If possible, I would wait a month or two before I would enlist.
( )	( )	( )	10. I would go to war only if my friends went to war.
( )	( )	( )	11. I would refuse to participate in any way in war.
( )	( )	( )	12. I would disregard any possible exemptions and enlist immediately.
( )	( )	( )	13. I would not enlist but would give whatever financial aid I could.

Figure 5.3   The Attitudes Toward War Scale.

Source: Reproduced from "Attitudes Toward Defensive, Cooperative, and Aggressive War" by D. D. Day and O. F. Quackenbush, 1942, *Journal of Social Psychology, 16,* 11–20. Copyright © 1942. Used by permission of the Helen Dwight Reid Educational Foundation, Heldref Publications, 1319 Eighteenth Street NW, Washington, DC 20036-1802.

Table 5.1   Scale Values for the Questionnaire in Figure 5.3

Statement	Scale value	Statement	Scale value
1	2.5	8	5.9
2	7.5	9	4.6
3	0.8	10	5.1
4	7.9	11	8.2
5	2.5	12	1.4
6	8.4	13	3.5
7	6.3		

Note: The scale values are median scores (or midmost values), based on the responses of 15 men and 35 women to each particular item (Shaw & Wright, 1967).

defensive war (median = 8.05, or midway between the scale values of 7.9 for Statement 4 and 8.2 for Statement 11).

How Do I Prepare Items for a Questionnaire or an Interview?

In developing a questionnaire—as much as in developing an interview (discussed next)—pilot testing is absolutely essential. This testing enables the researcher to determine whether the items are worded properly, for example, whether terms like *approve* and *like* (or *disapprove* and *dislike*) are being used as synonyms or whether there are differences in implication. Suppose that a company president wants to examine a team of workers' opinions of the quality of a manager's job performance, and the president directs that a fixed-choice item be phrased as follows: "How do you feel about the manager? ____I like him. ____I dislike him." The item is useless because it does not distinguish between liking and approving. It is possible to like someone without approving of his or her job performance, and vice versa (Bradburn, 1982).

If you were assigned the job of writing questions, you would also have to be sure that the wording and presentation of your items do not lead the respondent into giving an unrealistically narrow answer. A poor question will produce a very narrow range of responses or will be misunderstood by respondents. Take the following item: "Do you approve of the way the manager is handling her duties? ____ Yes. ____No." Respondents might approve of the way she handled one crisis but not another, or they might disapprove of the way she handled the dress code but not the rumor about possible layoffs. Thus, a number of different items are needed to cover the various issues on which you want an opinion about the manager's effectiveness, and the issues must be spelled out if you are to avoid misunderstanding on the part of the respondents. Suppose the dress code crisis was resolved amicably, but the layoff crisis involved union confrontations. You need a separate question, or set of questions, regarding each situation and whether the respondent approved or disapproved of the way each was handled.

You must also avoid asking *leading questions* (i.e., questions that "lead" the respondent to answer in a particular way), because they can constrain responses and produce biased answers. An example of a leading question is "Do you agree that the manager has an annoying, confrontational style? ____Yes. ____No." The phrasing of the question practically directs the respondent to be overly negative or critical. How should the question be properly phrased? It depends on what you are trying to find out. However, in coming up with an alternative, you want to be sure that the new question is not worded so as to produce another meaningless answer: "Do you agree with the manager's work philosophy? ____Yes. ____No." What would a "yes" or "no" really tell you? You need to be more precise and specific, and also to do some probing to get meaningful information.

Problems such as these can be identified during the pilot testing and can often be resolved with rewording or with a set of probing items instead of a single item. The issue of whether to use open-ended or more structured items (or a combination of both) can also be answered by pilot testing. Like personality measures, the questionnaires used by many survey researchers come in a variety of open and fixed-choice formats. The latter may, for example, comprise multiple-choice, yes-no, either-or, or acceptable-unacceptable items. A fill-in-the-blank form is useful when more specific, unprompted responses are sought. Of course, these structured forms are effective only if the material to be covered allows this amount of simplification.

In your pilot testing, you might think about asking exploratory questions such as "What did the whole item mean to you?" "What was it you had in mind when you said '_____'?" "Consider the same item this way, and tell what you think of it: _____." "You said '_____,' but would you feel differently if the question read '_____'?" (Converse & Presser, 1986, p. 52). It is also important that the answers elicited reflect what the respondent really feels or believes. As a rule, people have not thought very much about most issues that do not affect them directly; their answers may reflect a superficial understanding, or they may try to "put on a good face." Thus, survey researchers may also ask the respondent how he or she feels about a topic (e.g., "How *deeply* do you feel about it?"). In this way, they attempt to determine whether the respondent believes what he or she has reported (Labaw, 1980). Still another technique is to ask respondents to rate their confidence in their answer so that they reveal how much they are guessing.

If you plan to use open-ended questions, a general method that was designed to prevent vague, rambling, irrelevant responses is the **critical incident technique** (Flanagan, 1954). It involves having the respondent describe an observable action the purpose of which was fairly clear to the respondent and the consequences sufficiently definite to leave little doubt about its effects. A typical use of this technique would begin with the interviewer saying something like "We are making a study of [specific activity], and we believe you are especially well qualified to tell us about this activity." The interviewer next asks, "What would you say is the primary purpose of [specific activity]?" and "How would you summarize the general aim of this activity?" Then the respondent is asked to think of the last time he or she was personally involved in this activity and to describe exactly what transpired. For example, a team of researchers used this technique in a study of company managers in the United States and India who were interviewed as part of an investigation of how managers cope with destructive rumors (DiFonzo, Bordia, & Rosnow, 1994). Managers were asked to describe as concretely and fully as possible an actual situation that had been important to their company in which they had been required to confront a harmful or a potentially harmful rumor. The data revealed some circumstances in which rumor control strategies are likely to succeed and that were also found to be consistent with empirically based theorizing. If you would like to use this method, we suggest you read an article by John Flanagan (1954), the inventor of the critical incident technique, which gives a more detailed example and a rationale for the procedure.

How Are Face-to-Face and Telephone Interviews Done?

We turn now to the **face-to-face interview**, but first, we should say a few words about the relative advantages of interviews and questionnaires. Questionnaires are useful because (a) they can be efficiently administered to large numbers of people (e.g., in mail surveys, assuming that they'll be mailed back to you); (b) they are relatively economical (since a mail survey eliminates travel time and cost); and (c) they provide a type of "anonymity" (i.e., instead of meeting the researcher face to face, the respondent returns the completed survey, for example, to an impersonal research center). The face-to-face interview is useful because (a) it provides an opportunity to establish rapport with people and to stimulate the trust and cooperation needed to probe sensitive issues; (b) it provides an opportunity to clarify questions (if participants are confused); and (c) it allows flexibility in determining the wording and sequence of questions by giving the researcher greater control (e.g., by letting the interviewer determine on the spot the amount of probing required).

Just as researchers who use questionnaires need to do pilot testing, researchers who use an **interview schedule** (i.e., a script containing the questions to be asked in the interview) must try it out before actually implementing the study. This pilot testing and all the planning that precedes it typically involve four steps: (a) stating the objectives of the research (the questions and hypotheses to be addressed); (b) formulating a plan to recruit the interviewees; (c) structuring the interview schedule; and (d) testing it and making appropriate revisions. The first step is self-explanatory. The second step is simply a matter of defining the population to which we want to generalize, and then devising a plan for recruiting a representative sample from that population (discussed in more detail in Chapter 9). In the final step (pilot testing), we interview a few people from the target population and listen *analytically* to their responses to each item (e.g., Downs, Smeyak, & Martin, 1980). Good interviewers have good listening skills; that is, they are patient, hear the facts, and do not jump in or interrupt before the person being interviewed has developed an idea (Weaver, 1972).

The third step (structuring the interview schedule) needs a little more explanation because it involves writing the items and checking each one for relevancy, determining ranges of responses for some fixed-choice items, and establishing the best sequence and wording of questions. Each question must be carefully considered for its bearing on the specific hypotheses or exploratory aims of the research. Because fatigue or boredom is apt to set in after an hour or more of being interviewed (less than an hour for some respondents), the interview schedule may require the pruning of undesirable or unnecessary items. If we need to know income levels, we need to decide on ranges of responses rather than bluntly ask for an exact amount. If we are planning to ask questions that rely on people's memories (e.g., critical incident questions), we want to make sure that we are not making unrealistic demands. One researcher who has studied and written extensively about memory errors in survey research mentioned that the best jogs to a person's memory about a particular event are those that help the person to differentiate the event from others that might be brought to mind (Tourangeau, 2000). However, this same researcher cautioned that even the best cues to help people recall experiences cannot trigger the retrieval of a memory that was not fully or accurately stored in the person's memory in the first place.

The sequence in which sets of questions should be presented also needs to be established. Specific questions appear to be less affected by what preceded them than are general or broadly stated questions (Bradburn, 1982; Schuman & Presser, 1996). When sensitive issues are touched on, it is usually better to ask these questions at the end of the interview. Some people may view questions about their age, education, and income as an invasion of their privacy. When asked at the beginning of an interview, questions like these may interfere with the establishment of trust. Even when they are asked at the end of the interview, it is helpful to preface such questions with a reassuring statement. In one study, the interviewer was unusually candid: "Some of the questions may seem like an invasion of your privacy, so if you'd rather not answer any of the questions, just tell me it's none of my business" (C. Smith, 1980). The researcher also needs to work out the best wording of the items to ensure that all the interviewees readily understand the wording in equivalent ways. The final step (the pilot testing) should reveal what jargon and expressions are inhibitors and facilitators of communication. Especially important is the phrasing of the opening question, which should show the person immediately that the interviewer is pursuing the stated purpose. As noted in Chapter 3, we also want to be as open and honest as possible in our communications with our respondents, just as we want them to be open and forthcoming in their responses.

Beginning in the 1960s, several factors led many researchers in the United States to turn to the **telephone interview** and the mail survey as substitutes for the face-to-face interview method. Among the factors contributing to this shift were (a) the increased costs of conducting face-to-face interviews (because interviewing is a labor-intensive activity); (b) the invention of random digit-dialing methods for random sampling of telephone households; and (c) the development of computer-assisted methods of recording responses, in which questions are flashed on a computer screen and the interviewer directly keys in responses for computer scoring (Rossi, Wright, & Anderson, 1983).

Like all research methods, telephone interviewing has both advantages and disadvantages (Downs et al., 1980; Lavrakas, 1987; P. V. Miller & Cannell, 1982). Among the advantages are that it allows a quick turnaround (i.e., information can be obtained more promptly than by a face-to-face interview or a mail survey). It has also been reported that refusal rates are usually lower in telephone interviewing because it is not necessary to allow a stranger into one's home. Among the disadvantages are that interviewing is restricted, first, to households that own a telephone and, then, to those that answer the telephone (instead of having an answering machine or caller ID constantly on duty to screen calls). A further disadvantage is that fewer questions (and less probing questions) can be asked because it is harder to establish rapport than in a face-to-face interview and people are more impatient to conclude a telephone interview.

Generally speaking, whether telephone or face-to-face interviewing is used, the same procedures are followed in developing an interview schedule and training the interviewers. One difference, however, is that telephone interviewers have less time to establish rapport; the person called can always immediately hang up without listening to the introduction. If the person does not immediately hang up, then a strategy used to foster "commitment" on the part of the person is to point out the important goals of the research and to use positive feedback to reinforce what the researcher perceives as good responding: "Thanks . . . this is the sort of information we are looking for in this research . . . it's important to us to get this information . . . these details are helpful" (P. V. Miller & Cannell, 1982, p. 256).

How Are Behavioral Diaries Used in Research?

As we said before, a nagging problem in self-report measures is that autobiographical questions may yield inaccurate answers when the participants are asked to rely on memory (e.g., how often they have done something or how much of something they have bought or consumed). Some examples are "How many weeks have you been looking for work?" and "How much have you paid for car repairs over the previous year?" As noted in Box 5.2, problems surface because the storing of events in memory is fallible, memory is porous, recall is limited, and people fill in the gaps of what they cannot retrieve (H. B. Bernard & Killworth, 1970, 1980; Reed, 1988; D. L. Schacter, 1999; A. A. Stone et al., 2000; Tourangeau, 2000; Webber, 1970; Zechmeister & Nyberg, 1982). Suppose we want to study lying in everyday life. If we ask people to estimate, for example, the number of "little white lies" they tell each day, the results can hardly be considered valid because of all the factors mentioned above and also the respondents' possible wish to give a socially desirable response.

An innovative tool that is thought by its users to overcome the various memory problems is the **behavioral diary** (Conrath, 1973; Wickesberg, 1968). The basic procedure is to ask people to keep diaries of certain events at the time they occur. As an illustration, social psychologists Bella M. DePaulo and Deborah A. Kashy, and their coworkers, used this method in studies of the lies that college students tell (DePaulo & Kashy, 1998; DePaulo, Kashy, Kirkendol, Wyer, & Epstein, 1996; Kashy & DePaulo, 1996). The participants in this research were asked to keep meticulous records of their lying. Assuming that the records they turned in were themselves truthful, the findings were quite revealing. For example, people who indicated they had told more lies were also found to be more manipulative and more concerned about self-presentation and, not surprisingly, to have told more self-serving lies.

As another illustration, Mihaly Csikszentmihalyi and Reed Larson (1984) used this tool to study teenagers' day-to-day lives. The participants in this study were 75 teenagers who were given beepers and were then signaled at random by the researchers. When the beeper went off, the teenager was supposed to record his or her thoughts and feelings at that moment. Figure 5.4 shows a week in the life of one participant. This person had hoped to spend her first year after high school studying abroad but learned that she would not be allowed to go. The scale at the top shows a continuum from self-reported bad to good moods, and the zig-zagged line reveals that this person's mood fluctuated tremendously as she tried to cope with everyday events. Clearly, she was happiest when with friends and unhappiest when alone.

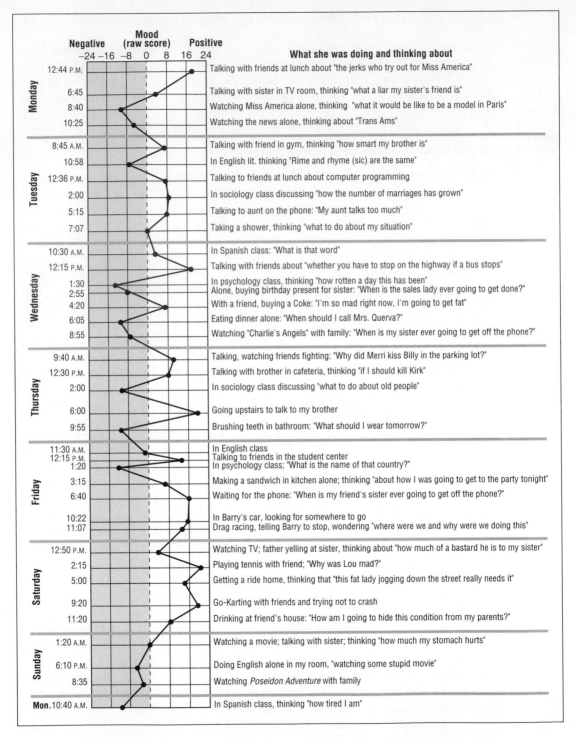

Figure 5.4 The self-recorded diary record of a week in the life of one teenage subject.

Researchers who use this method assume that such a diary gives more reliable data than questionnaires or interviews that elicit answers to autobiographical questions. To evaluate this assumption, a team of researchers (Conrath, Higgins, & McClean, 1983) collected data from managers and staff personnel in three diverse organizations (a manufacturer of plastic products, an insurance brokerage company, and a large public utility). Each participant was instructed to keep a diary of 100 consecutive interactions, beginning on a specific date and at a specific time. The instructions were to list the other party to the interaction, the initiator of the activity, the mode of interaction, the elapsed time, and the process involved. The diary was constructed in such a way that the participant could quickly record all this information with no more than four to eight check marks next to particular items. At a later time, each participant was asked to answer a questionnaire covering the same interactions.

The data from all the behavioral diaries and questionnaires were compared afterward. If one person reported talking to others, the researchers checked the diaries and questionnaires of those others to see whether they had also reported that activity. In this way, a separate measure of reliability was obtained for the behavioral diary and for the questionnaire data (i.e., concerning the reporting of specific events at the time of the events as opposed to a later time). The results were that the questionnaire data (the recalls from autobiographical memory) were less reliable than the behavioral diary data. In spite of these encouraging results, other researchers have challenged the accuracy of diary information and have argued that the participants may be overly attentive to events that "stick out" in their minds and may underreport other behavior (Maurer, Palmer, & Ashe, 1993). Nonetheless, it is another interesting method that, in conjunction with observational methods, might be used to triangulate on the behavior in question.

Summary of Ideas

1. Four fundamental issues in the use of *self-report measures* concern (a) the truthfulness of what people report, especially when the information is personal and sensitive; (b) the ethical and potentially risky implications of such information, particularly when the researchers have not been professionally trained; (c) the validity of information that depends on remembering some past event (Schacter's "seven sins of memory" in Box 5.2); and (d) the comparison of people's scores when individual sensitivities or thresholds of response are so different that cue words on rating scales mean different things to different people.

2. Two forms of self-report measures are those that allow respondents to express their feelings and impressions quite spontaneously *(open-ended)* and those that use a structured format with precoded response options *(fixed-choice);* the general advantages and limitations of open-ended measures are essentially the reverse of the advantages and limitations of fixed-choice measures.

3. The *Big Five factors* of personality (OCEAN) are openness to experience, conscientiousness, extraversion, agreeableness, and neuroticism (Box 5.3).

4. The *Rorschach inkblot test* and the *TAT* (which are both open-ended measures) operate on the principle that, in the spontaneous responses that come to mind, respondents will project some unconscious aspect of their life experience and emotions onto ambiguous stimuli. The *MMPI* (which

has a fixed-choice format) contains hundreds of statements to which the respondent answers true or false.

5. Three kinds of popular rating scales are the *numerical* (in which the numbers may be implicit or explicit), the *forced-choice* (which was developed to overcome the *halo effect*), and the *graphic* (resembling a thermometer that may or may not be segmented).

6. Other *rating errors* (besides the halo effect) include the *error of leniency,* the *error of central tendency,* the *logical error in rating,* and the *acquiescent response set*—each of which can be controlled in a particular way by the choosing or modifying of a numerical or graphic rating scale.

7. The *semantic differential,* which is a multidimensional *segmented graphic scale,* is designed to measure attitudes about the subjective meaning of things, usually in terms of the dimensions of *evaluation, potency,* and *activity* (Figure 5.1).

8. *Likert's method of summated ratings* is used to construct a one-dimensional numerical attitude scale (e.g., the Socialized Medicine Attitude Scale in Figure 5.2). *Thurstone's method of equal-appearing intervals* is another traditional procedure that is used to construct one-dimensional attitude scales (e.g., attitudes about three kinds of war in Figure 5.3).

9. The purpose of pilot-testing a *questionnaire* or *interview schedule* is to enable the researcher to fine-tune the data collection instrument and procedures. The four steps in developing an interview schedule are (a) working out the objective; (b) formulating a general strategy of data collection; (c) writing the questions and establishing the best sequence; and (d) pilot-testing the material.

10. The *critical incident technique* is a way of focusing open-ended responses by concentrating on an actual incident and asking the respondent a series of very specific questions.

11. *Telephone interviews* have become popular because they are more cost-efficient than *face-to-face interviews* and can also be implemented easily with *random digit-dialing* and computer-assisted interviewing and data-recording methods.

12. The *behavioral diary* records events as they happen, and there is no need to rely on longer term recall (e.g., the study about lying and the study of teenagers' day-to-day lives).

Key Terms

acquiescent response set p. 106
behavioral diary   p. 117
ceiling effect   p. 106
central tendency bias   p. 106
critical incident technique p. 114
cue words   p. 103
evaluation apprehension p. 97
face-to-face interview   p. 114
fixed-choice (structured) items   p. 99
floor effect   p. 106
forced-choice scales   p. 104

graphic scales   p. 104
halo effect   p. 104
interview schedule   p. 115
leniency bias   p. 105
Likert scales   p. 108
logical error in rating   p. 106
method of equal-appearing intervals   p. 111
Minnesota Multiphasic Personality Inventory (MMPI) p. 101
norm-referenced   p. 98
numerical scales   p. 103
open-ended items   p. 99
projective test   p. 101

rating errors   p. 105
rating scales   p. 103
Rorschach test   p. 101
self-report measures   p. 95
semantic differential method p. 107
standardized measures p. 95
summated ratings method p. 108
telephone interview   p. 116
Thematic Apperception Test (TAT)   p. 101
Thurstone scales p. 111

Multiple-Choice Questions for Review

1. A researcher at Southwestern University decides to use self-report methods in his study of caffeine use. His survey contains the following item: "In the past week, did you drink any coffee? Yes or no." This item is an example of (a) a fixed-choice question; (b) an open-ended question; (c) a neutrally worded question; (d) a negatively worded question.

2. A researcher at Baylor is conducting a study of the self-concept of college students. His survey contains the following item: "In your own words, please describe your self-concept. In other words, what kind of person are you?" This item is an example of (a) a negatively worded question; (b) an open-ended question; (c) a neutrally worded question; (d) a fixed-choice question.

3. A researcher at Case Western Reserve gives a participant an ambiguous picture of people in a social situation and asks the participant what the people in the picture are doing, what they are thinking, and what they will be doing in the future. This is an example of a (a) fixed-choice format question; (b) reverse-scored question; (c) projective test; (d) none of the above.

4. Some research participants are likely to agree with almost any question that is asked of them. This tendency is generally referred to as (a) an acquiescent response set; (b) an affirmation bias; (c) a nonnegation bias; (d) an affirmation tendency.

5. To avoid problems with the "halo effect," a researcher might want to use (a) forced-choice scales; (b) graphic rating scales; (c) equal-appearing interval scales; (d) segmented graphic scales.

6. Observers often assume that, if a person is physically attractive, he or she also has many other positive qualities, including being intelligent and outgoing. This is an example of (a) the error of central tendency; (b) the halo effect; (c) the error of misperception; (d) none of the above.

7. According to research on the semantic differential method, which of the following is a useful dimension of subjective meaning? (a) potency; (b) activity; (c) evaluation; (d) all of the above

8. Which of the following is also known as the method of summated ratings? (a) the semantic differential method; (b) the Thurstone method; (c) the Likert method; (d) the equal-appearing intervals method

9. Which of the following is also known as the method of equal-appearing intervals? (a) the semantic differential method; (b) the Thurstone method; (c) the Likert method; (d) the graphic rating method

10. A researcher at Rhode Island College wants to ask subjects the following question during an interview: "Describe as fully and concretely as possible a real situation that was important to you in which you acted in some way that was a cover for your true feelings." This is an example of (a) a self-recorded diary; (b) the critical incident technique; (c) the semantic differential method; (d) an interview schedule.

Discussion Questions for Review

1. An Austin Peay student wants to develop numerical and graphic items to measure attitudes about abortion. What advice would you give the student on how to get started?

2. A Central Michigan student is asked by the instructor to tell which rating error each of the following descriptions represents: (a) rating too positively someone you know; (b) tending to respond in an affirmative direction; (c) not using the extremes of a scale; (d) rating a central trait and other traits in the same way. Do you know the answers? Do you also know how to control for each of these errors?

3. A Northwestern University student who has a job selling used cars is thinking about developing a questionnaire to explore the motivations of people who buy and don't buy used cars. What methodological pointers would you give the student?

4. A student at Wheaton College in Norton, Massachusetts, wants to develop a Thurstone scale to measure attitudes about eliminating final exams for graduating seniors. Describe the steps she will need to take in developing this scale.

5. The student in Question 4 has a boyfriend who is a psychology major at Brown University. He tells her that he is planning to develop a Likert scale to measure the same attitudes. Do you know the difference between these two approaches?

6. A student at the City University of New York wants to use the semantic differential to study people's reactions to certain *New York Times* advertisements. If you were this student, how would you design this instrument?

7. A student with a dual major in psychology and political science at Ohio Wesleyan, who is running for student body president, reads *The Selling of the President,* in which the author, Joe McGinniss, wrote about the use of the semantic differential by advertising researchers who worked for Richard M. Nixon when he began assembling a team for his 1968 presidential campaign. The researchers traveled all through the United States asking people to evaluate the presidential candidates (Nixon, Hubert Humphrey, and George Wallace). They then plotted an "ideal presidential curve" (i.e., a line connecting the points that represented what the researchers thought would be the ideal candidate) and compared the candidates' profiles with this ideal. The Ohio Wesleyan student is also running against two rivals and wonders whether it might be possible to do a similar study. What methodological pointers would you give her?

8. A student at the University of South Africa, a correspondence university, works in a company that wants to study the morale of its employees. The student thinks it might be instructive to ask a sample of the employees one or two critical incident questions. How should they be worded?

9. A Haverford College student is asked by his instructor to state, in one succinct sentence, the major advantage of the behavioral diary method over using a questionnaire. How should he answer?

Answers to Review Questions

Multiple-Choice Questions

1. a	**3.** c	**5.** a	**7.** d	**9.** b
2. b	**4.** a	**6.** b	**8.** c	**10.** b

Discussion Questions

1. Define the aspects of attitudes about abortion you want to cover with your measure, and be sure the items are easily understood. Decide how many response categories you want to use in your numerical and segmented graphic scales.

2. Leniency bias, acquiescent response set, central tendency bias, and halo effect (or logical error in rating), respectively. The section on rating errors gives suggestions on how to control for each of these rating concerns.

3. Most of the chapter contributes to an answer to this question, but you might begin with the answer to discussion Question 1 above.

4. Have a large number of judges sort a large number of items into 11 piles numbered 1 to 11 in order of item favorableness. Compute the median rating of favorableness of each item, and select the items for the final scale on the basis of (a) the judges' agreement on each item's degree of favorableness and (b) the items' being spread fairly evenly throughout the range of attitudes from

1 to 11. The format of the final attitude scale might resemble the sample scale in Figure 5.3 (the sample scale values are shown in Table 5.1).

5. The major difference is that the Likert 5-point (or 7-point or 9-point) items are used only if they correlate highly enough with the total score. A sample scale based on the Likert method is shown in Figure 5.2.

6. Select a sample of bipolar cue words from the lists in this chapter that seem to best represent the evaluative, potency, and activity dimensions. Sample instructions are shown in Figure 5.1.

7. Instead of supposing what the ideal candidate might be like, it might be better to ask respondents which characteristics of candidates would elicit their votes.

8. One wording might be: "Describe in detail a situation in which you felt pleased and proud to be an employee of the company. What led up to the situation, and what was its outcome?" The same question might well be asked again, this time with "unhappy and ashamed" substituted for "pleased and proud."

9. It has been shown to lead to more accurate data.

CHAPTER 6

Reliability and Validity in Measurement and Research

Preview Questions

- What is the difference between validity and reliability?

- What are random and systematic errors?

- What is the purpose of retest and alternate-form reliability?

- What is internal-consistency reliability, and how is it increased?

- What is acceptable test-retest and internal-consistency reliability?

- How do I measure the reliability of judges?

- How is reliability related to replication and external validity?

- How are content and criterion validity defined?

- How is construct validity assessed in test development?

- What are four types of validity in experimental design?

What Is the Difference Between Validity and Reliability?

The purpose of this chapter is to explain different applications of two important criteria of how well measurements and certain research designs fulfill their functions. **Validity** is one of these criteria. In the most general terms, it shows how well the measure or design does what it purports to do. The measure in question might be a psychological test of some kind, a group of judges who rate things, a functional MRI scanner for monitoring brain activity, or any other instrument or measuring tool. Consider an aptitude test that is designed to predict whether applicants to law school will succeed if admitted. We would be interested in the test's *criterion validity,* as it would tell us how well scores on the test are correlated with the particular criterion of success used to assess it. We would also be interested in the test's *construct validity,* as it provides insurance that we are measuring the concept (or *construct*) in question. There are other uses of validity that are of interest to us as well, such as the test's *content validity,* or how adequately it has sampled the universe of content it purports to measure.

The concept of validity also has several different uses in research design, and in the following chapters we will examine specific experimental and nonexperimental designs and how well each fulfills its function. Suppose a new report found a statistically significant correlation between the living habits and the health outcomes in a particular society and implied that the relationship was causal. Because we can think of a *plausible rival hypothesis,* we are skeptical about the *internal validity* of this study. Quite apart from the causal relationship, we would also be interested in the generalizability (or *external validity*) of the observed association between living habits and health outcomes. That is, we would still want to know how dependable the data are, for example, whether the correlational findings can be replicated and generalized across different societies. In this chapter, we have much more to say about these and the other kinds of validity previewed in Table 6.1.

Table 6.1   Types of Reliability and Validity

Reliability

Alternate-form reliability: The degree of relatedness of different forms of the same test.
Internal-consistency reliability: The overall degree of relatedness of all items in a test or all raters in a judgment study (also called *reliability of components*).
Item-to-item reliability: The reliability of any single item on average (analogous to *judge-to-judge reliability,* which is the reliability of any single judge on average).
Test-retest reliability: The degree of temporal stability (relatedness) of a measuring instrument or test, or the characteristic it is designed to evaluate, from one administration to another; also called *retest reliability.*

Validity

Construct validity: The degree to which the conceptualization of what is being measured or experimentally manipulated is what is claimed, such as the constructs that are measured by psychological tests or that serve as a link between independent and dependent variables.
Content validity: The adequate sampling of the relevant material or content that a test purports to measure.
Convergent and discriminant validity: The grounds established for a construct based on the convergence of related tests or behavior (convergent validity) and the distinctiveness of unrelated tests or behavior (discriminant validity).
Criterion validity: The degree to which a test or questionnaire is correlated with outcome criteria in the present (its *concurrent validity*) or the future (its *predictive validity*).
External validity: The generalizability of an inferred causal relationship over different people, settings, manipulations (or treatments), and research outcomes.
Face validity: The degree to which a test or other instrument "looks as if" it is measuring something relevant.
Internal validity: The soundness of statements about whether one variable is the cause of a particular outcome, especially the ability to rule out *plausible rival hypotheses.*
Statistical-conclusion validity: The accuracy of drawing certain statistical conclusions, such as an estimation of the magnitude of the relationship between an independent and a dependent variable (the *effect size*) or an estimation of the degree of statistical significance of a particular statistical test.

Reliability is the second important criterion. In the most general terms, it implies consistency or stability, but it may also imply dependability. The concept of external validity (noted above) can be said to be a bridge between reliability and validity, because external validity implies not only generalizability but also whether, for example, an observed causal relationship can be replicated with different participants and in different settings. By stability, we mean, for example, that if we measure a person's IQ as 110 in January, we would expect to obtain a similar score when we test the person again in December. That is, we expect the person's IQ score to be steady over this period of time, though we anticipate seeing some random fluctuations in the IQ scores (discussed next). We would also be interested in the reliability of the test as a whole (its *internal-consistency reliability*), or how well all of the items in the test "hang together." If we are using judges to make ratings, we want to know how coherent all their ratings are as a group (*their* internal-consistency reliability) as well as the average reliability of any *single* judge (the *judge-to-judge reliability*). These and other applications of the concept of reliability, which are discussed in this chapter, are also previewed in Table 6.1.

All these types of validity and reliability may seem confusing at this point, but what each connotes and how they are all interrelated will become clearer as you delve deeper into this chapter. Generally speaking, if the measure we want to use is unreliable, it is often less likely to be valid. However, it is quite possible for a measure to be reliable and *not* be valid with regard to a specific criterion. For example, it is possible to imagine that individuals blink their eyes roughly the same number of times a minute under a variety of circumstances (the measure has high reliability), but we cannot predict someone's IQ or success in law school from the person's eye-blink rate (i.e., it is neither a valid measure of IQ nor a forecaster of grades in law school). When assessing various measuring tools of behavioral research (whether they are based on physical measures, test items, judges' ratings, etc.), researchers usually prefer validity and reliability to be as high as possible. The bottom line criterion is always validity, however, because it rarely serves the researcher's objectives to have a highly reliable measure that correlates with nothing of any consequence.

What Are Random and Systematic Errors?

Before we turn to the specialized uses of reliability and validity listed in Table 6.1, there are two other important concepts that are not only related to reliability and validity but also relevant to the statistical procedures discussed in later chapters. These are the concepts of random error and systematic error. **Random error** (often described as *noise*) is the name for chance fluctuations, or haphazard errors. **Systematic error**, on the other hand, is the name for fluctuations that are not random but are slanted in a particular direction (thus, another name for systematic error is *bias*). In classical test theory, the idea is that the scores obtained (also called the *raw scores* or *observed scores*) comprise the theoretically "true scores" (the actual or "real" values) plus random errors (called *errors of measurement*). Errors of measurement are understood as randomly pushing the raw scores up and

BOX 6.1 The Logic of Classical Test Theory

In the language of classical test theory, if we use the symbol Y_o to represent an observed (or raw) score on some dependent measure, Y_t for the true score, and e for random error, the relationship among these variables can be expressed as $Y_o = Y_t + e$. This model presumes that the variability of true scores and their random errors of measurement are independent of each other (i.e., they are uncorrelated). If you have had a course in statistics, you know that one popular measure of variability is the variance (σ^2) of a set of scores (discussed in Chapter 10). The classical model is based on the idea that the variance of observed scores (σ_o^2) is equal to the variance of true scores (σ_t^2) plus their random error variance of measurement (σ_e^2), that is, $\sigma_o^2 = \sigma_t^2 + \sigma_e^2$. Thus, the proportion of variance due to true scores (σ_t^2/σ_o^2) plus the proportion of variance due to their random errors of measurement (σ_e^2/σ_o^2) must equal 1. The smaller the random error variance (i.e., the less noise), the more reliable the raw scores will be and, therefore, the more precise our estimate of any particular true score should be.

down around the true scores. The greater these random fluctuations (i.e., the more noise there is), the less consistent or dependable (i.e., the less reliable) the raw scores are (see also Box 6.1).

Random errors are not confined to psychological measures; they are characteristic of all measurements, no matter how well controlled and precisely calibrated the instruments. As an illustration, the National Bureau of Standards in Washington, DC, checks the weights and measures used in the United States by comparing them with prototypes that are owned by the bureau. One prototype, the standard weight of 10 grams (the weight of two nickels), is designated as NB10. This prototype, which was acquired around 1940, has been weighed approximately once a week ever since. At each weighing, an attempt has been made to control all the factors known to affect the results (like air pressure and temperature), but still there have been fluctuations. In one series of five weighings of NB10, for example, the results were:

9.999591 grams

9.999600 grams

9.999594 grams

9.999601 grams

9.999598 grams

As you can see, although the first four digits are identical, the last three digits are shaky. As careful and precise as these measurements were, we can see errors of measurement in the form of chance fluctuations (random error) (Freedman, Pisani, Purves, & Adhikari, 1991).

As an illustration of systematic error (or bias), suppose the measuring instrument is off by a known percentage. Because all the results will be biased by the same percentage, we can easily correct for it. However, imagine a situation in which we know the direction but not the amount of the bias. For example, suppose we buy a bunch of grapes from a grocer who has an annoying habit of putting his thumb on the scale every time he weighs something, thus inflating the cost of our grapes (but we don't know by exactly how much). A systematic error may also occur quite innocently. Suppose your sample of subjects consists only of men, but you want to generalize your results to both women and men. Systematic error due to a biased sample may jeopardize the generalizability of your conclusions.

Another way of thinking about the difference between systematic and random errors is that random errors are likely to cancel one another, on the average, over many repeated measurements (i.e., they are likely to have an average of about zero). Systematic errors, on the other hand, do not cancel one another and do affect all measurements in roughly the same way (i.e., they do *not* have an average of about zero). Thus, if we want a single, unbiased estimate of the true weight of NB10, all we need do is calculate the arithmetic mean of all the different values, on the assumption that (a) the random errors will cancel out, and (b) the measurement apparatus is unbiased (i.e., there is no systematic error). In the case of the dishonest grocer with the heavy thumb, perhaps we could figure out how much his thumb on the scale inflates what he weighs. Simply by using another scale to weigh several bunches of grapes that he weighed, we can use the average difference in values to estimate the bias imposed by his heavy thumb. But imagine we have two scales, and we know that one is consistently too high and the other is inconsistent all the time. Which scale is better? We would prefer using the first scale, because a little bias is better than a lot of random error when we know the amount of bias and can adjust for it (Stanley, 1971).

What Is the Purpose of Retest and Alternate-Form Reliability?

As noted in Table 6.1, one type of reliability is **test-retest reliability** (also simply referred to as **retest reliability**). Suppose you want to use a psychological test or other assessment procedure to empirically examine some prediction of interest. Test-retest reliability is an estimate of the degree of fluctuation of the instrument, or of the characteristic it is designed to measure, from one administration to another. If it is a standardized test (such as an IQ test, or a personality test like the MMPI), you should be able to find out about its test-retest reliability in your literature search. You can also estimate the test-retest reliability by administering the instrument to a sample of people and then administering it again to the same people later on. The test-retest reliability can be represented by a correlation coefficient between the scores on the test administered at those two different times.

We will have more to say about correlation in Chapter 11, but if you have had a course in statistics, you know that the basic measure of association is the Pearson *r* correlation coefficient. If you are unfamiliar with the Pearson *r*, or need your memory of correlation jogged a little, all you need to know at this point is that the

Pearson *r* measures the strength of association (i.e., the degree of relatedness) of two variables, such as height and weight. One characteristic of the Pearson *r* is that it ranges from −1.0 through 0 to +1.0. A value of 0 means that the two variables being correlated have no linear relation, for example, that taller people are not heavier (or lighter) on average than shorter people. A value of +1.0 means that the two variables have a perfect positive relation: As the scores on one variable increase, there are perfectly predictable increases in the scores on the other variable. A value of −1.0 means the opposite: As the scores on one variable increase, there are perfectly predictable decreases in the scores on the other variable. Knowing these characteristics of the Pearson *r*, what would you want the correlation (*r*) to be between the scores at the initial testing and at the retesting if you are thinking about using a particular instrument in your research?

The answer is that you would probably want the *r* to be a positive value as high as possible, as the higher the test-retest coefficient, the more dependable or temporally stable the instrument. By *temporal stability* or *dependability* in this example, we mean that those who scored high initially scored high on retest, and that those who scored low initially scored low on retest. Thus, the retest reliability depends on maintaining one's *relative* position from initial test to retest; it is not affected by changes in *everyone's* scores from pretest to retest. If everyone earns, for example, 10 points more on retest because of practice effects (or 10 points less on retest because of fatigue effects), the retest reliability correlation is not affected even though the scores have changed quite a bit from pretest to retest. If you are measuring something that you believe is very stable over time, the closer the *r* is to +1.0, the more impressive is the temporal stability of the measuring instrument. On the other hand, if you are measuring a volatile or very changeable variable (such as mood), you will expect much lower test-retest reliability if there have been changes in circumstances affecting that variable. That is, you want a measuring instrument that is *sensitive* to the volatility or change. Thus, published reports of the test-retest reliability of an instrument ordinarily indicate not only the interval over which the retesting was done, but also the nature of the sample on which the test-retest reliability is based.

However, a common concern when people take the same test twice is that the test-retest *r* may be artificially inflated because of their familiarity with the test items. One way to prevent this kind of inflation is to create two statistically and theoretically comparable forms of the test with different items that measure the same content. Not all tests have more than one form, but many of the most popular ones do. If the forms are reliable, higher scores on one form should be associated with higher scores on the other forms as well. The correlation coefficient is again used to assess the reliability of the sets of scores, that is, their **alternate-form reliability**. Suppose we want to test vocabulary skills. We can randomly draw several samples of words from the dictionary and let each random sample constitute one form of our test. The correlation between each form with another form at a particular time is one indication of alternate-form reliability (Guilford, 1954). Other indications are that the forms have similar variances as well as similar intercorrelations with theoretically relevant criteria (Gulliksen, 1950; Nunnally & Bernstein, 1994).

Before we turn to another important application of reliability, we want to reiterate the conceptual difference between the simple correlations we have just discussed. In the case of test-retest reliability, the correlation is between scores on the same form administered to the same people at different times. Thus, it can be understood as a measure (or coefficient) of *stability*. In the case of alternate-form reliability, the correlation is between scores on different forms that were administered to the same people at approximately the same time. Thus, it is conceptualized as a measure (or coefficient) of *equivalence*. The situation becomes more complicated, however, if the correlation is between one form of the test at Time 1 and another form at Time 2, which is called a *cross-lag correlation*. We will have more to say about it later in this book (Chapter 8), but you may have (correctly) surmised that a cross-lag correlation can be affected by instability, nonequivalence, or both.

What Is Internal-Consistency Reliability, and How Is It Increased?

Internal-consistency reliability is a general expression that refers to the degree of relatedness of the individual items on a test. As it tells us how well the separate items (or *components* of the test) "hang together," it is also called the **reliability of components**. There are several ways of estimating this reliability. One traditional approach (illustrated below) is to use the Spearman-Brown formula, which in turn is based on the average intercorrelation of all the items symbolized as r_{ii} to denote the mean item-to-item Pearson (r) correlation. Two other traditional approaches, which you may come across in your reading, are K-R 20 and Cronbach's alpha coefficient, which are described briefly in Box 6.2. It has been demonstrated

---

BOX 6.2 K-R 20 and Cronbach's Alpha

K-R 20 gets it name from its originators, G. F. Kuder and M. W. Richardson (1937), and the *20* comes from its being their 20th-numbered equation. K-R 20 is useful when the test items are scored dichotomously, for example, scored 1 if marked correctly and 0 if not marked correctly. **Cronbach's alpha**, named after Lee J. Cronbach (1951), is not restricted to dichotomously scored items. If you have had a course in statistics, you may recall that another name for the p value is *alpha*. That alpha, which refers to the probability of a Type I error (discussed in Chapter 12), is not the same thing as Cronbach's alpha, which refers only to the degree of internal-consistency reliability. It is beyond the scope of this text to give examples of how K-R 20 or Cronbach's alpha are calculated, but if you are interested, you will find a detailed discussion in our advanced methods text (Rosenthal & Rosnow, 2008). However, the same rule applies whether we use K-R 20, Cronbach's alpha, or the Spearman-Brown formula we are using: The more comparable items there are in a test and the longer the test, the greater its internal-consistency reliability is.

that when all the item variances are equal, the estimates of internal-consistency reliability obtained from the two methods in Box 6.2 and the Spearman-Brown formula should be identical (Li & Wainer, 1998). In this discussion, we use the capital letter R to denote an estimate of internal-consistency reliability (to emphasize that it refers to the composite, or overall, measure of reliability), and we use the superscript SB to indicate that the estimation procedure is based on the Spearman-Brown formula (R^{SB}).

To illustrate, suppose you have made up a three-item questionnaire in which people are to indicate their agreement or disagreement with three attitudinal statements on a 5-point numerical scale from *strongly agree* to *strongly disagree*. You want to have a single summary score for each respondent based on your assumption that the items tap into conceptually related aspects of the attitudinal issue. You administer the questionnaire to a sample of people, score the results, and then correlate responses to Item 1 with responses to Item 2, Item 1 with Item 3, and Item 2 with Item 3. We can represent these Pearson correlations by the letter r with numerical subscripts indicating the specific items that were correlated with one another. Let us say you find $r_{12} = .45$ between Items 1 and 2; $r_{13} = .50$ between Items 1 and 3; and $r_{23} = .55$ between Items 2 and 3. Summing the values gives us $.45 + .50 + .55 = 1.50$. Dividing this total by the number of pairs (three pairs) tells us the *mean* item-to-item correlation ($r_{ii} = 1.50/3 = .50$), that is, the **item-to-item reliability**. Think of this value as the estimate of the *reliability of any single item on average*.

To estimate the internal-consistency reliability of the three-item test from the information at hand, we will use the **Spearman-Brown formula**. Created by Charles Spearman and William Brown, who came up with it independently (and simultaneously published their work in the same issue of the *British Journal of Psychology* in 1910), it can be written as

$$R^{SB} = \frac{nr_{ii}}{1 + [(n-1)r_{ii}]}$$

where n = the number of items in the test, and r_{ii} = the average intercorrelation of the items. To use the results noted above, we set n equal to 3 (because you have a three-item test) and r_{ii} equal to .50. Substituting in the formula above, we find

$$R^{SB} = \frac{3(.50)}{1 + [(3-1).50]} = \frac{1.5}{1 + 1.0} = .75$$

The beauty of this formula is that we can try out different values of n and predict what the effect will be on the internal-consistency reliability when the length of the test is changed. Thus, the formula is also known as the Spearman-Brown *prophecy formula*. For example, suppose we were to use six items instead of three. Assuming that the average intercorrelation remains at $r_{ii} = .50$, we predict as follows:

$$R^{SB} = \frac{6(.50)}{1 + [(6-1).50]} = .86$$

What if we wanted to further increase the length of our test, going to nine items? With $n = 9$ and the same average intercorrelation, our prophecy is:

$$R^{SB} = \frac{9(.50)}{1 + [(9 - 1).50]} = .90$$

There is not much difference between .90 and .86. However, what is striking is that we can keep on improving the internal-consistency reliability by steadily adding new items, as long as the average item-to-item correlation (r_{ii}) remains unchanged. If the new items are not as relevant or as reliable as items already in the test, then r_{ii} will be reduced, and if this reduction is great enough, the internal-consistency reliability will be reduced (Li, Rosenthal, & Rubin, 1996). Items with very low test-retest reliability will increase the error of measurement and reduce the internal-consistency reliability (Wainer & Thissen, 1993). Of course, we cannot add items forever, because there is a psychological limit to how long a test should be. If we make the test too long, the respondents will become fatigued and lose their concentration.

What Are Acceptable Test-Retest and Internal-Consistency Reliabilities?

Just how many items are optimal to achieve the reliability we want, without making the test or questionnaire so cumbersome as to burden respondents or give them headaches? There is no simple answer. The acceptable range depends on the context in which the instrument is to be used and the objective of the research. For example, if we need an instrument with a high degree of test-retest reliability, we might not settle for a test-retest correlation less than .80. And yet, there are many acceptable instruments with test-retest correlations below .80, including many medical tools for detecting or diagnosing illness (e.g., the instrument used for measuring blood pressure). Scores on many medical tests vary as a function of feelings of anxiety, changes in one's diet, and so on. Besides asking your instructor for guidance, you can develop a sense of the optimal test length in any particular case by looking up test reviews in sourcebooks (such as the *Mental Measurements Yearbook*) or by perusing the *Directory of Unpublished Experimental Mental Measures* (e.g., Goldman & Mitchell, 2003) for relevant measures.

To give you a context, the test-retest *r* on the Scholastic Assessment Test (SAT) for essay scores in the humanities is usually between .3 and .6, and for chemistry, it is usually between .6 and .8 (Braun & Wainer, 1989). In the previous chapter, we described the Minnesota Multiphasic Personality Inventory (MMPI) and the Rorschach inkblot test. Using the information they found in articles between 1970 and 1981, a team of psychologists (Parker, Hanson, & Hunsley, 1988) compared the internal consistency and test-retest reliability of these instruments and another well-known psychological test, the Wechsler Adult Intelligence Scale (WAIS). Developed by David Wechsler (a clinical psychologist who was connected with New York's Bellevue Hospital for many years), the WAIS is the most widely used individually administered intelligence test for adults. It is divided into verbal and performance subtests, the verbal part depending more on school-related abilities than the performance part. Parker et al. estimated that the average internal-consistency reliability was .87 for the overall WAIS, .84 for the MMPI, and .86 for the Rorschach test. They also estimated the average test-retest correlation at .82 for the overall WAIS, .74 for the MMPI, and .85 for the Rorschach. Internal-consistency reliability is usually expected to be higher than test-retest reliability, unless the test-retest intervals are very short. Parker et al.'s findings, then, are consistent with that expectation, though in the case of the Rorschach the difference is hardly noticeable. Only limited claims can be made about multidimensional instruments, such as the Rorschach and the MMPI, but the typical level of criterion-related validity of the Rorschach has been estimated at $r = .29$, and of the MMPI at $r = .30$, based on a comparative meta-analysis (Hiller, Rosenthal, Bornstein, Berry, & Brunell-Neuleib, 1999). These values contradict earlier claims of higher mean validity coefficients for the same instruments (Atkinson, 1986; Parker et al., 1988).

More is known about the reliability (and the validity) of the WAIS, the MMPI, and the Rorschach than about most other psychological tests in current use, but we do not want to leave you with the idea that these three tests are without controversy. For example, the limitations of projective tests as tools in diagnosing psychopathology have been debated, including the use of the TAT (e.g., Sharkey & Ritzler, 1985) and the Rorschach (Garb, Wood, Lilienfeld, & Nezworski, 2005). In an extensive review article, Garb et al. (2002) specifically cautioned clinicians not to take the Rorschach at face value in diagnosing psychopathology, as the use of certain standard norms for interpreting Rorschach protocols sometimes leads to diagnoses in which relatively normal individuals are identified as having severe psychopathology. Regarding the values noted by Hiller et al. (1999) for the criterion-related validity of the Rorschach ($r = .29$) and the MMPI ($r = .30$), they may actually be about as high as can be expected for personality tests (see Cohen, 1988, p. 81). There is also an extensive literature on intelligence testing arguing that other aptitudes besides those measured by the WAIS are characteristic of other forms of intelligence (e.g., Ceci, 1990, 1996; H. Gardner, 1983, 1986, 1993; H. Gardner, Kornhaber, & Wake, 1996; Sternberg, 1985, 1990, 1997; Sternberg & Detterman, 1986).

Far less is known about the reliability and validity of the two attitude questionnaires discussed in Chapter 5. Regarding the Thurstone questionnaire designed to measure attitudes toward defensive, cooperative, and aggressive war (Figure 5.3 on p. 112), the developers of this scale (Day & Quackenbush, 1942) reported only its internal-consistency reliability, which was in the .80 to .87 range for all three referents measured. For the Likert questionnaire measuring socialized-medicine attitudes (Figure 5.2, p. 110), all we know is that its internal-consistency reliability was reported by its developer (Mahler, 1953) to be .96. However, this 20-item questionnaire is interesting for another reason having to do with alternate-form reliability because the test in Figure 5.2 actually comprises two comparable 10-item forms, with alternate-form reliability in the .81 to .84 range.

How Do I Measure the Reliability of Judges?

As mentioned in Chapter 4, reliability is also a basic consideration in observational studies that use judges or raters. To cite an instance, in a procedure used by developmental psychologists to study attachment behavior in infants and the maternal responses, the judges code positive and negative actions in a number of situations.

Table 6.2   Ratings and Intercorrelations for Three Judges

A. Judges' ratings

| | Judges | | |
Mothers	A	B	C
Smith	5	6	7
Jones	3	6	4
Brown	3	4	6
Kelly	2	2	3
Blake	1	4	4

B. Judge-to-judge correlations

$r_{AB} = .645$
$r_{AC} = .800$
$r_{BC} = .582$
$r_{jj} = .676$

Note: We typically report correlations to two decimal places, but when we are going to use correlations in further calculations, it is often helpful to use three decimal places.

They do this coding, for example, when the mother and the infant are together, when the mother leaves the infant in the presence of a stranger, when the mother returns, and when the infant is left alone (Ainsworth, Blehar, Waters, & Wall, 1978; de Wolff & Van Ijzendoorn, 1997; Main & Solomon, 1990). Suppose a developmental researcher has three judges (A, B, and C) code the maternal behavior of five mothers (Smith, Jones, Brown, Kelly, and Blake) in one situation on a 7-point scale from *very secure* (1) to *very anxious* (7). The hypothetical results are shown in Part A of Table 6.2. After calculating the correlations between all pairs of judges (A with B; A with C; and B with C), the researcher obtains the mean of these correlations. The results are given in Part B of Table 6.2, in which the mean correlation is $r_{jj} = .676$ (the subscript *j* stands for "judge"). This correlation is the **judge-to-judge reliability**, or the *reliability of any single judge on average.*

We would also like to know the reliability of the group of three judges as a whole, that is, the internal-consistency reliability. We find it by using the Spearman-Brown formula, now expressed as

$$R^{SB} = \frac{nr_{jj}}{1 + [(n-1)r_{jj}]}$$

where n = the number of judges, and r_{jj} = the average judge-to-judge reliability. Substituting in the formula gives us

$$R^{SB} = \frac{3(.676)}{1 + [(3-1).676]} = \frac{2.028}{1 + 1.352} = .862$$

We now know that the reliability of the three judges' ratings as a whole (their internal-consistency reliability) is .862 and that the reliability of any single judge is .676 (the average judge-to-judge reliability). We would report both reliabilities and, of course, label each to avoid reader misunderstandings. Suppose we want to predict the amount by which internal-consistency reliability will increase if we use one more judge whose ratings are also correlated approximately .68 with those of the other judges. We find our prediction by substituting in the Spearman-Brown formula, with the number (n) of judges now 4 instead of 3 and the average reliability (r_{jj}) rounded to .68:

$$R^{SB} = \frac{4(.68)}{1 + [(4 - 1).68]} = .895$$

Using four instead of three judges is predicted to boost the internal-consistency reliability from .86 to roughly .90, assuming the judge-to-judge reliability is not reduced by the addition of this fourth judge.

Table 6.3 shows the Spearman-Brown internal-consistency estimates for values of n ranging from 1 to 20 judges. This same table can be used when we are interested not in judges, but in items for a test. When $n = 1$, we see that internal-consistency reliability (R^{SB}) is equivalent to the reliability of a single judge (r_{jj}), or a single test item (r_{ii}). To illustrate the use of this table, consider the following situations:

1. Given an obtained or estimated mean reliability, r_{jj}, and a sample of n judges, what is the approximate Spearman-Brown internal-consistency estimate, R^{SB}, of the mean of the judges' ratings? The value of R^{SB} is read from the table at the intersection of the appropriate row (n) and column (r_{jj}). Suppose we want to work with a variable believed to show a mean reliability of $r_{jj} = .50$ and can afford only four judges. We believe we should go ahead with our study only if the internal-consistency reliability (R^{SB}) will reach or exceed .75. Shall we go ahead? The answer is yes, because the table shows $R^{SB} = .80$ for an n of 4 and an r_{jj} of .50.

2. Given the value of the obtained or desired internal-consistency reliability, R^{SB}, and the number of judges actually available, n, what will be the predicted value of the mean reliability, r_{jj}? The table is entered in the row corresponding to the n of judges available and is read across until the value of R^{SB} closest to the one desired is reached; the value of r_{jj} is then read as the corresponding column heading. Suppose we will settle for internal-consistency reliability no less than $R^{SB} = .90$ and we have a sample of $n = 20$ judges available. For each of the variables to be rated by these judges, what should be the judges' minimally acceptable average individual reliability? From this table we see the answer is $r_{jj} = .30$.

3. Given an obtained or estimated mean reliability, r_{jj}, and the obtained or desired internal-consistency reliability, R^{SB}, what is the approximate number of judges (n) required? The table is entered in the column corresponding to the mean reliability, r_{jj}, and is read down until the value of R^{SB} closest to the one desired is reached; the value of n is then read as the corresponding row title. For example, we know our choice of variables to have a mean reliability of

| Table 6.3 | Estimation of Spearman-Brown Reliability (R^{SB}) Based on Number (n) of Judges or Test Items and Mean Judge-to-Judge (r_{jj}) or Item-to-Item (r_{ii}) Reliability |

Mean judge-to-judge (r_{jj}) or item-to-item (r_{ii}) reliability

N	.05	.10	.15	.20	.25	.30	.35	.40	.45	.50	.55	.60	.65	.70	.75	.80	.85	.90	.95
1	.05	.10	.15	.20	.25	.30	.35	.40	.45	.50	.55	.60	.65	.70	.75	.80	.85	.90	.95
2	.10	.18	.26	.33	.40	.46	.52	.57	.62	.67	.71	.75	.79	.82	.86	.89	.92	.95	.97
3	.14	.25	.35	.43	.50	.56	.62	.67	.71	.75	.79	.82	.85	.88	.90	.92	.94	.96	.98
4	.17	.31	.41	.50	.57	.63	.68	.73	.77	.80	.83	.86	.88	.90	.92	.94	.96	.97	.99
5	.21	.36	.47	.56	.62	.68	.73	.77	.80	.83	.86	.88	.90	.92	.94	.95	.97	.98	.99
6	.24	.40	.51	.60	.67	.72	.76	.80	.83	.86	.88	.90	.92	.93	.95	.96	.97	.98	.99
7	.27	.44	.55	.64	.70	.75	.79	.82	.85	.88	.90	.91	.93	.94	.95	.97	.98	.98	.99
8	.30	.47	.59	.67	.73	.77	.81	.84	.87	.89	.91	.92	.94	.95	.96	.97	.98	.99	.99
9	.32	.50	.61	.69	.75	.79	.83	.86	.88	.90	.92	.93	.94	.95	.96	.97	.98	.99	.99
10	.34	.53	.64	.71	.77	.81	.84	.87	.89	.91	.92	.94	.95	.96	.97	.98	.98	.99	.99
12	.39	.57	.68	.75	.80	.84	.87	.89	.91	.92	.94	.95	.96	.97	.97	.98	.99	.99	1.0
14	.42	.61	.71	.78	.82	.86	.88	.90	.92	.93	.94	.95	.96	.97	.98	.98	.99	.99	1.0
16	.46	.64	.74	.80	.84	.87	.90	.91	.93	.94	.95	.96	.97	.97	.98	.98	.99	.99	1.0
18	.49	.67	.76	.82	.86	.89	.91	.92	.94	.95	.96	.96	.97	.98	.98	.99	.99	.99	1.0
20	.51	.69	.78	.83	.87	.90	.92	.93	.94	.95	.96	.97	.97	.98	.98	.99	.99	.99	1.0

.40, and we want to achieve an internal-consistency reliability of .85 or higher. How many judges must we allow for in our preparation of a research budget? The answer is $n = 9$ judges.

4. This table can be used equally well in estimating the increase in internal-consistency reliability of tests when new, relevant items are added. In that case, we redefine the n of judges as the n of items, r_{ii} as the average intercorrelation of items (i.e., the item-to-item reliability), and R^{SB} as the Spearman-Brown internal-consistency estimate with n items. In the previous section, we gave the example of a three-item test (i.e., $n = 3$) with an average item-to-item correlation of $r_{ii} = .50$; the researcher wanted to estimate the overall effect of using three, six, or nine items. The table is entered in the column corresponding to this mean reliability, and we then read down the column until we reach the Spearman-Brown value closest to the one desired. Let us say we want to achieve internal-consistency reliability of $R^{SB} = .90$ or higher. How many new, relevant items will we need? When we read across the row, the answer is $n = 9$.

How Is Reliability Related to Replication and External Validity?

We turn now to the concept of validity, beginning with an application that is some-times a source of confusion, as it encompasses aspects of both reliability and valid-ity. Called **external validity** by Campbell and Stanley (1963), in its most recent iteration it was defined specifically as referring to "inferences about the extent to which a *causal relationship* [our emphasis] holds across variations in persons, settings, treatments, and outcomes" (Shadish, Cook, & Campbell, 2002, p. 82). It is one of four types of validity that many behavioral and social researchers presume play a role in causal inference (statistical-conclusion validity, construct validity, and internal validity are the other three), though for now we will concentrate only on external validity and its relevance to the importance of **replication**. Just as we are interested in the dependability of measurements, we are also interested in the dependability of causal generalizations in experimental research (or external validity) based on replicable findings.

We will have more to say about the logic of causal inference in experimental research in the next chapter, but suppose we obtain a particular result at one point in time in a psychology or educational or child development experiment. We want to know not only whether it will stand up over time, but also whether it is generalizable across different kinds of participants and different investigators (see also Box 6.3). Or suppose we have successfully conducted not one, but a series of experiments on learning or cognition, and although the causal results are reliable, the subjects in these experiments were psychology students. Can we assume that the same results will apply to a general population that is not as literate or as well educated? Suppose the research subjects in a biomedical experiment are male volunteers. Can we generalize to all women, or even to all men, including those who, if asked, would decline the invitation to participate in research? Or suppose we use one standard treatment in all experiments designed to study a particular phenomenon. Can we assume that the causal result will hold up across other treatment variations in other settings? These are the kinds of questions that external validity addresses.

BOX 6.3   The Problem of Correlated Replicators

In the evaluation of a set of replication studies, it is often assumed that the replications are independent of one another. But what does "independence" really mean? The usual minimum requirement is that the study participants be different persons. But what about the independence of the people who conducted the research? Are 10 replications conducted by one investigator as independent of one another as 10 replications each of which is conducted by a different investigator? One way to address this concern is to separate the replications into subsets (a procedure called *blocking*) and to compare the different subsets. For example, we might block on the particular interests of the investigators (Do they hold similar views, or are they at odds with one another?) or their background and training (Are they all affiliated in some way?). Once such characteristics have been identified, it is possible to assign a set of weights to the results that reflect some theoretically defined degree of independence, and to use these weights in our analysis (Rosenthal & Rosnow, 2008).

In fact, the *same* experiment can never be "exactly" duplicated, because at the very least the participants will be older. Thus, researchers think of all replications, even the ones most closely modeled on the original study, as *relative replications* (Cook & Campbell, 1979; R. Rosenthal, 1990c; Shadish et al., 2002; Sidman, 1960). In the case of external validity, the issue is whether the size of the effect (or *effect size*, discussed in detail in later chapters) of an independent variable (X) on a dependent variable (Y) is similar in both the original and the replication study. One convenient way to operationalize the concept of effect size is by computing the correlation between membership in the experimental or control group (coded, for example, as 1 vs. 0) and scores on Y. Effect size correlations that scatter around zero tell us that not much is going on between X and Y in either study. However, suppose we want to replicate an experiment in which the effect size was $r_{XY} = .50$ (the subscripts indicate that the correlation is between variable X and variable Y, also often symbolized in lower case as r_{xy}), and say the effect size in our replication attempt is $r_{XY} = .40$. The two correlations are positive, far from zero, and not that far apart, leading us to conclude that the replication attempt was successful. We can also compare the two effect sizes statistically (using a procedure described in Appendix C) to learn how likely it is that the differences found are due to simple chance variation.

Although we said that replications are possible only in a relative sense, we can think of a distribution of possible replications in which their overall variability is a function of the degree of similarity to the original study that characterizes each possible replication. If researchers choose the study designs of their replications to be as similar as possible to the study being replicated, they may be more true to the original ideal of replication but they may also pay a price. That price is *limited generalizability* across other variations in settings and treatments. Broadly speaking, the threats to the external validity of causal inferences that experimenters generally worry about fall into two categories (Shadish et al., 2002): (a) variables that *were not* in the experiment (variations in persons, settings, and treatments) and (b) those that *were* in the experiment (operationalizing the variable of interest too narrowly, or using a specialized group of participants, or conducting the research in a setting that is quite unlike the circumstances to which we want to generalize). Because it is impossible to rule out every possible threat to external validity, researchers must be sensitive to the limitations of their study designs and must not make false or imprudent causal generalizations.

How Are Content and Criterion Validity Defined?

Before turning to the three other applications of the concept of validity in experimental research (construct validity, statistical-conclusion validity, and internal validity), we will first examine its application in instrument (e.g., test) construction. We said that *validity* refers to the degree to which a test or measuring instrument actually does what it purports to do. This assessment is considered the most important criterion in instrument construction and typically involves accumulating evidence in three categories, called *content validity, criterion validity,* and *construct validity.* Test developers are expected to provide this information so that test users know the capabilities and limitations of each instrument before using it, and so that test takers are not misled or their time and effort wasted when they are administered these instruments. In this section, we will discuss content and criterion validity, and in the following section we will focus on construct validity in instrument construction (later in this chapter, we discuss construct validity in experimental design). Before we begin, however, another type of validity that you may come across in your reading is **face validity**; the term simply means whether the test seems on the surface (or "face") to be measuring something relevant. It should not be confused with content validity, as face validity refers not to what the test measures but only to how it looks. The idea of face validity is that if a test does not *appear* to be relevant, some respondents may not take it seriously (Anastasi & Urbina, 1997). Of course, there are many tests (projective tests such as the Rorschach and the TAT) that purposely do not contain a clue to what they are measuring.

Content validity means that the test or questionnaire items represent the kinds of material (or content areas) they are supposed to represent, usually a basic consideration in the construction phase of any test or questionnaire. Thus, reporting that a test or questionnaire has "good content validity" means that it adequately covers all major aspects of the content areas that are relevant. For example, when the MMPI was developed, the researchers tried to select a range of statements that would be endorsed in a certain direction by each of several different clinical groups. For this purpose, they began by developing a set of specifications, with the idea that the items could then be judged against these specifications. In this way, they hoped to differentiate among a number of different clinical conditions by including a wide range of items that tapped different content areas. To assess whether the test items were consistent with the original specifications, they called on expert judges to make subjective evaluations of the relevance or appropriateness of each item to assessing different content areas.

Less formal methods can be used in other situations. For instance, suppose an instructor is making up a final exam and wants it to have content validity. The instructor may start simply by asking, "What material should my students be able to master after studying the readings and taking my course?" The instructor makes a list of the material the exam should cover and then creates questions to represent this material. As students we have all experienced exams with poor content validity. They are the ones about which we say, "The instructor never mentioned this material, and it appeared in a two-line footnote in the appendix!" Thus, content validity has little to do with statistical aspects of the test or questionnaire (Cronbach & Quirk, 1971). The instructor is not interested in items that are highly intercorrelated, because such high intercorrelation would impose restrictions on the range of material the instructor wants the test to cover. Also, a test that is content-valid one semester is not necessarily going to be content-valid when the course is taught again, because there may be a new textbook or the instructor may have updated the lectures. The instructor must also make sure that all items can be easily understood, so that if a student gives the wrong answer, it is not because of some "irrelevant difficulty" but because the student did not know the right answer (Cronbach & Quirk, 1971, p. 168).

Criterion validity has more to do with statistical aspects of the test, as it refers to the degree to which the test or questionnaire is correlated with one or more outcome criteria (a variable with which the instrument should be reasonably correlated). For example, suppose researchers want to develop a test of college aptitude. They might use as their criterion the successful completion of the first year of college or maybe the grade point average (GPA) after each year of college. If they are developing a test to measure anxiety, they might use as their criterion the pooled judgments of a group of highly trained clinicians who rate the degree of anxiety of each person to whom the researchers administer the test. In assessing criterion validity, researchers select the most sensitive and meaningful criterion in the present (called **concurrent validity**) or future (called **predictive validity**) and then correlate performance on the test or questionnaire with that criterion.

For example, clinical diagnostic tests are ordinarily assessed for concurrent validity, as the criterion of the patient's "real" diagnostic status is in the present with respect to the test being validated. The concurrent validity of shorter forms of longer tests is also typically evaluated, the longer test being used as the criterion. The practical advantage to researchers of using a criterion in the present is that it is less expensive and less time-consuming than using a criterion that is in the future. It also controls for any possible complicating effect of temporal instability (Anastasi & Urbina, 1997). Frequently, researchers must consider the validity of the criterion itself. Suppose a researcher wants to develop a short test of anxiety that will predict the scores on a longer test of anxiety. The longer test serves as the researcher's criterion, and the new short test may be relatively valid with respect to the longer test. But the longer test may be of dubious validity with respect to some other criterion (e.g., clinicians' judgments). In other words, criteria must often be evaluated with respect to other criteria, but there are no firm rules (beyond the use of logic and the consensus of other researchers in that area) about what constitutes an "ultimate" criterion.

All the same, predictive validity also plays an important role in measurement. Tests of college aptitude are normally assessed for predictive validity because the criteria of graduation and GPA are of the future. The aptitude test scores are saved until the future-criterion data become available, and the test scores are then correlated with the future-criterion data. The resulting correlation coefficient serves as an index of criterion validity. GPA tends to be a fairly reliable criterion, but clinicians' judgments (e.g., about complex behavior) may be a less reliable criterion. Previously, we showed how the internal-consistency reliability of pooled judgments can be increased if more judges are used, assuming they are similar to the other judges. In the same way, we can increase the internal-consistency reliability of pooled clinical judgments simply by adding similar clinicians to the group whose pooled judgments are going to serve as the criterion (R. Rosenthal, 1973, 1982, 1987).

How Is Construct Validity Assessed in Test Development?

More sophisticated views of the validation of tests require that researchers be sensitive not only to the correlation between their measures and some appropriate criterion, but also to the correlation between their measures and some "inappropriate" criterion. Suppose that a researcher in clinical psychology develops a new test of psychological adjustment, which she wants to use in a field experiment. She does some pilot studies to ensure the validity of the new test. In one aspect of the pilot work, she has expert clinicians rate the psychological adjustment of a group of clients who have just been given the test. When she finds that the test scores correlate positively and substantially with the pooled judgment of the expert clinicians, she can correctly interpret this correlation as an attractive outcome of a concurrent validation effort.

However, suppose she also gives the clients a standard test of verbal aptitude and finds that their scores on this test and on her new test of psychological adjustment correlate positively and substantially with one another. Should she conclude that the new test is a reasonably valid measure of psychological adjustment, of verbal aptitude, of both, or of neither? This question is difficult to answer, but she can not claim on the basis of such results to understand the new test very well. It is not intended, after all, to be a measure of verbal aptitude. In short, the new test has good concurrent validity but fails to discriminate: It does not correlate differentially with criteria for different types of observation. This *ability to discriminate* is a vital characteristic of **construct validity** in test development, which in turn is considered the most "fundamental and all-inclusive validity concept, insofar as it specifies what the test measures" (Anastasi & Urbina, 1997, p. 114). To put it another way, construct validity has to do with what a test *really* does assess. In current usage, content and criterion validity provide valuable information in their own right but are generally regarded as improving our understanding of the construct assessed by the test.

How one should establish the construct validity of a test has been explored for years in psychology. One traditional approach is to use logical analysis, and another procedure involves manipulating the respondents' experience before the test or during the test to see whether the manipulation will produce differences in responding as the construct would imply (Cronbach & Quirk, 1971). In a seminal article, Donald T. Campbell and Donald W. Fiske (1959) proposed a way of formalizing the construct validation procedure. To achieve this statistically, they suggested that researchers use two kinds of validation evidence: (a) testing for *convergence* across different measures or manipulations of the same behavior (**convergent validity**) and (b) testing for *distinctiveness* between measures or manipulations of related but conceptually different traits or behaviors (**discriminant validity**). For example, finding that a new test of psychological adjustment correlates positively and substantially with expert clinicians' ratings would be seen as convergent validation evidence. Finding that the new test correlates positively and substantially with a test of verbal aptitude (which is distinct from the construct of psychological adjustment) would be seen as contrary to the necessary discriminant validation evidence. Recently, measures besides simple correlation have been applied to the quantification of construct validity (Westen & Rosenthal, 2003).

To give you a clearer sense of the process of construct validation, we turn to a landmark program of research by personality psychologists Douglas Crowne and David Marlowe, in which a number of different strategies were used, including logical analysis, correlation, and laboratory studies. The original purpose of this research was to develop a psychological scale that would measure *socially desirable responding*. As noted in the previous chapter, in this type of behavior people respond in ways that make them look good (rather than give their most candid and honest responses). As their work progressed, Crowne and Marlowe realized that the scale they were building might be assessing a more general personality variable, which they termed the *need for social approval* to reflect the idea that people differ in their need to be thought well of by others. In developing this scale—called the Marlowe-Crowne Social Desirability (MCSD) Scale—the researchers not only wanted to measure the degree to which people vary on the need-for-approval dimension independent of their level of psychopathology, but also to validate the need-for-approval construct.

Crowne and Marlowe began by considering hundreds of personality test items (including a few from the MMPI) that could be answered "true" or "false." To be included, an item had to reflect socially approved behavior but also had to almost certainly be untrue (behavior too good to be true). In addition, answers to the items could not have any implications of psychological abnormality or psychopathology. By having a group of psychology graduate students and faculty judge the social desirability of each item, Crowne and Marlowe developed a set of items that would reflect behavior that was too virtuous to be probable, but that would not be primarily influenced by personal maladjustment. The final form of the MCSD scale, which consisted of 33 items chosen by item analysis and ratings by experienced judges (Crowne, 1979; Crowne & Marlowe, 1964), showed a high degree of relationship to those variables with which the scale scores were expected to converge (i.e., convergent validation evidence). For example, high scorers on the final MCSD scale preferred low-risk behaviors and avoided being evaluated by others. The final form also showed only a low degree of relationship to those variables with which the scale was expected not to converge. For example, correlations with measures of psychopathology were smaller in magnitude than was the case for an earlier developed scale of social desirability, a result implying that the MCSD scale was a better measure of social desirability because it was not confounded by psychopathology. Also encouraging was an impressive correlation ($r = .88$) between the responses of a group of people who were tested 1 month apart (i.e., evidence of test-retest reliability).

These were promising beginnings for the MCSD scale, but it remained to be shown that the concept of need for social approval (and the scale developed to measure it) was meaningful beyond predicting responses on other paper-and-pencil measures. As part of their program of further validating their new scale and the construct that was its basis, the researchers undertook an ingenious series of studies relating scores on the MCSD scale to subjects' behavior in non-paper-and-pencil test situations. Crowne and Marlowe reasoned that "dependence on the approval of others should make it difficult to assert one's independence, and so the approval-motivated person should be susceptible to social influence, compliant, and conforming" (Crowne, 1991, p. 10). A series of relational studies produced results that were generally consistent with this logical expectation. For example, in the first of these studies, the subjects began by completing various tests, including the MCSD scale, and then were asked to get down to the serious business of the experiment. This "serious business" required them to (a) pack a dozen spools of thread into a small box, (b) unpack the box, (c) repack the box, (d) unpack the box, and so on for 25 minutes while the experimenter appeared to be timing the performance and making notes about them. After these dull 25 minutes had elapsed, the participants were asked to rate how "interesting" the task had been, how "instructive," and how "important to science" and how much they wanted to participate in similar studies in the future. Those persons who scored above the mean on social desirability said they found the task more interesting, more instructive, and more important to science and were more eager to participate again in similar studies than those persons who had scored below the mean. In other words, just as Crowne and Marlowe had predicted, the people higher in the need for social approval were more compliant and said nicer things to the experimenter about the task that he had set for them.

In still other research, Crowne and Marlowe used a variant of Asch's (1952) conformity procedure (described in Chapter 1). That is, a group of people are required to make judgments on specific issues, and all the confederates make the same uniform judgment, one that is quite clearly in error. Conformity was defined as the real subject's "going along with" the majority in his or her own judgment rather than giving the objectively correct response. In one study, Crowne and Marlowe had the real subject listen to a tape recording of knocks on a table and then report his or her judgment of the number of knocks. Each subject was led to believe that he or she was the fourth participant. To create this illusion, the experimenter played for the subject the tape-recorded responses of three prior participants to each series of knocks that was to be judged. The earlier three participants were the confederates, and they all gave an incorrect response in 12 of 18 trials. It was therefore possible to count the number of times out of 12 that the real subject yielded to the wrong but unanimous majority. The results were consistent with Crowne and Marlowe's hypothesis that the approval-motivated person is conforming: The subjects who had scored higher in the need for social approval went along with the majority judgment more than did the subjects who scored lower in the need for social approval.

Many additional studies were performed by these and other investigators (e.g., Allaman, Joyce, & Crandall, 1972; Crowne, 1979; Crowne & Marlowe, 1964; Paulhus, 1991; Weinberger, 1990), and some of the follow-up studies produced different results. In current usage, the word *need* in Crowne and Marlowe's *approval need* construct is no longer fashionable (Paulhus, 1991), and researchers have also suggested relabeling the construct *evaluative dependence* (Millham & Jacobson, 1978) or simply calling it *approval motivation* (Strickland, 1977). These developments are consistent with the course of any successful research program, in which researchers build on, and attempt to improve our understanding of, the earlier seminal work. However, the main point of this example is to pull together some of the ideas that we have discussed in this chapter and to illustrate a systematic approach to construct validity. If you are interested in seeing the final form of the

MCSD scale, it is reproduced in Robinson, Shaver, and Wrightsman's (1991) *Measures of Personality and Social Psychological Attitudes* (another useful resource for available tests in the public domain), along with commentary by D. L. Paulhus on related measures.

What Are Four Types of Validity in Experimental Design?

As noted earlier, the concepts of *external validity* and *construct validity* are two of four types of validity that are of major interest to experimenters, the other two being *statistical-conclusion* and *internal validity*. To review briefly, *external validity* is synonymous with "generalizability," and in the case of experimental design, with "causal generalization." That is, it refers to "whether a causal relationship holds over variations in persons, settings, treatments, and outcomes" (Shadish et al., 2002, p. 21). To borrow an example given by Shadish et al., suppose we are reading the results of an experiment on the effects of a kindergarten Head Start program to improve the reading ability of poor African American children in grammar schools in a particular city. The generalizability issue might be whether similar causal effects would result with poor Hispanic or other poor children in another city.

We know that *construct validity* is concerned with the conceptualization of variables. In research in which causal generalizations are the primary objective, construct validity refers to the validity of the hypothetical idea linking the independent (X) and dependent (Y) variables, but it also refers to the conceptualization of X and Y. An illustration was Latané and Darley's (1968, 1970) experiments (in Chapter 2) using the construct of "diffusion of responsibility" to explain why the more witnesses there are to an emergency (X), the less likely it is that any one of them will offer help (Y). Among the more common threats to construct validity are vagueness in defining or operationalizing the concepts or variables of interest. For example, what precisely is meant by "diffusion of responsibility," "witnesses," and an "emergency"? In the case of the idea of diffusion of responsibility, another relevant question is how well conceptualized this "theoretical scaffolding" between X and Y is (Cronbach & Meehl, 1955).

Although in the past some leading psychologists had claimed that it is quite possible to do research without using constructs, Shadish et al. (2002) argued that it is a logical impossibility for three reasons. First, researchers need constructs to connect the operations they use in their studies to pertinent theory and to the way that causal generalization will be used in practice. Not using constructs to connect operations is like speaking in gobbledygook, that is, without any substance or meaning. Second, constructs shape our perceptions and, because they also invariably have rich connotations, invite discourse and debate that stimulate further ideas for operationalizing and measuring these constructs. Third, the "creation and defense of basic constructs" is the essence of what science is about (Shadish et al., 2002, p. 65). In chemistry, the periodic table is a basic construct. In physics, the atom is another basic construct. In psychology, there are countless constructs that are considered essential (the *self*, the *body, groups, society, culture, environment, evolution,* and on and on). Indeed, the very idea of a *construct* is itself a basic construct in our thinking, and that we can talk about it in a meaningful way is further tacit evidence of the validity of Shadish et al.'s argument.

Another major application of validity in research is called **statistical-conclusion validity** because it refers to whether certain statistical conclusions are well grounded, such as conclusions about the size of the effect (i.e., the correlation between treatment and outcome, or between the independent variable and the dependent variable) or conclusions about the effect size's statistical significance (Shadish et al., 2002). For example, when a statement is made about a correlation, the question pertaining to statistical-conclusion validity is whether there is a likely relationship between two variables or whether some observed statistical association is due merely to chance fluctuations. When experimenters are interested in making a causal inference (i.e., that X causes Y), they first need to show that the presumed cause and the presumed effect actually occur together (i.e., that they *covary*). A "real" causal relationship may be occurring, but the statistical circumstances may not be conducive to observing (or "detecting") it at the given level of significance (more about this topic in later chapters).

The final type of validity in experimental research, **internal validity**, is concerned with ruling out **plausible rival hypotheses**. As defined by Shadish et al. (2002), the term *internal validity* refers specifically to whether an observed covariation between X and Y truly reflects a causal relationship from X to Y. There are a number of threats to internal validity, some of which we will discuss in the following chapter. To anticipate, suppose a team of students (one male student and one female student) decide to conduct an experiment on verbal learning. Their particular interest is in the causal effect of stress, in the form of loud noise, on the learning of certain prose material. In order to divide the work fairly, the students flip a coin to determine which of them will run the subjects in the stress condition and which of them will run those in the no-stress condition. The problem is that, even if these researchers find the hypothesized relationship, they cannot ascribe it to the experimental stress, because there are plausible rival hypotheses. One rival hypothesis is that the results are due to experimenter differences (e.g., personality and gender differences). This rival hypothesis could have been ruled out if each of the students had run half the subjects in the stress condition and half the subjects in the no-stress condition. Such a design would prevent the methodological *confounding* (or intermixing) of the effects of stress and the effects of plausible experimenter differences and, in turn, would strengthen the internal validity of the argument.

If you are confused about the difference between internal validity and construct validity, one way to separate them in your mind is to remember that *ruling out plausible rival hypotheses* is the essential characteristic of internal validity. That is, *internal validity* refers to whether we can logically rule out competing explanations for the observed covariation between the presumed independent variable (X) and the presumed effect of X on the dependent variable (Y). Construct validity, on the other hand, concerns the validity of the concepts we use in our measurements and causal explanations. Whenever you ask what is *really* being measured (e.g., "What does this test really measure?") or what is *really* being investigated (e.g., "What is this experiment really investigating?"), you are asking about construct validity rather than about

BOX 6.4 Being Wrong Versus Being in a Weak Position

Judith A. Hall (1984), whose ideas about what makes a good researcher were discussed in Chapter 1, has also proposed a good intuitive distinction among the four kinds of validity in experimental research. When either construct or internal validity is poor, researchers may be actively misled because they are at risk of making causal inferences that are plain "wrong." When either statistical-conclusion or external validity is poor, researchers are at risk of being in a "weak position" to make *any* causal inferences or sweeping conclusions because limits are imposed on what can be learned or what can be generalized to other situations.

internal validity. Stated another way, construct validity addresses whether the concepts being measured or manipulated are properly identified (i.e., whether we have a clear conception of what we are measuring or manipulating), and internal validity is whether a variable other than X (the causal variable we *think* we are studying) may have caused Y to occur (see also Box 6.4).

Summary of Ideas

1. Generally speaking, *validity* refers to the degree to which something does (or is) what it claims to do (or to be), whereas *reliability* refers to consistency, stability, or dependability.

2. All measurements are subject to *random errors* (frequently described as *noise*), which are chance fluctuations that are presumed to cancel out, on the average, over many repeated measurements. By contrast, *systematic error* (also called *bias*) pushes measurements in one direction.

3. According to the logic of classical test theory, observed (raw) scores comprise the true scores and their random errors of measurement (Box 6.1).

4. *Test-retest reliability,* or simply *retest reliability* (a measure of *stability*), is the correlation between scores on a test given to the same people on two different occasions. *Alternate-form reliability* (a measure of *equivalence*) is the correlation between scores on different forms of the same test given to the same people at approximately the same time.

5. *Internal-consistency reliability* is the overall degree of relatedness of the components of a test (also called *reliability of components*) or a group of judges. One way to measure it is to use the *Spearman-Brown formula,* which is based on the average item-to-item or judge-to-judge correlation and the number of items or judges (Table 6.3). Other useful measures of internal-consistency are *K-R 20* and *Cronbach's alpha coefficient* (Box 6.2), which (along with the Spearman-Brown procedure) give similar results when the item variances are equal.

6. The degree of reliability of widely used tests (e.g., the MMPI, the Rorschach, and the WAIS) gives some indication of what convention specifies as acceptable reliability.

7. *External validity,* one of four major types of validity in causal inference based on empirical research, is the dependability of causal generalizations across persons, settings, treatment, and outcome variations.

8. To say that a replication attempt was successful generally implies that the research procedure was modeled on the original study, the overall pattern of results was similar, and the effect sizes (e.g., the correlation between the independent variable, X, and the dependent variable, Y) of the studies were fairly similar.

9. Validity in test development usually means accumulating evidence in three categories: (a) *content-related validity;* (b) *criterion-related validity* (e.g., *predictive, concurrent*); and (c) *construct validity* (based, for example, on *convergent* and *discriminant validity,* as illustrated by Crowne and Marlowe's validation of the construct of "approval need" and the MCSD scale they created to measure it).

10. Besides *external validity* and *construct validity,* two other major types of validity of interest to experimenters are *statistical-conclusion validity* (whether certain statistical conclusions are well grounded, such as the effect size and the p value) and *internal validity* (whether plausible rival hypotheses can be ruled out).

Key Terms

alternate-form reliability
  p. 129
concurrent validity   p. 140
construct validity   p. 141
content validity   p. 139
convergent validity   p. 141
criterion validity   p. 140
Cronbach's alpha   p. 130
discriminant validity   p. 141
external validity   p. 136
face validity   p. 139
internal-consistency
  reliability   p. 130

internal validity   p. 145
item-to-item reliability (r_{ii})
  p. 131
judge-to-judge reliability (r_{jj})
  p. 134
K-R 20   p. 130
plausible rival hypotheses
  p. 145
predictive validity   p. 140
random error   p. 126
reliability   p. 126
reliability of components
  p. 130

replication   p. 137
retest reliability   p. 128
Spearman-Brown prophecy
  formula   p. 131
statistical-conclusion validity
  p. 145
systematic error   p. 126
test-retest reliability   p. 128
validity   p. 124

Multiple-Choice Questions for Review

1. Random error is error that (a) isn't worth worrying about; (b) is always in the same direction; (c) has an average of about zero; (d) is also known as *bias*.

2. Broadly speaking, _____ refers to the consistency or stability of measurement. (a) validity; (b) modulation; (c) reliability; (d) invalidity

3. A researcher at Wheelock College administers a test of chronic anxiety. One month later, she administers the same questionnaire and finds that scores on the two administrations of the test correlate highly ($r = .85$). This outcome demonstrates the _____ of the test. (a) internal validity; (b) internal-consistency reliability; (c) external validity; (d) test-retest reliability

4. A researcher at Roosevelt University constructs a five-item measure of attitudes toward national health insurance. The average intercorrelation among the items is $r_{ii} = .40$. Using the Spearman-Brown equation, he calculates that $R^{SB} = .77$. This researcher has calculated the _____ of the attitude scale. (a) internal validity; (b) internal-consistency reliability; (c) test-retest reliability; (d) convergent validity

5. In the question above, in which the researcher determined that $R^{SB} = .77$, what is the reliability of the scale as a whole? (a) .77; (b) .50; (c) .40; (d) cannot be determined from the information given

6. One intelligence test has two separate forms. Both measure intelligence, but they contain different questions. A researcher at Eastern University in Radnor, Pennsylvania, finds that the scores of students on Form A correlate highly with their scores on Form B ($r_{AB} = .92$). This correlation demonstrates the _____ reliability of the test. (a) internal consistency; (b) external consistency; (c) test-retest; (d) alternate-form

7. In determining whether one study replicates the results of another, scientists often examine _____, which are statistics that reflect the magnitude of the relationship between X and Y. (a) significance levels; (b) alpha coefficients; (c) effect sizes; (d) data on the manipulation checks

8. "A test should correlate with theoretically related external variables; for example, the SAT should correlate with grade point average." This statement defines _____ validity. (a) statistical-conclusion; (b) content; (c) consistency; (d) criterion

9. "A test should not correlate with variables from which it is theoretically distinct." This statement defines _____ validity. (a) convergent; (b) content; (c) discriminant; (d) criterion

10. The generalizability of the causal results of a study is referred to as the _____ of the study. (a) internal validity; (b) external validity; (c) construct validity; (d) discriminant validity

Discussion Questions for Review

1. An Emory University student is trying to make her mark in the field of psychology by developing a new scale measuring fear of public speaking. How might she assess her scale's predictive and construct validity?

2. On a quiz, a University of Toronto student is asked how we know that the Marlowe-Crowne scale (MCSD) measures need for social approval. What is the answer?

3. A University of Houston student has piloted his observational study using two judges and has found a moderate judge-to-judge reliability ($r_{jj} = .50$). Because he wants to achieve a higher overall reliability, he is distressed by the prospect of having to modify his coding criteria and training procedures. Another student suggests, "Don't bother with all that. Simply add two more judges to improve the internal-consistency reliability." Would you consider the second student's advice sound?

4. A Pennsylvania State University researcher wants to study the effects of the texture of toys on the frequency with which toddlers touch them. She uses the following toys: a brown teddy bear, a smooth blue plastic ball, a green wooden cube, and an orange corduroy-covered rattle. She finds that male toddlers are more likely to touch the ball and the cube than the teddy bear and the rattle, whereas female toddlers are more likely to touch the teddy bear and the rattle than the other two toys. When she reports the results, a member of the audience raises the possibility that male toddlers must therefore prefer hard, less variegated textures to soft, more variegated textures, whereas female toddlers show the reverse preference. What is one rival hypothesis that would also be consistent with the researcher's results? How might the rival hypothesis be ruled out?

5. A Northeastern University researcher wants to build a 20-item test to measure need for power. She assigns several students to use the Spearman-Brown formula to measure the internal-consistency reliability of her new test based on data recently collected from a large sample. They tell her that $R^{SB} = .50$ and that the mean interitem reliability (r_{ii}) equals .40. She asks them to check their work. Why?

6. A student at the State University of New York at Binghamton is interested in assessing a new 20-item scale of optimism-pessimism. How should she assess the reliability of this scale? The student is also advised by her instructor to measure several different traits using several different methods to demonstrate empirically the convergent and discriminant validity of the new scale. Why did the instructor give this advice?

7. A student at Bridgewater State College weighs a 10-pound object 5 times and obtains readings on the scale of 14, 8, 7, 10, and 11 pounds. Describe the systematic error and the random errors characterizing the scale's performance.

Answers to Review Questions

Multiple-Choice Questions

1. c	**3.** d	**5.** a	**7.** c	**9.** c
2. c	**4.** b	**6.** d	**8.** d	**10.** b

Discussion Questions

1. By showing that her scale correlates substantially with future symptoms of fear when people are asked to speak in public (predictive and convergent validity). In addition, the new scale should not correlate substantially with such less relevant variables as height, spatial relations abilities, and political party preference (discriminant validity). Convergent and discriminant validity are aspects of construct validity.

2. Because it correlates highly with behaviors defined as reflecting high need for social approval, but not as highly with behaviors not reflecting high need for approval.

3. Yes, because a total of four judges will yield an internal-consistency reliability of .80 when the typical judge-to-judge reliability is .50 (see Table 6.3).

4. Perhaps female toddlers prefer more complex shapes than do male toddlers. A new study might add four new stimuli: a smooth, hard teddy bear and rattle, and a soft, fuzzy ball and cube. If the plausible rival hypothesis is correct, female toddlers will prefer the new smooth, hard teddy bear and rattle to the new fuzzy ball and cube. Considering all eight stimuli, then, female toddlers will prefer the four complexly shaped stimuli, whereas male toddlers will prefer the four simply shaped stimuli if the rival hypothesis is accurate. Still another rival hypothesis is that the color differences of the toys determine the frequencies with which toddlers touch them. To address this alternative, similar toys would have to be created in different colors, such as wooden cubes that are brown, blue, green, and orange but are identical in all other respects.

5. Because Table 6.3 shows that, for 20 items, a mean item-to-item reliability of .40 is associated with an internal-consistency reliability of .93, not .50.

6. The test-retest reliability can be computed from administering the test twice to the same people (for example, 4 weeks apart) and computing the correlation between the two administrations. The internal-consistency reliability can be computed from correlating all the items with each other and then applying the Spearman-Brown formula to the average intercorrelation of the items (or using Table 6.3) to get the overall internal-consistency reliability. The reason for administering several different measures is that the student can show convergent validity with the measures with which her new scale should correlate substantially and discriminant validity with the measures with which her new scale should not correlate substantially.

7. There is no systematic error because the average reading is accurate (10 pounds). The random errors are +4, −2, −3, 0, and +1 on the five readings, or errors of +40%, −20%, −30%, 0%, and +10%, respectively, a not very precise performance.

CHAPTER 7

Randomized Experiments and Causal Inference

Preview Questions

- What is the purpose of doing randomized experiments?
- How is random assignment accomplished?
- What are between-subjects and within-subjects designs?
- What are factorial designs and Latin square designs?
- Why is causality said to be "shrouded in mystery"?
- On what grounds do scientists infer causality?
- What is the formative logic of experimental control?
- What is meant by *preexperimental designs*?
- What circumstances jeopardize internal validity?
- How can I control for demand characteristics and expectancy effects?

What Is the Purpose of Doing Randomized Experiments?

Inferring causality is both an evolutionary necessity and something we all do constantly. Yet, as one scholar observed, it is "a notion shrouded in mystery, controversy, and caution" (Pearl, 2000, p. 331). In this chapter, we will examine that assertion within the context of randomized designs and the logic of causal inference when using such designs. We will also mention what statistical procedures are frequently used to analyze the designs described in this chapter as well as suggest, in some cases, an alternative approach for asking focused questions of data. If you have not taken a statistics course or can hardly remember the difference between the t test and the F test, you can think of these abbreviated discussions as an introduction to the various data-analytic procedures discussed in detail in the final six chapters of this book. In the preceding chapter, we noted the difference between random error (*noise*) and systematic error (*bias*), and we will conclude with a discussion of subject-related and experimenter-related sources of systematic error that can produce *artifacts* in the research (and are not limited to randomized experiments).

In **randomized experiments**, the allocation of sampling units to groups or conditions is done by a process of **random assignment** (also called **randomization**) so that, for example, each person in a population of subjects has an equal probability of being chosen at every draw. In Jane Doe's sample report in Appendix A, her study takes the form of an experimental design in which the units are randomly assigned to one of two conditions. In biomedical research, randomized experiments (often called *trials*) are considered the "gold standard" of causal inference, although this does not mean that they are guaranteed to be flawless (see Box 7.1). Perhaps the most famous randomized biomedical trial was the 1954 Salk vaccine study (Meier, 1988, p. 3). The purpose of this study was to quantify the effect of inoculating over 200,000 young children with the Salk poliomyelitis vaccine as opposed to a placebo (consisting of a simple salt solution) given to over 200,000 other children (Francis et al., 1955). A prominent statistician pointed out a number of serious flaws in the implementation of the study but nevertheless concluded there was "convincing evidence for the effectiveness of the vaccine" (Brownlee, 1955, p. 1010). We return to the results of this landmark study later in this book, but what would you guess was the correlation between (a) receiving or not receiving the Salk vaccine and (b) not contracting or contracting polio? (We ask you this question to get you thinking about *effect size correlations;* the answer is given later in this chapter.)

Previously, we used the term *experiment* in a broad sense rather than restricting it only to randomized experiments (e.g., Galileo's, Newton's, and Foucault's

---

BOX 7.1 Imperfect Randomized Trials

Just as the value of gold can fluctuate, randomized trials (the *gold standard* of causal inference in biomedical research) can also fluctuate with regard to their potential value. In his book on causality, Judea Pearl (2000) noted several potential problems. First, perfect control is often hard to achieve because patients who suspect that they are in a placebo control group may attempt to obtain the experimental drug on their own from other sources. Second, patients who experience adverse reactions to an experimental drug may, without telling the researchers, decide to reduce their assigned dosage. Third, assigning patients with a terminal illness to a placebo group could have legal ramifications, as they are being denied access to a potentially lifesaving drug or an experimental treatment. (As we mentioned in Chapter 3, one option in many cases is to give the control group the best available treatment, so the comparison is between the experimental drug or treatment and the best available alternative.) Fourth, simply knowing that randomization is being used may make some patients wary of volunteering and could jeopardize the generalizability of the results if the volunteers' response to the treatment is different from the possible response of those who did not volunteer.

demonstration experiments in Chapter 1), and in the next chapter, we will give examples of single-case experiments and other nonrandomized designs. Traditionally, there are three reasons for using random assignment. One is that, as conceived by the statisticians who invented it, random assignment provides a safeguard against the possibility of researchers' subconsciously letting their opinions or preferences influence which sampling units will receive any given treatment (Gigerenzer et al., 1989). The term *sampling units* is simply a general way of referring to the participants, subjects, groups, or objects being studied (i.e., the units sampled from the population), though these units might also be animals, schools, countries, or agricultural crops. The term *treatment* is commonly used both as a general name for the manipulation or intervention and as a way of referring to the conditions to which sampling units are allocated. For example, in the Salk vaccine trial, the vaccine was the treatment that children in the experimental group received and children in the control group did not receive (but instead received a placebo treatment).

A second reason, which is the one that most experimenters would give, is that random assignment distributes the characteristics of the sampling units over the experimental and control conditions in a way that will not bias the outcome of the experiment (Kirk, 2000). There is no absolute guarantee, however, for it is always possible (especially when sample sizes are small) that some unintended or uncontrolled variable related to the dependent variable will affect the outcome in one condition more than another. Imagine a randomized psychological experiment with five people each in the experimental group and the control group. Suppose that, by sheer coincidence, two subjects who are unusually tense happen to end up in the experimental group (rather than one ending up in the experimental group and the other in the control group). If it also happened that tenseness is somehow an extraneous confounding variable in this case, it would be a suspected threat to the internal validity of the study. Random assignment does not guarantee equality in the characteristics of the sampling units assigned to different conditions, but the idea is to give each unit at each draw an equal chance of being assigned to a particular condition.

The third reason, which is also the one that psychological statisticians and textbooks in statistics underscore, is that random assignment permits the computation of statistics that require certain characteristics of the data (Kirk, 1995, 2000; Maxwell & Delaney, 2000). In particular, it provides a mechanism to derive probabilistic properties (p values) of estimates based on the data by controlling for extraneous variables (D. B. Rubin, 1974). However, suppose we want to study the effects of high dietary cholesterol on human longevity. It would be an ethical absurdity to think that we could randomly assign people to a high-cholesterol diet in order to see how many more would die than those assigned to a low-cholesterol diet. In observational studies based on very large samples, one option (discussed in the next chapter) is to use a procedure that reduces relevant characteristics of the "naturally treated" and "untreated" individuals to a single composite variable and then estimate the "treatment effect" by comparing the results in subclassifications of this variable (Rosenbaum & Rubin, 1983; D. B. Rubin, 1973; Rubin &

Thomas, 1996). Another option (also discussed in the next chapter) is a longitudinal study in which we measure a cohort of people periodically for many years in order to identify variables or conditions correlated with illness.

How Is Random Assignment Accomplished?

Statisticians speak of random assignment *rules* (or plans). For example, suppose a researcher has designed an experiment with two conditions (treatment and control), and each condition and set of measurements is to be presented in the form of a booklet. On the surface, the booklets look the same, but the booklet given to the experimental group incorporates a manipulation not contained in the booklet the control group receives. One possible randomization rule in this case would be to presort the booklets into pairs so each pair contains an experimental and a control booklet. The first subject gets Booklet A or B (which can be decided by a flip of a coin), and the next subject gets the other booklet. For the next two subjects this procedure is repeated, so the experimenter ends up with an equal number of subjects in each of two conditions. An alternative assignment rule is to arrange the booklets so that, of every 4 or 6 or 8 booklets, half are As and half are Bs (again determined by coin flips). If the study can be implemented on a computer, the computer can be programmed to do the random assignment and also to tabulate the results.

As another illustration, suppose that patients in one condition of a clinical trial receive a new drug and that those in the second condition receive a placebo. We assign the patients in equal numbers to these two conditions by, first, writing each person's name on a slip of paper and then "blindly" drawing *pairs* of names. We can have a calculator or computer spit out random digits and then decide which member of a pair will receive the new drug. For each pair, for example, we can randomly pick one member and, if the digits 1, 3, 5, 7, or 9 turn up, assign that person to the experimental group (and if 0, 2, 4, 6, or 8 turn up, assign the person to the control group). The other member of the pair is always assigned to the other group.

Here's one more example: Suppose we wanted to assign 40 subjects at random to either an experimental or a control condition. For this illustration, we use the table of random digits on p. 205, from which the following 120 single-digit integers were taken:

10097	32533	76520	13586	34673
37542	04805	64894	74296	24805
08422	68953	19645	09303	23209
99019	02529	09376	70715	38311
12807	99970	80157	36147	

Suppose we decide to read across and down the first five-digit column (10097, 37542, 08422, 99019, etc.) and again have the numbers 1, 3, 5, 7, 9 designate the participants to be randomly assigned to the experimental group (and 0, 2, 4, 6, 8 designate those in the control group). Thus, we assign Subject 1 to the experimental group (1), Subjects 2 and 3 to the control group (0, 0), Subjects 4 through 8 to the experimental group (9, 7, 3, 7, 5), Subjects 9 through 15 to the control group (4, 2, 0, 8, 4, 2, 2), Subjects 16 and 17 to the experimental group (9, 9), Subject 18 to the control group (0), Subjects 19 and 20 to the experimental group (1, 9), and so forth.

What Are Between-Subjects and Within-Subjects Designs?

When the subjects are exposed to one condition each, this arrangement is known as a **between-subjects design**. For example, Jane Doe's experimental design may be described as a "two-group between-subjects design." The basic design is illustrated in Part A of Table 7.1, where we see that 5 subjects receive Condition A and 5 other subjects receive Condition B. Another statistical name for the between-subjects design is **nested design**, because the subjects are "nested" within their own groups or conditions. A traditional way of analyzing two-condition between-subjects designs is by a t test for independent samples (discussed in Chapter 13). In biomedical trials, the outcome is often a dichotomous measure (e.g., die vs. live, or sick vs. well), and the data (frequencies) are arranged in a 2 × 2 table where the rows are the two levels of the independent variable (treatment absent vs. treatment present), the columns are the two levels of the outcome variable (die vs. live, or sick vs. well), and the cell values are independent frequencies (or *counts*). A typical statistical test would be the chi-square (χ^2) procedure on the independent frequencies (discussed in Chapter 15).

Table 7.1	Examples of Between- and Within-Subjects Designs

A. Between-subjects (nested) design

Condition A	Condition B
Subject 1	Subject 2
Subject 3	Subject 4
Subject 5	Subject 6
Subject 7	Subject 8
Subject 9	Subject 10

B. Within-subjects (crossed) design

Condition A	Condition B
Subject 1	Subject 1
Subject 2	Subject 2
Subject 3	Subject 3
Subject 4	Subject 4
Subject 5	Subject 5
Subject 6	Subject 6
Subject 7	Subject 7
Subject 8	Subject 8
Subject 9	Subject 9
Subject 10	Subject 10

Later in this book, we discuss statistical procedures called *contrasts,* which specifically ask focused questions of data. Contrasts compare observed group means with predicted weights, called **lambda weights (λ)**, with the stipulation that those weights must sum to zero (i.e., $\Sigma\lambda = 0$, where Σ, the upper-case Greek letter *sigma,* tells us to sum the lambdas). Suppose we predict that the experimental group will surpass the control group on the outcome measure. We can express this prediction by lambda weights of $+1$ and -1 for the experimental and control group, respectively. Of course, between-subjects designs are not limited to two groups, and lambda weights are not limited to plus-and-minus 1. Suppose we want to study the effects of nutrition on the academic performance of children who will be randomly assigned to four different conditions. One group of children will receive a hot lunch daily, another group will receive free milk, a third group will get a vitamin supplement, and the fourth group ("zero control group") will get nothing extra. Our prediction is that the observed group means will be highest in the hot lunch group (Group 1), followed by the free milk group (Group 2), then followed by the vitamin group (Group 3), and lowest of all in the zero control group (Group 4). In other words, we predict $M_1 > M_2 > M_3 > M_4$, where M denotes the group mean, the subscript indicates the particular group, and the symbol $>$ stands for "greater than." We can express this prediction by lambda weights of $+3$, $+1$, -1, -3 for Groups 1, 2, 3, 4, respectively. We return to this example later in this book (Chapter 14) and show how a contrast t or F test is computed to compare the four observed group means and their respective lambda weights in this 1×4 design (i.e., one dimension with four levels).

Suppose all the subjects receive *both* Condition A and Condition B. This basic design is illustrated in Part B of Table 7.1, where we see that all 10 subjects receive A and then B. This arrangement is called a **within-subjects design**. The t test is the usual procedure for analyzing such data, but this time we would use a t test for nonindependent samples (discussed in Chapter 13). Because the subjects' reactions are measured after each condition, this is also called a **repeated-measures design**. Another name for the basic within-subjects design is a **crossed design**, because the subjects are thought of as "crossed" by conditions (i.e., observed under two or more conditions) rather than nested within them. Within-subjects designs are also not limited to two groups. Say we want to study the degree to which students' performance on a cognitive task improves over time (i.e., over repeated occasions of measurement). Suppose we hypothesize that, on a certain cognitive task, students will improve by an equal amount each time they perform the task over four occasions that are 1 month apart (i.e., $M_1 < M_2 < M_3 < M_4$, where $<$ stands for "less than"). We can express this prediction by lambda weights of -3, -1, $+1$, $+3$ for Occasions 1, 2, 3, 4, respectively. (We return to this case in Chapter 14 and show how a contrast F test is computed.)

What Are Factorial Designs and Latin Square Designs?

When we think of the conditions as arranged (or *arrayed*) along a continuum or single dimension, it is described as a *one-factor* or *one-way design,* where the term *factor* is a general name for the overarching variable of interest (the independent

Table 7.2	Two-by-Two Factorial Design	
	Manipulated conditions	
Gender	Drug	Placebo
Women	A	B
Men	C	D

variable). Suppose, however, that women and men are randomly assigned to a drug or a placebo group. We now have a two-factor design with two *levels* of the variable of gender (women and men) and two levels of the variable of treatment (drug vs. placebo). This arrangement, called a **factorial design**, is depicted in Table 7.2. Because there are two levels of each of two factors, we describe the arrangement as a 2×2 factorial design (where "2×2" is read as "two by two") or a 2^2 factorial design.

When analyzing the results of studies that take the form of factorial designs, we also have several options (discussed in Chapter 14). Suppose that, referring to the symbols in Table 7.2, we predict Group A will be most responsive on the dependent measure, and that there will be no differences among Groups B, C, and D. In other words, our prediction is $M_A > M_B = M_C = M_D$, which we can express by lambda weights of $+3, -1, -1, -1$ for Groups A, B, C, D, respectively. The basic design is a 2×2 factorial, but for our data analysis we would think of it as a 1×4 and compute a contrast comparing the observed means and our λ weights. If we have no prediction or hunch, the standard way of analyzing the data is to compute a 2×2 analysis of variance (ANOVA), in which we analyze (a) the between-group variation of the women and men (the two levels of the *row factor* in Table 7.2), (b) the between-group variation of the drug versus the placebo (the two levels of the *column factor*), and (c) the interaction of these two factors (i.e., the interaction of the two levels of the row factor with the two levels of the column factor). None of these three results, however, will precisely test our prediction of $M_A > M_B = M_C = M_D$. In sum, it is not the conceptual framework of the research design that should dictate how we analyze the data; instead, our hypothesis or prediction or question of interest should guide our decision.

Suppose that, instead of a factorial design with two between-subjects factors, we have a within-subjects design with repeated treatments and measurements on men and women. Now we have a more complex design, in which one factor is between subjects (men and women) and the other is within subjects (repeated treatments and measurements). This design is called a *mixed factorial design,* and the traditional data analysis is explained in our advanced text (R. Rosenthal & Rosnow, 2008). However, this design does raise another issue. In within-subjects designs with repeated treatments and measurements, a potential problem is that the *order* in which the treatments are administered to the same subjects may be confounded with the treatment effect. Suppose the treatment conditions are administered to young children who are immediately measured after each treatment (i.e., a repeated-measures design). The children may be nervous when first measured, and they may perform poorly. Later on, they may be less nervous, and they may perform better. To address the problem

Table 7.3	A Latin Square Design			
	Order of administration			
	1	2	3	4
Sequence 1	A	B	C	D
Sequence 2	B	C	D	A
Sequence 3	C	D	A	B
Sequence 4	D	A	B	C

of systematic differences between successive treatments (or measurements), we use **counterbalancing**, that is, rotating the sequences. Some children will randomly receive Condition A before Condition B, and the others will randomly receive B before A.

A specific statistical design that has counterbalancing built in is called the **Latin square design**. It is characterized by a square array of letters (representing the treatment conditions) in which each letter appears once and only once in each row and in each column. Illustrated in Table 7.3 is a Latin square representing a case in which four treatments (A, B, C, D) are administered to all subjects in a counterbalanced pattern. Subjects randomly assigned to Sequence 1 will receive treatments in the sequence A, then B, then C, and finally D. In Sequences 2 through 4, treatments are administered in different sequences, BCDA, CDAB, and DABC, respectively. In Chapter 14, we illustrate the analysis of this type of design by the F statistic. You will also find more detailed discussions of Latin square designs in Keppel (1991), Kirk (1995), Maxwell and Delaney (2000), and R. Rosenthal and Rosnow (2008).

We can also have a randomized design with more than two factors and more than two levels within each factor, although it may stretch the number of subjects rather thinly. For example, if all we have to work with is 24 subjects, in a two-group between-subjects design with equal sample sizes, there will be 12 subjects in each group. But if we have a 3×4 factorial design and the same number of subjects, there will be 12 conditions and 2 subjects in each condition. Suppose we have a randomized factorial design with three between-subjects factors (A, B, C) and two levels of each factor. We now have eight pertinent sources of variation to look into: (a) between levels of Factor A; (b) between levels of Factor B; (c) between levels of Factor C; (d) interaction of levels of Factor A with levels of Factor B; (e) interaction of levels of Factor A with levels of Factor C; (f) interaction of levels of Factor B with levels of Factor C; and (g) interaction of all three factors. One final point is that, although we have mentioned only t and F tests, a data analysis is usually incomplete without a report of the sizes of the effects and the interval estimates for these effect sizes (more about this later in this book).

Why Is Causality Said to Be "Shrouded in Mystery"?

Earlier, we quoted the statement that causality is "a notion shrouded in mystery, controversy, and caution" (Pearl, 2000, p. 331). Yet, when we turn the key in a car's ignition, we know this action *causes* the motor to get going. We also know, for example, that gorging on fatty foods will cause us to put on weight. So what's the big mystery? The answer goes back to the 18th-century Scottish philosopher David Hume, and it "shook up causation so thoroughly that it has not recovered to this day" (Pearl, 2000, p. 336). However, before we turn to Hume's work, we need to define the particular kind of causality we are talking about. In the 4th century B.C., Aristotle identified four kinds of causality, which he called material, formal, final, and efficient. **Material causality** refers to the substance or substances necessary for the movement of something or the coming into being of a specific event. **Formal causality** refers to the plan or development that gives meaning to the event. **Final causality** (also called *teleologic,* which means the action is "goal-directed") refers to the objective or purpose of the event. And **efficient causality** refers to the activating force that was responsible for the event.

For example, imagine the flight of a curve ball thrown by a pitcher at a baseball game. The batter swings and misses, and we ask ourselves, "What *caused* the ball to break that way?" First, if we mean the *material cause,* then the answer, according to the physics of baseball (R. K. Adair, 1990), is that the roughness on the surface of the ball and the nature of fluid flow are the material cause of the ball's unusual movement. A ball with a smooth surface tends to have a smooth flight, especially if it passes through air at a speed of less than 50 miles per hour. A ball with rough seams that is traveling at a speed over 50 miles per hour encounters turbulence, particularly when it is thrown in a special way to take advantage of the nature of airflow. Second, if we mean the *formal cause,* it is the "idea" of "throwing a curve ball" as formally initiated in the mind of the catcher, who then communicated the idea to the pitcher, who thought "curve ball" up to the moment that the ball was released. Third, if we mean the *final (or teleological) cause,* it is the "objective" of having a ball break as it nears the plate so that the batter will be unable to hit the pitch squarely. Fourth, if we mean the *efficient cause,* it is the "act" of throwing the ball that causes it to travel at an optimal velocity and causes its trajectory to deviate from the original horizontal direction of motion.

How may we translate these four "causes" in the case of human behaviors? For human development, for instance, we may say that (a) cellular structure is the *material cause* (i.e., the "stuff" of development); (b) DNA or genetics is the *formal cause* (i.e., the biological blueprint); (c) physiological maturation is the *final cause* (i.e., the "end purpose" or goal); and (d) parenting as an environmental variable is the *efficient* (i.e., activating or instigating) *cause.* To some degree, all four kinds of causality are of interest to different behavioral and social scientists, but it was the fourth type of causality (efficient causality) that Hume was interested in, and the one that most scientists generally have in mind when they talk about a manipulated treatment producing a certain effect (i.e., *causing* something else to occur). Hume argued that efficient causality is nothing more than an illusion conditioned by sensory repetitions and the association of ideas. He described the case of a man hanging securely from a high tower in a cage of iron. Although there is no way that the man will fall, he nevertheless trembles in fear because his mind is conditioned (a modern term, not Hume's) to associate "fall and descent" with "harm and death"—which psychologists now call an "illusory correlation" (Fiedler, 2000).

Hume argued that no matter how deeply we think about causality or how closely we look into a situation, the causal connection is never visible or palpable. What could be a more perfect example, he asked, than a billiard ball that is lying on a table with another ball rapidly moving toward it? They strike, and the ball previously at rest is set in motion. We conclude that one ball *caused* the other to move, but all we can actually see is that "the two balls touched one another before the motion was communicated, and that there was no interval betwixt the shock and the motion. . . . Beyond these three circumstances of contiguity, priority, and constant conjunction, I can discover nothing in this cause. . . In whatever shape I turn this matter, and however I examine it, I can find nothing farther" (Hume, 1739–1740/1978, pp. 649–650). Furthermore, that an event precedes another event and predicts the second event well is hardly a reason to conclude that the prior event is the *cause* of the second event. Monday precedes Tuesday, just as night precedes day, but we would not say that Monday *causes* Tuesday or that night *causes* day. Hume was aware that the rooster's crow stands in prior constant conjunction to the sunrise but does not *cause* the sun to rise (Pearl, 2000, p. 336). How, then, do modern scientists deal with this conundrum?

On What Grounds Do Scientists Infer Causality?

In current thinking, scientists seem to boil down the criteria of efficient causality to Hume's "three circumstances of contiguity, priority, and constant conjunction" and the further stipulation that it is possible to rule out plausible rival causal explanations. We describe these criteria, collectively, as (a) covariation, (b) temporal precedence, and (c) internal validity. By *covariation*, we mean a fusion of what Hume called "contiguity" and "constant conjunction," but with the qualification that the conjunction between cause and effect is not necessarily constant, but *likely* or *probable*. By *temporal precedence*, we mean what Hume called "priority," the assumption that the cause always precedes the effect. And by *internal validity* (discussed in the previous chapter), we mean that the scientist attempts, on logical and empirical grounds, to rule out rival explanations for the conjunction. (See also Box 7.2.)

First, the scientist looks for evidence that the independent variable (X) and the dependent variable (Y) are mutually related (covary). That is, the scientist asks whether the presence (and absence) of X (the presumed cause) is actually associated with the presence (and absence) of Y (the presumed effect). Finding that X and Y show a satisfactory correlation, we have evidence of **covariation**. What constitutes a "satisfactory" correlation? That is not an easy question to answer. If I push you and you fall down, obviously there is a high degree of association between the two events. However, in taking a pill to lower cholesterol or to prevent cancer or a heart attack, the statistical association is likely to be far smaller, and yet it still might qualify as a "satisfactory correlation" in a clinical trial. Later in this book, we illustrate this idea with small correlations between X and Y that are considered enormously meaningful in randomized clinical trials. To anticipate a little, remember our asking you to guess the correlation between receiving or not receiving

---

BOX 7.2 Hume's "Rules"

In his classic work entitled *A Treatise of Human Nature,* David Hume (1739–1740/ 1978, pp. 173–175) listed eight "rules by which to judge causes and effects." They include the assumption that "the cause and effect must be contiguous in space and time," and also that "there must be a constant union betwixt the cause and effect" (what we mean by *covariation*). What we mean by *temporal precedence,* Hume stated as "the cause must be prior to the effect." Hume went on to explain how the perception of causation can be understood as the product of observations of contiguous events that occur in a certain temporal sequence. "Causality" is in the mind's eye, he thought, or as Pearl (2000) eloquently stated, for Hume the idea of a causal connection was "a learnable habit of the mind, almost as fictional as optical illusions and as transitory as Pavlov's conditioning" (p. 336). Many cognitive neuroscientists today would probably argue that we are "prewired" by the evolution of human nature to perceive causal connections, for it is hard to imagine how we could hope to survive without causal inferences and causal generalizations, even if they are merely mental and sociocultural constructions.

---

the Salk polio vaccine and not contracting or contracting polio in the landmark 1954 clinical trial? You may be surprised to know that the correlation was only .011 (Rosnow & Rosenthal, 2003). This small effect size r was not because the vaccine was ineffective (in fact, it is decidedly effective) but because polio was not a common event in the samples studied.

Although causation implies covariation, covariation does not imply causation. Hence, the second criterion of causality is evidence that Y did not occur until after X occurred—or what Hume called "priority" and we term **temporal precedence**. Because a later event cannot very well be the cause of an earlier one, we look for evidence that X came before Y. In relational research it is often hard to obtain incontrovertible evidence of temporal precedence, because we are looking at X and Y in retrospect (i.e., looking back at them). We have more to say about this issue in the next chapter, but sometimes it can be argued on logical grounds, even retrospectively, that X must have come before Y. Suppose we find satisfactory evidence of covariation between sex and adult height and want to say which came first in a linear chain of cause and effect. Common sense leads us to conclude that, if there is a causal connection between these two variables, then sex determines adult height rather than that adult height determines sex, because a person's sex is biologically established at conception. Still, temporal precedence and covariation are hardly enough for us to conclude that one variable is the cause (or even the partial cause) of the other. The barometer falls before it rains, but a falling barometer does not *cause* the rain (Pearl, 2000, p. 336). What is also needed is a plausible model of the presumed causal relationship between X and Y and, in turn, logical and evidentiary ways to rule out plausible rival explanations for the association between X and Y.

Thus, the third criterion is to figure out ways to anticipate and rule out threats to **internal validity**. Still, humans are not clairvoyant, and therefore there is a human limit on how successful this effort can be. That is, we cannot anticipate all rival explanations because we cannot look into the future. That qualification notwithstanding, beginning with the theoretical work of Donald T. Campbell and Julian C. Stanley (1963), followed by that of Thomas D. Cook and Campbell (1979), and more recently that of William R. Shadish, Cook, and Campbell (2002), psychological methodologists have compiled lists of the conditions that conceivably undermine internal validity (and also statistical-conclusion validity, construct validity, and external validity). We will give a sense of this theoretical work shortly, but the bottom line is that proceeding even within the more limited framework of the three criteria of covariation, temporal precedence, and internal validity, researchers find they must settle for the most pertinent and compelling evidence *available,* even if that evidence is inconclusive. Thus, causal inference is always subject to some degree of uncertainty. This uncertainty is not surprising, as we know that all ideas and methods are limited in some ways.

What Is the Formative Logic of Experimental Control?

Although some degree of uncertainty is a constant in science, just as it is in everyday life, the idea in performing randomized controlled experiments is that it should be possible to tease out patterns of causal relations. The logical rationale for this assumption derives from what, in the discipline of philosophy of science, is known as **Mill's methods**, the name given to certain logical propositions that were popularized by the 19th-century English philosopher John Stuart Mill. Two of Mill's methods—called *agreement* and *difference*—together provide the formative logical basis of experimental control. The fundamental idea, in principle, is that when two independent groups are comparable in all respects except for some intervention or manipulated variable that is operating in one group but not in the other, the intervention or manipulated variable is implicated as the probable causal agent responsible for observed differences between the two groups on the dependent measures. To see where this basic idea came from, we need to understand what Mill meant by the method of agreement and the method of difference.

First, the **method of agreement** states, "If X, then Y," X symbolizing the presumed cause and Y the presumed effect. The statement means that, if we find two or more instances in which Y occurs, and if only X is present on each occasion, it follows that X is a **sufficient condition** of Y. Calling X a sufficient condition means that it is *adequate* (i.e., capable or competent enough) to bring about the effect. Stated another way, an effect will be present when this sufficient cause is present. In baseball, we would say there are several sufficient conditions for getting the batter to first base, such as getting a hit (X_1), being walked by the pitcher (X_2), being struck by a pitch (X_3), or the catcher's not holding onto the ball after a third strike and failing to tag the runner or toss him out at first base (X_4).

Second, the **method of difference** states, "If not-X, then not-Y." The statement implies that if the presumed effect (Y) does not occur when the presumed cause (X) is absent, then X is a **necessary condition** of Y. Calling X a necessary condition means that it is *indispensable;* that is, X is absolutely essential to bring about the effect. Stated another way, the effect will be absent when the necessary cause is absent. To win in baseball (Y), it is *necessary* for your team to score more runs than the other team (X); not scoring any runs (not-X) will always result in not winning (not-Y).

To take these ideas one step further, suppose that X represents a new and highly touted tranquilizer, and Y represents a change in measured tension. We give people who complain of tension a certain dosage of X, and they show a reduction in measured tension. Can we conclude from this before-and-after observation that the tranquilizer caused the reduction in tension? Not yet, because even if we repeatedly find that giving X is followed by tension reduction, we imply only that X is a sufficient condition of Y. What we seem to need is a **control group** with which to compare the reaction in the first group. For our control group, we need a group of comparable individuals to whom we do not give drug X. If these people show no tension reduction, we have implied that X may be a necessary condition of Y.

We can diagram this simple randomized design as follows, and we see that it corresponds precisely to Mill's methods of agreement and difference:

Experimental group	**Control group**
If X, then Y	If not-X, then not-Y

Can we now conclude that taking the drug led to tension reduction? Yes, but with the stipulation that "taking the drug" implies something more than getting a chemical into the bloodstream. "Taking the drug" means among other things (a) having someone give the person a pill; (b) having someone give the person the attention that goes with pill giving; (c) having the person believe that relevant medication has been administered; and (d) having the ingredients of the drug find their way into the person's blood system.

Usually, when testing a drug in a randomized clinical trial, the researcher is interested only in the patients' reactions to the active ingredients of the medication. The researcher does not care whether the patients will feel better if they merely *believe* they are being helped, because this fact (i.e., the power of suggestion) has already been established. But if researchers know about the power of suggestion, how are they to separate the effects of the drug's ingredients from the effects of pill giving, of the patients' expectations of being helped, and of other factors that may be sufficient conditions of Y? The answer is by the choice of a different (or additional) control group. So this time, we use not a group given nothing, but a *placebo control group* given something that differs only in lacking the ingredients whose effects we would like to know. The general finding, incidentally, is that placebos are often effective and sometimes even as effective as the far more expensive drug for which they serve as the control (see also Box 7.3).

BOX 7.3 "I Shall Please"

The term *placebo* means in Latin "I shall please," and it is now widely recognized that *placebo effects* (i.e., the "healing" effects of inert substances or nonspecific treatments) are ubiquitous in clinical practice and research, including the healing effects of a placebo on angina, blood pressure, the common cold, cough, fever, panic disorder, headache, psoriasis, insomnia, pain, rheumatoid arthritis, and warts; even placebo vaccines have an effect (Turkkan & Brady, 2000). If people are told they are receiving a placebo, there is less placebo effect. Also, if they receive a real treatment but *believe* it to be a placebo, the treatment is usually less effective (White, Tursky, & Schwartz, 1985). Although expectations and the context of the situation play an important role in the placebo effect, the biobehavioral mechanism mediating the healing remains unexplained. But there is speculation that it may involve a classical conditioning interaction of the central nervous system and particular organ systems (Turkkan & Brady, 2000).

What Are Preexperimental Designs?

So far in this chapter, we have looked at different randomized experimental designs. Campbell and Stanley (1963) also described what they called **preexperimental designs** that, they argued, are so deficient in control that they are especially vulnerable to causal misinterpretations. Suppose that children who are administered a new educational intervention designed to improve their concentration are also given an achievement test after the intervention. This preexperimental design is called a **one-shot case study**, symbolized as X-O, where X = exposure to an event or experimental variable, and O = an observation or measurement. The problem with this design is that no allowance is made for a comparison with the reactions of children who did not receive the new intervention. Also, because there was no pretreatment measure, we have no idea what each child's level of performance on the achievement test might have been before the intervention. On the other hand, this design is reminiscent of a demonstration experiment in chemistry, in which X might be mixing chemical reagents in a test tube, and O is our observation of the reaction.

Useful guidance on the analysis of one-shot case study designs are Siegel and Castellan's (1988) and Higgins's (2004) texts. For example, suppose the achievement test had true-false and multiple-choice-type items, and the response options were equally likely to be chosen by chance alone in each case. One data-analytic possibility is to assess whether the distribution of observed responses for each item deviates from chance. Still another procedure, not discussed in the texts above, provides an index symbolized as Pi (Π) that converts the proportion of correct answers in multiple-choice-type tests to the proportion made *as if* there had been two equally likely choices (R. Rosenthal & Rubin, 1989). The index Π allows us to summarize the overall performance so we can compare performance on items made up of varying numbers of alternatives per item. There is a discussion of Π in our advanced text (R. Rosenthal & Rosnow, 2008). The point here is simply that, even for the most limited designs, there are frequently informative procedures for analyzing the data. A preferable option in this case, of course, is to redesign the study from scratch so we have a randomized controlled experimental design rather than a one-shot preexperimental design.

Campbell et al. suggested that, if we really are limited to a single sample but can make a small design recommendation, at least a small improvement on the one-shot case study is to measure the subjects before and after exposure to the treatment. Called a **one-group pre-post design**, this preexperimental design is symbolized as O-X-O. Still, the problem is that, without a non-X comparison condition, we cannot rule out uncontrolled events between X and O. However, it may be possible to have a within-subjects control condition. Suppose you have a skin rash that, the doctor tells you, is contact dermatitis produced by an allergic reaction to some substance that you are overly sensitive to. To figure out what substance produces that reaction, the doctor gives you an allergen patch test. A patch with tiny substances on it, each one numbered, is attached to your skin, and you are told to wear the patch for a couple of days to see whether your skin reacts to any of the substances. The patch also has a "negative-control" spot, that is, a place with nothing on it. Its purpose is to enable the doctor to control for the patch itself, that is, to detect whether the patch material irritates your skin. (The doctor is doing what, in the next chapter, is called a *single-case experiment*.)

What Circumstances Jeopardize Internal Validity?

Previously, we noted that, beginning with Campbell and Stanley's seminal work, methodologists have given considerable thought to potential threats to different forms of validity in randomized and nonrandomized designs (Cook & Campbell, 1976, 1979; Shadish et al., 2002). To help us set the stage for this discussion, Table 7.4 repeats in Parts A and B the one-shot case study and one-group pre-post design. Part C is a between-subjects design, in which the symbol R denotes that a random assignment procedure is used. As a further illustration of this design, say we are interested in studying whether giving middle-school students a lesson on the rules of correct spelling will improve their spelling ability. We design an experiment in which we assign the children to either an experimental group or a control group at random. We then teach those in the experimental group (Group I) the rules of correct spelling (X) and do not teach these rules to the children in the control group (Group II). Using the logic of Mill's methods, we compare the mean scores of these two groups by an independent *t* test. Since the groups are presumed to be similar in all pertinent characteristics except for the experimental treatment (X), any observed difference between them on the outcome measurement (O) should be due to the experimental treatment (X). This between-groups design is also known as an *after-only* (or *posttest-only*) *design* because no measurements were made before the experimental treatment was implemented (i.e., there was no *pretesting* of the children).

Table 7.4	Five Design Options

A. One-shot case study design

One group			X	O

B. One-group pre-post design

One group		O	X	O

C. After-only randomized between-subjects design

Group I	R		X	O
Group II	R			O

D. Before-after randomized between-subjects design

Group I	R	O	X	O
Group II	R	O		O

E. Solomon design (composite of C and D above)

Group I	R		X	O
Group II	R			O
Group III	R	O	X	O
Group IV	R	O		O

However, suppose we are also interested in knowing how the children responded before they were randomly placed in those two groups, because we think we need a *baseline* to tell us exactly how much improvement occurred on the average, or how much improvement occurred in each child. Instead of an after-only design, we use a *before-after design* (or *pre-post design*) as shown in Part D of Table 7.4. We begin by pretesting the children on a list of words of equal difficulty by having them spell the words. We then teach half of the children at random (Group I) the rules of spelling (X) and do not teach these rules to the other group (Group II), and afterward we test the children on the same list of words. Because we used random assignment, we assume the two groups scored about the same (i.e., on the average) on the pretest, but we have a way of checking on this assumption (i.e., we simply compare the pretest means). We also have another data-analysis option in that we can compute for each child a *difference score* based on the child's posttest-minus-pretest score, and we can then use our one-sample *t* test on these scores. A positive difference score would tell us that there was an achievement gain in spelling; a negative difference would tell us the opposite. We are mildly curious to find out whether there was a gain in the control group, which received nothing of substance but did take the same spelling test twice (a practice effect?). For this purpose, we can calculate the size of the one-sample effect from the one-sample *t* test (Rosenthal & Rosnow, 2008, Ch. 13).

Table 7.5	The Solomon Design (in Part E of Table 7.4) as a 2 × 2 Factorial Design	
	Treatment?	
Pretest?	Yes	No
No	Group I	Group II
Yes	Group III	Group IV

Richard L. Solomon (1949) argued that a possible problem with the before-after design is that merely pretesting the subjects in the experimental treatment group might "sensitize" them to that treatment and, in turn, distort the outcome in this group. He suggested controlling for this "sensitization effect" by using the four-group design in Part E of Table 7.4, now known as the **Solomon design**. It is actually a composite of the designs in Parts C and D, and, as Table 7.5 shows, the Solomon design can also be conceptualized as a 2 × 2 factorial design. Group I is not pretested but undergoes the experimental treatment. Group II gets only the posttest. Group III is pretested and retested and receives the same experimental treatment as Group I. Group IV is both pretested and retested but does not get the experimental treatment.

The Solomon design is predicated on the assumption that randomization will produce four groups that are similar to begin with. If this assumption is not met, Solomon's suggested interpretation of the results are suspect, because we instead have what (in Chapter 8) is called a *nonequivalent groups design*. Assuming all groups are similar in terms of pretreatment characteristics and performance, one idea is that we can estimate the pretreatment performance in Groups I and II (the unpretested groups) using the average value of the pretest in Groups III and IV. In other words, without actually pretesting Groups I and II, we can make a reasonable guess of the *average* pretest scores in both groups. This guess requires a leap of faith, because we cannot be *absolutely* sure what the mean pretest performance in the unpretested groups would have been. Even if the average value of the pretest in Group III is identical to that in Group IV, we can only *assume* that these values are close to those that would have been obtained by Groups I and II. The larger the sample sizes and the more skillfully implemented the random assignment, the more confidence we can have in this analytic procedure. However, even if the average pretest values in Groups III and IV differ greatly (which can easily happen when sample sizes are small or when randomization is not properly implemented), there is still a possibility that the unknown pretest scores in Groups I and II would have been similar to the mean of Groups III and IV.

A second idea is that, from our estimation of the average pretest performance levels in Groups I and II, we can enrich our understanding of the average posttest performance in these groups. That is to say, we can now interpret the average pre-to-post benefit of the experimental treatment without having subjected the experimental and control groups to pretesting. Of course, our estimation is just a comparison of the mean performance scores in Groups I and II (on the assumption

Table 7.6	Causal Events Affecting the Outcome Measure in the Solomon Design			
Causal event	Group I	Group II	Group III	Group IV
Pretest	No	No	Yes	Yes
Treatment	Yes	No	Yes	No
Sensitization	No	No	Yes	No
Extraneous effects	Yes	Yes	Yes	Yes

of comparability on the pretests because of the use of randomization). Our hypothesis was that the spelling ability performance of Group I would surpass that of Group II on the posttest.

Finally, a third idea of Solomon's was that this design can both reveal any "sensitization" effect and its direction. Table 7.6, which helps us explain Solomon's reasoning, shows what he viewed as four plausible causal events affecting the outcome measure in each group. Notice that the outcome in Group I can be affected by the experimental treatment and any unaccounted-for variables (called *extraneous effects*). The outcome in Group II can be affected only by extraneous effects, as there was no pretest and no experimental treatment. The outcome in Group III can be affected by the pretest and the treatment—and therefore by "sensitization"—and by any extraneous effects. Group IV can be affected by the pretest and extraneous effects. Solomon reasoned that to isolate the effect of sensitization, we need only subtract the posttest means of the four groups as follows: $(M_I - M_{II}) - (M_{III} - M_{IV})$. First, we do the subtractions within the parentheses, and then we subtract what remains in the right set of parentheses from what remains in the left set. That is, we first subtract the posttest mean of Group II from the posttest mean of Group I, which will cancel out the extraneous effects and leave the treatment effect. Next, we subtract the posttest mean of Group IV from the posttest mean of Group III, which will cancel out the pretest and extraneous effects and leave the treatment and sensitization effects. When we subtract what remains on the right from what remains on the left, what is left over is the "sensitization" effect. If the between-differences value is close to zero, we will conclude that there is little or no sensitization effect, whereas finding a positive or a negative value would indicate an obtained directional effect of sensitization (cf. Entwisle, 1961; Lana, 1959, 1969; Rosnow & Suls, 1970; Solomon & Howes, 1951; Solomon & Lessac, 1968).

This brings us to the four threats to internal validity that we mentioned earlier. First, the term **history** implies a plausible source of error attributable to an uncontrolled event that occurs between the premeasurement (the pretest) and the postmeasurement (the posttest) and that can bias the postmeasurement. History is a threat to internal validity when the inferred causal relationship is confounded by the irrelevant, uncontrolled event. Suppose we are testing a new educational treatment designed to improve the concentration of students in a public school setting and a sudden snowstorm results in an unexpected cancellation of classes. The preexperimental designs in Part A and Part B of Table 7.4 would not allow us to isolate the effects on motivation of a school closing, or to assess that factor apart from the effects of the new educational treatment designed to improve concentration. The Solomon design, as well as its two component designs in Parts C and D of Table 7.4, do allow us to assess this factor.

Second, **maturation** refers to certain intrinsic changes in the research participants, such as their growing older, wiser, stronger, or more experienced between the premeasurement and the postmeasurement. Maturation becomes a threat to internal validity when it is not the variable of interest but the inferred causal relationship is nevertheless confounded by the presence of these changes. Imagine a study in which the posttest is given 1 year after the pretest. If the students' concentration has improved as a result of their getting older, so that they have become better at the task, neither of the preexperimental designs in Table 7.4 will tell us whether the gains are due to the students' maturing or to their being subjected to a particular educational treatment. The Solomon design (or either of the component designs in Table 7.4) controls for maturation bias by randomization.

Third, **instrumentation** refers to the intrinsic changes in the measuring instruments, such as deterioration. Instrumentation is a threat to internal validity when an effect may be due to unsuspected changes in the instruments over time. In the case of our educational treatment, we might ask whether the effect is due to instability (i.e., deterioration) of the achievement test or to changes in the students that are caused by the treatment. Suppose the "instruments" are actually judges who are asked to rate the students. Over time, judges may become better raters of student concentration, in which case the confounding is due not to instrument deterioration but to instrument improvement. Instrumentation bias is not a relevant issue in the X-O design in Part A of Table 7.4 because the test is administered only once, but it is both relevant and uncontrolled in the O-X-O design in Part B, and relevant but specifically identifiable (controlled) in the Solomon design and its component designs in Parts C and D.

Fourth, **selection** also refers to the subjects or participants, but in this case, the threat to internal validity comes from the selection of the participants for their assignment to particular treatments. Selection is a threat to internal validity when there are important, unsuspected differences between the participants in each condition. In the X-O design there is no way of knowing beforehand anything about the state of the participants because they are observed or measured only after the treatment has been administered. The addition of an observation before the treatment in the O-X-O design results in an improvement over the X-O design; it enables us to ascertain the prior state of the participants. The Solomon design and its two component designs in Table 7.4 control for selection bias by randomization.

How Can I Control for Demand Characteristics and Expectancy Effects?

In Chapter 4, the terms *reactive* and *nonreactive* were used to distinguish measurements or observations that do (reactive) from those that do not (nonreactive) affect the behavior being measured or observed. When an engineer carefully takes the dimensions of a large piece of metal, we do not suppose that the act of measurement will have an effect on the metal. Similarly, when a biologist observes the movements of a paramecium, we do not expect the paramecium to change its behavior when the scientist is looking at it through a microscope. However, one may be less sure of the risks of reactive observation when humans, or some other animals, are the object of study. For example, one behavioral researcher reported that experienced observers in an animal lab could judge which of several experimenters had been handling a rat by the animal's behavior while running a maze or when being picked up (Christie, 1951). Another researcher observed that a dog's heart rate would drop dramatically simply because a certain experimenter was present (Gantt, 1964).

The term used to refer to this problem is **artifact**, which in this context means a finding that results from conditions other than those intended by the experimenter (e.g., Blanck, 1993; Fiske, 2000; Orne, 1959; R. Rosenthal, 1966; R. Rosenthal & Rosnow, 1969; Rosnow, 2002; Rosnow & Rosenthal, 1997; Rosnow, Strohmetz, & Aditya, 2000; Strohmetz, 2006). Artifacts are not simply serendipitous findings, however, but findings resulting from uncontrolled conditions that may jeopardize the validity (internal, construct, and external) of the researcher's conclusions about what went on in the study or about the implications of the results. In the remainder of this chapter we will touch on some of the work in this area (called the *social psychology of the experiment*), beginning with artifacts that are associated with the role and motivations of the research subject (subject-related artifacts) and then turning to experimenter-related artifacts. The artifact problem is that what one researcher interprets as a causal relation between X and Y another researcher may theorize to be the plausible relation between some uncontrolled subject-related or experimenter-related artifact and Y (cf. J. G. Adair, 1973; Danziger, 1988; Gniech, 1976; R. Rosenthal & Rosnow, 1969, 1975b; I. Silverman, 1977; Strohmetz & Rosnow, 1994; Suls & Rosnow, 1988). Students interested in a detailed overview of this problem will find such a discussion in our book entitled *People Studying People* (Rosnow & Rosenthal, 1997).

Pioneering work in the social psychology of the experiment was done by Martin T. Orne, whose interests in subject-related artifacts grew out of his research on hypnosis. Observations in that research led him to theorize that the trance manifestations that people exhibit on entering hypnosis are partly determined by their motivation to "act out" the role of a hypnotized person. Both their preconceptions of how a hypnotized person ought to act and the cues communicated by the hypnotist of how the subjects should behave, called **demand characteristics**, were viewed by Orne (1962, 1969, 1970) as plausible determinants of the subjects' expectations concerning how this role was to be enacted. In particular, Orne postulated that typical volunteers for psychology experiments have a tendency to act out the role of the "good subject," that is, the participant who is sensitive to demand characteristics and tries to give experimenters what they seemingly want to find. The extent to which some research participants will comply with demand characteristics can sometimes surprise even the experimenter. At one point in his research on hypnosis, Orne (1962) tried to devise a set of dull, meaningless tasks that nonhypnotized persons either would refuse to do or would try for only a short time. One task was to add thousands of rows of two-digit numbers. Five and a half hours after the subjects began, the experimenter gave up! When subjects were told to tear each worksheet into a minimum of 32 pieces before going on to the next, they *still* persisted.

In Chapter 5, we spoke of Milton Rosenberg's (1969) view of the human participants in psychological research as usually being apprehensive about being evaluated, a condition that he called *evaluation apprehension*. Although Rosenberg argued that typical subjects are motivated to "look good" rather than to help the cause of science (Orne's view), Rosenberg and Orne agreed that typical subjects frequently find meaning in even the most meaningless cues (as illustrated by the case noted above). Orne theorized that most research subjects (especially those who volunteer for research participation) reason that, no matter how trivial and inane the task outwardly seems (such as adding thousands of rows of two-digit numbers), the experimenter must surely have an important scientific purpose that justifies their experimental participation. Feeling that they have a stake in the outcome of the study, the "good subjects" believe that they are making a useful contribution to science by complying with the demand characteristics of the experiment, Orne argued. The puzzle is to figure out whether there are artifact-producing demand characteristics in a given experiment.

To help us in this quest, Orne (1962, 1969) proposed that **quasi-control subjects** be used. These are research subjects who are asked to step out of their traditional roles and to serve as "coinvestigators" (that is, rather than as "objects of study" for the experimenter to investigate). Such subjects are drawn from the same population as the experimental and control subjects, but the quasi-control subjects are asked to reflect on the context in which the experiment is being conducted. They then free-associate about how the situation might have influenced their behavior if they were in the experimental group. For example, the participation of a few subjects in the experimental group may be terminated at different points during the course of the study. They then become quasi-control subjects who are carefully interviewed about what they thought to be the demand characteristics of the experiment. The key to the success of the quasi-control method is that these individuals will be forthcoming with the interviewer. Thus, it is often helpful to have someone other than the experimenter do the interviewing so that the quasi-control subjects clearly perceive that, for them, the experiment is over and they really are "coinvestigators."

On the other side of the artifact coin are experimenter-related artifacts, that is, sources of bias (or systematic error) resulting from uncontrolled intentions or actions of the experimenters. A number of such sources have been identified (R. Rosenthal, 1966), though the one we describe here is particularly intriguing because it occurs when people's expectations unwittingly serve as self-fulfilling prophecies. When the "prophet" is the experimenter and the subjects' behavior is at issue, the self-fulfilling prophecy is called an **experimenter expectancy effect**. In one early study of experimenter expectancy, a dozen student experimenters were each given five rats that were to be taught to run a maze with the aid of visual cues (R. Rosenthal & Fode, 1963). Half the students were told their rats had been specially

---

BOX 7.4 Blindfolding to Ensure "Blindness"

The principle of ensuring "blindness" may also be applicable to the role of other participants in the research. For example, psychologists Kathy Hirsh-Pasek and Roberta Michnick Golinkoff (1993, 1996) used a novel method to study language comprehension in infants and toddlers, a model that the researchers called the "preferential looking paradigm." Suppose we want to study noun comprehension to find out how early in their lives infants and toddlers are able to distinguish a shoe from a hat. An infant is seated on a blindfolded parent's lap approximately $2\frac{1}{2}$ feet away from a pair of television monitors. By means of a concealed speaker, the word *shoe* is sounded at the same time that one of the monitors shows a shoe and the other monitor shows a hat. A camera records the child's preferential looking behavior over a series of trials using many different pairs of stimuli. Blindfolding the parent eliminates the possibility of the parent's unintentionally signaling the correct responses.

---

bred for maze-brightness, and the remaining students were told their rats had been specially bred for maze-dullness. Actually, there were no differences in the rats; they had been randomly labeled as "maze-bright" or "maze-dull." At the end of the experiment, however, there were observable differences. The rats run by experimenters who expected maze-bright behavior did, in fact, perform better than the rats run by experimenters who expected maze-dull behavior. When the study was repeated, this time in a series of learning experiments, each conducted in a Skinner box (R. Rosenthal & Lawson, 1964), similar results were observed. Allegedly brighter rats performed better than allegedly duller rats did. We should emphasize that the experimenters' expectations acted on the actual performance of the animals, not simply on the perception of the animals' performance. In addition, neither of these studies showed any evidence that the experimenters were trying to generate false data (i.e., there was no evidence of cheating).

One strategy for dealing with the experimenter expectancy problem is to use **blind experimenters,** that is, experimenters who are unaware of ("blind" to) which subjects are to receive the experimental treatment and which the control treatment. The idea here is that, if the experimenters do not know what treatment the subject receives, they are unlikely to communicate expectancies about the nature of that treatment. The necessity of keeping the experimenters blind (i.e., unaware) is well recognized in randomized drug trials. No randomized drug trial is taken completely seriously unless it has followed elaborate **double-blind procedures,** in which neither the subjects nor the experimenters know who is in the experimental and control groups. (See also Box 7.4.)

Another approach to the experimenter expectancy problem is to use a factorial design that not only assesses whether an expectancy effect is present but also allows

---

Table 7.7	The Expectancy Control Design

A. Basic 2 × 2 factorial design

| | Expectancy conditions | |
Treatment conditions	Experimental treatment	Control treatment
Experimental	Group A	Group B
Control	Group C	Group D

B. Burnham's (1966) study of discrimination learning in rats

| | Expectancy conditions | | |
Treatment conditions	Lesioning of brain	No lesioning	Row means
Lesioning of brain	46.5	49.0	47.75
No lesioning of brain	48.2	58.3	53.25
Column means	47.35	53.65	

---

a direct comparison of that effect with the phenomenon of theoretical interest. Called an **expectancy control design**, this approach usually takes the form of the 2 × 2 factorial arrangement shown in Part A of Table 7.7. Group A represents the condition in which the experimental treatment is administered to subjects by data collectors who expect the occurrence of the experimental effect in this group. Group D represents the condition in which the absence of the experimental treatment is associated with data collectors who expect the nonoccurrence of the experimental effect in this group. Ordinarily, researchers are interested in the experimental effect unconfounded with experimenter expectancy; the addition of the appropriate expectancy control groups permits the researchers to evaluate the experimental effect separately from the expectancy effect. Subjects in Group B receive the experimental treatment but are contacted by data collectors who do not expect an experimental effect in this group. The subjects in Group C do not receive the experimental treatment but are contacted by data collectors who expect an experimental effect.

You can see that it is an expensive design, because it calls for many data collectors who are randomly assigned to the four cells. However, it has been used in a number of experimental situations. Illustrative of its use in animal research is an early study reported by J. R. Burnham (1966), with the results in Part B of Table 7.7. Each of about two dozen student-experimenters ran one rat in a discrimination task in a T-maze (i.e., a runway with the starting box at the base and the goal at one end of the crossbar). Portions of the brains of approximately half the rats had been surgically removed (*lesioned*). The remaining rats had received only sham surgery, which involved a cut through the skull but no damage to brain tissue (so that it was impossible for the student-experimenters to tell which rats had actually undergone brain lesioning). The purpose of the study was explained to the student-experimenters as an attempt to learn the effects of lesions on discrimination learning. Expectancies were manipulated by the labeling of each rat as "lesioned" or "unlesioned." Some of the really lesioned rats were labeled accurately as lesioned, but some were falsely labeled as unlesioned. Similarly, some of the really unlesioned rats were labeled accurately as unlesioned, but others were falsely labeled as lesioned.

By comparing the means in the row and column margins, we get an idea of the relative effectiveness of the surgical and the expectancy treatments. The higher these scores, the better was the rats' performance in that row or column. Note that rats that had been surgically lesioned did not perform as well as those that had not been lesioned. Note also that rats that were *believed* to have been lesioned did not perform as well as those that were believed to be unlesioned. The logic of this design is that it enables the researcher to compare the magnitude of the effect of experimenter expectancy with the magnitude of the effect of actual removal of brain tissue. In this case, the two effects were similar in magnitude. Of course, we are not limited to comparing the differences in row means and column means, and previously in this chapter we mentioned how it is possible to compare all four cell means by computing a contrast that compares group means with predicted lambda weights.

Summary of Ideas

1. *Randomized experimental studies* are characterized by the assigning of subjects to treatments so as to guard against potential sources of allocation bias by giving each sampling unit an equal chance of being assigned to any group or condition, but this method does not guarantee equality of the different groups or conditions (also Box 7.1).

2. *Randomization* (i.e., *random assignment*) procedures include coin flipping and using random numbers to allocate the sampling units or treatment conditions in an unbiased way.

3. *Between-subjects designs* (*nested designs*) and *within-subjects designs* (*crossed designs*) are distinguished, respectively, by whether each sampling unit is observed once or more than once.

4. Designs may also have more than one dimension (*factorial designs*), and there are also combinations (mixed factorial designs) as well as *counterbalanced* repeated measures designs (*Latin square designs*).

5. Aristotle described four kinds of causality: *material, formal, efficient, and final.* Subsequently, inspired by Hume's "rules by which to judge causes and effects" (Box 7.2), scientific thought about efficient causality has coalesced around three fundamental criteria, which we described as *covariation, temporal precedence, and internal validity* (though causal inference is always subject to some degree of uncertainty).

6. The logic of using a control condition in two-group between-subjects designs embodies *Mill's methods of agreement and difference.*

7. *Preexperimental designs,* as illustrated by the one-shot case study (X-O) and the one-group pre-post study (O-X-O), make no effort to control for threats to internal validity.

8. Four threats to internal validity are called *history, maturation, instrumentation,* and *selection.* We discussed their potential confounding effects in the two preexperimental designs, an after-only randomized design, a before-after randomized design, and the *Solomon design* (created to tease out "sensitization" effects).

9. *Artifacts* are findings that result from conditions other than those intended (and controlled for) by the experimenter. Subject-related artifacts may be due to *demand characteristics,* which might be ferreted out by the use of *quasi-controls.*

10. *Experimenter expectancy* may cause the experimenter's working hypothesis to become a self-fulfilling prophecy. *Blind procedures* are used to control for expectancy effects, and *double-blind procedures* are the gold standard in biomedical trials. An *expectancy control design* is used to isolate and compare the expectancy effect with the effect of the main independent variable (e.g., Burnham's study of discrimination learning in rats).

Key Terms

artifact   p. 169
between-subjects design
  p. 154
blind experimenters   p. 171
control group   p. 162
counterbalancing   p. 157
covariation   p. 159
crossed design   p. 155
demand characteristics
  p. 169
double-blind procedures
  p. 171
efficient causality   p. 158
expectancy control design
  p. 172
experimenter expectancy
  effect   p. 170
factorial design   p. 156
final causality   p. 158
formal causality   p. 158

history   p. 167
instrumentation   p. 168
internal validity   p. 161
lambda (λ) weights   p. 155
Latin square design   p. 157
material causality   p. 158
maturation   p. 168
method of agreement
  p. 161
method of difference   p. 162
Mill's methods   p. 161
necessary condition   p. 162
nested design   p. 154
one-group pre-post design
  (O-X-O)   p. 164
one-shot case study (X-O)
  p. 163
preexperimental designs
  p. 163

quasi-control subjects
  p. 170
random assignment
  p. 151
randomization   p. 151
randomized experiments
  p. 151
repeated-measures design
  p. 155
selection   p. 168
Solomon design
  p. 166
sufficient condition
  p. 161
temporal precedence
  p. 160
within-subjects design
  p. 155

Multiple-Choice Questions for Review

1. Which of the following is considered a defining characteristic of randomized clinical trials in medical research? (a) random sampling of subjects; (b) random assignment of subjects to the experimental conditions; (c) use of a placebo-control group; (d) use of a quasi-control group

2. Randomization is (a) selecting a sample at random from a larger population; (b) manipulating a random sample of variables within an experiment; (c) ensuring that each subject has an equal chance of being assigned to any condition; (d) randomly determining which experimenter will conduct which experimental condition.

3. Which of the following was a type of cause identified by Aristotle? (a) final; (b) efficient; (c) formal; (d) all of the above

4. To conclude that X causes Y, scientists must be able to rule out plausible rival hypotheses. This is called the criterion of (a) covariation; (b) temporal precedence; (c) internal validity; (d) material causation.

5. Philosopher J. S. Mill stated, "If *X*, then *Y*." This is known as Mill's method of (a) agreement; (b) disagreement; (c) difference; (d) covariation.

6. Which of the following is a common threat to internal validity? (a) maturation; (b) covariation; (c) time-series data; (d) none of the above

7. Campbell et al.'s name for a research design in which there is only one group, and that group is measured only after the treatment, is the (a) Solomon design; (b) one-shot case study; (c) one-group pre-post study; (d) factorial design.

8. A study is conducted in which there is only one group, and that group is measured both before and after the treatment. This design is vulnerable to which of the following threats to internal validity? (a) history; (b) maturation; (c) selection; (d) all of the above

9. Which of the following research designs allows the scientist to examine the possibility of pretest sensitization? (a) Solomon four-group design; (b) one-shot case study; (c) one-group pre-post design; (d) factorial design

10. Cues given off by an experimental procedure and context that communicate to participants how they should behave are called (a) artifacts; (b) demand characteristics; (c) experimenter expectancy effects; (d) none of the above.

Discussion Questions for Review

1. A Colby College student wants to evaluate the effectiveness of a popular method of boosting self-esteem called "I'm-better-than-OK therapy." In this therapy, clients read pop psychology books, compliment themselves while looking in a mirror, and have group touch-a-lot sessions. What kind of control group(s) would you recommend?

2. A Villanova University student believes that positive reinforcement increases self-esteem. To test this hypothesis, she administers a self-esteem scale to 40 other students and correlates the scores with their grade point averages. Can you think of any limitations in this research design?

3. An Auburn University student tells his participants that he is interested in identifying the characteristics associated with good leadership skills. He then administers two measures titled Social Intelligence Survey and Interpersonal Problem-Solving Ability. Do you see any potential problem in this method?

4. A student at the University of New Mexico wants to prove that eating chocolate chip cookies will cure depression. What basic requirements of inference would he have to meet, according to J. S. Mill?

5. An American University student wants to use an expectancy control design to assess a program offering individual tutoring to enhance students' performance on achievement tests. How might she set up this design?

6. A manufacturer of pain relievers wants to market what seems to be a revolutionary new product: a near-cure for the common cold. Researchers in the R & D division select 1,000 persons to participate in a test study. Each participant is observed for 6 months. For the first 3 months, baseline data are collected. For the last 3 months, the participants take a weekly dose of the common-cold cure. Sure enough, 15% of the participants contract a cold during the first 3 months, whereas only 5% do so in the second 3 months. The investigators rush their findings to the company president, who must decide whether the data are convincing enough for the product to be put on the market. Can you think of any weakness in the research design?

7. On a quiz, University of Arkansas students are asked how the Solomon design teases out the effect of "sensitization"? What is the answer? The same students are also asked to define the following threats to internal validity: history, maturation, selection, and instrumentation. Do you know the answers?

8. A Howard University medical student designs an experiment to test the effects of a new drug. In consultation with her faculty mentor, she decides to include both a placebo control and a zero control group. Do you know the difference?

Answers to Review Questions

Multiple-Choice Questions

1. b	**3.** d	**5.** a	**7.** b	**9.** a
2. c	**4.** c	**6.** a	**8.** d	**10.** b

Discussion Questions

1. A placebo control group might be used to which clients are randomly assigned. This placebo control group would receive a pseudomethod of boosting self-esteem, for example, reading material believed to be irrelevant to self-esteem and watching irrelevant movies. The clients assigned to this placebo control group should believe that their "treatment" will have beneficial effects to the same degree as do the clients assigned to the "real" treatment.

2. Because the positive reinforcement (grades) was not experimentally manipulated, there is no basis for her concluding that it "caused" the self-esteem scores even if there is a positive correlation between self-esteem and GPA. Self-esteem may as well "cause" grades, or some other variable may "cause" both grades and self-esteem.

3. Telling participants the hypothesis and the names of the measuring instruments is likely to result in strong demand characteristics.

4. According to Mill's methods, the student would have to show that eating chocolate chip cookies is followed by a reduction in depression (method of agreement) and that not eating chocolate chip cookies is not followed by a reduction in depression (method of difference).

5. The basic plan could be implemented by use of the following four conditions, analogous to those shown in Table 7.7:

	Expectancy	
Actual treatment	Experimental	Control
Tutoring	A	B
Control	C	D

6. As in all one-group pre-post studies, history, maturation, and instrumentation all threaten the internal validity of the research.

7. The Solomon design allows researchers to use the subtraction-difference procedure to compare the difference between the experimental and control groups obtained when pretests have and have not been used. The four threats to internal validity were described as part of Campbell et al.'s analysis in this chapter.

8. A placebo-control group offers a treatment-like condition that serves to control for subjects' beliefs or expectations about the efficacy of any treatments that might be administered. A zero-control group is characterized by the absence of any intervention, "real" or "pseudo" (placebo).

CHAPTER 8

Nonrandomized Research and Causal Reasoning

Preview Questions

- How is causal reasoning attempted in the absence of randomization?
- What is the "third-variable" problem?
- How can causal effects be studied in nonequivalent groups?
- What are time-series designs and "found experiments"?
- What within-subjects designs are used in single-case experiments?
- How are correlations interpreted in cross-lagged panel designs?
- What is the purpose of longitudinal research using cohorts?

 ## How Is Causal Reasoning Attempted in the Absence of Randomization?

Causal reasoning is a fundamental aspect of human intelligence that has long been of interest to psychologists as well as philosophers. Cognitive psychologists have, for example, studied how people reason (e.g., Evans, Newstead, & Byrne, 1993; Johnson-Laird & Byrne, 1991), child psychologists have studied the developmental trajectory of causal reasoning (e.g., Ceci, 1990, 1996; H. Gardner, 1983, 1993, 1999), and social and organizational psychologists have explored the capacity to make causal distinctions in interpersonal situations (e.g., Aditya & House, 2002; Aditya & Rosnow, 2002; Rosnow, Skleder, Jaeger, & Rind, 1994). In the previous chapter, we saw how researchers do randomized controlled experiments in an attempt to create the equivalence they need to make causal inferences. Such experiments, though they are the gold standard of biomedical research, are not always possible, however.

Suppose you have been bitten by a dog. You go to a doctor, who prescribes a tetanus shot and an oral antibiotic. You ask the doctor to give the tetanus shot in the arm that has been bitten so that you have the use of your other arm. But the doctor points out that if she did so and you had a reaction to the tetanus, she would not be able to separate it from the possible continued reaction to the dog bite, which could, in the worst-case scenario, also cause the arm to swell. For this reason, she gives the shot in your "good arm" so any swelling due to an allergy to the tetanus will not be confounded with a possible reaction to the dog bite. Her causal reasoning is in some ways suggestive of the simplest single-case experiment (discussed later in this chapter). As in any such experiment, the doctor's "single-case experiment" will be based on **prospective data**; that is, she will collect data by following your reaction forward in time.

Prospective data are also commonly used in longitudinal research (also discussed later in this chapter), the defining characteristic of such research being that individuals are observed and measured repeatedly through time. For example, an important longitudinal study, known as the Framingham heart study, was started by the U.S. Public Health Service in 1948. Responding to concerns about the soaring coronary disease rate in the United States, this study has observed and measured several thousand residents of Framingham, Massachusetts. The findings have helped to improve our understanding of risk factors that predict cardiovascular disease. In 1960, cigarette smoking was first revealed to be a risk factor, and in 1961, high blood pressure was revealed to be another risk factor. The correlational findings in this study have led to randomized clinical trials that have confirmed the preventive approach to combating heart disease by exercising, not smoking, lowering harmful cholesterol, and reducing stress, blood pressure, and obesity (National Heart Institute, 1966).

The purpose of this chapter is to sample several major families of nonrandomized designs that are frequently used for generalized causal inference, including nonequivalent-groups designs, interrupted time-series designs, cross-lagged panel designs, and, as noted above, longitudinal and single-case experimental designs. Sometimes the data are collected back in time; these are called **retrospective data**. To give an epidemiological example, we turn to the basic data in Table 8.1 (adapted

Table 8.1 Causal Reasoning With Retrospective Data

Persons	Ate burger	Ate tuna sandwich	Ate fries	Ate salad	Drank shake	Got food poisoning
Mimi	Yes	No	Yes	No	No	Yes
Gail	No	No	No	Yes	Yes	No
Connie	No	No	Yes	No	No	No
Jerry	No	Yes	No	Yes	No	No
Greg	No	Yes	No	No	Yes	No
Dwight	No	No	No	Yes	No	No
Nancy	Yes	No	Yes	Yes	No	Yes
Richard	No	Yes	Yes	Yes	No	No
Kerry	No	No	No	Yes	No	No
Michele	Yes	No	Yes	Yes	Yes	Yes
John	Yes	No	Yes	Yes	No	Yes
Barbara	Yes	No	No	No	No	Yes

Source: Based on a similar example in *Logic and Philosophy: A Modern Introduction* (6th ed.) by H. Kahane, 1989, Wadsworth.

from an illustrative case noted by Kahane, 1989), which shows that of 12 people who ate at a fast-food restaurant, 5 of them (Mimi, Nancy, Michele, John, and Barbara) got food poisoning (Y). The causal problem is to determine the reason (X) for their getting sick when all we have is circumstantial evidence of covariation and temporal precedence. The challenge is to try to emulate the causal reasoning of Mill's methods in order to arrive at causal hypotheses that are as sound as possible within the limitations of the database (Cook & Campbell, 1979; Shadish et al., 2002).

Table 8.1 indicates that Michele had a milk shake, though we cannot think of a way that the milk shake might have caused food poisoning. Moreover, Gail and Greg also had milk shakes, and they did not get sick or even get an upset stomach. Of the 5 people who got sick, 3 (Nancy, Michele, and John) ate a salad, and it is possible that it contained spoiled dressing that did not taint any other salads. Of the 5 people who got sick, the table shows that 4 ate greasy french fries, which could have produced stomach upsets, but Connie and Richard also ate french fries and were not affected. The most striking finding in this table is that all those who got sick ate a rare hamburger (which no one else ordered). It is easy to imagine how a rare hamburger might have contained bacteria that were not destroyed in the cooking process. What should we conclude?

On the surface, the one common factor is the rare hamburger. But the owner now tells us that one of the food handlers was feeling ill the day these people were served. That food handler worked for a while, but then he asked to be excused after complaining of feeling dizzy and nauseous. Is it possible that the food handler was the culprit? Suppose he touched some but not all of the foods eaten that day. Maybe he passed on his germs in this way. His possible handling of Mimi's and Barbara's hamburger, Nancy's salad dressing, and Michele's and John's fries would be another factor common to all the cases. Using the logic of Mill's methods of agreement and difference, it is possible, in other words, that these particular foods were the *sufficient conditions* to bring about poisoning (Y), but that this food handler's handling of them (X?) was the *necessary* condition.

Once we think about this situation some more, we believe we can safely rule out the food handler because he must have touched many more items than those implicated above. If he were the cause (X), then others who ate at the restaurant should have become ill (Y). Maybe they did and just did not report it, but all we have is Table 8.1. It shows that 7 people did not get food poisoning (not-Y) even though they ate some of the same things the others ate (X), except for the rare hamburger (the true X?). Only the burger was absent in every reported case in which there was no food poisoning. On the basis of this circumstantial evidence, we now hypothesize that the burger was the necessary and sufficient condition (X) that brought about food poisoning (Y). Perhaps there are also variables that *moderate* the relationship between X and Y (more about moderator variables in Appendix C) or, in this case, decrease the relationship between X and Y (since everyone who ate the burger got the food poisoning). (We return to these results in Chapter 11, where we will show how the association between eating the burger and becoming sick can be quantified by a special case of the Pearson r correlation.) (See also Box 8.1.)

BOX 8.1 Quasi-Experimental Research

Campbell and Stanley (1963) coined the expression **quasi-experimental research** to describe all the different types of nonrandomized research for generalized causal inference discussed in this chapter. The term *quasi-experimental* should not be viewed as a snubbing (or put-down) of this research, however, as *quasi* merely means "resembling." Campbell and Stanley's reasoning was that this research often resembles randomized experimental research because quasi experiments have outcome measures, sampling units, and something comparable to the experimental treatment (i.e., an *intervention*), but what identifies them as quasi-experimental is that they do not randomly assign individual units to treatment conditions.

What Is the "Third-Variable" Problem?

Although we know that causality implies correlation (i.e., that X, the presumed cause, and Y, the presumed effect, covary), in nonrandomized research finding that X and Y covary does not tell *why* they are related. In the previous chapter, we explained that, besides covariation and temporal precedence, another requirement of causal inference is the exclusion of plausible rival hypotheses for the observation that X and Y covary. One possibility in nonrandomized research is that a "third variable" that is correlated with both X and Y is the reason X and Y covary; this is called the **third-variable problem**. For example, one author mentioned the positive correlation between (X) the size of children's feet and (Y) their spelling ability (Paulos, 1991). Should we therefore, he asked, use foot stretchers to increase children's spelling scores? The answer, of course, is no, because it is not the length of children's feet that is the causal factor but the fact that children with bigger feet are also usually older, and older children are better educated and therefore spell better. In other words, a third variable (age) that is correlated with *both* X and Y can also account for the correlation *between* X and Y.

As a practical illustration of this problem, imagine that we have discovered an outbreak of strange medical symptoms and want to explain them in causal terms. Time is of the essence, but we do not want to mislead, and possibly cause further harm, by making a spurious causal inference. We begin by drawing a representative sample of those afflicted and then interview them, with the aim of finding some event they have in common. Suppose we find that all have been taking a new prescription drug whose side effects have not been fully established. We now suspect that the new drug may be the cause of the symptoms. The most direct way to dispel our suspicion would be to design an experiment in which we take a sample of asymptomatic people (i.e., people without the particular symptoms) and randomly give half of them the suspected drug and give a placebo to the other half. Although this "gold standard trial" would allow us to compare these two groups of people to see whether those given the new drug are more likely to develop the strange symptoms, the ethical cost of such a study would be too high. We cannot expose people to a drug we have good reason to suspect is harmful.

As a realistic alternative, we can track down patients who were originally diagnosed as having the same illness or disease for which the new drug was prescribed for some patients. We compare those who were given the new drug by their physicians with those patients whose physicians did not prescribe the new drug. If only those given the new drug have developed the strange medical symptoms, the new drug would seem to be more seriously implicated as the causal agent. However, its causal role is still not fully established, because those patients given the new drug may differ on some unknown variable (a "third variable") from those not given the drug. That is, using the same logic we used when thinking about rival hypotheses in randomized experiments (threats to internal validity), we think it is plausible that not the new drug but an unknown correlate of being given the new drug might be the causal variable.

Suppose in our exploratory research we discover that not all patients who took the new drug were given the same dosage levels. Another strategy would correlate the dosage levels with the outcome variable. If it turns out that patients on larger dosages suffer more severely from the strange medical symptoms, would this evidence implicate the drug more strongly as the cause of those symptoms? Unfortunately, the answer is the same as the one above, which is that we still cannot be sure about the causal role of the new drug, as those given larger dosages may have initially been more severely ill. Thus, we wonder whether the *severity* of the illness for which different dosages of the drug were prescribed, rather than the drug itself, might be the unknown variable (the "third variable") that is responsible for the strange medical symptoms.

How have we done so far? "Not very well," you might answer. To establish temporal precedence, we need to show that taking the new drug preceded the strange medical symptoms. Unless our medical records go back far enough, we may not be able to prove that the symptoms did not occur until after the drug was taken. The covariation assumption requires us to show that the new drug is related to the strange medical symptoms. However, even if we can show that taking the new drug is correlated with the mysterious symptoms, it might be argued that, in order to be susceptible to the drug, a patient already had to be in a given state of distress. According to this argument, it is not the new drug, or *not only* the drug, that is related to the strange symptoms. If the patients who were in a state of distress were the only ones given the new drug, it is possible that the patients' state of distress determined the particular group in which they found themselves.

Despite the difficulty of clear inference in this example, we might still be convinced by strong circumstantial, though inconclusive, correlational evidence. If patients taking the new drug are more likely to show the strange medical symptoms, if those taking more of the new drug show more of the symptoms, and if those taking it over a longer period of time show more of the symptoms, we would be reluctant to say that the new drug is *not* the cause of the symptoms. Even if we are unwilling to say that the new drug was definitely at the root of the strange medical symptoms, at least on the basis of the type of correlational evidence outlined above, it might be prudent to act "as though" it were. On this basis, perhaps we can design a randomized experiment using primates to try to simulate the strange medical symptoms, because we now have a causal model with which to work. Still, failure to produce the symptoms in primates would not rule out a causal relationship in human patients.

How Can Causal Effects Be Studied in Nonequivalent Groups?

One family of nonrandomized designs, called **nonequivalent-groups designs**, are traditionally between-subjects designs in which the sampling units (subjects, groups, etc.) are allocated to experimental and control groups by means other than randomization and are observed or tested before and after the experimental treatment. Imagine we want to investigate the effect of a new therapy for treating hyperactive children. If this is a randomized experiment, we would use an unbiased procedure to assign the hyperactive children to a treated experimental group or an untreated control group. However, suppose that circumstances beyond our control dictate that we must use two intact groups: one group of children at School A and one group at School B. We can flip a coin to decide which school will be the experimental group, but we cannot randomly assign the individual children *within* each school to the two groups (see also Box 8.2).

BOX 8.2 Wait-List Control Groups

If in some cases the reason we cannot use a random assignment procedure is concerns about depriving the control group of the experimental treatment, we might propose a randomized design with a **wait-list control group**. Such a design can also have other benefits. Here is an example of a randomized design with a wait-list control group:

Group 1	R	O	X	O	O
Group 2	R	O		O	X	O

where R = random allocation of the participants to groups or treatment conditions; O = observation or measurement; and X = treatment or intervention. Those subjects assigned to Group 1 receive the experimental treatment during a regular period of the experiment, and (assuming the treatment was found to be beneficial) those assigned to Group 2 (the control condition) are given the experimental treatment sometime after the period of the experiment. If we measure Group 1 after the treatment and again after Group 2 receives it, and we compare these results with those in Group 2, then a further benefit of the design is that we have information about the immediate and delayed effect of the treatment as well as a replication of the immediate effect.

The children in the two schools will be observed and measured at the beginning and the end of the study according to this diagram:

School A	NR	O	X	O
School B	NR	O		O

where X = treatment or intervention, O = observation or measurement, and NR = nonrandomized allocation of subjects to conditions. The problem is that School A may be different from School B in a way that systematically biases the results when we compare one intact group (from School A) with another intact group (from School B). Though we have a nonequivalent-groups design, there is a statistical way of improving this situation if (a) the samples are large enough and (b) there are relevant subgroups that are well stocked with sampling units.

This statistical procedure, called *subclassification on propensity scores,* reduces all of the variables on which the "treated" and "untreated" subjects differ into a single composite variable (Rosenbaum & Rubin, 1983; D. B. Rubin, 2006). This composite variable, called a **propensity score**, is a summary statistic of all the differences on all variables on which the "treated" and "untreated" subjects differ. The actual procedure requires a computer program (D. B. Rubin, 2006) and is beyond the scope of this book, but Table 8.2 provides a summary illustration (D. B. Rubin, 2006, p. 43). In Part A of the table are the data from a study (Cochran, 1968) of the death rates for nonsmokers (N), cigarette smokers (C), and cigar and pipe smokers (CP) in each of three databases (Canada, the United Kingdom, and the United States). Note that the death rates are highest for the cigar and pipe smokers (CP) and lower for the nonsmokers (N) and cigarette smokers (C) in all three of the samples. In fact, the death rates of nonsmokers (N) and cigarette smokers (C) in the United States sample are identical, which would suggest that cigarette smoking is not harmful to health!

Part B of the table, however, shows substantial discrepancies in the average age of each subpopulation. Because age and mortality are correlated, age in this example is a confounding variable. We would need to adjust for the average differences

---

Table 8.2   Comparing Death Rates for Nonsmokers (N), Cigarette Smokers (C), and Cigar and Pipe Smokers (CP) in Three National Databases

	Canada			United Kingdom			United States		
	N	C	CP	N	C	CP	N	C	CP
A. Death rates per 1,000 person years									
	20.2	20.5	35.5	11.3	14.1	20.7	13.5	13.5	17.4
B. Average age in years									
	54.9	50.5	65.9	49.1	49.8	55.7	57.0	53.2	59.7
C. Adjusted death rates based on at least nine subclasses of age in each subpopulation									
	20.2	29.5	19.8	11.3	14.8	11.0	13.5	21.2	13.7

in age before reaching any conclusions about death rates of nonsmokers (N), cigarette smokers (C), and cigar and pipe smokers (CP). To adjust for age, each subpopulation is subdivided into age categories of roughly equal size. The next step is to compare the death rates within these age categories. The final step is to adjust the death rates by averaging over the age-group-specific comparisons to get overall estimates of the death rates. Part C of Table 8.2 shows the final results of this analysis. In this case, the adjusted death rates are based on dividing the subpopulations into nine or more subcategories of roughly equal size. Now we see very clearly that the death rate is consistently highest among the cigarette smokers and lowest in the nonsmoking U.S. database and lowest in the cigar and pipe smoking Canadian and United Kingdom databases.

What Are Time-Series Designs and "Found Experiments"?

In **time-series designs**, the defining characteristic is the study of variation across some dimension over time. When the effects of some intervention or "treatment" are inferred from a comparison of the outcome measures obtained at different time intervals before and after the intervention, the data structure is called an **interrupted time-series design**. The term *time series* means there is a data point for each point in time, and an *interrupted* time series means there is a dividing line at the beginning of the intervention (a line analogous to the start of the "treatment"). For example, Gottman (1979) described how certain cycles of social behavior might be studied in the context of a time-series design. He mentioned earlier work by Kendon (1967) showing that when two people converse, there are cycles of gazing and averting gazing at one another as a function of who is speaking. The person who begins speaking has a tendency to look away from the listener and then to increase eye-to-eye contact toward the end of the speech, which is an implicit signal for the listener to begin looking away and speaking. This cycle, Gottman thought, is suggestive of cycles of sine and cosine waves. Another example of cycles is regular repetitions of brain waves when people are awake, drowsy, or in different stages of sleep.

The statistical analysis of time-series designs has its own terminology and can be quite complex (e.g., Cryer, 1986; Judd & Kenny, 1981; Gottman, 1981), but we will give a simplified application that was inspired by the work of sociologist David P. Phillips. He referred to his studies as "found experiments" because they are essentially *found* (or discovered) in naturally occurring situations (cf. Phillips & Glynn, 2000). In one such set of studies, Phillips explored the clustering of imitative suicides after a series of televised news stories and televised movies about suicide (see Phillips, Lesyna, & Paight, 1992, for a review). The variations in the results were difficult to explain, however. For example, a New York City study found that teenage suicides had increased after three televised fictional films about suicide (Gould & Shaffer, 1986), but a follow-up study (Phillips & Paight, 1987) in California and Pennsylvania did not find an increase in teenage suicides after the same three films were televised. In a study in Austria, Phillips and

Carstensen (1986) found evidence of what seemed to be copycat imitations of suicides in news stories.

In Vienna, Austria, there was a sharp increase in the number of subway suicides in 1984. Persuaded by the evidence generated by Phillips and others, the Austrian Association for Suicide Prevention, Crisis Intervention, and Conflict Resolution argued that there might be a connection between this increase and the then heavy emphasis in newspaper stories on subway suicides. The organization drew up media guidelines and convinced two large-circulation Viennese newspapers to curtail the publicity given to subway suicides. The change in policy occurred in June 1987, and Figure 8.1 shows time-series data indicating a dramatic reduction in subway suicides and suicide attempts after this policy was enacted (Sonneck, Etzersdorfer, & Nagel-Kuess, 1994). Using the symbols that we used earlier (X for treatment or intervention; O for observation or measurement), we can diagram this interrupted time-series design as:

$$O\ O\ O\ O\ O\ O\ O\ X\ O\ O\ O\ O\ O$$

where O is the number (or frequency of occurrence) of subway suicides and suicide attempts in a particular calendar year, and X is the intervention of the media curtailment agreed to by the leading newspapers.

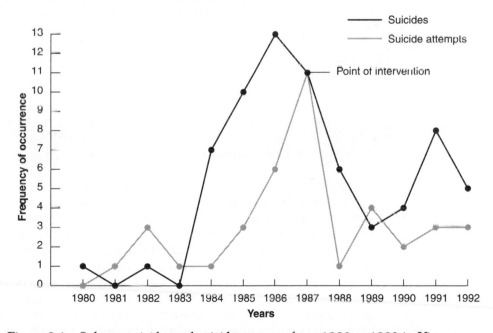

Figure 8.1   Subway suicides and suicide attempts from 1980 to 1992 in Vienna, Austria.

Source: Based on data in G. Sonneck, E. Etzersdorfer, and S. Nagel-Kuess, "Imitative Suicide on the Viennese Subway," *Social Science and Medicine*, 1994, 38, p. 454. Copyright © 1994. Reprinted with permission of Elsevier Science.

What Within-Subjects Designs Are Used in Single-Case Experiments?

A family of nonrandomized designs that is also a mainstay of behavior modification research is **single-case experimental research** (also called *small-N experimental research* and *N-of-1 experimental research*). Traditionally, following the lead of Campbell and Stanley (1963), these designs are conceptualized as a subcategory of interrupted time-series designs. Characteristic of all single-case experimental designs is that they incorporate "treatments" (interventions) that are manipulated and controlled for within a repeated-measures design. What distinguishes them from other experimental and nonexperimental designs is that, in single-case experiments, (a) only one sampling unit is studied, or only a few units are studied; (b) repeated measurements are taken of the unit (a within-subjects design); and (c) random assignment is rarely used. It would, of course, be impossible to assign a single subject at random to the various treatment procedures; instead, the occasions (at intervals of days, weeks, or months) may be assigned at random to the various treatment procedures, and the results are then compared (Hineline & Lattal, 2000).

Although the sampling unit in a single-case design is frequently a single subject (human or animal), it may be a group, such as an assembly line, a class of students, a shift of workers in a plant, or a set of hungry pigeons (see Box 8.3). In one study, the unit was the offensive backfield on a football team of 9- to 10-year-olds; the purpose of the single-case experiment was to test a schedule of feedback

BOX 8.3 Superstition in the Pigeon and the Financial Market

In a fascinating single-case study by B. F. Skinner (1948a), the unit was eight hungry pigeons. The birds were housed in cages in which there was a food hopper (containing grain) that swung into and away from the cage at regular intervals. A timing mechanism automatically moved the hopper into the cage so that all the pigeon had to do was reach into the hopper and eat. But six of the birds developed "superstitious" movements, in that whatever they had been doing in the moment when they were first rewarded with food became imprinted. One pigeon made counterclockwise motions about the cage before taking the grain; another performed a tossing motion of the head; and others persisted in making pendulum-type motions of the head and body or brushing movements toward the floor. Some behavioral economists theorize that this behavior is similar to what goes on in financial markets, where people infer causal connections between two occurrences when, in fact, there is no causal link (Fuerbringer, 1997).

to improve their execution of plays (Komaki & Barnett, 1977). In another case, the sampling unit was a community, and the objective was to encourage drivers to obtain and use child safety seats by presenting them with coupons they could exchange for a seat and training in its use (Lavelle, Hovell, West, & Wahlgren, 1992). In another study, a single-case design was used to evaluate the Great American Smokeout campaign's effect on smoking behavior in a large urban hospital (Hantula, Stillman, & Waranch, 1992).

Single-case experimental designs are often used in educational, clinical, and counseling settings to evaluate the effects of operant conditioning interventions (e.g., I. H. Iversen & Lattal, 1991; Johnston & Pennypacker, 1993a, 1993b; Kazdin, 1992). In operant conditioning (described in Chapter 2), one way to strengthen behavior is to reward the behavior, and one way to weaken behavior is to use extinction (no longer rewarding the response). Such designs use as a **behavioral baseline** the observations of a consistent pattern in the subject's behavior before the experimental treatment (or intervention). That is, a relatively stable pattern of behavior before the treatment or intervention serves as a kind of "pretest" with which details about the pattern of behavior after the treatment can be compared. In this way, the unit (e.g., the subject or group) serves as its own control in a within-subjects design.

As an illustration, a team of psychologists used a single-case design to track the effects of interventions used in the classroom to shape the behavior of a child named Robbie (R. V. Hall, Lund, & Jackson, 1968). The results of this study are shown in Figure 8.2. During the baseline period (a class spelling period), the psychologists

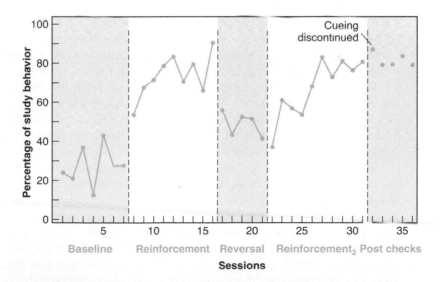

Figure 8.2   Robbie's study behavior record.

Source: Reproduced from R. V. Hall, D. Lund, and D. Jackson, "Effects of Teacher Attention on Study Behavior," *Journal of Applied Behavior Analysis,* 1968, *1,* pp. 1–12. Used by courtesy of R. Vance Hall and the *Journal of Applied Behavior Analysis.*

recorded that Robbie's study behavior was consistently low, ranging from a low point of about 15% of the time to a high point of slightly over 40%, with an average of about 25%. The rest of the time, they observed, Robbie's behavior was disruptive: He snapped rubber bands, played with toys in his pocket, slowly drank his milk and played with the milk carton, and laughed with those around him. Almost 55% of his teacher's attention was absorbed by this disruptive behavior.

The psychologists believed that the teacher's attention was actually maintaining Robbie's disruptive behavior. To modify his poor behavior, they decided to use a twofold intervention: (a) ignoring the nonstudy and disruptive behavior (extinction) and (b) attending to the appropriate study behavior (positive reinforcement). Whenever he engaged in 1 minute of continuous study, the observer would quietly signal the teacher and she would come over and compliment Robbie, saying such things as "Good work, Robbie." The second part of Figure 8.2 shows Robbie's increased study behavior during the nine sessions of this stage of the experiment. Then, to verify the effect of the teacher's attention, the consequences were reversed. The teacher ignored Robbie, remaining with the group. Robbie's study behavior decreased to about 50% over these sessions. When reinforcement was restored, Robbie's study behavior increased to and leveled off at about 75%. A checkup over the following weeks, when the teacher continued to praise Robbie's study behavior, showed that Robbie continued to study. Robbie's spelling performance also improved, with a jump from fewer than 5 words correct out of 10 to 9 correct out of 10.

Instead of Xs and Os, single-case researchers use a different notation system to represent their specific designs. The basic model is called an **A-B-A design**, which evolved out of an even simpler prototype, the **A-B design** (which is the simplest of all single-case designs). In the A phase, no treatment (or intervention) is in effect, and in the B phase, a treatment (or intervention) is operating. The first A in the A-B-A and A-B designs is, therefore, the baseline period. Once the researcher observes steady, continuous behavior in the baseline phase, the treatment (B) is introduced. In other words, the researcher is observing and recording the behavior repeatedly within all phases of the design: the A phase and the B phase. In an A-B design, the dependent variable is measured repeatedly throughout the baseline and intervention phases of the study. In the A-B-A design, the treatment is withdrawn at the end of the B phase and the behavior is measured; that is, there are repeated measures before the treatment, during the treatment, and then when the treatment has been withdrawn.

A number of other single-case designs are used in clinical intervention assessment. In the **A-B-BC-B design**, for example, the B and C are two different therapeutic interventions. The symbols tell us that the individual's behavior is measured or observed (a) before the introduction of either intervention, (b) during Intervention B, (c) during the combination of Intervention B and Intervention C, and (d) during B alone. The purpose of this design is to evaluate the effect of B both in combination with C and apart from C. Notice in this case that the sequence ends with a treatment phase, the reason being that, if the intervention is beneficial, the researcher does not want to end the study on a negative note.

Still another basic variant is the **A-B-A-B design**. The strategy again ends in a treatment phase of B, but this model provides two occasions (B to A and then A to B) for demonstrating the positive effects of the intervention (Hersen & Barlow, 1976). Returning to the illustrative study in Figure 8.2, we can see that it is a simple variant on this design, that is, an **A-B-A-B-A design**. Robbie's behavior was observed (a) before the reinforcement intervention, (b) during the intervention, (c) after removal of the intervention, (d) during its restoration, and (e) after the desired behavior had been shaped by the prior intervention. The advantage of this design is that it allows us to compare Robbie's behavior during different phases, although, as noted, it does not control for threats to internal validity (such as the instrumentation problem). Although the interpretation of single-case results typically depends on visual inspection, there are also statistical techniques for testing predictions in the evaluation of within-subjects results (e.g., Kazdin, 1976; Kratochwill & Levin, 1992; R. Rosenthal & Rosnow, 1985; R. Rosenthal, Rosnow, & Rubin, 2000). (See also Box 8.4.)

BOX 8.4 Randomization in Single-Case Research

On occasion, single-case researchers use designs that are hard to distinguish from randomized experimental designs. An example is a study done by psychologists at the University of Notre Dame (Anderson, Crowell, Hantula, & Siroky, 1988), in which the unit consisted of workers in a student-managed bar. The bar was a haunt of many students and faculty members, but the state board of health threatened to close it after citing health problems (e.g., pervasive accumulations of grease, as well as garbage disposal areas strewn with debris). The psychologists agreed to try to modify the behavior of the students who worked at the bar, and they used a variant on what is called the **A-B-C design**. In this case, the B phase consisted of exposing the workers to a task clarification treatment, and the C phase was a feedback period. What is particularly striking about this single-case research is that the researchers allocated the workers to three groups at random in an effort to control for the delay of feedback. The A phase was the baseline period, in which the workers' usual behavior was recorded. During the B phase, all the workers were instructed in how to work more neatly, and a set of criteria was posted for all to see (e.g., put refrigerated items in the refrigerator, pick up garbage in the men's bathroom, clean bar utensils, and wipe off all games). A week later, each worker in Group 1 was given feedback, which continued for 2 more weeks. The feedback treatment in Group 2 did not begin until 1 week after it had been initiated in Group 1, and the feedback in Group 3 was initiated a week later. Thus, it was possible to compare the effects of immediate and delayed feedback in this combination of a between-subjects (delay of feedback) and within-subjects (A-B-C) design. The result of the behavior modification effort was that sanitary conditions in the bar improved markedly, so much that it was not closed (to the gratification of the students and the researchers).

How Are Correlations Interpreted in Cross-Lagged Panel Designs?

A **cross-lagged panel design** is called *cross-lagged* because some of the data points are treated as temporally "lagged" (delayed) values of the outcome variable. It is called a *panel design* because, in social survey terminology, a *panel study* is another name for a **longitudinal study** (a study that examines the change in a person or a group of people over an extended period of time), and the roots of this design are in longitudinal investigations in sociological survey research (Lazarsfeld, 1978). Figure 8.3 shows the simplest cross-lagged design, where A and B denote two variables, each of which has been measured individually at two successive time periods. The figure shows paired correlations, where the symbol r denotes correlation, and the subscripts are the correlated variables. You will recall that the Pearson r can range from -1.0 (a perfect negative relationship) through 0 (no relationship) to $+1.0$ (a perfect positive relationship). Let us see what each of the correlations in Figure 8.3 tells us.

We will start with r_{A1A2} and r_{B1B2}, which refer to the correlation, respectively, between A at Time 1 and A at Time 2 and between B at Time 1 and B at Time 2. Both these correlations are like **test-retest correlations** that tell us the reliability of each A and B over two time periods. Next, there are r_{A1B1} and r_{A2B2}, which refer to the correlation, respectively, between A and B at Time 1 and A and B at Time 2. These correlations are called **synchronous correlations** (*synchronous* means that A and B are observed or measured in the same period); when we compare them, these two correlations tell us the reliability of the association between A and B over the two time periods. Finally, there are r_{A1B2} and r_{B1A2}, which refer to the correlation, respectively, between A at Time 1 and B at Time 2 and between B at Time 1 and A at Time 2. Both of these correlations are **cross-lagged correlations** that

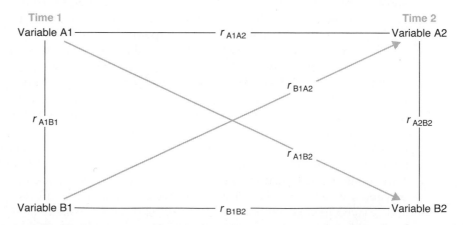

Figure 8.3   **Design for cross-lagged and other correlations between Variables A and B.**

Source: From p. 99 in *Essentials of Behavioral Research: Methods and Data Analysis* (2nd ed.), by Robert Rosenthal and Ralph L. Rosnow. © 1991. Reprinted by permission of The McGraw-Hill Book Companies.

show the relationships between two sets of data points, where one point is treated as a lagged value of the outcome variable.

The causal question concerns whether A is a more likely cause of B than B is of A, or whether A causes B to a greater extent than B causes A. The logic used to arrive at the answer is that, given equally reliable test-retest correlations (r_{A1A2} and r_{B1B2}) and synchronous correlations equal in magnitude (r_{A1B1} and r_{A2B2}), comparing the cross-lagged correlations (r_{A1B2} and r_{B1A2}) will enable us to conclude which is the more likely causal direction, or which variable (A or B) shows the preponderance of causal influence, assuming there is any causal relation. Thus, we suspect that A is a more likely (or more important) "cause" of B than B is of A if r_{A1B2} is appreciably higher than r_{B1A2}. On the other hand, we suspect that B is a more likely (or more important) "cause" of A than A is of B if r_{B1A2} is appreciably higher than r_{A1B2}. An example will show how this design is used and will also illustrate the hidden problem of *confounded hypotheses* (competing confounded pairs of hypotheses).

Figure 8.4 is taken from a correlational study by Kidder, Kidder, and Snyderman (1976). The correlations are based on archival data in the *FBI Uniform Crime Reports* for 1968–1969; the variables noted are the number of police (A) and the number of burglaries (B) in 724 U.S. cities during each year. Looking first at the test-retest correlations (.86 and .89), we see that both the number of police and the number of burglaries were quite reliable during this 2-year period. In other words, cities with a lot of police in 1968 had a lot of police in 1969, and also cities with a lot of burglaries in 1968 continued to have a lot of burglaries in 1969. The synchronous correlations of .47 and .39 between number of police and number of burglaries for 1968 and 1969, respectively, were substantial in magnitude.

At first glance, our intuition says that burglaries may cause an increase in the number of police. The problem of confounded hypotheses is that it might just as well be hypothesized that police increase burglaries, because the more police there

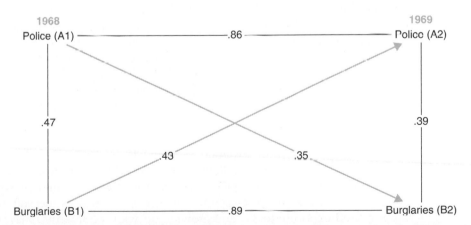

Figure 8.4   Correlation of number of police and number of burglaries per capita measured in 1968 and 1969 in 724 cities.

Source: Adapted from L. H. Kidder, R. L. Kidder, and P. Snyderman, 1976, by permission of L. H. Kidder.

are available, the more opportunities there are to keep thorough records of all the burglaries reported. That is, when there are not many police, some reported burglaries may go unrecorded. The cross-lagged correlations do not allow us to definitively rule out either competing hypothesis and, in fact, provide some support for both (.43 and .35). If you think carefully, you are sure to come up with other rival hypotheses. There are statistical ways of trying to rule out rival causal hypotheses in cross-lagged designs, but they also are not without problems (Campbell & Stanley, 1963; Kenny, 1979; Pelz & Andrew, 1964; Rogosa, 1980; Rozelle & Campbell, 1969). Although the cross-lagged panel strategy is no longer as popular as it once was, some leading methodologists continue to emphasize its usefulness as an exploratory procedure in the analysis of longitudinal data (Campbell & Kenny, 1999; cf. Kenny & Campbell, 1984, 1989).

What Is the Purpose of Longitudinal Research Using Cohorts?

Earlier in this chapter, we mentioned the Framingham heart study as an example of longitudinal research. You will recall that the defining characteristic of this kind of research is that individuals are observed or measured repeatedly through time. This design contrasts with a **cross-sectional design**, in which outcomes are measured for each individual during one period. Suppose we wanted to study the life course of some variable of interest. It is simpler, and certainly less costly, to sample different age groups during one time period than to try to follow individuals throughout their lives. However, the vital question is whether the cross-sectional results will give as accurate an account of the life course of the variable as a longitudinal study in which we follow a group of people throughout their lives.

For example, suppose we do a cross-sectional survey in 2007 to study the maturational effects of some variable of interest in people born in 1957, 1967, 1977, 1987, and 1997. The aim of our survey is to develop a growth curve of the outcomes of interest in people who are 10, 20, 30, 40, and 50 years old. Each of these age groups is called a **cohort**, a sociological term that means any group sharing a given trait, usually age. Thus, a group of people born around the same time and having had similar life experiences constitutes a cohort. In this case, there is a 10-year difference between the cohort born in 1957 and the cohort born in 1967. Usually a *generation* is defined as 20 years, so a "generation gap" generally implies a 20-year difference between cohorts (e.g., between the cohort born in 1957 and the cohort born in 1977).

The problem with our cross-sectional design is that those who are 40 in 2007 may have had different life experiences at age 10 (in 1977) from those who are 10 years old in 2007. That is, it is likely that children who are born and grow up in one period have life events quite different from those of children who are born and grow up in another period. Some experiences (such as the children's schooling, repeated exposure to TV, and growing up with the Internet) may, in turn, systematically alter what is considered "normal" in the two groups. The problem is that a possible confounding of cohort and maturation is hidden in a design that fails to look at several cohorts longitudinally. If life experiences are associated

| Table 8.3 | Percentages of Women in the Netherlands With No Religious Affiliation According to Age and Time Period |

	Period 1 (1909)	Period 2 (1929)	Period 3 (1949)	Period 4 (1969)
Age 20–30	Cohort 4 4.8	Cohort 5 13.9	Cohort 6 17.4	Cohort 7 23.9
Age 40–50	Cohort 3 3.1	Cohort 4 11.9	Cohort 5 17.2	Cohort 6 22.0
Age 60–70	Cohort 2 1.9	Cohort 3 6.7	Cohort 4 11.9	Cohort 5 19.4
Age 80–	Cohort 1 1.2	Cohort 2 3.8	Cohort 3 6.6	Cohort 4 12.2

Note: An example of a cross-sectional design is shown by the vertical analysis (Period 4), and an example of a longitudinal design is shown by the diagonal analysis (Cohort 4).

Source: Reproduced from "Age, Cohort and Period: A General Model for the Analysis of Social Change" by J. A. Hagenaars and N. P. Cobben, 1978, *Netherlands Journal of Sociology, 14,* pp. 58–91. Used by permission of J. A. Hagenaars and Elsevier Science Publishers.

with the variable of interest, we may draw spurious conclusions about maturational effects by relying solely on a cross-sectional design.

Table 8.3 illustrates how the relationship between maturation (age) and another variable may be misinterpreted because of a reliance on the results of cross-sectional studies instead of on the results of longitudinal studies of cohorts. This table shows the results of a study done in the Netherlands by Jacques A. Hagenaars and Niki P. Cobben (1978), in which data were compiled on the percentages of women with no religious affiliation, by age and time period. The results are shown for seven different cohorts (generations) of women in the Netherlands. The values in the vertical rectangle beneath Period 4 provide the basic data for a cross-sectional analysis, and the values in the parallelogram for Cohort 4 provide the basic data for a longitudinal analysis. Notice that the trends are opposite in these two sets of values and therefore lead to completely opposite conclusions.

A graph showing this difference appears in Figure 8.5; it allows us to compare the cross-sectional data for Period 4 (1969) with the longitudinal data for Cohort 4 in Table 8.3. The cross-sectional curve would mislead us to the conclusion that, with the passing of years and the approach of the end of life, religious observance increased (i.e., the percentage of nonaffiliation decreased) in these women. By contrast, the cohort curve tells us that the opposite is true: Religious observance actually decreased (i.e., the percentage of nonaffiliation increased) in these women as they became older.

Researchers who generally use longitudinal designs—including animal researchers (e.g., Fairbanks, 1993)—also attempt, whenever possible, to examine several cohorts cross-sectionally and longitudinally. In this way they learn about cohort changes as

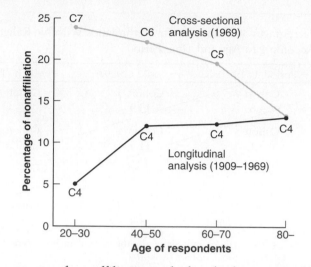

Figure 8.5 **Percentages of nonaffiliation with church of women in the Netherlands, as shown by a cross-sectional design in 1969 and a longitudinal design from 1909 to 1969.** Cohorts are symbolized as C7 (Cohort 7), C6 (Cohort 6), and so forth.

Source: Reproduced from J. A. Hagenaars and N. P. Cobben, "Age, Cohort and Period: A General Model for the Analysis of Social Change," *Netherlands Journal of Sociology,* 1978, *14,* pp. 58–91. Used by permission of J. A. Hagenaars and Elsevier Science Publishers.

well as age group changes as a function of period. Other informative uses of longitudinal designs are possible, but each is limited in certain predictable ways, and the data analysis is usually complex because it must deal with various methodological issues (e.g., Diggle, Liang, & Zeger, 1996). You will find a further discussion of a number of these designs and related issues in our advanced text (Rosenthal & Rosnow, 2008). However, as stated earlier, it is prudent to use several strategies that allow convergence on the question or phenomenon of interest. Each approach and procedure is always limited in some way, but the idea is to use methods whose strengths and weaknesses will compensate for one another.

Summary of Ideas

1. The observed data in nonrandomized research may be *prospective* (collected as behavior or a reaction is followed forward in time, as in the anecdote about the doctor treating a patient for a dog bite) or *retrospective* (collected back in time, e.g., as extracted from historical records in the epidemiological study of the cause of food poisoning).

2. *Quasi-experimental research* (the general term for the families of nonrandomized research in this chapter) resembles randomized experimental research in some respects but does not use random assignment (Box 8.1).

3. The *third-variable problem* in nonrandomized research is that an uncontrolled or unmeasured variable that is correlated *with X* (a presumed causal variable) and *Y* (the presumed effect of *X*) may account for the association between *X* and *Y*, so that this "third variable" is the actual determinant of both *X* and *Y* (e.g., age as a determinant of foot size and spelling ability, and the case of the strange medical symptoms).

4. In nonequivalent-groups designs with large relevant subgroups, comparability of the "treated" and "untreated" subjects may be achieved by subclassification on *propensity scores* (e.g., the study of nonsmokers, cigarette smokers, and pipe and cigar smokers in three large databases).

5. The use of *wait-list controls* may overcome objections to a randomized design if the objections are based on the ethical cost of depriving control subjects of the benefits of the treatment given to the experimental subjects (Box 8.2).

6. *Interrupted time-series designs* compare the "effects" of an intervention in the situation before and after it occurs (e.g., the Vienna subway study).

7. *Single-case experimental designs* come in many different forms (e.g., *A-B-BC-B* and *A-B-A-B*); the unit of study may be an *N* of 1 (e.g., the study of Robbie) or a few subjects (Skinner's study of superstition in pigeons in Box 8.3) or several groups of individuals with one of the treatments randomized (the *A-B-C* study in Box 8.4).

8. In the *cross-lagged panel approach*, some data points are treated as temporally delayed values, and the *cross-lagged correlations* are analyzed along with the *test-retest* and the *synchronous correlations* for the direction of causation (e.g., the retrospective data study of the number of police and the number of burglaries).

9. *Longitudinal research* means that the variable of interest is observed in such a way as to uncover changes that occur over time, such as studying the "life course" of some variable.

10. In studies in which age is the independent variable, a *cross-sectional analysis* of a life course variable may lead to spurious conclusions (e.g., women's religiosity in the Netherlands).

Key Terms

A-B design   p. 188
A-B-A design   p. 188
A-B-A-B design   p. 188
A-B-A-B-A design (the Robbie study)   p. 189
A-B-BC-B design   p. 188
A-B-C design   p. 189
behavioral baseline   p. 187
cohort   p. 192
cross-lagged correlations p. 190
cross-lagged panel design p. 190

cross-sectional design   p. 192
interrupted time-series design   p. 184
longitudinal study   p. 190
nonequivalent-groups designs   p. 182
propensity score   p. 183
prospective data   p. 178
quasi-experimental research p. 180
retrospective data   p. 178
single-case experimental research   p. 186

synchronous correlations (in cross-lagged panel designs) p. 190
test-retest correlations (in cross-lagged panel designs) p. 190
third-variable problem p. 180
time-series designs   p. 184
wait-list control group p. 182

Multiple-Choice Questions for Review

1. Which of the following is definitely not characteristic of quasi experimental designs? (a) experimental group; (b) randomization; (c) control group; (d) repeated measurement

2. A researcher at North Carolina State University develops a new treatment program for alcoholism. He allows the participants to choose whether they want to be in the experimental group or the control group. This is an example of a (a) true experimental design; (b) nonequivalent-groups design; (c) time-series design; (d) cohort design.

3. In large-sample nonequivalent-groups designs, the comparability of "treated" and "untreated" subjects (a) may be improved by subclassification on propensity scores; (b) is also going to be suspect whatever we do; (c) is no worse than in a similar randomized experiment; (d) all of the above.

4. One type of research design involves measuring a single variable on many separate occasions and assessing the impact of interventions on this variable. This type of design is called a (a) correlational design; (b) cohort design; (c) cross-sectional design; (d) time-series design.

5. A behavioral therapist at Northeastern University is working with autistic children. He decides first to observe their baseline levels of disruptive behavior and then to observe their behavior several times after administering his intervention. He then removes his intervention to determine whether the disruptive behavior will return to baseline levels. This type of design can be described as an (a) A-B design; (b) A-B-C design; (c) A-B-A design; (d) A-B-A-C design.

6. A study examining changes in individuals over an extended period of time is called a (a) longitudinal study; (b) quasi-longitudinal study; (c) nonequivalent-groups design; (d) time-series study.

7. A researcher at the University of Montana conducts a study on the relationship between watching TV (Variable A) and violent behavior (Variable B). She measures both variables at two points in time. She calculates the correlation between watching TV at Time 1 and watching TV at Time 2. This is an example of a(n) _____ correlation. (a) internal validity; (b) test-retest; (c) synchronous; (d) cross-lagged

8. The same researcher calculates the correlation between watching TV at Time 2 and violent behavior at Time 2. This is an example of a(n) _____ correlation. (a) internal consistency; (b) test-retest; (c) synchronous; (d) cross-lagged

9. In the study above, this researcher also calculates the correlation between watching TV at Time 1 and violent behavior at Time 2. This is an example of a(n) _____ correlation. (a) internal validity; (b) test-retest; (c) synchronous; (d) cross-lagged

10. The same researcher finds that $r_{A1B2} = .30$ and $r_{B1A2} = .02$. These results suggest that (a) it is more likely that watching TV causes violent behavior; (b) it is more likely that violent behavior causes TV watching; (c) there is no causal relationship between watching TV and violent behavior; (d) watching TV and violent behavior have reciprocal causal effects.

Discussion Questions for Review

1. A University of Toledo student wants to assess the possible causal relationship between therapist approval, which is expressed in tone of voice, and degree of patient progress. Using a sample of 45 therapist-patient dyads, he measures these variables at the beginning and end of treatment. From the results shown below, what do you think he will conclude?

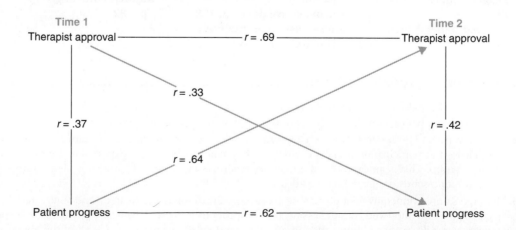

2. Using a cross-sectional design, an Oklahoma University student found a lower degree of androgyny in women aged 40–45 than in women aged 20–25. What confounding variable prevents him from concluding that androgyny decreases with age? Can you think of a better way to do the study?

3. A Catholic University student wants to do a time-series analysis of the effects of assassination attempts against U.S. presidents but cannot decide on the dependent variable. What dependent variable would you advise her to track, and how would you suggest she locate the kind of data she needs for such a study?

Answers to Review Questions

Multiple-Choice Questions

1. b	3. a	5. c	7. b	9. d
2. b	4. d	6. a	8. c	10. a

Discussion Questions

1. Since (a) the test-retest correlations are similar to each other, (b) the synchronous correlations are similar to each other, and (c) the cross-lagged correlations differ appreciably from each other (.64 versus .33), it might be reasonable for him to conclude a preponderance of causal influence of the patient progress variable over the therapist approval variable.

2. The cohort of women is confounded with their age, so the student cannot tell whether age or cohort differences or both are reflected in the obtained differences. For example, it may be that the women aged 40–45 have been showing an *increasing* degree of androgyny as they developed from age 20–25 to age 40–45. A longitudinal design of the type shown in Table 8.3 would be a better way to do this study.

3. Some dependent variables that may reflect presidential assassination attempts are stock market figures, mental-health-facility-usage data, gun-control legislation activity, the number of people announcing for elective positions, views of the United States reflected in the foreign press, and changes in party affiliation. Reference librarians can help her find the government and other documents that carry the needed information. These documents are also a rich source of ideas for other dependent variables for which data are available.

CHAPTER 9

Survey Research and Subject Recruitment

Preview Questions

- What are opportunity and probability samples?
- What is meant by *bias* and *instability* in survey research?
- Why is bias in sampling such an elusive concept?
- How can I do simple random sampling?
- What are stratified random sampling and area probability sampling?
- What did the *Literary Digest* case teach pollsters?
- What are point estimates and interval estimates?
- What are the benefits of stratification?
- How is nonresponse bias handled in survey research?
- What are the typical characteristics of volunteer subjects?
- How is volunteer bias in opportunity samples managed?

What Are Opportunity and Probability Samples?

In the two preceding chapters, we examined the logic and limitations of various randomized and nonrandomized designs for empirical studies. As a leading statistician remarked, "In a sense all studies lie on a continuum from irrelevant to relevant with respect to answering a question" (D. B. Rubin, 1974, p. 699). For example, a randomized experiment in a college setting may have a restricted sample of subjects but more control over the variables of interest. On the other hand, a non-equivalent-groups experiment in a natural setting may allow less control over the manipulated treatment (or intervention) but may be less constrained as to the participants. In this chapter, we turn our attention to the selection of research participants. When experimenters are interested in learning about human nature in general, they often use **opportunity samples**, the first units that are available, rather than use special sampling procedures to select the participants. By contrast, survey researchers would say that, as they are interested in generalizing their findings to a very specific larger pool (**population**) of people, respondents from *sampling lists* (or *sampling frames*) identify the relevant units or subgroups in the population. If they use opportunity samples, spurious results and misleading conclusions may compromise their work.

For example, pollsters often use survey designs to map out some specified population's opinions on important societal issues, such as a community's fears of crime or its choice of political candidates. Similar methods are sometimes used in epidemiological research, forensic research, economic research, and many other areas. When health officials wanted to find out about national trends in cases of tuberculosis contracted on the job, they did surveys of hospitals to count employees reported to have TB (Kilborn, 1994). As the federal courts became inundated with mass torts involving asbestos cases (averaging 1,140 per month in 1990, or one third of the federal criminal caseload), one solution was to sample asbestos cases from the larger pool within a court's jurisdiction. The assessed damages in randomly chosen cases from each of five disease categories were then applied to each larger pool (Saks & Blanck, 1992). More recently, when researchers wanted to study the prevalence of psychological resilience after a traumatic event, they did a probability sample of New Yorkers in the 6 months following the September 11, 2001, terrorist attack on the World Trade Center and observed that resilience was present in two thirds of the sample and never fell below one third even among highly exposed individuals with posttraumatic stress disorder (Bonanno, Galea, Bucciarelli, & Vhahov, 2006).

Instead of questioning every member of the population (which is usually impossible), this type of research focuses on a segment (or **sample**) that is believed to be typical of the population. How can researchers be certain that the segment is **representative** (or typical) of the population? How can they be certain, for example, that the percentage of fear of crime in the sample is typical of the percentage in a whole specified population, or know that the reported TB cases in sampled hospitals are representative of trends in all similar hospitals, or know that a sample of a couple thousand New York residents adequately represents the broader New York population? They can compare the sample with the most recent census data, though it is well known that census data are problematic because it is impossible to contact every member of the population. Thus, the answer is that researchers who use a sample can never be 100% sure of their results. They can make a reasonable guess, however, by first developing an accurate sampling frame that defines the target population and then relying on a carefully designed blueprint (the **sampling plan**) to select the sample by means of probability sampling. The term **probability sampling** implies that randomness enters into the selection process (i.e., random selection) at some stage so that the laws of mathematical probability apply; **probability** refers to the mathematical chance of an event's occurring. Examples of probability are the likelihood of getting "heads" when you flip a coin once (1 chance in 2) or getting a 2 when you throw a die once (1 chance in 6).

Although survey studies take many different forms, all use sampling plans in which some method of probability sampling determines the random selection of the subjects. Such plans enable the researcher to assume reasonably—but with no guarantee of being correct—that the sample is representative of its population. However, practical problems may impose limits on the representativeness of the sample. Even in the most carefully conducted survey, not everyone in the sample can be reached and, of those who are actually contacted, not everyone will agree to participate. For example, in the study of psychological resilience after the September 11 terrorist attack, a random digit-dialing approach was used to contact members of the sample. When the number of completed and partial interviews was summed and this total was divided by the sum of all numbers that were either eligible as residential telephone numbers or of unknown eligibility, the response rate was estimated to be 34% (Bonanno et al., 2006). Later in this chapter, we will discuss how survey researchers confront the nonresponse problem, and also how experimenters who use opportunity samples of volunteer subjects cope with the problem of volunteer bias. We will begin, however, by describing some basic concepts in survey sampling and then illustrate the logic of probability sampling plans. (Remember not to confuse *random selection* with *random assignment*. As we explained earlier, random assignment is the unbiased allocation of units to groups or conditions; its purpose is to control differences in the groups or conditions to be compared.)

What Is Meant by Bias and Instability in Survey Research?

Survey research is done not only by private organizations (the Gallup Organization and Louis Harris & Associates, among others), but by individual researchers working alone or with ties to private organizations (e.g., the Research Triangle Institute in North Carolina), and in the United States at university-based institutes that can implement face-to-face and telephone interviewing in national probability surveys (such as the University of Chicago's National Opinion Research Center, the University of Michigan's Institute for Social Research, and Temple University's Institute for Survey Research). Although this research takes many different forms, all valid survey research is characterized by sampling plans in which every element, or sampling unit, in the population has a known nonzero probability of being selected at each draw. Two important statistical requirements of a probability sampling plan are (a) that the sample values be unbiased and (b) that there be stability in the samples.

To be **unbiased**, the values produced by the sample must, on average, coincide with the "true" values of the population—though we can never actually be sure that this requirement has been met in a given study unless we already know those values. **Stability** means that there is not much variability (or spread) in the sample values. Stability is estimated by statistical procedures such as the variance and the standard deviation (which are described in the next chapter). Figure 9.1 will help you to understand these two technical requirements more clearly. In the design, the O is a particular sampling unit, the X represents the true population mean, and the horizontal line represents the underlying continuum on which the relevant values are determined. The beauty of sampling theory is that it can be applied not only to individual respondents but also to teams in a population of teams

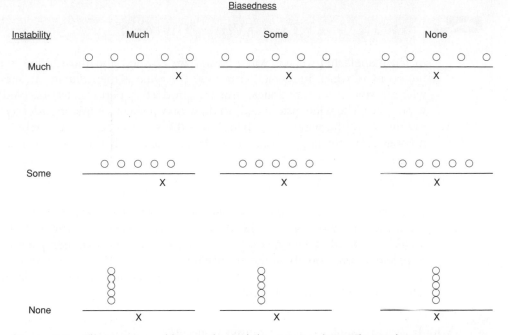

Figure 9.1   Illustrations of bias and instability in sampling. The circles represent sampling units located on some dimension, and X represents the population mean.

Source: From p. 208 in *Essentials of Behavioral Research: Methods and Data Analysis* (2nd. ed.) by Robert Rosenthal and Ralph L. Rosnow. Copyright © 1991. Reprinted by permission of The McGraw-Hill Book Companies.

(e.g., Little League baseball teams), or to products on an assembly line, or to any other specified population of animate or inanimate units.

Suppose we want to estimate the number of widgets made by assembly-line workers in a given period. In Figure 9.1, we now think of O as a work team's output, X is the value that we are trying to estimate (i.e., the true population value, or number of widgets, on the average, that are made by all the teams of assembly-line workers). The distance between the true population value and the midpoint of the sampling units indicates the amount of **bias** (i.e., systematic error). The spread (variability) among the sampling units indicates their degree of instability. We see that the amount of instability is constant within each row, going from a high amount of instability (or spread) in row 1 to no instability in row 3. The amount of bias is constant in each column, going from a high bias in column 1 to zero bias in column 3. Thus, in the three cases in column 3, the sample values are balanced around the population mean, but with much instability in row 1, some in row 2, and none in row 3. In the three cases in row 3, there is no instability, but there is much bias in column 1, some in column 2, and none in column 3. The hypothetical case at the intersection of row 3 and column 3 represents the best of all situations, though it is unlikely that we will ever find such complete agreement.

BOX 9.1 The Wine Taster

In the manufacture of red wine, grapes are crushed and the residue is put into huge vats in which fermentation occurs. The wine is then drawn off into barrels, where fermentation continues, and the product is periodically sampled by the wine taster. The wine taster needs to draw only a small sample in order to evaluate the quality of the wine in the barrel. It is the same in survey research: The more homogeneous the population, the smaller the sample that needs to be drawn.

Generally speaking, the more *homogeneous* (alike) the members of the population are, the fewer of them need to be sampled (see also Box 9.1). If all widget makers are exactly alike (the case in row 3, column 3), *any* sampling unit will provide complete information about the population as a whole. The more *heterogeneous* (dissimilar) the different teams are, the more sampling units we will need to ensure a sample of the full range of dissimilarity.

Why Is Bias in Sampling Such an Elusive Concept?

We said that we can never really know "for sure" whether there is bias in the results. However, there *is* one way to know for certain, and that is to examine every single member of the population and the sample *at the same time* the sampling is done. If the pattern of replies in the sample exactly matches the pattern of replies in the population, we know for certain that there is no sampling bias in the survey sample. Later in this chapter, we give an illustration where we are, in fact, able to sample from a completely known population of values. Of course, this procedure, practically speaking, makes no sense because we have no need of a sample if we know the responses of everyone in the population.

It is also sometimes said that election forecasting allows us to know for certain whether a sample is biased because we can compare the predicted results with the actual results. However, the problem is that we are comparing data obtained at one point in time with the results at another point in time. Still, a well-designed and carefully executed selection process involving probability sampling can produce data that are remarkably close to the election results. For example, Gallup Survey records in U.S. presidential elections show discrepancies that are extremely small. In the 1996 election, the final election poll conducted by the Gallup Organization for *USA Today* and CNN, using 1,448 "likely voters" who were sampled on November 3–4, 1996, predicted that Bill Clinton would win 48%, Robert Dole 40%, and Ross Perot 6% of the vote. The prediction that Clinton would top Dole by 8% was right on the mark, and the specific vote predictions were close to the actual election result of 49% for Clinton, 41% for Dole, and 8% for Perot (Kagay, 1996). Polls conducted close to the election are usually better predictors than early polls, but there is no guarantee that voters will not change their minds between the poll and the election. In the 1996 election, many early polls reported a landslide 15 percentage point lead by Clinton, which may have made some Clinton supporters complacent and therefore less likely to show up to vote. In the 2000 election, the final difference between George W. Bush and Al Gore was razor thin in some states, and not surprisingly, final polls were in some disagreement about which candidate would ultimately be the victor.

In the 2004 presidential election, most of the polls taken in the final days just before the election had George W. Bush winning the popular vote by a percentage point or two, and those polls that did not were usually within the margin of error of plus-or-minus 3 percentage points. The research firms that designed the exit polling system used by news organizations in the 2004 election mistakenly showed John Kerry leading, however. One suspected reason for this glitch was that half the surveyors were 34 or younger, and it appears that they were more successful in securing interviews with Kerry supporters as they left polling places than with Bush supporters (Steinberg, 2005).

How Can I Do Simple Random Sampling?

The basic prototype of probability sampling is called **simple random sampling**. The *simple* tells us that the sample is selected from an undivided population, and *random* means that the sample is to be chosen by a process that will give every sampling unit in the population the same chance of being selected at each draw (see also Box 9.2). In order for this to occur, the selection of one unit must have

BOX 9.2 Randomness and Aimlessness

Don't confuse randomness with *aimlessness,* or "hit-or-miss" sampling, which, in fact, can seldom be called random. You can prove the difference to yourself by asking a friend to write down "at random" several hundred one-digit numbers from 0 to 9. Afterward, tabulate the 0s, 1s, 2s, and so on. If the numbers were truly random, there would be few obvious sequences, and each digit would occur approximately 10% of the time. You will find, however, that the results are inconsistent with the hypothesis of randomness. You will see obvious sequences, and some digits will occur with high frequency, whereas others will appear hardly at all (Wallis & Roberts, 1956). Interestingly, however, psychologist Allen Neuringer, using a single-case experimental strategy, was able to reinforce pigeons in making left-right choices that looked pretty random (Neuringer, 1992). He then used feedback to reinforce individual Reed College students to generate sequences of numbers that also closely resembled random sequences (Neuringer, 1996; Neuringer & Voss, 1993).

no influence on the selection of other units. In simple random sampling, a further requirement is that we have knowledge of the existence of all the units in the population (such as a list of names of everyone in the population). The idea is to draw units (e.g., names) one at a time until we have as large a sample as we require. The actual method of selecting people might consist of throwing dice, having a computer draw units at random, using a table of random digits, or even spinning a roulette wheel or drawing capsules from an urn. In doing phone interviewing (described in Chapter 5), random digit dialing is used to include people with unlisted numbers; the researcher selects the first three digits according to the geographic area of interest and then uses a computer program to select the last four digits.

Procedures such as drawing capsules from an urn provide the least complex approach, but they are not without potential problems. A famous case illustrating the hazards of inadequate randomization occurred in 1970. The previous year, while the war in Vietnam was in progress, the U.S. Congress had passed a bill allowing the use of a random lottery to select conscripts for the armed forces. To give each individual an equal chance of being selected or not selected, the planners decided to pick birthdays out of an urn. The 365 days of the year were written on slips of paper and placed inside tiny cylindrical capsules. Once all the capsules were inside the urn, it was shaken for several hours, and then the capsules were removed, one by one. However, the results were found to be biased in spite of the precautions taken to ensure an unbiased sample: The birth dates in December tended to be drawn first, those in November next, then those in October, and so on. The reason was that the January capsules were put in the urn first, the February capsules next, and so forth, and layers were formed with the December capsules on top. Even shaking the urn for several hours did not ensure a thorough mixing of the capsules (Broome, 1984; Kolata, 1986).

The use of a table of random digits, such as Table 9.1, helps us to avoid such pitfalls. The 2,250 digits in this list came from a million random digits that were generated by an electronic roulette wheel programmed to produce a random frequency pulse every tiny fraction of a second (Rand Corporation, 1955). As a check on the hypothesis of impartiality, the computer counted the frequency of 0s, 1s, 2s, and so on in the final results. A probability method that is impartial would produce an approximately equal number of 0s, 1s, 2s, and so on in the overall table of a million random digits. This equality is exactly what was observed. In Chapter 7, we showed how to use the random numbers in this table to allocate subjects to experimental and control conditions (i.e., how to do random assignment).

To see how you might use this table if you were doing a survey (i.e., a random selection), imagine you want to conduct a public opinion poll, and you decide to interview 10 men and 10 women individually after choosing them at random from a list of 96 men and a list of 99 women. You begin by numbering the population of men consecutively from 01 to 96 and the population of women from 01 to 99. You are now ready to use the random digits in Table 9.1. To do so, you put your finger blindly on a starting position. You can start anywhere in the table and then move your finger in any direction, as long as you do not pick a set of numbers because they "look right" or avoid a set of numbers because they "don't look right." Suppose you

2,250 Random Digits

Rows	1–5	6–10	11–15	16–20	Columns 21–25	26–30	31–35	36–40	41–45	46–50
1	10097	32533	76520	13586	34673	54876	80959	09117	39292	74945
2	37542	04805	64894	74296	24805	24037	20636	10402	00822	91665
3	08422	68953	19645	09303	23209	02560	15953	34764	35080	33605
4	99019	02529	09376	70715	38311	31165	88676	74397	04436	27659
5	12807	99970	80157	36147	64032	36653	98951	16877	12171	76833
6	66065	74717	34072	76850	36697	36170	65813	39885	11199	29170
7	31060	10805	45571	82406	35303	42614	86799	07439	23403	09732
8	85269	77602	02051	65692	68665	74818	73053	85247	18623	88579
9	63573	32135	05325	47048	90553	57548	28468	28709	83491	25624
10	73796	45753	03529	64778	35808	34282	60935	20344	35273	88435
11	98520	17767	14905	68607	22109	40558	60970	93433	50500	73998
12	11805	05431	39808	27732	50725	68248	29405	24201	52775	67851
13	83452	99634	06288	98083	13746	70078	18475	40610	68711	77817
14	88685	40200	86507	58401	36766	67951	90364	76493	29609	11062
15	99594	67348	87517	64969	91826	08928	93785	61368	23478	34113
16	65481	17674	17468	50950	58047	76974	73039	57186	40218	16544
17	80124	35635	17727	08015	45318	22374	21115	78253	14385	53763
18	74350	99817	77402	77214	43236	00210	45521	64237	96286	02655
19	69916	26803	66252	29148	36936	87203	76621	13990	94400	56418
20	09893	20505	14225	68514	46427	56788	96297	78822	54382	14598
21	91499	14523	68479	27686	46162	83554	94750	89923	37089	20048
22	80336	94598	26940	36858	70297	34135	53140	33340	42050	82341
23	44104	81949	85157	47954	32979	26575	57600	40881	22222	06413
24	12550	73742	11100	02040	12860	74697	96644	89439	28707	25815
25	63606	49329	16505	34484	40219	52563	43651	77082	07207	31790
26	61196	90446	26457	47774	51924	33729	65394	59593	42582	60527
27	15474	45266	95270	79953	59367	83848	82396	10118	33211	59466
28	94557	28573	67897	54387	54622	44431	91190	42592	92927	45973
29	42481	16213	97344	08721	16868	48767	03071	12059	25701	46670
30	23523	78317	73208	89837	68935	91416	26252	29663	05522	82562
31	04493	52494	75246	33824	45862	51025	61962	79335	65337	12472
32	00549	97654	64051	88159	96119	63896	54692	82391	23287	29529
33	35963	15307	26898	09354	33351	35462	77974	50024	90103	39333
34	59808	08391	45427	26842	83609	49700	13021	24892	78565	20106
35	46058	85236	01390	92286	77281	44077	93910	83647	70617	42941
36	32179	00597	87379	25241	05567	07007	86743	17157	85394	11838
37	69234	61406	20117	45204	15956	60000	18743	92423	97118	96338
38	19565	41430	01758	75379	40419	21585	66674	36806	84962	85207
39	45155	14938	19476	07246	43667	94543	59047	90033	20826	69541
40	94864	31994	36168	10851	34888	81553	01540	35456	05014	51176
41	98086	24826	45240	28404	44999	08896	39094	73407	35441	31880
42	33185	16232	41941	50949	89435	48581	88695	41994	37548	73043
43	80951	00406	96382	70774	20151	23387	25016	25298	94624	61171
44	79752	49140	71961	28296	69861	02591	74852	20539	00387	59579
45	18633	32537	98145	06571	31010	24674	05455	61427	77938	91936

Source: From *A Million Random Digits with 100,000 Normal Deviates*, 1955, New York: Free Press. Reprinted by permission of the Rand Corporation.

put your finger on the first five-digit number in row 5, column 1. Beginning with this number, 12807, you will read across the line two digits at a time, selecting the men numbered 12, 80, 79, 99, and so on, until you have randomly chosen the 10 male interviewees. You do the same thing, beginning at another blindly chosen point, to select the 10 female interviewees. If you have fewer than 10 persons on each list, you will need to read only one digit at a time. If you have between 100 and 999 persons on your list, you will need to read three digits at a time, and so forth.

Suppose you choose the same two-digit number more than once, or suppose you choose a two-digit number not represented by any member of the population. In either case, you go on to the next two-digit number in the row (that is, unless you are sampling with replacement, as discussed next). What if your population is so small that you are forced to skip many numbers in the table because they are larger than the largest number of people in your population? For example, what if there are 450 people in the population and you want to select 50 people at random? Because the population is numbered from 001 to 450, you will have to skip approximately one half the three-digit numbers in the section of the table you have chosen (i.e., those from 451 to 999). As a simple solution (also acceptable in terms of randomness), you may mentally subtract 500 from any number in the range from 501 to 999. This additional option will result in fewer unusable selections.

Another option in some situations is sampling with or without replacement. **Sampling with replacement** means that the selected names are placed in the selection pool again and may be reselected on subsequent draws. Thus, every unit in the population continues to have the same probability of being chosen every time a number is read. To do sampling with replacement, we have to select items one at a time. For example, suppose the sampling units are days of the year sealed in tiny capsules in an urn stirred so completely that there are no layers or nonrandom clusters. We simply select a capsule, read it, and put it back, so that the same capsule may be selected more than once.

In **sampling without replacement**, a previously selected name cannot be reselected and must be disregarded on any later draw. The population shrinks each time you remove a name, but all the names remaining still have the same likelihood of being drawn on the next occasion. For example, if you scoop a handful of capsules, record each, and then discard those you picked, this would be sampling without replacement. Either option is technically acceptable, but survey researchers usually prefer sampling without replacement because they do not want to use the same sampling units twice or more. For example, the wine taster (Box 9.1) who draws and then spits out a small sample of wine is also doing simple random sampling without replacement. We wouldn't have it any other way!

What Are Stratified Random Sampling and Area Probability Sampling?

Simple random sampling is useful when the population is known to be homogeneous or when its precise composition is unknown. When we know something about the exact composition, there is a more efficient method of sampling, in which we sample from the different substrates of the population. Professional polling organizations typically use this approach to probability sampling, that is, randomly selecting sampling units (persons or households) from several subpopulations (termed *strata* or *clusters*) into which the population is divided. For example, if we know the population is 60% female and 40% male (a ratio of 3 to 2), and that gender is a pertinent variable, we can improve our sampling procedure by selecting subsamples proportionate in size to this 3:2 ratio of females to males.

Called **stratified random sampling**, this procedure is a very efficient way of probability sampling. That is, a separate sample is randomly selected from each homogeneous stratum (or "layer") of the population. The stratum means are then statistically weighted to form a combined estimate for the entire population. In a survey of political opinions, for example, it might be useful to stratify the population according to party affiliation, gender, socioeconomic status, and other meaningful categories related to voting behavior. This method ensures that we have enough women, men, Democrats, Republicans, and so on to draw descriptive or correlational conclusions about each respective subgroup. We will have more to say about this method of sampling shortly.

A popular variant of this sampling strategy is called **area probability sampling**, because the population is divided into geographic areas (i.e., population clusters or strata). This method is applicable to any population divisible into meaningful geographic areas related to the variables of interest. For example, depending on the variables of interest, meaningful geographic areas might be people living in urban neighborhoods, Inuits in igloos, or nomads in tents. The assumption is that, within each of the areas, the sampling units will have the same probability of being chosen. The sampling procedure can be more complicated than those described above, but the method is cost-effective because the research design can be used repeatedly with only minor modifications. Suppose a polling organization needs an area probability sample of 300 out of 6,000 estimated housing units in a city, and a good list of all the dwellings in the entire city does not exist (and would be too costly to prepare). Using a city map, the pollsters can instead obtain a sample of dwellings by selecting small clusters of blocks.

To do this in the simplest case, they divide the entire map of the city into blocks of equal size and then select 1 of, say, every 20 blocks for the sample. If they define the sample as the housing units located within the boundaries of these equal-sized sample blocks, the probability of selection for *any* unit is the selection of its block—which is set at 1/20 to correspond to the desired sampling rate of 300/6,000 (Kish, 1965). In other cases, researchers categorize the blocks by taking into account their size or some other factor of interest and then treat this factor as a stratum to sample in a specific way. The procedure can become more complicated as the area gets bigger, but the key requirements are to ensure (a) that all areas will have some chance of selection and (b) that the units within the areas are chosen impartially (Fowler, 1993). For the same plan to be used again, all that must be altered are the randomly selected units within each area.

What Did the *Literary Digest* Case Teach Pollsters?

The late George Gallup, the pioneering survey researcher who founded the Gallup Survey, once noted some of the methodological lessons learned by survey researchers going back to 1936 (Gallup, 1976). That year, Franklin D. Roosevelt (the Democratic presidential candidate) was running against Governor Alfred Landon of Kansas (the Republican candidate). Most people thought Roosevelt would win easily, but a pseudoscientific poll conducted by a current events magazine, the *Literary Digest,* predicted that Landon would win an overwhelming victory. What gave the prediction credence was that the *Digest* had successfully predicted the winner in every presidential election since 1916. Moreover, this time, it announced it had based its prediction on a sample of 2.4 million respondents!

The magazine got these 2.4 million by generating a nonrandom sample of 10 million people from sources like telephone directories, automobile registration lists, and club membership lists; straw vote ballots were then mailed to each name. The lists had actually been compiled for solicitation purposes, and advertising was included with the straw vote ballot (D. Katz & Cantril, 1937). One problem was that few people in 1936 had a telephone (only one in four households), owned a car, or belonged to a club, so that the final list was biased in favor of wealthy Republican households. Another problem was that there was a large number of nonrespondents, and subsequent analyses suggest that had they responded, the results might have been very different.

As it turned out, the election voting was split pretty much along economic lines, the more affluent voting for Landon and the less affluent voting for Roosevelt. The *Digest* predicted that Landon would win by 57% to Roosevelt's 43%, but the election results were Roosevelt 62% and Landon 38% (Freedman et al., 1991). The *Digest* could actually have used the information that the sample was top-heavy in upper-income Republicans to correct its estimate, but it deliberately ignored this information. Instead, the *Digest* proudly (but naively) proclaimed that the "figures had been neither weighted, adjusted, nor interpreted." After making the largest error ever made by political prognosticators in a presidential election, the *Digest* (which had been in financial trouble before the election) declared bankruptcy.

A lesson learned from this episode is that, if we seek to generalize to an entire population our findings of percentage differences in a sample, the sampling plan and its execution must be properly implemented in a precise scientific way, and sampling weights must be used to correct for potential biases. Yet, similar pseudoscientific public opinion polls are conducted daily by many "news shows" that pose a yes-or-no or multiple-choice question about some current controversial issue and invite the viewers to e-mail their opinions. The external validity of the reported results is so low as to render any generalization useless, as in all likelihood those who respond are not only nonrepresentative of the general population but also nonrepresentative of even the regular viewing audience. In one case, a television station skipped its polling one night and still received 20 calls voting "yes" and 38 voting "no" (Rosnow & Rosenthal, 1970, p. 239). It may be "entertaining" to see the results of such polls, but what they truly reveal is the naïveté of those conducting the polls and/or the audience that believes them.

George Gallup was just getting started during the days of the *Literary Digest* flop. Using his own polling method, he was able to predict that Roosevelt would win (although Gallup was off by 6 percentage points)—as well as to predict what the *Literary Digest* results would be. His method, called **quota sampling**, was an early precursor of current methods; it assigned a quota of people to be questioned and let the questioner build up a sample that was roughly representative of the population. The interviewer would be given ranges of variables and told to identify by sight people who seemed to fit this quota. For example, an interviewer might be told to talk to so many people of ages 21–35, 36–55, and 56 or over. We do not know how much of this interviewing took place on busy street corners and at trolley stops rather than in house-to-house canvassing, but bias might be introduced simply as a consequence of the interviewed individuals' being more accessible than others (Rossi et al., 1983). Now, of course, we would use random selection procedures instead of leaving the selection of units to the judgment of the questioner. However, another lesson that Gallup and others in the 1930s learned from the *Literary Digest* episode was that large numbers do not, in and of themselves, increase the representativeness or the predictive accuracy of a sample.

Because of that experience, the methodology of survey sampling has been improved in other ways as further unexpected problems have been encountered and additional lessons learned. In the congressional election of 1942, for example, pollsters had not reckoned with voter turnout, which was at an all time low because people were changing their places of residence to work in war factories or to enter the military. Gallup's polls correctly predicted that the Democrats would retain control of the House of Representatives, but the margin of victory turned out to be much closer than either he or any other pollsters had predicted. The important lesson learned this time was to give far more attention to the factor of voter turnout in making predictions. In the 1948 presidential election, Harry S Truman, by luring Democratic defectors back into the fold during the last 2 weeks before Election Day, turned the tide against his Republican opponent, Thomas E. Dewey. However, many public opinion polls predicted that Dewey would win. This time, Gallup and other pollsters learned the lesson that political polling had to be done as close to Election Day as possible (see also Box 9.3).

After 1948, the Gallup Survey (and other respected polls) adopted area probability sampling, in which election districts are randomly selected throughout the nation, and then randomly chosen households within these districts are contacted by interviewers. The use of this procedure, and the lessons learned from the mistakes made in the *Literary Digest* episode and its aftermath, quickly brought about further improvements. By 1956, the Gallup Survey, based on a little more than 8,000 respondents, was able to predict with a margin of error of only 1.7% that Dwight D. Eisenhower would be reelected president. The *margin of error* means that, in this case, the prediction (based on the laws of mathematical probability) was that the anticipated percentages would fall within an interval bound by plus-and-minus 1.7 percentage points.

BOX 9.3 Push Polls

Don't confuse the legitimate type of polling with what are called *push polls*—an insidious form of negative political campaigning that is designed to push opinions in a particular direction rather than scientifically sample them. Push polls use rumors, gossip, lies, innuendoes, and half-truths to manufacture negative voter attitudes by posing questions like "Would you be more or less likely to vote for [name of candidate] if you knew he/she had been arrested/failed to pay child support/failed to pay income taxes/falsified his/her resume?" If you are asked questions like these in a telephone "interview," ask about the sponsors of the survey and how the information is being used. The American Association for Public Opinion Research (AAPOR) has campaigned against push polling, including issuing repeated warnings to the public and the media about the iniquity of these pseudoscientific polls. You can help in combating push polls by finding out the name and location of the organization doing the "interviewing" and reporting this information to the AAPOR by e-mail at AAPOR-info@goAMP.com.

Poll watchers now expect an error of no more than 2 or 3 percentage points in national elections, if the probability sampling plan is properly implemented.

What Are Point Estimates and Interval Estimates?

The margin of error is an example of an interval estimate, whereas survey researchers are also interested in making point estimates of population values. **Point estimates** tell us about some typical characteristic of the target population. For instance, in a probability survey of a college population, we might want a point estimate of the number of seniors who plan to continue their education after graduating. Examples noted earlier in this chapter were the average number of widgets made by assembly-line workers, the number of cases of tuberculosis contracted on the job, and the frequency of psychological resilience in New Yorkers after the September 11, 2001, terrorist attack on the World Trade Center. **Interval estimates**, on the other hand, tell us how much the point estimates are likely to be in error (e.g., because of variability in the composition of the population).

Suppose we do a simple random survey of 100 college students out of a population of 2,500 graduating seniors at a certain university. Each student is asked, "Do you plan to continue your education after you graduate from college, by going on to graduate school, business school, medical school, dental school, or law school?" In answer to our question, 25 of them reply yes. In order to make a point estimate of the population value, we simply multiply the sample proportion replying yes (.25) by the total number of students in the population (2,500). The result leads us to estimate that the true (but unknown) number of graduating seniors planning to continue their education is 625.

How "approximate" is this estimate? Computing a **confidence interval** will give us the answer, as it will tell us the probability that the estimated population value is correct within plus-or-minus some specified interval. Suppose we want to say with 95% confidence (i.e., 95 chances in 100) that the estimated population value of 625 is correct within plus-or-minus some specified interval (called a *95% confidence interval*). In our polling a sample (*n*) of 100 graduating seniors, we found that .25 (symbolized as *prop,* for proportion) of that sample planned to continue their education. To obtain an approximate 95% confidence interval around *prop,* we compute

$$\text{Lower limit} = prop - 2\sqrt{\frac{prop\,(1 - prop)}{n}}$$

and

$$\text{Upper limit} = prop + 2\sqrt{\frac{prop\,(1 - prop)}{n}}$$

In this example, $n = 100$, $prop = .25$, and $1 - prop = .75$, so

$$2\sqrt{\frac{prop\,(1 - prop)}{n}} = 2\sqrt{\frac{(.25)(.75)}{100}} = .09$$

with a resulting lower limit of $.25 - .09 = .16$, and an upper limit of $.25 + .09 = .34$. Applying these proportions to the population (*N*) of 2,500 yields $.16(2,500) = 400$ as the lower limit, and $.34(2,500) = 850$ as the upper limit of our approximate 95% confidence interval for the number of graduating students planning to continue their education. (In Chapters 10 and 12, we will show how to compute confidence intervals for other important values.)

What Are the Benefits of Stratification?

In the illustration above, we randomly selected individual sampling units, using the population of graduating seniors as a single heterogeneous cluster. In most cases of survey research, sampling several strata or clusters is more efficient if the population can be separated into more homogeneous strata. As an illustration of the benefits of stratification, and also a further illustration of an unbiased sampling plan, suppose we want to use probability sampling to estimate the average hourly production of widgets by teams of assembly-line workers. To keep this example simple, we will imagine that the entire population consists of four such teams and that the mean number of widgets produced per hour is as follows:

Team A	11.5
Team B	12.5
Team C	13.0
Team D	19.0
	14.0 (true population value)

Adding the average hourly production rates (11.5 + 12.5 + 13.0 + 19.0 = 56.0) and dividing by 4 (56.0/4 = 14.0) tells us that the true population value is 14.0. But for this example, we ask, "How accurate an estimate of the true population value will we obtain by simple random sampling or stratified random sampling?" Finding the answer to this question will reveal what an **unbiased sampling plan** is.

We must initially decide on the size of the sample (the n) we wish to use to estimate the population value. To keep it simple, we will define the sample size as any two teams selected at random ($n = 2$). For example, were we to randomly select Team A and Team B, we would get a point estimate of 12.0, computed as (11.5 + 12.5)/2 = 12.0. How good is this estimate? The answer, called the **error of estimate**, is defined in this case as the closeness of 12.0 to the true population value of 14.0. We figure this answer out by subtracting the population value from the sample mean, or 12.0 − 14.0 = −2.0. In other words, this particular sample underestimates the true population by 2.0 (the negative difference tells us it is an underestimate; a positive difference would indicate an overestimate). Table 9.2 lists all possible combinations of two-member samples, the estimates derived from them, and the error of estimate for each sample. The average of the errors of estimate (when we take account of their signs) gives the *bias* of the general sampling plan. Not surprisingly, we see (at the bottom of the last column) that the general sampling plan is unbiased (even though there is error associated with individual sample values).

In stratified random sampling (to which we now turn), we begin by dividing the population into a number of parts. We then randomly sample independently in each part. To get started, notice that the last column in Table 9.2 shows that every simple random sample containing Team D overestimates the population value, and that every random sample without this team underestimates it. If we had reason to suspect this fact before the sampling, we could make use of such information to form strata so that a heterogeneous population is divided into two parts, each of which is fairly homogeneous (Snedecor & Cochran, 1989). One stratum will consist of Teams A, B, and C, and the second stratum will consist of Team D alone, as Table 9.3 shows. This table helps us to see clearly why this general sampling plan is called *unbiased* and also to see the advantages of stratification in probability sampling.

Table 9.2 Results for All Possible Simple Random Samples of Size Two

Sample	Sample values	Estimate of population value	Error of estimate
Team A, Team B	11.5, 12.5	12.00	−2.00
Team A, Team C	11.5, 13.0	12.25	−1.75
Team A, Team D	11.5, 19.0	15.25	+1.25
Team B, Team C	12.5, 13.0	12.75	−1.25
Team B, Team D	12.5, 19.0	15.75	+1.75
Team C, Team D	13.0, 19.0	16.00	+2.00
Total		84.00	0.00
Mean		14.00	0.00

			Weighted	Estimate of	Error of
Sample	Stratum 1	Stratum 2	sample values	population value	estimate
1	Team A	Team D	34.5, 19.0	13.375	−0.625
2	Team B	Team D	37.5, 19.0	14.125	+0.125
3	Team C	Team D	39.0, 19.0	14.500	+0.500
Total				42.000	0.000
Mean				14.000	0.000

Table 9.3 Results for All Possible Stratified Random Samples of Size Two

Starting with the first row, notice under "Weighted sample values" that Team A's score is $11.5 \times 3 = 34.5$, whereas Team D's score is not weighted (19.0). The reason we weight Team A's score by multiplying it by 3 is that it is one of three members of Stratum 1. By the same reasoning, we did not weight Team D's score because it is the sole occupant of Stratum 2. To compute the scores under "Estimate of population value," we add Team A's weighted score to Team D's unweighted score and then divide by the total number of members, or $(34.5 + 19.0)/4 = 13.375$. We obtain the "Error of estimate" by subtracting the true population mean from this result, or $13.375 - 14.0 = -0.625$ (which indicates that the Team A + Team D sample underestimates the true population value by a small amount). This table shows the results of all possible stratified random samples of size two. Again, we find (not unexpectedly) that the general sampling plan is unbiased in that the average of the errors of estimate (bottom of last column) is zero.

By comparing the results in Tables 9.2 and 9.3, you will see in quantitative terms the advantages of separating selections from strata of the population. The most extreme errors in Table 9.2 range from −2.00 to +2.00, a difference of 4.00. By contrast, the most extreme errors in Table 9.3 range from −0.625 to +0.500, a difference of 1.125. Notice that fewer samples are possible of size two in Table 9.3 than in Table 9.2. In summary, the error of an individual sample is greater in simple random sampling of a heterogeneous population than in stratified random sampling of that same population divided into more homogeneous strata, in this case by a magnitude of $4.00/1.125 = 3.56$, or more than three times the size. And the potential for error is also greater in simple random sampling than in stratified random sampling. Some forethought (and reliable information, of course) is needed about possible mean differences when one is dividing the population into more homogeneous strata; this forethought can pay off handsomely in the utility of stratification.

How Is Nonresponse Bias Handled in Survey Research?

Nonresponse bias is error due to nonparticipation. For example, a growing problem in the use of polling methods is that, as people become concerned more about issues of privacy, random samples become harder to obtain because more and more people hang up the phone in response to telephone polls. However, there are also other reasons for nonparticipation, such as when people are not at home

	First wave	Second wave	Third wave	Total nonrespondents	Total population
Basic data:					
a. Number of respondents	300	543	434	1,839	3,116
b. Percentage of population	10	17	14	59	100
c. Mean trees per respondent	456	382	340	290	329
Cumulative data:					
d. Mean trees per respondent (Y_1)	456	408	385		
e. Mean trees per nonrespondent (Y_2)	315	300	290		
f. Difference ($Y_1 - Y_2$)	141	108	95		
g. Percentage of nonrespondents (P)	90	73	59		
h. Bias = $(P)(Y_1 - Y_2)$	127	79	56		

Table 9.4 Example of Bias Due to Nonresponse in Survey Research

Source: From *The Volunteer Subject,* by R. Rosenthal and R. L. Rosnow, 1955; p. 4. Copyright © 1975. Reprinted by permission of John Wiley & Sons. Based on data from Finkner (1950) and Cochran (1963).

because both adults work, or because the person who answers the phone is simply too busy. A typical answer by one person who turned down a telephone request to interview her about where she shops was "It was 7 o'clock, I was putting the kids to bed, and it was zoo time around here, which is when these people call" (Rothenberg, 1990, p. 1). Statisticians and survey researchers have devoted considerable effort to studying the effects of nonresponse bias. Not only might this bias result in a smaller **effective sample size** (the size of the actual final sample) than the researcher planned on for statistical reasons (discussed in a later chapter), but the accuracy of estimates of population values may be jeopardized as well.

Table 9.4 illustrates in quantitative terms the basic idea of nonresponse bias, and it also illustrates one way that researchers who use mailed questionnaires may attempt to reduce this bias by sending out questionnaires more than once. The data in this table are based on three waves of questionnaires that were mailed out to peach growers in North Carolina (Finkner, 1950). It is unusual to have data about both the respondents and the nonrespondents. But when we have such relevant information on all members of the population surveyed, we can use it to compare those who respond with those who don't respond. In this study, one variable was the number of peach trees owned, and data were available for the entire population of growers for just this variable. At least for this variable, then, we can quantify the amount of the bias due to nonresponse remaining after the first, second, and third mailings (Cochran, 1963, 1977).

The first three rows of Table 9.4 provide all the basic data in this study, in the form of (a) the number of respondents to each wave of questionnaires and the number of nonrespondents; (b) the percentage of the total population (3,116) represented by each wave of respondents and nonrespondents; and (c) the mean number of trees owned by the respondents in each wave. To calculate the effective sample size after each mailing, we cumulate the number of respondents to that point. Thus, the effective sample size is 300 after the first mailing; 300 + 543 = 843 after two mailings; and $843 + 434 = 1,277$ after three mailings. To convert the values in row a into the percentages in row b, we divided the row a values by the total population size and multiplied by 100 to change a proportion into a percentage. For example, dividing the number of respondents to the first mailing by the total population value gives us $300/3,116 = .096$, which, when rounded to .10 and multiplied by 100, tells us that 10% of the growers responded to the first mailing.

The remaining five rows of data are based on the cumulative number of respondents after the first, second, and third mailings. For each wave, five items of information are provided: (d) the mean number of peach trees owned by the respondents up to that point in the survey; (e) the mean number of trees owned by those not yet responding; (f) the difference between these two values; (g) the percentage of the population not yet responding; and (h) the magnitude of the bias (defined in terms of peach trees owned) up to that point in the survey. The bottom row (h) shows that, with each successive wave of respondents, there was a decrease in the magnitude of the bias (a fairly typical result in such cases). The implication is that increasing the effort to recruit the nonrespondents should lessen the bias of the point estimates.

Knowing the magnitude and direction of the nonresponse bias can help us adjust our estimate of the generalizability of the results. To make this adjustment, we need to have information about the nonrespondents as well as the respondents on some variable that is related to our area of interest. Without this information, we can compute the proportion of population participants (P) and the statistic of interest (the point estimate) for the respondents (Y_1), but we cannot compute the statistic of interest (the corresponding point estimate) for those people who did not respond (Y_2). We may be in a position to suspect bias but may be unable to give an estimate of its magnitude. We will come back to this problem in a moment (in our discussion of volunteer bias), but (as Table 9.4 implies) one way to reduce nonresponse bias may be to try to increase the rate of response of the likely nonrespondents.

In the case of mail surveys, more nonrespondents may be drawn into the subject sample by one or more follow-up mailings or reminders. Survey researchers who do mail surveys often advise telephoning the nonrespondents if the response rate is still not satisfactory. Professional pollsters attempt to increase the initial rate of participation by using various kinds of incentives and attention-getting techniques, such as using special delivery as opposed to ordinary mail, using hand-stamped rather than postage-permit envelopes, and sometimes including a courtesy gift at the time of the request for participation (Linsky, 1975). In Chapter 5, we discussed the creation of questionnaires; to increase response rates, it is important that the instructions be clear, that the items be easy to read and the layout attractive, and that the task of answering questions not be burdensome (Fowler, 1993; Tryfos, 1996). In the case of telephone surveys, we may be able to increase response rates by sending an informative advance letter that spells out the importance of the study, by pilot-testing probing questions to ensure that the persons contacted will not feel intimidated by them or by the uses to which the data will be put, and by training our interviewers and screening out bad ones. One or more follow-up telephone calls on evenings and weekends may also improve the response rate (Fowler, 1993; Tryfos, 1996), assuming the calls are not perceived as intrusive and bothersome.

What Are the Typical Characteristics of Volunteer Subjects?

So far, we have focused on the prototypical survey study. We turn now to a problem similar to nonresponse bias that occurs in other research (e.g., experimental research) in which the participants are individually recruited. As we noted earlier, experimenters do not usually concern themselves with the particulars of a probability sampling plan when recruiting their subjects but instead use opportunity samples. One reason for their lack of concern is that it is often impossible to work within the confines of a probability sampling plan. A second reason is that, even when random subject selection is feasible, many experimenters assume that "people are people" in terms of the psychological factors or mechanisms they are studying. That is, the assumption is that, as long as people are randomly assigned to treatment conditions, it should make little difference whether those assigned to the experimental and control groups are volunteer subjects or a random sample of some specified population. In some cases, using strictly volunteer subjects can, however, lead to biased conclusions (discussed in the next section); using random assignment would not address this problem (see also Box 9.4).

You may be wondering how anyone can know how volunteer subjects are different from nonvolunteers, inasmuch as nonvolunteers are, by definition, unavailable. One technique used to study the characteristics and reactions of volunteers and nonvolunteers is to recruit the research subjects from a population for which information is available on everyone in the population (e.g., biographical data and psychological test results). Requests for research volunteers are then made some time later (sometimes years later), and those who volunteer are compared with those who do not volunteer on relevant items of information. For instance, most colleges routinely administer psychological tests and questionnaires to all incoming students during an orientation period. The results, assuming they

BOX 9.4 The Ubiquitous Volunteer

When scientists recruit volunteers for randomized trials involving risk (e.g., an experiment testing the effects of different diets on cholesterol), those people already at high risk may be most likely to volunteer. However, volunteer bias is not limited to experimental studies. Suppose a cable TV company randomly selects subscribers to be interviewed in a telephone survey. The dissatisfied subscribers may be more likely to participate because they have grievances they want to voice (Tryfos, 1996). The question is how to generalize from these volunteers to the target population.

Table 9.5	Characteristics of the Typical Research Volunteer

1. Better educated
2. Higher social class
3. Higher IQ scores
4. Higher need for social approval
5. More sociable
6. More arousal-seeking
7. More unconventional
8. More often female
9. Less authoritarian

are ethically obtainable by the researchers (who, i.e., having received the IRB's permission, as discussed in Chapter 3), can be used not only to compare those who volunteer with those who do not volunteer for a certain psychological experiment or other type of study later that same year, but also to compare the respondents with nonrespondents to an alumni-organization questionnaire sent out years later.

Table 9.5, which is based on an analysis of hundreds of studies comparing volunteers and nonvolunteers, contains a summary list of nine general characteristics of typical volunteers for research participation (R. Rosenthal & Rosnow, 1975b). The characteristics in this table are ranked in the descending order of their approximate reliability based on the data that we examined in that analysis. The list of characteristics has been simplified to make it easier to refer to when we return to these characteristics in the next section, but all are context-dependent to some degree. The following are examples:

1. Volunteer subjects tend to be better educated than nonvolunteers, especially in studies in which personal contact between investigator and respondent is not required.

2. Volunteers are characteristically higher in social class status than nonvolunteers, but only defined by the respondents' own status rather than by parental status.

3. People who volunteer for somewhat less typical types of research (e.g., hypnosis, sensory isolation, sex research, and small-group and personality research) typically score higher on IQ tests than nonvolunteers do.

4. Volunteers tend to be higher than nonvolunteers in need for social approval (i.e., the variable studied by Marlowe and Crowne, discussed in Chapter 6).

5. Volunteers are typically more sociable than nonvolunteers, according to their responses on personality tests.

6. Volunteers tend to be more arousal-seeking than nonvolunteers, especially when the volunteering is for studies involving stress, sensory isolation, or hypnosis.

7. Volunteers tend to be more unconventional than nonvolunteers, especially when the volunteering is for studies of sexual behavior.

8. Women are more likely to volunteer for research in general, but they are less likely than men to volunteer for physically and emotionally stressful research (e.g., electric shock, high temperature, sensory deprivation, and interviews about sexual behavior).

9. Volunteers tend to be less authoritarian than nonvolunteers (a characteristic implying that volunteers are typically less rigid thinkers and are likely to put a high value on individual freedom).

How Is Volunteer Bias in Opportunity Samples Managed?

In studying this topic, we have used the term **volunteer bias** to refer to systematic error resulting when the responses of people who volunteer differ from how individuals in the general population would respond (R. Rosenthal & Rosnow, 1975b; Rosnow & Rosenthal, 1997). On the basis of knowing that research volunteers, compared to nonvolunteers, may be brighter (Item 3), higher in approval need (Item 4), less authoritarian (Item 9), and so on, we can sometimes predict the direction of the potential volunteer bias. Imagine that a researcher wants to assess experimentally the validity of a new teaching procedure that is purported to make young children less rigid in their thinking. The researcher asks parents and teachers to volunteer their children or pupils as participants in the investigation because, realistically, it is impossible to draw a random sample for participation. The researcher expects that the children who are volunteered will (like adults who volunteer themselves) be low in authoritarianism (Item 9). Because people who are low in authoritarianism are also likely to be less rigid thinkers, the researcher suspects that using volunteered children will lead to a more conservative assessment of the new teaching procedure than if it were possible to use a randomly selected subject sample (i.e., to use probability sampling). The reason is that both the experimental and the control groups will already be unusually low on the dependent variable (rigidity of thinking). Knowing this, however, the researcher can have greater confidence in the evidence for the causal relationship to which the results of this study point, because that relationship is likely to be even greater in the general population.

We can also imagine predicting the opposite type of inferential error in another situation. Suppose a manager wants to find out how persuasive an advertisement is before recommending its use in a heavily funded television campaign. The manager hires a research consulting firm to pilot-test the advertisement. The firm does so on volunteer subjects, who are assigned at random to an experimental group that sees the advertisement or a control group that sees something else that will fill the same amount of time. The manager (who took psychological methods in college and knows about the characteristics of volunteer subjects) suspects that the consultants' volunteer subjects are probably relatively high in approval need (Item 4), and he also knows (from taking a course in personality psychology) that people who are high in approval need are likely to be more influenced than those who are low in approval need. Putting this information together, the knowledgeable manager reasons that the consultants' results may overestimate the effect of the advertising campaign. That is, because the volunteers may have overreacted to the treatment in the experimental group, the predicted effect of the advertising campaign in the more general population may be exaggerated to some (unknown) degree by the pilot-study results.

Knowing that biased conclusions are possible in a given situation, researchers can try to avoid this problem. For example, the use of volunteer subjects may lead to biased conclusions in the standardization of a new test. In Chapter 5, we noted that many standardized tests are norm-referenced. That is, each person's score can be compared with those of a normative reference group by means of a table of values representing the typical performance of a given group. These *norms* provide a standard of comparison so that we can see how much any person's score deviates from the average of a large group of representative individuals. For example, if you plan to apply to law school, you will want to know how much your score on the Law School Admission Test (LSAT) deviates from the scores of other highly qualified college students with similar career plans. In the next chapter, we will explain how to interpret a "standard score," but what is more relevant here is that a crucial assumption of researchers in developing norms for new tests is that the resulting values are representative of the target population. For example, the developers of the LSAT have such information on everyone in the target group because everyone in the group must take this test. However, suppose a researcher uses volunteer subjects to standardize a brand-new intelligence test but wants to use the test and the resulting norms in a population consisting of typical volunteers *and* nonvolunteers. Because of Characteristic 3, our best guess is that the researcher's estimates of population norms will be inflated values, since volunteers can be expected to score higher on intelligence tests than nonvolunteers in the same population. The researcher needs to think of some noncoercive way of encouraging nonvolunteers to participate in the research.

Previously, we summarized some techniques used to stimulate participation by typical nonrespondents in survey research. Researchers can use a number of other incentives to stimulate participation by typical nonvolunteers (R. Rosenthal & Rosnow, 1975b; Rosnow & Rosenthal, 1997). Increasing such participation should, in turn, lessen the likelihood of subject selection bias by drawing a more representative subject sample. For example, one recruitment technique is to explain to the potential subjects *why* they will find the research interesting and worthwhile. This approach is based on the finding that persons more interested in the research are more likely to participate (R. Rosenthal & Rosnow, 1975b). A second technique is to explain the research in a way that is nonthreatening, so that potential participants are not put off by fears of unfavorable evaluation (i.e., by their evaluation apprehensions). The basis of this technique is another set of findings that persons who expect to be unfavorably evaluated by the investigator are less likely to volunteer, and those who expect to be favorably evaluated are more likely to volunteer. Some other empirically based techniques for stimulating research participation are emphasizing the scientific importance of the research, offering small courtesy gifts to potential participants for taking the time to consider participating, and avoiding unnecessary procedures that may be perceived as psychologically or biologically stressful.

A hasty reading of these techniques may give the impression that they are designed only to increase rates of participation. However, there is another, more subtle, benefit. When we tell our prospective participants as much as possible about the significance of the research, avoid doing unnecessary psychologically or biologically stressful research, and so on, it follows that we probably put more care and thought into our planning to ensure that the study would withstand the scrutiny of critical evaluations. In effect, we are treating the participants as if they are another "granting agency"—which in a sense they are, granting us their time and cooperation. Thus, another benefit of these techniques is that they provide incentives to us, the researchers, to be ethically responsible and humane when we decide what kind of research to do and how to do it (Blanck et al., 1992; R. Rosenthal, 1994b; Rosnow, 1997).

Whatever your research project, whether it involves a survey, a randomized experiment, a single-case experiment, or some other strategy of collecting data directly from people, the final step before implementing the study is to pilot-test the materials. For example, suppose we want to study a sensitive topic and are concerned that people will be reluctant to tell the truth (e.g., Lee, 1993). We might pilot-test more than one version of the questionnaire or interview schedule. If we are concerned about nonresponse bias, we might test different recruitment procedures. Interestingly, even when conducting the actual survey, researchers use embedded randomized experiments on subsets of the sample, which can provide an opportunity to pilot-test different recruitment methods to help prevent incurably flawed data in future research (e.g., Fienberg & Tanur, 1989; Schuman & Presser, 1996; Tanur, 1994). As the old saying goes, an ounce of prevention is worth a pound of cure.

Summary of Ideas

1. *Opportunity samples* use the first units that are available, whereas *probability sampling plans* use a random procedure for selecting a *sample* that is expected to be representative of the target *population*. However, to be absolutely sure that a sample is representative, we would have to know the true population value in advance, in which case (practically speaking) there would be no reason to study the sample.

2. A *biased* sample overestimates or underestimates the true population value. An *unstable* sample is characterized by sampling units that vary greatly from one another. Generally speaking, the more homogeneous the population is, the fewer the sampling units needed.

3. In *simple random sampling,* the sample is selected from an undivided population (or from a relatively homogeneous stratum), and each unit has the same chance of being selected on any draw. Two options are (a) *sampling with replacement* and (b) *sampling without replacement* (e.g., the wine taster).

4. *Area probability sampling* is a variant of *stratified random sampling* in which the strata are geographic clusters.

5. The *Literary Digest* case (and its aftermath) taught political pollsters that (a) valid sampling must be done in a precise, scientific way that uses random selection (not, e.g., *quota sampling*); (b) large samples do not, in and of themselves, ensure representativeness; and (c) polling close to Election Day usually yields better predictions, but attention to voter turnout (or the predicted turnout) is

important. "Push polls" (Box 9.3), an insidious form of political campaigning, are bogus "polls" designed to manufacture negative voter attitudes.

6. *Point estimates* predict typical population characteristics, where *interval estimates* tell us how much the point estimates are likely to be in error. *Confidence intervals* tell us the probability that the estimated population value is correct within some specific interval.

7. As the widget example illustrated, both the error of estimate of an individual sample and the likelihood of making that error tend to be greater in simple random samples than in stratified random samples.

8. In survey research that uses a probability sampling plan, bias due to nonresponse is likely to diminish with each successive wave of respondents (e.g., in the survey of peach growers). Other ways to reduce nonresponse bias in survey research include (a) using reminders and follow-up communications; (b) personalizing the contact; and (c) offering an incentive to respond.

9. On practical, ethical, and theoretical grounds (e.g., the idea that people are similar), behavioral experimenters generally use opportunity samples of volunteer subjects.

10. The typical volunteer subject (compared to the typical nonvolunteer) is (a) better educated; (b) higher in social class status; (c) higher in IQ; (d) higher in need for social approval; (e) higher in sociability; (f) more arousal-seeking; (g) more unconventional; (h) more often female; and (i) less authoritarian. Knowing the relationship between these characteristics of volunteer subjects and the variable of interest, we can sometimes predict the direction of volunteer bias in experimental and nonexperimental studies.

11. Procedures for stimulating subject participation (e.g., telling people as much as possible about the significance of the research and avoiding stressful manipulations) also provide incentives to researchers to act ethically and humanely.

12. Pilot-testing the research materials can produce valuable information that will help us avoid making certain costly, intractable mistakes.

Key Terms

area probability sampling
 p. 207
bias   p. 201
confidence interval   p. 211
effective sample size   p. 214
error of estimate   p. 212
interval estimates   p. 210
nonresponse bias   p. 213
opportunity samples   p. 198
point estimates   p. 210
population   p. 199

probability   p. 199
probability sampling   p. 199
quota sampling   p. 209
representative   p. 199
sample   p. 199
sampling plan   p. 199
sampling without
 replacement   p. 206
sampling with replacement
 p. 206

simple random sampling
 p. 203
stability   p. 200
stratified random
 sampling   p. 207
unbiased   p. 200
unbiased sampling plan
 p. 212
volunteer bias   p. 218

Multiple-Choice Questions for Review

1. Which of the following is most commonly used in public opinion polling? (a) random selection; (b) random assignment; (c) random processing; (d) opportunity sampling

2. A _____ is the total group of participants in which one is interested; a _____ is a segment of the total group that will be studied more closely. (a) universe of subjects, population; (b) population, sample; (c) sample, population; (d) sample, microsample

3. The true population mean is 4. A sample is chosen with the following values: 2, 3, 4, 5, 6. This sample is (a) unbiased; (b) biased; (c) random; (d) nonrandom.

4. The true population mean is 4. Sample A has the following values: 3, 4, 4, 5. Sample B has the following values: 0, 4, 4, 8. Compared to Sample B, Sample A is more (a) unbiased; (b) biased; (c) stable; (d) random.

5. A sampling plan is created in which each member of the population has an equal probability of being selected. This is called a(n) _____ plan. (a) quota sampling; (b) simple random sampling; (c) stratified random sampling; (d) area probability sampling

6. A public opinion pollster divides the population into subpopulations of males and females, and of Democrats and Republicans. She then takes a random sample from each of these subpopulations. This approach is called (a) area probability sampling; (b) stratified random sampling; (c) simple random sampling; (d) quota sampling.

7. A researcher concludes that 1,000 students at a particular college plan to go to graduate school. This is an example of a(n) (a) reliable measure; (b) interval estimate; (c) point estimate; (d) judge's rating.

8. The same researcher states that it is 95% likely that between 900 and 1,100 students at the college plan to go to graduate school. This is an example of a(n) (a) observation measure; (b) confidence interval estimate; (c) point estimate; (d) judge's rating.

9. In some circumstances, people who agree to participate in survey research are noticeably different from people who refuse to participate. This problem is sometimes called (a) lack of randomization; (b) sampling without replacement; (c) instability in sampling; (d) nonresponse bias.

10. Compared to nonvolunteers, those who typically volunteer to participate in psychological research tend to be (a) less authoritarian; (b) higher in arousal-seeking; (c) more sociable; (d) all of the above.

Discussion Questions for Review

1. Do you know the answer to the following questions asked of a University of Vermont student? Given a true population mean of 12 and the following subjects' scores, (a) which group is measured with greatest stability, and (b) which group is the most biased?

Group 1	Group 2	Group 3
10	10	9
11	12	12
12	14	15
13	16	18

2. Fed up with studying for midterms, four Smith College students—Susan, Valerie, Ellen, and Jane—decide to throw darts at Susan's encyclopedia, which contains one volume for each letter of the alphabet. Because the word *midterm* begins with the letter M, the M volume is chosen as the target. Each person gets three darts. Susan hits the M volume every time; Valerie hits the N volume every time; Ellen hits the L volume, the M volume, and the N volume once each; and Jane hits the M volume, the N volume, and the O volume once each. Assuming that each volume of the encyclopedia is the same size, interpret the performance of each person in terms of bias and instability.

3. A Virginia Polytechnic Institute student is interested in the relationship between IQ and sociability. He designs a questionnaire to study this relationship and sends it out to hundreds of people. Twenty percent of the people complete and return the questionnaire. What is a possible source of bias in the results this student will obtain? How would you improve on his design?

4. A University of Kansas student is asked by his instructor to think up experimental cases in which the difference between typical volunteer subjects and nonvolunteers might lead the researcher (a) to overestimate the effectiveness of the experimental treatment and (b) to underestimate the effectiveness of the experimental treatment. Can you help the student? Can you also think of how these situations might be remedied?

5. A University of Michigan student wants to sample the opinions of all graduating seniors on various issues. However, because the graduating class is so large, she decides it would be best to sample a representative group rather than try to contact every one of the graduating seniors. Describe the steps she should take to develop a representative sampling plan, as well as some further steps she might take to deal with the problem of nonresponse bias.

6. A Cabrini College student wants to conduct an interview study using married adults who frequent the King of Prussia shopping mall. Because she is worried about volunteer bias, she would like to make every reasonable effort to obtain as representative a sample as she possibly can. What can she do to encourage people to participate in her study?

Answers to Review Questions

Multiple-Choice Questions

1. a	3. a	5. b	7. c	9. d
2. b	4. c	6. b	8. b	10. d

Discussion Questions

1. Group 1 is measured with the greatest stability; its subjects' scores range only from 10 to 13, whereas Groups 2 and 3 range from 10 to 16 and from 9 to 18, respectively. The means of Groups 1, 2, and 3 are 11.5, 13.0, and 13.5, respectively; therefore, the mean of Group 3 is the most biased.

2. Susan showed no bias with respect to the target volume (her average hit was M, the target volume) and no instability (she hit the same volume each time). Valerie showed a one-volume-away bias, hitting N on average, instead of volume M; she showed no instability, hitting the same volume each time. Ellen showed no bias (her average volume hit was M, the target volume, but she showed a three-volume instability, hitting three adjacent volumes). Jane showed a one-volume-away bias, hitting volume N on average instead of volume M; she showed a three-volume instability, hitting three adjacent volumes. We can summarize the results as follows:

	Bias	No bias
Some instability	Jane	Ellen
No instability	Valerie	Susan

3. Since volunteers or respondents tend to be more intelligent and more sociable than the general population, the correlation between IQ and sociability found in this self-selected sample may be quite different from the correlation we would find in the general population. One way to improve on the design might be to use follow-up questionnaires to increase the representativeness of the sample. Another way to improve on the design might be to try to locate data archives that include data from almost all of a given target population, for example, a college sample all of whom were tested at the time of admission or orientation.

4. In a study of the effects of a placebo on self-reported happiness, volunteers might show a larger placebo effect (i.e., the difference between the placebo and the no-treatment conditions) than nonvolunteers because volunteers are more likely to want to please the experimenter. In a study of the effects of a treatment designed to increase sociability, volunteers might show a smaller treatment effect than nonvolunteers because volunteers might already score so much higher on sociability that it might be hard to show further changes. Any procedures reducing volunteer bias would help reduce these potential problems.

5. She might draw a random sample of graduating seniors and contact them several times to reduce nonresponse bias. If she knew what characteristics were likely to be highly correlated with responses to her questionnaire, she might do her random selection within the various strata formed by her subdividing the sample into relatively more homogeneous subgroups.

6. She can try to make her appeal for volunteers as interesting, nonthreatening, and rewarding as possible.

CHAPTER 10

![Chapter 10 banner graphic]

Summarizing the Data

Preview Questions

- How is visual integrity ensured when results are graphed?
- How are frequencies displayed in tables, bar graphs, and line graphs?
- How do stem-and-leaf charts work?
- How are percentiles used to summarize part of a batch?
- How is an exploratory data analysis done?
- How does asymmetry affect measures of central tendency?
- How do I measure how "spread out" a set of scores is?
- What are descriptive and inferential measures?
- How do I compute a confidence interval around a population mean?
- What is distinctive about the normal distribution?
- Why are z scores called *standard scores,* and how are they used?

How Is Visual Integrity Ensured When Results Are Graphed?

In this chapter, we review some older and newer procedures that will help you summarize and evaluate tendencies of the data. Some procedures will be applicable as you analyze your results and write a report, but you should also find them useful beyond the bounds of this course. For instance, once you understand the logic of frequency distributions, summary measures of central tendency and variability, descriptive and inferential measures, and standard (z) scores, you will be in a stronger position to evaluate claims made on the basis of such information. In the following chapters, we will show how these concepts also provide the basic ingredients of other important data-analytic procedures (see also Box 10.1).

It is said that a picture is worth a thousand words, and this statement often seems true when one is representing and interpreting research data. Thus, we begin by showing some ways of graphing results to reveal tendencies of the data. With computer programs, it is easy to recast quantitative data into a visual display, though it is important not to overcomplicate the results, as confusion and clutter will elicit vacant staring rather than easy comprehension. A properly done visual

BOX 10.1 What If You're Using a Computer Program?

If you are learning to use a computer to run a statistics program (such as SPSS, SAS, SYSTAT, or Minitab), you will find that most of the quantitative methods described here are among the most common statistical tools. When you understand the logic of these methods, you will have a better sense of what your computer churns out. You will also find that most methods described in this book are simple enough to allow you to work out the examples on a pocket calculator that can compute the standard deviation and variance of a sample (S, S^2) and a population (σ, σ^2). If your budget permits, you will find calculators that can compute correlations and t tests directly. Some calculators give precise p values (so you won't have to search out a table of values), and some can be programmed with your favorite formulas.

display will be informative and easy to understand. Edward R. Tufte (1983), a statistician specializing in such designs, suggested that to ensure visual integrity and easy comprehension by viewers, writers need to keep in mind the three criteria of all good visual displays: clarity, precision, and efficiency. *Clarity* means representing data in a way that is closely integrated with their numerical meaning. *Precision* means representing the data exactly, and not exaggerating numbers. *Efficiency* means presenting the data in a reasonably compact space, so the viewer or reader is encouraged to think about their substance and is not distracted by unnecessary details.

One of Tufte's (1990) mantras is that "confusion and clutter are failures of design, not attributes of information" (p. 53). He mentioned a visual artifact that an eminent design artist (Albers, 1969) described as "one plus one equals three or more." That is, information clumsily layered on other information in a visual representation presents a constant danger that viewers will perceive more facts than the data actually support. The point, Tufte cautioned, is not to fault the viewer for a lack of understanding, but to avoid this situation by thinking hard about how to represent the data clearly, precisely, and efficiently. (Figuratively speaking, of course, sometimes it does seem true that one plus one equals more than the sum of its parts, as in the behavior of a mob or the baking of a cake.) Another statistician, Howard Wainer (1997), added that "the most important component of a memorable graph is the information it contains" (p. 148). The surest ways to exhibit data badly are to crowd the display with irrelevancies and to use a type font that is hard to read, a text full of jargon, or numbers that overburden people with irrelevant or unimportant information (Wainer, 1997).

Table 10.1 Palatability Evaluation by 50 Tasters of Two Food Products		
Score	Control product	New product
−3	1	0
−2	3	1
−1	8	2
0	17	11
+1	15	16
+2	5	13
+3	1	7

Source: From *Statistics: A Guide to the Unknown* (3rd ed.) by J. M. Tanur et al. Copyright © 1972 Holden Day. Reprinted by permission of Brooks/Cole a division of Thomson Learning: www. thomsonrights. Fax 800-/30-2215.

How Are Frequencies Displayed in Tables, Bar Graphs, and Line Graphs?

When researchers want to emphasize visually the overall pattern of the data, they often decide to use a **frequency distribution**. Such a display shows the number of times that each score or other unit of observation occurs in a set of data. A frequency distribution usually takes the form of a chart (e.g., a bar graph or a line graph), but frequencies can also be displayed in a tabular format. For example, Table 10.1 shows the frequency distribution of a set of evaluations of a new food product (after Street & Carroll, 1989). This aspect involved a palatability evaluation, in which the researchers had 50 people taste and evaluate the new food product and a competitive food product (a control) already on the market. Instead of a rating scale with words such as *terrible, very poor, poor, average, good, very good,* and *excellent,* the participants were given a variation of the pictorial scale in Figure 10.1. In the scoring of the results, each of the faces was assigned a number (or score) in the sequence −3, −2, −1, 0, +1, +2, +3, with −3 implying the "least agreeable" and +3 being "most agreeable." Table 10.1 shows the *frequency* (the number) of tasters who chose each option in the face scale. For example, in the top row of Table 10.1, we see that only one participant rated the control product −3 and that no one gave the new product this "least agreeable" (−3) rating.

Figure 10.2 recasts the results clearly and efficiently as two **bar graphs**, where the height of the solid bars represents the number (frequency) of tasters who chose each option. Notice that the implicit scale values appear on the horizontal axis (called the **x axis**) and the number of tasters appears on the vertical axis (called the **y axis**). Another name for the horizontal (x) axis is the **abscissa**; another name for the vertical (y) axis is the **ordinate**. (To keep these names straight, remember that the "abscissa sits," or rests on the bottom.) Comparing the two bar graphs allows us immediately to see that the new food product was rated, in general, as more agreeable than the control product. Notice that the

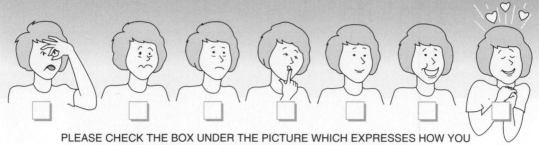

PLEASE CHECK THE BOX UNDER THE PICTURE WHICH EXPRESSES HOW YOU
FEEL TOWARD THE PRODUCT YOU HAVE JUST TASTED.

Figure 10.1   Pictorial taste-test scale (the scores −3 to +3 were assigned the figures from left to right) used in a palatability evaluation study.

Source: From p. 166 in *Statistics: A Guide to the Unknown* (3rd ed.), by J. Tanur et al. Copyright © 1972 Holden Day. Reprinted with permission of Brooks/Cole a division of Thomson Learning: www.thomsonrights. Fax 800-730-2215.

tallest bar in the control product group represents tasters who chose the 0 option, whereas the tallest bar in the new product group represents those who chose the +1 option.

Bar graphs are especially useful for representing categories of responses and frequencies (or proportions) within those categories. An efficient way of graphing *changes* in the frequency (or proportion) of scores over time is **line graphs**. An example was shown in Chapter 8, where Figure 8.1 (page 185) is a line graph of up-and-down change in the frequency of subway suicides and suicide attempts from 1980 to 1992 in Vienna, Austria. To find the year in which the number of suicides or suicide attempts was greatest, we simply find the highest point and then look at the abscissa to read the year. The value of the visual display in Figure 8.1 is not only that it shows the increases and decreases at a glance, but that it also allows us to compare the change over time in two line graphs (shown together) before and after the intervention.

How Do Stem-and-Leaf Charts Work?

No hard-and-fast rule requires that frequency distributions always resemble the types discussed above. Another alternative, called the **stem-and-leaf chart** (invented by John W. Tukey), provides a clear, precise, and efficient technique for displaying and interpreting a "batch" of data. A stem-and-leaf chart is a hybrid between a table and a graph inasmuch as it presents original numbers and simultaneously gives an economic summary view of them. It does not involve any elaborate statistical theory; instead, it relies on the creative imagination of the researcher who decides to use it, perhaps in order to do an exploratory data analysis (as illustrated later in this chapter) or to test a prediction or working hypothesis (Chambers, Cleveland, Kleiner, & Tukey, 1983; Emerson & Hoaglin, 1983; Tukey, 1977).

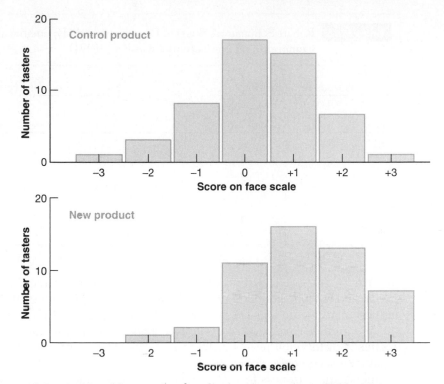

Figure 10.2   A pair of bar graphs that display the results in Table 10.1.

To illustrate how a stem-and-leaf chart is constructed, suppose we ask 15 students to rate a famous rapper, known for his social statements and wry political observations, on a scale from 0 ("the most shallow") to 100 ("the most profound"), and we get the following results: 66, 87, 47, 74, 56, 51, 37, 70, 82, 66, 41, 52, 62, 79, 69. Figure 10.3 shows a stem-and-leaf of these ratings. The stems are the first digits of these two-digit numbers, and the leaves are the second digits. There are two scores concentrated in the 80s (82 and 87), three scores in the 70s (70, 74, and 79), four scores in the 60s (62, 66, 66, and 69), and so forth. The beauty of the stem-and-leaf is that it allows us to see the batch as a whole and to note (a) whether the data set is symmetrical, (b) how spread out the scores are, (c) whether any scores

Stems	Leaves
8	2 7
7	0 4 9
6	2 6 6 9
5	1 2 6
4	1 7
3	7

Figure 10.3   A stem-and-leaf chart of students' ratings of a famous rapper.

Table 10.2	Robert Schumann's Bouts of Depression and Hypomania and His Compositional Productivity (Weisberg, 1994)

Periods of depression		Periods of hypomania	
Year	Number of compositions	Year	Number of compositions
1830	1	1829	1
1831	1	1832	4
1839	4	1840	25
1842	3	1843	2
1844	0	1849	28
1847	5	1851	16
1848	5		

are outside the batch, (d) whether there are small and large concentrations of scores, and (e) whether there are any gaps (Emerson & Hoaglin, 1983). Thus, stem-and-leaf charts score high on the criteria of clarity, precision, and efficiency.

As a further illustration of the use of stem-and-leaf in research, we turn to the frequency distribution results in Table 10.2, based on a correlational study done by cognitive psychologist Robert W. Weisberg (1994). Weisberg was interested in an old theory that madness fosters creativity, and he decided to test this theory in the case of the prolific German composer Robert Schumann (1810–1856). Schumann suffered from manic-depression (now called bipolar disorder) and eventually committed suicide. Weisberg first compiled a complete list of Schumann's musical compositions, then noted those compositions that experts considered works of genius, and also documented the specific years in which Schumann suffered from depression or hypomania (a mild form of mania, characterized by elation and quickness of thought). Weisberg found no support for the idea that madness fostered brilliance in Schumann's work. However, Table 10.2 shows that he had a tendency to produce more compositions when he was in a hypomanic than when he was in a depressive state. Another way of representing these data is shown in Figure 10.4, which plots the rates in adjoining stem-and-leaf charts. Called a **back-to-back stem-and-leaf chart**, this arrangement lets us see at a glance that the rates are spread out more for hypomania than for depression, and that the rates during bouts of depression are concentrated in a single stem.

Depression	Stems	Hypomania
	2	5 8
	1	6
5 5 4 3 1 1 0	0	1 2 4

Figure 10.4   A back-to-back stem-and-leaf chart of Schumann's number of compositions during his bouts of depression and hypomania (based on Table 10.2).

How Are Percentiles Used to Summarize Part of a Batch?

So far, the charts we have looked at were used to display *all* the data, but researchers also find it useful to summarize *part* of the batch. For example, there is often a practical value in knowing the point in the distribution below and above which a certain percentage of scores falls, called the **percentile**: 25% of the scores fall below the 25th percentile, 75% of the scores fall below the 75th percentile, and so on. When producing stem-and-leaf charts, for example, researchers also usually accompany the charts with a quantitative summary of the data that includes a listing of the scores falling at the 25th, 50th, and 75th percentiles.

In many cases, it is highly useful to know the location of the typical score and the spread of scores around that location. We turn to measures of spread in a moment, but one very useful measure of typical location is the 50th percentile, also called the **median** (symbolized as *Mdn*). It is one of several popular measures of **central tendency**, which tells us that it is one measure of the location of central or typical values. The median is the score above and below which half the scores fall. In other words, the median is the midmost score in a distribution of scores. For example, when the total number of scores (symbolized as N) is an odd number, the median is simply the middle score. Thus, in the series 2, 3, 3, 4, 4, 5, 6, 7, 7, 8, 8, the *Mdn* = 5 because it is in the middle, leaving five scores below it (2, 3, 3, 4, 4) and five scores above it (6, 7, 7, 8, 8).

When the number of scores is an even number (so that there are two midmost scores), the median is computed as half the distance between the two middle numbers. In the series 2, 3, 3, 4, 4, 7, the *Mdn* = 3.5, halfway between the 3 and the 4 at the center of the set of scores. Tied scores can create a small problem, however. In the series 1, 2, 3, 3, 3, what do we regard as the median? One solution is to imagine such a series as perfectly ranked so that, for example, the series 1, 2, 3, 3, 3 is seen as made up of a 1, a 2, a "small" 3, a "larger" 3, and a "still larger" 3. The assumption is that using a more precise measurement procedure would have allowed us to break the ties. In the series 1, 2, 3, 3, 3, we regard the "small 3" as the median, because there are two scores below this particular 3 and two above it. In reporting this result, however, we would simply state, "*Mdn* = 3."

An easy way to locate the median (the 50th percentile) is to multiply $N + 1$ (where N is again the total number of scores in the ordered set) by .50. In the back-to-back stem-and-leaf in Figure 10.4, Schumann's annual rate of musical compositions was 0, 1, 1, 3, 4, 5, 5 scores when he was depressed. The median is given by .50($N + 1$), which is .50(7 + 1) = 4th score in the set of seven ordered scores, or *Mdn* = 3 compositions. Similarly, Schumann's rate of compositions was 1, 2, 4, 16, 25, 28 scores when he was hypomanic. The median rate is given by .50(6 + 1) = 3.5th score in this set. That is, the median is halfway between the number 4 and the number 16, or *Mdn* = 10.

We can also use this procedure to locate other percentiles. The 75th percentile is .75($N + 1$), and the 25th percentile is .25($N + 1$). In the 0, 1, 1, 3, 4, 5, 5 set, the 75th percentile is .75(8) = 6th score, or 5 compositions. The 25th percentile in this set is .25(8) = 2nd score, that is, 1 lone composition. In the 1, 2, 4, 16, 25, 28 set, the 75th percentile is .75(7) = 5.25th score (i.e., 25% of the distance between the 5th and 6th scores), which gives 25.75 compositions. For these same six scores, the 25th percentile is .25(7) = 1.75th score (i.e., 75% of the distance between the 1st and 2nd scores), which is 1.75 compositions. The distance between the 25th and 75th percentiles is called the **interquartile range**. In the 1, 2, 4, 16, 25, 28 set, the interquartile range reveals that, when Schumann was in a hypomanic state, the middle 50% of his annual work was between 1.75 and 25.75 compositions.

How Is an Exploratory Data Analysis Done?

Previously, we mentioned that the stem-and-leaf can be used not only to do hypothesis testing (known as **confirmatory data analysis**), but also to do exploratory data analysis. **Exploratory data analysis** is detective work because we are looking for clues, and to do it properly, we must look in the right place (Tukey, 1977). Therefore, we would not stop with a visual display of the overall batch of data but would also look for patterns in parts of the batch. Let us see how to do this using only the stem-and-leaf chart and the calculation of percentiles.

In the previous chapter, we referred to research on volunteer characteristics. As part of that research, a number of investigators were interested in what kind of volunteers become "no-shows" (i.e., people who fail to show up for their scheduled research appointments). Suppose we want to estimate the typical number of subjects we need to volunteer to ensure that at least 40 will show up. Some years ago, we explored a variation on this question in a literature review of 20 available studies that had reported the proportion of no-shows (R. Rosenthal & Rosnow, 1975b). Those proportions are listed in the stem-and-leaf chart in Figure 10.5. The proportion of no-shows (reading from top to bottom) was .42 in one study, .41 in another study, .40 in another study, .38 in another study, and so forth. To continue our detective work, we will compute the 25th, 50th (*Mdn*), and 75th percentiles on these data.

Reading now from the lowest to the highest score in Figure 10.5, the sequence of values is as follows:

1. .03	**6.** .19	**11.** .32	**16.** .37
2. .10	**7.** .24	**12.** .36	**17.** .38
3. .12	**8.** .30	**13.** .36	**18.** .40
4. .14	**9.** .30	**14.** .37	**19.** .41
5. .16	**10.** .31	**15.** .37	**20.** .42

and the location of the median in this ordered series is the .50(20 + 1) = 10.5th score. That is, the median is halfway between the 10th score (.31) and the 11th score (.32), or *Mdn* = .32 (i.e., .315 rounded to the nearest even value).

The location of the 25th percentile score is given by .25(N + 1), and therefore .25(21) = 5.25th score (i.e., 25% of the distance between the 5th and 6th scores), which gives us .17. The location of the 75th percentile score is .75(N + 1), which we calculate as .75(21) = 15.75th score, 75% of the distance between the 15th and

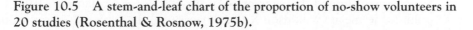

Stems	Leaves
.4	0 1 2
.3	0 0 1 2 6 6 7 7 7 8
.2	4
.1	0 2 4 6 9
.0	3

Figure 10.5   A stem-and-leaf chart of the proportion of no-show volunteers in 20 studies (Rosenthal & Rosnow, 1975b).

16th scores. In this case, the 15th and 16th scores are both .37, so 75% of the distance between them is zero, and therefore the 75th percentile = .37. To summarize this stem-and-leaf chart in certain key values of the distribution, we would report that (a) the maximum value = .42; (b) the 75th percentile = .37; (c) the *Mdn* (50th percentile) = .32; (d) the 25th percentile = .17; and (e) the minimum value = .03.

What have we learned? The interquartile range (the distance between the 25th and 75th percentiles) reveals that the 50% of the studies that were midmost have values between .17 and .37. From the fact that the median no-show rate of volunteers is .32, we now have a recommendation: If we are counting on 40 volunteer participants to show up for our research, we should schedule about 60 (i.e., one third of 60 = 20, and 60 − 20 = 40), or one-half more research subjects than we absolutely need. Of course, this recommendation is based on the assumption that the results in Figure 10.5 are, in fact, typical and that the median no-show rate is still about the same. In fact, other, more recent, findings by Aditya (1996) do seem to support this assumption; he found that the median no-show rate had remained relatively unchanged (still about one third).

How Does Asymmetry Affect Measures of Central Tendency?

Besides the median, another informative measure of central tendency is the **mode**. It is the score, or category of scores, that occurs most often. In the series 3, 4, 4, 4, 5, 5, 6, 6, 7, the mode = 4. The series 3, 4, 4, 4, 5, 5, 6, 7, 7, 7 has two modal scores (at values 4 and 7) and is thus described as *bimodal* (having two modes). For the stem-and-leaf chart in Figure 10.5, we would refer to the modal *category* as the ".30s" (stem of .3 and leaves of 0, 0, 1, 2, 6, 6, 7, 7 ,7, 8). Sometimes, there is no distinct mode, in which case it is better to use another measure to describe the central tendency of the data, such as the median or the ordinary mean.

The ordinary mean (or *arithmetic mean*), called the **mean** for short, is generally symbolized in psychology research reports as *M* (American Psychological Association, 2001). However, an older symbol that some textbooks use for the arithmetic mean is $\overline{X}$. Whether you see *M* or $\overline{X}$, the arithmetic mean is the sum of the scores (ΣX) divided by the total number (*N*) of scores in a set (or *n* for a subset of scores, that is, a sample of scores). Thus, the formula for the mean is

$$M = \frac{\Sigma X}{N}$$

BOX 10.2 The Mean as the Center of Gravity

You can think of the mean as the "center of gravity" of a distribution of numbers. Suppose you turned the stem-and-leaf on its side and balanced it. The balance point is the mean (Wilkinson & Engelman, 1996). In Table 10.1, how would you calculate the "balance point" (the mean) of the scores for each of the two food products? You could add up the 50 scores (i.e., −3 to +3 ratings) in each group and divide by 50, which gives $M = .22$ for the control product and $M = 1.18$ for the new product. A shortcut for finding the mean of these scores is to multiply each score by its frequency, sum the results, and divide by N.

where Σ (the uppercase Greek letter sigma) tells us to "sum" the X scores. In the series 1, 2, 3, 3, 3, the sum of the scores is 12, the number of scores is 5, and therefore, $M = 12/5 = 2.4$. For the stem-and-leaf values in Figure 10.5, the mean is calculated as the sum of the reported proportions (5.65) divided by 20, which gives $M = .28$ (i.e., .2825 rounded to .28) as the mean proportion of no-shows (see also Box 10.2).

Reporting more than one measure of central tendency will give readers a clearer idea of the distribution of the data set. When the distribution of scores is symmetrical, the median and the mean give the same value. The mode is a good way to show that there were many identical scores, and the median is useful when there are extreme high or low scores, because it is unaffected by only a few extreme scores. When scores are tightly bunched, the mean is close to all the scores, though averaging in a few extremely high or extremely low scores may give a misleading picture of the central tendency of the data set.

Figure 10.6 further illustrates these relationships. The (b) curve displays a **symmetrical distribution**, which means there is a correspondence in arrangement

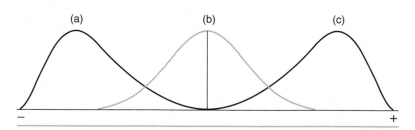

Figure 10.6   Illustrations of symmetry and asymmetry. Only distribution (b) is symmetrical, in that both sides of the middle line are identical. When the long, pointed tail is toward the positive end (i.e., a long right tail) as represented by (a), the distribution is said to be positively skewed. When the long, pointed tail is toward the negative end (i.e., a long left tail) as illustrated by (c), the distribution is said to be negatively skewed.

on the opposite sides of the middle line. When the right side is not the reverse of the left side of the distribution, we have an **asymmetrical distribution**. When the mean of the distribution is much larger than the median, the stretched-out tail points conspicuously toward the positive end (in a **positively skewed distribution**), as shown by the (a) curve. When the mean is smaller than the median, the stretched-out tail points toward the negative end (in a **negatively skewed distribution**), as shown by the (c) curve. The (b) curve also shows what we meant when we said that, in a symmetrical (or nonskewed) distribution, the median and the mean have the same value.

Suppose that a few scores lie far outside the normal range. These far-out scores are called **outliers**. When a distribution of scores is strongly asymmetrical because of outliers, researchers often prefer a **trimmed mean** to an ordinary mean because an ordinary mean is very sensitive to extreme values. Trimming implies giving the data set a "light haircut" by cutting off not just the one or more outliers from one side, but the same percentage of scores from both ends of the series of scores. Consider, for example, a strongly asymmetrical series: -20, 2, 3, 6, 7, 9, 9, 10, 10, 10. The -20 is an outlier that clearly disrupts the homogeneity of the series. To expunge outliers fairly, we trim an equal number of scores at each end. In this case, trimming one score from each end leaves 2, 3, 6, 7, 9, 9, 10, 10. What if we had not given the series such a haircut? Would leaving the outlier in have distorted the average by very much? It depends on how the "average" is defined. The trimmed mean = 7.0 and the untrimmed mean = 4.6, so the answer is yes in the case of the ordinary mean (M). The median is unaffected by trimming, so for these scores $Mdn = 8$ with or without trimming. The mode, which may be affected by trimming, is 10 for the scores before trimming but is bimodal at 9 and 10 after trimming (see also Box 10.3).

BOX 10.3   Unusual Scores and "Wild Scores"

Medians and trimmed means protect us in certain cases from possibly misleading interpretations based on very unusual scores. For example, if we calculated the benefits of a proposed tax plan for 10 families and found 9 of them with a $100 benefit and 1 with a $9,100 benefit, the mean benefit of $1,000 would be highly unrepresentative of the "typical benefit" compared to the trimmed mean, the median, or (in this case) even the mode. Medians and trimmed means also protect us somewhat against the intrusion of certain scores recorded erroneously (called *wild scores*). Imagine the series 4, 5, 5, 6, 6, 6, 7, 7, 8, of which the mean, median, mode, and trimmed mean are all 6. However, suppose we erred and entered the data as 4, 5, 5, 6, 6, 6, 7, 7, 80. Our new (erroneous) mean would now be 14, although our median or trimmed mean would remain unaffected.

How Do I Measure How "Spread Out" a Set of Scores Is?

Besides knowing the central tendency (or "typical value") of a set of scores, researchers also want to know how "spread out" the scores are (i.e., they want to know the *interval estimate,* as it is called in Chapter 9). That is, they also want to know how far the scores deviate from the value of the central tendency measure. Just as there are different measures of central tendency, there are also several different measures of what is alternatively described as *spread, dispersion,* or *variability.* For example, we mentioned the interquartile range (i.e., the distance between the 25th and 75th percentiles), which tells us the variability characteristic of the middle 50% of the scores. Other measures of spread include the range (crude and extended), the variance, and the standard deviation.

We will start with the ordinary **range** (or **crude range**), which is simply the difference between the highest and lowest scores. If you are administering a scale, you will want to report the *potential* crude range as well as the *observed* (or obtained) range. If the potential crude range is very narrow, it may be impossible to produce appreciable differences among the participants; that is, there is a flaw in the design. On the other hand, it does not follow that simply having a very wide potential range will automatically result in a substantial observed range. The way we interpret the range depends on the purpose of the study and the nature of the instruments used. For example, if you used a scale consisting of 20 five-point items, each item scored from 1 to 5, the potential crude range is from 20 to 100. You would report the potential crude range (CR) as being the highest score (H) minus the lowest score (L), or potential $CR = H - L = 80$ points. Using the same method, you would also report the crude range for the observed scores.

A further distinction is made between the crude range and the **extended range** (sometimes called the **corrected range**). In the series 2, 3, 4, 4, 6, 7, 9, the crude range is the highest score minus the lowest score, or $CR = 9 - 2 = 7$. The extended range (ER) assumes that, in more precise measurements, a score of 9 will fall somewhere between 8.5 and 9.5 and that a score of 2 will fall somewhere between 1.5 and 2.5. To adjust for this possibility, we think of the extended range in this case as running from a high of 9.5 to a low of 1.5. The extended range is then $9.5 - 1.5 = 8$. The extended range thus adds a half unit at the top of the distribution and a half unit at the bottom of the distribution, or a total of 1 full unit, and can be computed as $ER = (H - L) + 1$. The crude range and the extended range tell us about the extreme scores in a set of scores, whereas the next two measures of spread—the variance and the standard deviation—are based on information from all the scores.

The **variance** of a set of scores tells us the deviation from the mean of the scores, but instead of using deviation values directly, it squares the deviations and averages them. In other words, it is the mean of the squared deviations of the scores (X) from their mean (M). The variance of a set of scores is also commonly referred to as the **mean square** (i.e., the mean of the squared deviations), and you will see this term again in our discussion of the F test (which is used in the statistical procedure known as *analysis of variance*). The symbol used to denote the variance of a population is σ^2 (read as "sigma-squared"), and the formula used to calculate the population variance is

$$\sigma^2 = \frac{\Sigma(X - M)^2}{N}$$

where the numerator instructs us to sum the squared deviations of the individual scores from the mean of the set of scores, and the denominator tells us to divide that sum by the total number of scores.

The **standard deviation** is by far the most widely used and reported of all measures of spread around the average. Symbolized as σ, the standard deviation of a population is the square root of the population variance. That is,

$$\sigma = \sqrt{\sigma^2}$$

or calculated from the original data as

$$\sigma = \sqrt{\frac{\Sigma(X - M)^2}{N}}$$

Thus, another name for the standard deviation is the **root mean square**, which is shorthand for the square root of the mean of the squared deviations, as the equation above shows.

If you do not have a calculator that allows you to compute the standard deviation and the variance directly from "raw" (i.e., obtained) scores (and are not using a computer with a statistics package), it is still easy to compute these values with the calculator you use to balance your checkbook. Table 10.3 shows the summary data you need to calculate the variance and standard deviation of the set of raw scores in the first column. You compute the population variance and standard deviation in five easy steps:

Step 1 (in the first column) is to add up the six raw scores ($\Sigma X = 30$), and then to find their mean by dividing the sum by the number of scores ($M = 30/6 = 5$).

Table 10.3 Summary Data for Computing the Variance and the Standard Deviation

Raw scores	$X - M$	$(X - M)^2$
2	−3	9
4	−1	1
4	−1	1
5	0	0
7	2	4
8	3	9
$\Sigma X = 30$	$\Sigma(X - M) = 0$	$\Sigma(X - M)^2 = 24$
$M = 5$		

Step 2 (in the second column) is to subtract the mean from each raw score. As a check on your arithmetic, you will find that these deviation scores sum to zero, that is, $\Sigma(X - M) = 0$.

Step 3 (in the last column) is to square the deviation scores in column 2, and then to add up the squared deviations, which gives $\Sigma(X - M)^2 = 24$.

Step 4 is to compute the population variance (σ^2) by substituting the value obtained in Step 3 in the numerator, and the number of scores in the denominator, which gives you

$$\sigma^2 = \frac{\Sigma(X - M)^2}{N} = \frac{24}{6} = 4$$

Step 5 is to find the standard deviation, either by obtaining the square root of the value in Step 4, that is,

$$\sigma = \sqrt{4} = 2$$

or by direct substitution in the formula noted earlier, that is,

$$\sigma = \sqrt{\frac{\Sigma(X - M)^2}{N}} = \sqrt{\frac{24}{6}} = 2$$

What Are Descriptive and Inferential Measures?

Another distinction is that made between descriptive and inferential measures. Suppose we are interested in the variability of the batting averages of a favorite baseball team. We collect the scores of *all* the players and then compute the standard deviation using the formula described above. In this case, the formula used for measuring variability is characterized as a **descriptive measure** because it describes a *complete population* of scores or events, with Greek letters (not italicized) used to symbolize the particular measure (e.g., σ or σ^2).

As discussed in the previous chapter, researchers are also interested in generalizing from a sample of known scores or events to a population of unknown scores or events, which may be finite or infinite (see Box 10.4). Suppose we were interested in the variability of major-league baseball players' batting averages. We collect a sample of scores and then make inferences about the variability of scores in the population from which they were drawn. The equation we now use to measure variability is characterized as an **inferential measure**, with roman type (italicized) used to symbolize the particular measure (e.g., S or S^2).

Except for the denominator and the symbol (Greek or roman), the descriptive and inferential formulas for computing variances (σ^2 and S^2)—and, therefore, standard deviations (σ and S)—are similar. In the descriptive formulas for variances and standard deviations, the numerator value is divided by N (as previously shown). In the inferential formulas, the numerator value is divided by $N - 1$ (because it can be shown statistically that, with repeated sampling, this procedure gives the most accurate inferences). Thus, if you want to estimate the variance

BOX 10.4 Finite and Infinite

In the baseball example, we are dealing with both a finite sample and a finite population. *Finite* means that all the units or events can, at least in theory, be completely counted. *Infinite,* on the other hand, means "boundless" or "without limits." Suppose, based on samples of sand that have been randomly collected, we want to make a generalization about the variability of all the sand at Atlantic City, New Jersey. Here, we are attempting to make an inference from a finite sample to a population of unknown "events" that is regarded as infinite (because of ecological changes and so on).

(σ^2) of a population from a sample, you use the statistic S^2 (referred to as the **unbiased estimator of the population value of σ^2**) and the following formula:

$$S^2 = \frac{\Sigma(X - M)^2}{N - 1}$$

where N is the sample size. And if you want to estimate the σ of a population from a sample, you use the statistic S and the following formula:

$$S = \sqrt{S^2} = \sqrt{\frac{\Sigma(X - M)^2}{N - 1}}$$

For example, if you think of the 6 raw scores in the first column of Table 10.3 (scores of 2, 4, 4, 5, 7, 8) as a sample from a larger population, and you want to generalize from this sample of $N = 6$ scores to the larger population, you compute

$$S^2 = \frac{\Sigma(X - M)^2}{N - 1} = \frac{24}{5} = 4.8$$

and

$$S = \sqrt{4.8} = 2.19$$

How Do I Compute a Confidence Interval Around a Population Mean?

In our discussion of survey research (Chapter 9), we introduced the idea of confidence interval estimates, which tell us about the degree to which the point estimates are likely to be in error. The most commonly reported confidence interval estimate (symbolized as CI) is the 95% CI. This interval runs from a value below our obtained point estimate to a value above it, both values having been chosen so that there is a 95% probability that the true (but unknown) population value falls between the lower and upper limits. Because confidence intervals tell us how accurately or precisely we have estimated some quantity (e.g., a specific number of people, a proportion of a population, or a population mean), they are valuable pieces of information to have in a research report. Thus, we turn now to a procedure for obtaining confidence limits around an estimate of a population mean. (In a later chapter, we will describe a procedure for obtaining confidence limits around an estimate of a population effect size.)

Three quantities are required to compute a 95% CI around an obtained estimate of a population mean: N, S, and $t_{(.05)}$, where N is the number of scores upon which the observed mean (M) is based, and S is the standard deviation of the N scores obtained, computed again as

$$S = \sqrt{\frac{\Sigma(X - M)^2}{N - 1}}$$

If you have had a course in statistics, you know that t is the symbol for Student's t test (discussed in Chapter 13), but for this application, all you will need to know is how to find the value of $t_{(.05)}$. Looking at Table B.2 in Appendix B (page 394), you see, at the very top, a row labeled "two-tailed" and a value of ".05" in the fourth column. You know you are looking at the right column if you see 12.706 as the first value (corresponding to what in the far left is labeled "$df = 1$") and 1.960 as the last value (corresponding to "$df = \infty$" and ∞ is the symbol for infinity). We explain these terms in a later chapter, but for this application the df (which stands for *degrees of freedom*) is defined as $N - 1$ (the number of sample scores minus 1). We obtain the quantity $t_{(.05)}$ from Table B.2 by looking down the column headed ".05 two-tailed," until we reach the row label indicating the number of df on which our obtained mean was based (i.e., $N - 1$).

Consider again the data of Table 10.3, in which $N = 6$ raw scores. These scores are 2, 4, 4, 5, 7, 8, with mean (M) = 5 and (as calculated in the previous section) $S = 2.19$. We find that $t_{(.05)} = 2.57$, because $df = N - 1 = 5$, and Table B.2 shows the value 2.57 at the intersection of the column headed ".05 two-tailed" and the row labeled 5 df. To obtain a 95% confidence interval around the estimated population mean, we find

$$\text{Lower limit} = M - \frac{(t_{(.05)})(S)}{\sqrt{N}}$$

and

$$\text{Upper limit} = M + \frac{(t_{(.05)})(S)}{\sqrt{N}}$$

For our example in Table 10.3, we find

$$\text{Lower limit} = 5 - \frac{(2.57)(2.19)}{\sqrt{6}} = 5 - 2.30 = 2.70$$

CI (%)	x	$t_{(x)}$ (for $df = 5$)
99.9	.001	6.87
99	.01	4.03
95	.05	2.57
90	.10	2.02
80	.20	1.48

Table 10.4 Values of x and $t_{(x)}$ (for $df = 5$) for Five Different Confidence Intervals

and

$$\text{Upper limit} = 5 + \frac{(2.57)(2.19)}{\sqrt{6}} = 5 + 2.30 = 7.30$$

Because we computed a 95% CI around the obtained estimate of the population mean, we would state that "there is a 95% probability that the estimated population mean falls between 2.70 and 7.30."

Although 95% confidence intervals are the most commonly used, we can choose any size CI we like. We need only replace the quantity $t_{(.05)}$ with the quantity $t_{(x)}$, where $x = 1$ minus the desired CI. Table 10.4 shows the values of x and $t_{(x)}$ (for $df = 5$) for five different confidence intervals. Values of $t_{(x)}$ are larger for the more demanding confidence intervals (99% and 99.9%), as we would expect in general, but these values of $t_{(x)}$ are especially large (4.03 and 6.87) because of the small sample size in our example ($N = 6$).

What Is Distinctive About the Normal Distribution?

When scores on a variety of types of measures (intelligence test scores, physical performance measures, scores on an attitude scale, and so forth) are collected by means of a representative sampling procedure, the distribution of these scores often forms a curve that has a distinct bell-like shape (as shown in Figure 10.7).

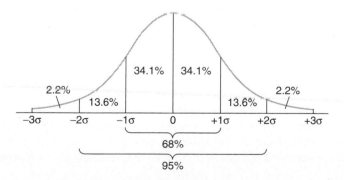

Figure 10.7   The normal distribution divided into standard deviation units.

This curve is called a **normal distribution** because of the large number of different kinds of measurements that are assumed to be ordinarily ("normally") distributed in this manner.

The normal distribution is particularly useful in providing a mathematical description of populations because it can be completely described from our knowledge of just the mean and the standard deviation. For example, we can say that
roughly two thirds of the area of the normal distribution is within one standard deviation of the mean, and so on. Specifically (as represented in Figure 10.7), 68.3%
of normally distributed scores fall between -1σ and $+1\sigma$; 95.4% fall between -2σ
and $+2\sigma$; and 99.7% fall between -3σ and $+3\sigma$. Even though over 99% of the
scores fall between -3σ and $+3\sigma$, the left and right tails of the normal curve never
do touch down on the abscissa; instead, they stretch into infinity.

One reason the normal distribution is so useful is that, by some simple arithmetic, we can translate raw scores obtained by different measures into standard deviation units. Not only does this process make the different scores comparable, but
we can usually estimate what proportion of normally distributed scores in the population can be found in any region of the curve. Because so many measurements
are distributed normally in the population, the statistics derived from this bell-
shaped curve are also very important in the testing of hypotheses. We will return to
this topic in Chapter 12, but let us see how you might translate a raw score into a
standard deviation unit, or a standard score.

Why Are *z* Scores Called *Standard Scores,* and How Are They Used?

A normal curve with a mean set equal to 0 and the standard deviation set equal to
1 is described as a **standard normal curve**. Any individual raw score can be put
through a statistical translation (referred to as **transformation**) into a **standard
score** corresponding to a location on the abscissa of a standard normal curve. A
standard score (called a **z score**) expresses, in standard deviation units, the raw
score's distance from the mean of the normative group. We make the transformation by subtracting the mean of the group (M) from the individual raw score (X),
and then dividing this difference by the standard deviation (σ) of the normative
group, that is

$$z \text{ score} = \frac{X - M}{\sigma}$$

For example, scores on the Scholastic Assessment Test (SAT) have a normative
group mean of 500 and a standard deviation of 100. Suppose you want to transform an individual raw score of 625 into a *z* score with a distribution mean of 0
and a standard deviation of 1. You simply calculate as follows:

$$z = \frac{625 - 500}{100} = 1.25$$

and find that the raw score of 625 corresponds to a z score of 1.25, which tells you how far above the mean (in terms of the standard deviation of the distribution) this score is. To transform the z score back to the original raw score, you multiply the z score by σ and add it to M:

$$X = (z \text{ score}) (\sigma) + M = (1.25)(100) + 500 = 625$$

Table B.1 in Appendix B (see page 393) provides a listing of z scores (standardized normal deviates). The z column (with rows ranging from .0 to 4.0) lists z values to one decimal place. The remaining columns (.00 to .09) carry z to two decimal places. The body of the table shows the proportion of the area of the normal distribution that includes and is to the right of (i.e., above) the value of any particular z on the abscissa. You can use this information to estimate the proportion of normally distributed scores in the population that is higher (or lower) than the raw score of 625 (corresponding to a z score of 1.25) on the SAT. Given $z = 1.25$, you simply locate the intersection that corresponds to 1.2 (row 13) and .05 (column 6). That value is .1056, which estimates the proportion of SAT scores including and higher than an obtained score of 625 in the normative group of students taking the SAT. Multiply .1056 by 100 to transform the proportion into a percentage, which tells you that 10.56% of those tested ordinarily score as high as 625 or higher. Subtracting this percentage from 100 tells you how many ordinarily score lower than 625 (i.e., $100 - 10.56 = 89.44\%$ score lower).

Note that the title of Table B.1 refers to "one-tailed" p values. We will have more to say about "one-tailed" (or "one-sided") significance levels in other chapters, but basically the term means that we are concentrating on one part of the normal distribution. In the case of a positive z score, we are focusing on the part from the midpoint (0) to the end of the right tail. If the z were a negative score, we would be concentrating on the part from the midpoint to the end of the left tail. In summary, then, a positive z score is above the mean; a negative z score is below the mean; and a zero z score is at the mean.

The beauty of reporting z scores is that scores on different tests or instruments need not be normally distributed to be transformed into z scores and then compared in terms of this common metric. For example, by calculating z scores for height and weight, you can tell whether a person is taller than he or she is heavy, relative to others in the normative distribution of height and weight. However, only if they are distributed approximately normally in the population can you estimate from a z score how many scored above or below a given z score. You can do so for SAT scores because they are approximately normally distributed in the population.

As a practical illustration of the utility of z scores, imagine that an instructor has two measures of course grades on five male and five female students, as shown in Table 10.5. One set of scores (X_1) is based on an essay exam of 50 points with $M = 21.2$ and $\sigma = 11.69$, and another (X_2) is based on a multiple-choice exam of 100 points with $M = 68.8$ and $\sigma = 17.47$. The instructor transforms the raw scores into standard scores, with the results shown in the z_1 and z_2

Table 10.5	Raw and Standard Scores on Two Exams				
Student ID and gender	Exam 1		Exam 2		Average of z_1 and z_2 scores
	X_1 score	z_1 score	X_2 score	z_2 score	
1 (M)	42	+1.78	90	+1.21	+1.50
2 (M)	9	−1.04	40	−1.65	−1.34
3 (F)	28	+0.58	92	+1.33	+0.96
4 (M)	11	−0.87	50	−1.08	−0.98
5 (M)	8	−1.13	49	−1.13	−1.13
6 (F)	15	−0.53	63	−0.33	−0.43
7 (M)	14	−0.62	68	−0.05	−0.34
8 (F)	25	+0.33	75	+0.35	+0.34
9 (F)	40	+1.61	89	+1.16	+1.38
10 (F)	20	−0.10	72	+0.18	+0.04
Sum (Σ)	212	0	688	0	0
Mean (M)	21.2	0	68.8	0	0
SD (σ)	11.69	1.0	17.47	1.0	0.98

columns. For example, on Exam 1 Student 1 received a raw score of 42, which the instructor converts to a z score by computing $(42 − 21.2)/11.69 = 1.78$. Student 1's score on Exam 1 is almost 2 standard deviations above the mean, but Student 2's score on the same exam is approximately 1 standard deviation *below* the mean.

The z scores take this information into account, allowing the instructor to make easy comparisons within and across students. Here, the instructor counted the two exams equally to get the average score (in the last column), but it is easy enough to weight them. Suppose she had wanted to count the second exam twice as much as the first exam; she would double the z scores for Exam 2 before averaging the two exams and then divide by 3 instead of 2. Notice also that the standard deviation (SD) at the bottom of the last column is not 1.0; the reason is that the averages of two or more z scores are not themselves distributed as z scores with $\sigma = 1.0$. If the instructor wanted the averages of these z scores to be distributed as z, she would first have to z-score these averages.

Summary of Ideas

1. Clarity, precision, and efficiency are important criteria of graphic integrity when we want to represent numerical data in a visual display.

2. In a *frequency distribution*, a set of scores is arranged according to the incidence of occurrence either in a table or in a figure such as a *bar graph* or, if we want to show change over time, a *line graph*.

3. In a *stem-and-leaf chart,* the original data are preserved with any desired precision so that we can visually detect the symmetry, spread, and concentration of the batch as well as any outliers.

4. A *percentile* locates a score in a distribution by defining the point below which a given proportion (or percentage) of the cases falls. The *interquartile range* is the distance between the 25th and 75th percentiles.

5. The *median* (*Mdn,* or 50th percentile) is the midmost score of a distribution.

6. The *mode* is the score (or the batch of scores in a stem-and-leaf chart) occurring with the greatest frequency.

7. The *mean* (*M*) is the arithmetic average of a set of scores.

8. In a *symmetrical distribution,* the median and the mean have the same value. *Trimmed means* are useful when distributions are strongly *asymmetrical,* and (like medians) they can often protect us against the intrusion of "wild scores" (Box 10.3).

9. The *range* is the distance between the highest and lowest scores (the *crude range*), sometimes *extended* (also called *corrected*) to increase precision.

10. The *variance* (or *mean square*) is the average squared distance from the mean of all the scores.

11. The *standard deviation* (or *root mean square*) is the square root of the variance.

12. *Descriptive measures* (e.g., σ and σ^2) are used to calculate population values, and *inferential measures* (*S* and S^2) are used to estimate population values based on a sample of values.

13. A *confidence interval* (CI) around an estimated population mean tells us how accurately we have estimated the mean within certain lower and upper limits.

14. The *normal distribution* is a bell-shaped curve that is completely described by the mean and the standard deviation.

15. We calculate *standard scores* (*z scores*) by *transforming* raw scores to standard deviation units.

16. Standard scores permit the comparison (and averaging) of scores from different distributions of widely differing means and standard deviations.

Key Terms

abscissa   p. 227
asymmetrical distribution
   p. 235
back-to-back stem-and-leaf
   chart   p. 230
bar graphs   p. 227
central tendency   p. 231
confirmatory data analysis
   p. 232
corrected range   p. 236
crude range   p. 236
descriptive measure   p. 238
exploratory data analysis
   p. 232
extended range   p. 236
frequency distribution
   p. 227

inferential measure   p. 238
interquartile range   p. 232
line graphs   p. 228
mean (*M*)   p. 233
mean square (S^2)   p. 236
median (*Mdn*)   p. 231
mode   p. 233
negatively skewed
   distribution   p. 235
normal distribution
   p. 242
ordinate   p. 227
outliers   p. 235
percentile   p. 231
positively skewed
   distribution   p. 235
range   p. 236

root mean square   p. 237
standard deviation   p. 237
standard normal curve
   p. 242
standard score (*z*)   p. 242
stem-and-leaf chart   p. 228
symmetrical distribution
   p. 234
transformation   p. 242
trimmed mean   p. 235
unbiased estimator of the
   population value of σ^2
   p. 239
variance   p. 236
x axis   p. 227
y axis   p. 227
z score   p. 242

Multiple-Choice Questions for Review

1. A graph in which the horizontal axis contains the score values, and in which the vertical axis reflects the frequency of a given score, is called a (a) stem-and-leaf chart; (b) cascade plot; (c) data summary graph; (d) frequency distribution.

2. Participants in a study at Iona College are asked to take a test of anxiety. Forty percent of the subjects receive scores lower than 12 on this test. For this sample, the value 12 is considered the (a) mean; (b) 40th percentile; (c) 60th percentile; (d) median.

3. Which of the following is considered a measure of central tendency? (a) mean; (b) 50th percentile; (c) mode; (d) all of the above

4. In a data set consisting of 0, 0, 0, 2, 2, 8, what is the mode? (a) 0; (b) 1; (c) 2; (d) 8

5. In the data set shown above, what is the M? (a) 0; (b) 1; (c) 2; (d) 8

6. In the same data set, what is the Mdn? (a) 0; (b) 1; (c) 2; (d) 8

7. Consider the following set of data points: 0, 1, 2, 3, 4. What is the crude range of these scores? (a) 2.5; (b) 0; (c) 4; (d) 5

8. Formulas that are used to calculate information about a population are called _____. (a) popular; (b) descriptive; (c) inferential; (d) none of the above

9. A standard normal distribution has a mean of _____ and a standard deviation of _____. (a) 0, 1; (b) 1, 0; (c) 1, 1; (d) cannot be determined from this information

10. A DePaul researcher administers an attitude scale to a group of I/O students. The average score is 2, and the standard deviation is 2. Suppose that you receive a score of zero. What is your z score? (a) 2; (b) −2; (c) 0; (d) −1

Discussion Questions for Review

1. A University of Oregon student conducted a study on anxiety in 11 business executives. Their scores on a standardized test of anxiety were 32, 16, 29, 41, 33, 37, 27, 30, 22, 38, and 33. Can you reconstruct the student's stem-and-leaf chart for these scores? What is the median of these scores, and what are the extended range and the interquartile range?

2. A Fordham University student is interested in studying ways of cutting down noise pollution in Manhattan. Her first step is to buy a machine that will measure the loudness of various sounds. In order to decide which machine to buy, she tests four brands against a standard tone of 85 decibels for five trials each, with the results shown below. Assuming that all the machines have the same price, which should be her first choice?

	Machine A	Machine B	Machine C	Machine D
	76	84	83	85
	82	87	89	81
	78	83	91	93
	84	85	77	89
	80	86	105	77
M	80	85	89	85
S	3.16	1.58	10.49	6.32

Oops . . . she finds that the manufacturer has discontinued her first-choice brand. Which machine would you recommend as a second choice, and why?

3. A Haverford College student recorded the following scores: 22, 14, 16, 24, 13, 26, 17, 98, 11, 9, and 21. What measure of central tendency would you advise him to calculate? Why?

4. A Florida State University student was looking at her grades for the midterm and the final exam. On the midterm she got a score of 58 and the class mean was 52 with a standard deviation of 12. On the final she got a score of 110; the class mean was 100 with a standard deviation of 30. On which test did she do better?

5. A Brandeis University student calls home to tell his family that he just received a score of 2 on a new IQ test. As they wonder why they are spending so much money on his tuition, he reassures them that 2 is his z score. What percentage of the population did he score above?

6. A University of Missouri professor has three sections with three graduate assistants—Tom, Dick, and Harry—each of whom has six students. The time has come to grade papers. In order to ensure uniform grading standards across the sections, the professor instructs the assistants to give an average score of 8.0 (equivalent to B−) on a scale of 1 to 12 (where 1 represents a grade of F, and 12 represents a grade of A). The assistants submit the following sets of grades:

Tom	Dick	Harry
12	8	7
6	8	7
5	10	8
5	7	5
8	8	6
12	7	9

The professor calls in Harry and says, "You have not followed my instructions. Your scores are biased toward having your section do better than it is supposed to." Calculate the means of each section, and then argue the truth or falsity of the professor's accusation. The professor next calls in Tom and Dick and says, "Although both of your sections have a mean grade of 8.0, Tom's scores look more spread out." Calculate, and then compare, the standard deviation of the scores in the sections to decide whether the professor is right. Which is a better grade (relative to one's own section), a 5 in Tom's section or a 7 in Dick's section?

7. Compute the σ, σ^2, S, and S^2 on the no-show data in the stem-and-leaf chart shown in Figure 10.5 (p. 233).

Answers to Review Questions

Multiple-Choice Questions

1. d	3. d	5. c	7. c	9. a
2. b	4. a	6. b	8. b	10. d

Discussion Questions

1. The stem-and leaf plot is

Stem	Leaf
4	1
3	0 2 3 3 7 8
2	2 7 9
1	6

The median score can be found from $.5(N + 1) = .5(12) = 6$. Because the sixth score is 32, that is our median. The extended range is the crude range $(41 - 16)$ plus 1 unit, or $25 + 1 = 26$. The interquartile range is from the $.25(N + 1)$th to the $.75(N + 1)$th score, or from 27 to 37.

2. Her first choice is Machine B because it shows no bias and the least instability or variability. Her second choice might be Machine D because it shows no bias or Machine A because, although it shows a 5-decibel bias, it measures volume more consistently. As long as she remembers to correct for the 5-decibel bias, she might be well advised to get Machine A.

3. Because of the outlier score of 98, he should prefer the median or a trimmed mean to the ordinary mean. In this example, the mean of the 11 untrimmed scores is 24.6, whereas the median is only 17 and the trimmed mean (trimmed by 1 on each end) is 18.2.

4. She did better on the midterm, where the z score $= (58 - 52)/12 = .50$, than on the final, where the z score $= (110 - 100)/30 = .33$.

5. He scored above 97.7% of the normative population.

6. The professor is correct in thinking Harry's grading to be biased. However, the professor is wrong about the direction of the bias. Harry's average grade is a C+ (7) instead of a B− (8). The professor is correct in thinking Tom's grades are more spread out than Dick's grades. The three standard deviations are 3.00, 1.00, and 1.29 for Tom, Dick, and Harry, respectively. Students earning scores of 5 in Tom's section performed the same as those earning scores of 7 in Dick's section; in both cases, $z = -1.00$.

7. The answers are $\sigma = .115$, $\sigma^2 = .013$, $S = .118$, and $S^2 = .014$.

CHAPTER 11

Correlating Variables

Preview Questions

- What are different forms of correlations?
- How are correlations visualized in scatter plots?
- How is the product-moment r calculated?
- How is the Spearman rank correlation computed?
- How is dummy coding used in correlation?
- When is the phi coefficient used?

What Are Different Forms of Correlations?

You have seen that researchers view variables not in isolation, but instead as systematically and meaningfully associated with, or related to, other variables. In this chapter, we will elaborate on how, using a single number (called the **correlation coefficient**), you can indicate the strength of association between two variables (X and Y). In particular, we describe correlations that reflect the degree to which mutual relations between X and Y resemble a straight line (called **linearity**). The **Pearson r**, short for Karl Pearson's product-moment correlation coefficient, is the correlation coefficient of choice in such situations. Values of r of 1.0 (positive or negative) indicate a perfect linear relation (i.e., a fixed change in one variable is always associated with a fixed change in the other variable), while 0 indicates that neither X nor Y can be predicted from the other by use of a linear equation (see also Box 11.1). A positive r tells us that an increase in X is associated with an increase in Y, whereas a negative r indicates that an increase in X is associated with a decrease in Y.

We begin by examining what different values of r look like. Then we proceed through the steps in computing the correlation coefficient when the raw data have different characteristics, as previewed in Table 11.1. The common names shown in the table communicate whether the values of X and Y are continuous or dichotomous, though *Pearson r* also is often used in a more general way to refer to any correlation computed as a product-moment r. **Continuous variable** simply means that it is possible to imagine another value falling between any two adjacent scores, and **dichotomous variable** means that the variable is divided into two discrete parts (it is also called a **discrete variable**, that is, a variable with two or more

BOX 11.1 Galton, Pearson, and r

In an earlier chapter, we mentioned Francis Galton's pioneering work. Galton was very intuitive about statistics, and he instinctively came up with a way of measuring the "co-relation" between two variables. At the time, one of his many projects concerned the relationship between traits of fathers and their adult sons. One day, while he was strolling around the grounds of a castle, it started to rain and Galton sought refuge in the recess of a rock by the side of the pathway. It was there, he later recalled, that, while thinking about his research, the notion of statistical correlation initially flashed across his mind. Though the word *correlation* was already in widespread use in physics, it is believed that Galton's initial spelling of "co-relation" may have been a way of distancing his notion from the commonly used word (Stigler, 1986, p. 297). Galton was constantly preoccupied with all kinds of projects, and thus, although the statistical concept for which he is best known is correlation, he did not develop the idea beyond its use in some of his research. The reason that *r* is called the *Pearson r* is that it was Karl Pearson (1857–1936) who perfected Galton's "index of co-relation" in a more mathematically sophisticated way (Stigler, 1986).

distinct or separate parts). For example, a researcher who studies the discrimination of pitch (the highness or lowness of a tone) might correlate changes in the frequency of sound waves (X) with the differing ability of individuals to discriminate the changes (Y). Both variables are continuous, in that we can imagine a score of 1.5 between 1 and 2, or 1.55 between 1.5 and 1.6. Suppose the researcher correlates the participants' gender with their abilities to discriminate pitch. Pitch discrimination is a continuous variable, but gender is a discrete variable that is dichotomous (i.e., divided into two separate parts).

Table 11.1 Four Forms of Karl Pearson's Product-Moment *r*

Common name	Characteristics of the data
Pearson r	Two continuous variables, such as the correlation of scores on the Scholastic Assessment Test (SAT) with grade point average (GPA) after 4 years of college
Spearman rho (r_s)	Two ranked variables, such as the correlation of the ranking of the top 25 college basketball teams by sports writers (Associated Press ranking) with the ranking of the same teams by college coaches (*USA Today* ranking)
Point-biserial $r(r_{pb})$	One continuous and one dichotomous variable, such as the correlation of subjects' gender with their performance on the SAT-Verbal
Phi coefficient (ϕ)	Two dichotomous variables, such as the correlation of subjects' gender with their "yes" or "no" responses to a specific question

Correlation (*r*-type) indices have other useful applications besides those discussed in this chapter. In the case of dichotomous variables, for example, we can create dichotomies in what is called a *median split,* by splitting variables at the median point (we will return to this idea when we discuss the *binomial effect-size display* in the next chapter). There is also a family of *r*-type effect size indices that we discuss in Chapter 14 when we turn to comparisons (*contrasts*) on more than two conditions. Other important applications that are beyond the scope of this book are discussed in our advanced text (R. Rosenthal & Rosnow, 2008). For example, in a *partial correlation,* we can measure the correlation between two variables when the influence of other variables on their relationship has been eliminated statistically. Because correlations usually shrink in magnitude when the sample shrinks in variability on either of the variables being correlated, it is also possible to use a statistical solution (proposed by Karl Pearson) to correct for this restriction of variability. The purpose of this chapter, however, is to amplify your working knowledge of the basics of computing and interpreting Pearson *r* correlations in the kinds of situations you are most likely to encounter.

How Are Correlations Visualized in Scatter Plots?

In addition to the graphics described in the preceding chapter, another informative visual display is called a **scatter plot** (or a *scatter diagram*). It takes its name from looking like a cloud of scattered dots. Each dot represents the intersection of a line extended from a point on the X axis (the horizontal axis, or abscissa) and a line extended from a point on the Y axis (the vertical axis, or ordinate). To illustrate, Table 11.2 repeats the data that we used at the end of the previous chapter to explain z scores, and we will continue to discuss these data in this chapter. For now, we will concentrate on the raw scores (the X_1 and X_2 scores) of these 10 students on the two exams. Figure 11.1 displays these scores in the form of a scatter plot.

Table 11.2 Raw and Standardized Data for Product-Moment Correlation

Student ID and gender	Exam 1		Exam 2		Product of z_1 and z_2 scores
	X_1 score	z_1 score	X_2 score	z_2 score	
1 (M)	42	+1.78	90	+1.21	+2.15
2 (M)	9	−1.04	40	−1.65	+1.72
3 (F)	28	+0.58	92	+1.33	+0.77
4 (M)	11	−0.87	50	−1.08	+0.94
5 (M)	8	−1.13	49	−1.13	+1.28
6 (F)	15	−0.53	63	−0.33	+0.17
7 (M)	14	−0.62	68	−0.05	+0.03
8 (F)	25	+0.33	75	+0.35	+0.12
9 (F)	40	+1.61	89	+1.16	+1.87
10 (F)	20	−0.10	72	+0.18	−0.02
Sum (Σ)	212	0	688	0	+9.03
Mean (*M*)	21.2	0	68.8	0	.90
SD (σ)	11.69	1.0	17.47	1.0	

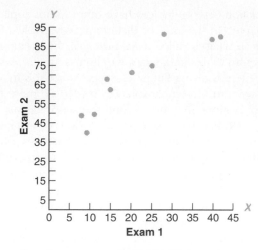

Figure 11.1   Scatter plot of raw scores in Table 11.2.

By way of comparison, Figure 11.2 shows additional scatter plots (each containing 50 dots) that represent different values of the correlation coefficient, including zero and near-perfect rs (see also Box 11.2). Now imagine a straight line through the dots in Figure 11.2. The higher the correlation is, the more tightly clustered along the line are the dots (and, therefore, the better is the linear predictability). Notice that the cloud of dots slopes up for positive correlations and slopes down for negative correlations, and that the linearity becomes clearer as the correlation becomes higher. From these

 BOX 11.2   The Third-Variable Problem Revisited

Of course, if we are interested in causality, even finding a perfect correlation will not rule out the possibility of a third-variable causal explanation of the observed relationship between X and Y (previously discussed in Chapter 8). As another example of the third-variable problem, there is a positive correlation between milk consumption and the incidence of cancer in various societies. The explanation for the correlation, however, is that people who live in relatively wealthy societies live longer, and increased longevity increases the likelihood of getting cancer. Indeed, any health practice (such as milk drinking) that increases longevity usually correlates positively with cancer incidence (Paulos, 1990). Another example is the small negative correlation observed between death rates and divorce rates (more divorce, less death) in various regions of the country. The third variable in this correlation is the age distribution of the various regions, as older married couples are less likely to divorce and more likely to die than younger couples (Paulos, 1990).

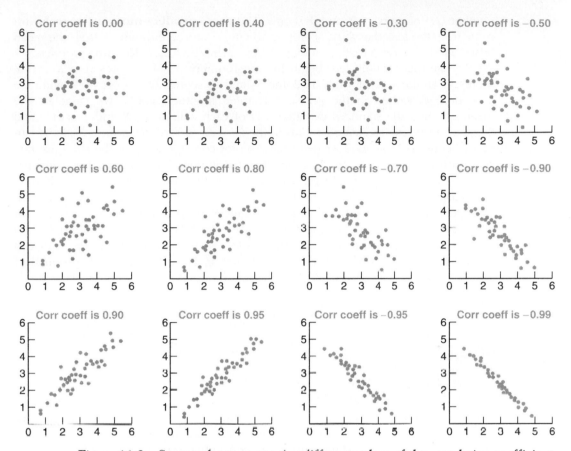

Figure 11.2   Scatter plots representing different values of the correlation coefficient.
Source: From Statistics (2nd ed., pp. 119, 121), by D. Freedman, R. Pisani, R. Purves, and A. Adhikari, 1991, New York: W. W. Norton. Reproduced by permission of D. Freedman and W. W. Norton.

diagrams, what would you guess is the size of the Pearson r represented by the data in Figure 11.1?

How Is the Product-Moment r Calculated?

There are many useful formulas for calculating different forms of the product-moment correlation coefficient (r). However, the following formula (which defines the Pearson r conceptually) can be used quite generally in most situations:

$$r_{xy} = \frac{\Sigma z_x z_y}{N}$$

This formula indicates that the linear correlation between two variables (X and Y) is equal to the sum of the products of the z scores of X and Y divided by the number (N) of pairs of X and Y scores. The name **product-moment correlation** came from the idea that the z scores (in the numerator) are distances from the mean (also called *moments*) that are multiplied by each other ($z_x z_y$) to form "products."

To use this formula, we begin by transforming the raw scores (the X and Y scores, or in the case of Table 11.2, the X_1 and X_2 scores) to z scores following the procedure described in the previous chapter. In other words, we calculate the mean (M) and the standard deviation (σ) of each column of X and Y scores and then substitute the calculated values in the $(X - M)/\sigma$ formula, where X is any student's score. In Table 11.2 we see such z scores corresponding to the students' raw scores on Exam 1 and Exam 2. Notice that, for Student 5, the z score for Exam 1 is identical to the z score for Exam 2, even though the raw scores are very different. The reason is that the z scores for Exam 1 were computed from the mean and standard deviation of Exam 1 (21.2 and 11.69, respectively), whereas the z scores for Exam 2 were computed from the mean and standard deviation of Exam 2 (68.8 and 17.47, respectively). Instead of averaging the z scores (as we did in the previous chapter for a different purpose), the last column in Table 11.2 gives the products of the z scores and their mean, showing that the rounded Pearson $r = .90$. That is,

$$r_{xy} = \frac{\Sigma z_x z_y}{N} = \frac{9.03}{10} = .903$$

where r_{xy} is, in this case, the correlation between X_1 and X_2 scores, and z_x and z_y are z-transformed X_1 and X_2 scores.

Although we use the conceptual formula above as a teaching tool in this chapter, it is far easier to obtain the Pearson r by using SPSS, SAS, SYSTAT, Minitab, or a calculator that allows you to punch a few buttons to compute r. But if all you have is the calculator you use to balance your checkbook, another way to compute the Pearson r (which is easier than using the conceptual formula above) is to use the following formula, which is based on raw scores rather than z scores:

$$r_{xy} = \frac{N\Sigma XY - (\Sigma X)(\Sigma Y)}{\sqrt{[N\Sigma X^2 - (\Sigma X)^2][N\Sigma Y^2 - (\Sigma Y)^2]}}$$

where N = the number of X and Y pairs of scores, and Σ directs us to sum a set of values. This formula may look difficult, but it is not hard to use. All you need are the sums of the scores and of the squared scores. To illustrate, Table 11.3 shows the basic data you need to compute r from the raw scores in Table 11.2. All that is different in Table 11.3 is that the scores on Exam 1 are symbolized as X scores and the scores on Exam 2 are symbolized as Y scores. Substituting the summary data of Table 11.3 into the formula above gives

$$r_{xy} = \frac{10(16,430) - (212)(688)}{\sqrt{[10(5,860) - (212)^2][10(50,388) - (688)^2]}} = \frac{18,444}{\sqrt{(13,656)(30,536)}} = .90$$

When using this formula, don't forget to take the square root of the denominator (see also Box 11.3).

	Exam 1		Exam 2		
Student	X	X^2	Y	Y^2	XY
1	42	1,764	90	8,100	3,780
2	9	81	40	1,600	360
3	28	784	92	8,464	2,576
4	11	121	50	2,500	550
5	8	64	49	2,401	392
6	15	225	63	3,969	945
7	14	196	68	4,624	952
8	25	625	75	5,625	1,875
9	40	1,600	89	7,921	3,560
10	20	400	72	5,184	1,440
Sum (Σ)	212	5,860	688	50,388	16,430

Table 11.3   Basic Data for Computing Pearson r from Raw Scores

How Is the Spearman Rank Correlation Computed?

As noted in Table 11.1, the four correlations discussed in this chapter are product-moment rs, and thus are simply special cases of the Pearson r that we have been discussing. Suppose the data are ranks rather than scores on a rating scale. The correlation coefficient is now called the **Spearman rho (r_s)**, but it is nothing

BOX 11.3   Linearity and Nonlinearity

Remember that the Pearson r is a measure of linearity. Though this r is close to 1, even a Pearson r near 0 does not automatically imply zero relationship between X and Y but only indicates there is no *linear relationship*. You need to inspect the scatter plot before ruling out the possibility of a nonlinear relationship. **Nonlinearity** can take many different forms (e.g., U-shaped, J-shaped, and wave-shaped curves). Suppose you are studying the relationship between age and the latency (delay) of some response, and you find that the latency decreases up to a certain age and then gradually increases. If you plot the results by means of a line graph, your curve showing this nonlinear relation will resemble a $\cup$ with age plotted on the abscissa (the X axis) and latency (delay) of response (from low to high) on the ordinate (the Y axis). Other examples of nonlinear relations include curves for learning, extinction, dark adaptation, and response rate as a function of the amount of reinforcement.

more than a Pearson r computed on numbers that happen to be in ranks. Ranked numbers are more predictable than unranked numbers because knowing only the number of pairs of scores (N) immediately tells us both the mean and the standard deviation of the scores obtained. A simple computational formula for correlations for scores that have been ranked is

$$r_s = 1 - \frac{6(\Sigma D^2)}{N^3 - N}$$

where 6 is a constant value, and D is the difference between the ranks assigned to the two scores representing each of the N sampling units.

To illustrate the use of this formula, Table 11.4 shows a portion of the data collected by Paul Slovic (1987) in his investigation of the perception of risk. He was interested in comparing the judgments people make when they are asked to characterize and evaluate hazardous activities and technologies. This table shows the overall rankings made by 15 experts on risk assessment and 40 members of the League of Women Voters (LWV). We see, for example, that the experts ranked motor vehicles as most hazardous (Rank 1) and skiing as least hazardous (Rank 30), but the LWV members ranked nuclear power as most hazardous (Rank 1) and vaccinations as least hazardous (Rank 30). Notice that the sums of the ranks are equal for the two variables (465). The column headed D lists the differences between the ranks. For instance, the difference in ranking of nuclear power is computed as $D = 1 - 20 = -19$. The sum of the D scores is always 0. The column headed D^2 shows such differences squared, so that $(-19)^2 = 361$.

To use the simple computational formula for the Spearman rho, we substitute the sum of the squared differences (indicated as 1,828 at the bottom of the column headed D^2) as follows:

$$r_s = 1 - \frac{6(\Sigma D^2)}{N^3 - N} = 1 - \frac{6(1,828)}{30^3 - 30} = .59$$

In interpreting rank correlations, we use the D scores and the ranks to help us interpret similarities and differences in the results. Here, a positive difference score tells us that the LWV members perceived the activity or technology as less risky than did the experts, whereas a negative difference score indicates the opposite conclusion. We see, for example, that the two groups of raters disagreed little about the high risks associated with motor vehicles, handguns, and motorcycles (D of +1 or −1). There was little disagreement about the much lower risk associated with power mowers ($D = -1$), but there was strong disagreement about nuclear power ($D = -19$), X-rays ($D = 15$), and mountain climbing ($D = -14$).

The equivalence of the Spearman r_s and the Pearson r computed from ranked data holds only when there are no ties in the ranking. If there are only a few ties, r_s will be quite similar to r. As there are no ties in Table 11.4 for either the LWV voters or the experts, we expect equivalence of the Spearman r_s and the Pearson

Table 11.4 Ordering of Perceived Risk for 30 Activities and Technologies

Activity or technology	League of Women Voters	Experts	D	D²
Nuclear power	1	20	−19	361
Motor vehicles	2	1	1	1
Handguns	3	4	−1	1
Smoking	4	2	2	4
Motorcycles	5	6	−1	1
Alcoholic beverages	6	3	3	9
General (private) aviation	7	12	−5	25
Police work	8	17	−9	81
Pesticides	9	8	1	1
Surgery	10	5	5	25
Firefighting	11	18	−7	49
Large construction	12	13	−1	1
Hunting	13	23	−10	100
Spray cans	14	26	−12	144
Mountain climbing	15	29	−14	196
Bicycles	16	15	1	1
Commercial aviation	17	16	1	1
Electric power (nonnuclear)	18	9	9	81
Swimming	19	10	9	81
Contraceptives	20	11	9	81
Skiing	21	30	−9	81
X-rays	22	7	15	225
High school and college football	23	27	−4	16
Railroads	24	19	5	25
Food preservatives	25	14	11	121
Food coloring	26	21	5	25
Power mowers	27	28	−1	1
Prescription antibiotics	28	24	4	16
Home appliances	29	22	7	49
Vaccinations	30	25	5	25
Sum (Σ)	465	465	0	1,828

Source: From "Perception of Risk," by P. Slovic, 1987, *Science, 236,* p. 281. Copyright © by American Association for the Advancement of Science. Reprinted with permission of Paul Slovic and the American Association for the Advancement of Science.

r computed from these ranked data. The needed data are in Table 11.5. For instance, to find the z score corresponding to the LWV's ranking of *nuclear power,* we computed

$$z = \frac{X - M}{\sigma} = \frac{1 - 15.50}{8.655} = -1.68$$

Table 11.5 Ranked and Standardized Data for Spearman Rho Correlation

Activity or technology	League of Women Voters		Experts		Product of z scores
	Rank	z score	Rank	z score	
Nuclear power	1	−1.68	20	+0.52	−0.87
Motor vehicles	2	−1.56	1	−1.68	+2.62
Handguns	3	−1.44	4	−1.33	+1.92
Smoking	4	−1.33	2	−1.56	+2.07
Motorcycles	5	−1.21	6	−1.10	+1.33
Alcoholic beverages	6	−1.10	3	−1.44	+1.58
General aviation	7	−0.98	12	−0.40	+0.39
Police work	8	−0.87	17	+0.17	−0.15
Pesticides	9	−0.75	8	−0.87	+0.65
Surgery	10	−0.64	5	−1.21	+0.77
Firefighting	11	−0.52	18	+0.29	−0.15
Large construction	12	−0.40	13	−0.29	+0.12
Hunting	13	−0.29	23	+0.87	−0.25
Spray cans	14	−0.17	26	+1.21	−0.21
Mountain climbing	15	−0.06	29	+1.56	−0.09
Bicycles	16	+0.06	15	−0.06	0.00
Commercial aviation	17	+0.17	16	+0.06	+0.01
Electric power	18	+0.29	9	−0.75	−0.22
Swimming	19	+0.40	10	−0.64	−0.26
Contraceptives	20	+0.52	11	−0.52	−0.27
Skiing	21	+0.64	30	+1.68	+1.08
X-rays	22	+0.75	7	−0.98	−0.74
High school and college football	23	+0.87	27	+1.33	+1.16
Railroads	24	+0.98	19	+0.40	+0.39
Food preservatives	25	+1.10	14	−0.17	−0.19
Food coloring	26	+1.21	21	+0.64	+0.77
Power mowers	27	+1.33	28	+1.44	+1.92
Prescription antibiotics	28	+1.44	24	+0.98	+1.41
Home appliances	29	+1.56	22	+0.75	+1.17
Vaccinations	30	+1.68	25	+1.10	+1.85
Sum (Σ)	465	0	465	0	17.82
Mean (M)	15.50	0	15.50	0	.59
SD (σ)	8.655	1.00	8.655	1.00	—

The last column of Table 11.5 shows the products of the z-scored ranks, with the sum and mean indicated at the bottom. That is,

$$r = \frac{\Sigma z_x z_y}{N} = \frac{17.82}{30} = .59$$

which, not surprisingly, is the same value we obtained using the simple computational formula for r_s.

The Spearman rho is typically used when the scores to be correlated are already in ranked form, as in the case that we have been discussing, or if you have judges rank a set of sampling units. The Spearman rho is also sometimes used to get a quick index of correlation when r_s is easy to compute by hand and r is hard and slow (see, e.g., Box 11.4). As another example, suppose we are working with raw scores that are continuous (such as the exam grades of the 10 students in Table 11.2) but we want to recast them as ranks and then compute a Spearman rho. Table 11.6 shows how we would do this. The students in Table 11.6 are now ranked from 1 (the highest raw score) to 10 (the lowest raw score), and again the

---

BOX 11.4 Using Rankings for Quick Estimates

Why use rankings when continuous data are available? In most cases, it is preferable to stay with the continuous data and use the Pearson r. However, suppose you want a quick estimate of the correlation between these six pairs of raw scores:

	Raw score for X	Raw score for Y	Rank of X	Rank of Y
Pair 1	73.8	801.76	2	1
Pair 2	186.2	732.90	1	2
Pair 3	44.4	539.57	3	3
Pair 4	38.6	206.11	4	5
Pair 5	37.5	210.56	5	4
Pair 6	21.8	159.33	6	6

Clearly, it would be tedious to calculate the Pearson r by hand from the raw scores. However, if you transform the raw scores into ranks and then calculate the Spearman rho on the basis of the (transformed) values in the last two columns, it is easier. But by sacrificing the continuity of the raw scores, you are also missing the fine distinctions. Still, in some situations, you may want to use rank ordering, such as when judges have no measuring instrument and must resort to rank ordering or when the raw scores include extreme outliers that may lead to misleading correlations (i.e., ranked scores never have extreme outliers).

Table 11.6	Raw Data from Table 11.2 Ranked for Spearman Rho Correlation					
	Exam 1		Exam 2			
Student	X_1 score	Rank	X_2 score	Rank	D	D^2
1	42	1	90	2	−1	1
2	9	9	40	10	−1	1
3	28	3	92	1	2	4
4	11	8	50	8	0	0
5	8	10	49	9	1	1
6	15	6	63	7	−1	1
7	14	7	68	6	1	1
8	25	4	75	4	0	0
9	40	2	89	3	−1	1
10	20	5	72	5	0	0
Sum (Σ)	212	55[a]	688	55[a]	0[b]	10

[a]Note that the sum of the ranks is equal for the two variables.
[b]Note that the sum of D is always 0.

D value is the difference between the ranks. The sum of the squared differences (indicated as 10 at the bottom of the column headed D^2) is simply substituted in the numerator of the Spearman rho formula:

$$r_s = 1 - \frac{6(\Sigma D^2)}{N^3 - N} = 1 - \frac{6(10)}{10^3 - 10} = .94$$

This is not the same correlation we got when working with the standardized raw scores ($r = .90$ in Table 11.2), but a slightly higher value ($r_s = .94$). The reason is that transforming the raw scores improved their symmetry, although transforming raw scores to ranks sometimes does lead to a lower correlation. Students often ask "Which is the 'right' correlation?"—the r based on the raw scores or the r or r_s based on the ranked scores? The answer is that they are *both right* and the only difference is that they are based on different values: continuous raw score values or ranks of scores. If there is an outlier in the distribution of continuous raw scores, correlating the scores may change the magnitude of r radically. In this case, we can use the trimming method (discussed in the previous chapter) and correlate the remaining continuous scores. If the sample is already quite small, however, we may prefer to rank the scores and then correlate those ranked scores (to avoid reducing the sample size any further). Whatever procedure we use, we should describe exactly what we did.

How Is Dummy Coding Used in Correlation?

Another case of the product-moment r is the **point-biserial correlation (r_{pb})**. The *point* means that scores for one variable are points on a continuum, and the *biserial* means that scores for the other variable are dichotomous. In many cases, the dichotomous scores may be arbitrarily applied numerical values, such as 0 and 1 or −1 and +1. The quantification of two levels of a dichotomous variable is called **dummy coding** when the numerical values 0 and 1 are used. Dummy coding is a tremendously useful method, for it allows us to quantify any variable that can be represented as dichotomous. For example, suppose you have performed an experiment in which there were two groups (an experimental and a control group) and you want to correlate group membership with scores on the dependent variable. To code group membership, you code 1 for experimental group and 0 for control group. Another dichotomous independent variable that can be easily recast into 1s and 0s is gender. Dichotomous dependent variables can also be dummy-coded by 1s and 0s, such as survival rate (live vs. die) or success rate (succeed vs. fail).

Going back to our earlier example in Table 11.2, suppose we want to compare males with females on Exam 1. The scores on that exam were as follows:

Males	Females
42	28
9	15
11	25
8	40
14	20

Although we see two groups of scores, this arrangement does not look like the typical one for a correlation coefficient, where we would expect to see *pairs* of X and Y scores. In this example, the scores on variable Y (exam scores) are shown, but X is hidden, the reason being that the group identification (male vs. female) implies the variable X scores.

The data arrangement rewritten in a form that looks more correlational is shown in Table 11.7. The first column shows the identification (ID) and gender information. Under "Exam 1," we see again the raw and standardized (z) scores for the first exam. Under "Student's gender," the first column shows the dummy-coded scores for gender, with the female students coded 1 and the male students coded 0. In this case, we would think of the dummy-coded variable as "femaleness" because 1 and 0 imply the presence and absence of femaleness, respectively. (If we had coded the male students 1 and the female students 0, we would then think of the dummy-coded variable as "maleness.") The next column under "Student's gender" shows the z scores after the dummy-coded values are standardized. For instance, to get the z score for Student 1's gender, we computed

$$z = \frac{X - M}{\sigma} = \frac{0 - 0.5}{0.5} = -1$$

where X = the dummy score of 0 for Student 1, M = the mean of the column of dummy scores ($M = 5/10 = 0.5$), and σ = the standard deviation (SD) shown at the bottom of that column (0.5).

| Student ID | Exam 1 | | Student's gender | | Product of |
and gender	Raw score	z score	Dummy code	z score	z scores
1 (M)	42	+1.78	0	−1	−1.78
2 (M)	9	−1.04	0	−1	+1.04
3 (F)	28	+0.58	1	+1	+0.58
4 (M)	11	−0.87	0	−1	+0.87
5 (M)	8	−1.13	0	−1	+1.13
6 (F)	15	−0.53	1	+1	−0.53
7 (M)	14	−0.62	0	−1	+0.62
8 (F)	25	+0.33	1	+1	+0.33
9 (F)	40	+1.61	1	+1	+1.61
10 (F)	20	−0.10	1	+1	−0.10
Sum (Σ)	212	0	5	0	+3.77
Mean (M)	21.2	0	0.5	0	.38
SD (σ)	11.69	1.0	0.5	1.0	

Table 11.7 Raw, Dummy-Coded, and Standardized Data for Point-Biserial Correlation

Notice that, as always, the z scores sum to zero. (Seeing a total score other than zero tells us there must be a computational or recording mistake.) Observe also that the standard deviation scores within the column of z scores are −1 for a dummy code of 0 and +1 for a dummy code of 1. This situation is always found when the number of 0 scores equals the number of 1 scores, but it is not always the case when the number of 0 scores does not equal the number of 1 scores. Finally, the sum of the products of the z scores (shown at the bottom of the last column of data) is +3.77. Dividing this value by the number of students ($N = 10$) yields the point-biserial correlation (r_{pb}) between femaleness and scores on Exam 1, that is,

$$r_{pb} = \frac{\Sigma z_x z_y}{N} = \frac{3.77}{10} = .38$$

The positive correlation tells us that the female students scored relatively higher on the exam than did the male students. If the correlation had been negative and of the same magnitude, it would have indicated that female students scored relatively lower on the exam than did male students.

When Is the Phi Coefficient Used?

Not infrequently in biomedical trials, both of the variables to be correlated are dichotomous. One variable (the independent variable) might be whether patients were randomly assigned to a drug group or a placebo group, and the other variable (the dependent variable) might be improvement rate (e.g., improved or not improved). As another illustration, in Chapter 8 we discussed a case in which people who had eaten a rare hamburger became sick. Looking again at Table 8.1 (on page 178),

Table 11.8 Dummy-Coded and Standardized Data for Phi Coefficient

Persons	Ate burger? Y = 1; N = 0	z score	Got food poisoning? Y = 1; N = 0	z score	Product of z scores
Mimi	1	+1.183	1	+1.183	1.400
Gail	0	−0.846	0	−0.846	0.716
Connie	0	−0.846	0	−0.846	0.716
Jerry	0	−0.846	0	−0.846	0.716
Greg	0	−0.846	0	−0.846	0.716
Dwight	0	−0.846	0	−0.846	0.716
Nancy	1	+1.183	1	+1.183	1.400
Richard	0	−0.846	0	−0.846	0.716
Kerry	0	−0.846	0	−0.846	0.716
Michele	1	+1.183	1	+1.183	1.400
John	1	+1.183	1	+1.183	1.400
Sheila	1	+1.183	1	+1.183	1.400
Sum (Σ)	5	0.00	5	0.00	12.012
Mean (M)	.417	0.00	.417	0.00	1.00
SD (σ)	.493	1.000	.493	1.000	.337

suppose we are interested in quantifying the relation between these two variables. We now have another special case of the product-moment r, called the **phi coefficient** (symbolized by ϕ, the lowercase Greek letter phi). In this case, both of the variables are dichotomous (with applied numerical values such as 0 and 1 or −1 and +1).

We can find the value of the phi coefficient (ϕ) in several different ways; two of them are shown here. The conceptual procedure, represented in Table 11.8, illustrates why we say that ϕ is another special case of the product-moment r. Under the "Ate burger?" heading, the first column shows the dummy-coded scores of Yes = 1 and No = 0. The next column shows the standardized scores (the z scores) corresponding to the dummy-coded values. For instance, we computed the z score corresponding to Mimi's 1 as

$$z = \frac{X - M}{\sigma} = \frac{1 - .417}{.493} = +1.183$$

Similarly, under the "Got food poisoning?" heading, the dummy coding is again Yes = 1 and No = 0, followed by the corresponding z scores.

The last column in Table 11.8 shows the mean of the product of the z scores as 1.00, and we report it as the phi (ϕ) coefficient because both variables are dichotomous, but we compute it as

$$r = \frac{\Sigma z_x z_y}{N} = \frac{12.012}{12} = 1.00$$

In other words, we have treated phi (ϕ) no differently from any product-moment r calculated on the basis of z scores. The positive correlation tells us that answering "yes" to the question "Ate burger?" is directly related to answering "yes" to the question "Got food poisoning?" and the 1.00 tells us that we can predict who got food poisoning perfectly from the knowledge of who ate a burger. If the 1.00 correlation were negative, there would be a perfect inverse relation between eating the burger and getting food poisoning. Thus, when interpreting phi coefficients, we must pay close attention to how the two dichotomous variables were dummy-coded and labeled.

There is an easier way to compute ϕ by using an alternative formula that takes advantage of the fact that the data can be represented in a 2×2 table of frequencies (or *counts*), also called a *chi-square contingency table* (more about chi-square in Chapter 15) or simply a *contingency table*. You will see this 2×2 format in Table 11.9, which shows that all five people who ate the burgers then got food poisoning and that the seven people who did not eat them remained well. Notice that the cells are labeled A, B, C, D. With this code, we now use the following formula to calculate the phi coefficient:

$$\phi = \frac{BC - AD}{\sqrt{(A + B)(C + D)(A + C)(B + D)}}$$

Substituting in this formula yields

$$\phi = \frac{(7)(5) - (0)(0)}{\sqrt{(7)(5)(5)(7)}} = \frac{35 - 0}{\sqrt{1,225}} = \frac{35}{35} = 1.00$$

which (not unexpectedly) is the same result that we obtained using the conceptual formula for the Pearson r.

We will have more to say about the point-biserial correlation (r_{pb}) and the phi coefficient (ϕ) in the following chapters, as r_{pb} and ϕ are also useful indices of the effect size. It is becoming increasingly important in empirical research that scientists report and interpret the effect size, and (as we show in the following chapters) correlation-type (r-type) indices are easily computed and readily interpreted in a wide variety of situations. However, the real-life importance of an effect size depends on the context of the research and the nature of the dependent variable. Nonetheless, knowing the size of the effect is another important piece of information that can help you decide whether it is meaningful in a practical or personal way.

Table 11.9 Contingency Table Coded for Computation of Phi Coefficient

Ate burger?	Got food poisoning? Yes	No	Totals
No	**A** 0	**B** 7	**(A + B)** = 7
Yes	**C** 5	**D** 0	**(C + D)** = 5
Totals	**(A + C)** = 5	**(B + D)** = 7	

Summary of Ideas

1. The *Pearson r* is a standard index of *linear* relationship, with the possible values running from −1.0 to +1.0 (Box 11.3).

2. *Scatter plots* let us visualize the clustering and slope of dots that represent the relationship between X and Y.

3. The Pearson *r*, defined as $(\Sigma z_x z_y)/N$, is called the *product-moment correlation* because z scores (i.e., standardized distances from the mean) are also known as *moments*.

4. The *Spearman rho* (r_s) is the Pearson *r* calculated on scores that happen to be in ranked form (e.g., the data on perceptions of risk) and is sometimes a quick estimate of correlation (Box 11.4).

5. Calculating *r* on the original unranked scores typically results in a value for the correlation different from calculating r_s on the ranks of the original scores, and calculating *r* on the original unranked scores is ordinarily preferred in most cases.

6. The *point-biserial correlation* (r_{pb}) is the Pearson *r* where one of the variables is *continuous* and the other is *dichotomous* (e.g., exam score and student's gender). *Dummy-coding* the dichotomous variable (e.g., female vs. male, live vs. die, or succeed vs. fail) allows us to calculate r_{pb} by the Pearson *r* formula.

7. The *phi coefficient* (ϕ) is the Pearson *r* where both variables are dichotomous (e.g., "Ate burger?" and "Got food poisoning?"). To calculate the correlation between two dichotomous variables, we can (a) dummy-code both variables (e.g., Yes = 1 and No = 0) and then use the corresponding z scores to compute the Pearson *r* or (b) compute ϕ directly from a 2×2 contingency table.

Key Terms

continuous variable p. 249
correlation coefficient p. 249
dichotomous variable p. 249

discrete variable   p. 249
dummy coding   p. 261
linearity   p. 249
nonlinearity   p. 255
Pearson *r*   p. 249
phi coefficient (ϕ)   p. 263

point-biserial correlation (r_{pb})   p. 260
product-moment correlation   p. 254
scatter plot   p. 251
Spearman rho (r_s)   p. 255

Multiple-Choice Questions for Review

1. A correlation coefficient reflects the degree of _____ relationship between two variables. (a) linear; (b) curvilinear; (c) any kind of; (d) positive

2. Correlation coefficients range from ____. (a) 0 to 1; (b) −1 to 0; (c) 1 to 10; (d) −1 to +1

3. A variable (such as gender) with two possible values is called a _____ variable. (a) continuous; (b) dichotomous; (c) quadratic; (d) linear

4. A graph is created in which the X variable is plotted along one axis and the Y variable is plotted along the other axis. Each data point is then represented as a dot in this graph. This kind of graph is called a (a) partial plot; (b) multivariate plot; (c) scatter plot; (d) median-split plot.

5. Another name for the Pearson *r* is the (a) Spearman rank correlation; (b) product-moment correlation; (c) phi coefficient; (d) point-biserial correlation.

6. Consider the following set of data:

X	z_x	Y	z_y	$z_x z_y$
8	1.34	16	1.34	1.80
6	0.45	12	0.45	0.20
4	−0.45	8	−0.45	0.20
2	−1.34	4	−1.34	1.80
Sum (Σ) 20	0.00	40	0.00	4.00

What is the correlation between X and Y? (a) .1; (b) −.1; (c) 1; (d) −1

7. A distance from a mean is called a(n) _____; the result of two numbers that are multiplied together is called a _____. (a) deviation, sum; (b) deviation, divisor; (c) error, multiplicative index; (d) moment, product

8. A correlation between two variables that are ranked is most specifically called a _____.
   (a) point-biserial correlation; (b) phi coefficient; (c) Pearson r; (d) Spearman rho

9. A student at Eastern Connecticut University hypothesizes that being female or male is related to one's position on abortion (measured as "prochoice" or "prolife"). To test this hypothesis, the correlation that the student is most likely to use is a (a) Spearman rho; (b) phi coefficient; (c) point-biserial correlation; (d) none of the above.

10. A student at the London School of Economics wants to determine whether political party affiliation (Labour or Conservative) is related to intelligence (measured by an IQ test that yields a series of continuous scores). To test this hypothesis, the student is most likely to use a (a) Spearman rho; (b) phi coefficient; (c) point-biserial correlation; (d) none of the above.

Discussion Questions for Review

1. A St. Bonaventure University researcher administers tests of IQ and reading ability to four high school students. In addition, their grade point averages are obtained from school records, with the following results:

	IQ	Reading	GPA
Student 1	105	13	2.6
Student 2	113	17	3.4
Student 3	87	10	2.0
Student 4	125	19	3.8

The correlation between IQ and reading ability is $r = .98$. Without doing any direct calculation, the researcher says he knows the correlation between reading and GPA. Do you know this correlation? What about the correlation between IQ and GPA—without any direct calculation?

2. Twenty subjects take part in a University of Minnesota study on the relationship between socioeconomic status (SES, coded as rich = 1, poor = 0) and shyness (coded as shy = 1, not shy = 0).

Given the results shown below, what is the correlation between these two variables? What specific type of Pearson correlation is this?

	SES	Shyness		SES	Shyness
Subject 1	0	1	Subject 11	0	0
Subject 2	0	1	Subject 12	1	1
Subject 3	0	0	Subject 13	0	0
Subject 4	0	1	Subject 14	1	0
Subject 5	1	1	Subject 15	0	1
Subject 6	0	0	Subject 16	1	0
Subject 7	1	1	Subject 17	1	0
Subject 8	1	0	Subject 18	1	1
Subject 9	0	1	Subject 19	0	1
Subject 10	1	0	Subject 20	1	0

3. A student at the University of Waterloo had two judges rate infants' fussiness, with the following results:

	Rater 1	Rater 2
Infant 1	60	30
Infant 2	40	50
Infant 3	30	60
Infant 4	50	40

The interjudge agreement, in terms of r, was not what the student had hoped for; it was $r = -1.0$. So he got himself two more raters, whose ratings were as follows:

	Rater 3	Rater 4
Infant 1	60	130
Infant 2	40	150
Infant 3	30	160
Infant 4	50	140

What is the agreement, in terms of r, between Raters 3 and 4?

4. A Georgia State University student has a job managing a 200-seat summer-stock theater that is filled to capacity on Saturday nights. To study the effect of staff courtesy on audience enjoyment, she asks the ticket taker to smile at randomly selected patrons. After the show, each member of the audience rates his or her enjoyment of the performance on a 7-point scale. Can you identify the independent and dependent variables and then figure out a way to calculate the correlation between them?

5. A student at California State University at Chico administered two tests to five subjects with the following results:

	Test A	Test B
Subject 1	1	4
Subject 2	2	3
Subject 3	3	2
Subject 4	4	1
Subject 5	5	100

Show a scatter plot of the relationship between the scores on Test A and Test B. Is there anything troubling about this plot? Can you adjust this problem by using a different version of a Pearson r? Show a scatter plot of the revised or transformed scores on Tests A and B. What is the correlation between the tests if you use (a) the original scores and (b) the revised or transformed scores?

6. Two students from Foothill College compared their obtained scatter plots. Which plot is associated with the higher correlation? How can you tell just from inspecting the scatter plots? What are the actual r values associated with each plot?

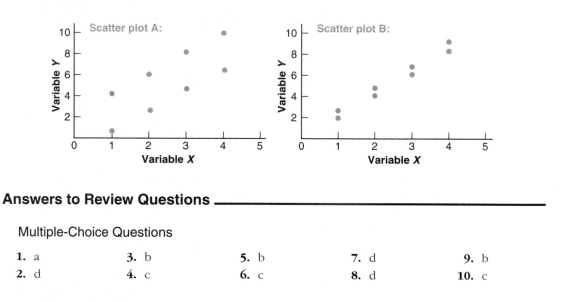

Answers to Review Questions

Multiple-Choice Questions

1. a	**3.** b	**5.** b	**7.** d	**9.** b
2. d	**4.** c	**6.** c	**8.** d	**10.** c

Discussion Questions

1. The correlation between reading ability and GPA is 1.00 because the z scores for reading and for GPA are identical. Careful inspection of the original reading and GPA scores shows that the GPA scores are always one fifth the size of the reading scores. If a variable (X) is multiplied by any constant (c), it yields a new variable (cX) that is correlated 1.00 with the original variable (X). The reason is that the old scores are multiplied by c, the old mean is multiplied by c, and the old σ is multiplied by c. Thus,

$$\text{old } z = \frac{X - M}{\sigma}$$

and in turn,

$$\text{new } z = \frac{cX - cM}{c\sigma} = \frac{X - M}{\sigma}$$

As reading ability and GPA have the same z scores, GPA z scores can be substituted for reading z scores, and GPA will be correlated .98 with IQ just as reading is correlated .98 with IQ. You can check this out by computing z scores for all three variables (IQ, reading, and GPA) and computing the correlations among these three variables.

2. The correlation is $-.20$, computed by ϕ, the two-dichotomous-variables version of the Pearson r. It can be computed by the z-score method or by the 2×2 contingency table method; that is,

$$\phi = \frac{\Sigma z_x z_y}{N}$$

or

$$\phi = \frac{BC - AD}{\sqrt{(A + B)(C + D)(A + C)(B + D)}}$$

3. The correlation between Raters 3 and 4 is also -1.00. We can compute that directly, or we can notice that Rater 3 rates identically to Rater 1 and that Rater 4 rates identically to Rater 2, except for adding a constant of 100 points to each of Rater 2's ratings. Adding a constant (c) to each score also adds the constant to the mean, so adding a constant to the raw scores does not change the z scores because

$$\text{old } z = \frac{X - M}{\sigma}$$

and

$$\text{new } z = \frac{(X + c) - (M + c)}{\sigma} = \frac{X - M}{\sigma}$$

4. The independent variable is smiling (scored 1) or not smiling (scored 0). The dependent variable is the rating of enjoyment. For the 200 patrons, we correlate the scores on the treatment variable (1 or 0) with the scores on the 7-point enjoyment scale.

5.

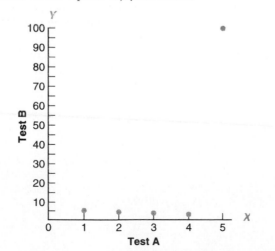

The score of 100 on Test B appears to be an outlier. We can solve the outlier problem by using ranks instead of scores:

Test A		Test B	
Score	Rank	Score	Rank
1	5	4	2
2	4	3	3
3	3	2	4
4	2	1	5
5	1	100	1

Our scatter plot based on ranks is

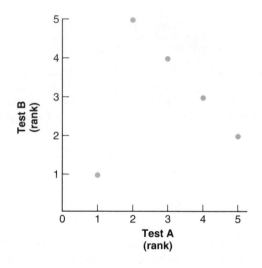

The correlation between Test A and Test B is .69 if we use the original scores; it is .00 if we use the ranks. A discrepancy that large is unusual and needs to be evaluated further before we can confidently say we "know" the correlation between Test A and Test B.

6. Scatter Plot B is associated with the higher correlation because its points are more tightly clustered around the straight-line relationship between variables X and Y. The correlation between variables X and Y is .75 for Scatter Plot A and .98 for Scatter Plot B.

CHAPTER 12

Statistical Significance, Effect Size, and Power Analysis

Preview Questions

- Why is it important to focus not just on p values?
- What is the reasoning behind null hypothesis significance testing?
- What do Type I and Type II errors imply in practical terms?
- How do I determine, interpret, and report the statistical significance of r?
- What is the purpose of the binomial effect-size display?
- How can I do a power analysis?
- How do I compute a confidence interval for an effect size r?
- What does computing Killeen's p_{rep} tell me?

Why Is It Important to Focus Not Just on p Values?

Besides describing data (Chapter 10) and measuring relationships (Chapter 11), researchers are usually interested in making comparisons using statistical tests such as t (Chapter 13), F (Chapter 14), and chi-square (Chapter 15). In randomized clinical trials, for instance, researchers compare the different groups to see whether there is a difference in success rates in the treatment versus the control group. In Chapter 10, we described another kind of study (a judgment study), in which the subjects rated the palatability of a new food product and a comparison food product already on the market. The new food was rated more favorably on the average (i.e., the mean) than was the comparison product. Because the researchers wanted to know whether the difference between the two means might be due to chance, they performed a test of statistical significance. Finding the probability (**p value**) associated with the observed difference to be quite small (less than .05), they concluded that the difference between means was "real" and not merely a result of chance (Street & Carroll, 1989). We will examine the reasoning behind this procedure, called **null hypothesis significance testing (NHST)**.

In recent years, there has been a growing realization that NHST is sometimes misunderstood or misused. For example, p values have sometimes been misconstrued as being indicative of the size, or even the importance, of the effect in question. However, finding that an obtained effect is statistically significant at some specified p level does not automatically reveal that the effect was sizable or important. Nor does the failure to obtain statistical significance at the desired p level tell us that there was no obtained effect, or that the obtained effect was trivial or unimportant. The p value of a significance test (e.g., t, F, or chi-square) is influenced not only by the size of the effect, but by the total number of units or observations (N). As either the size of the effect or the total N increases, the value of the significance test increases, and the p value decreases. Not only does finding a significant p not tell us whether the effect size, the N, or both were responsible in some way, but even if the effect size were responsible, there would still be a lingering question concerning what aspect of this measure was the contributing factor.

However, as researchers usually covet small p values, given an estimated effect size, one way to maximize the "power" of a significance test to detect an expected effect is to figure out in advance how many units (e.g., subjects) will be needed to achieve the desired p level. Similarly, a *power analysis* is sometimes done after nonsignificant results are obtained so that the *effective power* (i.e., the actual power) can be estimated. Later in this chapter, we will illustrate how to perform a power analysis. The essential point is that it is important to focus attention not just on p values but on other vital aspects of the results as well, such as the strength of the relationship between X and Y (the *effect size*) and the power of the statistical test used to detect that effect. In this chapter, we concentrate on the simplest correlational (r-type) index of effect size, symbolized here as $r_{\text{effect size}}$, and in the next chapter we describe another useful index of effect size based on the standardized difference between two group means (Cohen's d). One reason that we begin with the r-type index is that r-type effect size statistics are easy to calculate from t, F, and chi-square statistics, as explained in the following three chapters. Another reason is that r-type indices can be used in situations in which other indices (such as the standardized difference between two groups' means) would not be relevant, for example, where there are more than two groups and we have predicted a particular pattern of results involving *all* the groups (R. Rosenthal, Rosnow, & Rubin, 2000; Rosnow & Rosenthal, 1996, 2002, 2003). Another reason we start with the effect size r is that it lends itself to interpretation by a procedure described later in this chapter as the *binomial effect-size display* (or BESD).

What Is the Reasoning Behind Null Hypothesis Significance Testing?

To help you understand intuitively what NHST and some related concepts mean, we will borrow a simple analogy (Wainer, 1972). Imagine you are walking along the Atlantic City boardwalk when a shady character approaches you and whispers he has a quarter that he is willing to sell you for *only* five dollars. What makes the coin worth so much more than its face value? The answer, he tells you, is that this is a quarter with a special property. When properly used, this quarter can win you fame and fortune because it does not always come up heads

BOX 12.1 How Are Probabilities Determined?

One characteristic of probabilities is that if all outcomes are *independent* (i.e., one outcome is not influenced by any other), the sum of all the probabilities associated with an event is equal to 1. For example, when you throw a die, there are six possibilities, and (unless the die is loaded) the probability of any particular outcome is 1/6, or .167. Therefore, summing all of the independent probabilities gives us $.167 \times 6 = 1.00$. Or instead of throwing a die, suppose you have two fair coins and flip both at the same time. There are four possible combinations of heads (H) and tails (T): HH, HT, TH, TT. In determining probabilities, the general rule is to count the total number of possible outcomes and then to count the number of outcomes that yield the event you are interested in. The probability of that event is the ratio of the number you are looking for (the favorable event) to the total number of outcomes. For example, the probability (p) of two heads (out of the four possible events) can occur in only one way (HH) and is therefore 1 divided by 4, so $p = .25$. The probability of only one head (out of these four possible events) can occur in two ways (HT or TH) and is therefore 2 divided by 4, so $p = .5$.

and tails with equal regularity. Instead, one outcome is more likely than the other. A smart person can, when flipping the coin, bet on the outcome and win a fortune, he says. "It might sound like a cock-and-bull story," he adds, "but flip the coin and see for yourself."

If the coin is not what the boardwalk huckster says it is, getting a head or a tail is the result purely of chance. That is, if the coin is an ordinary one, then the probability of heads or tails is always one chance in two (see also Box 12.1). Thinking empirically, you accept his challenge and decide to test whether the probability of heads does or does not equal the probability of tails. You flip the coin once and heads appears. You flip the coin again, and again it comes up heads. Suppose you flip the coin nine times and each time it comes up heads. Would you believe him now? If your answer is yes, would you believe him if, in nine tosses, the coin had come up heads eight times and tails once? This is the essential question in NHST. You can be as stringent as you like in setting a rejection criterion, but you *may* eventually pay for this decision by rejecting what you perhaps should not.

The concepts and reasoning involved in NHST evolved out of the ideas and arguments of different statisticians; for a fascinating historical overview, read Gigerenzer et al.'s (1989) *The Empire of Chance*. Let us state these ideas more precisely. When you decide to test whether the probability of heads "does or does not" equal the probability of tails, two hypotheses are implied. One is that the quarter is unbiased (i.e., the probability of heads *does* equal the probability of tails), and the second is that the coin is biased (i.e., the probability of heads *does not* equal the probability of tails). Think of the "experiment" of tossing a coin as a way of trying to determine which of these hypotheses you cannot logically reject. In statistical terms, the name for the first hypothesis is the **null hypothesis** (symbolized as H_0), and the name for the second hypothesis is the **alternative hypothesis** (symbolized as H_1). That is,

H_0 *(null hypothesis):* The probability of heads equals the probability of tails in the long run (i.e., the coin is not biased).

H_1 *(alternative hypothesis):* The probability of heads is not equal to the probability of tails in the long run (i.e., the coin is biased).

Notice that the two hypotheses are *mutually exclusive;* that is, when one hypothesis is true, the other must be false. Experimenters who do NHST are usually interested in testing the specific H_0 (i.e., no difference) against a general H_1 (i.e., some difference). For example, in a between-subjects design with an experimental and a control group, the null hypothesis generally implies no difference in the success rate between the experimental group and the control group (e.g., no difference in survival rates, performance rates, or however else the "success rate" may be defined). The idea behind NHST is to try to reject H_0 and yet be reasonably sure that you will not be wrong in doing so. Hence, there are two kinds of decision risks of general concern in NHST, called *Type I* and *Type II errors.*

A **Type I error** implies that the decision maker mistakenly rejected the null hypothesis (H_0) when it is, in fact, true and should not have been rejected. A **Type II error** implies that the decision maker mistakenly failed to reject the null hypothesis when it is, in fact, false and should have been rejected. The risk (or probability) of making a Type I error is called by three different names: **alpha (α)**, the **significance level**, and the **p value**. The risk (or probability) of making a Type II error is known by one name: **beta (β)**. To make the most informed decision, researchers who do NHST would, of course, like to know what each risk is in a given case, so that they can balance these risks in some way. Let us return with this newfound knowledge to the analogy of the boardwalk huckster with the coin for sale.

Suppose you decide that you do not want to be wrong more than 1 time out of 20, which is called the *5% significance level* (see also Box 12.2). You flip the coin 9 times and get 8 heads and 1 tail. To make an informed decision, you need to know about the chances of obtaining this result or a result even more extreme. That is, you need to know the probability of obtaining this result (or a more extreme result) if the null hypothesis (H_0) is true. Therefore, you think, "If this probability is less than 1/20 (i.e., $p < .05$), I will reject the null hypothesis and buy the coin; if not (i.e., $p > .05$), I will not buy the coin." Because it can be shown that the probability of 8 or 9 heads in 9 tosses is less than 1 out of 20 (p approximately .02, or 1 out of 50), you decide to reject the null hypothesis and buy the coin (assuming you have no pangs of conscience about purchasing a crooked coin and using it to win bets). In other words, you are doing so for two reasons: (a) because the resultant probability leads you to reject the null hypothesis of a fair coin, with 50%

> ## BOX 12.2 The 5% Solution
>
> The ultimate day-to-day decision about what is a reasonable risk is a personal one. But as you do your literature search, you will notice that many researchers use the .05 significance level as a critical demarcation point for deciding whether to reject the null hypothesis. The conventional wisdom behind this procedure goes something like this: The logic begins, more or less, with the proposition that one does not want to accept an alternative hypothesis that stands a fairly good chance of being false (i.e., one ought to avoid Type I errors). The logic goes on to state that one either accepts an alternative hypothesis as probably true (not false) or rejects it, concluding that the null is too likely for one to regard *it* as rejectable. The .05 alpha is seen by many scientists as a good "fail-safe" standard because it is convenient (most statistical tables show 5% values) and stringent enough to protect us from too often concluding that the null hypothesis is false when it is actually true.

heads, at your chosen significance level (or alpha) of 5%, and (b) because you believe that the alternative hypothesis (i.e., the coin is biased) is tenable and that the data (i.e., 8 heads and 1 tail, or 89% heads instead of 50%) support this hypothesis.

What Do Type I and Type II Errors Imply in Practical Terms?

The analogy we used is actually a simplified one, not exactly a true representation of what goes on in NHST. One reason the coin example falls short is that it is not a "relational event." That is, there is only one variable: the result of the coin toss. The researcher who does NHST, however, usually wants to know the probability of claiming that two variables (X and Y) are related when, in fact, they are unrelated, or that the average "success rate" of one group (e.g., the experimental group) has surpassed that of another group (the control group). In practical terms, then, Type I error can be understood as mistakenly claiming a relationship that does not truly exist, and it is the likelihood of this risk that initially most interests researchers who rely on NHST. The question that they want answered is "What is the probability of a Type I error?"

Although most researchers who do NHST are not indifferent to the probability of making a Type II error (i.e., failing to claim a relation that truly does exist), many of them do tend to attach greater psychological importance to the risk of making a Type I error than to the risk of making a Type II error. Of course, we also give greater weight to some decision risks than to others (see Box 12.3), but the reason the researcher attaches greater weight to the risk of making a Type I error is explained in Table 12.1. In the context of the coin example, the risk of making a "Type I error" would imply an *error of gullibility,* or

BOX 12.3 Innocent or Guilty?

Imagine that a man is being tried for a brutal murder, and suppose that, if convicted, he is likely to be executed. As a member of the jury, you have to vote on whether he is innocent or guilty of the charges against him. If you vote "guilty" and in fact he is not guilty, you may be sending an innocent man to be executed. If you vote "innocent" and in fact he is not innocent, you could be turning a brutal murderer loose in the community. In the United States, it is generally accepted that convicting an innocent person is a more serious risk than permitting a guilty person to go free. The lesson? Just as most scientists who do NHST do not weight Type I and Type II errors equally, in everyday life we also give greater weight to some decision risks than to others.

being fleeced by the huckster's claim that an ordinary coin is biased. A "Type II error" implies *blindness,* or the failure to perceive that a not-so-ordinary coin is *really* biased as claimed. Although this analogy is a long stretch, the fact is that researchers are taught to believe that it is far worse to risk being "gullible" than it is to risk being "blind" to a real relationship. Some philosophers characterize this choice as the "healthy skepticism" of the scientific method (Axinn, 1966; Kaplan, 1964).

To show how Type I and Type II error risks are conceptualized in the tactical language of NHST, we turn to Table 12.2. For researchers, the null hypothesis is usually the assumption that no relationship between two variables is present in the population from which a sample was drawn, or that there is no difference in "success rates" in the different groups or conditions. The researcher considers the possibility of making a Type I error whenever a true null hypothesis is tested. As defined by the upper-left cell in this table (which corresponds to the "gullibility" cell of Table 12.1), a Type I error results when the researcher mistakenly rejects the null hypothesis by incorrectly claiming a relationship that does not exist. As defined by the lower-right cell of Table 12.2 (which corresponds to

Table 12.1 Analogies of Type I and Type II Errors

	True state	
Your decision	The coin is unbiased	The coin is biased
The coin is biased (i.e., it won't come up heads and tails equally)	"Type I" (gullibility risk)	No error of inference
The coin is unbiased (i.e., it is an ordinary coin)	No error of inference	"Type II" (blindness risk)

| Table 12.2 | Implications of the Decision to Reject or Not to Reject the Null Hypothesis (H_0) |

	True state	
Scientist's decision	H_0 is true	H_0 is false
To reject H_0	Type I error	No error of inference
Not to reject H_0	No error of inference	Type II error

the "blindness" cell of Table 12.1), a Type II error results when the researcher mistakenly accepts the null hypothesis by failing to claim a relationship that does exist.

How Do I Determine, Interpret, and Report the Statistical Significance of *r*?

Especially when the *p* value is low enough to justify rejecting the null hypothesis, you increase your information about the results by also knowing the effect size. Thus, you need to know not only how to determine the *p* value, but also how to estimate the effect size. We will have much more to say about estimating effect sizes in the remaining chapters, but let us see how you would determine the statistical significance of the effect size *r* and then report what you found. Table 12.3, which contains a portion of a larger table in Appendix B (see Table B.5 on p 402), shows the *p* levels associated with different values of *r*. The first column lists $N - 2$ (where *N* is the total number of units or observations, for example, the number of subjects), and the other columns indicate the *p* levels (i.e., Type I error risks). Notice that both one-tailed and two-tailed *p* levels are given and that the two-tailed *p* values are always twice the size of the one-tailed. The **two-tailed *p* value** is frequently used when the alternative hypothesis (H_1) did *not* specifically predict in which side (or tail) of the probability distribution the significance would be detected. **One-tailed *p* values** are used when the alternative hypothesis requires the significance to be in one tail rather than in the other tail. However, many researchers traditionally ignore this distinction and report only two-tailed *p* values, which, although a conservative convention, is also acceptable in most cases.

As an illustration of how to read Table 12.3 (and Table B.5), suppose you conduct an exploratory study to examine the relationship between people's level of self-esteem (as measured by a standardized personality inventory) and the extent to which they are reported as engaging in gossip (measured by peer ratings). However, you are unsure of the direction this relationship will take because (based on your literature review) you think that a positive *or* a negative correlation is possible. The reason you are unsure is that some authors portray the inveterate gossip as a social isolate, the least popular member of a group, characterized by feelings of little self-worth, social anxiety, and a need for esteem from others, who gossips in order to become the center of attention and to obtain status or esteem from others.

| Table 12.3 | Significance Levels of r | | | | |

	Probability level (p)				
	.10	.05	.02	.01	two-tailed
$N - 2$	.05	.025	.01	.005	one-tailed
1	.988	.997	.9995	.9999	
2	.900	.950	.980	.990	
3	.805	.878	.934	.959	
4	.729	.811	.882	.917	
5	.669	.754	.833	.874	
10	.497	.576	.658	.708	
20	.360	.423	.492	.537	
30	.296	.349	.409	.449	
40	.257	.304	.358	.393	
50	.231	.273	.322	.354	
100	.164	.195	.230	.254	
200	.116	.138	.164	.181	
300	.095	.113	.134	.148	
500	.074	.088	.104	.115	
1,000	.052	.062	.073	.081	

Note: For a more complete table, see Appendix B, Table B.5. However, notice in Table B.5 that all p values are shown as two-tailed.

By contrast, other authors view the typical gossip as sensitive, curious, social, and involved, a person who gossips out of a need to control or manipulate those perceived to be subordinates. As you are unsure about hypothesizing a positive or a negative relationship, you decide the safe bet is to report a two-tailed p value.

Continuing with this example, suppose that, in a total N of 52 subjects, you find that the correlation between self-esteem and the tendency to gossip is $r = .33$. In your literature search, you noticed that effect size correlations of this magnitude were often referred to as "moderate" or "medium-sized" in psychology. That usage is based on the operational definitions proposed by Jacob Cohen (1988) for use with the power analysis tables he developed, where the operational definitions of "small," "medium," and "large" effect sizes for r were approximately .1, .3, and .5, respectively. However, as we will show in a moment, it should not be assumed that a "small" effect is one that is trivial or inconsequential, as the practical importance of an effect depends on the context and the nature of the dependent variable. That the effect size r you obtained was a positive value is consistent with the idea that high gossipers are also higher in self-esteem (whereas a negative r would have implied that the high gossipers were lower in self-esteem). To serve as a helpful (but not critical) alpha, let us assume you chose the conventional 5% significance level. Looking at the intersection of $N - 2 = 50$ and the column labeled .05 two-tailed in Table 12.3, you see that r must be at least .273 to be beyond the level of risk you chose in order to reject the null hypothesis. As this table shows, the obtained p is somewhere between .02 and .01 two-tailed. That is, $r = .33$ is larger than the listed value for $p = .02$ two-tailed ($r = .322$) and smaller than the listed value for $p = .01$ two-tailed ($r = .354$).

In reporting p values, many statisticians recommend providing the actual descriptive level of significance, because it carries more information that the phrases "significant difference" and "no significant difference at the .05 level." For example, the problem in reporting that there was "no significant difference at the .05 level" is that we have no idea whether the p was .06 (which is not very different from .05) or a value much greater than .05, such as .50 (which is no better than merely flipping a coin). If you are looking up p values in a statistical table, you may not have the option of reporting them precisely, in which case your most convenient option may be to report that p is less than (<) or greater than (>) the particular column value in the statistical table. But if you have the exact p value (e.g., from computer output or from a scientific calculator), you can use scientific notation to show a very small p value instead of reporting a string of zeros. For example, instead of reporting $p = .00000025$, you would report 2.5^{-7}, where the superscript -7 tells the reader to count 7 places to the left of the decimal in 2.5 and make that the decimal place.

Notice in Table 12.3 that a correlation can be significant at $p = .05$, no matter whether it is a very large correlation or a very small correlation. What counts most in this table is whether the "$N - 2$" is sufficiently large to allow us to detect the particular magnitude of r at the desired level of significance. For example, we see that even an r as small as .062 would be significant at $p = .05$ (two-tailed) with $N = 1,002$, but an r that is 9 times larger would not be significant at the same level with $N = 12$. Thus, only reporting that an effect size r was "significant" does not give us a clue to whether it was as small as .062 (in this table) or as large as 1.0. Furthermore, does it really make any sense to ignore or dismiss a sizable r that was not "statistically significant" ($p > .05$) because the total N was too small? Would it not be more prudent to try to replicate the study with a larger N before concluding that "nothing happened"?

What Is the Purpose of the Binomial Effect-Size Display?

In the following chapters, we will present easy-to-use formulas for obtaining $r_{\text{effect size}}$ from t, F, or chi-square. For now, let us examine how to transform the $r_{\text{effect size}}$ into a convenient display called the **BESD**, shorthand for **binomial effect-size display** (R. Rosenthal & Rubin, 1982b). The BESD is called a *display* because it converts the "success rates" in experimental and control groups into a 2×2 table; it is called a *binomial* (which means "two-term") display because two variables are displayed as dichotomous. To show how the BESD works, we refer to the results in a publicized clinical trial in which the independent variable was whether the subjects received an aspirin every other day, and the dependent variable was whether they experienced a heart attack.

This study reported that heart attack risk is "cut in half" by aspirin (Steering Committee of the Physicians' Health Study Research Group, 1988). Presumably, the

Table 12.4	Aspirin's Effect on Heart Attack

A. Myocardial infarction (MI) in placebo and aspirin conditions

Condition	Heart attack	No heart attack	Total
Placebo	189	10,845	11,034
Aspirin	104	10,933	11,037
Total	293	21,778	22,071

B. Binomial effect-size display of $r_{effect\ size}$ = .034

Condition	MI present	MI absent	Total
Placebo	51.7[a]	48.3[b]	100
Aspirin	48.3[b]	51.7[a]	100
Total	100	100	200

[a]Computed from 100(.500 + r/2).
[b]Computed from 100(.500 − r/2).

Source: Based on results reported in "Preliminary Report: Findings From the Aspirin Component of the Ongoing Physicians' Health Study," by Steering Committee of the Physicians' Health Study Research Group, 1988, *New England Journal of Medicine, 318,* pp. 262–264.

way aspirin works to reduce mortality from heart attack, or myocardial infarction (MI), is by promoting circulation even when fatty deposits have collected along the walls of the coronary arteries. That is, aspirin makes the transport of blood easier as the arteries get narrower. The finding that heart attack risk is "cut in half" was based on a 5-year investigation of 22,071 male physicians, approximately half of whom (11,037) were given an ordinary aspirin tablet (325 mg) every other day; the remainder (11,034) were given a placebo. Part of the results are shown in Table 12.4.

Part A of Table 12.4 shows the number of participants in each condition who did or did not have a heart attack. A chi-square (χ^2) test of the statistical significance of these frequencies (using a procedure described in Chapter 15) yielded a p value considerably smaller than the .05 significance level. It was "p is approximately .0000006" (or in scientific notation, 6.0^{-7}), which tells us that the value of the chi-square was very unlikely to be a fluke or a lucky coincidence. But when we calculate the effect size as a standard phi (ϕ) coefficient (using the procedure described in Chapter 11 for calculating phi on 2 × 2 tables of independent frequencies, or another procedure described in Chapter 15), the result is $r_{effect\ size}$ = .034. Before we dismiss this very small-sized r as inconsequential, let us also see what it means in terms of practical importance.

We said that the scientists reported that heart attack risk is cut in half by aspirin, and let us see how they arrived at this conclusion. In the placebo condition, 189 out of 11,034 subjects had a heart attack, which is 1.7% (i.e., 189/11,034 multiplied by 100). In the aspirin condition, 104 out of 11,037 subjects had a heart attack, which is 0.9% (i.e., 104/11,037 multiplied by 100). Dividing 0.9 by 1.7 yields .53, which (rounded) is why it was said that the risk of having a heart attack was cut in half. However, despite this good news, we see that the percentages are small, the reason being that relatively few people in the samples studied were actually in jeopardy of having a heart attack in the time frame of this study (1.3% of the 22,071 subjects). The question is how to represent the effect size r for the population as a whole and yet not exaggerate its implications.

No measure can capture the full picture, and therefore it is usually a good idea to explain the implications of medical (and other) results in more than one way. The BESD can be used for this purpose, as it is a standardized display that gives us an idea of the implications of an effect size indexed by a correlation coefficient. Part B of Table 12.4 shows what the effect size r would look like as a BESD. That is, it shows the effect size r to be a simple difference in outcome rates between the experimental (the aspirin) and control (the placebo) groups in a 2×2 table with rows and columns always totaling 100 (R. Rosenthal & Rubin, 1982b). Given a higher success rate in the experimental group than in the control group, the BESD is obtained from any effect size r simply by computation of the treatment success rate as $100(.50 + r/2)$ and the control condition success rate as $100(.50 - r/2)$. Because in this study $r/2$ is $.034/2 = .017$, the r of .034 yields an aspirin success rate (i.e., MI absent) of $100(.50 + .017) = 51.7$ and a placebo success rate of $100(.50 - .017) = 48.3$. The difference between these rates $(51.7 - 48.3 = 3.4)$ divided by 100 is .034, which is the effect size indexed by r.

Having the rows and columns always sum to 100 makes the values in the four cells easier to interpret and compare as proportions or percentages. This BESD tells us that about 3.4% of persons (in a theoretical population that was split into equal halves) who would probably have experienced a myocardial infarction (i.e., given these particular conditions) might not experience MI if they followed the aspirin regimen. The BESD preserves the effect size r and lets us see that it is equivalent to reducing the heart attack rate from 51.7% to 48.3% in a theoretical population in which half the people are given aspirin and half are not, and half have heart attacks and half do not. Remember, however, that the term *success rates* is simply a general expression; in this case, its operational definition was "MI absent versus MI present" (whereas the definition in other studies might be passed vs. failed, or improved vs. not improved, and so forth).

Many people (including many experienced researchers) might be surprised to learn that an effective biomedical intervention could be associated with an effect size r as small as .034, but certainly the practical importance of this finding is indisputable. In fact, effect size rs smaller than .10 are not at all unusual in biomedical trials. In Chapter 7, we mentioned the 1954 Salk vaccine randomized trial—"the biggest public health experiment ever" (Meier, 1988, p. 3)—in which over 200,000 children who were given the Salk poliomyelitis vaccine were compared with a control group of over 200,000 children who received a simple salt solution (Francis et al., 1955). There were serious problems with the design and implementation of the experiment, but it was nevertheless concluded that there was "convincing evidence for the effectiveness of the vaccine" (Brownlee, 1955, p. 1010). Interestingly, the effect size r of this "convincing evidence" was .011, which is even smaller than the effect size r in the aspirin study. Again, the reason for the small r is not that the

BOX 12.4   Effect Size Estimates

One result of our consideration of these small effect sizes is to make us more sanguine about the size of effects in the behavioral and social sciences. However, rather than rely on just one study for an effect size estimate, it is far more informative to use meta-analysis to summarize the results of a number of independent studies. For example, from a meta-analysis of 76 studies, Devine and Reifschneider (1995) estimated an average $r_{effect\ size}$ of .28 for the effect of psychoeducational care on adult hypertensives' blood pressure. In the area of social psychology, from a meta-analysis of 35 studies, Eagly, Ashmore, Makhijani, and Longo (1991) estimated an average r of .32 for the effect of physical attractiveness on attributions of social competence. Again in the area of social psychology, Richard, Bond, and Stokes-Zoota (2003) noted that the average of 322 meta-analyses of social psychological phenomena was $r = .21$. Effect sizes run the gamut from small to large, but they tend to be especially small (i.e., r values of .10 or smaller) in biomedical drug trials (R. Rosenthal & Rosnow, 2008, Table 11.8 on pp. 325–326). When preventive treatments are tested in such trials, small effect sizes are usually found because of the relatively rare occurrence of the disease. Since preventive treatments may have negative side effects, the ultimate goal would seem to be to identify people who are unlikely to benefit from the treatment, so that they are not needlessly put at risk of experiencing negative side effects.

Salk vaccine was ineffective (in fact, it was dramatically effective) but that polio was a relatively rare event in the samples studied (Rosnow & Rosenthal, 2003). (See also Box 12.4.)

In your literature search, you may have noticed that some researchers, when reporting the effect size, refer to a squared correlation coefficient. This value (r^2) is called the *coefficient of determination,* or *proportion of variation explained.* However, the terms *determination* and *explained* are used in a technical sense and, despite the names, do not mean that r^2 explains the causal relation between X and Y. They mean only that r^2 represents the fraction or proportion of the variability shared by X and Y. Although r^2 is useful in a number of more advanced statistical applications (R. Rosenthal & Rosnow, 2008), for two reasons we suggest that you always report the "non-squared r" whenever you mean the effect size. One reason is that squared r values lose their directionality, but directionality is usually of vital interest (i.e., "Is the treatment helping or hurting?" or "Is the correlation positive or negative?"). Second, squared r values can mask "small" effects that may be of great practical importance, and effect size indices of any size when squared are likely to be misconstrued as being much less important than is often true. For example, in the aspirin study, squaring $r_{effect\ size}$ would be like a magician making a rabbit disappear, since $(.034)^2 = .00$! But when we think of $r_{effect\ size} = .034$ as reflecting a 3.4% decrease in heart attacks (which was the interpretation given in Table 12.4), the effect size (r) takes on practical importance—especially if you can count yourself or a loved one among that percentage (R. Rosenthal, 1990a, 1990b). Similarly, in the Salk polio vaccine study, squaring $r = .011$ gives us $r^2 = .000$ or, to four decimal places, .0001.

How Can I Do a Power Analysis?

When the null hypothesis has not been rejected in a given study, the reason may be that there was not enough statistical power to reject it, as statistical *power* has to do with the sensitivity of the statistical test (such as t, F, or chi-square) in providing an adequate opportunity to reject the null hypothesis when it warrants rejection (e.g., J. Cohen, 1988; Keppel, 1991; Kirk, 1995; Kraemer & Thiemann, 1987; K. R. Murphy & Myors, 2004). The purpose of a **power analysis** is to learn whether there was a reasonable chance of rejecting the null hypothesis, and whether the power should be increased in any future study to increase the sensitivity of the statistical test.

To illustrate, suppose that young researcher Smith conducts an experiment (with $N = 80$) on productivity and finds that Managerial Style A is better than B (the old standard), with p less than .05 and $r_{effect\ size} = .22$. That is, Smith's results are statistically significant at the conventional 5% level. Old researcher Jones, the creator of Style B, is skeptical and asks his graduate students to try to replicate Smith's results using 20 available subjects. The graduate students, to Jones's perverse delight, report a failure to replicate Smith's results. Their obtained two-tailed p value, they gleefully tell Jones, is *greater* than .30. Before savoring his victory, Jones tells his graduate students to calculate the effect size of their result. They return with glum faces to report that their effect size is *identical* ($r_{effect\ size} = .22$) to Smith's.

In other words, Jones's students have found exactly what Smith found, even though the p values of the two studies are not very close. The problem is that the students were working with a level of statistical power that was too low to obtain the p value reported by Smith. Because of the smaller sample size of 20, their power to reject the null hypothesis at .05 two-tailed was about .15, whereas Smith's power of around .50 (using an N of 80) was more than three times as great. Still, even power of .50 is no better than a coin flip: 50:50!

You will recall that beta (β) is the probability of a Type II error (i.e., the probability of failing to claim a relationship that does exist). **Power** is simply $1 - \beta$, or the probability of not making a Type II error. In the language of NHST, *power* is the probability of rejecting the null hypothesis when it is false and needs rejecting. For any given statistical test of a null hypothesis (e.g., t, F, or χ^2), the power of the statistical test is determined by three components: (a) the level of risk of drawing a spuriously positive conclusion (i.e., the p level); (b) the size of the study (i.e., the sample size); and (c) the effect size. These three components are so related that when any two of them are known, the third can be determined. Thus, if you know the values for (a) and (c), you should be able to estimate how large a total N you need to achieve your desired level of statistical significance.

Table 12.5	Rounded Sample Sizes (Total N) Required to Detect Effects at $p = .05$ Two-Tailed												
	Effect size correlation (r)												
Power	.05	.10	.15	.20	.25	.30	.35	.40	.45	.50	.55	.60	.65	.70
.25	664	168	76	44	29	21	16	13	10	9	8	7	6	5
.50	1,538	386	172	97	63	44	33	25	20	16	14	11	10	8
.60	1,960	491	218	123	79	55	41	31	25	20	16	14	12	10
.70	2,469	617	274	154	99	68	50	38	30	24	20	16	14	12
.80	3,138	784	348	195	124	86	63	48	37	30	24	20	17	14
.85	3,589	896	397	222	142	98	71	54	42	34	27	22	19	16
.90	4,200	1,048	464	260	165	114	83	62	49	39	31	26	21	18
.95	5,193	1,295	573	320	203	140	101	76	59	47	38	31	25	21
.99	7,341	1,829	808	451	286	196	142	106	82	65	52	42	34	28

Source: Based on Arno Ouwehand's Power Calculator 2, available via UCLA Department of Statistics (http://calculators. stat.ucla.edu).

Table 12.5 provides a compact way of estimating the total number of subjects needed to detect different effect size rs at the .05 (two-tailed) significance level. Suppose you decide to work with power = .8 or better, because this happens to be a recommended level (J. Cohen, 1988), and say you anticipate finding a "small" effect ($r_{effect\ size} = .10$) based on your review of the relevant literature. Given this magnitude of effect ($r = .10$) and power (.8), Table 12.5 shows that you would need 784 subjects (i.e., total N) to reject the null hypothesis at .05 two-tailed. This is a lot of subjects! Had you chosen to work in an area with typically larger effects, your recruitment of subjects would have been made much easier. For example, with an effect size $r = .30$ and power = .8, the table shows that you would need 86 subjects total. Suppose the effect size was even larger. With $r_{effect\ size} = .50$, you would need a total N of only 30 subjects.

A complicating factor, however, is that if you are recruiting volunteer subjects, you know that not everyone who agrees to participate will actually show up. From our discussion in Chapter 10 (of how an exploratory data analysis might be done), you recall that, on the average, about a third of those who say they will participate as subjects may be no-shows. To be on the safe side, you may want to multiply your estimated sample size N by 1.5 on the (risky) assumption that a third of the volunteers will not show up. However, the good news is that, in addition to increasing the total N (which can be expensive and time-consuming), there are also other techniques to increase power. (In the next chapter, you will find a discussion of some other ways to improve the power of the t test.)

How Do I Compute a Confidence Interval for an Effect Size r?

Just as we were interested in confidence intervals for proportions (Chapter 9) and means (Chapter 10), we are also interested in confidence intervals for effect size rs.

Suppose you wanted to know the 95% confidence interval (CI) for an effect size r. You would proceed in four steps:

Step 1 is to consult Table B.6 in Appendix B (p. 403), which is used to transform the $r_{effect\ size}$ to a Fisher z_r (which is a log-based transformation of r). This transformaton changes the finite scale of r values (which range from -1.0 to $+1.0$) into a normal distribution without limits. To distinguish the Fisher z_r from the standard score z noted in previous chapters, we use the subscript "r" (not italicized) to remind you that this particular z is related to r.

Step 2 is to substitute the value of N in your study (i.e., the total sample size of your study) in the following expression:

$$\left(\frac{1}{\sqrt{N-3}}\right)1.96$$

where 1.96 is the standard score z for $p = .05$ two-tailed, and the other value defines the *standard error* of a Fisher z_r. You will find discussions of the standard error in statistics texts (see also R. Rosenthal & Rosnow, 2008), but in general, it refers to the standard deviation of a given statistic. (In the next chapter, where we describe the computational formula for the t test as resembling a "signal-to-noise" ratio, you can think of the standard error as the more technical definition of noise in the denominator of the t formula.)

Step 3 is to find the limits of the 95% CI by subtracting (to create the lower limit) the result in Step 2 from, and adding it (to create the upper limit) to, the Fisher z_r transformed effect size in Step 1.

Step 4 is to consult Table B.7 in Appendix B (p. 404) to transform these lower and upper z_r values back to $r_{effect\ size}$ values to define the 95% CI around the effect size r.

To illustrate, suppose we find that $r_{effect\ size} = .33$ based on a total sample size of $N = 80$, and we want to compute the 95% CI. The first step is to look in Table B.6 at the intersection of the row labeled .3 and the column labeled .03, where we find Fisher $z_1 = .343$. The second step is to substitute $N = 80$ in the expression, that is,

$$\left(\frac{1}{\sqrt{N-3}}\right)1.96 = \left(\frac{1}{\sqrt{77}}\right)1.96 = 0.2234$$

The third step is to subtract the result in Step 2 from the result in Step 1 to find the lower limit of z_r (i.e., $.343 - .2234 = .1196$, rounded to .12), and to add the result in Step 2 to the result in Step 1 to find the upper limit of z_r (i.e., $.343 + .2234 = .5664$, rounded to .57). The final step is to transform both results of Step 3 into effect size rs, which we do by consulting Table B.7. For $z_r = .12$, we see at the intersection of the row labeled .1 and the column labeled .02 that .119, rounded to .12, is the lower limit of our $r_{effect\ size}$ of .33. For $z_r = .57$, we see at the intersection of the row labeled .5 and the column labeled .07 that .515, rounded to .52, is the upper limit of our $r_{\text{effect size}}$ of .33. We can now say, with 95% confidence, that the population value of $r_{\text{effect size}}$ is between .12 and .52.

To see how the confidence interval is affected by smaller and larger Ns, suppose that the N is 20 instead of 80. Substituting in the expression in Step 2 gives

$$\left(\frac{1}{\sqrt{N-3}}\right)1.96 = \left(\frac{1}{\sqrt{17}}\right)1.96 = 0.4754$$

which, when we carry out the remaining calculations, results in a 95% CI from −.13 to .67. A negative effect size r means that the pattern of the observed effect is opposite that predicted, so in this case, the confidence interval is so wide that it includes unexpected as well as expected directional patterns. What if we increase the sample to 320? Substituting in the expression in Step 2 gives us

$$\left(\frac{1}{\sqrt{N-3}}\right)1.96 = \left(\frac{1}{\sqrt{317}}\right)1.96 = 0.1101$$

which, when we follow through with the remaining steps, yields a 95% CI from .23 to .42. Thus, we see that working with a smaller N widens the confidence interval, and that working with a larger N shrinks the confidence interval. Because we would prefer a narrower rather than a wider confidence interval, the lesson is to work with the largest reasonable N possible.

Also, you need not restrict yourself to a 95% CI if you prefer working with some other interval. The table below shows values of alpha (i.e., p levels), confidence intervals, and the corresponding standard score z for $p = .10$, .05, and .01 two-tailed:

alpha (α)	.10	.05	.01
Confidence interval (CI)	90%	95%	99%
2-tailed z	1.64	1.96	2.58

For example, if you prefer to work with a 90% CI, you substitute 1.64 for 1.96 in the expression in Step 2, and if you prefer a 99% CI, you substitute 2.58. Increasing the confidence interval from 95% to 99% will, in turn, widen the confidence interval, and vice versa. If you ask yourself how wide an interval you need to be 100% sure about some risky event, you will see intuitively why increasing the confidence level results in a wider confidence interval.

What Does Computing Killeen's p_{rep} Tell Me?

Finally, we want to mention a new statistic, called $\boldsymbol{p_{\text{rep}}}$, that Peter R. Killeen (2005) proposed as an alternative to NHST, particularly when the ability to replicate a research finding is of primary interest. Suppose you are interested in two experimental findings in two different areas, and you are thinking about trying to replicate one of them as a first step in a line of research. You would like to know which one has a greater chance of being replicated. Computing p_{rep} will tell you the probability of replicating the same direction of effect as reported in the original study, assuming you will be working with the same number of subjects and similar procedures as in the original study. The beauty of p_{rep} is that it can be estimated from the reported p value by

$$p_{rep} = \frac{1}{1 + \left(\dfrac{p}{1-p}\right)^{2/3}}$$

where p is the significance level.

Suppose you compute a statistical test (such as t, F, or chi-square) and find $p = .05$. Substituting in this formula yields

$$p_{rep} = \frac{1}{1 + \left(\dfrac{.05}{1-.05}\right)^{2/3}} = \frac{1}{1 + \left(\dfrac{.05}{.95}\right)^{2/3}} = \frac{1}{1.14} = .88$$

which tells you that your finding will replicate 88% of the time, where *replication* is defined as "an effect of the same sign as that found in the original experiment" (Killeen, 2005, p. 346). Table 12.6 lists p_{rep} values for significance (p) levels from .40 to .001. Notice that the probability of replication (p_{rep}) increases as the p value (i.e., the likelihood of Type I error) gets smaller and smaller. Multiplying the p_{rep} value by 100 yields an estimate of the percentage of time that the effect will replicate. Although p_{rep} is intended to be used primarily as a measure of robustness of individual studies, Killeen provided support for the statistic in some meta-analytic findings (meta-analysis is discussed in Appendix C) in which the median p_{rep} was similar to the percentage of replication reported in each meta-analysis.

Table 12.6 Probability of Replicating Directional Effect	
p value	Probability of replication (p_{rep})
.40	.57
.30	.64
.20	.72
.15	.76
.10	.81
.05	.88
.01	.96
.001	.99

Summary of Ideas

1. Three procedures discussed in this chapter that use statistics and probabilities are (a) *null hypothesis significance testing (NHST);* (b) *effect size* estimation (and the corresponding *BESD* and *confidence interval*); and (c) *power analysis.*

2. The probability of a particular favorable outcome is the number of favorable events divided by the total number of possible events (Box 12.1).

3. The *null hypothesis* (H_0) and the *alternative hypothesis* (H_1) are mutually exclusive: When one is true, the other must be false.

4. A *Type I error* is a mistake in rejecting H_0 when it is true, whereas a *Type II error* is a mistake in failing to reject H_0 when it is false. The probability of a Type I error is called *alpha* (α), the *significance level,* and the *p value;* the probability of a Type II error is called *beta* (β).

5. Traditionally, scientists have believed that it is worse to make a Type I error (i.e., an error of "gullibility") than to make a Type II error (i.e., an error of "blindness to a relationship").

6. When doing NHST, scientists try to see whether they can reject the null hypothesis and yet be reasonably sure that they will not be wrong in doing so (Box 12.2).

7. Failure to reject the null hypothesis does not automatically imply "no effect," and therefore statistical significance should not be confused with the presence or absence of an effect, or with the practical importance of an obtained effect.

8. The *binomial effect-size display (BESD)* represents the difference in "success rates" (e.g., the survival rate, cure rate, improvement rate, or selection rate) between the experimental and the control condition based on the strength of the effect size correlation ($r_{\text{effect size}}$).

9. *Power,* defined as $1 - \beta$, refers to the probability of not making a Type II error.

10. Given a particular estimated effect size r and a preferred level of power, we can use Table 12.5 to determine how large the total N must be to allow detection of the effect at $p = .05$ two-tailed.

11. To create a confidence interval around an $r_{\text{effect size}}$, the Fisher z_r transformation is used to locate upper and lower limits of the r, and then these Fisher z_r limits are translated back into the upper and lower limits of the $r_{\text{effect size}}$.

12. The smaller the N, or the higher the desired confidence (e.g., 99% instead of 95%), the wider is the confidence interval.

13. The p_{rep} statistic, which assumes the same number of subjects and a similar level of sampling error as in the original study, gives the probability of a same-direction replication.

Key Terms

alpha (α)   p. 274
alternative hypothesis
  (H_1)   p. 274
beta (β)   p. 274
binomial effect-size display
  (BESD)   p. 279
null hypothesis (H_0)   p. 274

null hypothesis significance
  testing (NHST)   p. 271
one-tailed *p* value   p. 277
p_{rep} p. 286
power ($1 - \beta$)   p. 283
power analysis   p. 283
p value   p. 271, 274

$r_{\text{effect size}}$ p. 272
significance level
  p. 274
two-tailed *p* value
  p. 277
Type I error   p. 274
Type II error   p. 274

Multiple-Choice Questions for Review

1. "There will be no difference between the experimental group and the control group." This statement is an example of a(n) (a) alternative hypothesis; (b) experimental hypothesis; (c) directional hypothesis; (d) null hypothesis.

2. "The experimental group will score higher than the control group." This statement is an example of (a) H_0; (b) H_1; (c) H_2; (d) H_3.

3. Rejecting the null hypothesis when it is true is called a (a) Type 0 error; (b) Type I error; (c) Type II error; (d) Type III error.

4. Failing to reject H_0 when it is false is called a (a) Type 0 error; (b) Type I error; (c) Type II error; (d) Type III error.

5. A Type II error can be thought of as an error of (a) imprecision; (b) deafness; (c) gullibility; (d) blindness.

6. Scientists usually consider a _____ error to be more serious than a _____ error. (a) Type I, Type II; (b) null hypothesis, alternative hypothesis; (c) alternative hypothesis, null hypothesis; (d) Type II, Type I

7. A student at Lincoln University conducts a study with 52 subjects and finds the correlation between authoritarianism and prejudice to be $r = .273$. According to Table 12.3, what is the two-tailed significance level associated with this correlation? (a) .10; (b) .05; (c) .01; (d) .001

8. Squaring r yields a statistic known as the (a) coefficient of determination; (b) binomial effect-size display; (c) proportion of variability unexplained; (d) none of the above.

9. A student at Central Arkansas University wants to conduct a study with power of .60 and, based on previous research, expects to get an effect size r of .20. According to Table 12.5, how many subjects should she obtain to reject the null hypothesis at the .05 level two-tailed? (a) 10; (b) 20; (c) 60; (d) 123

10. A student at the University of Alaska expects to find an effect size r of .40 but unfortunately can obtain only 25 subjects. According to Table 12.5, what will be the power (to reject the null hypothesis at the .05 level, two-tailed) of his study? (a) .20; (b) .25; (c) .30; (d) .50

Discussion Questions for Review

1. A Notre Dame University student manipulated the presence or absence of a confederate in a wheelchair to affect subjects' willingness to sign a petition urging more handicapped parking spaces for public and private buildings. The effect size of the result was $r_{effect\ size} = .40$. Can you create and interpret a BESD for this effect size?

2. A Gallaudet University student was asked by her professor to define the Type II error in the context of the aspirin study (Table 12.4) and to tell how it is related to the power of a test. Do you know the answer? Do you know what factors determine the power of a test of significance?

3. A panicking friend asks a University of Texas student for help with a project she is doing at Southern Methodist University on sex differences in scores on a new test of assertiveness. Her study will involve a randomly sampled group of males and a randomly sampled group of females. She tells the University of Texas student that effect sizes in this area of research have tended to be approximately $r_{effect\ size} = .20$. She wants to present her findings at the Southeastern Psychological Association meeting in New Orleans but worries that the study will not be accepted for presentation unless the group difference reaches a significance level (alpha) of $p = .05$ two-tailed. She also tells her University of Texas friend that the power level she is seeking for her study is .7. Given all this information, how many male and how many female subjects should the friend advise her to run?

4. A St. Lawrence University student does a study and gets $p = .05$. Exactly what does this p value tell him? What doesn't it tell him that is also important to know?

5. The first three students to complete their course research projects at Minot State University displayed their BESDs to the other students, to inspire them. All three students had developed new methods of teaching vocabulary. What $r_{effect\ size}$ was associated with each of the following BESDs?

Student A:

Method	Above average	Below average
New	75	25
Old	25	75

Student B:

Method	Above average	Below average
New	55	45
Old	45	55

Student C:

Method	Above average	Below average
New	35	65
Old	65	35

6. The Gallaudet University student in Question 2 is also asked by her professor to create a 95% confidence interval for the effect size correlation of .034 in the aspirin study. Do you know how to do it?

7. Dr. Sando, an experienced medical specialist, is consulted by a biomedical researcher who is interested in pursuing a particular line of research. The biomedical researcher wants to begin by replicating one of two earlier studies as a basis of her grant application, and she asks Dr. Sando which study, in his opinion, has the higher payoff potential. He advises her to compute the p_{rep} value for each study. What will doing so tell the biomedical researcher?

Answers to Review Questions

Multiple-Choice Questions

1. d	**3.** b	**5.** d	**7.** b	**9.** d
2. b	**4.** c	**6.** a	**8.** a	**10.** d

Discussion Questions

1. The BESD is shown below, and the interpretation is that the effect size amounts to a 40% difference between rates of petition signing in the wheelchair-present and in the wheelchair-absent condition. The percentages in the BESD are not the raw percentages (rates) in the actual data but are "standardized" so that the values in the margins are equalized (i.e., we assume that half the population was in each condition, and that half the population was in each outcome group).

Condition	Signing petition	Not signing petition	Total
Wheelchair present	70	30	100
Wheelchair absent	30	70	100
Total	100	100	200

2. A Type II error would have occurred if it had been concluded that there was a correlation of zero between taking aspirin and having a heart attack when that correlation was not really zero. The power of a test is the probability that results will be found significant at a given p value when the null hypothesis is false. Power is defined as $1 - \beta$, where β = the probability of making a Type II error. The power of a particular test of significance depends on the alpha (α) we set, the actual size of the effect being investigated, and the size of the sample.

3. In Table 12.5, the intersection of the column headed .20 and the row labeled .70 shows the required total N to be 154. Therefore, she should run 77 females and 77 males.

4. It tells him that only 5% of the time would he obtain a result that significant, or more significant, if the null hypothesis (H_0) were really true. It does not tell him about the size of the effect being studied.

5. Since r is simply the difference between the proportions successful in the treatment and the control conditions, the three rs are:

$$\text{Student A's results} \quad .75 - .25 = .50$$
$$\text{Student B's results} \quad .55 - .45 = .10$$
$$\text{Student C's results} \quad .35 - .65 = -.30$$

Notice that the result for Student C reflects a negative r; the new method is *worse* than the old.

6. Step 1 is to use Table B.6 (on p. 403) to get the Fisher z_r that corresponds to $r_{effect\ size} = .034$, and we find $z_r = .034$ (i.e., not different from r in this particular case). Step 2 is to substitute the N of 22,071 in the expression

$$\left(\frac{1}{\sqrt{N-3}}\right)1.96$$

which gives us .0132. Step 3 is to subtract this value from .034 to get the lower limit of z_r (.02 rounded), and to add the value to .034 to get the upper limit of z_r (.05). Step 4 is to use Table B.7 (on p. 404) to transform lower and upper limits of z_r to $r_{effect\ size}$. We can say that, with 95% confidence, the effect size r of aspirin is between .02 and .05 in the population from which the 22,071 subjects were randomly sampled.

7. Choosing the study with the higher p_{rep} will increase the payoff potential. Multiplying p_{rep} by 100 reveals the percentage of time that the directional result is likely to be replicated, that is, given similar sample sizes and similar procedures to those in the original study.

CHAPTER 13

The Comparison of Two Conditions

Preview Questions

- What do signal-to-noise ratios have to do with t tests?
- How do I compute an independent-sample t test?
- What can a table of p values for t teach me?
- How can I estimate $r_{\text{effect size}}$ from an independent-sample t?
- How can I estimate Cohen's d from an independent-sample t?
- How do I interpret Cohen's d for independent groups?
- How can I maximize the independent-sample t?
- How does a paired t test differ from an independent-sample t test?
- What are the statistical assumptions of the t test?

What Do Signal-to-Noise Ratios Have to Do With t Tests?

We have examined the logic of using statistics and probabilities to test hypotheses, and with this chapter we begin our discussion of the three most popular statistical tests: the t test (described in this chapter), the F test (Chapter 14), and the chi-square (χ^2) test (Chapter 15). The statistical test you choose is guided by the nature of the question or hypothesis in which you are interested. If you are interested in comparing the means of two groups (e.g., experimental and control groups), you will find the *t* **test** a convenient and powerful method (see also Box 13.1). It will allow you to test the likelihood that the population means represented by the two groups are equal (i.e., the null hypothesis), by setting up a signal-to-noise ratio. In this ratio, the *signal* is represented by the difference between the two means, and the *noise* is represented by the variability of the scores within the samples. The larger the signal is relative to the noise, the more likely the null hypothesis is to be rejected.

As an illustration of how t tests can be thought of as signal-to-noise ratios, suppose that a researcher is conducting an experiment on the effect of vitamins on the academic performance of children from families below the poverty level. In Chapter 7, we described the statistical design of this research as a between-subjects

BOX 13.1   Student's *t*

The *t* test is also called **Student's *t*** in honor of William Sealy Gosset, its inventor. Introduced in 1908 by Gosset, it "revolutionized the statistics of small samples" (Snedecor & Cochran, 1989, p. 54). Trained as a chemist, Gosset worked for Guinness, the Irish brewery. For security reasons, the staff members were prohibited from publishing their research, but Gosset quietly published under the pseudonym "Student." Before Gosset's development of the *t* test, researchers who did experiments in small samples with varying effects were in a quandary over how to generalize the effects to populations whose variability was unknown. Gosset's genius was to perceive a way of testing the equality of population means whose variability was unknown, given only the means and variability of samples (Gigerenzer et al., 1989). The preeminent statistician R. A. Fisher (1973) later wrote of Gosset's profound contribution that, "important as it was in itself, [it] was of far greater importance in inaugurating the first stage of the process by which statistical methods attained sufficient refinement to be of real assistance in the interpretation of data" (p. 4).

randomized design. The researcher has randomly assigned the children to an experimental group (which is administered vitamins at regular intervals) or to a control group (which receives a placebo). The experimenter's working hypothesis is that vitamins will have a positive effect on the children's academic performance, and the null hypothesis is that vitamins will have *no* effect on their academic performance. Table 13.1 and Figure 13.1 show two alternative outcomes of this experiment and help to illustrate the signal-to-noise idea.

We see that the means of the vitamin groups are identical ($M = 15$), as are the means of the control groups ($M = 10$). The only difference between Results A and Results B is that one set of results (B) is more variable. That is, the scores of B are less tightly bunched than the scores of A. When we compare the mean differences *between* the groups ($15 - 10 = 5$), it seems we should also take into consideration the amount of variability *within* the groups. That is, the 5 points of difference between the groups look larger to us when seen against the backdrop of the small

Table 13.1   Between-Subjects Design with Alternative Results A and B

	Results A		Results B	
	Vitamins	Control	Vitamins	Control
	13	8	9	4
	15	10	15	10
	17	12	21	16
Mean (*M*)	15	10	15	10

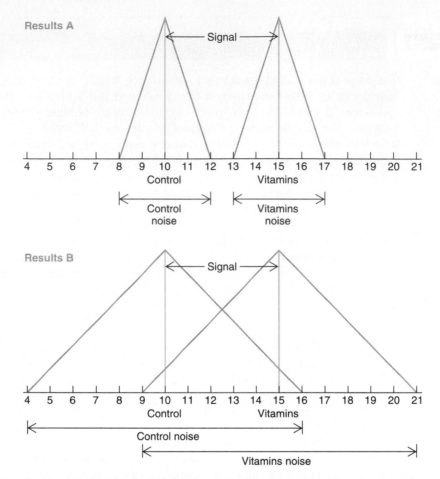

Figure 13.1 Graphic display of the data in Table 13.1. Note that Results A have no overlapping data but that Results B overlap from the scores of 9 to 16.

within-group variation of Results A than when seen against the backdrop of the larger within-group variation of B.

This is the way the **independent-sample *t* test** works. It is a test of statistical significance that examines the difference between two independent means (the *signal*) against the background of the within-group variability (the *noise*). The larger the difference between the means (i.e., the greater the signal), and/or the smaller the within-group variability for any given size of study (i.e., the less the noise), the greater will be the value of *t* (see also Box 13.2). Because large *t* values are associated with differences between means that are more statistically significant, researchers generally prefer larger *t* values. That is, larger *t* values have a lower level of probability (the *p* value or alpha) and, in turn, allow researchers to reject the null hypothesis that there is no difference between means. Later in this chapter, we

BOX 13.2 Shouting to Make Yourself Heard!

Suppose you are trying to conduct an intimate conversation in a noisy restaurant. You have to shout to make your words (the signal) understood over the background din (the noise). However, if there is not much noise, you can whisper and your communication will be easily picked up. By analogy, *t* tests are more sensitive to differences between groups (i.e., the signal) when the variability within groups (the din, or noise) does not overwhelm the magnitude of a real difference.

will discuss some design strategies during the planning phase of the research that will maximize the independent *t*.

How Do I Compute an Independent-Sample *t* Test?

In the example we have been considering, the two groups are presumed to be *independent* of one another; that is, the results in one group are not influenced by the results in the other group. This is also true of Mary Jones's experiment in Appendix A. Had she used a repeated-measures design, the two scores on each sampling unit would not be independent. We will explain the use of *t* tests with nonindependent data later in this chapter, but when we want to compare two independent samples, a general purpose formula for this *t* test is

$$t = \frac{M_1 - M_2}{\sqrt{\left(\dfrac{1}{n_1} + \dfrac{1}{n_2}\right)S^2}}$$

in which M_1 and M_2 are the means of the two independent groups; n_1 and n_2 are the number of units (the number of participants) in each of the two groups, and S^2 is what (in Chapter 10) was called the *unbiased estimator of the population variance*.

You will see the same formula repeated on the first page of the appendix of Mary Jones's report, along with her calculation of *t* based on the data she summarized in the body of her report (in her Table 1). You can also think of S^2 in the *t* formula above as the "pooled estimate" of the population variance (i.e., a single estimate of the variance associated with both populations from which these two samples were drawn), computed as

$$S^2 = \frac{\Sigma(X_1 - M_1)^2 + \Sigma(X_2 - M_2)^2}{n_1 + n_2 - 2}$$

where X_1 and X_2 are individual raw scores, and the other symbols are as defined above. If you want to try your hand with another set of data to check your understanding of these formulas, you can work with Mary Jones's raw scores.

| Table 13.2 | Basic Data for Calculating t for Results A and B in Table 13.1 |

Results A:

	Vitamin group				Control group		
	X_1	$X_1 - M_1$	$(X_1 - M_1)^2$		X_2	$X_2 - M_2$	$(X_2 - M_2)^2$
	13	−2.0	4.0		8	−2.0	4.0
	15	0.0	0.0		10	0.0	0.0
	17	+2.0	4.0		12	+2.0	4.0
Sum (Σ)	45	0	8.0		30	0	8.0
Mean (M)	15				10		
S	2.0				2.0		
S^2	4.0				4.0		
σ	1.6				1.6		

Results B:

	Vitamin group				Control group		
	X_1	$X_1 - M_1$	$(X_1 - M_1)^2$		X_2	$X_2 - M_2$	$(X_2 - M_2)^2$
	9	−6.0	36.0		4	−6.0	36.0
	15	0.0	0.0		10	0.0	0.0
	21	+6.0	36.0		16	+6.0	36.0
Sum (Σ)	45	0	72.0		30	0	72.0
Mean (M)	15				10		
S	6.0				6.0		
S^2	36.0				36.0		
σ	4.9				4.9		

Table 13.2 provides all the basic data needed to compute t by hand for the two sets of results in Table 13.1. Notice that the measures of spread at the bottom of Results A and B (i.e., S, S^2, and σ) clearly verify what we perceived when we inspected the data in Table 13.1, which is that the raw scores of Results B were more "spread out" than the scores of A. For each group, we computed the sum of the squares of the deviations of the scores from their mean, and we will now enter this information in the formula for the pooled estimate of the population variance.

With Results A we find

$$S^2 = \frac{\Sigma(X_1 - M_1)^2 + \Sigma(X_2 - M_2)^2}{n_1 + n_2 - 2} = \frac{8.0 + 8.0}{3 + 3 - 2} = \frac{16.0}{4} = 4.0$$

so

$$t = \frac{M_1 - M_2}{\sqrt{\left(\dfrac{1}{n_1} + \dfrac{1}{n_2}\right)S^2}} = \frac{15 - 10}{\sqrt{\left(\dfrac{1}{3} + \dfrac{1}{3}\right)4.0}} = \frac{5}{1.63} = 3.06$$

Performing the same calculations on Results B gives us

$$S^2 = \frac{\Sigma(X_1 - M_1)^2 + \Sigma(X_2 - M_2)^2}{n_1 + n_2 - 2} = \frac{72.0 + 72.0}{3 + 3 - 2} = \frac{144.0}{4} = 36.0$$

and

$$t = \frac{M_1 - M_2}{\sqrt{\left(\dfrac{1}{n_1} + \dfrac{1}{n_2}\right)S^2}} = \frac{15 - 10}{\sqrt{\left(\dfrac{1}{3} + \dfrac{1}{3}\right)36.0}} = \frac{5}{4.90} = 1.02$$

Not surprisingly, in view of the larger denominator in the t test for Results B (4.90) than for Results A (1.63), the value of t is larger for Results A than for B. We expected this effect because of the difference in variability (i.e., the difference in noise levels) between A and B. We can look up the approximate p values corresponding to these results in a suitable table, or if we have a good calculator handy or are working with a statistics program, we will be given the exact p values when we calculate the independent sample t test. (The information is also available online at an excellent Web site developed by the Department of Statistics at the University of California, Los Angeles: http://calculators.stat.ucla.edu.) As larger values of t are rarer events, we expect a smaller p to be associated with Results A than with Results B.

What Can a Table of p Values for t Teach Me?

Although it is convenient to think of t as a single test of statistical significance, you can also think of it as a family of curves (called the **t distribution**). The reason is that there is a different curve (each resembling the standard normal distribution) for every possible value of what are called the **degrees of freedom** (symbolized as df) of the t test. In the case that we have been considering (the independent-sample t test), the degrees of freedom are defined as $n_1 + n_2 - 2$ (see also Box 13.3). One of

BOX 13.3   Degrees of Freedom

The origin of degrees of freedom (df) has to do in a way with the standard deviation, which in turn depends on the deviations from the mean (i.e., the $X - M$ values). Suppose you have five raw (X) scores: 1, 3, 5, 7, 9, with $\Sigma X = 25$ and $M = 5$. The sum of the deviations from the mean has to be zero. That is, $\Sigma(X - M) = 0$ because $(1 - 5) + (3 - 5) + (5 - 5) + (7 - 5) + (9 - 5)$ equals zero. Knowing this, if you were given all but one value, you could easily find the missing value. In other words, one deviation in the group is not free to vary, so 1 df is eliminated. Therefore, with a batch of five scores, you have 4 df remaining. In the case of a t test on two independent samples, you lose 1 df for each group, so that $df = n_1 + n_2 - 2$.

Table 13.3			t Values Required for Significance at Various p Levels		
			Probability level (p)		
	.20	.10	.05	.01	two-tailed
df	.10	.05	.025	.005	one-tailed
1	3.08	6.31	12.71	63.66	
2	1.89	2.92	4.30	9.92	
3	1.64	2.35	3.18	5.84	
4	1.53	2.13	2.78	4.60	
5	1.48	2.02	2.57	4.03	
6	1.44	1.94	2.45	3.71	
8	1.40	1.86	2.31	3.36	
10	1.37	1.81	2.23	3.17	
15	1.34	1.75	2.13	2.95	
20	1.32	1.72	2.09	2.84	
25	1.32	1.71	2.06	2.79	
30	1.31	1.70	2.04	2.75	
40	1.30	1.68	2.02	2.70	
60	1.30	1.67	2.00	2.66	
80	1.29	1.66	1.99	2.64	
100	1.29	1.66	1.98	2.63	
1,000	1.28	1.65	1.96	2.58	
∞	1.28	1.64	1.96	2.58	

Note: For a more complete table, see Appendix B, Table B.2.

the great contributions of the inventor of the t test, W. S. Gosset (Box 13.1), was to figure out the curve for each number of degrees of freedom. Table 13.3 provides a summary of the most pertinent information from those curves for selected p values. This table gives us the areas found in one or both tails of the selected t curves. That is, for one-tailed p values, this table gives the areas found in the right-hand tail, and for two-tailed p values, it gives the areas found in both tails.

Looking carefully at Table 13.3, we see that for any level of p, the value of t required to reach that level is smaller and smaller as the degrees of freedom (df) increase. In addition, for any df, a higher t value is required to reach more extreme (smaller) p values. One way to think about t is that when the null hypothesis of "no difference" or "no effect" is true (i.e., when the means in the population do not differ), the most likely value of t is zero. However, even if the population mean difference were truly zero, we would often find nonzero t values by chance alone. Suppose the direction of the effect was predicted and, therefore, we decide to use the one-tailed p values. With $df = 8$, we would obtain a t value of 1.40 or greater (favoring the predicted outcome) about 10% of the time (i.e., one-tailed $p = .10$), or of 1.86 or greater about 5% of the time (one-tailed $p = .05$), or of 3.36 or greater about 0.5% of the time (one-tailed $p = .005$).

Notice also in Table 13.3 (and Table B.2 in Appendix B) that the values of t in each column become more stable as the degrees of freedom increase. The reason is that the t distribution gradually approximates the standard normal distribution as the size of the samples is increased. At 30 df, the t distribution is fairly close to that of the standard normal distribution. When df = infinity (∞), the t distribution gives values identical to those for the standard normal distribution. This information may come in handy if you decide to do a meta-analysis (described in Appendix C), as the implication is that you can look up the p levels of z values in the $df = \infty$ row of Table B.2.

We are now ready to look up our two t values, and this exercise will give you a further insight into what a statistics computer program, scientific calculator, or Web site gives you. We will assume that the direction of the effect was predicted, and we will use the more comprehensive listing found in Table B.2 (pp. 394–395). The rows show the degrees of freedom (df), which will be 4 for both sets of results because we eliminate 1 df in each group (i.e., df = 3 + 3 − 2 = 4) when computing an independent-sample t test. We put a finger on the row labeled 4 df and read across the columns until we find a value that is the same as or larger than the obtained value of t. For Results A, the t of 3.06 is larger than the value listed for p = .025 one-tailed (2.776) but smaller than the value listed for p = .01 one-tailed (3.747). Thus, the one-tailed p of t = 3.06 is less than .025 (i.e., $p < .025$ one-tailed) but greater than .01 (i.e., $p > .01$ one-tailed). For Results B, the t of 1.02 is larger than the value listed for p = .25 one-tailed (.741) but smaller than the value listed for p = .10 one-tailed (1.533). Thus, the one-tailed p for t = 1.02 with 4 df is < .25 but > .10.

You must decide for yourself whether you will regard any given t as an event rare enough to make you doubt that the null hypothesis is true. Still, you cannot simply decide, say, that "$p < .20$ is a reasonable risk" and then expect the instructor (or others) to automatically accept your decision. By tradition in psychology, most researchers who do NHST prefer the .05 significance level. By this standard, you would conclude that Results A are "statistically significant" and that Results B are "not statistically significant." Of course (as discussed in the previous chapter), you will also want to examine the effect sizes and confidence intervals (also possibly the BESDs), as you know that the p values alone fail to tell the whole story. Let us see how you would obtain this information either in your own research or from the reported t in a published report.

How Can I Estimate $r_{\text{effect size}}$ From an Independent-Sample t?

The procedure for estimating $r_{\text{effect size}}$ from a t test that compares two groups is simple enough to be performed on any calculator. In the cases we have been discussing, we used the independent (or two-sample) t test on a continuous dependent variable, so our effect size r will be the point-biserial correlation (r_{pb}) described in Chapter 11. That is, our $r_{\text{effect size}}$ can be understood as the correlation between dummy-coded experimental (1) and control (0) group membership and the dependent variable scores. This effect size r can be calculated from t by

$$r_{\text{effect size}} = \sqrt{\frac{t^2}{t^2 + df}}$$

where t^2 is the squared value of the independent-sample t test, and df is defined as $n_1 + n_2 - 2$.

Thus, in the case of Results A in Table 13.2, with $t = 3.06$ and $df = 3 + 3 - 2 = 4$, we find

$$r_{\text{effect size}} = \sqrt{\frac{t^2}{t^2 + df}} = \sqrt{\frac{(3.06)^2}{(3.06)^2 + 4}} = .84$$

which indicates a "jumbo-sized" effect. In the case of Results B, with $t = 1.02$ and the same df, we find

$$r_{\text{effect size}} = \sqrt{\frac{t^2}{t^2 + df}} = \sqrt{\frac{(1.02)^2}{(1.02)^2 + 4}} = .45$$

which indicates a substantial effect in spite of the failure of the test to achieve significance at the conventional 5% level. If you turn to the appendix of Mary Jones's report, you will see the same formula and other sample calculations.

We can now create a confidence interval around these effects by following the four easy steps in the previous chapter. To review, with 95% confidence and $r_{\text{effect size}} = .84$, the first step is to use Table B.6 (page 403) to identify the corresponding Fisher z_r, which in this case is 1.221. In Step 2, we substitute $N = 6$ in the expression

$$\left(\frac{1}{\sqrt{N-3}}\right)1.96 = \left(\frac{1}{\sqrt{6-3}}\right)1.96 = 1.1316$$

where 1.96 represents the 95% CI, although we can (as noted in the previous chapter) choose another confidence level if we wish. In Step 3, we subtract the value obtained in Step 2 from 1.221 to find the lower limit of z_r (0.0894, rounded to .09) and add 1.1316 to 1.221 to find the upper limit of z_r (2.3526, rounded to 2.35). In the final step, we use Table B.7 (page 404) to transform these lower and upper z_r values back into r values. In sum, we are 95% confident the $r_{\text{effect size}}$ in the population is between .09 and .98 (see also Box 13.4).

BOX 13.4 Crossing Over

Notice at the end of the Results section of Mary Jones's report that she discusses the fact that her 95% CI crossed over into the negative side. There is a special relationship between confidence intervals and the α levels on which they are based. Since the width of the confidence interval in percentage units is given by $(1 - \text{two-tailed } \alpha)100$, if an obtained effect size is found significant at the two-tailed α level or at $\alpha/2$ one-tailed, the end of the confidence interval closer to .00 will not cross over the .00 point (i.e., the interval will be entirely on the positive side of .00, or entirely on the negative side of .00). For example, if a 95% CI is entirely between +.00 and +1.00, or entirely between −.00 and −1.00, it will be significant at least at .05 two-tailed or .025 one-tailed. If a 90% CI is entirely between +.00 and +1.00, or entirely between −.00 and −1.00, it will be significant at least at .10 two-tailed or .05 one-tailed.

Table 13.4	BESDs for Results A in Table 13.2	

BESD for lower limit $r_{effect\ size} = .09$ (95% confidence):

	Improved	**Not improved**
Vitamins	54.5	45.5
Control	45.5	54.5

BESD for obtained $r_{effect\ size} = .84$:

	Improved	**Not improved**
Vitamins	92	8
Control	8	92

BESD for upper limit $r_{effect\ size} = .98$ (95% confidence):

	Improved	**Not improved**
Vitamins	99	1
Control	1	99

As noted in the previous chapter, had we worked with a much larger N or a less stringent confidence level (90% rather than 95%), the interval would not have been this wide. Applying what we discussed previously about BESDs, we can also now create such displays for the lower and upper limits surrounding the BESD for each obtained $r_{effect\ size}$. Table 13.4 shows the BESDs for the results we have seen, and it gives us a clearer sense of one aspect of the possible practical importance of the effect in question (because it is now encapsulated within the boundaries of the confidence interval). We see that the effect of taking vitamins is important at either extreme of the 95% CI.

How Can I Estimate Cohen's *d* From an Independent-Sample *t*?

Jacob Cohen (1969) proposed that, when the *t* test is used to compare two independent means, a useful "pure number" (i.e., free of the original measurement unit) index of the effect size can be expressed in standard deviation units as

$$d = \frac{M_1 - M_2}{\sigma_{pooled}}$$

known as **Cohen's *d***. That is, the difference between the two independent means is divided by the pooled population σ (i.e., the combined standard deviation of the experimental and control group scores), and

$$\sigma_{pooled} = S_{pooled}\left(\sqrt{\frac{df}{N}}\right)$$

We discuss the interpretation of *d* in the next section, but here we will illustrate the use of these formulas with the two sets of results in Table 13.2. A word of caution: In studies with very small samples, there is a danger that one or more outliers may inflate the denominator of the formula for d, causing d to be small even when there is a substantial difference between the two means (R. R. Wilcox, 2005). An outlier that is an error can frequently be dealt with by trimming (as discussed in Chapter 10), but a far-out score that is not an error is a strong reminder to explore the data further (R. Rosenthal & Rosnow, 2008, pp. 309–311). Whatever option the researcher decides on, it is important that the researcher explain what was done and why it was done.

For Results A in Table 13.2, we now solve for the pooled population σ by

$$\sigma_{\text{pooled}} = S_{\text{pooled}}\left(\sqrt{\frac{df}{N}}\right) = 2.0\left(\sqrt{\frac{4}{6}}\right) = 1.633$$

and then solve for Cohen's d by

$$d = \frac{M_1 - M_2}{\sigma_{\text{pooled}}} = \frac{15 - 10}{1.633} = 3.06$$

For Results B, we find

$$\sigma_{\text{pooled}} = S_{\text{pooled}}\left(\sqrt{\frac{df}{N}}\right) = 6.0\left(\sqrt{\frac{4}{6}}\right) = 4.90$$

and therefore

$$d = \frac{M_1 - M_2}{\sigma_{\text{pooled}}} = \frac{15 - 10}{4.90} = 1.02$$

There is, however, a far easier way to estimate d if we have the independent-sample t value. If the two samples are equal in size (i.e., $n_1 = n_2$), we can estimate d from

$$d = \frac{2t}{\sqrt{df}}$$

For Results A in Table 13.2, the independent sample t value was 3.06 with $df = 4$, which gives us

$$d = \frac{2t}{\sqrt{df}} = \frac{2(3.06)}{\sqrt{4}} = 3.06$$

For Results B, the t value was 1.02, again with $df = 4$, yielding

$$d = \frac{2t}{\sqrt{df}} = \frac{2(1.02)}{\sqrt{4}} = 1.02$$

When the two sample sizes are *not* equal, we need to modify the formula for obtaining d from t as follows:

$$d = \frac{2t}{\sqrt{df}}\left(\sqrt{\frac{\overline{n}}{n_{\text{h}}}}\right)$$

where $\bar{n}$ is the mean sample size, that is, $(n_1 + n_2)/2$. The value n_h is called the *harmonic mean sample size* and is computed as

$$n_h = \frac{2(n_1 n_2)}{n_1 + n_2}$$

In studies with equal sample sizes, the mean sample size $(\bar{n})$ is equal to the harmonic mean sample size (n_h), and the unequal-n formula is identical to the equal-n formula for estimating d from an independent-sample t.

How Do I Interpret Cohen's d for Independent Groups?

Cohen (1969, 1988) recognized that researchers might prefer to think of effect sizes in terms of r rather than d. If that is an option that you are considering, then you can interpret the r (in terms of the BESD) rather than the d. If you choose this option, you convert d into the point-biserial r in an unequal-n design by

$$r = \frac{d}{\sqrt{d^2 + 4\left(\dfrac{\bar{n}}{n_h}\right)}}$$

In an equal-n design, the formula simplifies to one given by Cohen (1988, p. 23) as

$$r = \frac{d}{\sqrt{d^2 + 4}}$$

To illustrate the unequal-n option, suppose group means of 6.0 and 4.8, σ_{pooled} of 2.0, and sample sizes of 85 and 15. First, we find d from

$$d = \frac{M_1 - M_2}{\sigma_{pooled}} = \frac{6.0 - 4.8}{2.0} = .6$$

and find n_h from

$$n_h = \frac{2(n_1 n_2)}{n_1 + n_2} = \frac{2(85 \times 15)}{85 + 15} = 25.5$$

Since $\bar{n} = (85 + 15)/2 = 50$, we find r from

$$r = \frac{d}{\sqrt{d^2 + 4\left(\dfrac{\bar{n}}{n_h}\right)}} = \frac{.6}{\sqrt{(.6)^2 + 4\left(\dfrac{50}{25.5}\right)}} = .21$$

If you decide to work with d, Cohen (1969, 1988) suggested some ways of interpreting the population distributions, assuming that the population distributions of the two groups being compared are normal (bell-shaped). He created a table in which you can look up this information (see Cohen, 1988, p. 22). One way, for example, is to think about the percentage (%) of nonoverlap or the percentage of overlap of the two distributions. Another way is to consider the percentage in one

| Table 13.5 | Rounded Values of Percentage Overlap and Nonoverlap, r, and r^2 for Different Values of Cohen's d | | | |

d	% overlap	% nonoverlap	r	r^2
0	100	0	.00	.00
.2 ("small")	85	15	.10	.01
.5 ("medium")	67	33	.24	.06
.8 ("large")	53	47	.37	.14
1.0	45	55	.45	.20
2.0	19	81	.71	.50
3.0	7	93	.83	.69
4.0	2	98	.89	.80

of the two populations that exceeds the same percentage in the other population. Still another option is the percentage in one population that the upper half of cases in the other population exceeds. All this information is available in Cohen's (1988) table and the accompanying discussion (p. 22). In our experience, most students find the first of these three options most intuitive, and thus Table 13.5 shows the rounded percentages of overlap and nonoverlap—and also the rounded values of r and r^2 corresponding to different values of d. For example, $d = .2$, which indicates that one of two means is two tenths of a standard deviation above the other, would correspond to an 85% overlap of the two population distributions; therefore, the gap (the nonoverlap) is $100 - 85 = 15\%$. Because the tails of normal distributions stretch into infinity, there is always some overlap when d is greater than 0 even if the gap is minimal. Even with Cohen's $d = 4.0$ (indicating that one of two means is 4 standard deviations above the other), there is still a 2% overlap.

Notice that d values of .2, .5, and .8 are labeled "small," "medium," and "large," respectively; Cohen coined these labels to make it more convenient to use his power tables. However, Cohen (1988) cautioned against taking these labels too literally or assuming that "small" implies "trivial." We mentioned previously that Cohen used the labels "small," "medium," and "large" as a convenient way of referring to r values of .1, .3, and .5, respectively. However, you can see in this table that there is not an exact correspondence between the labeling systems for d and r. Cohen's d of .2 ("small") does correspond with $r = .10$ ("small"), but Cohen's d of .5 ("medium") corresponds with $r = .24$, and Cohen's d of .8 corresponds with $r = .37$. Furthermore, as we noted in Chapter 12, reporting r^2 as a measure of effect size can be misleading, since "small" effects seem to virtually disappear when squared, and even very substantial effects (e.g., $d = 1.0$) seem misleadingly small when translated into r^2 (.20). Cohen (1988) counseled that "the *meaning* of any given [effect size] is, in the final analysis, a function of the context in which it is embedded" (p. 535). In the previous chapter, recall our discussion of aspirin's effect on preventing a heart attack and the Salk vaccine's effect on preventing polio, both of which were associated with effect sizes that, though small, were hardly trivial in terms of their health implications. It is important to keep this in mind when reporting and interpreting effect size indices.

One final point about d is that if you are planning to report it, it is advisable to report and interpret a confidence interval as well. The 95% confidence interval for Cohen's d on independent means is obtained by

$$95\% \text{ CI} = d \pm t_{(.05)}(S_{\text{Cohen's d}})$$

where $t_{(.05)}$ is the critical value of t at $p = .05$ two-tailed for $df = n_1 + n_2 - 2$, and $S_{\text{Cohen's d}}$ is the square root of the following (the variance of Cohen's d):

$$S^2_{\text{Cohen's d}} = \left[\frac{n_1 + n_2}{n_1 n_2} + \frac{d^2}{2(df)} \right] \frac{n_1 + n_2}{df}$$

Suppose $d = .50$, n_1 and n_2 are each 40, and thus $df = 40 + 40 - 2 = 78$, so we find

$$S^2_{\text{Cohen's d}} = \left[\frac{40 + 40}{(40)(40)} + \frac{(.50)^2}{2(78)} \right] \frac{40 + 40}{78} = .053$$

and therefore $S_{\text{Cohen's d}} = \sqrt{.053} = .230$. With $df = 78$, the critical value of $t_{(.05)}$ is 1.99. Substitution yields 95% CI $= .50 \pm 1.99(.230) = .50 \pm .458$, which indicates that there is a 95% probability that the population value of d falls between .042 and .958.

How Can I Maximize the Independent-Sample t?

As mentioned in the previous chapter, the t test, like any significance test, can be shown to consist of two components, one having to do with the effect size and the other with the size of the study (i.e., the number of sampling units). The way these two components come together is expressed by the following conceptual relationship:

Significance test = Size of effect × Size of study,

which tells us that t is the product of the effect size (defined, for example, as the effect size r or as Cohen's d) and the study size (defined, for example, as the total number of sampling units, or N). That is, the larger the effect size or the more subjects used, the greater will be the value of t. This conceptual relationship helps us to plan specific ways of maximizing the t test in a given situation (i.e., ways of strengthening the power of the t test).

For example, here is another formula in which t is mathematically broken down into an effect size and a study size component:

$$t = d \times \left[\frac{\sqrt{n_1 n_2}}{n_1 + n_2} \times \sqrt{df} \right]$$

where the effect size is defined as Cohen's d, and the study size is defined by the sample sizes of the two groups (n_1 and n_2). When the sample sizes are equal (i.e., $n_1 = n_2$), this formula simplifies to

$$t = d \times \frac{\sqrt{df}}{2}$$

When we think about these formulas, we can see that there are three ways of increasing the value of *t*.

First, because we know that *d* is defined as

$$d = \frac{M_1 - M_2}{\sigma_{\text{pooled}}}$$

one way to increase the value of *t* is to use a stronger treatment to drive the means of the two comparison groups further apart. For example, were we to investigate the effects of varying amounts of after-school tutoring, we might use 5-hours versus 2 hours of tutoring per week, but certainly not 5 minutes versus 2 minutes per week. Because this approach would maximize the value of $M_1 - M_2$ in the numerator of Cohen's *d* (i.e., the definition of the effect size component in the conceptual relationship), it would be a sensible design strategy.

A second way to maximize *t* is to decrease the variability of responses within the two groups, which we can do by decreasing the σ_{pooled} in the denominator of Cohen's *d* (again strengthening the power of *t*). This is exactly what happened in Results A of Table 13.2, in which the variability of response within groups ($\sigma = 1.6$) was substantially less than that in Results B ($\sigma = 4.9$). Two possible ways of decreasing the variability of response are (a) to standardize the research procedures to make them more uniform and (b) to recruit subject samples that are relatively homogeneous in those characteristics that are substantially correlated with the dependent variable. However, in using very homogeneous samples, we may trade generalizability (external validity) for statistical power (statistical conclusion validity).

Still a third way of strengthening the power of the *t* test is by increasing the total study size, which we discussed in the preceding chapter. Given a total available study size of *N* (where $N = n_1 + n_2$), it is also prudent to try to keep the sample sizes equivalent in the two groups (i.e., $n_1 = n_2$), as an unequal-*n* design may drain power, and the more unequal the sample sizes, the greater the drain (see R. Rosenthal & Rosnow, 2008, Table 13.1 on p. 384).

How Does a Paired *t* Test Differ From an Independent-Sample *t* Test?

So far, we have used *t* to compare the means of two *independent* groups. That is, we regarded the scores in one group as having no inherent relationship to the scores in the other group. However, suppose we measure the same subjects more than once (e.g., before and after they are exposed to a learning experience) and we want to compare the means of these two measures. Now the two groups of scores are no longer independent because of the repeated-measures (within-subjects) design. A less obvious example of samples that are not independent occurs when the two groups consist of children who are related by birth, and one member is assigned to Group 1 and the other to Group 2. The common family membership introduces a degree of prior relatedness between the scores in Group 1 and those in Group 2.

When samples that are not independent are compared by the independent *t* test, the value of the obtained *t* is biased (it is usually too small, but also sometimes

| Table 13.6 | Basic Data for Paired t Test | | | | | |

Family	Group 1 X_1 (girls)	Group 2 X_2 (boys)	Mean (M_X)	D	$D - M_D$	$(D - M_D)^2$
Smith	4	3	3.5	1	−1	1
Ross	6	4	5.0	2	0	0
Simpson	8	5	6.5	3	1	1
Jones	4	3	3.5	1	−1	1
Hill	6	4	5.0	2	0	0
Brown	8	5	6.5	3	1	1
Sum (Σ)	36	24	30.0	12	0	4
Mean (M)	6	4	5.0	2.0		

Note: The value of M_D is shown as 2.0 at the bottom of the column of differences (D) between Groups I and II (i.e., $D = X_1 - X_2$), and the value of $\Sigma(D - M_D)^2$ is shown as 4 at the bottom of the last column.

too large). To avoid this problem, we instead use a **paired t test** (also called a **one-sample t test**, a **correlated-sample t**, or a **matched-pair t**) for samples that are not independent. To illustrate this approach, we refer to the basic data in Table 13.6, which shows a hypothetical study in which girls were predicted to be more sociable than boys. The scores are the ratings of a judge on a 9-point scale of sociability. What makes this study appropriate for a paired t is that these are six *pairs* of girls and boys, each pair of children from a particular family. When we examine the judge's ratings over these pairs, we find that a child's sociability score is to some degree predictable from family membership. For instance, the column of means shows that the Smith and Jones children were judged (on the average) to be less sociable than the Simpson and Brown children.

In t tests for matched (or correlated) data, we perform our calculations on the difference score (D) for each pair of lined-up scores. We use the following formula:

$$t = \frac{M_D}{\sqrt{\left(\frac{1}{N}\right) S_D^2}}$$

in which M_D is the mean of the $D = X_1 - X_2$ scores; N is the number of D scores (i.e., the number of lined-up pairs); and S_D^2 gives us the unbiased estimate of the population value of σ_D^2, where

$$S_D^2 = \frac{\Sigma(D - M_D)^2}{N - 1}$$

and *df* is now defined as $N - 1$, where N is the number of paired scores. Thus, the paired, or one-sample, t subtracts the values of one of the correlated samples from the corresponding values of the other correlated sample, thereby creating a new *single* sample of difference scores.

Substituting the data in Table 13.6, we find

$$S_D^2 = \frac{\Sigma(D - M_D)^2}{N - 1} = \frac{4}{6 - 1} = .80$$

and

$$t = \frac{M_D}{\sqrt{\left(\frac{1}{N}\right)S_D^2}} = \frac{2.0}{\sqrt{\left(\frac{1}{6}\right).80}} = \frac{2.0}{.365} = 5.48$$

We can now look up p as a one-tailed value (because we predicted that girls would score higher than boys), also compute the effect size, and finally display the effect size as a BESD. For the p value, we turn to Table B.2 (pp. 394–395), but we now read across the row labeled 5 df (because the degrees of freedom for a single sample are defined as $N - 1$, or $6 - 1 = 5$). Our obtained t of 5.48 is larger than 4.773 but smaller than 5.893, so one-tailed $p < .0025$ but $> .001$.

When you use a calculator to compute statistics (as we did in this case), it is a good idea not to scrimp on the number of decimal places in the intermediate calculations, because rounding error can produce inaccurate results. By analogy, suppose you were a NASA engineer trying to figure out how much fuel would be needed to take a manned rocket to Mars. By rounding off the calculations, you might send the astronauts on an impossible mission. If you are puzzling over how many decimals to *report* in a statistical test, the convention is to report statistical tests (e.g., t, F, χ^2) to two decimal places. So in this case we would report $t = 5.48$. What about p values? As noted in the previous chapter, many statisticians report the actual descriptive level of significance, and we suggested using scientific notation when there is a string of zeros. In this case, where the actual descriptive level of significance is $p = .0014$, the scientific notation would be $p = 1.4^{-3}$ one-tailed; also seen from time to time is the notation $p = 1.4/10^3$.

When we calculate the effect size r from t using the formula given earlier in this chapter, we find

$$r_{\text{effect size}} = \sqrt{\frac{t^2}{t^2 + df}} = \sqrt{\frac{(5.48)^2}{(5.48)^2 + 5}} = .926$$

which leads us to conclude that we have another "jumbo-sized" effect in addition to a statistically significant one. Statistically, the interpretation of this value is more complex than the effect size r that we calculated from the independent t. Although it is beyond the scope of this book, you will find a detailed discussion in our advanced text (R. Rosenthal & Rosnow, 2008, pp. 398–400).

The estimation of confidence intervals for effect sizes in association with nonindependent means is currently a matter of debate, but Table 13.7 shows what the effect would look like as a BESD with equal totals in the margins. Once again, we see that the BESD sets the marginal totals at 100. In the upper-left and lower-right cells, the 96.3 value was calculated as

$$100(.50 + r/2) = 100(.50 + .926/2) = 96.3$$

Table 13.7	Binomial Effect-Size Display of Results in Table 13.6		
	Sociability		
Gender	More sociable	Less sociable	Total
Girls	96.3	3.7	100
Boys	3.7	96.3	100
Total	100	100	200

and in the upper-right and lower-left cells, the 3.7 value was calculated as

$$100(.50 - r/2) = 100(.50 - .926/2) = 3.7$$

The difference between 96.3 and 3.7, divided by 100, is the effect size r of .926. The cell values should not be mistaken for the actual frequencies that would be obtained in a random sample; they should instead be seen as standardized values because of the uniform totals that we imposed on the margins for ease of interpretation.

What Are the Statistical Assumptions of the t Test?

In the report in Appendix A, Mary Jones refers to an assumption of the t test as **homogeneity of variance**. There are additional assumptions of the t test (R. Rosenthal & Rosnow, 2008, pp. 401–403), but homogeneity of variance means that the population variance of the two groups is assumed to be equal. When this assumption is seriously violated, the p value may be off, and the effect size r calculated from t may also be inaccurate. How can you determine whether there has been a serious violation of the homogeneity-of-variance assumption? Mary describes one approach, which is to compare the highest and the lowest estimated population variance by means of the F test. Mary's use of this procedure led her to conclude that the homogeneity-of-variance assumption had, in fact, been violated, and she then used another procedure (called *Satterthwaite's method*) to adjust the degrees of freedom of her t test. The formulas she used are discussed at the end of her report.

However, we do want to note that the most commonly used procedures in this situation involve transformations of the raw data to make the variances more nearly equal, and afterward, the t test is computed on the transformed data. Among the most commonly used transformations are (a) the square root of each raw score, (b) the log transformation of each raw score, and (c) the reciprocal value of each score, all of which are discussed in detail in our advanced text (R. Rosenthal & Rosnow, 2008). Another alternative, which is convenient when transformations are not possible (e.g., if we were working with the published data of other researchers), or when a transformation is ineffective, is to replace the pooled S^2 in the denominator of the t

formula with the largest S^2. This is a serviceable but conservative procedure (R. Rosenthal & Rosnow, 1985), as the effect size estimated from t will be smaller (possibly a lot smaller) than the estimate obtained with Satterthwaite's method. To illustrate in the case of Mary Jones's Table 1, where the largest $S = 16,645.07$, and therefore $S^2 = 277,058,355.305$, recalculating t gives us

$$t = \frac{M_1 - M_2}{\sqrt{\left(\frac{1}{n_1} + \frac{1}{n_2}\right)S^2}}$$

$$= \frac{16,146.67 - 6,990.63}{\sqrt{\left(\frac{1}{15} + \frac{1}{16}\right)277,058,355.305}} = \frac{9,156.04}{5,982.20} = 1.53$$

which, with $df = n_1 + n_2 - 2 = 29$, has an associated one-tailed $p = .068$ and $r_{effect\ size} = .273$.

Summary of Ideas

1. The *t test* operates like a signal-to-noise ratio used to compare two means relative to the variability of scores within each group. The larger the signal is relative to the noise, the more likely the null hypothesis is to be rejected (Box 13.2).

2. The *independent-sample t* is used to compare two group means when the scores in one group are not influenced by the scores in the other group. The *degrees of freedom (df)* of the independent-sample t are defined as $n_1 + n_2 - 2$ because, in each group, one deviation from the mean is not free to vary (Box 13.3).

3. There is a different t curve (or distribution) for every possible value of the degrees of freedom of the t test, each curve resembling the standard normal distribution, which the t *distribution* gradually approximates as the size of the samples is increased. At 30 df, the t distribution is fairly close to that of the standard normal distribution.

4. To find a one- or two-tailed p for an obtained t, we need to know the degrees of freedom (df) as well as the value of t. Reporting a one-tailed p implies that we predicted in which side of the t distribution the p value would be situated.

5. Once we have created a confidence interval for the obtained $r_{effect\ size}$, we can create BESDs to represent the lower and upper limits (also Box 13.4).

6. Another common measure of effect size when the t test is used to compare two independent means is *Cohen's d*, which indexes the standardized difference between the two independent means. We showed how to convert d into r for equal and unequal sample sizes, how to obtain d from the independent t for equal and unequal sample sizes, and also how to interpret d and compute a confidence interval for it.

7. Like any significance test, the t test is made up mathematically of two components: the size of the effect times the size of the study. We can maximize the power of the independent-sample t by (a) drawing the means further apart (which increases the value of the effect size); (b) decreasing the variability within groups (also increasing the value of the effect size); and (c) increasing the effective size of the study (i.e., increasing the total N).

8. The *paired t* (also called the *correlated-sample t, matched-pair t,* and *one-sample t*) is used to compare the means of two groups that are not independent, in which case $df = N - 1$, where N is the total number of paired scores. Using the independent sample t in this situation yields a biased value of t (usually too small, but also sometimes too large).

9. Several assumptions are made in the use of t tests, and we discussed *homogeneity of variance* and how, when this assumption is violated, a serviceable but conservative procedure involves adjusting the t formula. Mary's report in Appendix A illustrates another corrective procedure (Satterthwaite's method).

Key Terms

Cohen's *d* p. 301
correlated-sample *t* p. 307
degrees of freedom (*df*)
  p. 297
homogeneity of variance
  p. 309

independent-sample *t* test
  p. 294
matched-pair *t* p. 307
one-sample *t* test
  p. 307
paired *t* test   p. 307

Significance test = Size of
  effect × Size of study
  p. 305
Student's *t* p. 293
t distribution   p. 297
t test   p. 292

Multiple-Choice Questions for Review

1. In a *t* test, the difference between the two means can be thought of as the (a) significance level; (b) noise; (c) signal; (d) none of the above.

2. In a *t* test, the variability of scores within samples can be thought of as the (a) significance level; (b) noise; (c) signal; (d) none of the above.

3. A student at Bryn Mawr College conducts a study with 5 subjects in the experimental group and 6 subjects in the control group. She then calculates a *t* test. How many degrees of freedom are associated with this test? (a) 4; (b) 5; (c) 6; (d) 9

4. A researcher at the University of Saskatchewan computes a *t* test for independent samples. There is a total of 8 subjects, and $t = 5$. What is the appropriate one-tailed p value? (a) <.05; (b) <.0025; (c) <.005; (d) <.001.

5. A very small p value (e.g., .001) automatically means that you have a (a) large effect; (b) moderate effect; (c) small effect; (d) cannot be determined from this information.

6. A student at Williams College conducts a study with an experimental group and a control group. There are 4 subjects in each group. He calculates that $t = 3$. The effect size is the square root of (a) 9/15; (b) 3/13; (c) 3/4; (d) 3/7.

7. Fill in the blanks in the following conceptual equation: Significance test = _____ × _____. (a) *t, r*; (b) *t,* Size of study; (c) Effect size, Size of study; (d) *r,* Effect size.

8. Which of the following can be used in maximizing *t*? (a) decreasing the difference between the means; (b) calculating *r* instead of *t*; (c) decreasing the variability within groups; (d) all of the above

9. Scores on two variables may not be independent because they were obtained (a) from the same subjects; (b) with a within-subjects design; (c) from brother-sister pairs from the same family; (d) all of the above.

10. A study is conducted in which scores were obtained from 4 subjects on two separate occasions. In other words, there are 8 total observations from 4 subjects. The data are analyzed by means of a paired *t* test. How many degrees of freedom will there be? (a) 3; (b) 4; (c) 7; (d) 8

Discussion Questions for Review

1. A Kent State University researcher hypothesizes that marijuana use decreases short-term memory. He brings five subjects to his laboratory. Each subject is given a test of short-term memory. Each subject is then given marijuana and administered another test of short-term memory. The results are given below (high scores indicate good memory):

	Test 1	Test 2
Subject 1	5	2
Subject 2	7	5
Subject 3	4	5
Subject 4	8	3
Subject 5	8	4

Can you set up the formula and insert the numbers that would be used to test the hypothesis that the scores on Test 2 are significantly lower than the scores on Test 1? What would be the degrees of freedom? If you found a significant difference and a large effect size, should you conclude that marijuana causes a decrease in short-term memory? Why or why not?

2. A Loyola University student conducted a study comparing the creativity scores of four biology and four history majors. The results were

Biology	History
4	7
6	3
3	5
3	6

Can you set up the formula that would be used to compute a t test? What would be the degrees of freedom? How would you compute and interpret the effect size?

3. An experimenter at the University of California at San Diego studied sex differences in nonverbal sensitivity. Her results showed that the women were significantly better than the men at decoding nonverbal cues, with $t = 2.34$, $df = 62$, $p < .05$ two-tailed, and $r_{effect\ size} = .28$. Pretend that the experimenter added an additional 60 subjects, randomly selected from the same population as the original sample. When the analysis is recalculated with the extra subjects, should the new t be larger, smaller, or about the same size? Should the p value be larger, smaller, or about the same size? Should $r_{effect\ size}$ be larger, smaller, or about the same size? Should the 95% confidence interval be wider, narrower, or about the same size?

4. A Santa Fe College student has developed a brief training program that increases sensitivity to nonverbal cues. He plans to compare it to a brief training program that increases sensitivity to people in general. He plans to randomly assign 10 subjects to each treatment, the subjects having been found through newspaper ads. He describes his plan to his professor, who suggests he think hard about trying to obtain a larger t than he is likely to get in the planned study. What might the student do to get a larger t?

Answers to Review Questions

Multiple-Choice Questions

1. c	**3.** d	**5.** d	**7.** c	**9.** d
2. b	**4.** b	**6.** a	**8.** c	**10.** a

Discussion Questions

1. The difference or change scores (D) for the five subjects are $-3, -2, +1, -5, -4$. The paired t can be computed from

$$t = \frac{M_D}{\sqrt{\left(\frac{1}{N}\right)S_D^2}} = \frac{[(-3) + (-2) + (+1) + (-5) + (-4)]/5}{\sqrt{\left(\frac{1}{5}\right)5.30}} = 2.53$$

obtaining S_D^2 from

$$S_D^2 = \frac{\Sigma(D - M_D)^2}{N - 1}$$

$$= \frac{[(-3) - (-2.6)]^2 + [(-2) - (-2.6)]^2 + [(+1) - (-2.6)]^2 + [(-5) - (-2.6)]^2 + [(-4) - (-2.6)]^2}{5 - 1}$$

$$= 5.30$$

The df are $N - 1 = 5 - 1 = 4$. Had we found a significant and large change in memory test scores, we would not be able to conclude that the change was due to marijuana use. There was no control group to rule out plausible rival hypotheses. Had we been able to compute the significance level and effect size, we would have used Table B.2 (on pp. 394–395) and found our t with 4 df to be significant at $p < .05$ one-tailed (but not quite significant at $p = .025$ one-tailed). The effect size would have been computed from

$$r_{\text{effect size}} = \sqrt{\frac{t^2}{t^2 + df}} = \sqrt{\frac{(2.53)^2}{(2.53)^2 + 4}} = .78$$

2. We would compute t from

$$t = \frac{M_1 - M_2}{\sqrt{\left(\frac{1}{n_1} + \frac{1}{n_2}\right)s^2}} = \frac{4.00 - 5.25}{\sqrt{\left(\frac{1}{4} + \frac{1}{4}\right)2.46}} = 1.13$$

The df would be $n_1 + n_2 - 2 = 6$, and the effect size could be computed from

$$r_{\text{effect size}} = \sqrt{\frac{t^2}{t^2 + df}} = \sqrt{\frac{(1.13)^2}{(1.13)^2 + 6}} = .42$$

a very substantial effect size though t is not significant ($p = .30$ two-tailed).

3. From the conceptual equation:

Significance test = Size of effect × Size of study,

we can see that increasing the size of the study would increase the value of the significance test, and the result would be a smaller (more significant) p value. However, the effect size would not be systematically affected by the addition of more subjects of the same type. To illustrate, we assume the following original ingredients of t:

$$t = \frac{2.585 - 2.000}{\sqrt{\left(\dfrac{1}{32} + \dfrac{1}{32}\right)1.00}} = 2.34$$

and $p = .023$ two-tailed, $r_{\text{effect size}} = .28$. We then add 60 subjects (30 to each group), yielding

$$t = \frac{2.585 - 2.000}{\sqrt{\left(\dfrac{1}{62} + \dfrac{1}{62}\right)1.00}} = 3.26$$

and $p = .0014$ two-tailed, $r_{\text{effect size}} = .28$. Therefore, with nothing changing but n_1 and n_2, we see that t increases, p decreases, and the $r_{\text{effect size}}$ remains unchanged. The 95% confidence interval will shrink with the additional subjects, as illustrated in the previous chapter.

4. The student might try three approaches. First, he might try to drive the means further apart by using a control group that is not as similar to the treatment group. Second, he might use participants who are more homogeneous than the people who answer newspaper ads. Third, he might use larger sample sizes for each condition.

CHAPTER 14

Comparisons on More Than Two Conditions

Preview Questions

- What is analysis of variance (ANOVA), and how are F and t related?

- How is variability apportioned in a one-way ANOVA?

- How are ANOVA summary tables set up and interpreted?

- How can I test for simple effects after an omnibus F?

- How is variability apportioned in a two-way ANOVA?

- How do I interpret main and interaction effects?

- How are a two-way ANOVA computed and a summary table set up?

- How do I compute a focused t or F on more than two groups?

- What do $r_{effect\ size}$, $r_{alerting}$, and $r_{contrast}$ tell me?

- How are contrasts on multiple repeated measures computed?

- How are Latin square designs analyzed?

What Is Analysis of Variance (ANOVA), and How are F and t Related?

Although it is generally true that the t test is often used whenever there are only two means to be compared, later in this chapter we will describe how this statistical test can be used to examine a predicted trend in more than two conditions. Another very popular statistic that you are bound to see in your literature search is the **F test**, which is the primary focus of this chapter. We will see that F tests are signal-to-noise ratios used to divide up variability in the procedure called **analysis of variance**, or **ANOVA** (see also Box 14.1). Even if you expect to use a computer to analyze your data, you will find that working through the examples in this chapter improves your understanding of the information provided by your computer program. Furthermore, some of the concepts and formulas in this chapter are so relatively new that they may not yet be available in your computer program, but they are simple enough to calculate by hand or by using the basic ingredients provided by your computer program.

BOX 14.1   Fisher, ANOVA, and the "Lady Tasting Tea"

The F test (or F ratio) takes its name from its inventor, Sir Ronald A. Fisher (1890–1962), a giant in the field of statistics, who also introduced a wide variety of other fundamental concepts. The F ratio is based on the *analysis of variance* (ANOVA), which Fisher originally used to separate the effects of different treatments on crop variations in agricultural experiments. In Chapter 10, we described the variance (S^2 or σ^2) as a measure of the spread of scores around the mean. ANOVA, when used in between-subjects (also referred to as *between-group*) comparisons, compares the spread of scores *between* the conditions ($S^2_{between}$) with the spread of scores *within* the conditions (S^2_{within}). Thus, in the F ratio of $S^2_{between}$ divided by S^2_{within}, you can think of $S^2_{between}$ as the *signal spread* and S^2_{within} as the *noise spread*. For a fascinating popular account of Fisher's work and how statistics revolutionized 20th-century science, see David Salsburg's *The Lady Tasting Tea* (2001). The title refers to a summer tea party of university professors, their wives, and some guests in Cambridge, England, in the late 1920s. One of the guests insists that tea tastes different depending on whether the tea is poured into the milk or the milk is poured into the tea, and Fisher proposes a strategy for testing the hypothesis and even works out the probabilities of different outcomes—although the results of the afternoon's tea tasting are never reported (Salsburg, 2001, pp. 3–4).

There is a relationship between F and t that is important to understand. Simply stated, squaring t always produces F, but taking the square root of F does not always produce t. The reason for this conundrum will become clearer as you read this chapter. For the moment, all you need to remember is that, when only two groups are to be compared, taking the square root of F always produces t. Thus, since squaring t always produces F, and you recall that the effect size of t used to compare two means is computed as

$$r_{\text{effect size}} = \sqrt{\frac{t^2}{t^2 + df}}$$

it follows that, whenever only two samples (or two groups) are to be compared, the effect size of F can be computed as

$$r_{\text{effect size}} = \sqrt{\frac{F}{F + df_{\text{within}}}}$$

where df_{within} refers to the degrees of freedom "within conditions," obtained from the df within each group and then adding them. When there are more than two samples (or conditions), the estimation of the "effect size" from F (and t) is more subtle, as we explain later in this chapter.

Because we cover a great deal of ground in this chapter, it is useful to have an overall sense of the content. We begin by explaining the logic of F tests and the analysis of variance in between-subjects designs, using as our illustration a randomized design with four independent groups. In the illustrative analysis, the F test is what we have called an *omnibus F* (for reasons that are explained shortly). The problem with omnibus statistical procedures is that they are vague and do not lend themselves to interpretable effect size indicators (such as r). Thus, we redirect our attention to more "focused" statistical tests that examine what the *APA Publication Manual* (2001, p. 26) refers to as "one-degree-of-freedom effects" (which we have described as *focused statistical procedures*). The first such procedure we illustrate is the use of t tests after an omnibus F. If we find it useful to think of the analysis in terms of a factorial design, then another option is to use F tests to address three one-degree-of-freedom effects. When we have a specific prediction involving more than two group means, a preferable procedure is to compute a contrast t or F test that addresses the prediction. Finally, we will turn to the use of contrasts with repeated measures.

In the previous chapter, we began with a hypothetical case to illustrate the signal-to-noise ratio of the t test. If we look at another example, we will see that the logic is essentially the same for analysis of variance. In this illustration, we imagine that an experimenter interested in the effects of nutrition on the academic performance of children decides to use a four-group instead of a two-group randomized design. One group of randomly assigned children gets a hot lunch daily, another group gets free milk, the third group gets a vitamin supplement, and the fourth group gets nothing extra. Once again, imagine two sets of results of this experiment, as represented by A and B in Table 14.1. We would

Table 14.1   Between-Subjects Design with Alternative Results A and B

Results A:

	Group 1 Zero	Group 2 Milk	Group 3 Vitamins	Group 4 Hot lunch
	8	10	13	17
	10	12	15	19
	12	14	17	21
Mean (M)	10	12	15	19

Results B:

	Group 1 Zero	Group 2 Milk	Group 3 Vitamins	Group 4 Hot lunch
	4	6	9	13
	10	12	15	19
	16	18	21	25
Mean (M)	10	12	15	19

describe A and B as 1 × 4 ("one by four") between-subjects designs because the configuration consists of four independent groups (or samples) in a one-way arrangement.

In examining these results, what conclusions would you be willing to draw on the basis of A compared to B? Notice that the outcome in the sample receiving no special nutritional bonus (Group 1) has an average of 10 units of academic performance, whereas the average performance of the sample receiving milk (Group 2) is 12, of that receiving vitamins (Group 3) is 15, and of that receiving hot lunches (Group 4) is 19. By applying the logic about the within-group variance described in the previous chapter, we find ourselves feeling more impressed by Results A than by Results B. In Results A, subjects never varied in their performance by more than 2 points from the average score of their group. The few points of difference between the mean scores of the four groups look larger when seen against the backdrop of the small within-group variation of Results A, but they look smaller when examined against the backdrop of the large within-group variation of Results B.

The analysis of variance provides us with a more formal comparison of the variation between the average results per condition and the average variation within different conditions. In this kind of analysis, as we see next, a ratio (the **F ratio**, or **F test**) is formed. In Chapter 13, we stated that one way to think about t is that if the null hypothesis were true, the most likely value of t would be 0. F ratios, on the other hand, usually have values close to 1.0 when the variation between conditions is not different from the variation within conditions (i.e., when H_0 is true); we explain later why this is so. The larger the F ratio becomes, the greater is the dispersion of group means relative to the dispersion of scores within groups. In other words, as with the t, researchers generally prefer larger F values because they are associated with smaller p levels.

How Is Variability Apportioned in a One-Way ANOVA?

The calculation of F tests is one purpose of the analysis of variance. A more general purpose is to divide up the variation of all the observations into a number of separate sources of variance. In this illustration of comparing the four samples in a one-way ANOVA, the total variation among the 12 scores is broken into two sources: (a) systematic variation between groups or conditions (the *signal* variation) and (b) error variation within groups or conditions (the *noise* variation).

It will be useful here to look again at the basic idea of variance:

$$S^2 = \frac{\Sigma(X - M)^2}{N - 1}$$

where S^2 is the unbiased estimate of the population value of σ^2, and N is the total number of units. As we mentioned in Chapter 10, the quantity S^2 is also called a **mean square** (abbreviated as *MS*) because when the sum of the squares—that is, $\Sigma(X - M)^2$—is divided by $N - 1$ (or *df*), the result is the squared deviation per *df*, representing a kind of average.

In the analysis of variance, we are especially interested in the numerators of our various S^2 values (e.g., for between conditions and for within conditions). This interest has to do with the additive property of the numerators, or the **sum of squares** (abbreviated as SS) of the deviations about the mean. These SS values add up to the total sum of squares in the following way:

$$\text{Total } SS = \text{Between-conditions } SS + \text{Within-conditions } SS$$

In one-way between-subjects designs, the analysis of variance requires the calculation of the between-conditions SS and the within-conditions SS. If you are using a calculator to work the examples in this chapter, you can compute the total SS as a check on your arithmetic. Before we start crunching numbers, let us look at the formulas for each of these three sums of squares.

First, the total SS is defined as the sum of squares of all the measurements' deviations from the grand mean. What goes into the total SS is given by the following formula:

$$\text{Total } SS - \Sigma(X - M_G)^2$$

where X is each observation and M_G is the grand mean (i.e., the mean of the condition means).

Second, the between-conditions SS is defined as the sum of squares of the deviations of the condition means from the grand mean, as given by the following formula:

$$\text{Between } SS = \Sigma[n_k(M_k - M_G)^2]$$

where n_k is the number of observations in the kth condition (and k is *any* particular condition), M_k is the mean of the kth condition, and M_G is again the grand mean.

Third, the within-conditions SS is defined as the sum of squares of the deviations of the measurements from their condition means, as given by the following formula:

$$\text{Within } SS = \Sigma(X - M_k)^2$$

where X is each observation and M_k is again the mean of the condition to which X belongs.

We will now use these formulas to compute an overall ANOVA on the scores of Results A in Table 14.1. Table 14.2 provides the basic data for this analysis, with the addition of two new symbols: M_k for the group or the condition mean and M_G for the grand mean. First, we compute the total sum of squares by

$$\text{Total } SS = \Sigma(X - M_G)^2$$

which instructs us to subtract the grand mean from each individual score and then add up the squared deviations:

$$
\begin{aligned}
\text{Total } SS = {} & (8 - 14)^2 + (10 - 14)^2 + (12 - 14)^2 \\
& + (10 - 14)^2 + (12 - 14)^2 + (14 - 14)^2 \\
& + (13 - 14)^2 + (15 - 14)^2 + (17 - 14)^2 \\
& + (17 - 14)^2 + (19 - 14)^2 + (21 - 14)^2 \\
= {} & 170
\end{aligned}
$$

<table>
<tr><td colspan="5">**Table 14.2** Data for ANOVA Based on Results A in Table 14.1</td></tr>
</table>

	Group 1 Zero	Group 2 Milk	Group 3 Vitamins	Group 4 Hot lunch
	8	10	13	17
	10	12	15	19
	12	14	17	21
M_k	10	12	15	19

$$M_G = \frac{10 + 12 + 15 + 19}{4} = 14$$

Next, we compute the between-conditions sum of squares by

$$\text{Between } SS = \Sigma[n_k(M_k - M_G)^2]$$

which instructs us to subtract the grand mean from each condition mean and then add up the weighted squared deviations:

$$\begin{aligned}
\text{Between } SS &= 3(10 - 14)^2 \\
&+ 3(12 - 14)^2 \\
&+ 3(15 - 14)^2 \\
&+ 3(19 - 14)^2 \\
&= 138
\end{aligned}$$

And finally, we compute the within-conditions sum of squares by

$$\text{Within } SS = \Sigma(X - M_k)^2$$

which instructs us to subtract the appropriate condition mean from each individual score and then add up the squared deviations:

$$\begin{aligned}
\text{Within } SS &= (8 - 10)^2 + (10 - 10)^2 + (12 - 10)^2 \\
&+ (10 - 12)^2 + (12 - 12)^2 + (14 - 12)^2 \\
&+ (13 - 15)^2 + (15 - 15)^2 + (17 - 15)^2 \\
&+ (17 - 19)^2 + (19 - 19)^2 + (21 - 19)^2 \\
&= 32
\end{aligned}$$

As a check on our arithmetic, we add the sum of squares between conditions to the sum of squares within conditions to make sure their total equals the total sum of squares, that is,

$$\begin{aligned}
\text{Total } SS &= \text{Between } SS + \text{Within } SS \\
170 &= \quad\quad 138 \quad\quad + \quad\quad 32
\end{aligned}$$

Table 14.3	Summary ANOVA for Results in Table 14.1				
Source	SS	df	MS	F	p
Between conditions	138	3	46	11.50	.003
Within conditions	32	8	4		

How Are ANOVA Summary Tables Set Up and Interpreted?

The results of a one-way ANOVA may be displayed in the form shown in Table 14.3. The rows label the source of variation, in this case the variation between and within conditions. Listed in the *SS* column are sum-of-squares values for each source of variation. The degrees of freedom (*df*) are listed in the next column (see also Box 14.2). As there were four independent conditions (symbolized as $k = 4$), three of the means were free to vary once the grand mean (M_G, or mean of the means) was determined. We define the degrees of freedom between conditions as

$$df_{between} - k - 1$$

which in this case is $df_{between} = 4 - 1 = 3$.

We obtain the degrees of freedom within conditions from the *df* within each condition (defined as $n - 1$) and then adding them. The reason we have $n - 1$ degrees of freedom within each condition is that all scores but one are free to vary within each condition once the mean of that condition is determined, and so we eliminate 1 *df* within each condition. Thus, the degrees of freedom within conditions are found by

$$df_{within} = N - k$$

BOX 14.2 Focused and Omnibus Tests and Effect Sizes

Previously, we alluded to the distinction between omnibus and focused statistical procedures. *F* tests with 1 *df* in the numerator are **focused statistical procedures** because they address specific statistical questions. *F* tests with numerator $df > 1$ are **omnibus statistical procedures** because they address diffuse (or unfocused) statistical questions. The rule of thumb is to report effect sizes for focused statistical procedures and not for omnibus statistical procedures, because effect size indicators are far more interpretable for focused procedures. Because all *t* tests are intrinsically focused, another rule of thumb is to report effect size indicators for all *t* tests. As you get deeper into this chapter, you will have a better understanding of the reason for this rule, and also of which *F* tests have numerator $df = 1$.

where N is the total number of measurements or sampling units and k is the number of conditions, giving us $df_{within} = 12 - 4 = 8$.

The total degrees of freedom (not shown in Table 14.3) are defined as the total number of measurements minus 1, that is,

$$df_{total} = N - 1$$

which gives us $df_{total} = 12 - 1 = 11$. After we have computed the $df_{between}$ and df_{within}, we can check our calculations by adding these df to see whether they agree with the df_{total}. In the present case, we have

$$df_{total} = df_{between} + df_{within}$$
$$11 \quad = \quad 3 \quad + \quad 8$$

The MS column shows the mean squares, which we find by dividing the sums of squares by the corresponding df. We divide 138 by 3 to get $MS_{between} = 46$, and we divide 32 by 8 to get $MS_{within} = 4$. These MS values can be seen as the amounts of the total variation (measured in SS) attributable to each df. The larger the MS for the between-conditions source of variance (the signal) relative to the within-conditions source of variance (the noise), the less likely becomes the null hypothesis of no difference between the conditions. If the null hypothesis were true, the SS variation per df should be roughly the same for the df between groups and the df within groups. The F value in the next column provides this information. We obtained this F by dividing the mean square between conditions by the mean square within conditions; the result is a signal-to-noise ratio of $F = 46/4 = 11.5$.

To review, F is called the F ratio to reflect the fact that it is a ratio of two mean squares (i.e., two variances, as noted in Box 14.1). The denominator mean square (i.e., the mean square for error) serves as a kind of base rate for noise level, or typical variation. The numerator (the signal) is a reflection of both the size of the effect and the size of the study. In other words, a numerator MS may be large relative to a denominator MS because (a) the effect is large, (b) the n per condition is large, or (c) both are large. Thus, large F values should not be automatically seen as indicating the presence of large effects. No effect size is noted because we compute the effect size of F only when the numerator $df = 1$, the situation we find when two conditions are being compared or, as described later in this chapter, when we are reporting a contrast F test on more than two groups.

The final value in Table 14.3 is the probability that an F of this size or larger, with this number of degrees of freedom (i.e., 3 in the numerator and 8 in the denominator), might occur if the null hypothesis of no difference among the means were true. In the previous chapter, we noted that there is a different distribution of t values for every possible value of the degrees of freedom. The situation for F is similar but more complicated, as for every F ratio there are *two* relevant df values to take into account. One is the degrees of freedom between conditions and the other is the degrees of freedom within conditions. For every combination of $df_{between}$ and df_{within}, there is a different curve. As is the case for t, small values of F are likely when the null hypothesis of no difference between conditions is true, but large values of F are unlikely and are used as evidence to suggest that the null hypothesis is probably false.

Another important difference between t and F curves was alluded to earlier, when we said that the expected value of t is 0 when the null hypothesis is true but that the expected value of F is approximately 1 when the null is true. The symmetrical bell shape of t curves means that they are centered at 0, with negative values running to negative infinity and positive values running to positive infinity. However, F curves are positively skewed, with values beginning at 0 and ranging upward to positive infinity. In other words, F is intrinsically one-tailed as a test of significance. When the null hypothesis is true, the expected value of F is $df/(df-2)$, where these are df for within conditions. For most values of df, then, the expected value of F when the null hypothesis is true is a little more than 1.0, as noted in Table 14.4.

Table 14.4 F Values Required for Significance at the .05 (Upper Entry) and .01 Levels

Degrees of freedom within conditions (denominator)	Degrees of freedom between conditions (numerator)						Expected value of F when H_0 is true
	1	2	3	4	6	∞	
1	161	200	216	225	234	254	
	4052	4999	5403	5625	5859	6366	—
2	18.5	19.0	19.2	19.3	19.3	19.5	
	98.5	99.0	99.2	99.3	99.3	99.5	—
3	10.1	9.55	9.28	9.12	8.94	8.53	
	34.1	30.8	29.5	28.7	27.9	26.1	3.00
4	7.71	6.94	6.59	6.39	6.16	5.63	
	21.2	18.0	16.7	16.0	15.2	13.5	2.00
5	6.61	5.79	5.41	5.19	4.95	4.36	
	16.3	13.3	12.1	11.4	10.7	9.02	1.67
6	5.99	5.14	4.76	4.53	4.28	3.67	
	13.7	10.9	9.78	9.15	8.47	6.88	1.50
8	5.32	4.46	4.07	3.84	3.58	2.93	
	11.3	8.65	7.59	7.01	6.37	4.86	1.33
10	4.96	4.10	3.71	3.48	3.22	2.54	
	10.0	7.56	6.55	5.99	5.39	3.91	1.25
15	4.54	3.68	3.29	3.06	2.79	2.07	
	8.68	6.36	5.42	4.89	4.32	2.87	1.15
20	4.35	3.49	3.10	2.87	2.60	1.84	
	8.10	5.85	4.94	4.43	3.87	2.42	1.11
25	4.24	3.38	2.99	2.76	2.49	1.71	
	7.77	5.57	4.68	4.18	3.63	2.17	1.09
30	4.17	3.32	2.92	2.69	2.42	1.62	
	7.56	5.39	4.51	4.02	3.47	2.01	1.07
40	4.08	3.23	2.84	2.61	2.34	1.51	
	7.31	5.18	4.31	3.83	3.29	1.80	1.05
∞	3.84	2.99	2.60	2.37	2.09	1.00	
	6.64	4.60	3.78	3.32	2.80	1.00	1.00

Note: For a more complete table, see Appendix B, Table B.3.

Table 14.4 enables us to locate the p value of a given F. A more comprehensive table can be found in Appendix B (see pp. 396–400). In Table 14.4, notice that the values of F required to reach the .05 and .01 levels decrease as the df_{within} value increases for any given $df_{between}$ value. Similarly, the critical values of F decrease as the $df_{between}$ value increases for any given df_{within}, except for the special cases of $df_{within} = 1$ or 2. For $df_{within} = 1$, there is a substantial increase in the F value required to reach the .05 and .01 levels as the $df_{between}$ value increases from 1 to infinity. For $df_{within} = 2$, only a very small increase in the F values is required to reach the .05 and .01 levels as the $df_{between}$ values increase from 1 to infinity. In practice, however, there are very few studies with large $df_{between}$ and only 1 or 2 df_{within}.

To look up our F of 11.50 in Table 14.4, we put a finger on the intersection of $df_{between} = 3$ and $df_{within} = 8$. The two values are 4.07 (the F value required for significance at $p = .05$) and 7.59 (the F value required for significance at $p = .01$). Because our obtained F is larger than 7.59, we know that the corresponding p must be less than .01. As indicated by Table B.3 on pp. 396–400, the actual p is approximately .003. Performing the same calculations on Results B in Table 14.1, we would find F to be 1.28 (again with 3 and 8 degrees of freedom). Looking up this value in Table B.3, we find it to be too small to be significant at even the .20 level. The actual p is approximately .35.

What do the more precise p values tell us? The p value of .003 for Results A implies that we would obtain an F of 11.50 or larger (for numerator $df = 3$ and denominator $df = 8$) only 3 in 1,000 times if we repeatedly conducted this study under the same conditions and if there really were no overall differences between the four groups (i.e., if the null hypothesis were true). The p value of .35 for Results B implies that we would obtain an F of 1.28 with 3 and 8 df once every 3 times if we conducted the study under *these* conditions over and over, and if the null hypothesis were true. In reporting the p value, there is no need to state that it is one-tailed, because this fact is implicit in F (see also Box 14.3).

BOX 14.3 Using t to Boost Power

The F tests we have looked at so far are all omnibus tests, and we cannot take the square root of an omnibus F and get t. But, as noted earlier, taking the square root of a focused F (i.e., F with numerator $df = 1$) gives us t. An interesting characteristic of F distributions is that the p values, although naturally one-tailed, translate into two-tailed p values in t curves. Suppose you have a focused F and find $p = .06$ in the predicted direction. If you plan to report t, you may have the option of reporting $p = .03$ one-tailed (because you predicted the direction) or $p = .06$ two-tailed (if you choose a more conservative p), but you do not have this option with F. There is, of course, not much difference between $p = .06$ and $p = .03$, except that they fall on either side of the coveted $= .05$.

How Can I Test for Simple Effects After an Omnibus F?

For the basic data in Table 14.2, knowing that the four groups differ significantly does not tell us whether milk helps in and of itself and whether vitamins help in and of themselves. To address these questions, we need to compare (a) the results in Group 2 with the results in Group 1 (the zero control) and (b) the results in Group 3 with the zero control. These comparisons are called **tests of simple effects**, and an easy way to do them is by t tests. Using the formula for comparing independent means given in the previous chapter, we continue to define S^2 as the pooled value (as described in the previous chapter), though we can now find this value simply from our ANOVA because it is the MS_{within} denominator of our F ratio.

To illustrate the test of simple effects using the results in Table 14.2, we substitute the values of Groups 1 and 3 in the general formula for the independent t test:

$$t = \frac{M_3 - M_1}{\sqrt{\left(\frac{1}{n_3} + \frac{1}{n_1}\right) S^2}} = \frac{15 - 10}{\sqrt{\left(\frac{1}{3} + \frac{1}{3}\right) 4}} = 3.06$$

where M_3 is the mean of Group 3; M_1 is the mean of Group 1; n_3 and n_1 are the sample sizes of these groups; and S^2 is the value of the within-conditions MS shown in Table 14.3. However, in testing this t for significance, we base our df not on $n_3 + n_1 - 2$ (as we did previously), but on df equal to the within-conditions SS (i.e., 8 df), since we are using a pooled estimate of S^2. Referring to Table B.2 (see pp. 394–395), we find the significance of $t = 3.06$ to be less than $p = .01$ but more than $p = .005$ one-tailed. The actual one-tailed p is approximately .008 (and the two-tailed $p = .016$, that is, .008 × 2).

Had we planned from the beginning to compute a specific t test, we could do so whether our overall F was significant or not. That is, we do not have to engage in a kind of "Simon says" game in which we seek "permission" from the p value associated with an omnibus test before we examine the effect of interest. However, if we are going to explore for large differences that we did not specifically predict, our t test results will be much more interpretable if our overall F is significant. The reason is that if we use a lot of t tests to go on a fishing expedition for significant differences, some of them will turn out to be significant by chance. One procedure that researchers sometimes use to try to avoid an excess of findings of significant t values when there are lots of possible t tests, or the t tests were unplanned, is to work with a more conservative level of significance, such as .01 instead of .05, or even .005 or .001 (all listed in Table B.2).

However, we recommend not placing all the emphasis on the significance level and paying more attention to the effect size and its corresponding confidence interval. To calculate the effect size correlation on our t, we use the same formula as before, but we define the degrees of freedom from the groups being compared, that is,

$$r_{effect\ size} = \sqrt{\frac{t^2}{t^2 + df}} = \sqrt{\frac{(3.06)^2}{(3.06)^2 + 4}} = .84$$

where df is based on the fact that there were 3 subjects in Group 3 and 3 subjects in Group 1, and therefore $df = n_3 + n_1 - 2 = 4$. The confidence interval (CI) is computed as before. In the BESD for this two-group comparison, the $r_{effect\ size}$ of .84 amounts to a difference in success rates of 8% to 92% between nonusers and users of vitamins, respectively (i.e., if half the population used vitamins and half the population showed improved performance).

How Is Variability Apportioned in a Two-Way ANOVA?

R. A. Fisher (Box 14.1) noticed that it is sometimes possible to rearrange a one-way design to form a two-way design of much greater power to reject certain null hypotheses. We turn now to an analysis of the simplest two-way design, one in which there are two levels of each factor (i.e., a 2 × 2 factorial). An example is essential, and we study again the hypothetical effects of nutrition on academic performance. However, we will slightly change the question we asked earlier about the differences among our four nutritional conditions. Instead we ask several questions:

1. What is the effect on academic performance of the intake of daily milk?
2. What is the effect on academic performance of the intake of daily vitamins?
3. What is the effect on academic performance of both milk and vitamins (i.e., the hot lunch includes both milk and vitamins)?
4. Is the effect of vitamins different when milk is also given from when milk is not given?
5. Is the effect of milk different when vitamins are also given from when vitamins are not given?

We can answer all these questions by using a two-way design of the kind shown in Table 14.5. Notice that this table uses the same scores as those in Table 14.2, which should give you further insight into the two-way factorial by comparing its summary ANOVA with the one-way ANOVA computed previously. Table 14.6 shows the group means of the sets of scores in Table 14.5. Table 14.6 also illustrates how this 2 × 2 design allows us to answer more questions than the omnibus ANOVA on the 1 × 4 design. For example, we can learn whether the effect

Table 14.5 Raw Scores of a Two-Way Design

Vitamin treatment	Milk treatment		Row means
	Present	Absent	
Present	17, 19, 21	13, 15, 17	17
Absent	10, 12, 14	8, 10, 12	11
Column means	15.5	12.5	14

Table 14.6	Means and Effects of Results in Table 14.5			
	Milk treatment			
Vitamin treatment	Present	Absent	Row means	Row effects
Present	19	15	17	+3.0
Absent	12	10	11	−3.0
Column means	15.5	12.5	14 (grand mean)	
Column effects	+1.5	−1.5		

of one of our factors is much the same for each of the two or more conditions of the other factor. As noted before, another name for the difference between group means is **simple effects**. In this example, a comparison of the differences between the simple effects tells us that there is a two-unit effect $(12 − 10 = 2)$ of milk when no vitamins are given, and that there is a four-unit effect $(19 − 15 = 4)$ of milk when vitamins are given. Similarly, there is a five-unit effect $(15 − 10 = 5)$ of vitamins when no milk is given and a seven-unit effect $(19 − 12 = 7)$ of vitamins when milk is given.

Another characteristic of factorial designs is that the subjects serve double duty, thereby increasing the power $(1 − \beta)$ to reject certain null hypotheses regarding overall effects if the null hypotheses are false. That is, more of the subjects available for the study are able to contribute to the major comparisons (milk vs. no milk; vitamins vs. no vitamins). In this case, half of all the subjects of the experiment are in the milk conditions instead of the quarter of all subjects that would be in the milk condition in a one-way design. Thus, half the subjects can be compared to the remaining half, who received no milk, so that all the subjects of the experiment shed light on the question of the effect of drinking milk. The overall effect (also called a **main effect**) of milk is assessed by a comparison of the milk and no-milk column means (15.5 and 12.5, respectively). At the same time that all of the subjects provide information on the milk comparison, they also provide information on the effect of vitamins. The main effect of vitamins is assessed by a comparison of the vitamin and no-vitamin marginal values in the rows (means of 17 and 11, respectively).

As described next, factorial designs also give us information about **interaction effects** (i.e., assuming they are really of interest to us). They represent the "leftover" combination of the independent variables after the removal of the main effects, and because they are leftover effects, they are called **residuals**. In the 2×2 example that we have been discussing, the interaction is designated as "rows × columns" (stated as "rows by columns") or "vitamins × milk" (stated as "vitamins by milk") to imply this combination. Once you fully understand these ideas, you will have a better sense of when you have actually hypothesized an interaction (in the statistical sense of ANOVA) and when all you are really interested in is the pattern of the group means, which we turn to later in this chapter.

How Do I Interpret Main and Interaction Effects?

To help explain further what main and interaction effects tell us in a factorial ANOVA, it is useful to begin by examining how the analysis of variance divides up the variance of all the observations into a number of separate sources of variance. We think of the group means (as well as the individual scores) as comprising a number of separate statistical components. In a two-way ANOVA (such as the 2 × 2 design in Tables 14.5 and 14.6), the group means (and individual measurements) can be broken into (a) the grand mean, (b) the row effects, (c) the column effects, (d) the interaction effects, and (e) error. We will start by examining how the first four components (the grand mean, the row effect, the column effect, and the interaction effect) are conceptualized in terms of an "additive model" (i.e., a model in which the components sum to the group means).

As noted previously, the *grand mean* (M_G) is the mean of all group means, or $(19 + 15 + 12 + 10)/4 = 14$. As shown in Table 14.6, the **row effect** for each row is the mean of that row (M_r) minus the grand mean:

$$\text{Row effect} = M_r - M_G$$

Thus, the row effects are computed as $17 - 14 = +3.0$ for vitamins present and $11 - 14 = -3.0$ for vitamins absent. The **column effect** of each column is the mean of that column (M_c) minus the grand mean:

$$\text{Column effect} = M_c - M_G$$

which gives us $15.5 - 14 = +1.5$ for milk present and $12.5 - 14 = -1.5$ for milk absent. Each set of effects sums to zero when totaled over all conditions, a result that is characteristic of all row, column, and interaction effects.

Not visible in Table 14.6 are the interaction effects (i.e., the residuals, or leftover effects). These effects are what remain after the grand mean, row effect, and column effect are subtracted from the group mean. In other words,

$$\text{Interaction effect} = \text{Group mean} - \text{Grand mean} - \text{Row effect} - \text{Column effect}$$

so for these data, the interaction effects for the vitamins-plus-milk group (VM), the vitamins-only group (V), the milk-only group (M), and the zero control (O) are computed as shown in Table 14.7. What can we learn about the results of our

	Group mean	−	Grand mean	−	Row effect	−	Column effect	=	Interaction
VM	19	−	14	−	3.0	−	1.5	=	0.5
V	15	−	14	−	3.0	−	(−1.5)	=	(−0.5)
M	12	−	14	−	(−3.0)	−	1.5	=	(−0.5)
O	10	−	14	−	(−3.0)	−	(−1.5)	=	0.5
Sum	56	−	56	−	0.0	−	0.0	=	0.0

Table 14.7 Interaction Effects Revealed When Group Means Are Decomposed

BOX 14.4   The Additive Model

We said that the idea of ANOVA is based on an *additive model;* that is, components sum to the group means. You can see this more clearly when you total all four conditions of the two-way table:

	Group mean	=	Grand mean	+	Row effect	+	Column effect	+	Interaction effect
VM	19	=	14	+	3.0	+	1.5	+	0.5
V	15	=	14	+	3.0	+	(−1.5)	+	(−0.5)
M	12	=	14	+	(−3.0)	+	1.5	+	(−0.5)
O	10	=	14	+	(−3.0)	+	(−1.5)	+	0.5
Sum	56	=	56	+	0.0	+	0.0	+	0.0

The conceptual advantage of the additive structure is that it provides a baseline that allows you to compare row, column, and interaction effects with one another. The statistical advantage is that it makes *F* tests possible.

experiment by studying this table? The grand mean tells us the general "level" of our measurements and is usually not of great intrinsic interest. The +3 and −3 row effects indicate that the groups receiving vitamins (VM and V) did better than those not receiving vitamins (M and O). The +1.5 and −1.5 column effects indicate that the groups receiving milk (VM and M) did better than those not receiving milk (V and O). The column of +0.5 and −0.5 interaction effects indicate that the group receiving *both* vitamins and milk (VM) and the group receiving *neither* vitamins nor milk (O) did better than the groups receiving *either* vitamins (V) *or* milk (M). But although it is slightly better from the viewpoint of the interaction effect alone to receive neither treatment, this statistical advantage in the interaction effect (i.e., 0.5) is more than offset by the statistical disadvantage in the row effect (i.e., −3.0) and the column effect (i.e., −1.5) to be receiving neither treatment. (See also Box 14.4.)

How Are a Two-Way ANOVA Computed and a Summary Table Set Up?

Earlier, when we analyzed the results of the present study as a one-way ANOVA, we computed the total sum of squares as

$$\text{Total } SS = \Sigma(X - M_G)^2 = 170$$

where X is each observation or measurement, and M_G is the mean of all the condition means. We computed the within-conditions SS as

$$\text{Within } SS = \Sigma(X - M_k)^2 = 32$$

where M_k is the mean of the group or condition to which each observation or measurement (X) belongs. For our two-way ANOVA, we may use the same (above) formulas, but we also need to compute the sums of the squares of the rows, the columns, and the interaction.

The sum of squares of the rows is defined as

$$\text{Row } SS = \Sigma[nc(M_r - M_G)^2]$$

where n is the number of observations in each condition; c is the number of columns contributing to the computation of M_r (the mean of the rth row); and M_G is again the grand mean. The sum of squares of the columns is defined as

$$\text{Column } SS = \Sigma[nr(M_c - M_G)^2]$$

where n is the number of observations in each condition; r is the number of rows contributing to the computation of M_c (the mean of the cth column); and M_G is the grand mean. And finally, the interaction sum of squares is defined as

$$\text{Interaction } SS = \text{Total } SS - (\text{Row } SS + \text{Column } SS + \text{Within } SS)$$

At the same time that we compute the formulas above, we can take apart the individual scores to help us understand better the various terms of the analysis of variance. The ANOVA summary is presented in Table 14.8, and Table 14.9 shows at an individual level where the SS values came from. The only new values in Table 14.8 are those for *error,* which for each subject is computed as the person's raw score minus the group mean. The term *error,* as it is used in this context, means that the size of the deviations of raw scores from their group mean reflects how "poorly" we have predicted scores from a knowledge of group or condition membership. Hence, a score shows a large error if it falls far from the mean of its group and a small error if it falls close to the mean of its group. We can now write *error* as

$$\text{Error} = \text{Score} - \text{Group mean}$$

Table 14.8   Two-Way ANOVA on Results in Table 14.5

Source	SS	df	MS	F	p	$r_{\text{effect size}}$
Vitamins (rows)	108	1	108	27.0	8.3^{-4}	.88
Milk (columns)	27	1	27	6.75	.03	.68
Interaction	3	1	3	0.75	.41	.29
Within error	32	8	4			

Table 14.9 Effects for Computing ANOVA on Results in Table 14.5

Group	Score	=	Grand mean	+	Row effect	+	Column effect	+	Interaction effect	+	Error
VM	17	=	14	+	3.0	+	1.5	+	0.5	+	(−2)
VM	19	=	14	+	3.0	+	1.5	+	0.5	+	0
VM	21	=	14	+	3.0	+	1.5	+	0.5	+	2
V	13	=	14	+	3.0	+	(−1.5)	+	(−0.5)	+	(−2)
V	15	=	14	+	3.0	+	(−1.5)	+	(−0.5)	+	0
V	17	=	14	+	3.0	+	(−1.5)	+	(−0.5)	+	2
M	10	=	14	+	(−3.0)	+	1.5	+	(−0.5)	+	(−2)
M	12	=	14	+	(−3.0)	+	1.5	+	(−0.5)	+	0
M	14	=	14	+	(−3.0)	+	1.5	+	(−0.5)	+	2
O	8	=	14	+	(−3.0)	+	(−1.5)	+	0.5	+	(−2)
O	10	=	14	+	(−3.0)	+	(−1.5)	+	0.5	+	0
O	12	=	14	+	(−3.0)	+	(−1.5)	+	0.5	+	2
ΣX	168	=	168	+	0	+	0	+	0	+	0
ΣX^2	2,522	=	2,352	+	108	+	27	+	3	+	32

Thus, for the VM subject in Table 14.5 who scored 17, Table 14.9 shows that we subtract 19 (the mean of this group) to get the error score of −2. Rearranging the relationship above, we have

$$\text{Score} = \text{Group mean} + \text{Error}$$

and since

Group mean = Grand mean + Row effect + Column effect + Interaction effect

it follows that

Score = Grand mean + Row effect + Column effect + Interaction effect + Error

as is also indicated by the column headings in Table 14.9.

Beneath each column in Table 14.9 are shown the sums of the listed values (ΣX) and the sums of squares of the listed values (ΣX^2), and we can now see where the SS values for Vitamins (rows), Milk (columns), Interaction, and Within error in Table 14.8 came from. Totaling all of the SS values in Table 14.8 gives 108 + 27 + 3 + 32 = 170, the total SS, previously defined as the sum of the squared deviations between every single score and the grand mean, that is, $(17 − 14)^2 + (19 − 14)^2 + \ldots + (12 − 14)^2 = 170$. In Table 14.9, subtracting the sum of the squared grand means (shown as 2,352) from the sum of the squared scores (shown as 2,522) gives us the same value (i.e., total SS = 2,522 − 2,352 = 170). Looking again at Table 14.3 reminds us that, in the one-way ANOVA, the total SS is allocated to two sources of variance: a between-conditions and a within-conditions source. In the move from a one-way to a two-way ANOVA, the within-conditions source of variance (i.e., the source attributable to error) remains unchanged (i.e., "Within error" or "Within conditions" $SS = 32$ in Tables 14.3, 14.8, and 14.9). However, the between-conditions source of variance in the one-way ANOVA (shown in Table 14.3 as 138) is, in the two-way table (Table 14.8), now broken down into three components: a row effect SS, a column effect SS, and an interaction effect SS.

Let us also compute these values using our formulas and the raw scores in Table 14.5. First, we obtain the row effect sum of squares from

$$\text{Row } SS = \Sigma[nc(M_r - M_G)^2]$$
$$= [(3)(2)(17 - 14)^2] + [(3)(2)(11 - 14)^2]$$
$$= 108$$

where Table 14.5 shows $n = 3$ scores in each group, $c = 2$ columns, row means (M_r) of 17 and 11, and a grand mean (M_G) of 14. The resulting value is, of course, the same value shown in Table 14.8 and in the bottom row of Table 14.9.

Next, we obtain the column effect sum of squares from

$$\text{Column } SS = \Sigma[nr(M_c - M_G)^2]$$
$$= [(3)(2)(15.5 - 14)^2] + [(3)(2)(12.5 - 14)^2]$$
$$= 27$$

where the only new values from Table 14.5 are $r = 2$ rows and the column means (M_c) of 15.5 and 12.5. Again, the resulting value is the same as that in Table 14.8 and in the bottom row of Table 14.9.

Finally, we obtain the sum of squares of the interaction from

$$\text{Interaction } SS = \text{Total } SS - (\text{Row } SS + \text{Column } SS + \text{Within } SS)$$

which gives us

$$\text{Interaction } SS = 170 - (108 + 27 + 32) = 3$$

and, as anticipated, it is the value shown in Table 14.8 and in the bottom row of Table 14.9.

The logic of computing the degrees of freedom of the two-way ANOVA is the same as that in the one-way analysis, but we must apportion the between-conditions df to the row main effect, the column main effect, and the interaction. The degrees of freedom for rows in Table 14.8 are

$$df_{\text{rows}} = r - 1$$

where r is the number of rows (thus, $df_{\text{rows}} = 2 - 1 = 1$). The degrees of freedom for columns are

$$df_{\text{columns}} = c - 1$$

where c is the number of columns (thus, $df_{\text{columns}} = 2 - 1 = 1$). The degrees of freedom for the interaction are

$$df_{\text{interaction}} = (r - 1)(c - 1)$$

which gives us $df_{\text{interaction}} = (2 - 1)(2 - 1) = 1$.

The degrees of freedom for the "Within error" are the same as those in Table 14.3, defined as

$$df_{within} = N - k$$

where N is the total number of observations or measurements and k is the number of groups or conditions (thus, $df_{within} = 12 - 4 = 8$). In other words, this is the number of subjects in each group or condition minus 1 totaled over all groups, or $df_{within} = (3-1) + (3-1) + (3-1) + (3-1) = 8$. As a check on the degrees of freedom, we compute the df of the total SS as $df_{total} = N - 1$ and find this result ($df_{total} = 12 - 1 = 11$) to be identical to the sum of the df in Table 14.8 (i.e., $1 + 1 + 1 + 8 = 11$).

As before, we obtain the mean square (MS) values in Table 14.8 by dividing the sums of squares by the corresponding df. That is, we divide 108 by 1 to get 108, and we divide 32 by 8 to get 4 (i.e., the amount of the total variation, measured in SS, attributable to each df). We compute the F ratios by dividing the mean squares for rows, columns, and interaction (the signals) by the mean square within conditions (the noise). Thus, we divide 108 by 4 to get 27.0, and we divide 27 by 4 to get 6.75, and we divide 3 by 4 to get 0.75.

Because F ratios with 1 df in the numerator are focused tests, we can indicate effect sizes by r-type measures. Since our F is a comparison of two groups, and in two-group comparisons we know that $\sqrt{F} = t$, we calculate the effect size of each F by the formula given at the beginning of this chapter:

$$r_{effect\ size} = \sqrt{\frac{F}{F + df_{within}}}$$

We interpret these results as we would any effect size correlation, including using the confidence interval and the BESD described in Chapter 11.

Table 14.8 shows precise values of p. The F of 6.75 for the effect of milk could have occurred by chance approximately 3 times in 100, and the F of 27.0 for the effect of vitamins could have occurred by chance far less often ($p = 8.3^{-4}$, or 8 times in 10,000), if the null hypothesis were true. By contrast, the F for interaction was so small ($F < 1$) that it could easily have arisen by chance. However, if the interaction were of interest, we would analyze it as before (i.e., as a comparison between the residuals of the diagonal cells). The effect sizes tell us that both milk and vitamins have a beneficial effect, and that more of the effect is attributable to vitamins than to milk. We can also calculate t tests of simple effects by using the procedure described previously.

How Do I Compute a Focused t or F on More Than Two Groups?

In a study in which more than 500 active psychological researchers were asked about the proper way to think about interaction effects in analysis of variance, about a third of them answered incorrectly, mistaking the pattern of the group means for the interaction residuals (Zuckerman, Hodgins, Zuckerman, & Rosenthal, 1993). However, you know that group means are made up of the grand mean, the row effect, the column effect, and the interaction (Box 14.4). The interaction effects

| **Table 14.10** | Summary ANOVA (Omnibus F) for Results A and B in Table 14.1 |

Results A:

Source	SS	df	MS	F	p
Between conditions	138	3	46	11.50	.003
Within conditions	32	8	4		

Results B:

Source	SS	df	MS	F	p
Between conditions	138	3	46	1.28	.35
Within conditions	288	8	36		

are what are left over after the removal of those other effects from the group means. The confusion may come from the common usage of *interaction* to imply a "combination of things," which is true of statistical interactions. But a statistical interaction in analysis of variance also has a specialized meaning, as you learned in the preceding discussion. If you are not interested in residuals but are interested in some predicted pattern of the group means in designs with more than two conditions, the most powerful and precise way to test your prediction is by a statistical procedure for asking focused questions of data (called a **contrast**).

To illustrate, we refer to the hypothetical data (A and B) that we presented earlier in this chapter (Table 14.1). The overall analysis of variance of each set (A and B) is summarized in Table 14.10. You now know that the reason the omnibus *F* is so much larger for Results A than for Results B is that the within-conditions variability is so much smaller in Results A than in B. However, saying there was "no difference" between the four groups in Results B would make no sense intuitively, because in Table 14.1 we clearly see a gradual increment in the scores from Group 1 to Group 4.

Suppose we had hypothesized a linear pattern of regularly increasing means from Group 1 to Group 4. Because we would get the same omnibus *F* no matter how the groups were arranged, the omnibus *F* would be a poor choice to test our hypothesis. A better choice would be to compute a contrast *t* or *F* that is specifically addressed to the predicted linear trend. To do so, we state our prediction in simple integers, called *lambda weights* (λ) in Chapter 7 (also called **contrast weights** in this chapter), the only stipulation being that the lambdas sum to zero (i.e., $\Sigma\lambda = 0$). Because we hypothesized an increasing linear trend in the four groups, we might choose λs of -3, -1, $+1$, $+3$ to represent our prediction. Next, we compare these lambda weights with the obtained scores using the following formula:

$$t_{contrast} = \frac{\Sigma M\lambda}{\sqrt{MS_{within}\left(\Sigma \frac{\lambda^2}{n}\right)}}$$

where M in the numerator refers to a specific condition mean; MS_{within} in the denominator refers to the within-conditions mean square in Table 14.10; n is the number of observations in a given condition; and λ refers to the contrast weight required by our prediction for that condition.

Using this formula with Results A, we find

$$t_{contrast} = \frac{(10)(-3) + (12)(-1) + (15)(+1) + (19)(+3)}{\sqrt{4\left[\frac{(-3)^2}{3} + \frac{(-1)^2}{3} + \frac{(+1)^2}{3} + \frac{(+3)^2}{3}\right]}}$$

$$= \frac{30}{\sqrt{(4)(6.667)}} = 5.809$$

which, with 8 df (the degrees of freedom for MS_{within}, or $N - k$), has an associated $p = .0002$ one-tailed (or in scientific notation, $p = 2.0^{-4}$ one-tailed). For Results B, applying this same formula yields

$$t_{contrast} = \frac{(10)(-3) + (12)(-1) + (15)(+1) + (19)(+3)}{\sqrt{36\left[\frac{(-3)^2}{3} + \frac{(-1)^2}{3} + \frac{(+1)^2}{3} + \frac{(+3)^2}{3}\right]}}$$

$$= \frac{30}{\sqrt{(36)(6.667)}} = 1.936$$

which, with 8 df, has an associated $p = .044$ one-tailed. The reason that we prefer these results to those in Table 14.10 is that the $t_{contrast}$ addresses the hypothesized linear trend, whereas the F tests in Table 14.10 are not focused on the predicted trend.

You will recall that squaring t always gives F. Thus, because squaring these two contrast t values produces contrast F values, we find that $F_{contrast} = (5.809)^2 = 33.74$ for Results A and that $F_{contrast} = (1.936)^2 = 3.75$ for Results B. To obtain the p levels of these F values, we consult Table B.3 with 1 and 8 degrees of freedom. Suppose we want to report a summary ANOVA table that shows the contrast F carved out of the between-conditions sum of squares. There are several ways to obtain the information we need. One option is to compute the contrast mean square ($MS_{contrast}$) from

$$MS_{contrast} = \frac{nL^2}{\Sigma\lambda^2}$$

where

$$L = M_1\lambda_1 + M_2\lambda_2 + M_3\lambda_3 + M_4\lambda_4$$

To illustrate with Results B, we solve for L as follows:

$$L = (10)(-3) + (12)(-1) + (15)(+1) + (19)(+3) = 30$$

and then substitute in the previous equation to find

$$MS_{contrast} = \frac{nL^2}{\Sigma\lambda^2} = \frac{3 \times (30)^2}{(-3)^2 + (-1)^2 + (+1)^2 + (+3)^2} = \frac{2,700}{20} = 135$$

Table 14.11	Linear Contrast Carved Out of ANOVA on Results B in Table 14.10				
Source	SS	df	MS	F	p
Between conditions	138	3	46	1.28	.35
Contrast	135	1	135	3.75	.089
Noncontrast	3	2	1.5	.04	
Within conditions	288	8	36		

We know that $MS = SS/df$, and since $df = 1$ for all contrasts, $MS_{contrast} = SS_{contrast}$.

Table 14.11 shows the linear contrast sum of squares that we carved out of the between-conditions sum of squares. The contrast F is $MS_{contrast}/MS_{within} = 135/36 = 3.75$, the same result as squaring the contrast t. New to this table is the noncontrast sum of squares (3), which is simply the remainder after subtraction of the contrast sum of squares (135) from the between-conditions sum of squares (138). The $F_{noncontrast}$ of .04 came from dividing the mean square noncontrast (1.5) by the mean square within (36).

What Do $r_{effect\ size}$, $r_{alerting}$, and $r_{contrast}$ Tell Me?

Because contrasts are focused tests, we can report an effect size index. We have several choices of r-type indices, each giving us a different perspective on the results. We will define three such indices: the effect size r, the alerting r, and the contrast r. Further discussion of these and several other useful indices can be found in our other work (R. Rosenthal & Rosnow, 2008; R. Rosenthal, Rosnow, & Rubin, 2000).

The **effect size r** (or $r_{effect\ size}$) is the correlation between each subject's score (Y) on the dependent measure and the contrast weight (λ) assigned to the condition to which the subject belongs. Thus, this index can also be denoted as $r_{Y\lambda}$, and it can be computed from the results in Table 14.11 by

$$r_{effect\ size} = r_{Y\lambda} = \sqrt{\frac{F_{contrast}}{F_{contrast} + F_{noncontrast}(df_{noncontrast}) + df_{within}}}$$

with terms defined in that table. Substituting in this equation, we find

$$r_{effect\ size} = \sqrt{\frac{3.75}{3.75 + .04(2) + 8}} = \sqrt{\frac{3.75}{11.83}} = .563$$

The **alerting r** (or $r_{alerting}$) is the correlation between the condition means (M) and their respective contrast (λ) weights and thus can also be denoted as $r_{M\lambda}$. It takes its name from the idea that it alerts us to trends of possible interest and, when squared, reveals the proportion of the sum of squares between conditions that can be accounted for by the contrast weights. It is easy enough to compute the alerting r if you have a calculator that gives you correlations when you punch in the raw scores and tap the correlation key. Table 14.12, which shows the alerting r

Table 14.12 Product-Moment r Between Group Means and Linear Contrast Weights for Results B in Table 14.1

Groups	Group means		λ weights		Product of z_1
	Mean	z_1 score	Lambda	z_2 score	and z_2 scores
1 (Zero)	10	−1.1795	−3	−1.3416	1.582
2 (Milk)	12	−0.5898	−1	−0.4472	.264
3 (Vitamins)	15	+0.2949	+1	+0.4472	.132
4 (Hot lunch)	19	+1.4744	+3	+1.3416	1.978
Sum (Σ)	56	0	0	0	3.956
Mean (M)	14	0	0	0	.989
SD (σ)	3.3912	1.0		2.2361	1.0	

calculated in the tabular format of Chapter 11, is a reminder that this r is simply a product-moment correlation. That is,

$$r_{M\lambda} = \frac{\Sigma z_1 z_2}{N} = \frac{3.956}{4} = .989$$

Squaring the alerting r gives us $(.989)^2 = .978$, which indicates the proportion of the between-conditions sum of squares that is accounted for by our linear contrast (see also Box 14.5).

BOX 14.5 Computing Contrasts From Omnibus F Tests

Suppose we read a research article about an experiment with more than two groups, and all that is reported is group means and an overall F with numerator $df > 1$ (i.e., an omnibus F, as described in Box 14.2). A linear relationship was predicted but never precisely tested. Given the information in that article, we can compute a contrast F in four easy steps and decide for ourselves whether the results were consistent with the linear prediction. Assume that (as in Results B in Table 14.1 and Table 14.10) the reported group means are 10, 12, 15, 19 and the omnibus F is 1.28. First, we create a set of contrast (λ) weights to represent the predicted trend, and say we choose weights of −3, −1, +1, +3. Second, we correlate these weights with their respective group means, getting an alerting r of .989. Third, we multiply the omnibus F by its numerator df and find the maximum possible value of any contrast F carved out of $SS_{between}$, which in this case is $F(3,8) = 1.28 \times 3 = 3.84$. The final step is to multiply the squared alerting r by the maximum-possible-contrast F to get the linear contrast F, so in this case we find $F_{contrast} = (.989)^2 \times 3.84 = 3.75$ (the same result as shown in Table 14.11).

When the alerting r approaches 1.0, we can use the following familiar formula to estimate $r_{\text{effect size}}$ from F:

$$r = \sqrt{\frac{F}{F + df_{\text{within}}}}$$

which we refer to more generally as the **contrast r** (or r_{contrast}) rather than (as in our discussion of two-group comparisons) the effect size r. The contrast r can be understood as a partial correlation between each subject's score (Y) on the dependent measure and the contrast weight (λ) assigned to the condition, with other between-condition variability removed. Thus, the contrast r can also be denoted as $r_{Y\lambda \cdot NC}$, where NC means that all the "noncontrast" variation has been removed (or partialed out). Because in two-group designs there is no noncontrast variation to be partialed out, $r_{\text{contrast}} = r_{\text{effect size}}$ in all two-group comparisons. In the case of Results B, where $r_{\text{alerting}} = .989$, and $r^2_{\text{alerting}} = .978$, we find

$$r_{\text{contrast}} = r_{Y\lambda \cdot NC} = \sqrt{\frac{F_{\text{contrast}}}{F_{\text{contrast}} + df_{\text{within}}}} = \sqrt{\frac{3.75}{3.75 + 8}} = .565$$

Not surprisingly, given the fact that r^2_{alerting} is near 1.0, the contrast correlation is nearly identical to the value of $r_{\text{effect size}}$ we saw before (i.e., .563).

In two-group designs, $r_{\text{effect size}}$ and r_{contrast} are identical, although when there are more than two groups, it is also possible for r_{alerting}, $r_{\text{effect size}}$, and r_{contrast} to have identical values. Usually, however, r_{contrast} is larger than $r_{\text{effect size}}$, and the difference is sometimes quite substantial. The value of r_{alerting} tends to be larger than $r_{\text{effect size}}$ and r_{contrast}, but it need not be so (R. Rosenthal, Rosnow, & Rubin, 2000; Rosnow & Rosenthal, 1996; Rosnow, Rosenthal, and Rubin, 2000). Using this entire family of effect size indices generally captures the different meanings of contrasts in a way that cannot be precisely communicated by any single measurement.

How Are Contrasts on Multiple Repeated Measures Computed?

So far in our discussion of statistical tests, whether those tests involved comparing two means (t tests) or more than two groups (F tests), each of our participants, or other units, contributed only a single score, measurement, or observation. However, it often happens in behavioral research that we must measure participants more than once to address the question of interest. Such research is called *intrinsically repeated-measures research* (R. Rosenthal, Rosnow, & Rubin, 2000). Suppose that we want to learn the degree to which students' performance on a cognitive task improves over time (i.e., over repeated occasions of measurement). There is no alternative to measuring the participants repeatedly (i.e., twice, or three times, or more, depending on our specific research question). Our theory might predict, for example, that on a particular cognitive task, the students will improve by an equal amount each time they perform the task over four measurement occasions, say, 1 month apart. Table 14.13 shows the results of a hypothetical study of three students, and Table 14.14 shows the summary ANOVA.

Table 14.13 Cognitive Performance Measured on Four Occasions

| Student | Occasion of Measurement | | | | Mean |
	First	Second	Third	Fourth	
1	1	3	7	5	4.0
2	0	6	2	4	3.0
3	2	4	6	8	5.0
Mean	1.00	4.33	5.00	5.67	4.0

As in any two-way ANOVA, Table 14.14 displays a row effect (between subjects in this example), a column effect (occasions in this example), and an interaction effect (an occasions × subjects interaction in this example). The mean square (*MS*) for subjects (4.00) tells us how far apart the three subjects' means are on average. The mean square for occasions (12.89) tells us how far apart the four occasions' means are on average. The occasions × subjects interaction mean square (3.56) tells us how different the subjects' effects are on different occasions or, equivalently, how different the occasions' effects are for different subjects; we can think of these results as the heterogeneity of the patterns or profiles of four scores among the three subjects. If all three subjects show identical patterns or profiles over the four occasions of measurement, the interaction *MS* equals zero. Figure 14.1 shows that the three patterns (or profiles) are not identical but do show some similarities. If they were identical, all three profiles would be completely parallel to one another over the four occasions of measurement. Figure 14.2 shows how the three profiles might look if there were no interaction at all.

Although the three profiles of Figure 14.1 are certainly different from one another, what they do have in common is that all three subjects' second, third, and fourth performance scores are higher than their first scores. That fact is consistent with our prediction that performance would improve with each successive measurement, but it is not quite the same as our prediction. We predicted that students would improve by an equal amount on each occasion of measurement. Using what we have learned about contrasts, we can create a contrast score for each subject. This contrast score, or *L* score, tells us the degree to which the subject behaved in accordance with our prediction. The *L* score is simply the sum of

Table 14.14 Analysis of Variance of Data of Table 14.13

Source	SS	df	MS	$F_{(3,6)}$	p
Between subjects	8.00	2	4.00	—	
Within subjects	60.00	9			
Occasions	38.67	3	12.89	3.62	.08
Occasions × subjects	21.33	6	3.56		

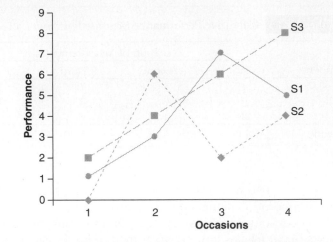

Figure 14.1   Profiles of three subjects' performance measured on four occasions.

the products of the contrast (λ) weights, multiplied by the subject's actual performance, or

$$L = \Sigma Y\lambda = Y_1\lambda_1 + Y_2\lambda_2 + \ldots + Y_k\lambda_k$$

We form the contrast (λ) weights for the occasions of measurement by writing down the value we predict and then subtracting the mean of the four predictions from each individual prediction to meet the requirement that, for any contrast, the sum of the λ weights must equal zero. Suppose our prediction was

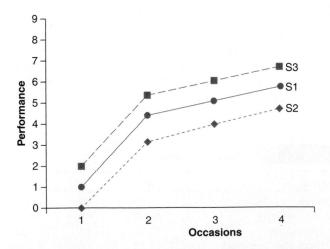

Figure 14.2   Profiles of three subjects' performance showing zero interaction.

that, over four occasions, the subjects' scores would go from 1 to 3 to 5 to 7. The mean of these four predicted values is 4, which we subtract from each of our four predicted values, obtaining λ weights of -3, -1, $+1$, $+3$. Then, for Subject 1 the L score is

$$L = \Sigma Y\lambda = 1(-3) + 3(-1) + 7(+1) + 5(+3) = 16$$

The analogous L scores for Subjects 2 and 3 are 8 and 20, respectively.

We can now compute a one-sample t test on these three L scores by using the following formula:

$$t_{(df)} = \frac{M_L}{\sqrt{\left(\frac{1}{N}\right) S_L^2}}$$

where M_L is the mean of the L scores, N is the number of subjects, S_L^2 is the variance of the L scores, and df refers to the degrees of freedom for the one-sample t test, usually $N - 1$. For the data of Table 14.13, we find

$$t_{(2)} = \frac{14.67}{\sqrt{\left(\frac{1}{3}\right) 37.33}} = 4.16$$

and $p = .027$ one tailed. For our effect size index, we compute

$$r_{\text{contrast}} = \sqrt{\frac{t^2}{t^2 + df}} = \sqrt{\frac{(4.16)^2}{(4.16)^2 + 2}} = .95$$

There is an alternative to the use of L scores in repeated-measures analyses as long as there are at least three occasions of measurement. We can use r values, the correlations of the repeated measures with their associated λ weights. For Subject 1, given the following data:

Occasion	1	2	3	4
Score (Y)	1	3	7	5
λ	-3	-1	$+1$	$+3$

we find that the product-moment correlation of Subject 1's scores (1, 3, 7, 5) with their associated λ weights (-3, -1, $+1$, $+3$) over the 4 occasions is $r = .80$. The analogous correlations for Subjects 2 and 3 are .40 and 1.00, respectively. We can now compute a one-sample t test on these three r values as follows:

$$t_{(df)} = \frac{\bar{r}}{\sqrt{\left(\frac{1}{N}\right) S_r^2}}$$

where $\bar{r}$ is the mean of the r values, N is the number of subjects, S_r^2 is the variance of the r values, and df refers to the degrees of freedom for the one-sample t test, usually $N-1$. For the data of Table 14.13, then,

$$t_{(2)} = \frac{.73}{\sqrt{\left(\frac{1}{3}\right).0933}} = 4.14$$

and $p = .027$ one-tailed. For our effect size index, we compute

$$r_{contrast} = \sqrt{\frac{t^2}{t^2 + df}} = \sqrt{\frac{(4.14)^2}{(4.14)^2 + 2}} = .95$$

In this example, the values of t, p, and $r_{contrast}$ are the same for the L scores and the r values, but it is possible for these values to differ markedly for L scores versus r values.

How Are Latin Square Designs Analyzed?

In the repeated-measures research we have considered so far, the research question itself *required* that each subject be measured two or more times (i.e., there were *intrinsically* repeated measures). In another very common use of repeated measures, it is *not required* in principle that a repeated-measures design be used. Such a design is used to increase the efficiency, precision, and statistical power of the study by administering several treatments to each of the subjects or other sampling units. We call this type of research *nonintrinsically repeated-measures research* (R. Rosenthal, Rosnow, & Rubin, 2000).

Suppose we want to compare the effectiveness of four treatment conditions for a rare disorder: a new treatment, the established or standard treatment, a placebo control, and a no-treatment (zero) control. But suppose we have available only four patients with the rare disorder. We could randomly assign one patient to each treatment condition, but we could learn little from that approach. We would never know whether differences in treatment outcome were due to differences in the four conditions of treatment or simply due to individual differences among the four patients. The treatment conditions would be entirely confounded with the patients' individual differences.

Perhaps we could administer all four treatments to all four patients as outlined in Table 14.15. All four patients would begin by having no treatment (say, for 1 month), then have a month of placebo treatment, then a month of the standard treatment, and then a month of the new treatment. This kind of repeated-measures design would give us 16 observations, 4 per treatment, instead of just 1 per treatment, but our results would still be confounded. This time the order of presentation (first vs. second vs. third vs. fourth) would be completely confounded with the treatment. We would never be able to disentangle the effects, for example, of being fourth-administered from the effects of the new treatment condition.

Table 14.15 Four Treatments Administered to Each of Four Patients

	Treatment occasion			
	1	2	3	4
Patients	None	Placebo	Old	New
Patient 1				
Patient 2				
Patient 3				
Patient 4				

There is something we can do to "unconfound" order effects from treatment effects. We can counterbalance our design by the use of the Latin square, previously described in Chapter 7. Table 14.16 shows the Latin square rearrangement of the four treatment conditions in Table 14.15. Our four treatments (labeled A, B, C, D) are all administered to each of the four patients, but each patient is given a different sequence of the four treatments. The sequences are arranged so that each treatment occurs once in each row (sequence), and once in each column (order). This arrangement allows us to learn of differences among the four treatments, differences among the four orders of presentation, and differences among the four sequences or subjects. In this design, sequences and subjects are confounded, but as we are rarely interested in either sequence or subject effects, this confounding poses no great problem.

Table 14.17 shows the results of a study of the type we have been discussing, and Table 14.18 summarizes the analysis of variance. We will not describe the details of this analysis here, but they are available in our advanced text (R. Rosenthal & Rosnow, 2008). Here it is enough to note that there is a substantial F for both the order effect and the treatment effect, but we also note that both F tests are omnibus tests, telling us little of what we really want to know about the treatment effect or the order effect. The most efficient way to investigate the treatment effects is to use the L scores method described in the preceding section. For each patient, we compute the appropriate L score. For example, if our prediction had been that a placebo would be a lot better than no treatment at all, and that the old

Table 14.16 Latin Square Design for the Conditions of Table 14.15

	Order of administration			
	1	2	3	4
Sequence 1	A	B	C	D
Sequence 2	B	C	D	A
Sequence 3	C	D	A	B
Sequence 4	D	A	B	C

Table 14.17 Data Obtained for the Latin Square of Table 14.16

	Order of administration				
	1	2	3	4	Σ
Sequence 1	2	7	10	7	26
Sequence 2	4	8	10	5	27
Sequence 3	6	9	5	8	28
Sequence 4	9	4	8	10	31
Σ	21	28	33	30	112

Treatment sums (each based on 4 scores)

A	B	C	D
16	27	34	35

treatment would be somewhat better than a placebo, and that the new treatment would be somewhat better than the old treatment, we might have predicted relative outcome scores of 2, 5, 6, 7, respectively, for no treatment, placebo, old treatment, and new treatment. The mean of these predicted scores is 5, a value we subtract from each predicted score to produce contrast (λ) weights that sum to zero.

In this example, then, our contrast weights are −3, 0, +1, +2, respectively. Subject 1 (who is listed as Sequence 1 in Table 14.17) has an L score of 18, computed as

$$L = \Sigma Y\lambda = 2(-3) + 7(0) + 10(+1) + 7(+2) = 18$$

Subjects 2, 3, and 4 have L scores of 13, 9, and 16, respectively. The t test examining our prediction yields

$$t_{(3)} = \frac{M_L}{\sqrt{\left(\frac{1}{N}\right)s_L^2}} = \frac{14}{\sqrt{\left(\frac{1}{4}\right)15.33}} = 7.15$$

Table 14.18 Analysis of Variance of the Data of Table 14.17

Source	SS	df	MS	$F_{(3,6)}$	p
Sequences	3.50	3	1.17	—	
Orders	19.50	3	6.50	4.11	.066
(Sequences × orders)	(67.00)	(9)	(7.44)		
Treatments	57.50	3	19.17	12.13	5.9^{-3}
Residual (S × O)	9.50	6	1.58		

and $p = 2.8^{-3}$ one-tailed. For our effect size index, we compute

$$r_{contrast} = \sqrt{\frac{t^2}{t^2 + df}} = \sqrt{\frac{(7.15)^2}{(7.15)^2 + 3}} = .97$$

a huge (and highly significant) effect size.

We could, of course, compute L scores for somewhat different predictions or hypotheses. For example, if our prediction had been simply that our two treatment conditions (old and new) would do better than our two control conditions (no treatment and placebo), we might have used contrast weights of $+1, +1, -1, -1$, respectively, for those four conditions. Had we examined that prediction, we would have found L scores of 8, 9, 2, 7 for Patients 1, 2, 3, 4, respectively, yielding $t_{(3)} = 4.18$, $p = .012$, and $r_{contrast} = .92$. Had we wanted to investigate the order effect, we could have done so in analogous fashion. For example, had we hypothesized that patients would tend to get better over time, we might have predicted a linear trend with contrast weights of $-3, -1, +1, +3$. Had we used these weights to investigate order effects, we would have found $t_{(3)} = 2.29$, $p = .053$, $r_{contrast} = .80$. We leave it to our readers to verify that these values are correct!

Summary of Ideas

1. The F test used in a between-conditions *analysis of variance (ANOVA)* is a ratio of the spread of mean scores around the grand mean (the signal) to the spread of scores within each condition (the noise) (also Box 14.1).

2. For the special case of the comparison of two groups, $F = t^2$, and in that particular case, we can calculate the effect size correlation for F as

$$r_{effect\ size} = \sqrt{\frac{F}{F + df_{within}}}$$

However, later in this chapter, we called this formula the *contrast r* when applied to focused tests on more than two groups, although in two-group comparisons $r_{contrast} = r_{effect\ size}$.

3. F tests with numerator $df = 1$ and all t tests are characterized as *focused statistical tests,* and F tests with numerator $df > 1$ are called *omnibus statistical tests* (Box 14.2).

4. When computing t tests on *simple effects* after the omnibus F, we define S^2 in the t formula as the MS within (i.e., the pooled error term) in the ANOVA summary table.

5. When computing effect size r values on simple effects after computing the omnibus F, we define df in the $r_{effect\ size}$ formula by the size of the groups being compared ($df = n_1 + n_2 - 2$).

6. In *factorial designs,* because two or more levels of each factor (independent variable) are administered in combination with two or more levels of every other factor, such factorial designs generally use sampling units more efficiently and address more questions than do ordinary one-way ANOVAs.

7. The *error* of individual scores (i.e., the deviation of each score from the mean of the group) represents the extent to which the score can be predicted from a knowledge of group membership.

8. The summary table for the factorial ANOVA differs from the summary table for the one-way ANOVA in reflecting the subdivision of the between-conditions SS into *main* and *interaction SS*.

9. The additive model is based on the idea that each group mean is the sum of the grand mean, the *row effect,* the *column effect,* and the *interaction effect.* The model thus provides a baseline that allows us to compare these effects with one another (Box 14.4).

10. *Interaction effects* in two-way ANOVA are the effects left over (*residuals*) after the row and column effects are removed from the group means. Removing the grand mean will reveal the pure residuals.

11. *Contrast t and F tests* are focused procedures that compare (*contrast*) an obtained pattern of means with a predicted pattern expressed in the form of lambda (λ) weights that sum to zero.

12. The $r_{alerting}$ effect size index is the correlation between the group means and their respective λ weights, and thus is also symbolized as $r_{M\lambda}$. The $r_{contrast}$ is the (partial) correlation between the scores on the dependent variable and their respective λ weights with noncontrast sources of variation removed, and thus it is also symbolized as $r_{Y\lambda \cdot NC}$.

13. Squaring the alerting r reveals the proportion of the between-conditions sum of squares that is accounted for by the particular contrast (λ) weights. If this value approaches 1.0, we can use the formula in (2) above to estimate $r_{effect size}$ from F. The alerting r is also useful in computing contrasts from reported group means and an omnibus F (Box 14.5).

14. In intrinsically repeated-measures research, we *must* measure the participants more than once to address the question of interest. We can use either the L score or the r value method to compute contrasts, but it is possible for contrast r values obtained from these two methods to differ markedly.

15. In nonintrinsically repeated-measures research, it is *not essential* that we use a repeated-measures design, but it increases efficiency, precision, and statistical power to do so. An example is the Latin square design described at the end of this chapter.

Key Terms

alerting r ($r_{alerting}$ or $r_{M\lambda}$) p. 336
analysis of variance (ANOVA) p. 315
column effect p. 328
contrast r ($r_{contrast}$ or $r_{Y\lambda \cdot NC}$) p. 338
contrast p. 334
contrast (λ) weights p. 334

effect size r ($r_{effect size}$ or $r_{Y\lambda}$) p. 336
focused statistical procedures p. 321
F ratio p. 318
F test p. 318
interaction effects p. 327
main effect p. 327
mean square (S^2, or MS) p. 318

omnibus statistical procedures p. 321
residuals p. 327
row effect p. 328
simple effects p. 327
sum of squares (SS) p. 319
tests of simple effects p. 325

Multiple-Choice Questions for Review

1. When comparing only two groups, $F =$ _____. (a) t; (b) $2t$; (c) t^2;(d) $t/2$
2. A "one-way ANOVA" has only one _____. (a) degree of freedom; (b) between-group SS; (c) variance; (d) treatment condition
3. S^2 is also called _____. (a) sum of squares; (b) σ^2; (c) F ratio; (d) mean square

4. Total $SS =$ _____ $SS +$ _____ SS. (a) Experimental; Control; (b) Dependent; Independent; (c) Between; Within; (d) all of the above

5. In a two-way factorial, the between $SS =$ _____. (a) Main effects SS; (b) Main effects SS + Interaction SS; (c) Main effects SS + Interaction SS + Error SS; (d) none of the above

6. A student at the University of Tennessee conducts an experiment with three groups. Each group contains four subjects. How many between-conditions degrees of freedom will there be? (a) 2; (b) 3; (c) 4; (d) 11

7. In the study above, what are the total degrees of freedom? (a) 2; (b) 3; (c) 4; (d) 11

8. A student at Southern Illinois University conducts a study with two groups and five subjects in each group. She calculates that $F = 5$. According to Table 14.4, what is the appropriate p value? (a) $p > .05$; (b) $p < .05$; (c) $p < .01$; (d) cannot be determined

9. A student at the University of Arizona conducts an experiment with four groups. He calculates an F test to examine the overall differences between the groups. He then computes t tests to compare each group to each of the others. These t tests are said to be tests of (a) within-subjects effects; (b) main effects; (c) repeated-measures effects; (d) simple effects.

10. Both F with numerator $df = 1$ and any t test are (a) focused tests; (b) unfocused tests; (c) omnibus tests; (d) diffuse tests.

Discussion Questions for Review

1. From a population of 50 male professional runners, an Ohio State researcher randomly assigns 10 to each of five groups. Each group receives a different brand of running shoe. The brands are coded A, B, C, D, E. Each member of a group receives a new pair of the top-of-the-line shoe made by a shoe company and then rates the shoe for comfort. Below are the mean comfort ratings (on a scale from 1 to 20) given to the different brands:

Brand	Rating
A	19
B	13
C	17
D	9
E	10

   Suppose the researcher performs an analysis of variance, and the within-shoe-brands mean square is 94, whereas the mean square for between-shoe-brands is 188. What is the value of the omnibus F testing the significance of the overall difference among the shoe brands? What are the associated degrees of freedom?

2. A University of Pittsburgh researcher has the following two sets of data, each of which contains three independent groups. The 12 subjects in each set were randomly assigned to the groups; 4 subjects were assigned to each group. The numbers are scores on some dependent measure.

Set A:

Group 1	Group 2	Group 3
2	5	11
3	5	10
2	4	9
1	6	10
Mean 2	5	10

Set B:

Group 1	Group 2	Group 3
9	11	23
−6	−10	10
4	0	−2
1	19	9
Mean 2	5	10

Which set of data is likely to yield a larger F ratio in an analysis of variance? How can you be sure?

3. A University of Colorado student obtains the following set of means in a study that measures the benefits of vacations in rural versus urban areas for participants who live in rural or urban areas. Higher numbers indicate greater benefits. Figure out the row effects, the column effects, and the interaction residuals, and then decide how they should be interpreted.

	Urban subjects	Rural subjects
Urban vacations	5	3
Rural vacations	11	1

4. A University of Maine student obtains the data shown in Table 14.2 and computes the ANOVA shown in Table 14.3. His primary interest, however, is in whether the scores of the hot lunch group on average are significantly better than the average scores of the remaining three groups. How would you advise him to address his question?

5. A McGill University student who computed a contrast F is advised by her instructor to look at the alerting r before estimating the effect size r from $\sqrt{(F)/(F + df)}$. Why?

6. A University of Maryland–Baltimore County student who used a repeated-measures design in his research is advised by his instructor to compute a contrast using L scores. What are they, and how can the student form a set of lambda weights?

Answers to Review Questions

Multiple-Choice Questions

1. c	3. d	5. b	7. d	9. d
2. b	4. c	6. a	8. a	10. a

Discussion Questions

1. An appropriate table of variance for this study is

Source	SS	df	MS	F	p
Between brands	752	4	188	2.0	.11
Within brands	4,230	45	94		

The researcher finds F from MS between divided by MS within and then finds df from $k - 1$ for numerator df and $N - k$ for denominator df. The researcher does not report $r_{\text{effect size}}$ because this is an omnibus F test (i.e., one with numerator $df > 1$).

2. Set A would yield a larger F because its within-condition variability is much smaller than that of Set B. Since the means of Sets A and B are equal, the MS between for Sets A and B are equal. Therefore, the results with the smaller MS within will yield the larger F.

3. The following table shows the means, row effects, and column effects (as in Table 14.6):

	Type of subjects			
Type of vacation	Urban (US)	Rural (RS)	Row means	Row effects
Urban (UV)	5	3	4	−1
Rural (RV)	11	1	6	+1
Column means	8	2	5	
			(grand mean)	
Column effects	+3	−3		

The interaction effects for each of the four conditions are computed from:

	Group mean	−	Grand mean	−	Row effect	−	Column effect	=	Interaction effect
UV, US	5	−	5	−	(−1)	−	3	=	(−2)
UV, RS	3	−	5	−	(−1)	−	(−3)	=	2
RV, US	11	−	5	−	1	−	3	=	2
RV, RS	1	−	5	−	1	−	(−3)	=	(−2)
Sum	20	−	20	−	0.0	−	0.0	=	0.0

If we disregard matters of statistical significance, these results show that the type of subjects made the largest difference, the type of vacation made the smallest difference, and the interaction made an intermediate amount of difference. The urban subjects benefited more than the rural subjects, the rural vacations were associated with greater benefits than were the urban vacations, and the interaction showed greater benefits for those vacationing in the setting in which they did *not* reside.

4. A t test following the F would address the question appropriately. The two means to be compared would be the hot lunch mean and the mean of the means of the remaining three groups, that is, $(10 + 12 + 15)/3 = 12.33$. The two required sample sizes, n_1 and n_2, would be the n for the hot lunch (i.e., 3) and the n for the children in the remaining three groups (i.e., $3 + 3 + 3 = 9$). As in the case of most t tests computed after the ANOVA, the S^2 used in computing t is the S^2 obtained from the ANOVA, the MS within. Thus

$$t = \frac{19 - 12.33}{\sqrt{\left(\frac{1}{3} + \frac{1}{9}\right)4}} = 5.00$$

and with $df = 8$, $p = .0005$. Whenever we compute t, or F with 1 df in the numerator, we want to know the effect size. So we compute the effect size correlation from

$$r_{\text{effect size}} = \sqrt{\frac{t^2}{t^2 + df}} = \sqrt{\frac{(5.0)^2}{(5.0)^2 + 8}} = .87$$

which is a jumbo-sized effect. An alternative way to address this question is by means of t_{contrast}, which in this case would involve contrast (λ) weights of $+3, -1, -1, -1$, reflecting our prediction that the mean of the hot lunch would be higher than the other three means, which in turn would not differ from each other. As we would expect, the value of t_{contrast} is identical to our sample t value of 5.00, that is,

$$t_{\text{contrast}} = \frac{\Sigma M\lambda}{\sqrt{MS_{\text{within}}\left(\Sigma\frac{\lambda^2}{n}\right)}} = \frac{19(+3) + 10(-1) + 12(-1) + 15(-1)}{\sqrt{4\left[\frac{(+3)^2}{3} + \frac{(-1)^2}{3} + \frac{(-1)^2}{3} + \frac{(-1)^2}{3}\right]}} = \frac{20}{\sqrt{16}} = 5.00$$

5. In the context of contrast analysis, the formula she wanted to use to estimate the effect size r from her contrast F is referred to more generally as the contrast r rather than the effect size r. However, it can be used to estimate the effect size r if the squared alerting r approaches 1, as it would imply that there is very little noncontrast variation to be concerned about.

6. L scores are the contrast scores for each subject in a repeated-measures contrast, defined as the sum of the products of the contrast (λ) weights multiplied by the subject's performance scores (the Y scores). A convenient way to form a set of λ weights is to write down your prediction in integers and then to subtract the mean from each integer. For example, if the student had predicted that the scores would go from 3 to 9 and then back to 3, he would subtract the mean of 5 from each predicted value, yielding λ weights of $-2, +4, -2$. Though not required, the student could simplify the computations a little by dividing the contrast weights by 2 to yield the simpler weights of $-1, +2, -1$.

CHAPTER 15

The Analysis of Frequency Tables

Preview Questions

- What is the purpose of chi-square (χ^2)?
- How do I compute 1-*df* chi-squares?
- How do I obtain the *p* value, effect size, and confidence interval?
- What is the relationship between 1-*df* χ^2 and phi?
- How do I deal with tables larger than 2 × 2?
- How do I take the margins into account?

What Is the Purpose of Chi-Square (χ^2)?

To review, in our discussion of the correlation coefficient (Chapter 11), we said that it could be viewed quite directly as a measure of the degree of relationship between two variables. As noted in Chapter 12, when the number of pairs of scores on which *r* is computed is small, a very large *r* (i.e., a substantial effect) can occur quite often by chance even if the true correlation is zero. For this reason, we would like to know for the effect size *r* not only its magnitude but also its confidence interval.

On the one hand, *r* tells us immediately how "big" a relationship there is between two variables, but not how unlikely it is to have occurred by chance. On the other hand, *t* and *F* tell us immediately (i.e., with the help of some tables or a computer program or a scientific calculator) how unlikely it is that a given relationship has occurred by chance, but not how "big" the effect is. However, by taking a simple additional step, described in Chapters 13 and 14, we can compute the size of the relationship that a large *t* or *F* has convinced us is unlikely to have occurred by chance. Thus, *r* gives us the size of the relationship and permits us a further assessment of statistical significance, whereas *t* and *F* give us statistical significance and permit us a further assessment of the size of the relationship.

The statistic we discuss in this final chapter is the **chi-square**, symbolized as χ^2 and pronounced "ki (rhymes with *eye*) square." Invented in 1900 by Karl Pearson (who also invented the product-moment *r*), it is a statistic that, like *t* and *F*, tells us

> ## BOX 15.1 Fisher as Detective
>
> In the 19th century, Gregor Mendel, the legendary Austrian botanist, performed experiments that became the basis of the modern science of genetics. Working with garden peas, he showed that their characteristics could be predicted from the characteristics of their "parents." In a famous piece of scientific detective work, R. A. Fisher (the inventor of the F test and the null hypothesis) later used the chi-square to ask whether Mendel's data may have been manipulated so that they would seem to be more in line with his theory. Fisher used the chi-square as a "goodness-of-fit" test of Mendel's reported findings compared with statistically expected values, and he found Mendel's data *too perfect* to be plausible. Fisher concluded that Mendel had been deceived by a research assistant, who knew what Mendel wanted to find and who manipulated the data *too* well.

(with the aid of a table, computer program, or scientific calculator) how unlikely it is that the relationship investigated has occurred by chance. Also like t and F, chi-square does not tell us immediately about the strength of the relationship between the variables (see also Box 15.1). Just as in the case of t and F, any given value of χ^2 is associated with a stronger degree of relationship when it is based on a smaller number of units or observations. In other words, a relationship must be quite strong to result in a large χ^2 (or t or F) with only a small number of research participants.

We compute χ^2 for tables of independent frequencies (also called *counts*), and therefore χ^2 can be thought of as a comparison of counts. It does its job of testing the relationship between two variables by assessing the discrepancy between the theoretically **expected frequency** (f_e) and the obtained or **observed frequency** (f_o). In other words, χ^2 differs from the other significance tests we have examined in that it can be used for dependent variables that are not scored or scaled. In all the earlier examples of t and F, participants' responses were recorded as scores in such a way that some could be regarded as so many units greater or less than other scores. Because χ^2 is a comparison of counts, it allows us to deal with categories of response that are not easily scaled, ordered, or scored.

One other important point is that chi-square, like F, can be a focused or an omnibus test. You will recall that all t tests are focused tests, whereas F tests with numerator $df = 1$ are focused and F tests with numerator $df > 1$ are omnibus tests. Chi-squares with 1 df are also focused tests, and those with $df > 1$ are omnibus tests. As effect sizes of focused tests are readily interpretable, we will explain not only how to compute the effect size r for a 1-df χ^2, but also strategies for interpreting χ^2 tables of counts when the $df > 1$.

How Do I Compute 1-*df* Chi-Squares?

Imagine we wanted to study the food preferences of students who belong to two eating clubs, the Junk Food Junkies (JFJ) and the Green Earthies (GE). We give each student a menu with a choice of one of two meals: a juicy grilled hamburger with onions, pickles, relish, and barbecue sauce on a sesame seed bun (called a Big Jack) or a grilled soyburger with lettuce and tomato on whole wheat bread. Table 15.1 provides the basic data for computing a simple chi-square from a 2 × 2 table. Membership in the clubs is thought of as the independent variable; each club member falls into one and only one of the four possible cells. In Section A, the observed frequencies are the number of students in that column (JFJ vs. GE eating club) who chose the alternative listed in that row. Suppose we had hypothesized that Junk Food Junkies will tend to prefer a Big Jack and that Green Earthies will tend to prefer a grilled soyburger. As this table shows, of the members of the Junk Food Junkies, 24 chose a Big Jack, and 12 chose the soyburger, and of the members of the Green Earthies, 13 chose a Big Jack, and 30 chose the soyburger.

The following general formula summarizes the steps we will take in applying chi-square to these data:

$$\chi^2 = \sum \frac{(f_o - f_e)^2}{f_e}$$

Table 15.1   Basic Data for 2 × 2 Chi-Square

A. Observed frequencies (f_o)

Food choice	JFJ	GE	Row sums
Big Jack	24	13	37
Soyburger	12	30	42
Column sums	36	43	79

B. Expected frequencies (f_e)

Food choice	JFJ	GE	Row sums
Big Jack	16.861	20.139	37.000
Soyburger	19.139	22.861	42.000
Column sums	36.000	43.000	79.000

C. $(f_o - f_e)^2 / f_e$ values

Food choice	JFJ	GE	Row sums
Big Jack	3.023	2.531	5.554
Soyburger	2.663	2.229	4.892
Column sums	5.686	4.760	10.446

where f_o is the observed frequency in each cell, and f_e is the expected frequency in that cell. This formula instructs us to sum the squared differences between the observed frequencies (f_o) and the expected frequencies (f_e) after first dividing each squared difference by the expected frequency. If the null hypothesis of no relationship between the rows and columns is true, we expect the f_o and f_e values to be similar in magnitude. In other words, observed frequencies that are substantially larger and smaller than the expected frequencies are needed to cast doubt on the null hypothesis, because the value of chi-square will be small when the difference $f_o - f_e$ is small.

To use this formula, we must first determine for each of the observed frequencies the number of "expected" entries, that is, the number that would be expected if the null hypothesis of no relationship between the independent and dependent variables were true. To calculate this expected frequency (f_e) for each cell, we multiply the column total by the row total where that row and that column intersect in that cell. We then divide this quantity by the grand total of entries. That is,

$$f_e = \frac{(\text{Column total})(\text{Row total})}{\text{Grand total}}$$

For example, the upper-left cell in Section A of Table 15.1 is at the intersection of the JFJ column and the Big Jack row. The appropriate totals multiplied together and divided by the grand total are $(36 \times 37)/79 = 16.861$. Section B gives all the expected frequencies computed in this way. These values, row by row, are

$$(36 \times 37)/79 = 16.861$$
$$(43 \times 37)/79 = 20.139$$
$$(36 \times 42)/79 = 19.139$$
$$(43 \times 42)/79 = 22.861$$

As a check on our arithmetic, notice that the row totals, the column totals, and the grand total of all the values in Section B are equal to the corresponding totals of the values in Section A. Substituting in the general formula for chi-square, we add up the $(f_o - f_e)^2/f_e$ values (i.e., for each cell, the square of the difference between the observed and expected frequency divided by the expected frequency), which gives us

$$\chi^2 = \sum \frac{(f_o - f_e)^2}{f_e} = \frac{(24 - 16.861)^2}{16.861} + \frac{(13 - 20.139)^2}{20.139} + \frac{(12 - 19.139)^2}{19.139} + \frac{(30 - 22.861)^2}{22.861}$$
$$= 3.023 + 2.531 + 2.663 + 2.229 = 10.446$$

The $(f_o - f_e)^2/f_e$ values for each cell also appear in Section C of Table 15.1 and are thus a reminder that the total of all those values is the chi-square.

Although the formula we have been using to compute χ^2 will work in any situation, there is an easier way to compute the 1-df chi-square directly from the observed frequencies (f_o) in a 2×2 table:

$$\chi^2_{(1)} = \frac{N(\text{BC} - \text{AD})^2}{(\text{A} + \text{B})(\text{C} + \text{D})(\text{A} + \text{C})(\text{B} + \text{D})}$$

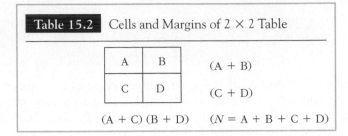

Table 15.2   Cells and Margins of 2 × 2 Table

A	B	(A + B)
C	D	(C + D)

(A + C) (B + D)   (N = A + B + C + D)

where the letters are defined in Table 15.2. For the observed frequencies in Part A of Table 15.1, we find

$$\chi^2_{(1)} = \frac{79[(13 \times 12) - (24 \times 30)]^2}{(37)(42)(36)(43)} = \frac{79(318,096)}{2,405,592} = 10.446$$

How Do I Obtain the p Value, Effect Size, and Confidence Interval?

As is true of t and F, there is also a different chi-square curve for every value of the degrees of freedom. The degrees of freedom (df) of chi-square are defined as

$$df = (\text{rows} - 1)(\text{columns} - 1)$$

that is, the number of rows minus 1 multiplied by the number of columns minus 1. The larger the value of χ^2, the less likely are the observed frequencies to differ from the expected frequencies only by chance. Table 15.3 gives a sample listing of χ^2 values with 1 to 5 degrees of freedom for $p = .10, .05,$ and $.01$. A more comprehensive listing can be found in Table B.4 (p. 401). Notice that χ^2 must be larger than the degrees of freedom to throw doubt on the null hypothesis.

In this example, the 1-df chi-square of 10.446 is larger than the largest value shown for $df = 1$ (6.64 for $p = .01$). The rounded p is approximately .001, which means that a chi-square value this large or larger would occur 1 time in 1,000 repeated samplings if the null hypothesis were true. That is, there is about 1 chance in 1,000 that a chi-square this large would occur if there really were no relationship between organizational membership and food preference (see also Box 15.2).

We now estimate the effect size. As these are frequency data in a 2 × 2 table, it should be obvious that we will estimate the effect size by the **phi coefficient (ϕ)**.

Table 15.3   Chi-Square Values for Significance at .10, .05, and .01

df	$p = .10$	$p = .05$	$p = .01$
1	2.71	3.84	6.64
2	4.60	5.99	9.21
3	6.25	7.82	11.34
4	7.78	9.49	13.28
5	9.24	11.07	15.09

BOX 15.2   Chi-Square and the Null Hypothesis

Reminiscent of F, all chi-square curves begin at zero and range upward to infinity. You will recall that the expected value of t is zero when the null hypothesis is true, and the expected value of F is $df/(df - 2)$, where df are for the denominator mean square (Table 14.4 in Chapter 14). For chi-square distributions, the expected value (when the null hypothesis of no relation is true) is equal to the df defining that chi-square distribution, that is, (rows $-$ 1)(columns $-$ 1). Thus, for chi-squares based on 2×2, 2×3, and 2×4 tables, the average value of the χ^2 obtained if the null hypothesis were true would be 1, 2, and 3, respectively. The maximum possible value of χ^2 is the total N.

In computing phi, we again use the following general formula that was introduced at the end of Chapter 11:

$$\phi = \frac{BC - AD}{\sqrt{(A + B)(C + D)(A + C)(B + D)}}$$

with the letters defined in Table 15.2. Substituting the data in Section A (observed frequencies) of Table 15.1, we find

$$\phi = \frac{(13 \times 12) - (24 \times 30)}{\sqrt{(37)(42)(36)(43)}} = \frac{-564}{1,551} = .36$$

Although we see that the numerator of this phi is negative because of the particular arrangement of the cell counts, we also see that Junk Food Junkiness (scored 1 or 0) is positively correlated with Big Jackness (scored 1 or 0). Because the findings are consistent with our hypothesis, we report the phi as a positive effect size (i.e., $r_{\text{effect size}} = .36$ is in the predicted direction). We can, if we wish, also transform the $r_{\text{effect size}}$ into a binomial effect-size display (BESD) with uniform row and column totals of 100 each.

And finally, we compute a 95% confidence interval around the observed effect using the procedure described in Chapter 12 (although we are not limited to a 95% confidence interval and can choose any level of confidence we feel comfortable with). To review, we first consult Table B.6 (p. 403) to convert our $r_{\text{effect size}} = .36$ into Fisher $z_r = .377$. Step 2 substitutes the value of $N = 79$ in the expression

$$\left(\frac{1}{\sqrt{N - 3}}\right) 1.96 = \left(\frac{1}{\sqrt{79 - 3}}\right) 1.96 = .2248$$

In Step 3, we subtract and add this value to the value in Step 1 to find the lower and upper limits of the Fisher z_r values. The lower limit is $.377 - .2248 = .1522$

(rounded to .15), and the upper limit is .377 + .2248 = .6018 (rounded to .60). In the final step, we convert these scores back into the metric of the effect size correlation using Table B.7 (p. 404). We have 95% confidence that the $r_{effect\ size}$ is between .15 and .54. Had the total sample size been larger, or had we decided to work with 90% confidence, the interval would have been narrower.

What Is the Relationship Between 1-*df* χ^2 and Phi?

If the sample size (N) is not too small ($N > 20$), and if the smallest expected frequency is not too small (e.g., less than 3 or so), we can test the significance of phi coefficients by chi-square tests, because

$$\chi^2 = (\phi^2)(N)$$

Having satisfied these assumptions in our present data set, we substitute in this equation and find

$$\chi^2 = (.3636^2)(79) = 10.444$$

which, not surprisingly, is the same value of chi-square that we obtained before (within rounding error).

Notice that the formula above serves as another example of the conceptual relationship described in Chapter 13, that is,

Significance test = Size of effect $\times$ Size of study

which reminds us that χ^2 (like t and F) is the product of the effect size and the study size. Hence, the larger the effect or the more sampling units in the chi-square table (i.e., the more participants in the study), the greater will be the value of the χ^2. This relationship underscores the importance of doing a power analysis, and it implies that, as in the case of t and F, a relationship must be very strong (i.e., the effect must be substantial) to result in a large chi-square value with only a small number of participants.

More often, we will compute the χ^2 first and then calculate the $r_{effect\ size}$, and as mentioned previously, we report the effect size only when working with chi-squares with $df = 1$. To find the value of the effect size correlation from the 1-*df* chi-square, we use the following formula:

$$\phi = \sqrt{\frac{\chi^2}{N}}$$

which is our operational definition of $r_{effect\ size}$ for any chi-square with $df = 1$. In our continuing example, substituting in this formula yields

$$r_{effect\ size} = \sqrt{\frac{\chi^2}{N}} = \sqrt{\frac{10.446}{79}} = .36$$

which, of course, is the same value of phi that we calculated previously (see also Box 15.3).

BOX 15.3 Computing Effect Sizes From News Reports of Clinical Trials

You can use these formulas to compute effect sizes from the limited information in newspaper stories about clinical trials. For example, a page-one story in the *New York Times* was headlined "Safe Therapy Is Found for High Blood-Clot Risk" (Grady, 2003). The story told of a clinical trial involving 508 patients who were at high risk of blood clots, half of whom had been given low-dose warfarin (Coumadin) and the other half, a placebo. "Of the 253 on placebos, 37 developed blood clots, as compared with only 14 of 255 on the drug" (p. A22). The drug was considered so beneficial that "the study itself was halted ahead of schedule by its sponsor, the National Heart, Lung and Blood Institute, because a safety board found such a benefit to treatment that it would have been unethical to keep giving placebos to people in the control group" (p. A1). What was the size of the obtained effect? From the reported information, we re-create the table of counts

Condition	Blood clot	No blood clot	Total
Placebo	37	216	253
Low-dose warfarin	14	241	255
Total	51	457	508

and calculate $\chi^2 = 11.7$, $p = .0006$, and $r_{\text{effect size}} = .15$. If you would like to learn more about how to calculate and interpret effect sizes in similar research, you will find further discussion in our other work (R. Rosenthal & Rosnow, 2008; Rosnow & Rosenthal, 2007).

How Do I Deal With Tables Larger Than 2 × 2?

When there are many cells in a table of counts, a statistically significant chi-square may be more difficult to interpret than in a 2 × 2 table. Table 15.4 illustrates this situation in a 2 × 4 table that we created by the addition of two new groups to Table 15.1. One new group (designated as PC) consists of 35 members of the Psychology

Table 15.4 Obtained Frequencies (f_o) for 2 × 4 Chi-Square

Food choice	PC	MC	JFJ	GE	Row sums
Big Jack	21	8	24	13	66
Soyburger	14	3	12	30	59
Column sums	35	11	36	43	125

Table 15.5	Expected Frequencies (f_e) and $(f_o - f_e)^2/f_e$ Values				

A. Expected frequencies (f_e)

Food choice	PC	MC	JFJ	GE	Row sums
Big Jack	18.480	5.808	19.008	22.704	66
Soyburger	16.520	5.192	16.992	20.296	59
Column sums	35	11	36	43	125

B. $(f_o - f_e)^2/f_e$ values

Food choice	PC	MC	JFJ	GE	Row sums
Big Jack	0.344	0.827	1.311	4.148	6.630
Soyburger	0.384	0.925	1.467	4.640	7.416
Column sums	0.728	1.752	2.778	8.788	14.046 (grand total)

Club, and the other new group consists of 11 members of the Mathematics Club (MC). The hypothesis is that psychology and mathematics students will be more like Junk Food Junkies than Green Earthies in choosing grilled beef over grilled soy.

Table 15.5 shows in Section A the expected frequencies (f_e) computed from the observed frequencies in Table 15.4. For example, in Table 15.4 we see that 21 of the 35 students who belong to the Psychology Club chose grilled beef. To obtain the expected frequency shown as 18.480 in Table 15.5, we multiply the appropriate row total (shown as 66 in Table 15.4) by the appropriate column total (35) and then divide the product by the total number of observations (125); the result is $(66 \times 35)/125 = 18.480$. Notice that the row and column sums in Section A of Table 15.5 are identical to the corresponding values in Table 15.4.

The calculation of the chi-square with $df = 3$ is accomplished by the general procedure and formula given earlier:

$$\chi^2 = \sum \frac{(f_o - f_e)^2}{f_e}$$

and the entries in Section B of Table 15.5 show the $(f_o - f_e)^2/f_e$ results used in this procedure. The value of this chi-square, then, is the grand total of these cell data, or 14.046. The p value of this chi-square (with 3 df) is .0028 (or in scientific notation, $p = 2.8^{-3}$).

The larger the value of the chi-square, the less likely are the observed frequencies to differ from the expected frequencies only by chance, and this chi-square is interestingly large. However, all it tells us is that *somewhere* in the data the observed frequencies depart noticeably from the expected values. In a way, it reminds us of the case of analysis of variance with $df > 1$ in the numerator of F. That is, a significant omnibus F tells us that there is some difference, but not where that difference may be found. To help us interpret chi-square tables with $df > 1$, several options are available.

One option is to inspect closely the $(f_o - f_e)^2/f_e$ results, as these results show which of the cells contributed most to the overall large chi-square. A large cell entry in such a table indicates that the cell in question is "surprising" to us given the magnitude of the row and column totals associated with that cell. That is, the cell is "unexpected" in terms of chance or likelihood—not necessarily in terms of our research hypothesis, however. In Table 15.5, the largest values in Section B suggest that Green Earthies reacted in a less likely way than would be expected by chance on the basis of the choices of the other three groups.

A second option for dealing with tables of counts larger than 2 × 2 is to subdivide them into smaller tables. In this procedure, called **partitioning of tables**, we compute additional chi-squares based on portions of the overall table. Either a prior theory or hypothesis or the nature of the obtained results can guide our judgment about which additional chi-squares to compute. The number and size of the subtables are guided by certain statistical rules, and the calculations also call for certain statistical adjustments. If you would like to learn more about partitioning large tables of counts, as well as other strategies for dealing with such tables, you will find a detailed discussion in our advanced text (R. Rosenthal & Rosnow, 2008).

For a third option, called **standardizing the margins** (Mosteller, 1968), all that you will need is a calculator and a little patience. This option (which is not as well known as the previous two) enables you to take the size of the row and column totals (or "margins") into account by setting all the row totals equal to each other and all the column totals equal to each other. This process is, however, different from a BESD, which sets the row and column margins equal to 100. To show how standardizing the margins is done, and also what it can tell us, we illustrate this method with our continuing example.

How Do I Take the Margins Into Account?

One of the problems of trying to understand the results in tables of counts larger than 2 × 2 is that our eye is likely to be fooled by the absolute magnitude of the frequencies displayed (the f_o data). Suppose we were to ask of the data in Table 15.4 which group of students is most overrepresented in the Big Jack category. Our eye notes that Psychology Club members (PC) and Junk Food Junkies (JFJ) have the greatest frequency of occurrence in that category. Thus, we might conclude that one of these groups is most overrepresented in the Big Jack category. Our conclusion would be in error, however. The reason is that we looked only at the interior of the table and not, at the same time, at the sums in the row and column margins.

A look at these margins suggests that the PC and JFJ groups *should* have larger obtained frequencies in the Big Jack category than the Mathematics Club members (MC) because the PC and JFJ groups have more members than the MC group. In addition, there are slightly more students in general in the Big Jack category than in the soyburger category. Taking all these margins into account simultaneously would show us that it is actually the MC students who are most overrepresented in the Big Jack category.

Table 15.6   Steps in Standardizing the Margins

A. Results "corrected" for unequal column margins in Table 15.4

Food choice	PC	MC	JFJ	GE	Row sums
Big Jack	.600	.727	.667	.302	2.296
Soyburger	.400	.273	.333	.698	1.704
Column sums	1.000	1.000	1.000	1.000	4.000

B. Results "corrected" for unequal row margins in A (above)

Food choice	PC	MC	JFJ	GE	Row sums
Big Jack	.261	.317	.291	.132	1.001
Soyburger	.235	.160	.195	.410	1.000
Column sums	.496	.477	.486	.542	2.001

C. Final "corrected" results

Food choice	PC	MC	JFJ	GE	Row sums
Big Jack	.517	.657	.589	.238	2.001
Soyburger	.483	.343	.411	.762	1.999
Column sums	1.000	1.000	1.000	1.000	4.000

D. Results in C (above) shown as deviations from an expected value of .500

Food choice	PC	MC	JFJ	GE	Row sums
Big Jack	+.017	+.157	+.089	−.262	+.001
Soyburger	−.017	−.157	−.089	+.262	−.001
Column sums	.000	.000	.000	.000	.000

In large tables of counts, "taking the margins into account" becomes a difficult matter without the use of systematic aids to eye and mind. Standardizing the margins allows us to adjust (or "correct") for the unequal column and row margins and thus provides us with a systematic procedure for taking the unequal margins into account. Table 15.6 illustrates the steps taken to adjust for the unequal column and row margins in Table 15.4.

Section A of Table 15.6 shows the results of the first step in this process, which divides each obtained frequency (in Table 15.4) by its column sum. To obtain the "corrected" values for 21 and 14 in Table 15.4, we divide each by 35. To obtain the "corrected" values for 8 and 3 in Table 15.4, we divide each by 11; and so on. These calculations give us the results in Section A of Table 15.6, where we can see that the column margins have been equalized but that the row margins remain very unequal. To adjust for the latter, we divide each of the new values in Section A by its row margin. To obtain the "corrected" values for .600, .727, .667, and .302, we divide each by 2.296. To obtain the "corrected" values for .400, .273, .333, and .698, we divide each by 1.704. The results appear in Section B of Table 15.6.

Section B has equalized the row margins, at least within rounding error, but the column margins are no longer equal. By now, we know what to do about that: Simply divide each entry of Section B by its new column margin. That process will equalize the column margins but *may* make our new row margins unequal. We repeat this procedure until further repetitions (called *iterations*) no longer affect the margins. For these data, the final results obtained by successive iterations are shown in Section C of Table 15.6, which shows margins equalized within rounding error and allows us to interpret the table entries without worrying about the confusing effects of variations in margins. It clearly shows that, in the Big Jack category, the Mathematics Club (MC) is overrepresented most, whereas in the soyburger category, the Green Earthies (GE) are the ones most overrepresented.

There is one additional step we can take to throw the results into bolder relief: We can show the cell entries as deviations from the values we would expect if there were no differences whatever among the groups in their representation in the Big Jack and soyburger categories. If there were no such differences, and given the margins of Section C, all the values in the table would be .500. In forming our final table, we subtract this expected value of .500 from each entry in Section C; the results are shown in Section D of Table 15.6.

The interpretation of Section D is fairly direct. Besides the big difference between the Green Earthies, who are overrepresented very heavily in the soyburger category, and all the other groups, which are more modestly overrepresented in the Big Jack category, there are other differences that help us to interpret our earlier results. For example, even though some of the sample sizes are too small to be very stable, we can also raise some tentative questions about differences among the three groups overrepresented in the Big Jack category. The Mathematics Club is substantially more overrepresented in the Big Jack category than the Psychology Club, which is virtually not overrepresented at all. The Junk Food Junkies fall almost exactly midway between the PC and MC groups in their degree of overrepresentation in the Big Jack category.

Because of the small sample sizes, the differences among these three groups (PC, MC, JFJ) are not significant statistically, but with larger sample sizes they might be. In any case, the purpose of the procedure of standardizing the margins is to highlight the differences among groups, whether these differences achieve statistical significance or not.

A Journey Begun

The *beginning* in the title of this book is intended to have a double meaning. It not only describes the level of the text but also conveys the idea of a journey. For some students, the journey embarked on at the start of this course is now complete. For others, the journey has just begun. In either case, it should be recognized that, particularly in some of their statistical aspects, the design of experiments and the comparison of research conditions constitute a very specialized and highly developed field. The purpose of Chapters 10–15 was to further your understanding of the logic and meaning of the statistical procedures and concepts associated with the application of the scientific method, an understanding that may have been initi-ated in a basic statistics course. A thorough knowledge of the characteristics of both the data obtained and the statistics used is assumed by professional re-searchers to be an essential aspect of sound scientific practice. Whether the conclu-sion of this chapter represents the start or the end of your journey in social or behavioral research, you should now have a deeper understanding of the applica-bility and limits of the scientific method. Many of the procedures you have learned about in these final chapters can be used to address questions you have about the scientific results reported in newspapers and magazines (or that you hear about in chat groups on the Internet) and to address many everyday questions that can be framed in ways that will allow you to reach beyond other people's conclusions and, using empirical reasoning, decide for yourself what is true.

Summary of Ideas

1. *Chi-square* (χ^2) is used to test the degree of agreement between the data actually obtained (or *the observed frequency*) and the data expected (*the expected frequency*) under a particular hypothesis (e.g., the null hypothesis).
2. The expected value of chi-square when the null hypothesis is true is equal to the degrees of free-dom defining the particular chi-square distribution.
3. The effect size r for 2×2 chi-squares (i.e., focused chi-squares) is phi (ϕ), which is computed directly from chi-square by

$$r_{\text{effect size}} = \phi = \sqrt{\frac{\chi^2}{N}}$$

and can be used, for example, to estimate effect sizes in news reports of clinical trials (Box 15.3).
4. We compute the confidence interval and use the BESD to interpret the effect size as described in previous chapters.
5. If the sample size is not too small, and if the smallest expected frequency is not too small, we test the significance of the effect size r by $\chi^2 = (\phi^2)(N)$, which also reflects the conceptual relationship that Significance test = Size of effect $\times$ Size of study.
6. As in the case of t and F, a relationship must be quite strong to result in a large chi-square with only a small number of sampling units (also Box 15.2).
7. One option in interpreting larger tables of counts is to examine the $(f_o - f_e)^2/f_e$ results, because they show which of the cells in the table of counts contributed most to the overall chi-square.
8. A second option is to *partition* the larger table of counts into smaller (e.g., 2×2) chi-square tables (discussed in our advanced text).
9. A third option is to *standardize the margins* (totals) by making all row margins equal and by, at the same time, making all column margins equal.

Key Terms

chi-square (χ^2)   p. 351
expected frequency (f_e)   p. 352

observed frequency (f_o)   p. 352
partitioning of tables   p. 360

phi coefficient (ϕ)   p. 355
standardizing the margins   p. 360

Multiple-Choice Questions for Review

1. Chi-square differs from significance tests such as t and F in that it is specifically designed for use when (a) there are multiple dependent variables; (b) there are multiple independent variables; (c) the dependent variables are not ordered, scored, or scaled beyond two levels; (d) none of the above.

2. Chi-squares are calculated from the differences between _____ and _____ frequencies. (a) expected, obtained; (b) theoretical, operational; (c) between, within; (d) none of the above

3. In the following 2 × 2 table, what is the expected frequency in the upper-left cell? (a) 1; (b) 4; (c) 19; (d) 25

	Democrats	Republicans
Males	4	1
Females	1	19

4. A student at Kutztown University examines a 2 × 2 table of counts and calculates the chi-square to be 6. According to Table 15.3, what is the appropriate p value? (a) $< .10$; (b) $< .05$; (c) $< .01$; (d) cannot be determined from this information

5. The same student examines a 4 × 2 table of counts and calculates the chi-square to be 6. According to Table 15.3, what is the appropriate p value? (a) $> .10$; (b) $< .10$; (c) $< .05$; (d) cannot be determined from this information

6. The effect size measure typically associated with 1-df chi-square is _____. (a) ϕ; (b) f_e; (c) f_o; (d) d

7. $\chi^2 = $ _____ × _____. (a) ϕ^2, N; (b) row total, column total; (c) rows $- 1$, columns $- 1$; (d) none of the above

8. Chi-square tables are also called tables of _____. (a) means; (b) ANOVAs; (c) counts; (d) unequaled margins

9. A study is conducted that yields a 3 × 4 chi-square table. The overall chi-square is found to be significant. To interpret the results more fully, the researcher decides to examine a table of $(f_o - f_e)^2/f_e$ scores. In this table, the cells with _____ numbers indicate "unexpected" results. (a) small; (b) positive; (c) no; (d) large

10. A study is conducted that yields a 3 × 4 chi-square table. To interpret the results more fully, the researcher uses a procedure setting the row and column totals equal to each other. This procedure is called (a) partitioning; (b) examining a table of $(f_o - f_e)^2/f_e$ scores; (c) standardizing the margins; (d) binary analysis.

Discussion Questions for Review

1. A clinical psychologist at the University of Alabama examines the relation of three types of psychopathology to socioeconomic status (SES) in 100 subjects. Her table of counts is

SES	Schizophrenic	Neurotic	Depressed
High	5	5	20
Medium	5	15	20
Low	10	10	10

How should she test the hypothesis that this table of counts is significantly different from what would be expected by chance if there were no relation between these variables? How many degrees of freedom will her statistic have? In what way will the p value she obtains address only incompletely her wish to examine the relationship between type of psychopathology and SES?

2. A Brigham Young University student obtained the following data, where the numbers are frequencies (counts). How should she plan to standardize the margins?

Annual carrot	Visual acuity		
consumption (lb.)	High	Average	Low
11–20	9	3	1
1–10	5	8	2
0	1	8	7

3. A researcher at Rochester Institute of Technology asks 10 engineering students each from the freshman, sophomore, junior, and senior classes whether they plan to attend graduate school. The results are

	Frosh	Sophs	Juniors	Seniors
Want advanced degree	7	6	3	1
Want out of school	3	4	7	9

How many degrees of freedom would the chi-square for this table have? How should the researcher calculate the expected frequencies? What is the nature of the relation between year in college and wanting an advanced degree?

4. Three students at the College of New Jersey each conduct the same study with the following results:

	χ^2 (1-df)	N	p
Student 1	2.00	20	.16
Student 2	3.00	30	.08
Student 3	4.00	40	.05

Student 3 claims a significant relationship between the two levels of her independent variable (0, 1) and the two levels of her dependent variable (0, 1). Students 1 and 2 chide her, saying that they have not found a significant effect and that her results are therefore undependable and unreplicable. How should Student 3 reply?

Answers to Review Questions

Multiple-Choice Questions

1. c	3. a	5. a	7. a	9. d
2. a	4. b	6. a	8. c	10. c

Discussion Questions

1. She would compute a χ^2 for which the df would be (rows − 1)(columns − 1) = (3 − 1)(3 − 1) = 4. Because her χ^2 is based on $df > 1$ (i.e., $df = 4$), its p value will tell her nothing about the nature of the relationship between type of psychopathology and SES. She should therefore consider inspecting the $(f_o - f_e)^2/f_e$ results, partitioning her table, and/or standardizing the margins.

2. Following the procedures of Table 15.6, she would arrive at this approximate solution:

Annual carrot	Visual acuity			
consumption (lb.)	High	Average	Low	Sum
11–20	.64	.20	.14	.98
1–10	.31	.45	.23	.99
0	.05	.34	.62	1.01
Sum	1.00	.99	.99	2.98

She can display these results as deviations from an expected value of .33 (i.e., the total of 3.00 divided by 9 cells = 3/9 = .33), yielding the following:

Annual carrot	Visual acuity			
consumption (lb.)	High	Average	Low	Sum
11–20	.31	−.13	−.19	−.01
1–10	−.02	.12	−.10	.00
0	−.28	.01	.29	.02
Sum	+.01	.00	.00	.01

These results show very clearly that high-visual-acuity subjects are relatively overrepresented among high carrot consumers, whereas low-visual-acuity subjects are relatively overrepresented among low carrot consumers. As a corollary, we see that high-visual-acuity subjects are underrepresented among low carrot consumers, whereas low-visual-acuity subjects are relatively underrepresented among high carrot consumers. Unless this was a randomized experiment, the student should be cautious about inferring causality. Although it is possible that eating more carrots leads to better visual acuity, it may also be that better visual acuity leads to finding more carrots in the darker regions of the refrigerator.

3. The df for this χ^2 are obtained from (rows − 1)(columns − 1) = (2 − 1)(4 − 1) = 3. The expected frequencies are obtained from

$$f_e = \frac{(\text{Row total})(\text{Column total})}{\text{Grand total}}$$

which, for these data, results in

	Frosh	Sophs	Juniors	Seniors
Want degree	4.25	4.25	4.25	4.25
Want out	5.75	5.75	5.75	5.75

With each advancing year, a greater proportion of students want out, a result shown clearly in the final results, in deviation form, of standardizing the margins:

	Frosh	Sophs	Juniors	Seniors
Want degree	.26	.20	−.10	−.36
Want out	−.26	−.20	.10	.36

Once again, we must be careful in our interpretation of the results. Because this is a cross-sectional study, we cannot distinguish differences in year at college from cohort differences (discussed in Chapter 8).

4. Student 3 should ask that all three students compute the effect size correlation that is associated with their results, using the following formula:

$$r_{\text{effect size}} = \phi = \sqrt{\frac{\chi^2}{N}}$$

When the three students compute their r values, they all find exactly the same magnitude of effect ($r_{\text{effect size}} = .316$). Student 3 shows thereby that the three studies agree with one another remarkably well.

APPENDIX A

Communicating Your Research Findings

Research Reports and Poster Presentations

For scientists in all fields, the research process is not complete until results have been reported in a peer-reviewed journal. Students are also required to report their research findings, but the primary audience is usually the instructor. It is rare for undergraduate students to try to have their research findings published, as the rejection rates of many peer-reviewed journals in psychology and related fields are daunting (70%, 80%, or even higher). Even professional researchers have experienced rejection, and they do not lightly encourage students to strike out on their own without the skilled guidance of an experienced hand. If, however, you are that rare individual encouraged by your instructor to submit a paper to a journal, then your instructor will also caution you about the precise style required for journal submissions. The standard of most (but not all) psychology journals in the United States is the *Publication Manual of the American Psychological Association* (hereafter called the APA manual), published by the American Psychological Association in 2001. The APA manual also has a Web site that you can visit to see what is new in APA style (www.apastyle.org).

The purpose of this appendix is not to show you how to prepare a journal manuscript, but to show you how to communicate your research findings in a written report for your instructor and, if applicable, in a poster presentation for a wider audience. It is becoming increasingly common for students to present their research results in poster presentations as well as in written reports. If you plan to present a poster at a local or regional meeting, it is important to familiarize yourself with any special requirements or guidelines of the sponsoring organization. The guidelines and tips that we list in this appendix were borrowed from Rosnow and Rosnow's *Writing Papers in Psychology: A Student Guide to Research Reports, Literature Reviews, Proposals, Posters, and Handouts* (2006). Although these guidelines are in the spirit of the APA manual, there are certain departures from strict APA style, such as an appendix for your raw data and calculations. The reason for this difference is that you are writing a paper for your instructor to evaluate and grade, and the needs of instructors are different from journal editors' requirements.

Getting Organized

Before we turn to the procedure of writing a report, we discuss the most difficult step for many students: getting started. Clearly, it would be advantageous to begin early to ensure that your task will not be rushed and that you will have ample time to revise and polish your work well before the due date. One reason that students have trouble getting going is that they are unclear about the assignment. Thus, before you do anything else, make sure you know what is expected of you. You can talk with other students to get their impressions, but that approach may stress you out even more. The best person for you to consult is the instructor, teaching assistant, or grader to make sure that you are on the right track.

Besides knowing the form of the final report, keep the following questions in mind as you get organized:

- When is the final report due?
- How will it be graded?
- Will there be an opportunity to obtain feedback as the project progresses?
- Is there a specified length for the final report?
- Are intermediate drafts or outlines required, and when are they due?
- Are sample reports available to provide a further idea of what is expected?

Questions about due dates are especially important because missing deadlines (just like unexcused absences on a job) is a sure way to elicit disapproval. If you are someone who has a hard time meeting deadlines, remember that instructors have heard all the excuses. Try keeping a pocket calendar of self imposed "deadlines" and checking it frequently to see what your tasks are over the next several days. If that approach fails, try posting scheduled dates and appointments over your mirror or desk, or anywhere else you routinely look.

To help you keep on schedule, you can jot down both self-imposed and assigned dates, such as

- Completion of preliminary literature search for proposal
- Completion of proposal for research
- Completion of ethics review
- Implementation of data collection
- Completion of data collection
- Completion of data analysis
- Completion of an outline for first draft
- Completion of first draft
- Completion of revised draft(s)
- Completion of final typed manuscript (and poster and handout, if required)

Sample Research Report

Exhibit A.1 shows what a research report submitted as a course requirement looks like. It is a good idea to study this annotated report before you continue. We will focus on each of the following eight parts and provide you with simple guidelines and tips:

Title page

Abstract

Introduction

Method

Results

Discussion

References

End material (e.g., tables, figures, appendixes)

Title Page

We turn now to the structure and form of your research report, beginning with the title page. Notice that the page number in the upper-right corner is accompanied (on every page) by the words "Biasing Effects." These words are called *page headers*, and their purpose is to make it easy for the instructor or grader to identify each manuscript page if any pages become separated. The APA rule is that page headers should consist of two or three words from the title. The other kinds of information shown on the title page of Mary's sample paper are her name (the *byline*), the number and name of the course or sequence for which the paper is being submitted, the name of the instructor, and the date the paper will be submitted.

Abstract

Although the *abstract* (or summary) appears on page 2, it is written after you have completed the rest of your paper, as it is a distillation of the important points covered in the body of your report. It tells the reader what your research is about in one succinct paragraph. In the sample report, Mary gives a synopsis of the background of her research, her hypothesis, the way she tested it, the results, and a very brief description of the way her discussion section will proceed. The APA rule is that abstracts not exceed 960 characters and spaces (approximately 120 words), but instructors are usually more lenient about the length of abstracts in student reports.

Remember that the purpose of the abstract is to let the instructor quickly anticipate what to expect in your report. With that objective in mind, here are some questions to guide you when planning your abstract:

- What was the problem that I studied or the objective of my study?
- What principal method did I use (a laboratory experiment, a survey questionnaire, judges as raters, etc.)?
- Who were the research participants (i.e., what were their pertinent characteristics)?
- What were the major results?
- What primary conclusions and implications appear in the discussion section?

Introduction

The introduction (the first section after the abstract page) has no lead (as the other sections do) but begins by repeating the full title of the paper (not the student's name, however). This section emphasizes linking ideas to past research and should lead into your

(*text continues on p. 382*)

The title is
succinct, yet
adequately
descriptive.

The student's
name and
contact infor-
mation ap-
pear below
the title.

Pages are
numbered
consecutively,
beginning
with the title
page, and
contain a
short
heading.

Biasing Effects 1

Biasing Effects of Knowledge of Drug-Testing

Results on Bail Judgments

Mary Jones

(e-mail address or other contact information)

Insert course
and instructor
and the date
the paper is
turned in.

(Number and Name of Course)

Instructor: Professor Bruce Rind

(Date the Research Report Is Submitted)

Exhibit A.1 Mary Jones's Research Report

Study on attractiveness

The abstract begins on a new page.

Biasing Effects 2

Abstract

This simulation experiment was inspired by legal arguments
about mandatory drug testing of all suspects on arrest.
One argument was that knowledge of this testing would
have biasing effects on bail judgments in legal
proceedings, whereas another argument was that drug use
information would have no prejudicial effects. Drawing
on correspondent inference theory, my hypothesis was that
harsher bail judgments are more likely when judges are
informed that the defendant has tested positive for drug
usage than when no testing information is made available.
The participants were college students, who were randomly
given one of two scenarios about a defendant who had been
arrested as a suspected burglar. The experimental scenario
told that the defendant's blood test while he was in
custody revealed that he had very recently used drugs. In
the control scenario, the drug test information was
omitted. The students were asked to imagine that they
were the bail judge and to set a dollar amount from \$0
to \$50,000. The data were analyzed by an independent-
sample t and afterward, because of heterogeneity of
variance, by Satterthwaite's adjusted t. Both results
were in the direction hypothesized and statistically
significant, and $r_{effect\ size}$ was .34. Methodological
limitations and ideas for follow-up research are
discussed.

Abstract is not indented.

The abstract tells why the research was important and worth doing, what was hypothesized, what the study involved, what the results were, and what else appears in the discussion.

Double spacing leaves one line between each line of type.

Although the left margin is even, the right margin is ragged.

Within the constraints of limited resources & time (thus)

Biasing Effects 3

Biasing Effects of Knowledge of Drug-Testing

Results on Bail Judgments

        McGuire (1997) listed various ways in which ideas for
research and theory arise, two of which are serendipity
and the resolution of conflicting views. Both played a
hand in the inspiration for this research. While watching
TV one evening, I was channel surfing when I happened to
see a discussion between lawyers who were arguing over
whether drug testing should be performed on all persons
arrested. One lawyer stated that mandatory drug testing
would be a valuable weapon for law enforcement officials
in fighting the drug war. Another lawyer countered that
mandatory drug testing could pose a threat to individual
rights because positive results would unfairly bias
judges' decisions on how much bail to impose, even in
cases in which there is no connection between the drug
usage and the crime committed. The first lawyer then
insisted that such information would have no effect on a
bail judge's decision. This difference in views (i.e.,
whether or not there might be a biasing effect on bail
judgments) whetted my curiosity. Attribution theory,
particularly an aspect known as correspondent inference
theory, provided a basis for a testable hypothesis.

        The main task of the bail judge is to set bail at a
level that will make it likely the defendant will appear
for trial. In making this decision, the judge will perhaps
consider factors suggestive of the defendant's traits,
with the idea that some traits should predict whether the
defendant will skip bail or show up for the trial.
Attribution theory is specifically concerned with factors
that influence how observers infer the traits of

Appendix A

Biasing Effects 4

particular actors (cf. Jones & Davis, 1965; Kelley, 1972) and how this trait information is used to make decisions or judgments regarding actors (Baron & Byrne, 1987). In this vein, Jones and Davis's correspondent inference theory provided a conceptual framework for the description of how observers go about inferring traits of actors. According to this theory, observers focus primarily on certain types of observed behavior to infer traits on the assumption that only certain actions are indicative of some traits. Three questions that observers ask themselves, according to Jones and Davis, are (a) Was the behavior freely chosen? (b) Did the behavior produce uncommon effects? and (c) Was the behavior low in social desirability?

The third question seemed especially relevant to the controversial issue of interest in this research. On the assumption that drug usage is generally held to be low in social desirability (i.e., in our society), it seemed to follow from correspondent inference theory that observers are likely to concentrate on this form of socially undesirable behavior in judging actors' traits. Once observers have inferred traits, they tend to use this knowledge to predict the actors' future behavior as well as to assess and guide their own actions, decisions, and judgments regarding those actors (Baron & Byrne, 1987). The hypothesis in this study was that having information about positive results from a drug test is likely to result in harsher bail judgments.

Method

Participants and Study Design

A sample of 31 male and female undergraduate students participated in this study. With the permission of the

Marginal notes:

Citations buttress the introduction.

Connecting points are lettered for clarity.

The introduction concludes with your hypotheses, or theoretical expectations, prior to your seeing the findings.

First-level headings are centered.

Second-level headings are flush left and italicized.

The introduction gives a concise history and background of the topic, and it leads to the question of interest.

An ampersand appears in parentheses, where *and* is used otherwise.

Biasing Effects 5

instructor and the consent of all the students who
participated, an experiment was conducted during a
scheduled class meeting. Students were randomly assigned to
either an experimental (n = 15) or a control (n = 16)
condition. Each student received a one-page questionnaire,
the questionnaires having been mixed together and then
administered to all the students simultaneously. At the
conclusion of the study, the students were fully debriefed.

The Questionnaire

The questionnaire asked for the respondent's age,
sex, year in college, grade point average (GPA), and
major. Next came the instruction to "please read the
following paragraph carefully, and then answer the
question that follows it." In the experimental condition,
the paragraph stated:

> A man was arrested as a suspected burglar. He fit
> the description of a man seen running from the
> burglarized house. While in custody the man
> submitted to a blood test, and it was determined
> that he had very recently used drugs.

In the control condition, the last sentence in the
scenario above was deleted, and the following sentence was
substituted:

> The man spent enough time in custody to receive two
> meals and make three phone calls.

Immediately after either scenario was the following item:
"If you were the bail judge, what bail would you set?
Choose a dollar amount from $0 to $50,000."

Results

The overall findings are given in Table 1, which
shows that the mean judgment of the students exposed to

Second-level heading is flush left in italics.

Block quotations are indented five to seven spaces from the left margin.

Centered first-level heading.

Sample sizes of subgroups are denoted by italicized lower-case n.

Brief quotations incorporated into the text are enclosed in double quotation marks.

The results are a major section of the text and thus follow without a page break.

Appendix A

Biasing Effects 6

the drug information was higher than the mean judgment of those exposed to the neutral scenario. The independent-sample t test on these data yielded $t = 2.08$, $df = 29$, $p = .023$ one-tailed, $r_{effect\ size} = .36$, and a 95% confidence interval around the effect size ranging from .01 to .63. One assumption when the t test is used to compare two means is that population variances of the samples are equal, but the variances shown in Table 1 are noticeably unequal. In a standard statistical procedure recommended by the instructor, the result of dividing the larger of the two variances (S^2) by the smaller of the two variances yielded $F(14, 15) = 9.0, p = 6.3^{-5}$, indicating heterogeneity of variance.

On the instructor's suggestion, two ways of dealing with heterogeneity of variance were considered: One involved transformation of the raw scores, and the other was a procedure known as Satterthwaite's method. The latter procedure was chosen (illustrated in Rosenthal, Rosnow, & Rubin, 2000), and the calculations are shown in the appendix at the end of this report. By this method, the t test is calculated in a slightly different way, and the degrees of freedom are adjusted. Both the t test result and the effect size r were similar to the results above, with $t = 2.03$, $df = 16$, $p = .03$ one-tailed, $r_{effect\ size} = .34$. The 95% confidence interval of the obtained effect size r ranged from $r = -.02$ to .62, also similar to the previous result above. The reason this confidence interval crosses slightly into the negative side is that a 95% confidence interval has .025 as the one-tailed p, and the obtained p in this case did not quite make the .025 (i.e., it was .03).

Margin notes:

Statistical test, degrees of freedom, significance, effect size, and confidence interval.

F with numerator $df > 1$ is an omnibus test; therefore, no effect size is reported.

Degrees of freedom are 14 for the numerator and 15 for the denominator of the F ratio.

Letters used as statistical symbols are italicized: t, F, n, df, S^2, p, and so forth.

Biasing Effects 7

Discussion

The discussion begins by reminding us of the study's purpose and the main findings.

One fundamental purpose of our criminal justice system is to be just and unbiased in all of its aspects. The results of my experiment were in the hypothesized direction, indicating that harsher bail judgments were more likely when the "judges" were informed that the defendant had tested positive for drug usage. This finding implies that the goal of being just and unbiased may be jeopardized if drug testing and the reporting of its results are mandated by law. This biasing effect can be avoided if judges are not given access to the results of the drug testing.

The discussion, as it is another major section of the text, does not require a break.

However, because I was unable to use real judges and had to use college students, the results may not be applicable to actual bail judges. Future research can be designed to address this problem of external validity and also to assess the participants' inferences of corresponding traits from socially undesirable behavior. It is interesting that, although the participants seemingly judged the suspect more harshly when the drug information was included, there was no logical connection between the drug usage and the burglary. Perhaps the participants were drawing on a stereotype to assume that the association was likely, because the media often report property crimes that are motivated by the need to get money to purchase drugs. Future research could use other crime scenarios that are not stereotypically associated with drugs to determine whether biasing effects occur and are general in nature. Finally, this paper does not address the legal issue that this kind of testing of someone "innocent until proved guilty" is possibly unconstitutional, that is, on the grounds that it is a violation of civil rights.

Mary gives the limitations of her study, and thus shows that she has a good understanding of the limited generalizability of her findings.

Biasing Effects 8

References

Book with
two authors.

Baron, R. A., & Byrne, D. (1987). *Social psychology: Understanding human interaction.* Boston: Allyn & Bacon.

Chapter in an
edited book
in a series of
volumes.

Jones, E. E., & Davis, K. E. (1965). From acts to dispositions: The attribution process in person perception. In L. Berkowitz (Ed.), *Advances in experimental social psychology* (Vol. 2, pp. 219-266). New York: Academic Press.

"Ed." for one
editor.

Kelley, H. H. (1972). Attribution in social interaction. In E. E. Jones, D. E. Kanouse, R. E. Nisbett, S. Valins, & B. Weiner (Eds.), *Attribution: Perceiving the causes of behavior* (pp. 1-26). Morristown, NJ: General Learning Press.

Page numbers
of chapter in
edited book.

"Eds." for
more than
one editor.

McGuire, W. J. (1997). Creative hypothesis generating in psychology: Some useful heuristics. *Annual Review of Psychology, 48,* 1-30.

Book with
three authors.

Rosenthal, R., Rosnow, R. L., & Rubin, D. B. (2000). *Contrasts and effect sizes in behavioral research: A correlational approach.* Cambridge, UK: Cambridge University Press.

The references begin on a new page.

Ampersand before the last author's name.

Journal titles and book titles are italicized, but not titles of articles or chapters.

Biasing Effects 9

Table number and title are flush left.

Table 1

Mean, Variability, and Number of Participants in Each Group

Measure	Experimental group	Control group
Mean	$16,146.67	$6,990.63
S	16,645.07	5,549.60
S^2	277,058,355.31	30,798,060.16
n	15	16

Where means are reported, an associated measure of variability is also reported.

Tables appear after the references in the APA style, each table on a separate page.

Tables are used to present information efficiently.

Appendix A

Appendix

The following table shows the raw scores (i.e., the individual bail judgments) of 31 college students who were
randomly assigned to an experimental or a control group:

Experimental group	Control group
$10,000	$10,000
12,500	4,000
2,000	5,000
50,000	350
20,000	5,000
200	15,000
500	500
30,000	5,000
2,000	500
10,000	1,500
5,000	10,000
10,000	10,000
50,000	20,000
30,000	5,000
10,000	10,000
–	10,000

Shown below are basic equations and my calculations,
starting with the independent-sample t test:

$$t = \frac{M_1 - M_2}{\sqrt{\left(\frac{1}{n_1} + \frac{1}{n_2}\right) s^2}} = \frac{16,146.67 - 6,990.63}{\sqrt{\left(\frac{1}{15} + \frac{1}{16}\right) 149,682,340.575}} = 2.08$$

and the effect size r computed from t:

$$r_{\text{effect size}} = \sqrt{\frac{t^2}{t^2 + df}} = \sqrt{\frac{(2.08)^2}{(2.08)^2 + 29}} = .36$$

Although these data are typed, check with your instructor about whether handwritten data and equations are permissible in the appendix of your report.

The appendix of the student's report begins on a new page.

Showing the raw data and the computations of the study helps the instructor to grade the paper fairly.

For the Satterthwaite-adjusted t, I used the following
equation found in Rosenthal, Rosnow, & Rubin (2000):

$$t_{\text{Satterthwaite}} = \frac{M_1 - M_2}{\sqrt{\dfrac{S_1^2}{n_1} + \dfrac{S_2^2}{n_2}}} = \frac{16{,}146.67 - 6{,}990.63}{\sqrt{\dfrac{277{,}058{,}355.305}{15} + \dfrac{30{,}798{,}060.16}{16}}} = 2.03$$

and

$$df_{\text{Satterthwaite}} = \frac{\left(\dfrac{S_1^2}{n_1} + \dfrac{S_2^2}{n_2}\right)^2}{\left[\dfrac{\left(\dfrac{S_1^2}{n_1}\right)^2}{n_1 - 1}\right] + \left[\dfrac{\left(\dfrac{S_2^2}{n_2}\right)^2}{n_2 - 1}\right]} = \frac{\left(\dfrac{277{,}058{,}355.305}{15} + \dfrac{30{,}798{,}060.16}{16}\right)^2}{\left[\dfrac{\left(\dfrac{277{,}058{,}355.305}{15}\right)^2}{15 - 1}\right] + \left[\dfrac{\left(\dfrac{30{,}798{,}060.16}{16}\right)^2}{16 - 1}\right]} = 16.90$$

The student
has included
an expla-
nation of a
particular
procedure,
including the
citation of an
advanced text
that she
consulted.

As indicated in Rosenthal et al. (2000), I truncated the
16.90 df to the next lower integer, 16. The t of 2.03, with
df = 16, has a p of .030 one-tailed. To obtain the effect
size r, I used the t value of 1.96 associated with the
adjusted p value noted above (p = .030 one-tailed) and
used the original degrees of freedom (29), as indicated in
Rosenthal et al.:

$$r_{\text{effect size}} = \sqrt{\frac{t^2}{t^2 + df}} = \sqrt{\frac{(1.96)^2}{(1.96)^2 + 29}} = .34$$

Appendix A

hypotheses or research questions. Basically, it describes the point of the research and also provides a framework for your later description of the method used. The idea of writing a strong introduction is to lead the reader to the thought, "Yes, of course, that's what this researcher *had* to do to test this hypothesis." Mary begins by describing a debate she happened to see on television, which puts her research in a practical light that is both compelling and socially significant. She develops her hypothesis in such a way that the method section (which follows) will seem a natural consequence of the introduction.

Here are some questions to help you plan the introduction:

- What got me thinking about this study?
- How did I come up with my working hypothesis, and what did I expect to find?
- What terms do I need to define for the reader who may be unfamiliar with this area?
- Do I need to define any terms for special reasons, because they are used differently in different contexts or because I use them in a new way?
- How does the study build on, or derive from, other studies?
- Is each of my hypotheses clearly explained and justified in terms of its logical basis?

Outlining is a good way to organize your thoughts before you begin writing. However, if you did not outline the introduction (or any other section) before you drafted it, a useful trick is to outline the introduction (or the whole paper) after it is written. Just list, in sentence fragments or phrases, the main ideas and what further ideas detail or substantiate those main ideas, also in sentence fragments or phrases. This process will show you whether you have proceeded logically or if there are any lapses in logic that need to be corrected.

Incidentally, notice that Mary uses the personal pronouns *I* ("I was channel surfing . . .") and *my* ("whetted my curiosity") in her opening paragraph. Not all instructors find this usage acceptable, however, preferring instead that students use the third person rather than the first person in attributing an action to themselves, for example, referring to yourself as "the experimenter" (third person) rather than as "I" (first person). The APA manual cautions (pp. 37–38), however, that using the third person "may give the impression that you did not take part in your own study."

Method

In the method section, you describe the procedures used and give a detailed account of the pertinent characteristics of the research participants. Although we use *subjects* and *participants* interchangeably, the APA manual suggests that you call the subjects of the study *participants, individuals, college students, children,* or *respondents,* because the term *subjects* strikes many people as "too impersonal." The APA manual's rule of thumb is to describe the participants at whatever is the appropriate level of specificity, but to be sensitive to the labels you choose.

A particular problem is avoiding sexist language in describing the participants. It would be a mistake, for example, to use the word *man* as a general term for both men and women, as the word creates a mental picture that is simply inaccurate (Dumond, 1990). On the other hand, if the subjects were only men, it would be misleading *not* to describe them by sex (and by other relevant distinguishing characteristics, such as age and level of education). When this issue first gained prominence some years ago, writers began to coin contrived words such as "s/he" and "he/she" to avoid sexist language when referring to both sexes. You can avoid awkward terms like these by using plural pronouns when you are referring to both genders. The basic rule, however, is not to mislead people by creating the wrong mental picture.

Notice in Mary's paper that the method section is divided into two parts, each with a side heading. She begins by describing the participants and giving an overall picture of the design of the study. She also tells how the two forms of her questionnaire were distributed so that both she and the participants were blind to which treatment any person received. She ends up noting that she debriefed the participants. She then gives a detailed description of the questionnaire she created. In other reports, the method section may need more than two parts, depending on how complicated the study is.

Notice also that Mary's paper uses two formats of headings: center and flush left. The center heading is used to separate the paper into major sections, is written in uppercase and lowercase letters, and is not italicized. To subdivide the parts of the method section, Mary uses subheadings placed at the left margin, italicized, and typed in uppercase and lowercase. If she had wanted to use a further level of subheadings, they would have been indented, underlined, and followed by a period, with the body of the text then immediately following the heading.

Results

You describe your data in the results section, beginning with the main findings, those most relevant to your hypotheses. Try to strike a balance between being discursive and being overly precise. You might, as Mary does, present the results in a table or a graphic (as described in Chapter 10). Notice that Mary's table appears on a separate page after her reference section, that it is numbered and labeled, and that this labeling includes specific row and column headings. Except for some reports of single-case studies (see the discussion of single-case studies in Chapter 8), you are usually not expected to show individual scores in this section.

Mary's results section tells how she analyzed the data to test her hypothesis. She reports the significance test, including that her p value is one-tailed, and mentions the effect size r and 95% confidence interval. She then mentions that she consulted with the instructor about an appropriate statistical procedure for dealing with heterogeneity of variance, and she gives these results as well. She also mentions that her calculations are shown in the appendix at the end of her report.

A trick to help you pull the results together before you start writing is to set down a list of your statistical findings. Divide the list into coherent sets of results, and then decide the sequence according to their order of importance or relevance to your hypotheses, questions, and objectives. Experienced authors try to anticipate the questions that readers may have, particularly those about ambiguous results that call for clarification or further analysis. Here are some questions to help you structure this section:

- What were the different results, and what is their order of importance or relevance?
- How can I describe what I found in a careful, detailed way that will make complete sense to someone who is not informed on this topic?
- Have I omitted any necessary details or included superfluous information?
- In reporting my statistical results, am I being sufficiently precise?

Appendix A

Discussion

In the discussion section, you synthesize and interpret the various parts of your report to form a cohesive unit from the facts you have gathered. Without being overly repetitive, Mary begins by reminding us of the background that she developed in the introduction. She recapitulates her original hypothesis, underscoring the logical continuity of her presentation. Had she gotten any unexpected results, this would be the place to note how serendipity again entered into her study. She writes "defensively" in that she plays her own devil's advocate by pointing out the limitations of her study. She also raises some potential implications and future directions of her research, thus communicating that she has thought about this area.

As you begin to structure this section, here are some questions to consider:

- What was the major purpose of this study, and were there any secondary objectives?
- How do my results relate to that purpose and those objectives?
- Were there any unexpected findings of interest, and how can I describe them to show their relevance to this project and to possible follow-up research?
- How valid and generalizable are my findings, and what are their limitations?
- What can I say about the wider implications of the results?

References

The title page and abstract are on separate pages, and the first page of the introduction (page 3 of Mary's paper) begins on a separate page, but the method, results, and discussion sections follow one another without any page breaks. The reference section also begins on a separate page, and you can now see why complete and accurate notes are crucial. This section is an alphabetized listing of all the sources of information on which you drew. Your notes (e.g., on an index card for each reference) or a running list of sorted references in a file on your computer will now provide the final list.

The APA manual requires you list only those references that you have actually discussed or cited. Mary's paper gives us examples of the style recommended by the APA in referencing books, journal articles, and chapters in edited books, and you will find many other examples in the APA manual as well as in Rosnow and Rosnow's (2006) manual. Here is a condensed list of APA rules about referencing:

- List authors' names in the exact order in which they appear on the title page of the publication and by last name, then first initial and middle initial.
- Authors' names are separated by commas; use an ampersand (&) before the last author.
- Give the year the work was copyrighted (the year and month for magazine articles and the year, month, and day for newspaper articles).
- For titles of books, chapters in books, and journal articles, generally capitalize only the first word of the title and of the subtitle (if any) as well as any proper names.
- Italicize (or underline) the title of a book or a journal and the volume number of a journal article.

- Give the city and state of a book's publisher, using postal abbreviations, but you do not need to list state abbreviations for Baltimore, Boston, Chicago, Los Angeles, New York, Philadelphia, and San Francisco.
- If you are listing a foreign city other than Amsterdam, Jerusalem, London, Milan, Moscow, Paris, Rome, Stockholm, Tokyo, or Vienna, list the country as well.

End Material

The APA manual stipulates that tables and figures be placed in the manuscript after the reference section. The traditional purpose of this placement was to make it easier for the copy editor and the printer to work with the typewritten copy. It is now a common practice, after a paper has been officially accepted for publication, to ask the author to submit a disk containing the manuscript along with a hard copy or to send the manuscript as an e-mail attachment. The copy editor then has the option of working with the disk, the hard copy, or the e-mail version. Many instructors no longer insist that tables and figures be placed after the reference section and are quite amenable to having them inserted inside the results section so that they appear along with the narrative that refers to them. Before you decide on placement, however, ask your instructor or grader if it is acceptable to put your tables or graphics inside the running narrative section.

As illustrated by Mary's paper, many instructors also recommend that the final section of the student's report be an appendix that displays raw materials not described fully in the method section. For example, if you have stimulus materials that can be photocopied, this is the place to include them. Mary's appendix shows not her questionnaire (which was described in the method section) but her raw data and gives some of the logic of the statistical procedures she used. The instructor can see that Mary's analyses were done properly and that she has a clear understanding of the procedures. Had there been an error, the purpose of including this appendix would be to allow the instructor to trace how far back a mistake in the data analysis goes. The student will not be penalized for making what might seem a mistake in interpretation or understanding when it is a less serious (but still to be avoided) typographical error or a recording mistake.

Writing and Revising

Now that you know what is expected, it is time to begin writing a first draft. A good way to start is to compose a *self-motivator statement* that you can refer to as a way of focusing your thoughts. Such a statement can be posted over your computer as a guidepost to keep you from wandering off on a tangent. Mary's motivator might be "what I know about whether disclosing the results of drug tests influences bail judgments in criminal proceedings."

If you are someone who has trouble getting started, one useful trick is to begin not at the beginning but with the section you feel will be easiest to write. Once the ideas begin to flow, you can tackle the introductory section. This approach will also bolster flagging spirits, because you can reread the sections that you have already written when you begin to feel a loss of energy or determination. Try not to fall into the trap of escaping by napping or watching television. If you recognize these counterproductive moves for what they are, you should be able to avoid them.

Here are some helpful hints to make the writing go more smoothly:

- Find a quiet, well-lighted place in which to write, and do your writing in 2-hour stretches.
- Double-space your first draft so you can get an idea of how long the final (double-spaced) paper will be.
- Double spacing will also give you room for legible revisions if you like to revise your work in the printed version (which we each like to do) as well as on a computer screen.
- Number your printed pages using a header. Number your pages even if you are writing on a note pad.
- Pace your work so that you can complete the first draft and let it rest for at least 24 hours before you revise and polish what will be your final draft.

Layout and Printing

After you have revised your paper and are satisfied with the final version, it is time to prepare it for submission. The final report must not contain any typographical errors or spelling mistakes. To help you catch misspellings, use a spell check. Be sure that the spell check has not missed any misspelled technical terms, however. It may also not catch typos such as a capital *I* when you meant to type *in*. Using the grammar check would probably catch this kind of mistake, but a grammar check can drive writers to distraction by querying every phrase and line they write. Put the printed paper aside for a day or two, and then look at it again with a fresh eye. This process is called *proofreading* or *proofing*, and it is a final step before you submit your paper.

It is a good idea to proof the paper more than once, because gremlins in a program sometimes introduce weird changes. Also, you will be surprised how elusive some typos are; you can stare at them and still not see them right away. Ask yourself:

- Are there omissions?
- Are there misspellings?
- Are the numbers correct?
- Are the hyphenations correct?
- Are all the references cited in the body of the paper listed in the reference section, and vice versa?

Make sure the print is dark enough to be easily read, as you do not want to frustrate the grader by submitting a paper with typescript so light or blurry that it taxes the eyes. Use 8½ × 11-inch white paper. The APA manual requires that there be at least 1-inch margins on all four sides of the page, that no typed line exceed 6½ inches, and that there be no more than 27 lines of text on the page. In a student paper, however, these criteria are flexible. Double-space the printout, and print on one side of the paper only, using a page header to number the pages consecutively (described before and illustrated in Mary's paper).

Be sure to back up your work routinely. You never know when somebody may playfully touch a couple of keys and erase all your hard work. It is also a good idea to print a hard copy of your work periodically, so you have a double guarantee that you will not lose it. When the clean, corrected final draft is completed, make an extra copy—just in case. The original is for the instructor, and the duplicate copy ensures that a spare will be readily available if a problem arises.

Notice that Mary's paper leaves the right margin *ragged* (i.e., uneven), which is also a requirement of the APA manual. If this were an article for submission to a journal, although your manuscript would have a ragged right margin, the printed version would appear *justified* (i.e., even on the left and right, as in this book). Now is the time to give your paper a final look, checking to see that all the pages are there and in order, and then to turn it in on schedule. Having adhered to these guidelines, you should feel the satisfaction of a job well done.

Creating a Poster

If you plan to present a poster at a professional meeting, check to see whether the association has particular requirements, such as the number of pages permitted. The poster board surface also varies from one sponsoring organization to another but is usually about 4 feet high and either 6 or 8 feet wide. To give you a general idea, Exhibit A.2 shows a template for a poster consisting of six pages. This is usually the bare minimum, so if you have room for additional pages you can plan on including further information. Because you are obviously limited in how much you can say in a six-page poster, it is important to bring along copies of a more complete report to give to anyone who asks for one. On the title page, note your e-mail address and mailing address so that people can get in touch with you if they want to.

Your choice of font size should be determined by the distance from which people will be viewing the posters. The font height should not be less than 3/8 inches, though you might use a bigger font for the title and authors (no less than 1 inch or, depending on distance, as much as 2–3 inches high). As one instructor cautioned his students: Be prepared for a cramped area with relatively poor lighting, and a lot of distracting sensory activity (Rosnow & Rosnow, 2006, p. 115). Here are further tips from Rosnow and Rosnow's manual:

- Use a typeface that is easy to read, such as Arial or Times New Roman, not a fancy one that has squiggles or loops.
- Stand back about 5 feet and see if you can read the poster; the font size should not be less than 24 points.
- Because viewers don't usually want to stand around and study a poster assiduously, use as few words as possible.
- Don't overcomplicate tables or figures, and don't use jargon or exotic terms that may be unfamiliar to viewers and turn them away.
- Make your graphics simple so that they are eye-catching, such as a good photo or a good picture.
- Use color for important highlights, but use it sparingly because you are reporting a scientific study, not creating a work of art.
- Try looking at your poster through the eyes of those you want to attract, and also try it out on your instructor and other students for feedback.

Exhibit A.3 shows a poster based on Mary's study and Exhibit A.2's six-page template. You can see that it captures the highlights of her study, but it still would be necessary to read the report to understand the study thoroughly. Thus, it is important to bring along copies of a more complete report rather than simply hand out copies of the poster. However, your handout report should not be the paper you wrote for your instructor, which would be much too long and filled with irrelevant details for poster viewers. The idea is to try to boil down your research to a one-page (single-sided or double-sided) handout with the information single-spaced. At the very least, your handout should report group means, sample sizes, and measurement error. Based on what you have learned in this course, you should also have a sense of what other basic information a reader will need to reanalyze your results.

In preparing these materials, the idea is to try to anticipate people's questions and to tell them enough so they can come to their own conclusions. For your poster, remember that you are trying to draw attention to your study and not put people off by a cluttered presentation. You also want to chat with people who are interested in learning more about your study.

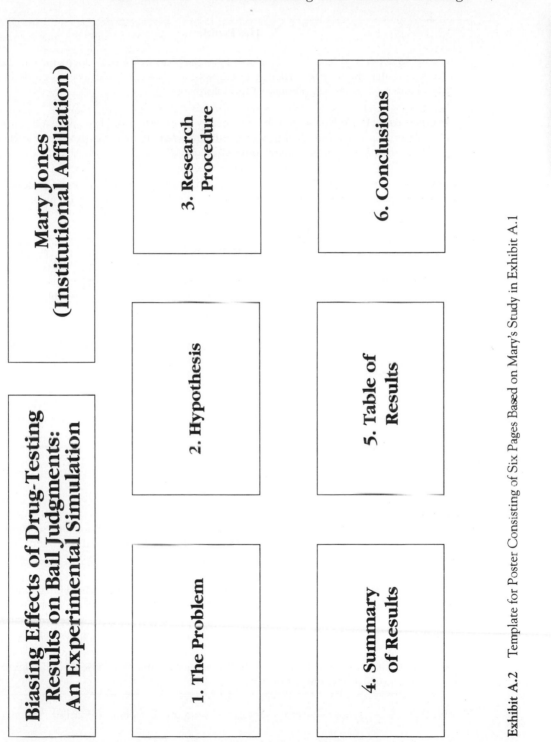

Exhibit A.2   Template for Poster Consisting of Six Pages Based on Mary's Study in Exhibit A.1

Appendix A

---

1. The Problem

Suppose someone arrested for suspicion of burglary is up for bail judgment and the judge knows that the suspect, when arrested, tested positive for drug use. Is the judge likely to order a harsher bail because of this information?

The crime control side has argued that mandatory drug testing of all suspects on arrest will have no biasing effects in legal proceedings, whereas the due process side has argued that drug information is likely to have prejudicial effects.

The purpose of this simulation experiment was to determine whether informing "judges" that the defendant has tested positive for drug usage will result in higher bail judgments.

---

2. Hypothesis

According to correspondent inference theory, observers focus mainly on certain types of observed behavior of an actor to infer traits because they believe that only certain behaviors are indicative of the actor's traits.

Once observers have inferred these traits, they use this information to predict the actor's future behavior and, in turn, to assess and to guide their own actions, decisions, and judgments regarding the actor.

On the basis of these assumptions, I hypothesized that providing "judges" with the defendant's positive results from a drug test would result in harsher bail judgments than when this information was unavailable.

---

3. Research Procedure

The "judges" in this experiment were 31 undergraduate students, who were randomly assigned to two conditions and asked to read one of two forms of a crime scenario. Both forms stated that "a man was arrested as a suspected burglar" and that "he fit the description of a man seen running from a burglarized house."

In the experimental condition, the story was that "while in custody the man submitted to a blood test, and it was determined that he had very recently used drugs." In the control condition, this information was omitted, and the story concluded with the statement that "the man spent enough time in custody to receive two meals and make three phone calls."

The students were asked to pretend to be the bail judge and to choose a dollar figure from $0 to $50,000 as the amount of bail.

Exhibit A.3   Mary Jones's Poster Presentation Using the Template in Exhibit A.3

4. Summary of Results

The results, shown in the table in Frame 5, indicated that the mean judgment of the experimental participants was higher than the mean judgment of the control participants, with $t(29) = 2.08$, one-tailed $p = .023$, $r_{effect\ size} = .36$.

Underlying the use of the t test is the assumption that the population variances are equal, but dividing the larger of the two associated variances (S^2) by the smaller of the two variances yielded $F(14, 15) = 9.0$, $p = 6.3^{-5}$, indicating heterogeneity of the population variances.

With the use of Satterthwaite's procedure, including adjustment of the degrees of freedom to make the t more accurate, the results were not much different: Satterthwaite $t(16) = 2.03$, one-tailed $p = .03$, $r_{effect\ size} = .34$. With 95% confidence, the population value of $r_{effect\ size}$ can be estimated as between $r = -.02$ and $.62$.

5. Mean, Variability, and Number of Participants

Measure	Experimental group	Control group
Mean	$16,146.67	$6,990.63
S	16,645.07	5,549.60
n	15	16

6. Conclusions

The results were consistent with the hypothesis that bail judgments would be biased in a harsher direction in the experimental than in the control condition. One possible implication of this finding is that our justice system's goal of being evenhanded and unbiased could be jeopardized if the results of mandatory drug testing were made available to judges before their bail judgments.

An important limitation of this study, however, is that the participants were college students, and thus, it might be argued that the results are not generalizable to actual bail judges. Another concern is whether the students' inferences of corresponding traits from socially undesirable behavior may have used stereotypes in assuming that there was a likely association between drug usage and the information in the burglary scenario.

Exhibit A.3   (*continued*)

APPENDIX B

Statistical Tables

Appendix B

Table B.1	z Values and Their Associated One-Tailed p Values								
				Second digit of z					
z	.00	.01	.02	.03	.04	.05	.06	.07	.08	.09
.0	.5000	.4960	.4920	.4880	.4840	.4801	.4761	.4721	.4681	.4641
.1	.4602	.4562	.4522	.4483	.4443	.4404	.4364	.4325	.4286	.4247
.2	.4207	.4168	.4129	.4090	.4052	.4013	.3974	.3936	.3897	.3859
.3	.3821	.3783	.3745	.3707	.3669	.3632	.3594	.3557	.3520	.3483
.4	.3446	.3409	.3372	.3336	.3300	.3264	.3228	.3192	.3156	.3121
.5	.3085	.3050	.3015	.2981	.2946	.2912	.2877	.2843	.2810	.2776
.6	.2743	.2709	.2676	.2643	.2611	.2578	.2546	.2514	.2483	.2451
.7	.2420	.2389	.2358	.2327	.2296	.2266	.2236	.2206	.2177	.2148
.8	.2119	.2090	.2061	.2033	.2005	.1977	.1949	.1922	.1894	.1867
.9	.1841	.1814	.1788	.1762	.1736	.1711	.1685	.1660	.1635	.1611
1.0	.1587	.1562	.1539	.1515	.1492	.1469	.1446	.1423	.1401	.1379
1.1	.1357	.1335	.1314	.1292	.1271	.1251	.1230	.1210	.1190	.1170
1.2	.1151	.1131	.1112	.1093	.1075	.1056	.1038	.1020	.1003	.0985
1.3	.0968	.0951	.0934	.0918	.0901	.0885	.0869	.0853	.0838	.0823
1.4	.0808	.0793	.0778	.0764	.0749	.0735	.0721	.0708	.0694	.0681
1.5	.0668	.0655	.0643	.0630	.0618	.0606	.0594	.0582	.0571	.0559
1.6	.0548	.0537	.0526	.0516	.0505	.0495	.0485	.0475	.0465	.0455
1.7	.0446	.0436	.0427	.0418	.0409	.0401	.0392	.0384	.0375	.0367
1.8	.0359	.0351	.0344	.0336	.0329	.0322	.0314	.0307	.0301	.0294
1.9	.0287	.0281	.0274	.0268	.0262	.0256	.0250	.0244	.0239	.0233
2.0	.0228	.0222	.0217	.0212	.0207	.0202	.0197	.0192	.0188	.0183
2.1	.0179	.0174	.0170	.0166	.0162	.0158	.0154	.0150	.0146	.0143
2.2	.0139	.0136	.0132	.0129	.0125	.0122	.0119	.0116	.0113	.0110
2.3	.0107	.0104	.0102	.0099	.0096	.0094	.0091	.0089	.0087	.0084
2.4	.0082	.0080	.0078	.0075	.0073	.0071	.0069	.0068	.0066	.0064
2.5	.0062	.0060	.0059	.0057	.0055	.0054	.0052	.0051	.0049	.0048
2.6	.0047	.0045	.0044	.0043	.0041	.0040	.0039	.0038	.0037	.0036
2.7	.0035	.0034	.0033	.0032	.0031	.0030	.0029	.0028	.0027	.0026
2.8	.0026	.0025	.0024	.0023	.0023	.0022	.0021	.0021	.0020	.0019
2.9	.0019	.0018	.0018	.0017	.0016	.0016	.0015	.0015	.0014	.0014
3.0	.0013	.0013	.0013	.0012	.0012	.0011	.0011	.0011	.0010	.0010
3.1	.0010	.0009	.0009	.0009	.0008	.0008	.0008	.0008	.0007	.0007
3.2	.0007									
3.3	.0005									
3.4	.0003									
3.5	.00023									
3.6	.00016									
3.7	.00011									
3.8	.00007									
3.9	.00005									
4.0	.00003									

Source: From *Nonparametric Statistics* (p. 247), by S. Siegel. New York: McGraw-Hill. Reprinted by permission of Mc-Graw-Hill, Inc.

Table B.2   *t* Values and Their Associated One-Tailed and Two-Tailed *p* Values

p / *df*	.50 / .25	.20 / .10	.10 / .05	.05 / .025	.02 / .01	.01 / .005	.005 / .0025	.002 / .001	
	.50	.20	.10	.05	.02	.01	.005	.002	two-tailed
	.25	.10	.05	.025	.01	.005	.0025	.001	one-tailed
1	1.000	3.078	6.314	12.706	31.821	63.657	127.321	318.309	
2	.816	1.886	2.920	4.303	6.965	9.925	14.089	22.327	
3	.765	1.638	2.353	3.182	4.541	5.841	7.453	10.214	
4	.741	1.533	2.132	2.776	3.747	4.604	5.598	7.173	
5	.727	1.476	2.015	2.571	3.365	4.032	4.773	5.893	
6	.718	1.440	1.943	2.447	3.143	3.707	4.317	5.208	
7	.711	1.415	1.895	2.365	2.998	3.499	4.029	4.785	
8	.706	1.397	1.860	2.306	2.896	3.355	3.833	4.501	
9	.703	1.383	1.833	2.262	2.821	3.250	3.690	4.297	
10	.700	1.372	1.812	2.228	2.764	3.169	3.581	4.144	
11	.697	1.363	1.796	2.201	2.718	3.106	3.497	4.025	
12	.695	1.356	1.782	2.179	2.681	3.055	3.428	3.930	
13	.694	1.350	1.771	2.160	2.650	3.012	3.372	3.852	
14	.692	1.345	1.761	2.145	2.624	2.977	3.326	3.787	
15	.691	1.341	1.753	2.131	2.602	2.947	3.286	3.733	
16	.690	1.337	1.746	2.120	2.583	2.921	3.252	3.686	
17	.689	1.333	1.740	2.110	2.567	2.898	3.223	3.646	
18	.688	1.330	1.734	2.101	2.552	2.878	3.197	3.610	
19	.688	1.328	1.729	2.093	2.539	2.861	3.174	3.579	
20	.687	1.325	1.725	2.086	2.528	2.845	3.153	3.552	
21	.686	1.323	1.721	2.080	2.518	2.831	3.135	3.527	
22	.686	1.321	1.717	2.074	2.508	2.819	3.119	3.505	
23	.685	1.319	1.714	2.069	2.500	2.807	3.104	3.485	
24	.685	1.318	1.711	2.064	2.492	2.797	3.090	3.467	
25	.684	1.316	1.708	2.060	2.485	2.787	3.078	3.450	
26	.684	1.315	1.706	2.056	2.479	2.779	3.067	3.435	
27	.684	1.314	1.703	2.052	2.473	2.771	3.057	3.421	
28	.683	1.313	1.701	2.048	2.467	2.763	3.047	3.408	
29	.683	1.311	1.699	2.045	2.462	2.756	3.038	3.396	
30	.683	1.310	1.697	2.042	2.457	2.750	3.030	3.385	
35	.682	1.306	1.690	2.030	2.438	2.724	2.996	3.340	
40	.681	1.303	1.684	2.021	2.423	2.704	2.971	3.307	
45	.680	1.301	1.679	2.014	2.412	2.690	2.952	3.281	
50	.679	1.299	1.676	2.009	2.403	2.678	2.937	3.261	
55	.679	1.297	1.673	2.004	2.396	2.668	2.925	3.245	
60	.679	1.296	1.671	2.000	2.390	2.660	2.915	3.232	
70	.678	1.294	1.667	1.994	2.381	2.648	2.899	3.211	
80	.678	1.292	1.664	1.990	2.374	2.639	2.887	3.195	
90	.677	1.291	1.662	1.987	2.368	2.632	2.878	3.183	
100	.677	1.290	1.660	1.984	2.364	2.626	2.871	3.174	
200	.676	1.286	1.652	1.972	2.345	2.601	2.838	3.131	
500	.675	1.283	1.648	1.965	2.334	2.586	2.820	3.107	
1,000	.675	1.282	1.646	1.962	2.330	2.581	2.813	3.098	
2,000	.675	1.282	1.645	1.961	2.328	2.578	2.810	3.094	
10,000	.675	1.282	1.645	1.960	2.327	2.576	2.808	3.091	
∞	.674	1.282	1.645	1.960	2.326	2.576	2.807	3.090	

(continued)

Table B.2 — t Values and Their Associated One-Tailed and Two-Tailed p Values

p / df	.001	.0005	.0002	.0001	.00005	.00002	two-tailed
	.0005	.00025	.0001	.00005	.000025	.00001	one-tailed
1	636.619	1,273.239	3,183.099	6,366.198	12,732.395	31,830.989	
2	31.598	44.705	70.700	99.992	141.416	223.603	
3	12.924	16.326	22.204	28.000	35.298	47.928	
4	8.610	10.306	13.034	15.544	18.522	23.332	
5	6.869	7.976	9.678	11.178	12.893	15.547	
6	5.959	6.788	8.025	9.082	10.261	12.032	
7	5.408	6.082	7.063	7.885	8.782	10.103	
8	5.041	5.618	6.442	7.120	7.851	8.907	
9	4.781	5.291	6.010	6.594	7.215	8.102	
10	4.587	5.049	5.694	6.211	6.757	7.527	
11	4.437	4.863	5.453	5.921	6.412	7.098	
12	4.318	4.716	5.263	5.694	6.143	6.756	
13	4.221	4.597	5.111	5.513	5.928	6.501	
14	4.140	4.499	4.985	5.363	5.753	6.287	
15	4.073	4.417	4.880	5.239	5.607	6.109	
16	4.015	4.346	4.791	5.134	5.484	5.960	
17	3.965	4.286	4.714	5.044	5.379	5.832	
18	3.922	4.233	4.648	4.966	5.288	5.722	
19	3.883	4.187	4.590	4.897	5.209	5.627	
20	3.850	4.146	4.539	4.837	5.139	5.543	
21	3.819	4.110	4.493	4.784	5.077	5.469	
22	3.792	4.077	4.452	4.736	5.022	5.402	
23	3.768	4.048	4.415	4.693	4.972	5.343	
24	3.745	4.021	4.382	4.654	4.927	5.290	
25	3.725	3.997	4.352	4.619	4.887	5.241	
26	3.707	3.974	4.324	4.587	4.850	5.197	
27	3.690	3.954	4.299	4.558	4.816	5.157	
28	3.674	3.935	4.275	4.530	4.784	5.120	
29	3.659	3.918	4.254	4.506	4.756	5.086	
30	3.646	3.902	4.234	4.482	4.729	5.054	
35	3.591	3.836	4.153	4.389	4.622	4.927	
40	3.551	3.788	4.094	4.321	4.544	4.835	
45	3.520	3.752	4.049	4.269	4.485	4.766	
50	3.496	3.723	4.014	4.228	4.438	4.711	
55	3.476	3.700	3.986	4.196	4.401	4.667	
60	3.460	3.681	3.926	4.169	4.370	4.631	
70	3.435	3.651	3.962	4.127	4.323	4.576	
80	3.416	3.629	3.899	4.096	4.288	4.535	
90	3.402	3.612	3.878	4.072	4.261	4.503	
100	3.390	3.598	3.862	4.053	4.240	4.478	
200	3.340	3.539	3.789	3.970	4.146	4.369	
500	3.310	3.504	3.747	3.922	4.091	4.306	
1,000	3.300	3.492	3.733	3.906	4.073	4.285	
2,000	3.295	3.486	3.726	3.898	4.064	4.275	
10,000	3.292	3.482	3.720	3.892	4.058	4.267	
∞	3.291	3.481	3.719	3.891	4.056	4.265	

Source: From "Extended Tables of the Percentage Points of Student's t-Distribution," by E. T. Federighi, 1959. *Journal of the American Statistical Association, 54,* pp. 683–688. Reprinted by permission of the American Statistical Association.

Appendix B

Table B.3 F Values and Their Associated p Values

df_2	df_1 p	1	2	3	4	5	6	8	12	24	∞
1	.001	405284	500000	540379	562500	576405	585937	598144	610667	623497	636619
	.005	16211	20000	21615	22500	23056	23437	23925	24426	24940	25465
	.01	4052	4999	5403	5625	5764	5859	5981	6106	6234	6366
	.025	647.79	799.50	864.16	899.58	921.85	937.11	956.66	976.71	997.25	1018.30
	.05	161.45	199.50	215.71	224.58	230.16	233.99	238.88	243.91	249.05	254.32
	.10	39.86	49.50	53.59	55.83	57.24	58.20	59.44	60.70	62.00	63.33
	.20	9.47	12.00	13.06	13.73	14.01	14.26	14.59	14.90	15.24	15.58
2	.001	998.5	999.0	999.2	999.2	999.3	999.3	999.4	999.4	999.5	999.5
	.005	198.50	199.00	199.17	199.25	199.30	199.33	199.37	199.42	199.46	199.51
	.01	98.49	99.00	99.17	99.25	99.30	99.33	99.36	99.42	99.46	99.50
	.025	38.51	39.00	39.17	39.25	39.30	39.33	39.37	39.42	39.46	39.50
	.05	18.51	19.00	19.16	19.25	19.30	19.33	19.37	19.41	19.45	19.50
	.10	8.53	9.00	9.16	9.24	9.29	9.33	9.37	9.41	9.45	9.49
	.20	3.56	4.00	4.16	4.24	4.28	4.32	4.36	4.40	4.44	4.48
3	.001	167.5	148.5	141.1	137.1	134.6	132.8	130.6	128.3	125.9	123.5
	.005	55.55	49.80	47.47	46.20	45.39	44.84	44.13	43.39	42.62	41.83
	.01	34.12	30.81	29.46	28.71	28.24	27.91	27.49	27.05	26.60	26.12
	.025	17.44	16.04	15.44	15.10	14.89	14.74	14.54	14.34	14.12	13.90
	.05	10.13	9.55	9.28	9.12	9.01	8.94	8.84	8.74	8.64	8.53
	.10	5.54	5.46	5.39	5.34	5.31	5.28	5.25	5.22	5.18	5.13
	.20	2.68	2.89	2.94	2.96	2.97	2.97	2.98	2.98	2.98	2.98
4	.001	74.14	61.25	56.18	53.44	51.71	50.53	49.00	47.41	45.77	44.05
	.005	31.33	26.28	24.26	23.16	22.46	21.98	21.35	20.71	20.03	19.33
	.01	21.20	18.00	16.69	15.98	15.52	15.21	14.80	14.37	13.93	13.46
	.025	12.22	10.65	9.98	9.60	9.36	9.20	8.98	8.75	8.51	8.26
	.05	7.71	6.94	6.59	6.39	6.26	6.16	6.04	5.91	5.77	5.63
	.10	4.54	4.32	4.19	4.11	4.05	4.01	3.95	3.90	3.83	3.76
	.20	2.35	2.47	2.48	2.48	2.48	2.47	2.47	2.46	2.44	2.43
5	.001	47.04	36.61	33.20	31.09	29.75	28.84	27.64	26.42	25.14	23.78
	.005	22.79	18.31	16.53	15.56	14.94	14.51	13.96	13.38	12.78	12.14
	.01	16.26	13.27	12.06	11.39	10.97	10.67	10.29	9.89	9.47	9.02
	.025	10.01	8.43	7.76	7.39	7.15	6.98	6.76	6.52	6.28	6.02
	.05	6.61	5.79	5.41	5.19	5.05	4.95	4.82	4.68	4.53	4.36
	.10	4.06	3.78	3.62	3.52	3.45	3.40	3.34	3.27	3.19	3.10
	.20	2.18	2.26	2.25	2.24	2.23	2.22	2.20	2.18	2.16	2.13
6	.001	35.51	27.00	23.70	21.90	20.81	20.03	19.03	17.99	16.89	15.75
	.005	18.64	14.54	12.92	12.03	11.46	11.07	10.57	10.03	9.47	8.88
	.01	13.74	10.92	9.78	9.15	8.75	8.47	8.10	7.72	7.31	6.88
	.025	8.81	7.26	6.60	6.23	5.99	5.82	5.60	5.37	5.12	4.85
	.05	5.99	5.14	4.76	4.53	4.39	4.28	4.15	4.00	3.84	3.67
	.10	3.78	3.46	3.29	3.18	3.11	3.05	2.98	2.90	2.82	2.72
	.20	2.07	2.13	2.11	2.09	2.08	2.06	2.04	2.02	1.99	1.95
7	.001	29.22	21.69	18.77	17.19	16.21	15.52	14.63	13.71	12.73	11.69
	.005	16.24	12.40	10.88	10.05	9.52	9.16	8.68	8.18	7.65	7.08
	.01	12.25	9.55	8.45	7.85	7.46	7.19	6.84	6.47	6.07	5.65
	.025	8.07	6.54	5.89	5.52	5.29	5.12	4.90	4.67	4.42	4.14
	.05	5.59	4.74	4.35	4.12	3.97	3.87	3.73	3.57	3.41	3.23
	.10	3.59	3.26	3.07	2.96	2.88	2.83	2.75	2.67	2.58	2.47
	.20	2.00	2.04	2.02	1.99	1.97	1.96	1.93	1.91	1.87	1.83

(continued)

Table B.3   *F* Values and Their Associated *p* Values

df_2	df_1 p	1	2	3	4	5	6	8	12	24	∞
8	.001	25.42	18.49	15.83	14.39	13.49	12.86	12.04	11.19	10.30	9.34
	.005	14.69	11.04	9.60	8.81	8.30	7.95	7.50	7.01	6.50	5.95
	.01	11.26	8.65	7.59	7.01	6.63	6.37	6.03	5.67	5.28	4.86
	.025	7.57	6.06	5.42	5.05	4.82	4.65	4.43	4.20	3.95	3.67
	.05	5.32	4.46	4.07	3.84	3.69	3.58	3.44	3.28	3.12	2.93
	.10	3.46	3.11	2.92	2.81	2.73	2.67	2.59	2.50	2.40	2.29
	.20	1.95	1.98	1.95	1.92	1.90	1.88	1.86	1.83	1.79	1.74
9	.001	22.86	16.39	13.90	12.56	11.71	11.13	10.37	9.57	8.72	7.81
	.005	13.61	10.11	8.72	7.96	7.47	7.13	6.69	6.23	5.73	5.19
	.01	10.56	8.02	6.99	6.42	6.06	5.80	5.47	5.11	4.73	4.31
	.025	7.21	5.71	5.08	4.72	4.48	4.32	4.10	3.87	3.61	3.33
	.05	5.12	4.26	3.86	3.63	3.48	3.37	3.23	3.07	2.90	2.71
	.10	3.36	3.01	2.81	2.69	2.61	2.55	2.47	2.38	2.28	2.16
	.20	1.91	1.94	1.90	1.87	1.85	1.83	1.80	1.76	1.73	1.67
10	.001	21.04	14.91	12.55	11.28	10.48	9.92	9.20	8.45	7.64	6.76
	.005	12.83	9.43	8.08	7.34	6.87	6.54	6.12	5.66	5.17	4.64
	.01	10.04	7.56	6.55	5.99	5.64	5.39	5.06	4.71	4.33	3.91
	.025	6.94	5.46	4.83	4.47	4.24	4.07	3.85	3.62	3.37	3.08
	.05	4.96	4.10	3.71	3.48	3.33	3.22	3.07	2.91	2.74	2.54
	.10	3.28	2.92	2.73	2.61	2.52	2.46	2.38	2.28	2.18	2.06
	.20	1.88	1.90	1.86	1.83	1.80	1.78	1.75	1.72	1.67	1.62
11	.001	19.69	13.81	11.56	10.35	9.58	9.05	8.35	7.63	6.85	6.00
	.005	12.23	8.91	7.60	6.88	6.42	6.10	5.68	5.24	4.76	4.23
	.01	9.65	7.20	6.22	5.67	5.32	5.07	4.74	4.40	4.02	3.60
	.025	6.72	5.26	4.63	4.28	4.04	3.88	3.66	3.43	3.17	2.88
	.05	4.84	3.98	3.59	3.36	3.20	3.09	2.95	2.79	2.61	2.40
	.10	3.23	2.86	2.66	2.54	2.45	2.39	2.30	2.21	2.10	1.97
	.20	1.86	1.87	1.83	1.80	1.77	1.75	1.72	1.68	1.63	1.57
12	.001	18.64	12.97	10.80	9.63	8.89	8.38	7.71	7.00	6.25	5.42
	.005	11.75	8.51	7.23	6.52	6.07	5.76	5.35	4.91	4.43	3.90
	.01	9.33	6.93	5.95	5.41	5.06	4.82	4.50	4.16	3.78	3.36
	.025	6.55	5.10	4.47	4.12	3.89	3.73	3.51	3.28	3.02	2.72
	.05	4.75	3.88	3.49	3.26	3.11	3.00	2.85	2.69	2.50	2.30
	.10	3.18	2.81	2.61	2.48	2.39	2.33	2.24	2.15	2.04	1.90
	.20	1.84	1.85	1.80	1.77	1.74	1.72	1.69	1.65	1.60	1.54
13	.001	17.81	12.31	10.21	9.07	8.35	7.86	7.21	6.52	5.78	4.97
	.005	11.37	8.19	6.93	6.23	5.79	5.48	5.08	4.64	4.17	3.65
	.01	9.07	6.70	5.74	5.20	4.86	4.62	4.30	3.96	3.59	3.16
	.025	6.41	4.97	4.35	4.00	3.77	3.60	3.39	3.15	2.89	2.60
	.05	4.67	3.80	3.41	3.18	3.02	2.92	2.77	2.60	2.42	2.21
	.10	3.14	2.76	2.56	2.43	2.35	2.28	2.20	2.10	1.98	1.85
	.20	1.82	1.83	1.78	1.75	1.72	1.69	1.66	1.62	1.57	1.51
14	.001	17.14	11.78	9.73	8.62	7.92	7.43	6.80	6.13	5.41	4.60
	.005	11.06	7.92	6.68	6.00	5.56	5.26	4.86	4.43	3.96	3.44
	.01	8.86	6.51	5.56	5.03	4.69	4.46	4.14	3.80	3.43	3.00
	.025	6.30	4.86	4.24	3.89	3.66	3.50	3.29	3.05	2.79	2.49
	.05	4.60	3.74	3.34	3.11	2.96	2.85	2.70	2.53	2.35	2.13
	.10	3.10	2.73	2.52	2.39	2.31	2.24	2.15	2.05	1.94	1.80
	.20	1.81	1.81	1.76	1.73	1.70	1.67	1.64	1.60	1.55	1.48

(continued)

Table B.3 F Values and Their Associated p Values

df_2	df_1 p	1	2	3	4	5	6	8	12	24	∞
15	.001	16.59	11.34	9.34	8.25	7.57	7.09	6.47	5.81	5.10	4.31
	.005	10.80	7.70	6.48	5.80	5.37	5.07	4.67	4.25	3.79	3.26
	.01	8.68	6.36	5.42	4.89	4.56	4.32	4.00	3.67	3.29	2.87
	.025	6.20	4.77	4.15	3.80	3.58	3.41	3.20	2.96	2.70	2.40
	.05	4.54	3.68	3.29	3.06	2.90	2.79	2.64	2.48	2.29	2.07
	.10	3.07	2.70	2.49	2.36	2.27	2.21	2.12	2.02	1.90	1.76
	.20	1.80	1.79	1.75	1.71	1.68	1.66	1.62	1.58	1.53	1.46
16	.001	16.12	10.97	9.00	7.94	7.27	6.81	6.19	5.55	4.85	4.06
	.005	10.58	7.51	6.30	5.64	5.21	4.91	4.52	4.10	3.64	3.11
	.01	8.53	6.23	5.29	4.77	4.44	4.20	3.89	3.55	3.18	2.75
	.025	6.12	4.69	4.08	3.73	3.50	3.34	3.12	2.89	2.63	2.32
	.05	4.49	3.63	3.24	3.01	2.85	2.74	2.59	2.42	2.24	2.01
	.10	3.05	2.67	2.46	2.33	2.24	2.18	2.09	1.99	1.87	1.72
	.20	1.79	1.78	1.74	1.70	1.67	1.64	1.61	1.56	1.51	1.43
17	.001	15.72	10.66	8.73	7.68	7.02	6.56	5.96	5.32	4.63	3.85
	.005	10.38	7.35	6.16	5.50	5.07	4.78	4.39	3.97	3.51	2.98
	.01	8.40	6.11	5.18	4.67	4.34	4.10	3.79	3.45	3.08	2.65
	.025	6.04	4.62	4.01	3.66	3.44	3.28	3.06	2.82	2.56	2.25
	.05	4.45	3.59	3.20	2.96	2.81	2.70	2.55	2.38	2.19	1.96
	.10	3.03	2.64	2.44	2.31	2.22	2.15	2.06	1.96	1.84	1.69
	.20	1.78	1.77	1.72	1.68	1.65	1.63	1.59	1.55	1.49	1.42
18	.001	15.38	10.39	8.49	7.46	6.81	6.35	5.76	5.13	4.45	3.67
	.005	10.22	7.21	6.03	5.37	4.96	4.66	4.28	3.86	3.40	2.87
	.01	8.28	6.01	5.09	4.58	4.25	4.01	3.71	3.37	3.00	2.57
	.025	5.98	4.56	3.95	3.61	3.38	3.22	3.01	2.77	2.50	2.19
	.05	4.41	3.55	3.16	2.93	2.77	2.66	2.51	2.34	2.15	1.92
	.10	3.01	2.62	2.42	2.29	2.20	2.13	2.04	1.93	1.81	1.66
	.20	1.77	1.76	1.71	1.67	1.64	1.62	1.58	1.53	1.48	1.40
19	.001	15.08	10.16	8.28	7.26	6.61	6.18	5.59	4.97	4.29	3.52
	.005	10.07	7.09	5.92	5.27	4.85	4.56	4.18	3.76	3.31	2.78
	.01	8.18	5.93	5.01	4.50	4.17	3.94	3.63	3.30	2.92	2.49
	.025	5.92	4.51	3.90	3.56	3.33	3.17	2.96	2.72	2.45	2.13
	.05	4.38	3.52	3.13	2.90	2.74	2.63	2.48	2.31	2.11	1.88
	.10	2.99	2.61	2.40	2.27	2.18	2.11	2.02	1.91	1.79	1.63
	.20	1.76	1.75	1.70	1.66	1.63	1.61	1.57	1.52	1.46	1.39
20	.001	14.82	9.95	8.10	7.10	6.46	6.02	5.44	4.82	4.15	3.38
	.005	9.94	6.99	5.82	5.17	4.76	4.47	4.09	3.68	3.22	2.69
	.01	8.10	5.85	4.94	4.43	4.10	3.87	3.56	3.23	2.86	2.42
	.025	5.87	4.46	3.86	3.51	3.29	3.13	2.91	2.68	2.41	2.09
	.05	4.35	3.49	3.10	2.87	2.71	2.60	2.45	2.28	2.08	1.84
	.10	2.97	2.59	2.38	2.25	2.16	2.09	2.00	1.89	1.77	1.61
	.20	1.76	1.75	1.70	1.65	1.62	1.60	1.56	1.51	1.45	1.37
21	.001	14.59	9.77	7.94	6.95	6.32	5.88	5.31	4.70	4.03	3.26
	.005	9.83	6.89	5.73	5.09	4.68	4.39	4.01	3.60	3.15	2.61
	.01	8.02	5.78	4.87	4.37	4.04	3.81	3.51	3.17	2.80	2.36
	.025	5.83	4.42	3.82	3.48	3.25	3.09	2.87	2.64	2.37	2.04
	.05	4.32	3.47	3.07	2.84	2.68	2.57	2.42	2.25	2.05	1.81
	.10	2.96	2.57	2.36	2.23	2.14	2.08	1.98	1.88	1.75	1.59
	.20	1.75	1.74	1.69	1.65	1.61	1.59	1.55	1.50	1.44	1.36

(continued)

Table B.3   F Values and Their Associated p Values

df_2	df_1 p	1	2	3	4	5	6	8	12	24	∞
22	.001	14.38	9.61	7.80	6.81	6.19	5.76	5.19	4.58	3.92	3.15
	.005	9.73	6.81	5.65	5.02	4.61	4.32	3.94	3.54	3.08	2.55
	.01	7.94	5.72	4.82	4.31	3.99	3.76	3.45	3.12	2.75	2.31
	.025	5.79	4.38	3.78	3.44	3.22	3.05	2.84	2.60	2.33	2.00
	.05	4.30	3.44	3.05	2.82	2.66	2.55	2.40	2.23	2.03	1.78
	.10	2.95	2.56	2.35	2.22	2.13	2.06	1.97	1.86	1.73	1.57
	.20	1.75	1.73	1.68	1.64	1.61	1.58	1.54	1.49	1.43	1.35
23	.001	14.19	9.47	7.67	6.69	6.08	5.65	5.09	4.48	3.82	3.05
	.005	9.63	6.73	5.58	4.95	4.54	4.26	3.88	3.47	3.02	2.48
	.01	7.88	5.66	4.76	4.26	3.94	3.71	3.41	3.07	2.70	2.26
	.025	5.75	4.35	3.75	3.41	3.18	3.02	2.81	2.57	2.30	1.97
	.05	4.28	3.42	3.03	2.80	2.64	2.53	2.38	2.20	2.00	1.76
	.10	2.94	2.55	2.34	2.21	2.11	2.05	1.95	1.84	1.72	1.55
	.20	1.74	1.73	1.68	1.63	1.60	1.57	1.53	1.49	1.42	1.34
24	.001	14.03	9.34	7.55	6.59	5.98	5.55	4.99	4.39	3.74	2.97
	.005	9.55	6.66	5.52	4.89	4.49	4.20	3.83	3.42	2.97	2.43
	.01	7.82	5.61	4.72	4.22	3.90	3.67	3.36	3.03	2.66	2.21
	.025	5.72	4.32	3.72	3.38	3.15	2.99	2.78	2.54	2.27	1.94
	.05	4.26	3.40	3.01	2.78	2.62	2.51	2.36	2.18	1.98	1.73
	.10	2.93	2.54	2.33	2.19	2.10	2.04	1.94	1.83	1.70	1.53
	.20	1.74	1.72	1.67	1.63	1.59	1.57	1.53	1.48	1.42	1.33
25	.001	13.88	9.22	7.45	6.49	5.88	5.46	4.91	4.31	3.66	2.89
	.005	9.48	6.60	5.46	4.84	4.43	4.15	3.78	3.37	2.92	2.38
	.01	7.77	5.57	4.68	4.18	3.86	3.63	3.32	2.99	2.62	2.17
	.025	5.69	4.29	3.69	3.35	3.13	2.97	2.75	2.51	2.24	1.91
	.05	4.24	3.38	2.99	2.76	2.60	2.49	2.34	2.16	1.96	1.71
	.10	2.92	2.53	2.32	2.18	2.09	2.02	1.93	1.82	1.69	1.52
	.20	1.73	1.72	1.66	1.62	1.59	1.56	1.52	1.47	1.41	1.32
26	.001	13.74	9.12	7.36	6.41	5.80	5.38	4.83	4.24	3.59	2.82
	.005	9.41	6.54	5.41	4.79	4.38	4.10	3.73	3.33	2.87	2.33
	.01	7.72	5.53	4.64	4.14	3.82	3.59	3.29	2.96	2.58	2.13
	.025	5.66	4.27	3.67	3.33	3.10	2.94	2.73	2.49	2.22	1.88
	.05	4.22	3.37	2.98	2.74	2.59	2.47	2.32	2.15	1.95	1.69
	.10	2.91	2.52	2.31	2.17	2.08	2.01	1.92	1.81	1.68	1.50
	.20	1.73	1.71	1.66	1.62	1.58	1.56	1.52	1.47	1.40	1.31
27	.001	13.61	9.02	7.27	6.33	5.73	5.31	4.76	4.17	3.52	2.75
	.005	9.34	6.49	5.36	4.74	4.34	4.06	3.69	3.28	2.83	2.29
	.01	7.68	5.49	4.60	4.11	3.78	3.56	3.26	2.93	2.55	2.10
	.025	5.63	4.24	3.65	3.31	3.08	2.92	2.71	2.47	2.19	1.85
	.05	4.21	3.35	2.96	2.73	2.57	2.46	2.30	2.13	1.93	1.67
	.10	2.90	2.51	2.30	2.17	2.07	2.00	1.91	1.80	1.67	1.49
	.20	1.73	1.71	1.66	1.61	1.58	1.55	1.51	1.46	1.40	1.30
28	.001	13.50	8.93	7.19	6.25	5.66	5.24	4.69	4.11	3.46	2.70
	.005	9.28	6.44	5.32	4.70	4.30	4.02	3.65	3.25	2.79	2.25
	.01	7.64	5.45	4.57	4.07	3.75	3.53	3.23	2.90	2.52	2.06
	.025	5.61	4.22	3.63	3.29	3.06	2.90	2.69	2.45	2.17	1.83
	.05	4.20	3.34	2.95	2.71	2.56	2.44	2.29	2.12	1.91	1.65
	.10	2.89	2.50	2.29	2.16	2.06	2.00	1.90	1.79	1.66	1.48
	.20	1.72	1.71	1.65	1.61	1.57	1.55	1.51	1.46	1.39	1.30

(continued)

Appendix B

Table B.3	F Values and Their Associated *p* Values

df_2	df_1 p	1	2	3	4	5	6	8	12	24	∞
29	.001	13.39	8.85	7.12	6.19	5.59	5.18	4.64	4.05	3.41	2.64
	.005	9.23	6.40	5.28	4.66	4.26	3.98	3.61	3.21	2.76	2.21
	.01	7.60	5.42	4.54	4.04	3.73	3.50	3.20	2.87	2.49	2.03
	.025	5.59	4.20	3.61	3.27	3.04	2.88	2.67	2.43	2.15	1.81
	.05	4.18	3.33	2.93	2.70	2.54	2.43	2.28	2.10	1.90	1.64
	.10	2.89	2.50	2.28	2.15	2.06	1.99	1.89	1.78	1.65	1.47
	.20	1.72	1.70	1.65	1.60	1.57	1.54	1.50	1.45	1.39	1.29
30	.001	13.29	8.77	7.05	6.12	5.53	5.12	4.58	4.00	3.36	2.59
	.005	9.18	6.35	5.24	4.62	4.23	3.95	3.58	3.18	2.73	2.18
	.01	7.56	5.39	4.51	4.02	3.70	3.47	3.17	2.84	2.47	2.01
	.025	5.57	4.18	3.59	3.25	3.03	2.87	2.65	2.41	2.14	1.79
	.05	4.17	3.32	2.92	2.69	2.53	2.42	2.27	2.09	1.89	1.62
	.10	2.88	2.49	2.28	2.14	2.05	1.98	1.88	1.77	1.64	1.46
	.20	1.72	1.70	1.64	1.60	1.57	1.54	1.50	1.45	1.38	1.28
40	.001	12.61	8.25	6.60	5.70	5.13	4.73	4.21	3.64	3.01	2.23
	.005	8.83	6.07	4.98	4.37	3.99	3.71	3.35	2.95	2.50	1.93
	.01	7.31	5.18	4.31	3.83	3.51	3.29	2.99	2.66	2.29	1.80
	.025	5.42	4.05	3.46	3.13	2.90	2.74	2.53	2.29	2.01	1.64
	.05	4.08	3.23	2.84	2.61	2.45	2.34	2.18	2.00	1.79	1.51
	.10	2.84	2.44	2.23	2.09	2.00	1.93	1.83	1.71	1.57	1.38
	.20	1.70	1.68	1.62	1.57	1.54	1.51	1.47	1.41	1.34	1.24
60	.001	11.97	7.76	6.17	5.31	4.76	4.37	3.87	3.31	2.69	1.90
	.005	8.49	5.80	4.73	4.14	3.76	3.49	3.13	2.74	2.29	1.69
	.01	7.08	4.98	4.13	3.65	3.34	3.12	2.82	2.50	2.12	1.60
	.025	5.29	3.93	3.34	3.01	2.79	2.63	2.41	2.17	1.88	1.48
	.05	4.00	3.15	2.76	2.52	2.37	2.25	2.10	1.92	1.70	1.39
	.10	2.79	2.39	2.18	2.04	1.95	1.87	1.77	1.66	1.51	1.29
	.20	1.68	1.65	1.59	1.55	1.51	1.48	1.44	1.38	1.31	1.18
120	.001	11.38	7.31	5.79	4.95	4.42	4.04	3.55	3.02	2.40	1.56
	.005	8.18	5.54	4.50	3.92	3.55	3.28	2.93	2.54	2.09	1.43
	.01	6.85	4.79	3.95	3.48	3.17	2.96	2.66	2.34	1.95	1.38
	.025	5.15	3.80	3.23	2.89	2.67	2.52	2.30	2.05	1.76	1.31
	.05	3.92	3.07	2.68	2.45	2.29	2.17	2.02	1.83	1.61	1.25
	.10	2.75	2.35	2.13	1.99	1.90	1.82	1.72	1.60	1.45	1.19
	.20	1.66	1.63	1.57	1.52	1.48	1.45	1.41	1.35	1.27	1.12
∞	.001	10.83	6.91	5.42	4.62	4.10	3.74	3.27	2.74	2.13	1.00
	.005	7.88	5.30	4.28	3.72	3.35	3.09	2.74	2.36	1.90	1.00
	.01	6.64	4.60	3.78	3.32	3.02	2.80	2.51	2.18	1.79	1.00
	.025	5.02	3.69	3.12	2.79	2.57	2.41	2.19	1.94	1.64	1.00
	.05	3.84	2.99	2.60	2.37	2.21	2.09	1.94	1.75	1.52	1.00
	.10	2.71	2.30	2.08	1.94	1.85	1.77	1.67	1.55	1.38	1.00
	.20	1.64	1.61	1.55	1.50	1.46	1.43	1.38	1.32	1.23	1.00

Source: Reproduced from Table V of R. A. Fisher and F. Yates, *Statistical Tables for Biological, Agricultural and Medical Research* (6th ed.), 1974, published by Longman Group UK Ltd., London (previously published by Oliver and Boyd Ltd., Edinburgh) and by permission of the authors and publishers. The 0.5% and 2.5% points are reproduced from "Tables of Percentage Points of the Inverted Beta (*F*) Distribution," *Biometrika*, Vol. 33 (April 1943), pp. 73–88, by permission of the Biometrika Trustees, Imperial College of Science, Technology, and Medicine, London, England.

Appendix B

Table B.4 χ^2 Values and Their Associated p Values

					Probability									
df	.99	.98	.95	.90	.80	.70	.50	.30	.20	.10	.05	.02	.01	.001
1	0^3157	0^3628	00393	0158	0642	.148	.455	1.074	1.642	2.706	3.841	5.412	6.635	10.827
2	.0201	.0404	.103	.211	.446	.713	1.386	2.408	3.219	4.605	5.991	7.824	9.210	13.815
3	.115	.185	.352	.584	1.005	1.424	2.366	3.665	4.642	6.251	7.815	9.837	11.345	16.268
4	.297	.429	.711	1.064	1.649	2.195	3.357	4.878	5.989	7.779	9.488	11.668	13.277	18.465
5	.554	.752	1.145	1.610	2.343	3.000	4.351	6.064	7.289	9.236	11.070	13.388	15.086	20.517
6	.872	1.134	1.635	2.204	3.070	3.828	5.348	7.231	8.558	10.645	12.592	15.033	16.812	22.457
7	1.239	1.564	2.167	2.833	3.822	4.671	6.346	8.383	9.803	12.017	14.067	16.622	18.475	24.322
8	1.646	2.032	2.733	3.490	4.594	5.527	7.344	9.524	11.030	13.362	15.507	18.168	20.090	26.125
9	2.088	2.532	3.325	4.168	5.380	6.393	8.343	10.656	12.242	14.684	16.919	19.679	21.666	27.877
10	2.558	3.059	3.940	4.865	6.179	7.267	9.342	11.781	13.442	15.987	18.307	21.161	23.209	29.588
11	3.053	3.609	4.575	5.578	6.989	8.148	10.341	12.899	14.631	17.275	19.675	22.618	24.725	31.264
12	3.571	4.178	5.226	6.304	7.807	9.034	11.340	14.011	15.812	18.549	21.026	24.054	26.217	32.909
13	4.107	4.765	5.892	7.042	8.634	9.926	12.340	15.119	16.985	19.812	22.362	25.472	27.688	34.528
14	4.660	5.368	6.571	7.790	9.467	10.821	13.339	16.222	18.151	21.064	23.685	26.873	29.141	36.123
15	5.229	5.985	7.261	8.547	10.307	11.721	14.339	17.322	19.311	22.307	24.996	28.529	30.578	37.697
16	5.812	6.614	7.962	9.312	11.152	12.624	15.338	18.418	20.465	23.542	26.296	29.633	32.000	39.252
17	6.408	7.255	8.672	10.085	12.002	13.531	16.338	19.511	21.615	24.769	27.587	30.995	33.409	40.790
18	7.015	7.906	9.390	10.865	12.857	14.440	17.338	20.601	22.760	25.989	28.869	32.346	34.805	42.312
19	7.633	8.567	10.117	11.651	13.716	15.352	18.338	21.689	23.900	27.204	30.144	33.687	36.191	43.820
20	8.260	9.237	10.851	12.443	14.578	16.266	19.337	22.775	25.038	28.412	31.410	35.020	37.566	45.315
21	8.897	9.915	11.591	13.240	15.445	17.182	20.337	23.858	26.171	29.615	32.671	36.343	38.932	46.797
22	9.542	10.600	12.338	13.041	16.314	18.101	21.337	24.929	27.301	30.813	33.924	37.659	40.289	48.268
23	10.196	11.293	13.091	14.848	17.187	19.021	22.337	26.018	28.429	32.007	35.172	38.968	41.638	49.728
24	10.856	11.992	13.848	15.659	18.062	19.943	23.337	27.096	29.553	33.196	36.415	40.270	42.980	51.179
25	11.524	12.697	14.611	16.473	18.940	20.867	24.337	28.172	30.675	34.382	37.652	41.566	44.314	52.620
26	12.198	13.409	15.379	17.292	19.820	21.792	25.336	29.246	31.795	35.563	38.885	42.856	45.642	54.052
27	12.879	14.125	16.151	18.114	20.703	22.719	26.336	30.319	32.912	36.741	40.113	44.140	46.963	55.476
28	13.565	14.847	16.928	18.939	21.588	23.647	27.336	31.391	34.027	37.916	41.337	45.419	48.278	56.893
29	14.256	15.574	17.708	19.768	22.475	24.577	28.336	32.461	35.139	39.087	42.557	46.693	49.588	58.302
30	14.953	16.306	18.493	20.599	23.364	25.508	29.336	33.530	36.250	40.256	43.773	47.962	50.892	59.703

Source: Reproduced from Table III of R. A. Fisher, *Statistical Methods for Research Workers* (14th ed.), 1973, copyright by Oxford University Press, England. Used by permission of Oxford University Press (originally published by Oliver and Boyd, Ltd.).

Table B.5   r Values and Their Associated p Values

(N − 2)	Probability level				
	.10	.05	.02	.01	.001
1	.988	.997	.9995	.9999	1.000
2	.900	.950	.980	.990	.999
3	.805	.878	.934	.959	.991
4	.729	.811	.882	.917	.974
5	.669	.754	.833	.874	.951
6	.622	.707	.789	.834	.925
7	.582	.666	.750	.798	.898
8	.549	.632	.716	.765	.872
9	.522	.602	.685	.735	.847
10	.497	.576	.658	.708	.823
11	.476	.553	.634	.684	.801
12	.458	.532	.612	.661	.780
13	.441	.514	.592	.641	.760
14	.426	.497	.574	.623	.742
15	.412	.482	.558	.606	.725
16	.400	.468	.542	.590	.708
17	.389	.456	.528	.575	.693
18	.378	.444	.516	.561	.679
19	.369	.433	.503	.549	.665
20	.360	.423	.492	.537	.652
22	.344	.404	.472	.515	.629
24	.330	.388	.453	.496	.607
25	.323	.381	.445	.487	.597
30	.296	.349	.409	.449	.554
35	.275	.325	.381	.418	.519
40	.257	.304	.358	.393	.490
45	.243	.288	.338	.372	.465
50	.231	.273	.322	.354	.443
55	.220	.261	.307	.338	.424
60	.211	.250	.295	.325	.408
65	.203	.240	.284	.312	.393
70	.195	.232	.274	.302	.380
75	.189	.224	.264	.292	.368
80	.183	.217	.256	.283	.357
85	.178	.211	.249	.275	.347
90	.173	.205	.242	.267	.338
95	.168	.200	.236	.260	.329
100	.164	.195	.230	.254	.321
125	.147	.174	.206	.228	.288
150	.134	.159	.189	.208	.264
175	.124	.148	.174	.194	.248
200	.116	.138	.164	.181	.235
300	.095	.113	.134	.148	.188
500	.074	.088	.104	.115	.148
1,000	.052	.062	.073	.081	.104
2,000	.037	.044	.052	.058	.074

Note: All p values are two-tailed in this table.

Source: From *Some Extensions of Student's t and Pearson's r Central Distributions*, by A. L. Sockloff and J. N. Edney, May 1972, Temple University Technical Report 72–5, Measurement and Research Center. Reprinted with the permission of Alan Sockloff.

Appendix B

Table B.6 Transformations of r to Fisher z_r

Second digit of r

r	.00	.01	.02	.03	.04	.05	.06	.07	.08	.09
.0	.000	.010	.020	.030	.040	.050	.060	.070	.080	.090
.1	.100	.110	.121	.131	.141	.151	.161	.172	.182	.192
.2	.203	.213	.224	.234	.245	.255	.266	.277	.288	.299
.3	.310	.321	.332	.343	.354	.365	.377	.388	.400	.412
.4	.424	.436	.448	.460	.472	.485	.497	.510	.523	.536
.5	.549	.563	.576	.590	.604	.618	.633	.648	.662	.678
.6	.693	.709	.725	.741	.758	.775	.793	.811	.829	.848
.7	.867	.887	.908	.929	.950	.973	.996	1.020	1.045	1.071
.8	1.099	1.127	1.157	1.188	1.221	1.256	1.293	1.333	1.376	1.422

Third digit of r

r	.000	.001	.002	.003	.004	.005	.006	.007	.008	.009
.90	1.472	1.478	1.483	1.488	1.494	1.499	1.505	1.510	1.516	1.522
.91	1.528	1.533	1.539	1.545	1.551	1.557	1.564	1.570	1.576	1.583
.92	1.589	1.596	1.602	1.609	1.616	1.623	1.630	1.637	1.644	1.651
.93	1.658	1.666	1.673	1.681	1.689	1.697	1.705	1.713	1.721	1.730
.94	1.738	1.747	1.756	1.764	1.774	1.783	1.792	1.802	1.812	1.822
.95	1.832	1.842	1.853	1.863	1.874	1.886	1.897	1.909	1.921	1.933
.96	1.946	1.959	1.972	1.986	2.000	2.014	2.029	2.044	2.060	2.076
.97	2.092	2.109	2.127	2.146	2.165	2.185	2.205	2.227	2.249	2.273
.98	2.298	2.323	2.351	2.380	2.410	2.443	2.477	2.515	2.555	2.599
.99	2.646	2.700	2.759	2.826	2.903	2.994	3.106	3.250	3.453	3.800

Source: Reprinted by permission from *Statistical Methods* (8th ed.), by G. W. Snedecor and W. G. Cochran © 1989 by Iowa State University Press, Ames, IA 50010.

Appendix B

| Table B.7 | Transformations of Fisher z_r to r |

z_r	.00	.01	.02	.03	.04	.05	.06	.07	.08	.09
.0	.000	.010	.020	.030	.040	.050	.060	.070	.080	.090
.1	.100	.110	.119	.129	.139	.149	.159	.168	.178	.187
.2	.197	.207	.216	.226	.236	.245	.254	.264	.273	.282
.3	.291	.300	.310	.319	.327	.336	.345	.354	.363	.371
.4	.380	.389	.397	.405	.414	.422	.430	.438	.446	.454
.5	.462	.470	.478	.485	.493	.500	.508	.515	.523	.530
.6	.537	.544	.551	.558	.565	.572	.578	.585	.592	.598
.7	.604	.611	.617	.623	.629	.635	.641	.647	.653	.658
.8	.664	.670	.675	.680	.686	.691	.696	.701	.706	.711
.9	.716	.721	.726	.731	.735	.740	.744	.749	.753	.757
1.0	.762	.766	.770	.774	.778	.782	.786	.790	.793	.797
1.1	.800	.804	.808	.811	.814	.818	.821	.824	.828	.831
1.2	.834	.837	.840	.843	.846	.848	.851	.854	.856	.859
1.3	.862	.864	.867	.869	.872	.874	.876	.879	.881	.883
1.4	.885	.888	.890	.892	.894	.896	.898	.900	.902	.903
1.5	.905	.907	.909	.910	.912	.914	.915	.917	.919	.920
1.6	.922	.923	.925	.926	.928	.929	.930	.932	.933	.934
1.7	.935	.937	.938	.939	.940	.941	.942	.944	.945	.946
1.8	.947	.948	.949	.950	.951	.952	.953	.954	.954	.955
1.9	.956	.957	.958	.959	.960	.960	.961	.962	.963	.963
2.0	.964	.965	.965	.966	.967	.967	.968	.969	.969	.970
2.1	.970	.971	.972	.972	.973	.973	.974	.974	.975	.975
2.2	.976	.976	.977	.977	.978	.978	.978	.979	.979	.980
2.3	.980	.980	.981	.981	.982	.982	.982	.983	.983	.983
2.4	.984	.984	.984	.985	.985	.985	.986	.986	.986	.986
2.5	.987	.987	.987	.987	.988	.988	.988	.988	.989	.989
2.6	.989	.989	.989	.990	.990	.990	.990	.990	.991	.991
2.7	.991	.991	.991	.992	.992	.992	.992	.992	.992	.992
2.8	.993	.993	.993	.993	.993	.993	.993	.994	.994	.994
2.9	.994	.994	.994	.994	.994	.995	.995	.995	.995	.995

Source: Reprinted by permission from *Statistical Methods* (8th ed.), by G. W. Snedecor and W. G. Cochran © 1989 by Iowa State University Press, Ames, IA 50010.

APPENDIX C

Introduction to Meta-Analysis

The Purpose of Meta-Analysis

It seems that almost every time we watch a television news broadcast or open a newspaper we learn about some new pharmaceutical study. We may be told that the study reported an effect in one direction but that other studies have reported an effect in the opposite direction or an effect that is close to zero. How do researchers resolve this conflicting evidence? Meta-analysis is the method of choice for providing a summary of all the research findings and identifying variables (called **moderator variables**) that may be responsible for increases or decreases in the degree of association between two events. The name **meta-analysis** (coined by Gene Glass, 1976) actually refers not to a single procedure for combining research findings and overcoming the equivocation of conflicting results, but to a collection of quantitative and graphic procedures. In using the term *research findings* in this context, meta-analysts typically are referring to effect size indices, which are the primary coin of the realm in meta-analysis.

In this appendix, we will give you a sense of some of the quantitative procedures that are used to compare and combine effect sizes and to estimate overall p values. We emphasize r-type indices because they can be used in situations in which other effect size indices would not make sense, but it is also common to see standardized difference indices (such as Cohen's d, described in Chapter 13) used in the meta-analysis of two group designs. If you would like to learn more about meta-analysis, you will find an engaging introduction in Hunt's *How Science Takes Stock* (1997) and in Cooper and Hedges's comprehensive *Handbook of Research Synthesis* (1994). There is also an overview of meta-analysis in a review article by R. Rosenthal and DiMatteo (2001) and further discussion in our advanced text (R. Rosenthal & Rosnow, 2008, Ch. 21). Although we focus only on the comparison and combination of two independent studies in this appendix, you will find procedures for comparing and combining any number of studies in texts and handbooks, including Chalmers and Altman (1995); Cook et al. (1994); H. Cooper (1998); Glass, McGaw, and Smith (1981); Hedges and Olkin (1985); Hunter and Schmidt (2004); Light and Pillemer (1984); Lipsey and Wilson (2001); R. Rosenthal (1991); and Wachter and Straf (1990).

Behavioral and social researchers not only have pioneered innovative procedures for use in meta-analysis but have embraced this approach to reveal moderator variables in a wide variety of areas. For example, social psychologist Alice H. Eagly (1978) used the methodology of meta-analysis to discover a fascinating moderator variable. Textbooks had long asserted that women were more conforming and more easily influenced than men, presumably because socialization processes had taught men to be independent thinkers, a cultural value that was seldom as suitable for women. Hypothesizing that the historical period in which the results were collected might be a moderator of the association between gender and influenceability, Eagly's meta-analysis revealed a pronounced difference in the association between gender and influenceability in the research published before 1970 from that found in research published during the era of the women's movement in the 1970s. In contrast to the older research, which found greater influenceability among females than among males, the later studies uncovered few gender differences in influenceability.

The first step in a meta-analysis is to define the independent and dependent variables of interest. The next step is to collect the relevant studies systematically and to collate them by defining specific categories of information. The ensuing steps use both quantitative and graphical procedures (e.g., stem-and-leaf charts) to examine the variability among the obtained effect sizes and use simple statistical formulas to make estimates of the average effect sizes and to determine the significance levels of the combined effects. Meta-analysts seek to develop a meaningful mosaic that reveals patterns in the data and, with the help of moderator variables, can explain seemingly contradictory results. Thus, meta-analysis helps researchers to develop a cumulative picture of the research results in a particular area rather than to rely on a single study or on a traditional narrative, nonquantitative review in attempting to understand a phenomenon. Meta-analysis also encourages a deeper understanding of each study, because each study has to be read carefully for the essential information needed.

Comparing Two Effect Sizes

Suppose we believe that two studies are conceptually similar, but we also want to compare their effect sizes as further insurance that they constitute a homogeneous set. First, we give the values of $r_{\text{effect size}}$ the same sign if both studies show effects in the same direction, but we give them different signs if the results are in the opposite direction. Second, we find for each $r_{\text{effect size}}$ value the Fisher z_r, which (as you learned in Chapter 12) is the log transformation of r found in Table B.6 (p. 403). Third, we substitute in the following formula to get the standard normal deviate (z) corresponding to the difference between the Fisher z_r scores:

$$z \text{ of difference} = \frac{z_{r1} - z_{r2}}{\sqrt{\dfrac{1}{N_1 - 3} + \dfrac{1}{N_2 - 3}}}$$

where z_{r1} and z_{r2} are the log transformations found in Step 2 for the $r_{\text{effect size}}$ values of Studies 1 and 2, respectively, and N_1 and N_2 are the total sample sizes of Studies 1 and 2, respectively. The final step is to look up the result in Table B.1 (p. 393), which gives us the associated one-tailed p of the z of difference. Let us try some examples.

Example 1. Suppose you have used 100 subjects to try to replicate an experiment that, when you computed the effect size on the reported t (using the procedure described in Chapter 13), yielded $r_{\text{effect size}} = .50$ based on only 10 subjects. In your study, you found $r_{\text{effect size}} = .31$, but your result was in the opposite direction of the one previously reported. You code your effect as negative to reflect the fact that it is in the opposite direction, and then you consult Table B.6 (p. 403) to find the Fisher z_r corresponding to each $r_{\text{effect size}}$. For $r = .50$, you find $z_r = .549$ in Table B.6 at the intersection of the .5 row and the .00 column. For $r = -.31$, you find $z_r = .321$ at the .3 row and the .01 column intersection, and you code the result as $-.321$ because it is based on your empirical finding, which was in the opposite direction of the earlier result.

Next, from the previous formula, you compute

$$z \text{ of difference} = \frac{(.549) - (-.321)}{\sqrt{\dfrac{1}{7} + \dfrac{1}{97}}} = \frac{.870}{.391} = 2.22$$

as the z of the difference between the two effect sizes. Looking up the p value associated with $z = 2.22$ in Table B.1 (p. 393), you find $p = .0132$ one-tailed, which you can round to .01 one-tailed or .03 two-tailed (i.e., $.0132 \times 2 = .03$ rounded). The p value is small enough to convince you that your result differs from the original one, and as the difference between the r values is obviously large as well as significant statistically, you decide that they cannot simply be combined without careful thought and comment. In describing the results of both studies considered together, you would report the differences between them and give a tentative explanation for the differences.

Example 2. Alternatively, suppose your result is in the same direction as the original one and of a similar magnitude, and you have used the same number of subjects. This time, imagine that the original $r_{\text{effect size}} = .45$ ($N = 120$) and your $r_{\text{effect size}} = .40$ ($N = 120$). Following the same procedure as in Example 1, you find in Table B.6 the z_r values corresponding to the effect size r values to be .485 and .424, respectively. From the preceding formula you compute

$$z \text{ of difference} = \frac{.485 \quad .424}{\sqrt{\dfrac{1}{117} + \dfrac{1}{117}}} = \frac{.061}{.131} = .47$$

as your obtained z of the difference. In Table B.1 you find the p associated with $z = .47$ to be .3192 one-tailed. Here, then, is an example of two studies that do not disagree significantly in their estimates of the size of the relationship between X and Y and are quite similar in magnitude. They can now be routinely combined by means of a simple meta-analytic technique, as shown next.

Combining Two Effect Sizes

Given two effect size r values that can be combined on conceptual and statistical grounds, we find the typical (or average) effect size by using the following formula:

$$\bar{z}_r = \frac{z_{r1} + z_{r2}}{2}$$

We afterward transform the resulting Fisher z_r into the metric of an effect size correlation. In this formula the denominator is the number of z_r scores in the numerator. The resulting value is an average Fisher z_r (symbolized here as $\bar{z}_r$, where the bar over the z_r signifies that it is a mean value). Example 3 shows how this number crunching proceeds.

Example 3. In Example 2, one $r_{\text{effect size}}$ = .45 and the other $r_{\text{effect size}}$ = .40 (both coded as positive to show that both results were in the predicted direction). You found the Fisher z_r scores corresponding to the effect size r values to be .485 and .424, respectively. From the formula above you compute

$$\bar{z}_r = \frac{.485 + .424}{2} = .45$$

as the average Fisher z_r. Finally, looking in Table B.7 (p. 404), you find that a Fisher z_r of .45 is associated with an r of .422, which is the $r_{\text{effect size}}$ estimate of the two studies combined.

Obtaining an Overall Significance Level

Although meta-analysts are generally more interested in effect sizes than in p values, they might be interested in the overall statistical significance of a set of comparable studies. It is an easy matter to combine the p values and get an overall estimate of the probability that the p values might have been obtained if the null hypothesis of no relationship between X and Y were true. We first obtain an accurate p value for each study (accurate, say, to two digits, not counting zeros before the first nonzero value, such as p = .43 or .024 or .0012). That is, if t (with 30 df) = 3.03, we code p as .0025, not as p < .05. Extended tables of the t distribution may be helpful here (such as Table B.2 on pp. 394–395), but more helpful still is a computer program or a good calculator that gives accurate p values at the touch of a couple of buttons. For each p, the meta-analyst finds z (not the Fisher z_r, but the standard normal deviate z in Table B.1 of Appendix B). Both p values should also be one-tailed, and we give the corresponding z values the same sign if both studies show effects in the same direction, but different signs if the results are in the opposite direction.

In our continuing example of working with two studies, the formula used to combine the two z values is as follows:

$$\text{Combined } z = \frac{z_1 + z_2}{\sqrt{2}}$$

That is, the sum of the two z values when divided by the square root of the number of z values combined yields a new z. This new z corresponds to the p value of the two studies combined if the null hypothesis of no relationship between X and Y were true.

Example 4. As an illustration, suppose we assume that Studies A and B are a combinable set with results in the same direction, but neither is statistically significant. One p is .121, and the other is .084. Their z values are 1.17 and 1.38, respectively. From the preceding formula we have

$$\text{Combined } z = \frac{1.17 + 1.38}{\sqrt{2}} = \frac{2.55}{1.41} = 1.81$$

as our combined z. The p associated with this combined z is .035 one-tailed (or .07 two-tailed).

Detective-Like Probing of Reported Data

For our illustrations of meta-analytic comparisons and combinations of effect size r and p values, we have concentrated on the case of only two results. Meta-analysts often work with many more results to be coded, compared, and combined, however. The procedures used are quite similar in spirit to the procedures described above, and you will find descriptions in the texts cited earlier—and also some tips on how to estimate effect sizes when published reports provide only limited details. Even from very limited information, it is often possible to re-create the original summary ANOVA table and to compute our own contrasts and effect sizes from the reconstituted summary (e.g., Rosnow & Rosenthal, 2007). There are also examples in the chapters in this text, such as computing an effect size index from a reported t test (Chapter 13), or computing a contrast from a reported omnibus F test (Box 14.5 in Chapter 14) and then computing your own r-type effect size indices (Chapter 14), or computing effect sizes from news reports of biomedical trials (Box 15.3 in Chapter 15).

Sometimes all that is reported are statistical test results for which there is no formal index of effect size available, but an exact probability is reported. This is often true for what are called nonparametric statistics (Higgins, 2004; Siegel & Castellan, 1988). Suppose a study in which four children were taught by a new educational method (the treatment) and five children were taught by an old (control) method. All four of the treated children were ranked higher than any of the five control children, and the non-parametric test (the Mann-Whitney U) had an exact p of .008 one-tailed. We simply find the value of t corresponding to the exact p and df and then substitute in the following familiar formula:

$$r_{equivalent} = \sqrt{\frac{t^2}{t^2 + df}}$$

where the result is indicated as $r_{equivalent}$ because it is analogous to $r_{effect\ size}$ between the treatment indicator (e.g., with the treatment dummy-coded 1 and the control coded 0) and the continuous outcome measure (i.e., a point-biserial r) with $N/2$ units in each group (Rosenthal & Rubin, 2003). In this example, where $p = .008$ and $N = 9$, the t value for 7 degrees of freedom is 3.16, and substituting in the formula above gives us $r_{equivalent} = .77$.

The File Drawer Problem

Because many journal editors are reluctant to accept "nonsignificant" results, researchers' file drawers may contain unpublished studies that failed to yield significant results (Bakan, 1967; Sterling, 1959). If there were a substantial number of such studies in the file drawers, the meta-analyst's evaluation of the overall significance level might be unduly optimistic. One solution to this **file drawer problem** is to calculate the number of studies averaging null results that would be required to nudge the significance level for *all* studies (retrieved and unretrieved combined) to the less coveted side of $p = .05$ (R. Rosenthal, 1979, 1983, 1991). If the overall significance level computed on the basis of the retrieved studies can be brought down to $p > .05$ by the addition of just a few more null results, then the original estimate of p is clearly *not robust* (i.e., not resistant to the file drawer threat).

Table C.1	Tolerances for Future Null Results		
	Original average significance level		
Retrieved studies	.05	.01	.001
1	1	2	4
2	4	8	15
3	9	18	32
4	16	32	57
5	25	50	89
6	36	72	128
7	49	98	173
8	64	128	226
9	81	162	286
10	100	200	353
15	225	450	795
20	400	800	1,412
25	625	1,250	2,206
30	900	1,800	3,177
40	1,600	3,200	5,648
50	2,500	5,000	8,824

Note: Entries in this table are the total number of old and new studies required to bring an original average p of .05, .01, or .001 down to an overall $p > .05$ (i.e., just barely to "nonsignificance").

Table C.1 illustrates the results of such calculations. It shows a table of *tolerance values* in which the rows represent the number of retrieved (i.e., meta-analyzed) studies and the columns represent three different levels of the average statistical significance of the retrieved studies. The intersection of any row and column shows the sum of old and new studies required to bring the p for all studies (retrieved *and* unretrieved) down to the level of being barely "nonsignificant" at $p > .05$.

Suppose we have meta-analyzed 8 studies and found the average (not the combined, but the mean) p value to be .05. The 64 in Table C.1 tells us that it will take an additional 56 unretrieved studies averaging null results to bring the original average $p = .05$ based on 8 studies ($64 - 8 = 56$) down to $p > .05$. As a general rule of thumb, it has been suggested that we regard as robust any combined results for which the tolerance level reaches $5(k) + 10$, where k is the number of studies retrieved (R. Rosenthal, 1991). In our example of 8 studies retrieved, this means that we will be satisfied that the original estimate of $p \leq .05$ is robust if we think that there are fewer than an additional $5(8) + 10 = 50$ studies with null results squirreled away in file drawers. Because this table shows a tolerance for an additional 56 studies, we conclude that the original estimate is robust.

The Counternull Statistic

The procedures we have discussed in this appendix should also be useful to you if you have done a study and also its replication, or if you are replicating an older study. One final point, however, is that if the results of your study include both an estimate of the effect size and (when possible) an interval estimate, you will have better protected yourself against Type I and Type II error. In Chapter 12, we described how to create a confidence interval around $r_{\text{effect size}}$, and in Chapter 13, we showed how to do the same thing for Cohen's d on two independent groups. Another way of protecting yourself against Type II error (the error of failing to reject the null hypothesis when it is false) is to consider the counternull value of the effect size whenever you have a p value that is nonsignificant and are about to conclude that "nothing happened" statistically. This value, called the **counternull statistic** (R. Rosenthal & Rubin, 1994) is a kind of "confidence interval" except that it involves the null hypothesis and the *obtained p* value. In the case of $r_{\text{effect size}}$, given a null value of zero, the counternull value can usually be estimated as

$$ r_{\text{counternull}} = \sqrt{\frac{4r^2}{1 + 3r^2}} $$

where $r_{\text{counternull}}$ is the point-biserial r (R. Rosenthal & Rubin, 1994; Rosnow & Rosenthal, 1996).

For example, suppose you do a t test and find $p = .115$ one-tailed, although the effect size r is far from zero, say, $r - .30$ (which is quite respectable). Before concluding there was "no effect," you will want to do a power analysis to see how much "effective power" your t test actually had (discussed in Chapter 12). In addition, substituting in the formula above, you find

$$ r_{\text{counternull}} = \sqrt{\frac{4r^2}{1 + 3r^2}} = \sqrt{\frac{(4)(.30^2)}{1 + (3)(.30^2)}} = .53 $$

which means that, although it is true that your $r_{\text{effect size}}$ of .30 did not differ significantly from .00, it is no more true than that your $r_{\text{effect size}}$ of .30 does not differ significantly from .53. Thus, were you to conclude that there was "no effect" based on $r = .30$ and $p = .115$, your conclusion would be seriously in error because the counternull value (.53) implies a large effect size as the upper limit of the "null-counternull interval," which in this example is a 77% confidence interval.

Appendix C

Glossary

Note: Indicated in parentheses is the primary chapter(s) or appendix where most of the following appear either as Key Terms (listed at the end of the chapter and indicated in boldface within the chapter) or are defined as important concepts or common terms.

A-B design Simplest single-case design, in which the dependent variable is measured throughout the pretreatment or baseline period (the A phase) and the treatment period (the B phase). (8)

A-B-A design Single-case design in which there are repeated measures before the treatment (the A phase), during the treatment (the B phase), and then with the treatment withdrawn (the final A phase). (8)

A-B-A-B design Single-case design in which there are two types of occasions (B to A and A to B) for demonstrating the effects of the treatment variable. (8)

A-B-A-B-A design Single-case design in which there are repeated measures before, during, and after treatment (the B phase). (8)

A-B-BC-B design Single-case design in which there are repeated measures before the introduction of the treatments (the A phase), then during Treatment B, during the combination of Treatments B and C, and, finally, during Treatment B alone; the purpose of the design is to tease out the effect of B both in combination with C and apart from C. (8)

A-B-C design General term for single-case design in which B and C are two different treatments. (8)

abscissa The horizontal axis of a distribution. (10)

abstract Brief, comprehensive summary of the content of a report or paper. (Appendix A)

accidental plagiarism Unwittingly falling into plagiarism. (3)

account for conflicting results One of several possible hypothesis-generating heuristics. (2)

acquiescent response set The tendency of an individual to go along with any request or attitudinal statement. (5)

active deception (deception by commission) Actively misleading the research participants, such as giving them false information about the purpose of the research, or having them unwittingly interact with confederates. (3)

additive model Statistical model in which the components sum to the group means in ANOVA. (14)

ad hoc hypothesis A conjecture or speculation developed on the spot to explain a result. (1)

aesthetic aspect of science The beauty or elegance of scientific theories, experiments, or other facets. (1)

after-only design Research design in which the subjects are measured after the treatment but not before; also called a *posttest-only design*. (7)

alerting r ($r_{alerting}$) The correlation between group means (M) and contrast (λ) weights; also designated as $r_{M\lambda}$. (14)

alpha (α) Probability of a Type I error. (12)

alpha coefficient See *Cronbach's alpha*.

alternate-form reliability The correlation between two forms of a test with different items that are measuring the same attribute. (6)

alternative hypothesis (H_1) The working hypothesis or the experimental hypothesis (that is, as opposed to the null hypothesis in null hypothesis significance testing). (12)

analogical thinking Reasoning by analogy. (2)

analogies and metaphors Devices used to explain or describe one thing in terms of another. (1, 2)

analysis of variance (ANOVA) Subdivision of the total variance of a set of scores into its components. (7, 14)

ancestry search Tracking "ancestral" citations of published work. (2)

ANOVA See *analysis of variance.*

"anything goes" philosophy of science Feyerabend's view that doing research involves a "let's-try-it-and-see" attitude, where anything that works is permissible. (4)

APA American Psychological Association.

APA manual *Publication Manual of the American Psychological Association.* (1, Appendix A)

a priori method The use of individual powers of pure reason and logic as a basis of explanation (Charles Peirce). (1)

APS Association for Psychological Science.

archival material A relatively permanent repository of data or material. (4)

area probability sampling A type of survey sampling in which the subclasses are geographic areas. (9)

arithmetic mean (*M*) The simple average of a set of values. (10)

artifact A specific threat to validity, or a confounded aspect of the scientist's observations. (7)

asymmetrical distribution A distribution of scores in which there is not an exact correspondence in arrangement on the opposite sides of the middle line. (10)

autonomy The person's "independence," in the context of research ethics; also refers to a prospective participant's right as well as ability "to choose" whether to participate in the study or to continue in the study. (3)

back-to-back stem-and-leaf chart The back-to-back plots of distributions in which the original data are preserved with any desired precision. (10)

back translation See *translation and back translation.*

bar graphs Distributions where the bars represent the number (frequency) of scores. (10)

before-after design A research design in which the subjects are measured before and after treatment; also called a *pre-post design.* (7)

behavior What someone does or how someone acts. (1)

behavioral baseline A comparison base, operationally defined as the continuous, and continuing, performance of a single unit in single-case research. (8)

behavioral diary Data collection technique in which the research participant keeps a record of events at the time they occur. (5)

behavioral science A general term that encompasses scientific disciplines in which empirical inquiry is used to study motivation, cognition, and behavior. (1)

Belmont Report The name given to a study developed by a national commission in 1974 to protect the rights and welfare of participants in biomedical and behavioral research. (3)

beneficence The "doing of good," which is one of the guidelines of the discussed ethical principles. (3)

BESD See *binomial effect-size display.*

beta (β) Probability of a Type II error. (12)

between-subjects design Statistical design in which the sampling units are exposed to one treatment each. (7)

bias Net systematic error. (6, 7, 9)

Big Five factors (OCEAN) The collective name for five broad domains of individual personality: (a) openness to experience, (b) conscientiousness, (c) extraversion, (d) agreeableness, and (e) neuroticism. (5)

bimodal A distribution showing two modes. (10)

binomial effect-size display (BESD) Procedure for the display of the practical importance of an effect size correlation ($r_{effect\ size}$) of any magnitude. (12)

bipolar rating scales Rating scales in which the ends of the scales are extreme opposites. (5)

blind experimenters Experimenters who are unaware of which participants are in the experimental and control conditions. (7)

byline The author's name as it appears on the title page of an article. (Appendix A)

causal inference The act or process of inferring that *X* causes *Y*. (7)

causation The relation of cause to effect. (7)

ceiling effect Situation in which the amount of change that can be produced is limited by the upper boundary of the measure. (5)

central tendency Location of the bulk of a distribution; measured by means, medians, modes, and trimmed means. (10)

central tendency bias A type of response set in which the respondent is reluctant to give extreme ratings and instead rates in the direction of the mean of the total group. (5)

certificate of confidentiality A formal agreement between the investigator and the government agency sponsoring the research that requires the investigator to keep the data confidential. (3)

chi-square (χ^2) A statistic used to test the degree of agreement between the frequency data actually obtained and those expected under a particular hypothesis (e.g., the null hypothesis). (15)

closed (structured, fixed-choice, or precoded) measures See *structured items*.

clusters See *strata*.

coefficient of determination (r^2) Proportion of variance shared by two variables. (12)

cognitive heuristics Information-processing rules of thumb. (1)

Cohen's d Index of effect size in standard deviation units. (13)

coherence The extent to which things (e.g., components of a theory or hypothesis) "stick together" logically. (2)

cohort A collection of individuals who were born in the same period, or a generation. (8)

column effect Column mean minus grand mean. (14)

composite reliability The aggregate reliability of two or more items or judges' ratings. (6)

concealed measurement The use of hidden measurements, such as a hidden recording device that eavesdrops on conversations. (4)

conceptual definitions See *theoretical definitions*.

concurrent validity The extent to which test results are correlated with some criterion in the present. (6)

confidence interval The upper and lower bounds of a statistic, where confidence is defined as $1 - \alpha$. (9, 10, 12, 13)

confidentiality Protection of research participants' or survey respondents' disclosures against unwarranted access. (3)

confirmatory data analysis Analysis of data for the purpose of testing hypotheses. (10)

confounded Mixed or confused.

confounded hypotheses (in panel designs) The inability to separate the effect attributed to one hypothesis from the effect attributed to another hypothesis in cross-lagged panel designs. (8)

construct Abstract variable, formulated from ideas or images, that serves as an explanatory concept. (2)

construct validity A type of test or research validity that addresses the psychological qualities contributing to the relationship between X and Y. (6)

content analysis A method of decomposing written messages and pictorial documents. (4)

content validity A type of test validity that addresses whether the test adequately samples the relevant material. (6)

contingency table A table of frequencies (counts) coded by row and column variables. (11)

continuous variable A variable for which we can imagine another value falling between any two adjacent scores. (11)

contrast r ($r_{contrast}$) The pure correlation between scores on the dependent variable (Y) and the lambda (λ) coefficients after the removal of any other patterns in the data; also designated as $r_{Y\lambda \cdot NC}$. (14)

contrasts Statistical procedures that address specific questions or predictions in the data, such as testing for a particular trend in the results. (14)

contrast weights See *lambda weights*.

contrived observation Unobtrusive observation of the effects of some variable that was introduced into a situation. (4)

control group A condition with which the effects of the experimental or test condition are compared. (7)

convergent validity Validity supported by a substantial correlation of conceptually similar measures. (6)

corrected range See *extended range*.

correlated replicators Nonindependent replicators. (6)

correlated-sample t See *paired t*.

correlational research Another common name for relational research, that is, research in which two or more variables or conditions are measured and related to one another. (1)

correlation coefficient An index of the degree of association between two variables, typically Pearson r or related product-moment correlation. (11)

correspondence with reality The extent to which a hypothesis agrees with accepted truths based on reliable empirical findings. (2)

counterbalancing A procedure in which some subjects receive Treatment A before Treatment B, and the others receive B before A (e.g., in Latin square designs). (7, 13)

counternull statistic A measure of the non-null magnitude of the effect size that is supported by the same amount of evidence as the null value of the effect size. (Appendix C)

counts Frequencies. (11, 15)

covariation The principle that, in order to demonstrate causality, what is labeled as the "cause" should be shown to be positively correlated with what is labeled as the "effect." (7)

criterion validity The extent to which a measure correlates with one or more criterion variables. (6)

critical incident technique Open-ended method that instructs the respondent to describe an observable action the purpose of which is fairly clear to the respondent and the consequences of which are sufficiently definite to leave little doubt about its effects. (5)

Cronbach's alpha A measure of internal consistency reliability, proposed by L. J. Cronbach. (6)

crossed design Another name for the basic within-subjects design, because the subjects can be said to be "crossed" by treatment conditions. (7)

cross-lagged correlations Correlations of the degree of association between two sets of variables, of which one is treated as a lagged (time-delayed) value. (6, 8)

cross-lagged panel design Relational research design using cross-lagged correlations, cross-sectional correlations repeated over time, and test-retest correlations. (8)

cross-sectional design Research that compares subjects on one or more variables at one point in time. (8)

crude range Highest score minus lowest score. (10)

cue words Guiding labels that define particular points or categories of response. (5)

debriefing Disclosing to participants the nature of the research in which they have participated. (3)

deception by commission See *active deception*.

deception by omission See *passive deception*.

decision-plane model A two-dimensional schema of the risks and benefits of doing research. (3)

degrees of freedom (*df*) The number of observations minus the number of restrictions limiting the observations' freedom to vary. (13)

demand characteristics M. T. Orne's term for the mixture of hints and cues that govern the participant's perception of (a) his or her role as research subject and (b) the experimenter's hypothesis. (3, 7)

dependent variable A variable the changes in which are viewed as dependent on changes in one or more other variables. (2)

descriptive measures Measures such as σ and σ^2 that are used to calculate population values. (10)

descriptive research An empirical investigation in which the objective is to map out a situation or set of events. (1)

df See *degrees of freedom*.

dichotomous variable A variable that is divided into two classes. (11)

discovery phase H. Reichenbach's general term for the origin, creation, or invention of ideas for investigation. (2)

discrete variable A variable taking on two or more distinct values. (11)

discriminant validity Validity supported by a lack of correlation between conceptually unrelated measures. (6)

dispersion Spread or variability. (10)

double-blind procedures Procedures in which neither the experimenter nor the participants know who has been assigned to the experimental and control groups. (7)

double deception A deception embedded in what the research participant thinks is the official debriefing. (3)

drunkard's search The mistake of looking for something in a convenient but not particularly relevant place. (1)

dummy coding Giving arbitrary numerical values (often 0 and 1) to the two levels of a dichotomous variable. (11)

effective power The actual power (i.e., $1 - \beta$) of the statistical test used. (12)

effective sample size The net equivalent sample size that the researcher ends up with. (9)

effect size A concept originally developed by J. Cohen, which typically refers to the magnitude of an experimental outcome or to the strength of relationship between two variables (e.g., an independent and a dependent variable). (12)

effect size r ($r_{\text{effect size}}$) The magnitude of an experimental effect (i.e., the size of the relation between X and Y, also designated as $r_{Y\lambda}$ in contrast analysis. (7, 12, 13, 14, Appendix C)

efficient causality The idea that a propelling or instigating event or condition sets some other event in motion or alters another condition to some degree. (7)

empirical Controlled observation and measurement. (1)

empirical reasoning A use of logic and evidence. (1)

equivalence, coefficient of The correlation between alternate measures of the same condition. (6)

error Fluctuation in measurements; also deviation of a score from the mean of the group or condition. (6, 14)

error of estimate Closeness of estimate to actual value. (9)

errors of measurement Random errors in classical test theory. (6)

ethical guidelines Principles intended to help researchers decide what aspects of a study might pose an ethical problem and, in general terms, how to avoid it. (3)

ethics The system of moral values by which behavior is judged. (3)

evaluation apprehension M. J. Rosenberg's term for the subject's emotional discomfort about possibly being negatively evaluated or not positively evaluated. (5, 7)

evaluation, potency, and activity Three primary dimensions of subjective meaning, which are typically measured by a semantic differential. (5)

expectancy control design An experimental design in which the expectancy variable operates separately from the independent variable of interest. (7)

expected frequency (f_e) Counts expected under specified row and column conditions if certain hypotheses (e.g., the null hypothesis) are true. (15)

expedited review The evaluation of proposed research without undue delay. (3)

experimental group A group or condition in which the subjects undergo a manipulation or some other experimental intervention. (7)

experimental hypothesis The experimenter's working hypothesis; also an alternative to the null hypothesis. (2)

experimental research An empirical investigation in which the objective is a causal explanation. (1)

experimenter expectancy bias Another name for the experimenter expectancy effect. (2, 7)

experimenter expectancy effect An experimenter-related artifact that results when the hypothesis held by the experimenter leads unintentionally to behavior toward the subjects that, in turn, increases the likelihood that the hypothesis will be confirmed. (2, 7)

exploratory data analysis Searching in the data for relationships, patterns, clues, leads, or insights. (10)

exploratory research An empirical investigation guided more by general questions than by specific hypotheses. (2)

extended range (corrected range) Crude range plus one unit. (10)

external validity The degree of generalizability. (6)

extraneous effect The result of an unaccounted-for variable. (7)

F_{contrast} The symbol used in this book to denote an F test (with numerator $df = 1$) that is used to address a focused prediction involving more than two groups or conditions. (14)

$F_{\text{noncontrast}}$ The result of dividing the mean square noncontrast by the mean square within, which is then used to compute an effect size r for $F_{\text{effect size}}$. (14)

face-to-face interview An interview in which the interviewer and the respondent directly interact with one another face to face. (5)

face validity The extent to which a test seems on its surface to be measuring what it purports to measure. (6)

factor A general name for a variable, the independent variable. (7)

factorial design A research design with more than one factor and two or more levels of each factor. (7)

fair-mindedness Impartiality. (3)

falsifiability (refutability) The principle (advanced by K. Popper) that a theoretical assertion is scientific only if it is stated in such a way that it can, if incorrect, be refuted by some empirical means. (2)

field experiments Experimental research that is done in a naturalistic setting. (4)

file drawer problem The concern that a substantial number of studies with nonsignificant results are tucked away in file drawers. (Appendix C)

final causality An emphasis on the end goal or objective (Aristotle). (7)

finite Term applied when all the units or events can, at least in theory, be completely counted. (10)

Fisher z_r The log transformation of r, as shown in Table B.6. (12, Appendix C)

fixed-choice measures. See *structured items.*

floor effect A condition in which the amount of change that can be produced is limited by the lower boundary of the measure. (5)

focused chi-square χ^2 with 1 df. (15)

focused statistical procedure Any t test, 1-df χ^2, or F with numerator $df = 1$. (14)

forced-choice scales Measures that use an item format requiring the respondent to select a single item (or a specified number of items) from a presented set of choices, even when the respondent finds no choice or more than one of the choices acceptable. (5)

formal causality Emphasis on the implicit form or meaning of something (Aristotle). (7)

found experiments D. P. Phillips's term for naturally occurring experiments. (8)

frames Sampling lists. (9)

F ratio Ratio of mean squares that are distributed as F when the null hypothesis is true, where F is a test of significance used to judge the tenability of the null hypothesis of no relationship between two or more variables (or of no difference between two or more variabilities). (14)

free-text searching Using terms that seem intuitively relevant in information retrieval. (2)

frequency distribution A chart that shows the number of times each score or other unit of observation occurs in a set of scores. (10)

F test See *F ratio.*

fugitive literature Hard-to-find literature. (2)

full-text database Information databank that contains the entire work, not just an abstract. (2)

good subject Participant who is overly sensitive to and compliant with demand characteristics. (7)

grand mean (M_G) The mean of means, or the mean of all observations. (14)

graphic scales Rating scales in the form of a straight line with cue words attached. (5)

halo effect A response set in which the bias results from the judge's overextending a favorable impression of someone, based on some central trait, to the person's other characteristics. (5)

harmonic mean sample size (n_h) The reciprocal of the arithmetic mean of sample sizes that have been transformed to their reciprocals. (13)

heterogeneous Dissimilarity among the elements of a set. (9)

heuristic Something general (e.g., a rule of thumb) that provokes interest and further thought. (2)

history A plausible threat to internal validity when an event or incident that takes place between the premeasurement and the postmeasurement contaminates the results of research not using randomization. (7)

homogeneity of variance Equality of the population variance of the groups to be compared. (13)

homogeneous Similarity among the elements of a set. (9)

hyperclaim An exaggerated assertion or conclusion. (3)

hypothesis Research idea that serves as a premise or supposition that organizes facts and guides observations. (2)

hypothesis-generating heuristics W. J. McGuire's term for strategic rules of thumb for coming up with research ideas and predictions. (2)

improve on older ideas One of several possible hypothesis-generating heuristics. (2)

independent-sample t test The t statistic, created by W. S. Gosset, used to compare samples that are independent. (13)

independent variable A variable on which the dependent variable depends; in experiments, a variable that the experimenter manipulates to determine whether there are effects on another variable. (2)

inferential measure A measure such as S and S^2 that is used to estimate population values based on a sample of values. (10)

infinite Boundless, or without limits. (10)

informants Term sometimes used (particularly in sociology) to describe research respondents. (4)

informed consent The procedure in which prospective subjects, who have been told what they will be getting into, give their formal consent to participate in the research. (3)

institutional review board (IRB) A group set up to make risk-benefit analyses of proposed studies. (3)

instrumentation A plausible threat to internal validity that occurs when changes in the measuring instrument (e.g., deterioration of the instrument) bias the results of research not using randomization. (7)

intensive case study In-depth examination of a particular incident, individual, phenomenon, etc. (2)

interaction effects (residuals) In factorial designs, condition means minus grand mean, row effects, and column effects. (14)

interaction of independent variables The mutually moderating effects of two or more independent variables. (2)

interactions See *interaction of independent variables*.

intercoder reliability The extent to which raters or judges who do coding of data are in agreement. (4)

interitem correlation (r_{ii}) The relationship of responses to one item with the responses to another item. (6)

internal-consistency reliability Reliability based on the intercorrelation among components of a test, such as subtests or all the individual test items. (6)

internal validity The degree of validity of statements made about whether X causes Y. (6, 7)

interquartile range The difference between the 75th and 25th percentiles. (10)

interrupted time-series design Time-series design punctuated by an intervention. (8)

interval estimates The extent to which point estimates are likely to be in error. (9)

intervention An experimental treatment.

interview schedule A script that contains the questions the interviewer will ask. (5)

intrinsically repeated measures Measurements that *must* be repeated to address the question of interest. (14)

introspection The subject's reflection on his or her sensations and perceptions. (5)

IRB See *institutional review board*.

item analysis A procedure used for selecting items (e.g., for a Likert attitude scale). (5)

item-to-item reliability (r_{ii}) The relationship of responses to one item with those to another item. (6)

iterations Repetitions, as in standardizing the margins of a large table of counts. (15)

judges Coders, raters, decoders, or others who assist in describing and categorizing ongoing events or existing records of events. (4)

judge-to-judge reliability (r_{jj}) The relationship of one judge's responses to those of another judge. (6)

judgment study The use of observers (judges or raters) to scale, sort, or rate certain variables (e.g., observable behavior). (4)

justification phase Reichenbach's term for the defense or confirmation of hypotheses, theories, or other proposed explanations. (2)

K-R 20 A measure of internal-consistency reliability, developed by Kuder and Richardson. (6)

lambda (λ) weights Values that sum to zero and are used to state a prediction. (7, 14)

Latin square design A specific repeated-measures design with built-in counterbalancing. (7, 14)

lazy writing The writing in papers saturated with quoted material that, with a little more effort, could be paraphrased. (3)

leading questions Questions that can constrain responses and produce biased answers. (5)

leftover effects See *residual effects*.

leniency bias A type of rating error in which the ratings are consistently more positive than they should be. (5)

Lie (L) Scale A set of items in the MMPI that were designed to identify respondents who are deliberately trying to appear "better" than they believe they are. (5)

Likert scales Attitude scales constructed by the method of summated ratings, developed by R. Likert. (5)

linearity Relationship between two variables that resembles a straight line. (11)

line graphs Visual displays of changes in the frequency or proportion of scores over time. (10)

literature search Retrieval of background information. (2)

logical error in rating   A type of response set in which the judge gives similar ratings for variables or traits that are only intuitively related. (5)

longitudinal study   Research in which the same subjects are studied over a period of time. (8)

main effect   The effect of an independent variable apart from its interaction with other independent variables. (14)

margin of error   Interval within which an anticipated value is expected to occur. (9)

margins   Row and column (marginal) total values. (12)

Marlowe-Crowne Social Desirability Scale (MCSD scale)   A standardized test that measures social desirability responding and need for social approval. (6)

matched-pair *t*   See *paired t*.

matching   The pairing of sampling units on certain relevant variables. (7)

material causality   Emphasis on the composition or substance of which something is made (Aristotle). (7)

maturation   A plausible threat to internal validity that occurs when results not using randomization are contaminated by the participants' having, for instance, grown older, wiser, stronger, or more experienced between the pretest and the posttest. (7)

MCSD   See *Marlowe-Crowne social desirability scale*.

Mdn   See *median*.

mean (*M*)   The arithmetic average of a set of scores. (10)

mean square (S^2), or *MS*   Variance. (10, 14)

mean square for error   Variance used as the denominator of *F* ratios. (14)

median (*Mdn*)   The midmost score of a distribution. (10)

meta-analysis   The use of quantitative and graphic methods to summarize a group of similar studies. (12, Appendix C)

metaphor   A word or phrase applied to a concept or phenomenon it does not literally denote. (1, 2)

metaphorical themes   Thematic analogies that allow a particular view of the world. (2)

method of agreement   If *X*, then *Y*—which implies that *X* is a sufficient condition of *Y* (J. S. Mill). (7)

method of authority   The acceptance of an idea as valid because it is stated by someone in a position of power or authority (C. Peirce). (1)

method of difference   If not-*X*, then not-*Y*—which implies that *X* is a necessary condition of *Y* (J. S. Mill). (7)

method of equal-appearing intervals   An attitude-scaling technique, developed by L. L. Thurstone, in which values are obtained for items on the assumption that the underlying intervals are equidistant; also called a *Thurstone scale*. (5)

method of self-report   The procedure of having the research participants describe their own behavior or state of mind (e.g., used in interviews, questionnaires, and behavioral diaries). (5)

method of tenacity   Clinging stubbornly to an idea because it seems obvious or is "common sense" (C. Peirce). (1)

methodological pluralism   The use of multiple methods of controlled observation in science. (1)

methodological triangulation   The approach of "zeroing in" on a pattern by using multiple but imperfect perspectives. (4)

microworld simulations   The use of computer-generated environments to simulate real-world settings. (4)

Milgram experiments   A set of experiments performed by Stanley Milgram in which he investigated the willingness of participants to give "electric shocks" to another subject, who was actually a confederate. (3)

Mill's methods   Logical methods (or propositions) popularized by the 19th-century English philosopher J. S. Mill, exemplified by the method of agreement and the method of difference. (7)

minimal risk   Studies in which the likelihood and extent of harm to subjects are no greater than those typically experienced in everyday life; such studies are generally eligible for an expedited review. (3)

Minnesota Multiphasic Personality Inventory (MMPI)   A structured personality test containing hundreds of statements that reflect general health, sexual attitudes, religious attitudes, emotional state, and so on. (5)

mixed factorial design   A design with two or more factors, with at least one between and one within subjects. (7)

MMPI   See *Minnesota Multiphasic Personality Inventory*.

mode   The score occurring with the greatest frequency. (10)

moderator variables   Conditions that alter the relationship between X and Y. (2, Appendix C)

MS   See *mean square*.

MS$_{contrast}$ The contrast mean square, which is equivalent to the contrast sum of squares. (14)

mutually exclusive   Describing the condition: If A is true, then not-A is false. (12)

N   The total number of scores in a study; the number of scores in one condition or subgroup is denoted as n.

naturalistic observation   Research that looks at behavior in its usual natural environment. (4)

necessary condition   A requisite or essential condition. (7)

need for social approval   The desire to be positively evaluated, or approved of. (6)

negatively skewed distribution   An asymmetrical distribution in which the pointed end is toward the left (i.e., toward the negative tail). (10)

nested design   Another name for the basic between-subjects design, because the subjects are "nested" within their own treatment conditions. (7)

network analysis   See *social network analysis*.

NHST   See *null hypothesis significance testing*.

N-of-1 experimental research   Another name for single-case experimental research. (8)

noise   Random error, or the variability within the samples. (6, 13, 14)

nonequivalent-groups designs   Nonrandomized research in which the responses of a treatment group and a control group are compared on measures collected at the beginning and end of the research. (8)

nonintrinsically repeated measures   Repeated-measures research in which it is not actually essential to use repeated measures, but their use increases the efficiency, precision, and power of the study. (14)

nonlinearity   Relationship between two variables that does not resemble a straight line. (11)

nonmaleficence   Not doing harm, which is one of the guidelines of the discussed ethical principles. (3)

nonreactive observation   Any observation that does not affect what is being observed. (4)

nonresponse bias   Systematic error that is due to nonresponse or nonparticipation. (9)

nonskewed distribution   A symmetrical distribution. (10)

normal distribution   A bell-shaped curve that is completely described by its mean and standard deviation. (10)

norm-referenced   Indicating that a standardized test has norms (i.e., typical values), so that a person's score can be compared with the scores of a reference group. (5)

norms   Tables of values representing the typical performance of a given group. (9)

no-shows   People who fail to show up for their scheduled research appointments. (10)

null-counternull interval   Range from the null value to the counternull value of the effect size. (Appendix C)

null hypothesis (H_0)   The hypothesis to be nullified; usually states that there is no relationship between two or more variables. (12)

null hypothesis significance testing (NHST)   The use of statistics and probabilities to evaluate the null hypothesis. (12)

numerical scales   Rating scales in which the respondent works with a sequence of defined numbers. (5)

observed frequency (f_o)   Counts obtained in specific rows and columns. (15)

observed scores   Raw scores.

observer bias   The systematic overestimation or underestimation of observable events. (4)

Occam's razor   The principle that explanations should be as parsimonious as possible (William of Occam, or Ockham). (2)

omnibus chi-square χ^2 with $df > 1$. (15)

omnibus statistical procedures F with numerator $df > 1$, or χ^2 with $df > 1$. (14)

one-group pre-post design (O-X-O)   A preexperimental design in which the reactions of only one group of subjects are measured before and after exposure to the treatment. (7)

one-sample t test   See *paired t*.

one-shot case study (X-O)   A preexperimental design in which the reactions of only one group of subjects are measured after the event or treatment has occurred. (7)

one-tailed p value   The p value associated with a result supporting a prediction of a specific direction of a research result, e.g., $M_A > M_B$ or the sign of r is positive. (10, 12)

one-way design A statistical design in which two or more groups comprise a single dimension. (7, 14)

open-ended items Questions or statements that offer the respondent an opportunity to express feelings, motives, or behaviors spontaneously. (5)

operational definitions The meaning of a variable in terms of the operations used to measure it or the experimental methods involved in its determination. (2)

operations Empirical conditions. (2)

opportunity samples The selection of subjects because they are available and convenient to recruit. (9)

ordinate The vertical axis of a distribution. (10)

outliers Scores lying far outside the normal range. (10)

p_{rep} P. R. Killeen's statistic for estimating the replicability of an obtained effect. (12)

page header Two or three words from the title that are typed in the upper-right corner of the manuscript. (Appendix A)

paired t **(correlated-sample** t**, or matched-pair** t**, or one-sample** t**)** The t test computed on nonindependent samples. (13)

panel study Another name for a longitudinal study. (8)

paradoxical incident An occurrence characterized by seemingly self-contradictory aspects. (2)

parsimony The degree to which the propositions of a theory are "sparing" or "frugal"; see also *Occam's razor*. (2)

partial concealment Observation in which the researcher conceals only who or what is being observed. (4)

participant observation Studying a group or a community from within by recording behavior as its occurs. (4)

partitioning of tables Subdividing larger chi-square tables into smaller tables (e.g., into 2 × 2 tables). (15)

passive deception (deception by omission) The withholding of certain information from the subjects, such as not informing them of the meaning of their responses when they are given a projective test or not telling them the full details of the study. (3)

payoff potential Subjective assessment of the likelihood that the idea will be corroborated. (2)

Pearson r Standard index of linear relationship. (11)

peer-reviewed journals Journals in which articles submitted for publication undergo reviews by experts in the field. (1)

percentile A point in a distribution of scores below and above which a specified percentage of scores falls. (10)

phi coefficient (ϕ) Pearson r where both variables are dichotomous. (11, 15)

physical traces Material evidence of behavior. (4)

pilot testing The evaluation of some aspect of the research before the study is implemented.

placebo A substance without any pharmacological benefit given as a pseudomedicine to a control group. (3, 7)

placebo control group A control group that receives a placebo. (7)

placebo effects The "healing" effects of inert substances or nonspecific treatments. (7)

plagiarism Representing someone else's work as one's own. (3)

plausible rival hypotheses Propositions, or sets of propositions, that provide a reasonable alternative to the working hypothesis. (6)

point-biserial correlation (r_{pb}) Pearson r where one of the variables is continuous and the other is dichotomous. (11)

point estimates Estimates of particular (usually average) characteristics of the population (e.g, the number of times an event occurs). (9)

population The universe of elements from which sample elements are drawn, or the universe of elements to which we want to generalize. (9)

positively skewed distribution An asymmetrical distribution in which the pointed end is toward the right (i.e., the positive tail). (10)

posttest-only design See *after-only design*.

power ($1 - \beta$) In significance testing, the probability of not making a Type II error. (12)

power analysis Estimation of the effective power of a statistical test, or of the sample size needed to detect an obtained effect given a specified level of power. (12)

power of a test The probability, when using a particular test statistic (e.g., t, F, χ^2), of not making a Type II error. (12)

precoded items Fixed-choice items. (5)

predictive validity The extent to which a test can predict future outcomes. (6)

preexperimental designs D. T. Campbell and J. C. Stanley's term for research designs in which there is such a total absence of control that they are of minimal value in establishing causality. (7)

pre-post design See *before-after design*.

preratings The ratings made before an experimental treatment. (2)

pretest The measurement made before an experimental manipulation or intervention. (5)

pretest sensitization The confounding of pretesting and X, the independent variable of interest. (7)

probability The mathematical chance of an event's occurring. (9, 12)

probability sampling The random selection of sampling units so that the laws of mathematical probability apply. (9)

product-moment correlation Standard index of linear relationship, or Pearson r. (11)

projective test A psychological measure that operates on the principle that the subject will project some unconscious aspect of his or her life experience and emotions onto ambiguous stimuli in the spontaneous responses that come to mind (e.g, the Rorschach test and the Thematic Apperception Test). (5)

prospective data Information collected by following the subject's behavior or reaction forward in time. (8)

propensity score A single composite variable that summarizes differences between "treated" and "untreated" subjects on a number of different variables. (8)

proportion of variation explained See *coefficient of determination*.

proposal See *research proposal*.

prospective data The data are collected forward in time. (8)

pseudoscience Bogus claims masquerading as scientific facts. (1)

PsycARTICLES The American Psychological Association's full-text database of APA journal articles. (2)

psychophysics The study of the relationship between physical stimuli and our experience of them. (1)

PsycINFO The American Psychological Association's main informational database. (2)

push polls An insidious form of negative political campaigning disguised as opinion polling but designed to push opinions in a particular direction. (9)

p value Probability value or level obtained in a test of significance. (12)

qualitative research Studies in which the raw data exist in a nonnumerical form. (4)

quantitative research Studies in which the raw data exist in a numerical form. (4)

quasi-control subjects Research participants who are asked to reflect on the context in which an experiment is conducted and to speculate on the ways in which the context may influence their own and other subjects' behaviors (M. T. Orne). (7)

quasi-experimental research D. T. Campbell and J. C. Stanley's term for study designs that resemble an experimental design (in that there are treatments, outcome measures, and experimental units), but in which there is no random assignment to create the comparisons from which treatment-caused changes can be inferred in randomized designs. (8)

quota sampling A procedure that assigns a quota of people to be interviewed and lets the questioner build up a sample that is roughly representative of the population. (9)

r^2 See *coefficient of determination*.

$r_{alerting}$ See *alerting r*.

$r_{contrast}$ See *contrast r*.

$r_{counternull}$ See *counternull statistic*.

$r_{effect size}$ See *effect size r*.

random assignment, rule of The plan according to which random allocation is implemented. (1, 7)

random digit dialing Procedure in which the researcher selects the first three digits of telephone numbers and uses a computer program to select the last digits at random. (9)

random error The effects of uncontrolled variables that cannot be specifically identified; such effects are, theoretically speaking, self-canceling in that the average of the errors will equal zero in the long run. (6)

randomization (random assignment) Random allocation of sampling units to treatment conditions. (7)

randomized experiments Experimental designs that use randomization. (1, 7)

randomized trials Another name for randomized biomedical experiments. (1, 7)

random sampling Selecting a sample by chance procedures and with known probabilities of selection. (1, 9)

random selection Another name for random sampling. (1)

range Distance between the highest and lowest score. (10)

rater biases Another name for systematic rating errors or response biases. (5)

rating errors Errors in responses on rating scales. (5)

rating scales The common name for a variety of measuring instruments on which the observer or judge gives a numerical value (either explicitly or implicitly) to certain judgments or assessments. (5)

raw scores Observed (obtained) scores.

reactive observation An observation that affects what is being observed or measured. (4)

refutability A synonym for *falsifiability*. (2)

relational research An empirical investigation in which the objective is to identify relationships among variables. (1)

reliability The extent to which observations or measures are consistent or stable. (6)

reliability of components Another name for internal-consistency reliability. (6)

repeated-measures design Statistical design in which the sampling units generate two or more measurements. (7, 14)

replicate To repeat or duplicate. (1)

replication The duplication of a scientific observation, usually an experimental result. (6)

representative Typical, such as when the segment is representative (or typical) of the larger pool. (9)

research proposal What you propose to study and how you plan to go about it. (2)

residuals Leftover effects when appropriate components are subtracted from scores or means. (14)

residuals See *interaction effects, row effects,* and *column effects.*

response biases Systematic errors in responding. (5)

retest reliability Another name for test-retest reliability. (6)

retrospective data Information collected by going back in time. (8)

rhetoric The language of a given field, which in science encompasses the proper use of technical terms. (1)

rhetoric of justification Persuasive or explanatory terminology. (1)

risk-benefit analysis An evaluation of the ethical risks and benefits of proposed studies. (3)

rival hypotheses Competing hypotheses. (4)

rival interpretations Plausible explanations that provide reasonable alternatives to working hypotheses. (4)

root mean square See *standard deviation.*

Rorschach test A projective test that consists of a set of inkblots on pieces of cardboard. (5)

row effect Row mean minus grand mean. (14)

r-type indices Correlational effect size measures.

Rushton study A field experiment, conducted in a mining company, that raised the issue of fair-mindedness. (3)

sample A subset of the population. (9)

sampling frames Lists of sampling units, also called *sampling lists.* (9)

sampling plan A design, scheme of action, or procedure that specifies how the participants are to be selected in a survey study. (9)

sampling units The elements that make up the sample. (9)

sampling without replacement A type of random sampling in which a previously selected name cannot be chosen again and must be disregarded in any later draw. (9)

sampling with replacement A type of random sampling in which the selected names are placed in the selection pool again and may be reselected in subsequent draws. (9)

Satterthwaite's method A procedure used to make t tests more accurate when suitable transformations are unavailable or ineffective. (13, Appendix A)

scatter diagram See *scatter plot.*

scatter plot (scatter diagram) A visual display of the correlation between two variables that looks like a cloud of scattered dots. (11)

SCI Science Citation Index—a reference database on the Web of Science. (2)

scientific method General expression for the methodology of science, or a systematic research approach or outlook emphasizing the use of empirical reasoning. (1)

scientific notation   A compact way of reporting numbers with many decimal places.

secondary observation   Information that is twice removed from the source. (4)

segmented graphic scale   A rating scale in the form of a line that is broken into segments. (5)

selection   A plausible threat to the internal validity of research not using randomization when the kinds of research subjects selected for one treatment group are different from those selected for another group. (7)

self-fulfilling prophecy   R. Merton's term for a prediction that is fulfilled because those aware of the prediction then act accordingly. (1, 7)

self-report measures   See *method of self-report.*

semantic differential method   C. E. Osgood et al.'s rating procedure, in which subjective meaning is judged in terms of several dimensions, usually evaluation, potency, and activity. (5)

seminal theories   Conceptualizations that shape or stimulate further work. (2)

sensitization effect   The effect of a pretest on subjects' reactions to the experimental treatment (R. L. Solomon). (7)

serendipity   Making a desirable discovery by accident. (2)

signal   Information. (13, 14)

signal-to-noise ratio   A ratio of information to lack of information, for example, the ratio of the variability between samples (the signal) to the variability within the samples (the noise). (13, 14)

significance level   The probability of a Type I error. (12)

Significance test = Size of effect × Size of study   The basic conceptual form of all significance tests. (13, 15)

simple effects   Differences between group or condition means. (14)

simple observation   Unobtrusive observation of events without any attempt to affect them. (4)

simple random sampling   A sampling plan in which the participants are selected individually on the basis of a randomized procedure. (9)

single-case experimental research   Studies using repeated-measures designs in which $N = 1$ subject or 1 group. (2, 8)

size of the study   The number of sampling units or some index of that number. (13)

small-N experimental research   Studies using repeated-measures designs in which the treatment effect is evaluated within the same subject or a small number of subjects. (8)

socially desirable responding   The tendency to respond in ways that seem to elicit a favorable evaluation. (5, 6)

social network analysis (SNA)   The use of visual and quantitative techniques to map networks of interpersonal communication or social interactions. (4)

social psychology of the experiment   The study of the ways in which subject-related and experimenter-related artifacts operate. (7)

Social Science Citation Index (SSCI)   A reference database on the Web of Science. (2)

Solomon design   A four-group experimental design, developed by R. L. Solomon, as a means of isolating pretest sensitization effects without contamination by pretesting. (7)

Spearman-Brown prophecy formula   A traditional equation that measures the overall internal-consistency reliability of a test from a knowledge of the reliability of its components. (6)

Spearman rho (r_s)   Pearson r computed on scores in ranked form. (11)

spread   Dispersion or variability. (10)

stability   The extent to which a set of measurements does not vary. (9)

standard deviation (root mean square)   An index of the variability of a set of data around the mean value in a distribution. (10)

standardized measures   Measurements (e.g., of ability, personality, judgment, and attitude) requiring that certain rules be followed in the development, administration, and scoring of the measuring instrument. (5)

standardizing the margins   F. Mosteller's procedure for setting all row totals equal to each other and all column totals equal to each other in large tables of counts. (15)

standard normal curve   Normal curve with mean = 0 and $\sigma = 1$. (10)

standard score (z score)   Score converted to a standard deviation unit. (10)

statistical conclusion validity   The relative accuracy of drawing statistical conclusions. (6)

statistical power   See *power.*

stem-and-leaf chart The plot of a distribution in which the original data are preserved with any desired precision (J. W. Tukey). (10)

strata (clusters) Subpopulations (or layers) in survey sampling. (9)

stratified random sampling Probability sampling plan in which a separate sample is randomly selected within each homogeneous stratum (or layer) of the population. (9)

structured items Response items with fixed options. (5)

Student's *t* The pen name used by the inventor of the *t* test, W. S. Gosset, was "Student." (13)

subclassification on propensity scores Using propensity scores to form matched subgroups of "treated" and "untreated" subjects (D. B. Rubin). (8)

sufficient condition A condition that is adequate to bring about some effect or result. (7)

summated ratings method A method of attitude scaling, developed by R. Likert, that uses item analysis to select the best items. (5)

sum of squares (*SS*) The sum of the squared deviations from the mean in a set of scores. (14).

symmetrical distribution A distribution of scores in which there is an exact correspondence in arrangement on the opposite sides of the middle line. (10)

synchronous correlations In panel designs, correlations of the degree of relationship of variables at a point in time. (8)

syndrome A set of symptoms.

systematic error The effect of uncontrolled variables that often can be specifically identified; such effects are, theoretically speaking, not self-canceling (in contrast to the self-canceling nature of random errors). (6, 7)

systematic observational research Observational research that is guided or influenced by preexisting questions or hypotheses. (4)

$t_{contrast}$ The symbol used in this book to denote a *t* test that is used to address a focused question or hypothesis in a comparison of more than two groups or conditions. (14)

tally sheets Recording materials for counting frequencies.

target population The population to which we want to generalize findings and conclusions. (1)

TAT See *Thematic Apperception Test*.

t distribution Family of curves, each resembling the standard normal distribution, for every possible value of the *df* of the *t* test. (13)

teleological causality The cause when the action is goal-directed.

telephone interview A survey interview conducted by phone rather than face to face. (5)

temporal precedence The principle that the "cause" must be shown to have occurred before the "effect." (7)

test-retest correlations Correlations that represent the stability of a variable over time. (6, 8)

test-retest reliability The degree of consistency of a test or measurement, or the characteristic it is designed to measure, from one administration to another. (6)

tests of simple effects Significance tests of the difference between two groups or two condition means in a multigroup design. (14)

Thematic Apperception Test (TAT) A projective test, developed by H. A. Murray, consisting of a set of pictures, usually of people in different life contexts. (5)

theoretical (conceptual) definition The meaning of a variable in abstract or conceptual terms. (2)

theoretical ecumenism The use of more than one relevant theoretical perspective, in order to foster a relatively holistic picture. (1)

theory A set of proposed explanatory statements connected by logical arguments and by explicit and implicit assumptions. (2)

third-variable problem A condition in which a variable correlated with *X* and *Y* is the cause of both. (8, 11)

three Rs principle (of humane animal experimentation) The argument that scientists should (a) *reduce* the number of animals used in research, (b) *refine* their animal experiments so that the animals suffer less, and (c) *replace* animals with other procedures whenever possible. (3)

Thurstone scale See *method of equal-appearing intervals*.

time-series designs Studies in which the effects of an intervention are inferred from a comparison of the outcome measures obtained at different time intervals before and after the intervention. (8)

transformation Conversion of data to another mathematical form. (10)

translation and back translation Process in which questionnaire items and instructions are translated from the source to the target language and then independently translated back into the source language. The researcher compares the original with the twice-translated version to see whether anything important was lost in the translations. (4)

treatments The procedures or conditions of an experiment. (7)

trials Biomedical term for randomized experiments. (7)

trimmed mean The mean of a distribution from which a specified highest and lowest percentage of scores has been dropped. (10)

t test A test of significance used to judge the tenability of the null hypothesis of no relationship between two variables. (13)

Tuskegee study Notorious study, from 1932 to 1973, of the course of syphilis in more than 400 low-income African American men in Tuskegee, Alabama; they were told only that they had "bad blood" and were not given penicillin when, in 1947, it was found to be an effective treatment for syphilis.

two-by-two factorial design ANOVA design with two rows and two columns. (7)

two-tailed p value The p value associated with a result supporting a prediction of a nonspecific direction of a research result; e.g., either $M_A > M_B$ or $M_B > M_A$ or the sign of r is either positive or negative. (12)

two-way design (two-way factorial) ANOVA design in which each entry in the table is associated with a row variable and a column variable. (14)

two-way factorial See *two-way design*.

Type I error The error of rejecting the null hypothesis when it is true. (12)

Type II error The error of failing to reject the null hypothesis when it is false. (12)

unbiased Describes the outcome when the average of the sample values coincides with the corresponding "true" population value. (9)

unbiased estimator of the population value of σ^2 A specific statistic usually written as S^2. (10,13)

unbiased sampling plan Survey design in which the range of the sample values coincides with the corresponding "true" population value.(9)

unipolar rating scales Rating scales in which one end represents a great deal of a quality and the other end represents a complete absence of that quality. (5)

unobtrusive observation Measurements or observations used to study behavior when the subjects are unaware of being measured or observed. (4)

unstructured measures See *open-ended measures*.

validity The degree to which what was observed or measured is the same as what was purported to be observed or measured. (6)

variability See *spread*.

variables Attributes of sampling units, events, or conditions that can take on two or more values, or observed or measured events or conditions that vary or are likely to vary. (2)

variance (mean square) The mean of the squared deviations of scores from their means in a population, or its unbiased estimate. (10)

varied replication Repeating (replicating) a previous study but with some new twist. (2)

visualization Seeing things in the "mind's eye"; also called *perceptibility* in this book. (1)

volunteer bias Systematic error resulting when participants who volunteer respond differently from the way individuals in the general population would respond. (9)

WAIS See *Wechsler Adult Intelligence Scale*.

wait-list control group A control group in which the subjects wait to be given the experimental treatment until after it has been administered to the experimental group. (8)

Wechsler Adult Intelligence Scale (WAIS) The most widely used of the individual intelligence tests; divided into verbal and performance scores. (6)

wild scores Extreme scores that result from computational or recording mistakes. (10)

within-subjects design Statistical design in which the sampling units (e.g., the research participants) generate two or more measurements. (7)

working hypothesis An empirically testable supposition. (2)

x **axis (abscissa)** The horizontal axis of a distribution. (10)

y **axis (ordinate)** The vertical axis of a distribution. (10)

yea-sayers Respondents who answer questions consistently in the affirmative. (5)

$\bar{z}_r$ The average Fisher z_r. (Appendix C)

zero control group A group that receives no treatment of any kind. (7)

z **score** See *standard score*.

References

Adair, J. G. (1973). *The human subject: The social psychology of the psychological experiment*. Boston: Little, Brown.

Adair, R. K. (1990). *The physics of baseball*. New York: Harper & Row.

Aditya, R. N. (1996). *The not-so-good subject: Extent and correlates of pseudovolunteering in research*. Unpublished M.A. thesis, Temple University Department of Psychology, Philadelphia.

Aditya, R. N., & House, R. J. (2002). Interpersonal acumen and leadership across cultures: Pointers from the GLOBE study. In R. E. Riggio, S. E. Murphy, F. J. Pirozzolo (Eds.), *Multiple intelligences and leadership* (pp. 215–240). Mahwah, NJ: Erlbaum.

Aditya, R. N., & Rosnow, R. L. (2002). Executive intelligence and interpersonal acumen: A conceptual framework. In B. Pattanayak & V. Gupta (Eds.), *Creating performing organizations: Interpersonal perspectives for Indian management* (pp. 225–246). New Delhi: Response/Sage.

Aiken, L. R., Jr. (1963). Personality correlates of attitude toward mathematics. *Journal of Educational Research, 56,* 576–580.

Ainsworth, M. D. S., Blehar, M. C., Waters, E., & Wall, S. (1978). *Patterns of attachment*. Hillsdale, NJ: Erlbaum.

Albers, J. (1969). *Search versus re-search: Three lectures by Josef Albers at Trinity College, April 1965*. Hartford, CT: Trinity College Press.

Allman, J. D., Joyce, C. S., & Crandall, V. C. (1972). The antecedents of social desirability response tendencies of children and young adults. *Child Development, 43,* 1135–1160.

Allport, G. W., & Postman, L. (1947). *The psychology of rumor*. New York: Holt, Rinehart & Winston.

American Association for the Advancement of Science. (1988). *Project on scientific fraud and misconduct*. Washington, DC: Author.

American Psychological Association. (1973). *Ethical principles in the conduct of research with human participants*. Washington, DC: Author.

American Psychological Association. (1982). *Ethical principles in the conduct of research with human participants*. Washington, DC: Author.

American Psychological Association. (1992). Ethical principles of psychologists and code of conduct. *American Psychologist, 47,* 1597–1611.

American Psychological Association. (2001). *Publication manual of the American Psychological Association* (5th ed.). Washington, DC: Author.

Anastasi, A., & Urbina, S. (1997). *Psychological testing* (7th ed.). Upper Saddle River, NJ: Prentice Hall.

Anderson, C. A., & Bushman, B. J. (1997). External validity of "trivial" experiments: The case of laboratory aggression. *Review of General Psychology, 1,* 19–41.

Anderson, D. C., Crowell, C. R., Hantula, D. A., & Siroky, L. M. (1988). Task clarification and individual performance posting for improving cleaning in a student-managed university bar. *Journal of Organizational Behavior Management, 9,* 73–90.

Arellano-Galdames, F. J. (1972). *Some ethical problems in research on human subjects*. Unpublished doctoral dissertation, University of New Mexico, Albuquerque.

Aronson, E., & Carlsmith, J. M. (1968). Experimentation in social psychology. In G. Lindzey & E. Aronson (Eds.), *The handbook of social psychology* (2nd ed., Vol. 2, pp. 1–79). Reading, MA: Addison-Wesley.

Asch, S. E. (1952). Effects of group pressure upon the modification and distortion of judgments. In G. E. Swanson, T. M. Newcomb, & E. L. Hartley (Eds.), *Readings in social psychology* (Rev. ed., pp. 393–401). New York: Holt, Rinehart & Winston.

Atkinson, L. (1986). The comparative validities of the Rorschach and MMPI: A meta-analysis. *Canadian Psychology, 27,* 238–247.

Atwell, J. E. (1981). Human rights in human subjects research. In A. J. Kimmel (Ed.), *Ethics of human subject research* (pp. 81–90). San Francisco: Jossey-Bass.

Axinn, S. (1966). Fallacy of the single risk. *Philosophy of Science, 33,* 154–162.

Babad, E. (1993). Pygmalion—25 years after interpersonal expectations in the classroom. In P. D. Blanck (Ed.), *Interpersonal expectations: Theory, research, and applications* (pp. 125–153). New York: Cambridge University Press.

Baenninger, R. (1987). Some comparative aspects of yawning in *Betta splendens, Homo sapiens, Panthera leo,* and *Papio sphynx. Journal of Comparative Psychology, 110,* 349–354.

Baenninger, R., Binkley, S., & Baenninger, M. (1996). Field studies of yawning and activity in humans. *Physiology and Behavior, 59,* 421–425.

Bailey, P., & Bremer, F. (1921). Experimental diabetes insipidus. *Archives of Internal Medicine, 28,* 773–803.

Bakan, D. (1967). *On method: Toward a reconstruction of psychological investigation.* San Francisco: Jossey-Bass.

Baldwin, W. (2000). Information no one else knows: The value of self-report. In A. A. Stone, J. S. Turkkan, C. A. Bachrach, J. B. Jobe, H. S. Kurtzman, & V. S. Cain (Eds.), *The science of self-report: Implications for research and practice* (pp. 1–7). Mahwah, NJ: Erlbaum.

Bales, R. F. (1950a). A set of categories for analysis of small group interaction. *American Sociological Review, 15,* 257–263.

Bales, R. F. (1950b). *Interaction process analysis: A method for the study of small groups.* Cambridge, MA: Addison-Wesley.

Bales, R. F. (1955). How people interact in conferences. *Scientific American, 192,* 18, 31–35.

Bales, R. F., & Cohen, S. P. (1979). *Symlog: A system for the multiple level observation of groups.* New York: Free Press.

Baltimore, D. (1997, January 27). Philosophical differences. *New Yorker,* p. 8.

Barker, P. (1996). *Psychotherapeutic metaphors: A guide to theory and practice.* New York: Brunner/Mazel.

Barrass, R. (1978). *Scientists must write.* London: Chapman & Hall.

Bartoshuk, L. (2002). Self-reports and across-group comparisons: A way out of the box. *APS Observer, 15:3,* 7, 26–28.

Bauer, M. I., & Johnson-Laird, P. N. (1993). How diagrams can improve reasoning. *Psychological Science, 4,* 372–378.

Baumrind, D. (1964). Some thoughts on ethics of research: After reading Milgram's "Behavioral Study of Obedience." *American Psychologist, 19,* 421–423.

Beck, A. T., Rush, A. J., Shaw, B. F., & Emery, D. (1979). *Cognitive therapy of depression.* New York: Guilford.

Beck, A. T., Steer, R. A., & Garbin, G. M. (1988). Psychometric properties of the Beck Depression Inventory. *Journal of Clinical Psychology, 40,* 77–100.

Beck, S. J., Beck, A., Levitt, E., & Molish, H. (1961). *Rorschach's test: Vol. 1. Basic processes.* New York: Grune & Stratton.

Bem, D. J. (1965). An experimental analysis of self-persuasion. *Journal of Experimental Social Psychology, 1,* 199–218.

Bem, D. J. (1972). Self-perception theory. In L. Berkowitz (Ed.), *Advances in experimental social psychology* (Vol. 6, pp. 1–62). New York: Academic Press.

Bergum, B. O., & Lehr, D. J. (1963). Effects of authoritarianism on vigilance performance. *Journal of Applied Psychology, 47,* 75–77.

Bernard, H. B., & Killworth, P. D. (1970). Informant accuracy in social network data, Part 2. *Human Communication Research, 4,* 3–18.

Bernard, H. B., & Killworth, P. D. (1980). Informant accuracy in social network data: 4. A comparison of clique-level structure in behavioral and cognitive network data. *Social Networks, 2,* 191–218.

Bersoff, D. M., & Bersoff, D. N. (2000). Ethical issues in the collection of self-report data. In A. A. Stone, J. S. Turkkan, C. A. Bachrach, J. B. Jobe, H. S. Kurtzman, & V. S. Cain (Eds.), *The science of self-report: Implications for research and practice* (pp. 9–24). Mahwah, NJ: Erlbaum.

Billow, R. M. (1977). Metaphor: A review of the psychological literature. *Psychological Bulletin, 84,* 81–92.

Biocca, F., & Levy, M. R. (Eds.). (1995). *Communication in the age of virtual reality.* Hillsdale, NJ: Erlbaum.

Blanck, P. D. (Ed.). (1993). *Interpersonal expectations: Theory, research, and applications.* New York: Cambridge University Press.

Blanck, P. D., Bellack, A. S., Rosnow, R. L., Rotheram-Borus, M. J., & Schooler, N. R. (1992). Scientific rewards and conflicts of ethical choices in human subjects research. *American Psychologist, 47,* 959–965.

Blanck, P., Schartz, H. A., Ritchie, H., & Rosenthal, R. (2006). Science and ethics in conducting, analyzing, and reporting disability policy research. In D. A. Hantula (Ed.), *Advances in social and organizational psychology* (pp. 141–159). Mahwah, NJ: Erlbaum.

Blumberg, M., & Pringle, C. D. (1983). How control groups can cause loss of control in action research: The case of Rushton coal mine. *Journal of Applied Behavioral Science, 19,* 409–425.

Bonanno, G. A., Galea, S., Bucciarelli, A., & Vhahov, D. (2006). Psychological resilience after disaster: New York City in the aftermath of the September 11th terrorist attack. *Psychological Science, 17,* 181–186.

Boorstein, D. J. (1985). *The discoverers.* New York: Vintage.

Bordia, P., & Rosnow, R. L. (1998). Rumor rest stops on the information highway: Transmission patterns in a computer-mediated rumor chain. *Human Communication Research, 25,* 163–179.

Borgatti, S. P., Everett, M. G., & Freeman, L. C. (2002). *Ucinet for Windows: Software for social network analysis.* Harvard, MA: Analytic Technologies.

Bradburn, N. M. (1982). Question-wording effects in surveys. In R. Hogarth (Ed.), *New directions for methodology of social and behavioral science: Question framing and response contingency* (No. 11, pp. 65–76). San Francisco: Jossey-Bass.

Braun, H. I., & Wainer, H. (1989). Making essay test scores fairer with statistics. In J. M. Tanur, F. Mosteller, W. H. Kruskal, E. L. Lehmann, R. F. Link, R. S. Pieters, & G. S. Rising (Eds.), *Statistics: A guide to the unknown* (3rd ed., pp. 178–187). Pacific Grove, CA: Wadsworth & Brooks/Cole.

Brehm, S. S., & Kassin, S. M. (1996). *Social psychology.* Boston: Houghton Mifflin.

Brehmer, B., & Dörner, D. (1993). Experiments with computer-simulated microworlds: Escaping both the narrow straits of the laboratory and the deep blue sea of the field study. *Computers in Human Behavior, 9,* 171–184.

Bridgstock, M. (1982). A sociological approach to fraud in science. *Australian and New Zealand Journal of Sociology, 18,* 364–383.

Brody, J. E. (2002, October 22). Separating gold from junk in medical studies. *New York Times,* p. F7.

Brooks-Gunn, J., & Rotheram-Borus, M. J. (1994). Rights to privacy in research: Adolescents versus parents. *Ethics and Behavior, 4,* 109–121.

Broome, J. (1984). Selecting people randomly. *Ethics, 95,* 38–55.

Brown, R. (1965). *Social psychology.* New York: Free Press.

Brown, W. (1910). Some experimental results in the correlation of mental abilities. *British Journal of Psychology, 3,* 296–322.

Brownlee, K. A. (1955). Statistics of the 1954 Polio vaccine trials. [Electronic version]. *Journal of the American Statistical Association, 272,* 1005–1013.

Burnham, J. R. (1966). *Experimenter bias and lesion labeling.* Unpublished manuscript, Purdue University, West Lafayette.

Buunk, B. P., & Gibbons, F. X. (Eds.). (1997). *Health, coping, and well-being: Perspectives from social comparison theory.* Mahwah, NJ: Erlbaum.

Campbell, D. T., & Fiske, D. W. (1959). Convergent and discriminant validation by the multitrait-multimethod matrix. *Psychological Bulletin, 56,* 81–105.

Campbell, D. T., & Kenny, D. A. (1999). *A primer on regression artifacts.* New York: Guilford.

Campbell, D. T., & Stanley, J. C. (1963). *Experimental and quasi-experimental designs for research.* Chicago: Rand McNally.

Cantor, N., & Kihlstrom, J. F. (1989). *Personality and social intelligence.* Englewood Cliffs, NJ: Prentice Hall.

Carr, K., & England, R. (Eds.). (1995). *Simulated and virtual realities: Elements of perception.* London: Taylor & Francis.

Ceci, S. J. (1990). *On intelligence...more or less: A bio-ecological treatise on intellectual development.* Englewood Cliffs, NJ: Prentice Hall.

Ceci, S. J. (1996). *On intelligence: A bioecologial treatise on intellectual development* (Expanded ed.). Cambridge: Harvard University Press.

Ceci, S. J., & Bruck, M. (1993). Suggestibility of the child witness: A historical review and synthesis. *Psychological Bulletin, 113,* 403–439.

Ceci, S. J., & Bruck, M. (1995). *Jeopardy in the courtroom: A scientific study of children's testimony.* Washington, DC: American Psychological Association.

Ceci, S. J., Peters, D., & Plotkin, J. (1985). Human subjects review, personal values, and the regulation of social science research. *American Psychologist, 40,* 994–1002.

Chalmers, I., & Altman, D. G. (1995). *Systematic reviews.* London: BJM Publishing Group.

Chambers, J. M., Cleveland, W. S., Kleiner, B., & Tukey, P. A. (1983). *Graphical methods for data analysis.* Pacific Grove, CA: Wadsworth.

Chandrasekhar, S. (1987). *Truth and beauty: Aesthetics and motivations in science.* Chicago: University of Chicago Press.

Cho, A. (2006). Math clears up an inner-ear mystery: Spiral shape pumps up the bass. *Science, 311,* 1087.

Christie, R. (1951). Experimental naiveté and experiential naiveté. *Psychological Bulletin, 48,* 327–339.

Clark, R. W. (1971). *Einstein: The life and times.* New York: World.

Cochran, W. G. (1963). *Sampling techniques* (2nd ed.). New York: Wiley.

Cochran, W. G. (1968). The effectiveness of adjustment by subclassification in removing bias in observational studies. *Biometrics, 24,* 295–313.

Cochran, W. G. (1977). *Sampling techniques* (3rd ed.). New York: Wiley.

Cohen, J. (1969). *Statistical power analysis for the behavioral sciences.* New York: Academic Press.

Cohen, J. (1988). *Statistical power analysis for the behavioral sciences* (2nd ed.). Hillsdale, NJ: Erlbaum.

Cohen, J. (1990). Things I have learned (so far). *American Psychologist, 45,* 1304–1312.

Cohen, J. (1994). The earth is round ($p < .05$). *American Psychologist, 49,* 997–1003.

Conant, J. B. (1957). Introduction. In J. B. Conant & L. K. Nash (Eds.), *Harvard case studies in experimental science* (Vol. 1, pp. vii-xvi). Cambridge: Harvard University Press.

Conrath, D. W. (1973). Communications environment and its relationship to organizational structure. *Management Science, 20,* 586–603.

Conrath, D. W., Higgins, C. A., & McClean, R. J. (1983). A comparison of the reliability of questionnaire versus diary data. *Social Networks, 5,* 315–322.

Converse, J. M., & Presser, S. (1986). *Survey questions: Handcrafting the standardized questionnaire.* Beverly Hills, CA: Sage.

Cook, T. D., & Campbell, D. T. (1976). The design and conduct of quasi-experiments and true experiments in field settings. In M. D. Dunnette (Ed.), *Handbook of industrial and organizational psychology* (pp. 223–326). Chicago: Rand McNally.

Cook, T. D., & Campbell, D. T. (1979). *Quasi-experimentation: Design and analysis issues for field settings.* Chicago: Rand McNally.

Cook, T. D., Cooper, H., Cordray, D. S., Hartmann, H., Hedges, L. V., Light, R. J., Louis, T. A., & Mosteller, F. (1994). *Meta-analysis for explanation: A casebook.* New York: Russell Sage Foundation.

Cooper, H. (1998). *Synthesizing research* (3rd ed.). Thousand Oaks, CA: Sage.

Cooper, H. M., & Hedges, L. V. (Eds.). (1994). *The handbook of research synthesis.* New York: Russell Sage Foundation.

Corsini, R. J. (Ed.). (1984). *Encyclopedia of psychology* (Vols. 1–4). New York: Wiley.

Crabb, P. B., & Bielawski, D. (1994). The social representation of maternal culture and gender in children's books. *Sex Roles, 30,* 69–79.

Crancer, J., Dille, J., Delay, J., Wallace, J., & Haybin, M. (1969). Comparison of the effects of marijuana and alcohol on simulated driving performance. *Science, 164,* 851–854.

Cronbach, L. J. (1951). Coefficient alpha and the internal structure of tests. *Psychometrika, 16,* 297–334.

Cronbach, L. J., & Meehl, P. E. (1955). Construct validity in psychological tests. *Psychological Bulletin, 52,* 281–302.

Cronbach, L. J. & Quirk, T. J. (1971). Test validity. In L. C. Deighton (Ed.), *Encyclopedia of education* (Vol. 9, pp. 165–175). New York: Macmillan & Free Press.

Crowne, D. P. (1979). *The experimental study of personality.* Hillsdale, NJ: Erlbaum.

Crowne, D. P. (1991). From response style to motive. *Current Contents: Social and Behavioral Sciences, 23*(30), 10.

Crowne, D. P., & Marlowe, D. (1964). *The approval motive: Studies in evaluative dependence.* New York: Wiley.

Cryer, J. D. (1986). *Time series analysis.* Boston: PWS-Kent.

Csikszentmihalyi, M., & Larson, R. (1984). *Being adolescent: Conflict and growth in the teenage years.* New York: Basic Books.

Danziger, K. (1988). A question of identity: Who participated in psychological experiments? In J. Morawski (Ed.), *The rise of experimentation in American psychology* (pp. 35–52). New York: Oxford University Press.

Darley, J. M., & Latané, B. (1968). Bystander intervention in emergencies. *Journal of Personality and Social Psychology, 8,* 377–383.

Davis, J. D., Gallagher, R. L., & Ladove, R. (1967). Food intake controlled by blood factors. *Science, 156,* 1247–1248.

Davison, G. C. (2000). Case study. In A. E. Kazdin (Ed.), *Encyclopedia of psychology* (Vol. 2, pp. 46–48). New York: Oxford University Press & American Psychological Association.

Day, D. D., & Quackenbush, O. F. (1942). Attitudes toward defensive, cooperative, and aggressive wars. *Journal of Social Psychology, 16,* 11–20.

DePaulo, B. M., & Kashy, D. A. (1998). Everyday lies in close and casual relationships. *Journal of Personality and Social Psychology, 74,* 63–79

DePaulo, B. M., Kashy, D. A., Kirkendol, S. E., Wyer, M. M., & Epstein, J. A. (1996). Lying in everyday life. *Journal of Personality and Social Psychology, 70,* 979–995.

Devine, E. C., & Reifschneider, E. (1995). A meta-analysis of the effects of psychoeducational care in adults with hypertension. *Nursing Research, 44,* 237–245.

De Vos, G. A., & Boyer, L. B. (1989). *Symbolic analysis cross-culturally: The Rorschach test.* Berkeley: University of California Press.

de Wolff, M. S., & Van Ijzendoorn, M. H. (1997). Sensitivity and attachment: A meta-analysis on parental antecedents of infant attachment. *Child Development, 68,* 571–591.

Diener, E. (2000). Subjective well-being. *American Psychologist, 55,* 34–43.

DiFonzo, N., & Bordia, P. (2006). Toward a dynamic social impact theory of rumor: Individual and network level factors in spread. In A. R. Pratkanis (Ed.), *The science of social influence.* New York: Psychology Press.

DiFonzo, N., & Bordia, P. (2007). *Rumor psychology: Social and organizational approaches.* Washington, DC: American Psychological Association.

DiFonzo, N., Bordia, P., & Rosnow, R. L. (1994). Reining in rumors. *Organizational Dynamics, 23,* 47–62.

DiFonzo, N., Hantula, D. A., & Bordia, P. (1998). Microworlds for experimental research: Having your (control and collection) cake and realism too. *Behavior Research Methods, Instruments, and Computers, 30,* 278–286.

Diggle, P. J., Liang, K.Y., & Zeger, S. L. (1996). *Analysis of longitudinal data* (reprinted with corrections). Oxford, UK: Oxford University Press.

Dorn, L. D., Susman, E. J., & Fletcher, J. C. (1995). Informed consent in children and adolescents: Age, maturation and psychological state. *Journal of Adolescent Health, 16,* 185–190.

Downs, C. W., Smeyak, G. P., & Martin, E. (1980). *Professional interviewing.* New York: Harper & Row.

Dumond, V. (1990). *The elements of nonsexist language.* New York: Prentice Hall.

Dunning, D., Heath, C., & Suls, J. M. (2004). Flawed self-assessment: Implications for health, education, and the workplace. *Psychological Science in the Public Interest, 5*(3), 69–106.

Eagly, A. H. (1978). Sex differences in influenceability. *Psychological Bulletin, 85,* 86–116.

Eagly, A. H., Ashmore, R. D., Makhijani, M. G., & Longo, L. C. (1991). What is beautiful is good, but …: A meta-analysis review of research on the physical attractiveness stereotype. *Psychological Bulletin, 110,* 109–128.

Ebbinghaus, H. (1885). *Über das Gedächtnis: Untersuchungen zur experimentellen Psychologie.* Leipzig, Germany: Duncker & Humblot.

Egan, T. (2003, January 3). Search for Bigfoot outlives the man who created him. *New York Times,* pp. A1, A16.

Emerson, J. D., & Hoaglin, D. C. (1983). Stem-and-leaf displays. In D. C. Hoaglin, F. Mosteller, & J. W. Tukey (Eds.), *Understanding robust and exploratory data analysis* (pp. 7–32). New York: Wiley.

Entwisle, D. R. (1961). Interactive effects of pretesting. *Educational and Psychological Measurement, 21,* 607–620.

Ericsson, K. A., & Simon, H. A. (Eds.). (1993). *Protocol analysis: Verbal reports as data* (Rev. ed.). Cambridge: MIT Press.

Esposito, J. L., Agard, E., & Rosnow, R. L. (1984). Can confidentiality of data pay off? *Personality and Individual Differences, 5,* 477–480.

Evans, J. St. B. T., Newstead, S. E., & Byrne, R. M. J. (1993). *Human reasoning: The psychology of deduction.* Hove, UK: Erlbaum.

Exline, J. J. (2002). Stumbling blocks on the religious road: Fractured relationships, nagging vices, and the inner struggle to believe. *Psychological Inquiry, 13,* 182–189.

Exner, J. E. (1993). *The Rorschach: A comprehensive system* (3rd ed., Vol. 1). New York: Wiley.

Fairbanks, L. A. (1993). What is a good mother? Adaptive variation in maternal behavior of primates. *Current Directions in Psychological Science, 2,* 179–183.

Federighi, E. T. (1959). Extended tables of the percentage points of Student's *t* distribution. *Journal of the American Statistical Association, 54,* 683–688.

Ferster, C. B., & Skinner, B. F. (1957). *Schedules of reinforcement.* New York: Appleton-Century-Crofts.

Festinger, L. (1954). A theory of social comparison processes. *Human Relations, 7,* 117–140.

Festinger, L. (1957). *A theory of cognitive dissonance.* Evanston, IL: Row Peterson.

Festinger, L. (1962). *A theory of cognitive dissonance.* Stanford, CA: Stanford University Press.

Festinger, L., Schachter, S., & Riecken, H. (1956). *When prophecy fails*. Minneapolis: University of Minnesota Press.

Feyerabend, P. (1988). *Against method* (Rev. ed.). London: Verso.

Fiedler, K. (2000). Illusory correlations: A simple associative algorithm provides a convergent account of seemingly divergent paradigms. *Review of General Psychology, 4,* 25–58.

Fienberg, S. E., & Tanur, J. M. (1989). Combining cognitive and statistical approaches to survey design. *Science, 243,* 1017–1022.

Fine, G. A., & Deegan, J. G. (1996). Three principles of Serendip: Insight, chance, and discovery in qualitative research. *Qualitative Studies in Education, 9,* 434–447.

Fine, G. A., & Turner, P. A. (2001). *Whispers on the color line: Rumor and race in America*. Berkeley: University of California Press.

Finkner, A. L. (1950). Methods of sampling for estimating commercial peach production in North Carolina. *North Carolina Agricultural Experiment Station Technical Bulletin, 91* (whole).

Fisher, R. A. (1960). *The design of experiments* (7th ed.). Edinburgh, Scotland: Oliver & Boyd.

Fisher, R. A. (1971). *The design of experiments* (8th ed.). New York: Hafner.

Fisher, R. A. (1973). *Statistical methods and scientific inference* (3rd ed.). New York: Hafner.

Fisher, R. A., & Yates, F. (1974). *Statistical tables for biological, agricultural, and medical research* (6th ed.). London: Longman.

Fisher, R. J. (1993). Social desirability bias and the validity of indirect questioning. *Journal of Consumer Research, 20,* 303–315.

Fiske, D. W. (2000). Artifact in assessment. In A. E. Kazdin (Ed.), *Encyclopedia of psychology* (Vol. 1, pp. 245–248). New York: Oxford University Press & American Psychological Association.

Flanagan, J. C. (1954). The critical incident technique. *Psychological Bulletin, 51,* 327–358.

Forrest, D. W. (1974). *Francis Galton: The life and work of a Victorian genius*. New York: Taplinger.

Fossey, D. (1981). Imperiled giants of the forest. *National Geographic, 159,* 501–604.

Fossey, D. (1983). *Gorillas in the mist*. Boston: Houghton Mifflin.

Foster, E. K., & Rosnow, R. L. (2006). Gossip and network relationships In D. C. Kirkpatrick, S. Duck, & M. K. Foley (Eds.), *Relating difficulty: The process of constructing and managing difficult interaction* (pp. 161–180). Mahwah, NJ: Erlbaum.

Fowler, F. J., Jr. (1993). *Survey research methods* (2nd ed.). Newbury Park, CA: Sage.

Francis, Jr., T., Korns, R. F., Voight, R. B., Boisen, M., Hemphill, F., Napier, J., & Tolchinsky, E. (1955). An evaluation of the 1954 poliomyelitis vaccine trials—Summary report. *American Journal of Public Health, 45*(5), 1–63.

Freedman, D., Pisani, R., Purves, R., & Adhikari, A. (1991). *Statistics* (2nd ed.). New York: Norton.

Frey, J. H. (1986). An experiment with a confidentiality reminder in a telephone survey. *Public Opinion Quarterly, 50,* 26–269.

Friedman, A. F., Lewak, R., Nichols, D. S., & Webb, J. T. (2001). *Psychological assessment with the MMPI-2*. Mahwah, NJ: Erlbaum.

Friedman, C. J., Johnson, C. A., & Fode, K. (1964). Subjects' descriptions of selected TAT cards via the semantic differential. *Journal of Consulting Psychology, 28,* 317–325.

Friedman, H. (Ed.). (1998). *Encyclopedia of mental health* (Vols. 1–3). San Diego, CA: Academic Press.

Fuerbringer, J. (1997, March 30). Why both bulls and bears can act so bird-brained: Quirky behavior is becoming a realm of economics. *New York Times,* Section 3, pp. 1, 6.

Funke, J. (1991). Dealing with dynamic systems: Research strategy, diagnostic approach and experimental results. *German Journal of Psychology, 16,* 24–43.

Gallup, G. (1976, May 21). *Lessons learned in 40 years of polling*. Paper presented before National Council on Public Polls.

Galton, F. (1869). *Hereditary genius*. London: Macmillan.

Gantt, W. H. (1964). Autonomic conditioning. In J. Wolpe, A. Salter, & L. J. Reyna (Eds.), *The conditioning therapies* (pp. 115–126). New York: Holt, Rinehart & Winston.

Garb, H. N., Wood, J. M., Lilienfeld, S. O., & Nezworski, M. T. (2002). Effective use of projective techniques in clinical practice: Let the data help with selection and interpretation. *Professional Psychology: Research and Practice, 33,* 454–463.

Garb, H. N., Wood, J. M., Lilienfeld, S. O., & Nezworski, M. T. (2005). Roots of the Rorschach controversy. *Clinical Psychology Review, 25,* 97–118.

Gardner, H. (1983). *Frames of mind: The theory of multiple intelligences*. New York: Basic Books.

Gardner, H. (1986). *The mind's new science: A history of the cognitive revolution*. New York: Basic Books.

Gardner, H. (Ed.). (1993). *Multiple intelligences: The theory in practice*. New York: Basic Books.

Gardner, H. (1999). *Intelligence reframed: Multiple intelligences for the 21st century*. New York: Basic Books.

Gardner, H., Kornhaber, M. L., & Wake, W. K. (1996). *Intelligence: Multiple perspective*. Ft. Worth, TX: Harcourt Brace.

Gardner, M. (1957). *Fads and fallacies in the name of science*. New York: Dover.

Garfield, E. (1989a). Art and science: 1. The art-science connection. *Current Contents, 21*(8), 3–10.

Garfield, E. (1989b). Art and science: 2. Science for art's sake. *Current Contents, 21*(9), 3–8.

Gazzaniga, M. S., & LeDoux, J. E. (1978). *The integrated mind*. New York: Plenum.

Gentner, D., Holyoak, K. J., & Kokinov, B. N. (Eds.). (2001). *The analogical mind: Perspectives from cognitive science*. Cambridge: MIT Press.

Gentner, D., & Markman, A. B. (1997). Structure mapping in analogy and similarity. *American Psychologist, 52,* 45–56

Gibson, E. J., & Walk, R. D. (1960, April). The visual cliff. *Scientific American, 202*(4), 64–71.

Gigerenzer, G. (1991). From tools to theories: A heuristic of discovery in cognitive psychology. *Psychological Review, 98,* 254–267.

Gigerenzer, G., Swijtink, Z., Porter, T., Daston, L., Beatty, J., & Krüger, L. (1989). *The empire of chance: How probability changed science and everyday life*. New York: Cambridge University Press.

Gilovich, T. (1991). *How we know what isn't so: The fallibility of human reason in everyday life*. New York: Free Press.

Glass, G. (1976). Primary, secondary, and meta-analysis of research. *Educational Researcher, 5,* 3–8.

Glass, G., McGaw, B., & Smith, M. L. (1981). *Meta-analysis in social research*. Beverly Hills, CA: Sage.

Gniech, G. (1976). *Störeffekte in psychologischen Experimenten*. Stuttgart: Kohlhammer.

Goldberg, L. R. (1993). The structure of phenotypic personality traits. *American Psychologist, 48,* 26–34.

Goldman, B. A., & Mitchell, D. F. (1995). *Directory of unpublished experimental mental measures* (Vol. 6). Washington, DC: American Psychological Association.

Goldman, B. A., & Mitchell, D. F. (2003). *Directory of unpublished experimental mental measures* (Vol. 8). Washington, DC: American Psychological Association.

Goldman, B. A., Mitchell, D. F., & Egelson, P. (Eds.). (1997). *Directory of unpublished experimental mental measures* (Vol. 7). Washington, DC: American Psychological Association.

Goldman, B. A., Osborne, W. L., & Mitchell, D. F. (1996). *Directory of unpublished experimental mental measures* (Vols. 4–5). Washington, DC: American Psychological Association.

Goldman, B. A., Saunders, J. L., & Busch, J. C. (1996). *Directory of unpublished experimental mental measures* (Vols. 1–3). Washington, DC: American Psychological Association.

Gombrich, E. H. (1963). *Meditations on a hobby horse*. London: Phaidon.

Gottman, J. M. (1979). Detecting cyclicity in social interaction. *Psychological Bulletin, 86,* 338–348.

Gottman, J. M. (1981). *Time-series analysis: A comprehensive introduction for social scientists*. Cambridge, UK: Cambridge University Press.

Gould, M. S., & Shaffer, D. (1986). The impact of suicide in television movies: Evidence of imitation. *New England Journal of Medicine, 315,* 690–694.

Grady, D. (2003, February 25). Safe therapy is found for high blood-clot risk. *New York Times,* pp. A1, A22.

Greco, M., Baenninger, R., & Govern, J. (1993). On the context of yawning: When, where, and why? *Psychological Record, 43,* 175–183.

Gross, A. E., & Fleming, I. (1982). Twenty years of deception in social psychology. *Personality and Social Psychology Bulletin, 8,* 402–408.

Gross, A. G. (1990). *The rhetoric of science*. Cambridge: Harvard University Press.

Guilford, J. P. (1954). *Psychometric methods* (2nd ed.). New York: McGraw-Hill.

Gulliksen, H. (1950). *Theory of mental tests*. New York: Wiley.

Hagenaars, J. A., & Cobben, N. P. (1978). Age, cohort and period: A general model for the analysis of social change. *Netherlands Journal of Sociology, 14,* 58–91.

Hall, J. A. (1984). *Instructor's manual to accompany Rosenthal/Rosnow: Essentials of behavioral research*. New York: McGraw-Hill.

Hall, R. V., Lund, D., & Jackson, D. (1968). Effects of teacher attention on study behavior. *Journal of Applied Behavior Analysis, 1,* 1–12.

Hantula, D. A. (Ed.). (2006). *Advances in social and organizational psychology*. Mahwah, NJ: Erlbaum.

Hantula, D. A., Stillman, F. A., & Waranch, H. R. (1992). Can a mass-media campaign modify tobacco smoking in a large organization? Evaluation of the Great American Smokeout in an urban hospital. *Journal of Organizational Behavior Management, 13,* 33–47.

Harré, R., & Lamb, R. (Eds.). (1983). *Encyclopedic dictionary of psychology*. Cambridge: MIT Press.

Harris, B. (1988). Key words: A history of debriefing in social psychology. In J. Morawski (Ed.), *The rise of experimentation in American psychology* (pp. 188–212). New Haven, CT: Yale University Press.

Härtel, C. E. J. (1993). Rating format research revisited: Format effectiveness and acceptability depend on rater characteristics. *Journal of Applied Psychology, 78,* 212–217.

Hartmann, G. W. (1936). A field experiment on the comparative effectiveness of "emotional" and "rational" political leaflets in determining election results. *Journal of Abnormal and Social Psychology, 31,* 99–114.

Haywood, H. C. (1976). The ethics of doing research...and of not doing it. *American Journal of Mental Deficiency, 81,* 311–317.

Hedges, L. V., & Olkin, I. (1985). *Statistical methods for meta-analysis*. New York: Academic Press.

Heise, G. A., & Miller, G. A. (1951). Problem solving by small groups using various communication nets. *Journal of Abnormal and Social Psychology, 46,* 327–331.

Hellweg, S. A. (1987). Organizational grapevines. In B. Dervin & M. J. Voigt (Eds.), *Progress in communication sciences* (Vol. 8, pp. 213–230). Norwood, NJ: Ablex.

Hersen, M., & Barlow, D. H. (1976). *Single-case experimental designs: Strategies for studying behavior change*. Oxford: Pergamon Press.

Higbee, K. L., & Wells, M. G. (1972). Some research trends in social psychology during the 1960s. *American Psychologist, 27,* 963–966.

Higgins, J. J. (2004). *Introduction to modern nonparametric statistics*. Belmont, CA: Wadsworth.

Hiller, J. B., Rosenthal, R., Bornstein, R. F., Berry, D. T. R., & Brunell-Neuleib, S. (1999). A comparative meta-analysis of Rorschach and MMPI validity. *Psychological Assessment, 11,* 278–296.

Hineline, P. H. (2005). The aesthetics of behavioral arrangements. *Behavior Analyst, 28,* 15–28.

Hineline, P. N., & Lattal, K. A. (2000). Single-case experimental design. In A. E. Kazdin (Ed.), *Encyclopedia of psychology* (Vol. 7, pp. 287–289). New York: Oxford University Press & American Psychological Association.

Hirsh-Pasek, K., & Golinkoff, R. M. (1993). Skeletal supports for grammatical learning: What infants bring to the language learning task. In C. Rovee-Collier & L. P. Lipsitt (Eds.), *Advances in infancy research* (Vol. 8, pp. 299–315). Norwood, NJ: Ablex.

Hirsh-Pasek, K., & Golinkoff, R. M. (1996). *The origins of grammar: Evidence from early language comprehension*. Cambridge: MIT Press.

Hodges, B. H., & Geyer, A. L. (2006). A nonconformist account of the Asch experiments: Values, pragmatics, and moral dilemmas. *Personality and Social Psychology Review, 10,* 2–19.

Hogan, R., Hogan, J., & Roberts, B. W. (1996). Personality measurement and employment decisions. *American Psychologist, 51,* 469–477.

Holyoak, K. J., & Thagard, P. (1997). The analogical mind. *American Psychologist, 52,* 35–44.

Hoover, K., & Donovan, T. (1995). *The elements of social scientific thinking* (6th ed.). New York: St. Martin's Press.

Houts, A. C., Cook, T. D., & Shadish, W., Jr. (1986). The person-situation debate: A critical multiplist perspective. *Journal of Personality, 54,* 52–105.

Hoyt, W. T. (2000). Rater bias in psychological research: When is it a problem and what can we do about it? *Psychological Methods, 5,* 64–86.

Hult, C. A. (1996). *Researching and writing in the social sciences*. Boston: Allyn & Bacon.

Hume, D. (1978). *A treatise of human nature*. Oxford: Oxford University Press. (Original work published 1739–1740).

Hunt, M. (1997). *How science takes stock: The story of meta-analysis*. New York: Russell Sage Foundation.

Hunter, J. E., & Schmidt, F. L. (2004). *Methods of meta-analysis* (2nd ed.). Thousand Oaks, CA: Sage.

Huprich, S. K. (Ed.). (2006). *Rorschach assessment of the personality disorders*. Mahwah, NJ: Erlbaum.

Imber, S. D., Glanz, L. M., Elkin, I., Sotsky, S. M., Boyer, J. L., & Leber, W. R. (1986). Ethical issues in psychotherapy research: Problems in a collaborative clinical trials study. *American Psychologist, 41,* 137–146.

Iversen, I. H., & Lattal, K. A. (1991). *Techniques in the behavioral and neural sciences: Vol. 6. Experimental analysis of behavior*. Amsterdam: Elsevier.

Iversen, L. L. (2000). *The science of marijuana*. Oxford: Oxford University Press.

Jaeger, M. E., & Rosnow, R. L. (1988). Contextualism and its implications for psychological inquiry. *British Journal of Psychology, 79,* 63–75.

Jammer, M. (1966). *The conceptual development of quantum mechanics*. New York: McGraw-Hill.

Janis, I. L., & Mann, L. (1965). Effectiveness of emotional role-playing in modifying smoking habits and attitudes. *Journal of Experimental Research in Personality, 1,* 181–186.

Johnson, G. (2002, September 24). Here they are, science's 10 most beautiful experiments. *New York Times,* Section F, p. 3.

Johnson-Laird, P. N. (1983). *Mental models: Towards a cognitive science of language, inference, and consciousness.* Cambridge: Harvard University Press.

Johnson-Laird, P. N., & Byrne, R. M. J. (1991). *Deduction.* Hove, UK: Erlbaum.

Johnston, J. M., & Pennypacker, H. S. (Eds.). (1993a). *Readings for strategies and tactics of behavioral research* (2nd ed.). Hillsdale, NJ: Erlbaum.

Johnston, J. M., & Pennypacker, H. S. (1993b). *Strategies and tactics of behavioral research* (2nd ed.). Hillsdale, NJ: Erlbaum.

Jones, E. E., & Gerard, H. B. (1967). *Foundations of social psychology.* New York: Wiley.

Jones, J. H. (1993). *Bad blood: The Tuskegee syphilis experiment* (Rev. ed.). New York: Free Press.

Judd, C. M., & Kenny, D. A. (1981). *Estimating the effects of social interventions.* Cambridge: Cambridge University Press.

Jung, C. G. (1910). Ein Beitrag zur Psychologie des Gerüchtes. *Zentralblatt für Psychoanalyse, 1,* 81–90.

Jung, C. G. (1959). A visionary rumor. *Journal of Analytical Psychology, 4,* 5–19.

Jung, J. (1969). Current practices and problems in the use of college students for psychological research. *Canadian Psychologist, 10,* 280–290.

Kagay, M. R.. (1996, December 15). Experts say refinements are needed in the polls. *New York Times,* p. 34.

Kahane, H. (1989). *Logic and philosophy: A modern introduction* (6th ed.). Belmont, CA: Wadsworth.

Kahneman, D., Slovic, P., & Tversky, A. (Eds.). (1982). *Judgment under uncertainty: Heuristics and biases.* New York: Cambridge University Press.

Kahneman, D., & Tversky, A. (1973). On the psychology of prediction. *Psychological Review, 80,* 237–251.

Kanner, L. (1943). Autistic disturbances of affective contact. *Nervous Child, 2,* 217–250.

Kaplan, A. (1964). *The conduct of inquiry: Methodology for behavioral science.* Scranton, PA: Chandler.

Kashy, D. A., & DePaulo, B. M. (1996). Who lies? *Journal of Personality and Social Psychology, 70,* 1037–1051.

Katz, D., & Cantril, H. (1937). Public opinion polls. *Sociometry, 1,* 155–179.

Kazdin, A. E. (1976). Statistical techniques for single-case experimental designs. In M. Hersen & D. H. Barlow (Eds.), *Single case experimental designs: Strategies for studying behavior change* (pp. 265–316). Oxford, UK: Pergamon Press.

Kazdin, A. E. (1980). *Research design in clinical psychology.* New York: Harper & Row.

Kazdin, A. E. (1992). *Research design in clinical psychology* (2nd ed.). Boston: Allyn & Bacon.

Kazdin, A. E. (Ed.). (2000). *Encyclopedia of psychology* (Vols. 1–8). New York: Oxford University Press & American Psychological Association.

Kelley, H. H., & Thibaut, J. W. (1969). Group problem solving. In G. Lindzey & E. Aronson (Eds.), *The handbook of social psychology* (2nd ed., Vol. 4, pp. 1–101). Reading, MA: Addison-Wesley.

Kelman, H. C. (1968). *A time to speak: On human values and social research.* San Francisco: Jossey-Bass.

Kendon, A. (1967). Some functions of gaze direction in social interaction. *Acta Psychologica, 26,* 1–47.

Kenny, D. A. (1979). *Correlation and causality.* New York: Wiley.

Kenny, D. A., & Campbell, D. T. (1984). Methodological considerations in the analysis of temporal data. In K. Gergen & M. Gergen (Eds.), *Historical social psychology* (pp. 125–138). Mahwah, NJ: Erlbaum.

Kenny, D. A., & Campbell, D. T. (1989). On the measurement of stability in over-time data. *Journal of Personality, 57,* 445–481.

Keppel, G. (1991). *Design and analysis: A researcher's handbook* (3rd ed.). Englewood Cliffs, NJ: Prentice Hall.

Kerner, O., et al. (1968). *Report of the National Advisory Commission on Civil Disorders.* New York: Bantam.

Kidder, L. H., Kidder, R. L., & Snyderman, P. (1976). *A cross-lagged correlational analysis of the causal relationship between police employment and crime rates.* Paper presented at the meeting of the American Psychological Association, Washington.

Kilborn, P. T. (1994, January 23). Alarming trend among workers: Surveys find clusters of TB cases. *New York Times,* pp. A1, A16.

Killeen, P. R. (2005). An alternative to null-hypothesis significance tests. *Psychological Science, 16,* 345–353.

Kimble, G. A. (1989). Psychology from the standpoint of a generalist. *American Psychologist, 44,* 491–499.

Kimmel, A. J. (Ed.). (1981). *Ethics of human subjects research.* San Francisco: Jossey-Bass.

Kimmel, A. J. (1988). *Ethics and values in applied social research*. Beverly Hills, CA: Sage.

Kimmel, A. J. (1991). Predictable biases in the ethical decision making of American psychologists. *American Psychologist, 46,* 786–788.

Kimmel, A. J. (1996). *Ethical issues in behavioral research: A survey*. Oxford, UK: Blackwell.

Kimmel, A. J. (2004). *Rumors and rumor control: A manager's guide to understanding and combating rumors*. Mahwah, NJ: Erlbaum.

Kimmel, A. J. (2006). From artifacts to ethics: The delicate balance between methodological and moral concerns in behavioral research. In D. A. Hantula (Ed.), *Advances in social and organizational psychology* (pp. 113–140). Mahwah, NJ: Erlbaum.

Kirk, R. E. (1995). *Experimental design: Procedures for the behavioral sciences* (3rd ed.). Pacific Grove, CA: Brooks/Cole.

Kirk, R. E. (2000). Randomized experiments. In A. E. Kazdin (Ed.), *Encyclopedia of psychology* (Vol. 6, pp. 502–505). New York: Oxford University Press & American Psychological Association.

Kish, L. (1965). *Survey sampling*. New York: Wiley.

Kleinmuntz, B. (1982). *Personality and psychological assessment*. New York: St. Martin's Press.

Kolata, G. B. (1986). What does it mean to be random? *Science, 231,* 1068–1070.

Kolodner, J. L. (1997). Educational implications of analogy: A view from case based reasoning. *American Psychologist, 52,* 57–66.

Komaki, J., & Barnett, F. T. (1977). A behavioral approach to coaching football: Improving the play execution of the offensive backfield on a youth football team. *Journal of Applied Behavior Analysis, 10,* 657–664.

Koshland, D. E., Jr. (1988). Science, journalism, and whistle-blowing. *Science, 240,* 585.

Kossinets, G., & Watts, D. J. (2006). Empirical analysis of an evolving social network. *Science, 311,* 88–90.

Kraemer, H. C., & Thiemann, S. (1987). *How many subjects? Statistical power analysis in research*. Newbury Park, CA: Sage.

Kragh, H. (2002, August). Paul Dirac: Seeking beauty. *Physics World,* pp. 27–31.

Kratochwill, T. R., & Levin, J. R. (Eds.). (1992). *Single-case research design and analysis: New directions for psychology and education*. Hillsdale, NJ: Erlbaum.

Kuder, G. F., & Richardson, M. W. (1937). The theory of estimation of test reliability. *Psychometrika, 2,* 151–160.

Kuhn, T. S. (1962). *The structure of scientific revolutions*. Chicago: University of Chicago Press.

Kuhn, T. S. (1977). *The essential tension*. Chicago: University of Chicago Press.

Labaw, P. (1980). *Advanced questionnaire design*. Cambridge, MA: ABT Books.

LaGreca, A. M. (Ed.). (1990). *Through the eyes of the child: Obtaining self-reports from children and adolescents*. Boston: Allyn & Bacon.

Lakoff, G., & Johnson, M. (1980). *Metaphors we live by*. Chicago: University of Chicago Press.

Lana, R. E. (1959). Pretest-treatment interaction effects in attitudinal studies. *Psychological Bulletin, 56,* 293–300.

Lana, R. E. (1969). Pretest sensitization. In R. Rosenthal & R. L. Rosnow (Eds.), *Artifact in behavioral research* (pp. 119–141). New York: Academic Press.

Lana, R. E. (1991). *Assumptions of social psychology: A reexamination*. Hillsdale, NJ: Erlbaum.

Lana, R. E., & Rosnow, R. L. (1972). *Introduction to contemporary psychology*. New York: Holt, Rinehart & Winston.

Lando, H. A. (1976). On being sane in insane places: A supplemental report. *Professional Psychology, 7,* 47–52

Lane, F. W. (1960). *Kingdom of the octopus*. New York: Sheridan House.

Latané, B., & Darley, J. M. (1968). Group inhibition of bystander intervention in emergencies. *Journal of Personality and Social Psychology, 10,* 215–221.

Latané, B., & Darley, J. M. (1970). *The unresponsive bystander: Why doesn't he help?* New York: Appleton-Century-Crofts.

Lavelle, J. M., Hovell, M. F., West, M. P., & Wahlgren, D. R. (1992). Promoting law enforcement for child protection: A community analysis. *Journal of Applied Behavior Analysis, 25,* 885–892.

Lavrakas, P. J. (1987). *Telephone survey methods: Sampling, selection, and supervision*. Beverly Hills, CA: Sage.

Lazarsfeld, P. F. (1978). Some episodes in the history of panel analysis. In D. B. Kandel (Ed.), *Longitudinal research for drug abuse* (pp. 249–265). New York: Hemisphere Press.

Leary, D. E. (Ed.). (1990). *Metaphors in the history of psychology*. Cambridge: Cambridge University Press.

Lee, R. M. (1993). *Doing research on sensitive topics*. London: Sage.

Levav, J., & Fitzsimons, G. J. (2006). When questions change behavior: The role of ease of representation. *Psychological Science, 17,* 207–213.

Lewin, T. (1994, January 7). Prize in an unusual lottery: A scarce experimental drug. *New York Times,* pp. A1, A17.

Lewis-Beck, M., Bryman, A., & Liao, T. F. (2003). *Encyclopedia of research methods for the social sciences.* Thousand Oaks, CA: Sage.

Li, H., Rosenthal, R., & Rubin, D. B. (1996). Reliability of measurement in psychology: From Spearman-Brown to maximal reliability. *Psychological Methods, 1,* 98–107.

Li, H., & Wainer, H. (1998). Toward a coherent view of reliability in test theory. *Journal of Educational and Behavioral Statistics, 23,* 478–484.

Light, R. J., & Pillemer, D. B. (1984). *Summing up: The science of reviewing research.* Cambridge: Harvard University Press.

Likert, R. A. (1932). A technique for the measurement of attitudes. *Archives of Psychology, 140,* 1–55.

Linsky, A. S. (1975). Stimulating responses to mailed questionnaires: A review. *Public Opinion Quarterly, 39,* 83–101.

Lipsey, M. W., & Wilson, D. B. (2001). *Practical meta-analysis.* Thousand Oaks, CA: Sage.

Liss, M. B. (1994). Child abuse: Is there a mandate for researchers to report? *Ethics and Behavior, 4,* 133–146.

Loomis, J. M., Blascovich, J., & Beall, A. C. (1999). Immersive virtual environments as a basic research tool in psychology. *Behavioral Research Methods, Instruments and Computers, 31,* 557–564.

Mahler, I. (1953). Attitude toward socialized medicine. *Journal of Social Psychology, 38,* 273–282.

Main, M., & Solomon, J. (1990). Procedures for identifying infants as disorganized/disoriented during the Ainsworth Strange Situation. In M. T. Greenberg, D. Cichetti, & E. M. Cummings (Eds.), *Attachment in the preschool years* (pp. 121–160). Chicago: University of Chicago Press.

Mann, L. (1967). The effects of emotional role playing on smoking attitudes and behavior. *Journal of Experimental Social Psychology, 3,* 334–348.

Mann, L., & Janis, I. L. (1968). A follow-up study on the long-term effects of emotional role playing. *Journal of Personality and Social Psychology, 8,* 339–342.

Mann, T. (1994). Informed consent for psychological research: Do subjects comprehend consent forms and understand their legal rights? *Psychological Science, 5,* 140–143.

Marks, G., & Miller, N. (1987). Ten years of research on the false-consensus effect: An empirical and theoretical review. *Psychological Bulletin, 102,* 72–90.

Martin, D. (2001, March 25). Charles Johnson, 76, proponent of flat earth. *New York Times,* p. 44.

Maurer, T. J., Palmer, J. K., & Ashe, D. K. (1993). Diaries, checklists, evaluations, and contrast effects in measurement of behavior. *Journal of Applied Psychology, 78,* 226–231.

Maxwell, S. E., & Delaney, H. D. (2000). *Designing experiments and analyzing data: A model comparison perspective.* Mahwah, NJ: Erlbaum.

McClelland, D. C., Atkinson, J. W., Clark, R. A., & Lowell, E. L. (1953). *The achievement motive.* New York: Appleton-Century-Crofts.

McCrae, R. R., & Costa, P. T., Jr. (1997). Personality trait structure as a human universal. *American Psychologist, 52,* 509–516.

McGuire, W. J. (1964). Inducing resistance to persuasion: Some contemporary approaches. In L. Berkowitz (Ed.), *Advances in experimental social psychology* (Vol. 1, pp. 191–229). New York: Academic Press.

McGuire, W. J. (1973). The yin and yang of progress in social psychology: Seven koan. *Journal of Personality and Social Psychology, 26,* 446–456.

McGuire, W. J. (1997). Creative hypothesis generating in psychology: Some useful heuristics. *Annual Review of Psychology, 48,* 1–30.

McGuire, W. J. (2006). Twenty questions for perspective epistemologists. In D. A. Hantula (Ed.), *Advances in social and organizational psychology* (pp. 329–358). Mahwah, NJ: Erlbaum.

McNemar, Q. (1946). Opinion-attitude methodology. *Psychological Bulletin, 43,* 289–374.

Medawar, P. B. (1969). *Induction and intuition in scientific thought* (Jayne Lectures for 1968). Philadelphia: American Philosophical Society.

Meier, P. (1988). The biggest public health experiment ever: The 1954 field trial of the Salk poliomyelitis vaccine. In J. M. Tanur, F. Mosteller, W. H. Kruskal, E. L. Lehmann, R. F. Link, R. S. Pieters, & G. R. Rising (Eds.), *Statistics: A guide to the unknown* (3rd ed., pp. 3–14). Pacific Grove, CA: Wadsworth.

Menges, R. J. (1973). Openness and honesty versus coercion and deception in psychological research. *American Psychologist, 28,* 1030–1034.

Merriam, S. B. (1991). *Case study research in education.* San Francisco: Jossey-Bass.

Merritt, C. B., & Fowler, R. G. (1948). The pecuniary honesty of the public at large. *Journal of Abnormal and Social Psychology, 43,* 90–93.

Merton, R. K. (1948). The self-fulfilling prophecy. *Antioch Review, 8,* 193–210.

Merton, R. K. (1968). *Social theory and social structure.* New York: Free Press.

Michener, W., Rozin, P., Freeman, E., & Gale, L. (1999). The role of low progesterone and tension as triggers of perimenstrual chocolate and sweets craving: Some negative experimental evidence. *Physiology and Behavior, 67*, 417–420.

Milgram, S. (1963). Behavioral study of obedience. *Journal of Abnormal and Social Psychology, 67*, 371–378.

Milgram, S. (1974). *Obedience to authority: An experimental view*. New York: Harper & Row.

Milgram, S. (1977). *The individual in a social world: Essays and experiments*. Reading, MA: Addison-Wesley.

Milgram, S., Mann, L., & Harter, S. (1965). The lost-letter technique: A tool of social research. *Public Opinion Quarterly, 29*, 437–438.

Mill, J. S. (1965). *A system of logic* (8th ed.). London: Longmans Green.

Miller, A. I. (1986). *Imagery in Scientific Thought: Creating 20th Century Physics*. Cambridge: MIT Press.

Miller, A. I. (1996). *Insights of Genius: Imagery and Creativity in Science and Art*. New York: Springer-Verlag.

Miller, G. A., & Newman, E. B. (1958). Tests of a statistical explanation of the rank-frequency relation for words in written English. *American Journal of Psychology, 71*, 209–258.

Miller, P. V., & Cannell, C. F. (1982). A study of experimental techniques for telephone interviewing. *Public Opinion Quarterly, 46*, 250–269.

Millham, J., & Jacobson, L. I. (1978). The need for approval. In H. London & J. E. Exner (Eds.), *Dimensions of personality* (pp. 365–390). New York: Wiley.

Mitchell, J. (1985). *Eccentric lives and peculiar notions*. New York: Harcourt Brace Jovanovich

Moher, D., Schulz, K. R., & Altman, D. G. (2001). The CONSORT statement: Revised recommendations for improving the quality of reports of parallel-group randomized trials. *Annals of Internal Medicine, 134*, 657–662.

Mook, D. G. (1983). In defense of external invalidity. *American Psychologist, 38*, 379–387.

Moreno, J. L. (1953). *Who shall survive?* New York: Beacon House.

Mosteller, F. (1968). Association and estimation in contingency tables. *Journal of the American Statistical Association, 63*, 1–28.

Murphy, K. R., Jako, R. A., & Anhalt, R. L. (1993). Nature and consequences of halo effect: A critical analysis. *Journal of Applied Psychology, 78*, 218–225.

Murphy, K. R., & Myors, B. (2004). *Statistical power analysis: A simple and general model for traditional and modern hypothesis tests* (2nd ed.). Mahwah, NJ: Erlbaum.

Myers, D. G. (2000). The funds, friends, and faith of happy people. *American Psychologist, 55*, 56–67.

National Commission for the Protection of Human Subjects of Biomedical and Behavioral Research (1979). *The Belmont report: Ethical principles and guidelines for the protection of human subjects of research*. Washington, DC: Government Printing Office.

National Heart Institute. (1966). *The Framingham heart study: Habits and coronary heart disease*. Public Health Service Publication No. 1515. Bethesda, MD: National Heart Institute.

Neuringer, A. (1992). Choosing to vary and repeat. *Psychological Science, 3*, 246–250.

Neuringer, A. (1996). Can people behave "randomly?" The role of feedback. *Journal of Experimental Psychology: General, 115*, 62–75.

Neuringer, A., & Voss, C. (1993). Approximating chaotic behavior. *Psychological Science, 4*, 113–119.

Nisbet, R. (1976). *Sociology as an art form*. London: Oxford University Press.

Nisbett, R. E., & Wilson, T. D. (1977). Telling more than we can know: Verbal reports on mental processes. *Psychological Review, 84*, 231–259.

Norwick, R., Choi, Y. S., & Ben-Shachar, T. (2002). In defense of self-reports. *APS Observer, 15*(3), 7, 24.

Nouri, H., Blau, G., & Shahid, A. (1995). The effect of socially desirable responding (SDR) on the relation between budgetary participation and self-reported job performance. *Advances in Management Accounting, 4*, 163–177.

Nunnally, J. C., & Bernstein, I. H. (1994). *Psychometric theory* (3rd ed.). New York: McGraw-Hill.

Offer, D., Kaiz, M., Howard, K. I., & Bennett, E. S. (2000). The altering of reported experiences. *Journal of the American Academy of Child and Adolescent Psychiatry, 39*, 735–743.

Omodei, M. M., & Wearing, A. J. (1995). The Fire Chief microworld generating program: An illustration of computer-simulated microworlds as an experimental paradigm for studying complex decision-making behavior. *Behavior Research Methods, Instruments, and Computers, 27*, 303–316.

Ones, D. S., Viswesvaran, C., & Reiss, A. D. (1996). Role of social desirability in personality testing for personnel selection: The red herring. *Journal of Applied Psychology, 81*, 660–679.

Oppenheimer, R. (1956). Analogy in science. *American Psychologist, 11,* 127–135.

Orne, M. T. (1959). The nature of hypnosis: Artifact and essence. *Journal of Abnormal and Social Psychology, 58,* 277–299.

Orne, M. T. (1962). On the social psychology of the psychological experiment: With particular reference to demand characteristics and their implications. *American Psychologist, 17,* 776–783.

Orne, M. T. (1969). Demand characteristics and the concept of quasi-controls. In R. Rosenthal & R. L. Rosnow (Eds.), *Artifact in behavioral research* (pp. 143–179). New York: Academic Press.

Orne, M. T. (1970). Hypnosis, motivation, and the ecological validity of the psychological experiment. In W. J. Arnold & M. M. Page (Eds.), *Nebraska Symposium on Motivation* (pp. 187–265). Lincoln: University of Nebraska Press.

Osgood, C. E., & Luria, Z. (1954). A blind analysis of a case of multiple personality using the semantic differential. *Journal of Abnormal and Social Psychology, 49,* 579–591.

Osgood, C. E., Suci, G. L., & Tannenbaum, P. H. (1957). *The measurement of meaning.* Urbana: University of Illinois Press.

Otten, M. W., & Van de Castle, R. L. (1963). A comparison of set "A" of the Holtzman inkblots with the Rorschach by means of the semantic differential. *Journal of Projective Techniques and Personality Assessment, 27,* 452–460.

Overman, E. S. (Ed.) (1988). *Methodology and epistemology for social science: Selected papers of Donald T. Campbell.* Chicago: University of Chicago Press.

Pargament, K. I. (2002). The bitter and the sweet: An evaluation of the costs and benefits of religiousness. *Psychological Inquiry, 13,* 168–181.

Parker, K. C. H., Hanson, R. K., & Hunsley, J. (1988). MMPI, Rorschach, and WAIS: A meta-analytic comparison of reliability, stability, and validity. *Psychological Bulletin, 103,* 367–373.

Parloff, D. N. (Ed.). (1995). *Ethical conflicts in psychology.* Washington, DC: American Psychological Association.

Paul, E. F., Miller, F. D., & Paul, J. (Eds.). (2000). *Why animal experimentation matters: The use of animals in medical research.* New Brunswick, NJ: Transaction Publishers.

Paulhus, D. L. (1991). Measurement and control of response bias. In J. P. Robinson, P. R. Shaver, & L. S. Wrightsman (Eds.), *Measures of personality and social psychological attitudes* (pp. 17–59). San Diego, CA: Academic Press.

Paulos, J. A. (1990). *Innumeracy: Mathematical illiteracy and its consequences.* New York: Vintage Books.

Paulos, J. A. (1991, April 24). Math moron myths. *New York Times OP-ED,* p. 25.

Pearl, J. (2000). *Causality: Models, reasoning, and inference.* Cambridge: Cambridge University Press.

Peirce, C. S. (1966). *Charles S. Peirce: Selected writings (Values in a universe of chance).* (P. P. Weiner, Ed.). New York: Dover.

Pelz, D. C., & Andrew, F. M. (1964). Detecting causal priorities in panel study data. *American Sociological Review, 29,* 836–848.

Pera, M., & Shea, W. R. (Eds.). (1991). *Persuading science: The art of scientific rhetoric.* Canton, MA: Science History.

Perloff, R. (2006). An Rx for advancing and enriching psychology. In D. A. Hantula (Ed.), *Advances in social and organizational psychology* (pp. 315–327). Mahwah, NJ: Erlbaum.

Pessin, J. (1933). The comparative effects of social and mechanical stimulation on memorizing. *American Journal of Psychology, 45,* 263–270.

Phillips, D. P., & Carstensen, M. S. (1986). Clustering of teenage suicides after television news stories about suicide. *New England Journal of Medicine, 315,* 685–689.

Phillips, D. P., & Glynn, L. M. (2000). Field study. In A. E. Kazdin (Ed.), *Encyclopedia of psychology* (Vol. 3, p. 370). New York: Oxford University Press & American Psychological Association.

Phillips, D. P., Lesyna, K., & Paight, D. J. (1992). Suicide and the media. In R. W. Maris, A. L. Berman, J. T. Maltsberger, & R. I. Yufit (Eds.), *Assessment and prediction of suicide* (pp. 499–519). New York: Guilford.

Phillips, D. P., & Paight, B. A. (1987). The impact of televised movies about suicide: A replicative study. *New England Journal of Medicine, 317,* 809–811.

Pierce, C. A., & Aguinis, H. (1997). Using virtual reality technology in organizational behavior research. *Journal of Organizational Behavior, 18,* 407–410.

Popper, K. R. (1934). *Logik der Forschung.* Vienna: Springer-Verlag

Popper, K. R. (1961). *The logic of scientific inquiry.* New York: Basic Books.

Popper, K. R. (1963). *Conjectures and refutations: The growth of scientific knowledge* (Rev. ed.). London: Routledge.

Popper, K. R. (1972). *Objective knowledge: An evolutionary approach*. Oxford: Oxford University Press.

Postman, L., Bruner, J. S., & McGinnies, E. (1948). Personal values as selective factors in perception. *Journal of Abnormal and Social Psychology, 43*, 142–154.

Powell, F. A. (1962). Open- and closed-mindedness and the ability to differentiate source and message. *Journal of Abnormal and Social Psychology, 65*, 61–64.

Principe, G. F., Kanaya, T., Ceci, S. J., & Singh, M. (2006). Believing is seeing: How rumors can engender false memories in preschoolers. *Psychological Science, 17*, 243–248.

Ragin, C. C. (1992). Introduction: Cases of "What is a case?" In C. C. Ragin & H. S. Becker (Eds.), *What is a case? Exploring the foundations of social inquiry* (pp. 1–17). Cambridge: Cambridge University Press.

Ragin, C. C., & Becker, H. S. (Eds.). (1992). *What is a case? Exploring the foundations of social inquiry*. Cambridge: Cambridge University Press.

Ramachandran, V. S. (Ed.). (1994). *Encyclopedia of human behavior* (Vols. 1–4). Orlando, FL: Academic Press.

Rand Corporation. (1955). *A million random digits with 100,000 normal deviates*. New York: Free Press.

Randhawa, B. S., & Coffman, W. E. (Eds.). (1978). *Visual learning, thinking, and communication*. New York: Academic Press.

Raudenbush, S. W. (1984). Magnitude of teacher expectancy effects on pupil IQ as a function of the credibility of expectancy induction: A synthesis of findings from 18 experiments. *Journal of Educational Psychology, 76*, 85–97.

Reed, S. K. (1988). *Cognition: Theory and applications* (2nd ed.). Pacific Grove, CA: Brooks/Cole.

Regis, E. (1987). *Who got Einstein's office? Eccentricities and genius at the Institute for Advanced Study*. Reading, MA: Addison-Wesley.

Reichenbach, H. (1938). *Experience and prediction*. Chicago: University of Illinois Press.

Richard, F. D., Bond, C. F., Jr., & Stokes-Zoota, J. J. (2003). One hundred years of social psychology quantitatively defined. *Review of General Psychology, 7*, 331–363.

Rind, B., & Bordia, P. (1996). Effect on restaurant tipping of male and female servers drawing a happy, smiling face on the backs of customers' checks. *Journal of Applied Social Psychology, 26*, 218–225.

Roberts, C. W. (Ed.). (1997). *Text analysis for the social sciences: Methods for drawing statistical inferences from texts and transcripts*. Mahwah, NJ: Erlbaum.

Roberts, R. M. (1989). *Serendipity: Accidental discoveries in science*. New York: Wiley.

Robin, H. (1993). *The scientific image: From cave to computer*. New York: W. H. Freeman.

Robinson, J. P., Shaver, P. R., & Wrightsman, L. S. (Eds.). (1991). *Measures of personality and social psychological attitudes*. San Diego, CA: Academic Press.

Rogosa, D. (1980). A critique of cross-lagged correlation. *Psychological Bulletin, 88*, 245–258.

Rokeach, M. (1960). *The open and closed mind*. New York: Basic Books.

Rosenbaum, P. R., & Rubin, D. B. (1983). The central role of the propensity score in observational studies for causal effects. *Biometrika, 70*, 41–55.

Rosenberg, M. J. (1969). The conditions and consequences of evaluation apprehension. In R. Rosenthal & R. L. Rosnow (Eds.), *Artifact in behavioral research* (pp. 279–349). New York: Academic Press.

Rosenhan, D. L. (1973). On being sane in insane places. *Science, 179*, 250–258.

Rosenthal, M. C. (1985). Bibliographic retrieval for the social and behavioral scientist. *Research in Higher Education, 22*, 315–333.

Rosenthal, M. C. (1994). The fugitive literature. In H. Cooper & L. V. Hedges (Eds.), *The handbook of research synthesis* (pp. 85–94). New York: Russell Sage Foundation.

Rosenthal, M. C. (2006). Retrieving literature for meta-analysis: Can we really find it all? In D. A. Hantula (Ed.), *Advances in social and organizational psychology* (pp. 75–92). Mahwah, NJ: Erlbaum.

Rosenthal, R. (1966). *Experimenter effects in behavioral research*. New York: Appleton-Century-Crofts.

Rosenthal, R. (1973). Estimating effective reliability in studies that employ judges' ratings. *Journal of Clinical Psychology, 29*, 342–345.

Rosenthal, R. (1976). *Experimenter effects in behavioral research* (Enlarged ed.). New York: Irvington.

Rosenthal, R. (1979). The "file drawer problem" and tolerance for null results. *Psychological Bulletin, 86*, 638–641.

Rosenthal, R. (1982). Conducting judgment studies. In K. R. Scherer & P. Ekman (Eds.), *Handbook of methods in nonverbal behavior research* (pp. 287–361). New York: Cambridge University Press.

Rosenthal, R. (1983). Meta-analysis: Toward a more cumulative social science. In L. Bickman (Ed.), *Applied social psychology annual* (Vol. 4, pp. 65–93). Beverly Hills, CA: Sage.

Rosenthal, R. (1985). From unconscious experimenter bias to teacher expectancy effects. In J. B. Dusek (Ed.), *Teacher expectancies* (pp. 37–65). Hillsdale, NJ: Erlbaum.

Rosenthal, R. (1987). *Judgment studies: Design, analysis, and meta-analysis.* Cambridge: Cambridge University Press.

Rosenthal, R. (1990a). Evaluation of procedures and results. In K. W. Wachter & M. L. Straf (Eds.), *The future of meta-analysis* (pp. 123–133). New York: Russell Sage Foundation.

Rosenthal, R. (1990b). How are we doing in soft psychology? *American Psychologist, 45,* 775–777.

Rosenthal, R. (1990c). Replication in behavioral research. *Journal of Social Behavior and Personality, 5,* 1–30.

Rosenthal, R. (1991). *Meta-analytic procedures for social research* (Rev. ed.). Newbury Park, CA: Sage.

Rosenthal, R. (1993). Interpersonal expectations: Some antecedents and some consequences. In P. D. Blanck (Ed.), *Interpersonal expectations: Theory, research, and applications* (pp. 3–24). Cambridge: Cambridge University Press.

Rosenthal, R. (1994a). Parametric measures of effect size. In H. Cooper & L. V. Hedges (Eds.), *The handbook of research synthesis* (pp. 231–244). New York: Russell Sage Foundation.

Rosenthal, R. (1994b). Science and ethics in conducting, analyzing, and reporting psychological research. *Psychological Science, 5,* 127–134.

Rosenthal, R. (1995a). Progress in clinical psychology: Is there any? *Clinical Psychology: Science and Practice, 2,* 133–150.

Rosenthal, R. (1995b). Writing meta-analytic reviews. *Psychological Bulletin, 118,* 183–192.

Rosenthal, R., & DiMatteo, M. R. (2001). Meta-analysis: Recent developments in quantitative methods for literature reviews. *Annual Review of Psychology, 52,* 59–82.

Rosenthal, R., & Fode, K. L. (1963). The effect of experimenter bias on the performance of the albino rat. *Behavioral Science, 8,* 183–189.

Rosenthal, R., Hall, J. A., DiMatteo, M. R., Rogers, P. L., & Archer, D. (1979). *Sensitivity to nonverbal communication: The PONS test.* Baltimore: Johns Hopkins University Press.

Rosenthal, R., & Jacobson, L. (1968). *Pygmalion in the classroom: Teacher expectation and pupils' intellectual development.* New York: Holt, Rinehart & Winston.

Rosenthal, R., & Lawson, R. (1964). A longitudinal study of experimenter bias on the operant learning of laboratory rats. *Journal of Psychiatric Research, 2,* 61–72.

Rosenthal, R., & Rosnow, R. L. (Eds.). (1969). *Artifact in behavioral research.* New York: Academic Press.

Rosenthal, R., & Rosnow, R. L. (1975a). *Primer of methods for the behavioral sciences.* New York: Wiley.

Rosenthal, R., & Rosnow, R. L. (1975b). *The volunteer subject.* New York: Wiley.

Rosenthal, R., & Rosnow, R. L. (1984). Applying Hamlet's question to the ethical conduct of research: A conceptual addendum. *American Psychologist, 39,* 561–563.

Rosenthal, R., & Rosnow, R. L. (1985). *Contrast analysis: Focused comparisons in the analysis of variance.* Cambridge: Cambridge University Press.

Rosenthal, R., & Rosnow, R. L. (1991). *Essentials of behavioral research: Methods and data analysis* (2nd ed.). New York: McGraw-Hill.

Rosenthal, R., & Rosnow, R. L. (2008). *Essentials of behavioral research: Methods and data analysis* (3rd ed.). Boston: McGraw-Hill.

Rosenthal, R., Rosnow, R. L., & Rubin, D. B. (2000). *Contrasts and effect sizes in behavioral research: A correlational approach.* Cambridge: Cambridge University Press.

Rosenthal, R., & Rubin, D. B. (1978). Interpersonal expectancy effects: The first 345 studies. *Behavioral and Brain Sciences, 3,* 377–386.

Rosenthal, R., & Rubin, D. B. (1979a). Comparing significance levels of independent studies. *Psychological Bulletin, 86,* 1165–1168.

Rosenthal, R., & Rubin, D. B. (1979b). A note on percent variance explained as a measure of the importance of effects. *Journal of Applied Social Psychology, 9,* 395–396.

Rosenthal, R., & Rubin, D. B. (1982a). Comparing effect sizes of independent studies. *Psychological Bulletin, 92,* 500–504.

Rosenthal, R., & Rubin, D. B. (1982b). A simple general purpose display of magnitude of experimental effect. *Journal of Educational Psychology, 74,* 166–169.

Rosenthal, R., & Rubin, D. B. (1989). Effect size estimation for one-sample multiple-choice type data: Design, analysis, and meta-analysis. *Psychological Bulletin, 106,* 332–337.

Rosenthal, R., & Rubin, D. B. (1994). The counternull value of an effect size: A new statistic. *Psychological Science, 5,* 329–334.

Rosenthal, R., & Rubin, D. B. (2003). $r_{equivalent}$: A simple general purpose display of magnitude of experimental effect. *Journal of Educational Psychology, 74,* 166–169.

Rosnow, R. L. (1980). Psychology of rumor reconsidered. *Psychological Bulletin, 87,* 578–591.

Rosnow, R. L. (1981). *Paradigms in transition: The methodology of social inquiry.* New York: Oxford University Press.

Rosnow, R. L. (1986). Shotter, Vico and fallibilistic indeterminacy. *British Journal of Social Psychology, 25,* 215–216.

Rosnow, R. L. (1991). Inside rumor: A personal journey. *American Psychologist, 46,* 484–496.

Rosnow, R. L. (1993). The volunteer problem revisited. In P. D. Blanck (Ed.), *Interpersonal expectations: Theory, research, applications* (pp. 418–436). New York: Cambridge University Press.

Rosnow, R. L. (1997). Hedgehogs, foxes, and the evolving social contract in psychological science: Ethical challenges and methodological opportunities. *Psychological Methods, 2,* 345–356.

Rosnow, R. L. (2001). Rumor and gossip in interpersonal interaction and beyond: A social exchange perspective. In R. M. Kowalski (Ed.), *Behaving badly: Aversive behaviors in interpersonal relationships* (pp. 203–232). Washington, DC: American Psychological Association.

Rosnow, R. L. (2002). Experimenter and subject artifacts. In N. J. Smelser & P. B. Baltes (Eds.), *International encyclopedia of the social and behavioral sciences.* Amsterdam: Pergamon.

Rosnow, R. L., Esposito, J. L., & Gibney, L. (1987). Factors influencing rumor spreading: Replication and extension. *Language and Communication, 7,* 1–14.

Rosnow, R. L., & Fine, G. A. (1974, August). Inside rumors. *Human Behavior,* pp. 64–68.

Rosnow, R. L., & Fine, G. A. (1976). *Rumor and gossip: The social psychology of hearsay.* New York: Elsevier.

Rosnow, R. L., & Georgoudi, M. (Eds.). (1986). *Contextualism and understanding in behavioral science.* New York: Praeger

Rosnow, R. L., Goodstadt, B. E., Suls, J. M., & Gitter, A. G. (1973). More on the social psychology of the experiment: When compliance turns to self-defense. *Journal of Personality and Social Psychology, 27,* 337–343.

Rosnow, R. L., & Rosenthal, R. (1970). Volunteer effects in behavioral research. In K. H. Craik, B. Kleinmuntz, R. L. Rosnow, R. Rosenthal, J. A. Cheyne, & R. H. Walters, *New directions in psychology* (No. 4, pp. 211–277). New York: Holt, Rinehart & Winston.

Rosnow, R. L., & Rosenthal, R. (1976). The volunteer subject revisited. *Australian Journal of Psychology, 28,* 97–108.

Rosnow, R. L., & Rosenthal, R. (1988). Focused tests of significance and effect size estimation in counseling psychology. *Journal of Counseling Psychology, 35,* 203–208.

Rosnow, R. L., & Rosenthal, R. (1989a). Definition and interpretation of interaction effects. *Psychological Bulletin, 105,* 143–146.

Rosnow, R. L., & Rosenthal, R. (1989b). Statistical procedures and the justification of knowledge in psychological science. *American Psychologist, 44,* 1276–1284.

Rosnow, R. L., & Rosenthal, R. (1991). If you are looking at the cell means, you're not looking at *only* the interaction (unless all main effects are zero). *Psychological Bulletin, 110,* 574–576.

Rosnow, R. L., & Rosenthal, R. (1995). "Some things you learn aren't so": Cohen's paradox, Asch's paradigm, and the interpretation of interaction. *Psychological Science, 6,* 3–9.

Rosnow, R. L., & Rosenthal, R. (1996). Computing contrasts, effect sizes, and counternulls on other people's published data: General procedures for research consumers. *Psychological Methods, 1,* 331–340.

Rosnow, R. L., & Rosenthal, R. (1997). *People studying people: Artifacts and ethics in behavioral research.* New York: W. H. Freeman.

Rosnow, R. L., & Rosenthal, R. (2002). Contrasts and correlations in theory assessment. *Journal of Pediatric Psychology, 27,* 59–66.

Rosnow, R. L., & Rosenthal, R. (2003). Effect sizes for experimenting psychologists. *Canadian Journal of Experimental Psychology, 57,* 221–237.

Rosnow, R. L., & Rosenthal, R. (2007). Assessing the effect size of outcome research. In A. M. Nezu & C. M. Nezu (Eds.), *Evidence-based outcome research: A practical guide to conducting randomized controlled trials for psychosocial interventions.* New York: Oxford University Press.

Rosnow, R. L., Rosenthal, R., & Rubin, D. B. (2000). Contrasts and correlations in effect size estimation. *Psychological Science, 11,* 446–453.

Rosnow, R. L., & Rosnow, M. (2006). *Writing papers in psychology: A student guide to research reports, literature reviews, proposals, posters, and handouts* (7th ed.). Belmont, CA: Thomson/Wadsworth.

Rosnow, R. L., Rotheram-Borus, M. J., Ceci, S. J., Blanck, P. D., & Koocher, G. P. (1993). The institutional review board as a mirror of scientific and ethical standards. *American Psychologist, 48,* 821–826.

Rosnow, R. L., Skleder, A. A., Jaeger, M. E., & Rind, B. (1994). Intelligence and the epistemics of interpersonal acumen: Testing some implications of Gardner's theory. *Intelligence, 19,* 93–116.

Rosnow, R. L., Strohmetz, D., & Aditya, R. (2000). Artifact in research. In A. E. Kazdin (Ed.), *Encyclopedia of psychology* (Vol. 1, pp. 242–245). New York: Oxford University Press & American Psychological Association.

Rosnow, R. L., & Suls, J. M. (1970). Reactive effects of pretesting in attitude research. *Journal of Personality and Social Psychology, 15,* 338–343.

Ross, L., Greene, D., & House, P. (1977). The "false-consensus effect": An egocentric bias in social perception and attribution processes. *Journal of Experimental Social Psychology, 13,* 279–301.

Rossi, P. H., Wright, J. D., & Anderson, A. B. (1983). Sample surveys: History, current practice, and future prospects. In P. H. Rossi, J. D. Wright, & A. B. Anderson (Eds.), *Handbook of survey research* (pp. 1–20). New York: Academic Press.

Rothenberg, R. (1990, October 5). Surveys proliferate, but answers dwindle. *New York Times,* pp. A1, D4.

Rozelle, R. M., & Campbell, D. T. (1969). More plausible rival hypotheses in the cross-lagged panel correlation technique. *Psychological Bulletin, 71,* 74–80.

Rozin, P., Fischler, C., Imada, S., Sarubin, A., & Wrzesniewski, A. (1999). Attitudes to food and the role of food in life in the U.S.A., Japan, Flemish Belgium and France: Possible implications for the diet-health debate. *Appetite, 33,* 163–180.

Rubin, D. B. (1973). The use of matched sampling and regression adjustment to control bias in observational studies. *Biometrics, 29,* 184–203.

Rubin, D. B. (1974). Estimating causal effects of treatments in randomized and nonrandomized studies. *Journal of Educational Psychology, 66,* 688–701.

Rubin, D. B. (2006). Estimating treatment effects from nonrandomized studies using subclassification on propensity scores. In D. A. Hantula (Ed.), *Advances in social and organizational psychology* (pp. 41–59). Mahwah, NJ: Erlbaum.

Rubin, D. B., & Thomas, N. (1996). Matching using estimated propensity scores: Relating theory to practice. *Biometrics, 52,* 249–264.

Rubin, Z. (1974). Jokers wild in the lab. In J. B. Maas (Ed.), *Readings in Psychology Today* (pp. 25–27). Del Mar, CA: CRM Books.

Russell, M. S., & Burch, R. L. (1959). *The principles of humane experimental technique.* London: Methuen.

Saks, M. J., & Blanck, P. D. (1992). Justice improved: The unrecognized benefits of aggregation and sampling in the trial of mass torts. *Stanford Law Review, 44,* 815–851.

Sales, B. D., & Folkman, S. (Eds.). (2000). *Ethics in research with human participants.* Washington, DC: American Psychological Association.

Salsburg, D. (2001). *The lady tasting tea: How statistics revolutionized science in the twentieth century.* New York: W. H. Freeman.

Saxe, L. (1991). Lying: Thoughts of an applied social psychologist. *American Psychologist, 46,* 409–415.

Schachter, S. (1968). Obesity and eating. *Science, 161,* 751–756.

Schacter, D. L. (1999). The seven sins of memory: Insights from psychology and cognitive neuroscience. *American Psychologist, 54,* 182–203.

Schaeffer, N. C. (2000). Asking questions about threatening topics: A selective overview. In A. A. Stone, J. S. Turkkan, C. A. Bachrach, J. B. Jobe, H. S. Kurtzman, & V. S. Cain (Eds.), *The science of self-report: Implications for research and practice* (pp. 105–121). Mahwah, NJ: Erlbaum.

Schuler, H. (1982). *Ethical problems in psychological research.* New York: Academic Press.

Schultz, D. P. (1969). The human subject in psychological research. *Psychological Bulletin, 72,* 214–228.

Schuman, H., & Presser, S. (1996). *Questions and answers in attitude surveys: Experiments on question form, wording, and content.* Thousand Oaks, CA: Sage.

Scott, W. A. (1968). Attitude measurement. In G. Lindzey & E. Aronson (Eds.), *The handbook of social psychology* (2nd ed., Vol. 2, pp. 204–272). Reading, MA: Addison-Wesley.

Scott-Jones, D., & Rosnow, R. L. (1998). Ethics and mental health research. In H. Friedman (Ed.), *Encyclopedia of mental health* (Vol. 2, pp. 149–160). Palo Alto, CA: Academic Press.

Sears, D. O. (1986). College sophomores in the laboratory: Influences of a narrow database on social psychology's view of human nature. *Journal of Personality and Social Psychology, 51,* 515–530.

Shadish, W. R., Cook, T. D., & Campbell, D. T. (2002). *Experimental and quasi-experimental designs for generalized causal inference.* Boston: Houghton Mifflin.

Sharkey, K. J., & Ritzler, B. A. (1985). Comparing diagnostic validity of the TAT and a new picture projection test. *Journal of Personality Assessment, 49,* 406–412.

Shaw, M. E., & Wright, J. M. (1967). *Scales for the measurement of attitudes*. New York: McGraw-Hill.

Sherman, S. J., Presson, C., & Chassin, L. (1984). Mechanisms underlying the false consensus effect: The special role of threats to the self. *Personality and Social Psychology Bulletin, 10*, 127–138.

Shermer, M. (1997). *Why people believe weird things: Pseudoscience, superstition, and other confusions of our time*. New York: W. H. Freeman.

Sidman, M. (1960). *Tactics of scientific research: Evaluating experimental data in psychology*. New York: Basic Books.

Sieber, J. E. (1982a). Deception in social research: 1. Kinds of deception and the wrongs they may involve. *IRB: A Review of Human Subjects Research, 3*, 1–2, 12.

Sieber, J. E. (Ed.). (1982b). *The ethics of social research* (Vols. 1–2). New York: Springer-Verlag.

Sieber, J. E. (1983). Deception in social research: 2. Factors influencing the magnitude of potential for harm or wrong. *IRB: A Review of Human Subjects Research, 4*, 1–3, 12.

Sieber, J. E. (1992). *Planning ethically responsible research*. Newbury Park, CA: Sage.

Sieber, J. E. (1994). Scientists' responses to ethical issues in science. In W. Shadish & S. Fuller (Eds.), *The social psychology of science* (pp. 286–299). New York: Guilford.

Sieber, J. E., & Saks, M. J. (1989). A census of subject pool characteristics and policies. *American Psychologist, 44*, 1053–1061.

Siegel, S. (1956). *Nonparametric statistics*. New York: McGraw-Hill.

Siegel, S., & Castellan, Jr., N. J. (1988). *Nonparametric statistics for the behavioral sciences* (2nd ed.). New York: McGraw-Hill

Sigall, H., Aronson, E., & Van Hoose, T. (1970). The cooperative subject: Myth or reality? *Journal of Experimental Social Psychology, 6*, 1–10.

Silverman, I. (1977). *The human subject in the psychological experiment*. New York: Pergamon.

Simonton, D. K. (2000). Archival research. In A. E. Kazdin (Ed.), *Encyclopedia of psychology* (Vol. 1, pp. 234–235). New York: Oxford University Press & American Psychological Association.

Singer, E., Hippler, H.-J., & Schwarz, N. (1992). Confidentiality assurances in surveys: Reassurance or threat? *International Journal of Public Opinion, 4*, 256–268.

Singer, E., Von Thurn, D. R., & Miller, E. R. (1995). Confidentiality assurances and response: A quantitative review of the experimental literature. *Public Opinion Quarterly, 59*, 66–77.

Skinner, B. F. (1938). *The behavior of organisms: An experimental analysis*. New York: Appleton-Century-Crofts.

Skinner, B. F. (1948a). Superstition in the pigeon. *Journal of Experimental Psychology, 38*, 168–172.

Skinner, B. F. (1948b). *Walden II*. New York: Macmillan.

Slife, B., & Rubinstein, J. (Eds.). (1992). *Taking sides: Clashing views on controversial psychological issues* (7th ed.). Guilford, CT: Dushkin.

Slovic, P. (1987). Perception of risk. *Science, 236*, 280–285.

Smart, R. G. (1966). Subject selection bias in psychological research. *Canadian Psychologist, 7a*, 115–121.

Smelser, N. J, & Baltes, P. B. (Eds.). (2002). *International encyclopedia of the social and behavioral sciences* (Vols. 1–26). Amsterdam: Pergamon.

Smith, C. (1980). *Selecting a source of local television news in the Salt Lake City SMSA: A multivariate analysis of cognitive and affective factors for 384 randomly-selected news viewers*. Unpublished doctoral dissertation, Temple University School of Communication, Philadelphia.

Smith, C. P. (Ed.) (1992), *Motivation and personality: Handbook of thematic content analysis*. Cambridge: Cambridge University Press.

Smith, M. B. (2000). Moral foundations in research with human participants. In B. D. Sales & S. Folkman (Eds.), *Ethics in research with human participants* (pp. 3–10). Washington, DC: American Psychological Association.

Smith, T. W. (1997, April 20). Punt, pass and ponder the questions. *New York Times*, p. 11.

Snedecor, G. W., & Cochran, W. G. (1989). *Statistical methods* (8th ed.). Ames: Iowa State University Press.

Snider, J. G., & Osgood, C. E. (Eds.). (1969). *Semantic differential technique: A sourcebook*. Chicago: Aldine.

Sockloff, A. L., & Edney, J. N. (1972). *Some extensions of Student's t and Pearson's r central distributions*. Technical Report 72–5. Temple University Measurement and Research Center, Philadelphia.

Solomon, R. L. (1949). An extension of control group design. *Psychological Bulletin, 46*, 137–150.

Solomon, R. L., & Howes, D. (1951). Word frequency, personal values, and visual duration thresholds. *Psychological Review, 58*, 256–270.

Solomon, R. L., & Lessac, M. S. (1968). A control group design for experimental studies developmental processes. *Psychological Bulletin, 70,* 145–150.

Sonneck, G., Etzersdorfer, E., & Nagel-Kuess, S. (1994). Imitative suicide on the Viennese subway. *Social Science and Medicine, 38,* 453–457.

Spearman, C. (1910). Correlation calculated from faulty data. *British Journal of Psychology, 3,* 271–295.

Sperry, R. W. (1968). Hemisphere deconnection and unity in conscious awareness. *American Psychologist, 23,* 723–733.

Stanley, B., Sieber, J. E., & Melton, G. B. (1987). Empirical studies of ethical issues in research: A research agenda. *American Psychologist, 7,* 735–741.

Stanley, J. C. (1971). Test reliability. In L. C. Deighton (Ed.), *The encyclopedia of education* (Vol. 9, pp. 143–153). New York: Macmillan & Free Press.

Steering Committee of the Physicians' Health Study Research Group. (1988). Preliminary report: Findings from the aspirin component of the ongoing physicians' health study. *New England Journal of Medicine, 318,* 262–264.

Steinberg, J. (2005, January 20). Study cites human failings in election day poll system. *New York Times,* A14.

Sterling, T. D. (1959). Publication decisions and their possible effects on inferences drawn from tests of significance—or vice versa. *Journal of the American Statistical Association, 54,* 30–34.

Stern, S. E., & Faber, J. E. (1997). The lost e-mail method: Milgram's lost-letter technique in the age of the Internet. *Behavior Research Methods, Instruments, and Computers, 29,* 260–263.

Sternberg, R. J. (1985). *Beyond IQ: A triarchic theory of human intelligence.* Cambridge: Cambridge University Press.

Sternberg, R. J. (1990). *Metaphors of mind: Conceptions of the nature of intelligence.* Cambridge: Cambridge University Press.

Sternberg, R. J. (1997). The concept of intelligence and its role in lifelong learning and success. *American Psychologist, 52,* 1030–1037.

Sternberg, R. J. (2000). Research dissemination. In A. E. Kazdin (Ed.), *Encyclopedia of psychology* (Vol. 7, pp. 76–80). New York: Oxford University Press & American Psychological Association.

Sternberg, R. J., & Detterman, D. K. (Eds.). (1986). *What is intelligence? Contemporary viewpoints on its nature and definition.* Norwood, NJ: Ablex.

Steuer, J. (1992). Defining virtual reality: Dimensions determining telepresence. *Journal of Communication, 42,* 73–93.

Stigler, S. M. (1986). *The history of statistics: The measurement of uncertainty before 1900.* Cambridge: Belknap/Harvard.

Stone, A. A., Turkkan, J. S., Bachrach, C. A., Jobe, J. B., Kurtzman, H. S., & Cain, V. S. (Eds.). (2000). *The science of self-report: Implications for research and practice.* Mahwah, NJ: Erlbaum.

Stone, P. (1997). Thematic text analysis: New agendas for analyzing text content. In C. W. Roberts (Ed.), *Text analysis for the social sciences: Methods for drawing statistical inferences from texts and transcripts.* Mahwah, NJ: Erlbaum.

Stone, P. (2000). Content analysis. In A. E. Kazdin (Ed.), *Encyclopedia of psychology.* New York: American Psychological Association & Oxford University Press.

Street, E., & Carroll, M. B. (1989). Preliminary evaluation of a new food product. In J. M. Tanur, F. M. Mosteller, W. H. Kruskal, E. L. Lehmann, R. F. Link, R. S. Pieters, & G. R. Rising (Eds.), *Statistics: A guide to the unknown* (3rd ed., pp. 161–169). Pacific Grove, CA: Wadsworth & Brooks/Cole.

Strickland, B. R. (1977). Approval motivation. In T. Blass (Ed.), *Personality variables in social behavior* (pp. 315–356). Hillsdale, NJ: Erlbaum.

Strohmetz, D. B. (2006). Rebuilding the ship at sea: Coping with artifacts in behavioral research. In D. A. Hantula (Ed.), *Advances in social and organizational psychology* (pp. 93–112). Mahwah, NJ: Erlbaum.

Strohmetz, D. B., & Rosnow, R. L. (1994). A mediational model of artifacts. In J. Brzeziński (Ed.), *Probability in theory-building: Experimental and non-experimental approaches to scientific research in psychology* (pp. 177–196). Amsterdam: Rudopi.

Stryker, J. (1997, April 13). Tuskegee's long arm still touches a nerve. *New York Times,* p. E4.

Student. (1908). The probable error of a mean. *Biometrika, 6,* 1–25.

Suls, J. M., Martin, R., & Wheeler, L. (2000). Three kinds of opinion comparison: The triadic model. *Personality and Social Psychology Review, 4,* 219–237.

Suls, J. M., & Miller, R. L. (Eds.). (1977). *Social comparison processes: Theoretical and empirical perspectives.* Washington, DC: Hemisphere.

Suls, J. M., & Rosnow, R. L. (1988). Concerns about artifacts in psychological experiments. In J. Morawski (Ed.), *The rise of experimentation in American psychology* (pp. 163–187). New York: Oxford University Press.

Susman, E. J., Dorn, L. D., & Fletcher, J. C. (1992). Participation in biomedical research: The consent process as viewed by children, adolescents, young adults, and physicians. *Journal of Pediatrics, 121,* 547–552.

Symonds, P. M. (1925). Notes on rating. *Journal of Applied Psychology, 9,* 188–195.

Tanur, J. M. (Ed.). (1994). *Questions about questions: Inquiries into the cognitive bases of surveys.* New York: Russell Sage Foundation.

Tanur, J. M., Mosteller, F., Kruskal, W. H., Lehmann, E. L., Link, R. F., Pieters, R. S., & Rising, G. R. (Eds.). (1989). *Statistics: A guide to the unknown* (3rd ed.). Pacific Grove, CA: Wadsworth & Brooks/Cole.

Taylor, S. J., & Bogdan, R. (1998). *Introduction to qualitative research: A guidebook and resources* (3rd ed.). New York: Wiley.

Tedlock, B. (2000). Ethnography and ethnographic representation. In N. K. Denzin & Y. S. Lincoln (Eds.), *Handbook of qualitative research* (2nd ed., pp. 455–486). Thousand Oaks, CA: Sage.

Thomas, C. B., Jr., Hall, J. A., Miller, F. D., Dewhirst, J. R., Fine, G. A., Taylor, M., & Rosnow, R. L. (1979). Evaluation apprehension, social desirability, and the interpretation of test correlations. *Social Behavior and Personality, 7,* 193–197.

Thurstone, L. L. (1929). Theory of attitude measurement. *Psychological Bulletin, 36,* 222–241.

Thurstone, L. L. (1929–1934). *The measurement of social attitudes.* Chicago: University of Chicago Press.

Tolman, E. C. (1959). Principles of purposive behavior. In S. Koch (Ed.), *Psychology: A study of a science* (Vol. 2, pp. 92–157). New York: McGraw-Hill.

Tourangeau, R. (2000). Remembering what happened: Memory errors and survey reports. In A. A. Stone, J. S. Turkkan, C. A. Bachrach, J. B. Jobe, H. S. Kurtzman, & V. S. Cain (Eds.), *The science of self-report: Implications for research and practice* (pp. 29–47). Mahwah, NJ: Erlbaum.

Treadway, M., & McCloskey, M. (1989). Effects of racial stereotypes on eyewitness performance: Implications of the real and rumored Allport and Postman studies. *Applied Cognitive Psychology, 3,* 53–63.

Trytos, P. (1996). *Sampling methods for applied research: Text and cases.* New York: Wiley.

Tufte, E. R. (1983). *The visual display of quantitative information.* Cheshire, CT: Graphics Press.

Tufte, E. R. (1990). *Envisioning information.* Cheshire, CT: Graphics Press.

Tukey, J. W. (1977). *Exploratory data analysis.* Reading, MA: Addison-Wesley.

Turk, D. C., & Melzack, R. (Eds.). (1992). *Handbook of pain assessment.* New York: Guilford.

Turkkan, J. S., & Brady, J. V. (2000). Placebo effect in research design. In A. E. Kazdin (Ed.), *Encyclopedia of psychology* (Vol. 6, pp. 210–212). New York: Oxford University Press & American Psychological Association.

Tversky, A., & Kahneman, D. (1974). Judgment under uncertainty: Heuristics and biases. *Science, 185,* 1124–1131.

U.S. Department of Health and Human Services. (1983). Protection of human subjects. *Code of Federal Regulations, 45,* Section 46.115.

VandenBos, G. R. (Ed.). (2007). *APA Dictionary of Psychology.* Washington, DC: American Psychological Association.

Vickers, B. (Ed.). (1996). *Francis Bacon: A critical edition of the major works.* Oxford: Oxford University Press.

Wachter, K. W., & Straf, M. L. (Eds.). (1990). *The future of meta-analysis.* New York: Russell Sage Foundation.

Wainer, H. (1972). Draft of Appendix for R. E. Lana & R. L. Rosnow's *Introduction to contemporary psychology.* New York: Holt, Rinehart & Winston.

Wainer, H. (1984). How to display data badly. *American Statistician, 38,* 137–147.

Wainer, H. (1997). *Visual revelations: Graphical tales of fate and deception from Napoleon Bonaparte to Ross Perot.* Mahwah, NJ: Erlbaum.

Wainer, H., & Thissen, D. (1993). Combining multiple-choice and constructed-response test scores: Toward a Marxist theory of test construction. *Applied Measurement in Education, 6*(2), 103–118.

Walker, C. J., & Blaine, B. (1991). The virulence of dread rumors: A field experiment. *Language and Communication, 11,* 291–298.

Walker, R. (2006, January 8). Cold call. *New York Times Magazine,* Section 6, p. 24.

Wallis, W. A., & Roberts, H. V. (1956). *Statistics: A new approach.* New York: Free Press.

Wasserman, S., & Faust, K. (1994). *Social network analysis: Methods and applications.* Cambridge: Cambridge University Press.

Weaver, C. (1972). *Human listening.* Indianapolis: Bobbs-Merrill.

Webb, E. J., Campbell, D. T., Schwartz, R. F., & Sechrest, L. (1966). *Unobtrusive measures: Nonreactive research in the social sciences.* Chicago: Rand McNally.

Webb, E. J., Campbell, D. T., Schwartz, R. F., Sechrest, L., & Grove, J. B. (1981). *Nonreactive measures in the social sciences* (2nd ed.). Boston: Houghton Mifflin.

Webber, R. A. (1970). Perception of interactions between superiors and subordinates. *Human Relations, 23,* 235–248.

Wechler, J. (Ed.). (1978). *On aesthetics in science.* Cambridge: MIT Press.

Weick, K. E. (1968). Systematic observational methods. In G. Lindzey & E. Aronson (Eds.), *The handbook of social psychology* (2nd ed., Vol. 2, pp. 357–451). Reading, MA: Addison-Wesley.

Weinberger, D. A. (1990). The construct validity of the repressive coping style. In J. L. Singer (Ed.)., *Repression and dissociation: Implications for personality theory, psychopathology, and health* (pp. 337–386). Chicago: University of Chicago Press.

Weiner, B. (1991). Metaphors in motivation and attribution. *American Psychologist, 46,* 921–930.

Weiner, I. B. (2003). *Principles of Rorschach interpretation.* Mahwah, NJ: Erlbaum.

Weisberg, R. W. (1994). Genius and madness? A quasi-experimental test of the hypothesis that manic-depression increases creativity. *Psychological Science, 5,* 361–367.

Werner, H. C., & Kaplan, B. (1963). *Symbol formation: An organismic-developmental approach to language and the expression of thought.* New York: Wiley.

Westen, D., & Rosenthal, R. (2003). Quantifying construct validity: Two simple measures. *Journal of Personality and Social Psychology, 84,* 608–618.

Wheeler, L., Martin, R., & Suls, J. (1997). The proxy model of social comparison for self-assessment of ability. *Personality and Social Psychology Review, 1,* 54–61.

White, D. M. (1950). The "gate keeper": A case study in the selection of news. *Journalism Quarterly, 27,* 383–390.

White, L., Tursky, B., & Schwartz, G. (Eds.). (1985). *Placebo: Clinical phenomena and new insights.* New York: Guilford Press.

White, T. L., Leichtman, M. D., & Ceci, S. J. (1997). The good, the bad, and the ugly: Accuracy, inaccuracy, and elaboration in preschoolers' reports about a past event. *Applied Cognitive Psychology, 11,* S37-S54.

Wickesberg, A. K. (1968). Communication networks in a business organization structure. *Journal of the Academy of Management, 11,* 253–262.

Wiggins, J. S. (Ed.). (1996). *The five-factor model of personality.* New York: Guilford Press.

Wilcox, B., & Gardner, D. (1993). Political intervention in scientific peer review: Research on adolescent sexual behavior. *American Psychologist, 48,* 972–983.

Wilcox, R. R. (2005). New methods for comparing groups: Strategies for increasing the probability of detecting true differences. *New Directions in Psychological Science, 14,* 272–275.

Wilkinson, L., & Engelman, L. (1996). Descriptive statistics. In L. Wilkinson (Ed.), *SYSTAT 9: Statistics I* (pp. 205–225). Chicago: SPSS Inc.

Wilkinson, L., and the Task Force on Statistical Inference. (1999). Statistical methods in psychology journals. *American Psychologist, 54,* 594–604.

Willis, G., Brittingham, A, Lee, L., Tourangeau, R., & Ching, P. (1999). *Response errors in children's surveys of immunization.* Vital and Health Statistics, Series 6, No. 8, Hyattsville, MD: National Center for Health Statistics.

Wolman, B. B. (Ed.). (1977). *International encyclopedia of psychiatry, psychology, psychoanalysis, and neurology* (Vols. 1–12). New York: Van Nostrand Reinhold.

Wood, J. (1989). Theory and research concerning social comparisons of personal attributes. *Psychological Bulletin, 106,* 231–248.

Woodrum, E. (1984). "Mainstreaming" content analysis in social science: Methodological advantages, obstacles, and solutions. *Social Science Research, 13,* 1–19.

Yin, R. K. (1989). *Case study research: Design and methods.* Newbury Park, CA: Sage.

Yonge, C. D. (Ed.). (1854). *The deipnosophists or the banquet of the learned of Athenaeus* (Vol. 1). London: Henry G. Bohn.

Zajonc, R. F. (1965). Social facilitation. *Science, 149,* 269–274.

Zechmeister, E. G., & Nyberg, S. E. (1982). *Human memory: An introduction to research and theory.* Monterey, CA: Brooks/Cole.

Zipf, G. K. (1935). *The psycho-biology of language.* Boston: Houghton Mifflin.

Zipf, G. K. (1949). *Human behavior and the principle of least effort.* Reading, MA: Addison-Wesley.

Zuckerman, M., Hodgins, H. S., Zuckerman, A., & Rosenthal, R. (1993). Contemporary issues in the analysis of data: A survey of 551 psychologists. *Psychological Science, 4,* 49–53.

Name Index

Shaffer, D., 184, 434
Shahid, A., 107, 439
Sharkey, K. J., 133, 444
Shaver, P. R., 144, 441
Shaw, B. F., 39, 429
Shaw, M. E., 111–112, 445
Shea, W. R., 11, 440
Sherman, S. J., 4, 445
Shermer, M., 5, 445
Sidman, M., 138, 445
Sieber, J. E., 17, 50, 65, 445–446
Siegel, S., 163, 393, 409, 445
Sigall, H., 17, 445
Silverman, I., 60, 169, 445
Simon, H. A., 96, 432
Simonton, D. K., 81, 445
Singer, E., 97, 445
Singh, M., 17, 441
Siroky, L. M., 189, 428
Skinner, B. F., 29–30, 45, 186, 432, 445
Skleder, A. A., 177, 444
Slife, B., 66, 445
Slovic, P., 13, 256–257, 436, 445
Smart, R. G., 17, 445
Smelser, N. J., 39, 445
Smeyak, G. P., 115–116, 432
Smith, C., 116, 445
Smith, C. P., 82, 445
Smith, M. B., 50, 445
Smith, M. L., 405, 434
Smith, T. W., 96, 445
Snedecor, G. W., 212, 293,
    403–404, 445
Snider, J. G., 107–108, 445
Snyderman, P., 191, 436
Sockloff, A. L., 102, 445
Solomon, J., 134, 438
Solomon, R. L., 87, 166–167, 445–446
Sonneck, G., 185, 446
Sotsky, S. M., 52, 435
Spearman, C., 131, 446
Sperry, R. W., 67, 446
Stanley, B., 50, 446
Stanley, J. C., 88, 128, 136, 161, 163,
    180, 186, 192, 430, 446
Steer, R. A., 39, 429
Steering Committee of the Physi-
    cians' Health Study Research
    Group, 279–280, 446
Steinberg, J., 203, 446
Sterling, T. D., 409, 446
Stern, S. E., 89, 446
Sternberg, R. J., 38, 133, 446
Steuer, J., 86, 446
Stigler, S. M., 250, 446
Stillman, F. A., 187, 434
Stokes-Zoota, J. J., 282, 441
Stone, A. A., 96, 117, 446
Stone, P., 82, 446
Straf, M. L., 405, 447
Street, E., 227, 271, 446

Strickland, B. R., 143, 446
Strohmetz, D., 169, 444, 446
Stryker, J., 51, 446
Student, 293, 446
Stuntz, P., xvi
Suci, G. L., 107, 440
Suls, J. M., 17, 41, 97, 167, 169, 432,
    443–444, 446, 448
Susman, E. J., 52, 432, 447
Swijtink, Z., 152, 273, 293, 434
Symonds, P. M., 105, 447

Tannenbaum, P. H., 107, 440
Tanur, J. M., 220, 227–228, 433, 447
Task Force on Statistical Inference,
    xiv, 448
Taylor, M., 97, 447
Taylor, S. J., 77, 447
Thagard, P., 11, 435
Thibaut, J. W., 4, 436
Thiemann, S., 283, 437
Thissen, D., 132, 447
Thomas, C. B., Jr., 97, 447
Thomas, N., 152–153, 444
Thorndike, R. L., 29–30
Thurstone, L. L., 111, 447
Tolchinsky, E., 151, 281, 433
Tolman, E. C., 18, 447
Tourangeau, R., 97, 115, 117, 447–448
Treadway, M., 37, 447
Troisi, J. R., II, xvi
Tryfos, P., 215–216, 447
Tufte, E. R., 226, 447
Tukey, J. W., xv, 228, 232, 447
Tukey, P. A., 228, 430
Turk, D. C., 96, 447
Turkkan, J. S., 96, 117, 163, 446–447
Turner, P. A., 31, 433
Tursky, B., 163, 448
Tversky, A., 13, 436, 447
Twain, M., 37

Urbina, S., 139–141, 428

Van de Castle, R. L., 102, 440
Van Hoose, T., 17, 445
Van Ijzendoorn, M. H., 134, 432
VandenBos, G. R., 39, 447
Vhahov, D., 199–200, 430
Vickers, B., 38, 447
Viswesvaran, C., 107, 439
Voight, R. B., 151, 281, 433
Von Thurn, D. R., 97, 445
Voss, C., 203, 439

Wachter, K. W., 405, 447
Wahlgren, D. R., 187, 437
Wainer, H., 226, 131–132, 272, 430,
    438, 447
Wake, W. K., 133, 434
Walk, R. D., 44, 434
Walker, C. J., 17, 89, 447

Walker, R., 6, 447
Wall, S., 134, 428
Wallace, J., 87, 431
Wallace, R. L., 5
Wallis, W. A., 203, 447
Waranch, H. R., 187, 434
Wasserman, S., 78, 447
Waters, E., 134, 428
Watts, D. J., 78, 437
Wearing, A. J., 86, 439
Weaver, C., 115, 447
Webb, E. J., 90, 447
Webb, J. T., 102, 433
Webber, R. A., 117, 448
Wechler, J., 10, 448
Wechsler, D., 132
Weick, K. E., 77, 88, 448
Weinberger, D. A., 143, 448
Weiner, B., 11, 448
Weiner, I. B., 101, 448
Weisberg, R. W., 230, 448
Wells, M. G., 17, 435
Werner, H. C., 28, 448
West, M. P., 187, 437
Westen, D., 141, 448
Wheeler, L., 41, 446, 448
White, D. M., 78, 448
White, L., 163, 448
White, T. L., 9, 448
Wickesberg, A. K., 117, 448
Wiggins, J. S., 100, 448
Wilcox, B., 56, 448
Wilcox, R. R., 302, 448
Wilkinson, L., xiv, 234, 448
Willis, G., 97, 448
Wilson, D. B., 405, 438
Wilson, T. D., 97, 439
Wolman, B. B., 39, 448
Wood, J., 41, 448
Wood, J. M., 133, 433
Woodrum, E., 83, 448
Wright, J. D., 116, 444
Wright, J. M., 111–112, 445
Wrightsman, L. S., 144, 441
Wrzesniewski, A., 43, 444
Wundt, W., 8
Wyer, M. M., 117, 432

Yates, F., 400, 433
Yin, R. K., 26, 448
Yonge, C. D., 7, 448

Zajonc, R. F., 28–29, 45, 448
Zechmeister, E. G., 117, 448
Zeger, S. L., 194, 432
Zipf, G. K., 17, 448
Zuckerman, A., 333, 448
Zuckerman, M., 333, 448

Subject Index

Sums of squares (SS) and degrees of freedom (df) in ANOVA:

$$\text{Total } SS = \Sigma(X - M_G)^2 \qquad df_{\text{total}} = N - 1$$

$$\text{Between } SS = \Sigma[n_k(M_k - M_G)^2] \qquad df_{\text{between}} = k - 1$$

$$\text{Within } SS = \Sigma(X - M_k)^2 \qquad df_{\text{within}} = N - k$$

Mean squares (MS) and F ratio in one-way ANOVA:

$$MS_{\text{between}} = \frac{\text{Between } SS}{df_{\text{between}}} \qquad MS_{\text{within}} = \frac{\text{Within } SS}{df_{\text{within}}} \qquad F = \frac{MS_{\text{between}}}{MS_{\text{within}}}$$

Row, column, and interaction SS and df in two-way ANOVA:

$$\text{Row } SS = \Sigma[nc(M_r - M_G)^2] \quad df_{\text{rows}} = r - 1$$

$$\text{Column } SS = \Sigma[nr(M_c - M_G)^2] \quad df_{\text{columns}} = c - 1$$

$$\text{Interaction } SS = \text{Total } SS - (\text{Row } SS + \text{Column } SS + \text{Within } SS) \quad df_{\text{interaction}} = (r - 1)(c - 1)$$

Mean squares (MS) and F ratios in two-way ANOVA:

$$MS_{\text{rows}} = \frac{\text{Row } SS}{df_{\text{rows}}} \qquad F_{\text{rows}} = \frac{MS_{\text{rows}}}{MS_{\text{within}}}$$

$$MS_{\text{columns}} = \frac{\text{Column } SS}{df_{\text{columns}}} \qquad F_{\text{columns}} = \frac{MS_{\text{columns}}}{MS_{\text{within}}}$$

$$MS_{\text{interaction}} = \frac{\text{Interaction } SS}{df_{\text{interaction}}} \qquad F_{\text{interaction}} = \frac{MS_{\text{interaction}}}{MS_{\text{within}}}$$

Contrast t on more than two independent groups:

$$t_{\text{contrast}} = \frac{\Sigma M\lambda}{\sqrt{MS_{\text{within}}\left(\Sigma \dfrac{\lambda^2}{n}\right)}}$$

$r_{\text{effect size}}$ *from contrast F on more than two independent groups:*

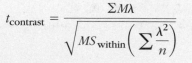

$$r_{\text{effect size}} = r_{Y\lambda} = \sqrt{\frac{F_{\text{contrast}}}{F_{\text{contrast}} + F_{\text{noncontrast}}(df_{\text{noncontrast}}) + df_{\text{within}}}}$$